A FIG

A FIGHTING RETREAT

The British Empire 1947–1997

Robin Neillands

Hodder & Stoughton

British Library Cataloguing in Publication Data

Neillands, Robin, 1935–
A fighting retreat
1. Great Britain – Armed forces – History – 20th century
2. Great Britain – Colonies – History – 20th century
3. Great Britain – Colonies – Defenses
I. Title
355′.009171241

ISBN 0 340 63520 7

Typeset by Hewer Text Composition Services, Edinburgh
Printed and bound in Great Britain by
Mackays of Chatham PLC., Chatham, Kent

Hodder and Stoughton
A division of Hodder Headline PLC
338 Euston Road
London NW1 3BH

DEDICATION

This book is dedicated to

Sergeant John Routledge, 40 Commando, Royal Marines
Died of wounds, Cyprus, December 1955

Colour Sergeant Jack Halford, BEM, 45 Commando, Royal Marines
Killed in action, Oman, June 1958

Sergeant 'Mac', MacFarlane, 42 Commando, Royal Marines
Killed in action, Limbang, Borneo, December 1962

They were friends of mine.

CONTENTS

LIST OF ILLUSTRATIONS

Helicopters and assault craft take 45, 42 and 40 Commando Royal Marines in to land at Port Said, November 1956. (*IWM*)

Assault ships closing in on the Suez Canal. (*Courtesy of T. Ashton*)

3 Commando Brigade Sniper looking down Rue Mahrousa, Port Said. (*Courtesy of T. Ashton*)

Marines of 45 Commando waiting to embark, Malta 1956. (*Courtesy of T. Ashton*)

Marines of 45 Commando Rifle Troop in Port Said, November 1956. (*Courtesy of T. Ashton*)

Commando carrier HMS Bulwark on exercise in the Mediterranean. (*Courtesy of E. Mather*)

Patrol of 45 Commando in the Radfan, Aden 1964. (*IWM*)

Machine gun platoon of the Seaforth Highlanders in Aden 1965. (*IWM*)

Soldier of First Battalion Parachute Regiment house-searching in Aden Colony. (*IWM*)

Soldiers of the Argyll and Sutherland Highlands in Crater, 1967. (*IWM*)

Gurkhas of the 2nd/2nd Gurkha Rifles board a Whirlwind helicopter, Borneo 1965. (*Gurkha Museum, Winchester*)

Gurkhas awaiting helicopters, Sarawak, November 1965. (*Courtesy of CJD Bullock*)

Transport One, Borneo. Gurkhas and a Whirlwind helicopter, 1966. (*IWM*)

Transport Two, Borneo. River patrol, 10th Gurkhas, 1965. (*IWM*)

British medical officer attends Iban baby, Sarawak 1964. (*IWM*)

Jungle fort, Borneo–Kalimantan frontier, 1964. (*IWM*)

Gurkhas manning GPMG, Borneo 1965. (*Courtesy of CJD Bullock*)

Private Smith, Gloucester Regiment, Belfast 1968. (*IWM*)

Corporal Les Smart of the 3rd Battalion, Light Infantry on the Peace Line, Belfast 1977. (*IWM*)

Riot in Belfast 1970. (*IWM*)

2nd Royal Anglians under attack in the Bogside, Londonderry 1981. (*IWM*)

San Carlos Water, May 1982. (*IWM*)

Paratroopers waiting to go ashore from *Norland*, 21 May 1982. (*IWM*)

Argentine prisoners and 2 Para soldiers, Goose Green. (*IWM*)

RFA *Galahad* ablaze after Argentine air attack, Fitzroy 1982. (*IWM*)

Parachute Regiment soldiers in Sussex Mountain, Falklands 1982. (*IWM*)

LIST OF MAPS

ACKNOWLEDGEMENTS

A book like this, an oral history of the last fifty years of the British Empire, could not have been written without a great deal of help from a large number of individuals and institutions. This help I would now like to acknowledge, for although I have tried to include as many accounts as possible, there was not space for them all.

As always, some people were particularly helpful and enthusiastic, and with this thought in mind my thanks must go first to David Evans, formerly of the King's African Rifles, for his encouragement in general, for his accounts of soldiering in Kenya during the Mau Mau time, for filling in a lot of background on his life as a District Officer in Kenya and for introducing me to other KAR officers, his comrades in the 26th KAR, Major Austin Maynard, Lieutenants David Williams and Christopher Minter.

Another helper was Spike Hughes of my old unit, Support Troop, 45 Commando, Royal Marines, so my thanks to Spike for his accounts of Cyprus and Suez 1956, and for finding other people who served in these campaigns and who now live in Spain. Thanks also to Jake Jacobs, of the Colonial Service, for his views on the complexity of the British Empire and for lending me his account of service in East Africa, and to D. F. B LeBreton, Secretary of the Overseas

Service Pensioners Association, for his help in finding people who had served in the Colonial Service throughout the Empire.

Thanks also to my old 'oppo', Terry Brown, late of 42 Commando, especially for the maps, and to my secretary of twenty-five years standing, Estelle Huxley, who combines a critical eye with a unique gift for reading my handwriting. Thanks go to Elizabeth Friend of the Empire and Commonwealth Museum, Bristol, and to the staff of many libraries and military museums in Britain and abroad for their assistance, encouragement and support.

Among these are the National Army Museum and the Imperial War Museum, London; the Army Air Corps Museum, Middle Wallop; the Parachute Museum, Aldershot; the Royal Marines Museum, Southsea; the Royal Engineers Museum, Chatham; the Gurkha Museum, Winchester. Also to the staff at the Red Fort, Delhi and the EOKA Museum, Nicosia, Cyprus. Thanks also to the Royal Commonwealth Society. Among many Regimental Secretaries, Brigadier A.I.H. Fyfe, DL, The Somerset Light Infantry and Lt.-Colonel E.J. Downham, MBE, BA. The Queen's Own Lancashire Fusiliers were especially helpful: To Lt.-Colonel Martin Scrase, MBE; to Alison Kearns, Archivist, The Red Cross Museum and Archives, Guildford; The Mechanics Institute and Circulating Library, Victoria, Australia; The National Archives, Nairobi; The Royal Commonwealth Society Archives; The Cambridge University Library. I should also like to thank the staff of the Commonwealth Secretariat, London.

Appeals for help, asking for those who had served in the Empire with 'a tale to tell or a memory to share' to come forward, were published by a great many newspapers and magazines and attracted a lot of accounts.

My thanks therefore to the Editors of *Pegasus*, the journal of the Parachute Regiment; *The Globe and Laurel*, journal of the Royal Marines; *The Sapper*, The Green Howards' Gazette; *The Kukri*, journal of the Brigade of Gurkhas; *Silver Bugle*, journal of The Light Infantry; *The Aberdeen Press and Journal*; Army Quarterly and Defence Journal; The Household Cavalry Regiment; Regimental Journal, The Devon and Dorset Regiment; *Tiger and Sphinx*, journal of The Gordon Highlanders; *Cumbria Magazine*; *The Straits Times*, Singapore; the *South China Morning Post*; *The Overseas Pensioner*; *The Manchester Evening News*; *Choice*; *The Lady*; *Lincolnshire Life* –

which produced a response from Australia; *The Oldie*; *The Eastern Daily Press*; *Western Morning News*; *Times of Malta*; *Soldier* Magazine; *Hawkeye*, the journal of the Army Air Corps; *The Standard*, Nairobi; *The Coventry Evening Telegraph*; *History Today*; *The Geographical Magazine*; The *Light Bob* Gazette; *The Beam*, Singapore; *The Life Guards Journal*; *The Tank Magazine*; *Derbyshire Life*; The Glider Pilot Regimental Association; *Regimental Journal*, The Royal Welch Fusiliers; The Air OP Officers Association.

Senior officers have been generous with their time, either in explaining their own campaigns or providing information on the background to the military operations of the British Army in a dozen colonial troublespots over the last fifty years. My thanks therefore to Field Marshal Lord Bramall and Field Marshal Lord Carver, both formerly Chiefs of the Defence Staff, to Lt.-General Sir Frank Kitson, GBE, KCB, MC, DL, for his accounts of Kenya during Mau-Mau, to Major General James Lunt, CBE, MA; to Major-General Peter Downward, CB, DSO, DFC, Governor of the Military Knights of Windsor for his account of his battalion of the Lancashire Regiment in Aden; to Major-General Sir Jeremy Moore MC and Bar for his accounts of Malaya, the Limbang operation in Borneo 1962 and the South Atlantic; and to Major-General Julian Thompson CB, OBE, another Royal Marine, for his accounts of soldiering in the Canal Zone, Northern Ireland and the Falklands War, and for reading the manuscript of this book.

Thanks go also to Brigadier Joe Starling MBE, MC, of 1Bn. The Suffolk Regiment and the Parachute Regiment, for tales of soldiering in Malaya, Aden and Northern Ireland; to Brigadier Christopher Bullock, OBE, MC, for his accounts of soldiering in Borneo with the 2/2nd Gurkha Rifles; and to Brigadier D.R. Green, CBE, MC, 10th Gurkha Rifles. Thanks also to Brigadier Freddie de Butts for his account of the last parade in India and his tales of warfare in Malaya and the Arabian Gulf; to Brigadier John Platt and to Brigadier B.C. Jackman OBE, MC, Gurka Rifles; to Lt.-Colonel A.S. 'Titch' Harvey MC and Bar, 5 Royal Gurkha Rifles and 6th Gurkhas, for his accounts of India and Malaya; to Colonel John Blashford Snell, MBE Royal Engineers; to Lt.-Colonel Ewen Southby-Tailyour, OBE, for his account of the Fitzroy tragedy and amphibious operations in the Falklands War of 1982; and to Major W. Shaw, MBE, The Royal Highland Fusiliers, Lt.-Colonel R.D. Strachan and Captain

C Harrison, The Gordon Highlanders, and Mr Harry Holder, The Royal Scots Fusiliers.

To Mr J. Ackerley, RAF, India and Pakistan; Mr Ian Aers, District Officer, Tanganyika; Mr John Anderson, planter, Malaya, 1951–86; Major J.C.T. Arnold, Royal Engineers, Suez 1956; Tony Aston, 45 Commando, for his photos of Cyprus and Suez; Mr Ray Ashworth, for his accounts of Aden, 1964–6; Jerry Bastin, REME, 1 Bn., The Parachute Regiment, Cyprus; Colin Bean (Private Sponge in 'Dad's Army') for his accounts of real-life soldiering in India, 1945–7; Miss Viviane Bell, Colonial Officer, Northern Rhodesia (Zambia) 1951–64; Corporal Tom Bell, RAF, Borneo, 1965–6; Colonel D.T.L. (Tim) Beath, 1 Bn., Somerset Light Infantry, for his account of the Somerset's Anti-Tank platoon at Suez in 1956; M.V. (Mark) Bentinck, Corps Historical Officer, Royal Marines; Major M.P.R. Barnes, Welsh Guards, Army Air Corps, Aden; and to a nun, Sister Barbara, OHP, for her letter on Africa.

To E.V. Berriman, 1st Bn., The Green Howards, for his account of jungle warfare in Malaya; Len Bishop, 846 Squadron, Fleet Air Arm, Borneo; Christopher Blake, for his account of service in Malaya and permission to quote from his book; William Broadway, Royal Engineers, Gambia and the Canal Zone; John Bowen, Malaya; Peggy D. Boxer, for her account of life in India; Roy Britton, Army Air Corps; Bill Broadway, Royal Engineers, West Africa; Terry Brown, 42 Commando RM. Malaya; Jack Brown, 4th Hussars, Malaya; Lt.-Colonel Burdick, The Devonshire Regiment, Kenya; J.A.N. Burra, Colonial Service, Palestine; Michael Busk, MC, Burma; George Butler, SAS and The Parachute Regiment, Malaya; to Colin Butcher, 2 Bn., The Parachute Regiment, Malaya, Borneo, and Northern Ireland, for his help on my visit to Brecon.

To Dr R.A. Callow, Colonial Service, Malaya; Colonel Patrick Carpenter, Gurkha Rifles, for his account of India at Partition; Marion Carswell, for her accounts of life in India; Anthony Carter, India; W.H. Cameron, Royal Fleet Auxiliary for his account of Suez 1956; Tony Carter, Royal Inniskilling Fusiliers for his account of India in 1947; Michael Clarke, Royal Air Force, Malaya; Graham W. Collins, The Kenya Survey; Sergeant David Cridge, B Co, 1 Bn. The Somerset Light Infantry, for his account of soldiering in Malaya during the Emergency; Alan Crocker, for his account of India; P.F.J. Corbett, Nigeria and

Angola; J. P. Cross, 1/1 Gurkha Rifles, North West Frontier and Pakistan.

To Percy Heath Dee, Coldstream Guards, Malaya; Ella Dix White, Egypt and Aden; Cliff Dowling, The Grenadier Guards, British Cameroons; Derek Duncan, 33 Parachute Light Regt., RA, for tales of the Canal Zone and Cyprus; Jim Durrant, Secretary, The Somersets in Malaya Reunion; Laura Eastwood, Kenya and Mau–Mau; W. English, The Parachute Regiment; Sergeant Fredrick P.J. Edge, Royal Signals, Malaya, 1953–5; Denis Edwards, 6th Airborne Div HQ, Palestine, 1947–8; J.L.D. Evans, OBE, Malaya.

Peter Faggatter, The Parachute Regiment, Palestine; Christopher Fairweather, 3rd Dragoon Guards, India; Colonel Ian Feild, for his account of Kenya; Major J.H. Featherstone, The British Legion, Malaga, Spain; Terence Foley, Royal Marines; Laurence John Foster, Department of Agriculture, Sarawak, Borneo; John Gardener, 22 SAS Regt., Malaya; Ralph Garwood, 1 Bn, The Suffolk Regiment; RSM Charles Golder and his wife, Doris Golder, for their fascinating accounts of the Canal Zone in 1951–4; Mike Gorrie, OBE, Singapore; Frank R. Graves, Royal Engineers, India, Malaya and Hong Kong.

To Mrs Anne Graham-Bell, for permission to quote from the account of her late husband Francis Graham-Bell, on Army Air Corps helicopter operations at Suez in 1956; Gerry Glaskin, Western Australia, Singapore and Malaya, 1949–58; Hugh Grant, 1 Bn., The Parachute Regiment, Cyprus; Major Tom Godwin, MBE, 1st Bn., The Parachute Regiment, for his accounts of Aden and Northern Ireland and Cyprus; Douglas Grey, Royal Engineers, Malaya; John Grebby, The Parachute Regiment, for his accounts of Jordon, 1958.

To Walter Gregory, of Trenton Ontario, 2nd Guards Brigade, Malaya; Colonel R.T.T. Gurdon, The Black Watch; Arnold Hadwin, 40 Commando, Palestine; Geraldine Hagan, Kenya, for sending my enquiry to *Jambo* magazine; David Ashley Hall for his accounts of Palestine in 1947; Cabby Harris, Canal Zone and Aden; Peter Hewitt, Colonial Police, Cyprus; Colonel L.J.L. Hill, India; F. Hughes, The Electricity Authority of Cyprus, 1952–8.

To Mike Jackson of Flying Wombat Music, Como, Western Australia; John James, 40 Commando, Royal Marines, Palestine; Daphne James, India; Reg Jinks, GHQ Signals, Delhi, for his tales of India; J.A. Jones, OBE, The Falkland Islands; Gordon Kirley,

Malaya; Major Harry Klein, Royal Engineers, Suez 56; Robert Joyce, 1 Bn., The Parachute Regiment, Cyprus; Brian Lancaster, Malaya; Les Lambert, 2 Bn., The Parachute Regiment, Suez 1956; Bambi Lewis, The British Red Cross, Kenya and Aden; John Loxton for his account of the Palestine Survey, 1937–46; Mr John Loch for permission to use extracts from his book, *My First Alphabet*, on his time in Malaya; Derek (Lou) Lucas, 40 Commando RM, Cyprus.

To Honor and Harry Maude, Gilbert and Ellis Islands, South Pacific; to D.J. McCaskill, 1 Bn., The Lancashire Fusiliers for his accounts of India in 1947; Donald S. McLean, Army Air Corps, Borneo; Ewen Macaulay, Pakistan; Marie Claire Marriot, The Gilbert and Ellis Islands; Captain J. Masters, MBE, for his account of Egypt and Cyprus; Geordie Mather, Royal Marines, for his accounts of soldiering in Borneo and Northern Ireland; Sergeant Denis Milborne, 5th Parachute Brigade Signals, Malaya, 1945; Mal Martin, Secretary, Suffolk Regt Old Comrades Association; Fredrick Munns, Royal Norfolks; Philip Mawhood for his tales from Tanganyika in 1964.

To Mr Ben Moger, for his wonderful account of the start of Mau–Mau in Kenya; Doreen Morrison, Melbourne, Australia, for her help over Rhodesia; John Morrison, 3 Para, Suez 1956; Sergeant J.R. Munro, The Light Infantry, Northern Ireland; Major Philip Neame, 2 Bn., The Parachute Regiment, Northern Ireland and The Falklands War, especially for his account of the battles at Goose Green and Wireless Ridge.

To Matthew Nash, The Black Watch, for help in finding contacts; Major Richard Nugee, Royal Artillery, for accounts on Northern Ireland; David Nicoll Griffith, Kenya; Jim O'Sullivan, Royal Army Pay Corps, India, 1947; Colonel Terence Otway and his son, Michael Otway, both of The Parachute Regiment, for accounts of service in India and Guyana; Ron Palmer, Royal Ulster Rifles, The Parachute Regimental Association; Pat Patrick, The Intelligence Corps, Cyprus; Flt.-Lieutenant, Brian Pearce, RAF, Oman; Major P.N. Pearson, 1 Bn., The Somerset Light Infantry, India; Major Victor Pegler, Royal Marines, once my Troop Sergeant in 45 Commando, for his accounts of Cyprus and Malaya; Mr Geoffrey Plummer, Cyprus, 1951–9.

To Edward Pond, 6th Airborne Division, for his account of Palestine; Major N.D. Poulson, Royal Marines, Cyprus; Lawrence Powers, King's Own Scottish Borderers, India; Captain R. A. Puddy,

M. M., 1 Bn., The Somerset Light Infantry, Malaya; June Powell, for her tales of India at Partition; P. J. Octoby, for his account of life in Cyprus; Rodney Pringle, The Canal Zone and Ghana.

To John F. Rankin, a National Service officer with The Black Watch in Kenya during Mau–Mau times, for permission to quote from his account 'A Subaltern's Diary'. This was written for his daughter Emma, '. . . to let her know what I got up to when I was your age'; all fathers might well do the same. To Eric Reed, Royal Engineers, Cyprus; J.T. Ted Relph, East Lancashire Regt, India 1947; Elizabeth Reynolds, India 1947; Gunner Bryan Ricketts, 33 Para Light Regt., Royal Artilery, for Cyprus and Suez 1956; Neville (Robbie) Robinson, 3 Para; Danny Rose, The Parachute Regiment, for his account of Palestine in 1948.

Thanks also to Michael Reynolds, Captain of Marines on HMS *Phoebe* for his accounts of Palestine in 1947–8; Michael Shaw for his memories of Palestine; J. Shortman, The Life Guards; Derek Snape, the Parachute Regiment and Lincolnshire Constabulary, attached to Cyprus Police; Ramnik Shah for his letter on Kenya.

To D.J. Sparrow, Royal Marines, for the account of his time in the Royal Marine Commandos in every part of the Empire; Michael A. Spry, for forwarding accounts of life in Rhodesia during the pre-Independence period; Corporal Alan Staff, 2 Bn., The Parachute Regiment, for his accounts of Cyprus and Suez 1956; Bob Tanner, 5th Parachute Brigade, Malaya 1945–6; Brian Tarpey, The Royal Marines Association, Malta GC.

To Dr Richard Underwood, Gilbert and Ellis Islands; Sheila Unwin for her lively account of the Tanganyika mutiny of 1964; I.L. Ward, from Auckland, New Zealand, Water Development Board, Cyprus; Micahel Wasilewski, a National Service officer in the 1/7th Gurkhas in Malaya; Harry Whitehead, 1 Bn., The Lancashire Fusiliers, for his tales of fighting in the Canal Zone, 1952–4 and for permission to quote extracts from his Kenya memoir, 'Jambo Askari'.

To John 'Patch' Williams, DCM, 2 Bn., The Parachute Regiment, for his account of the battle for Plaman Mapu, Borneo; Dennis Williams, 17 Field Squadron, Royal Engineers, Palestine; Lt.-Colonel Ian Wilson, Royal Engineers, for his accounts of Palestine and Cyprus; Mr Maurice J. Winter, planter, Malaya; Linda Wood, Aden Airlines, for her splendid and lively account of Aden 1963–7; Michael Wood,

Royal Artillery, for his account of India in 1947 and Hong-Kong in 1995.

I have tried hard to collect tales and memories from regimental officers, non-commissioned officers and private soldiers, as well as from those civilians, men and women, who served in the troublespots of the Empire as it came to an end and experienced the problems at first hand. Even where lack of space prevented an account from being included, their tales and memories were all useful, either as background to the story or as a check on other accounts, and most of them will be forwarded to the records at the Empire and Commonwealth Museum, Bristol.

INTRODUCTION

The British Empire: 1947–1997

'All Empire is little more than power in Trust'

John Dryden

This is a book about the last fifty years of the British Empire, from, 1947, when the British left India, to their departure from Hong Kong in 1997. The British Empire was very large and this book therefore concentrates on those parts where the British withdrawal was complicated by warfare, tribal or national conflict, or civil strife.

The original intention was to write a purely military history of the period, focusing on the troublespots: India at Partition, Palestine at the end of the Mandate, Malaya during the Emergency, Kenya during Mau-Mau, Cyprus during EOKA, the Canal Zone during the British withdrawal and the Suez operation of November 1956, Aden during the Radfan campaign and the British withdrawal, Borneo during the Indonesian Confrontation, the Troubles in Ireland from the Civil Rights marches of 1968–9 to the present day, and the most dramatic event in the period, the Falklands War of 1982, after a British Crown Colony was seized by Argentina.

That has remained the intention and that is the general thrust of the book, but in the course of researching and writing, it became obvious that the scope of the work must be extended, to cover the full background of the stories and all the elements involved.

The boundaries of this book are, firstly, that the text must involve the British Army – and such units as the Commando forces of the Royal Marines – and, secondly, that the events described must take place within a British Colony, Dependency, Trust Territory, Protectorate or Mandated Area – or in Northern Ireland.

Therefore, this book does not cover the campaigns of the British Army in Korea or anywhere else under the UN flag and will make only passing references to the involvement in Oman or the former Rhodesia (Zimbabwe), or places such as Belize or the West Indian islands where there was very little actual trouble before independence. Such limitations are necessary simply to keep the work to a reasonable size. Even within these constraints this book is twice as long as originally envisaged.

There are now fifty-two nations in the Commonwealth and the first point that ought to be made is that the majority of them achieved independence from Britain without any trouble at all. The countries and colonies featured in this book represent the exception, not the rule.

No one should assume from reading the accounts in this book that the British left the bulk of their former colonies under a hail of abuse, bricks and machinegun fire. Strife did come to many of the former colonies after the British left but that is another story.

During the research it also became obvious that the book could not start with the actual independence period and had to finish with at least a brief account of what happened in these countries after the British left. Each country had to be set in context, so how it was acquired and how it was composed, especially the internal racial, national, tribal or religious mix became part of the story, simply because those factors affected and compromised the British wish to withdraw and the local people's desire to manage their own affairs.

It also became apparent that the book could not be composed of purely military events or feature only Service personnel. Civilians were involved in every country, sometimes as victims, sometimes as policemen, often as planters or miners, managers, District Officers, nurses, air stewardesses, wives, and daughters.

The object of this book is to show what life in the Empire was like as it came to an end, as seen through the eyes of the people who were there, where possible told in the words of the people on the ground at the time. This did not only involve the soldiery. To give one example, daily life in Aden as the British withdrew is well and amusingly described by Linda Wood, then in her early twenties and a stewardess with Aden Airlines. It also became clear that the book had to tackle some broader issues affecting Empires in general and the British Empire as a whole, and so chapters have been added explaining how other Empires came into existence and how the British Empire in particular came to be formed. A closer examination of the issues soon revealed that the Empire was far more complicated than is commonly supposed and that the British rule, while sometimes oppressive, was generally benign. On the whole the British left their Empire well and ruled wisely while it existed.

This view is not always popular. There has been a certain amount of premature criticism from people tending to the view that the British Empire is something the British people should be ashamed of. There is little evidence to support that opinion. The massacre of civilian demonstrators by Brigadier Dyer in the Jallianwala Bagh at Amritsar in April 1919 is often quoted in this context and it was certainly a disgraceful affair. Between three and four hundred people were killed – Indian accounts say two thousand, which is clearly a wild exaggeration – and the Amritsar affair convinced many people, including Gandhi, that the British had outlived their welcome in India and must leave.

Amritsar cannot be excused but it is notable that few people can think of another such incident. The fact that it caused such outrage – Winston Churchill called it 'monstrous' – is an indication of how rare such events were and how greatly they were deplored by the British people . . . and the British Army.

Other national armies exist only to cow or terrorise the local population or their fellow citizens, but the British Army was never an instrument of oppression, at home or abroad. This book may paint a different picture of the old Imperialists from that commonly held today in certain quarters, a view often arrived at through ill-formed opinions or a distorted view of the facts.

In other histories I have written, accounts have been included from 'the other side', explaining how Britain's opponents viewed the campaign or battle in question. The letters that went out all over the world requesting memories or tales of the Empire were not targeted only at the British, and accounts from Indians, Malays, Chinese, Arabs, anyone who saw the end of Empire from 'the other side' or fought against the British Army would have been welcomed, but none came in.

The only Asian contributor was Ramnik Shah, a lawyer from Kenya, and his views are especially interesting, as they encapsulate several points of view on the 'End of Empire' period, on the hopes, the disappointments and the timing:

My most abiding memory of the End of Empire is connected with my return to Kenya after my studies in the UK. I arrived back on 11 December 1963, on the very eve of Independence.

When the plane landed in the brilliant sunshine of Nairobi on that warm morning, what stood out most vividly were the bright colours of the flags, bunting and balloons and other decorations in and around the airport. The whole place was vibrant with activity and bustle, noise and excitement, albeit controlled, patient and pleasant. Quite apart from cheerful African faces, it was the comings and goings of foreign dignitaries and their entourages, and of pressmen (in those days) which made a profound impression. Among the crowd of people I saw a frowning Robin Day with a TV camera crew, interviewing some VIP or other. All this made waiting at the Customs and Immigration all the more thrilling!

The journey from the airport to and through Nairobi reinforced these feelings of homecoming on a grand scale. There was a holiday atmosphere everywhere. You can imagine the effect on a young man like me, in my early twenties, on the threshold of one's career. Kenya, too, was on the brink of a new dawn and what lay ahead was a mixture of uncertainty and promise. While Asians and Europeans were naturally apprehensive about the future there could be no escaping the mood of celebration and everyone felt drawn into it.

The next few days were full of happenings and I vividly recall seeing them on TV with the Duke of Edinburgh taking centre stage on a few occasions. One particular personal memory I have is of Charles Rubia, the first African mayor of Nairobi, speaking impressively at one of these events, because within fifteen months or so I became his office neighbour and we shared the same corridor for some ten years!

Notwithstanding that my wife and I returned in 1974 to live in the United Kingdom for good, I have always been proud to have witnessed the coming of independence to Kenya, even though it was clear then and more so in retrospect, that the Kenyans were not 'ready' for it.

But surely 'readiness' in this context meant 'preparation', and historically Kenyan Africans were not groomed or trained – because of low expectations – to rule themselves. Many things went wrong there, but had stronger foundations been laid and had there been a recognition of the right to freedom and equality of opportunity, then Kenyans might have secured a better framework for self-government and practised it more effectively, considering the potential they have.

It is hard to disagree with any of that. The problem lies in the word 'historic'. British rule in Kenya lasted barely fifty years. During that time the British fought two World Wars, ran a vast Empire covering a quarter of the globe and, like other industrial nations, passed through sweeping changes and some very hard times.

Even if every settler had arrived in Kenya with no other thought in mind but to create a twentieth–century state, train the locals in the hard tenets of democratic government and then hand Kenya back to the indigenous people, he would have been hard pressed to complete the task in fifty years.

Ian Aers was among the last District Officers to serve in Tanganyika and recalls some incidents there in the decade before independence:

We arrived in 1948 – just thirteen years before independence – and spent the first tour on walking safaris with our two-year-old son. We often came to villages in the Serengeti where the locals had never seen a white child and touched him to make sure he was real. Tanganyika had been a German colony until after the Great War and I often used to ask the old men, the 'Wazee', what their rule had been like. The invariable reply was, 'It was hard but we knew where we were; with the British we are never sure.' In Tanganyika the DC had only a handful of police to maintain order in a district the size of Wales, so order was maintained through the tribal and village Chiefs.

There was a firm belief that when a murderer was hung, his blood was used as fuel in aeroplanes; in 1951 the Chiefs requested public hangings to prove to the people that blood was not taken. This belief was known as 'mumiani'. In 1960 – the year before independence – a surveyor driving a red Land Rover was hacked to death while using his surveying equipment, as he was thought to be practising 'mumiani'. The murderers were caught and I later held a tribal meeting, a Baraza, and read the riot act in Swahili. After the people had dispersed, my head messenger said to me, 'Bwana, did you know what the people expected?' He went on to explain that in German times, 'that tall tree there was used to hang the culprit and they expected you to do the same.'

I know that nowadays it is the in-thing to denigrate all us 'Colonialists' but we believe that, with the help of our wives, we did a difficult job well, and we have no regrets.

When independence in any part of the Empire is discussed, the size of the task must be stated and the local situation must be related to the Empire as a whole. The Colonial power had many places to think about and few local politicians anywhere in the Empire complained that they would not be able to handle their own affairs after independence.

More contributions from people in the former colonies would have been welcome as another usual source of information – history museums in other countries – proved equally fruitless this time around. Anyone who has seen how the End of Empire is described in the Red Fort at Delhi or visited the EOKA fighters' memorial museum in Nicosia will find the version of the facts presented there somewhat at odds with reality. Alan Staff, who served in Cyprus in 1956–7 as a Corporal with 2 Para (The 2nd Battalion, The Parachute Regiment), has been back to the island several times since:

I find most of the people very, very friendly, Greeks and Turks, but the Greeks have got some strange ideas as to what it was all about. That EOKA museum in Nicosia, with the car the Chief of Police used to smuggle people and arms about in, is a travesty of what really happened . . . and the idea that the EOKA could drive any British regiment, let alone 2 Para, out of anywhere is a laugh. If they will believe that, they will believe anything but it is no good talking to them. They have their version of the facts and that's that.

Two other contentious subjects – slavery and racism – have been raised by certain critics of the British and their Empire, so these subjects, too, might be mentioned briefly here. In both cases it is necessary to put the British role in context.

Slavery was a worldwide activity since Greek and Roman times and the British certainly played their part in both the slave trade and the keeping of slaves, especially in the West Indies, during the seventeenth and eighteenth centuries. However, the British were also in the forefront of moves to abolish the slave trade from the end of the eighteenth century, when the leading abolitionist was an Englishman, William Wilberforce.

Slave trading was prohibited throughout the British Empire in 1807 and slavery itself abolished in 1833. The Royal Navy was active in stamping out the slave trade, pursuing slavers in the Gulf and off the West African coast. When France and Spain were persuaded to abolish slavery in their colonies their slaveholders in the West Indies were compensated by the British taxpayer to the tune of £300,000 and £400,000 respectively. These were large sums in the middle decades of the nineteenth century. The American historian, Barbara Tuchman, has estimated that the cost of abolishing and fighting the slave trade in the nineteenth century cost the British taxpayer some £20 million, a fabulous sum in the last century.

Nor was it simply money. Those explorers who opened up Africa to the modern world in the late nineteenth century, Speke, Burton, Livingstone and the rest, were active against the Arab slavers, and their books, containing accounts of slaving activity in East and Central Africa, were a major factor in arousing and sustaining public revulsion against the slave trade. A British institution, the Anti-Slavery Society, the prototype of pressure groups, had a powerful voice in Victorian England, and was listened to in Parliament, at Court and in the Press.

Nor was anti-slavery action confined to the upper classes. During the American Civil War the cotton workers of Lancashire refused to handle cotton from the Southern States, saying they would rather be unemployed and starve than support the slave states of the Confederacy.

A desire to stamp out the slave trade also motivated many of the old Imperialists, men like General Charles Gordon, who died at the fall of Khartoum in 1885 having spent much of his life warring against the Arab slavers in the Sudan. Gordon's death – and the existence of the slave trade – was one of the chief factors that sent the British back to the Sudan in 1898, and having seized it they ruled the Sudan – the Anglo-Egyptian Sudan – wisely and well until they left 1956. It is now reported – in 1995 – that slavery has returned to the Sudan.

Accusations of British involvement in the slave trade have to be taken back to the Tudor or Stuart times to have much validity and should be balanced against the facts mentioned above. When the *entire* story is taken into account, the British role is not entirely shameful.

The issue of racism is more complex. To discriminate against anyone simply because of the colour of his or her skin is stupid and racist; few people today would argue with that. The complexity arises because in Empire times the British were no more racist than anyone else, and a good deal less racist than most. One thinks of the Indians with their caste system, or the attitude of Arabs to Africans in Arabia and their part in the slave trade or the massacre of Arabs by Africans in Zanzibar in 1964. People who single out the British Empire as uniquely culpable, and accuse her colonial servants of racism, are not on firm ground.

This does not excuse British racism but it puts it into context. Looking about the Empire, what seems at first sight to be racism – a fairly new concept incidentally – is often no more than an expression of class or cultural differences and a desire to be among one's own kind. The oft-quoted example of Empire racism is the refusal of British expatriates in the colonies to admit local people, even well-educated local people to their clubs. This seems intolerable until you ask an expatriate the reason:

Well, you can call it racism, I suppose. I certainly didn't think of it like that. Let me put it another way. I spent forty-two years of my life in Africa. I love the place and the people, and most of the people you will meet who worked out there will tell you the same; but I am English and at the end of the working day it was very nice to have a bath and go up to the club and spend a few hours among my own people, where I was not on parade, or on show, where I could tell a joke and not have to explain it or give unwitting offence. I just wanted a few hours at the end of the day among my own sort of people; surely that is not a crime?

Yes, I suppose if you had been to England and university and mixed with the British in pubs it was very hard to return to your own country and find you could not join the club and socialise with people who were happy to drink with you in England . . . but where do you stop? The clubs were set up and run and paid for by the expats for the expats, not to do down the locals. They had places where we were not welcome and vice versa. You may call it racism but I maintain that it was simply a way of getting among your own kind at the end of the day, nothing more.

General Sir Frank Kitson recalls the white settlers in Kenya during the Mau–Mau revolt in Kenya during the 1950s:

The word that summed up their attitude to the Africans is paternalistic. The older settlers had a mixed attitude. On the one hand, they wanted any Mau-Mau terrorist shot on sight. On the other hand if you picked up one of their boys, up to his neck in Mau-Mau, they were down on you like a flash, swearing that he was totally innocent and demanding his release at once, and no arguments. They had grown up with these people and simply would not believe they were involved in Mau-Mau, even if we had caught them red handed – and literally red-handed in some cases.

Time and again some settler would come storming into my office, ordering me to let his people go, and in the end I gave up arguing with them. I would say, 'Look, all right, you don't believe us. Fine. Your chap is in that tent over there. Go and talk to him yourself.'

Off they would go and hear the sorry tale, and more than once I have seen them come back with tears in their eyes, forced to believe that their people, Africans they had grown up with and who they thought of as friends, had been involved in cattle slashing and murder.

What the modern world sees as racism was more often the result of class discrimination. The colonists and expatriates who worked in the Empire were often less than kind to the lower orders from their own country. Every section of this book contains accounts where the 'expats' are treating the ordinary British soldiers like dirt.

'When we got to Dar-es–Salaam after the local soldiers had

mutinied,' recalls a Marine from 45 Commado, discussing the Tanganyika (Tanzania) rescue of January 1964, 'the local expats were all over us at first but it didn't last. Within a few days they would not even give us a lift if we were going into town and they tried to stop us going into some of the hotels and bars. The local Africans were all right, very friendly, and we got on fine with them.'

Another Royal Marine, Derek Lucas of 40 Commando, recalls clashing with the 'expats' in Cyprus:

'Scene: A Road Block. Enter an expat, driving. I hold up my hand and it begins:

"You can't search us, we're British."

"You do have your ID, don't you Sir?"

"Of course not. I'm British . . . lived here for years."

"Yes Sir, but where did you last park your car?"

"None of your business. Let me see the person in charge . . . Sergeant, this man is annoying us."

"Yes Sir, very sorry, Sir. If you could just step out of the car . . . Corporal, get the lads to empty the tank and check the spare wheel while I talk to this gentleman."

Result: plastic explosive inside the spare wheel. "Sir" was being used by EOKA as an innocent courier.'

The British troops in Cyprus eventually developed a routine for dealing with these 'stroppy bastards' at roadblocks.

Irate expatriate to tired soldier: 'No. I will NOT get out of the car. Look here, do you have any idea who I am?'

Tired soldier: 'Sarge . . . can you come over? Gentleman here doesn't know who he is.'

Not all the 'expats' were like this. Some were kindness itself to young men far from home, but far too many were arrogant and snobbish with the private soldiers. Neither were the British officers always willing to include their men in the social side of life in the Empire, as Private E. V. Berriman can confirm from his time in Malaya with the 1st Bn., The Green Howards:

Back at Raub, the Australians managing the mine sent us all an invitation, 'Come and have a Party'. The reply from battalion was that the officers would be delighted to attend. Back came a reply from the Aussies: 'Come off that old Pommie class-distinction lark. Either you ALL come or none of you come.' Needless to say, when it was at last decided that we would all go, I was 'chosen', to stay in camp and man the wireless set.

The British officers fared better but the NCOs and Other Ranks, the 'squaddies', were not welcome in expatriate clubs, even if their working hours were spent in the jungle or jebel, defending the members at the risk of their lives. In that respect at least, nothing had changed in the Empire since Kipling's day.

It's Tommy this, and Tommy that, and throw him out, the brute,
But it's 'Hero of his country' when the guns begin to shoot.

With all that said, the average British 'squaddie' had no real time for the local people, the 'Cyps', the 'Arabs', the 'wogs'. He got along with them well enough but had no particular interest in their culture or welfare. They were simply there, to do the 'dhobi' or serve tea and egg 'banjos', and might otherwise be ignored. Tony Carter recalls his time in India with the Inniskilling Fusiliers:

On the way to India we had lectures from the Ship Sergeant Major, the doctor and the Padre. The Sergeant Major told us that India was full of beggars, that we should not give them any money because most of them were richer than we were; they had been at it for generations and mutilated their children so they would have a better career as beggars. He also said that wogs were very weedy and if we hit one we should not hit too hard in case we killed him, in which case there would be trouble.

The M. O. told us that all the women were poxed to the eyebrows and we were to have nothing to do with them; our best girl friend was 'Miss Fist'. We should also take salt tablets and if we had to have a woman, use a condom. The padre gave us moral guidance, to remember our wives and girlfriends. 'My advice is to keep your hands in your pockets, one hand on your money, the other on your prick.' Thus prepared for an extended stay, the battalion arrived in India.

I promptly got dysentery and we all ended up at Dehra Dun. There I met two Indians, a laundry man – dhobi wallah – and a

Pathan tea seller – char wallah. One told me about Hinduism, the other about life on the North West Frontier. At the age of sixteen I had become a keen trades unionist, at the urging of a young man called Jim Callaghan, then a trades union official, and I got my information about India from 'New Ages', the newspaper of the Communist Party of India, which had news of trades union affairs in India.

The battalion then moved to Rawalpindi which had a large Anglo-Indian (mixed race) community. I got to know many of them because I got to know an English girl, daughter of a British officer in the Indian Army, and we would go to the Anglo-Indian Club because as an NCO I was not allowed in the Rawalpindi Club, which was for officers only. The Anglo-Indians did not mix socially with the British but were said to be very keen to get their daughter married to British soldiers.

I remember I was in the Orderly Room one day when a fellow sergeant requested permission to marry. The CO boomed out, 'Not to one of these half-chats, I hope, Sergeant?' My colleague said 'No' but of course she was.

The invariable term for an Indian was 'wog', unless you liked him, when you called him 'Johnny'. Other ranks were supposed to salute Indian officers but did not do so unless there was a British officer present. There were exceptions to the general rule, one of them being the lance-corporal in charge of the sweepers, who were all Untouchables. Bill, the lance-corporal, was very fond of his charges and spent hours drinking beer with them.

Through my girlfriend I met some members of the expatriate community. The 'expats' were not crudely racist, like the soldiers, and often got on well with individual Indians. Joyce's parents, though by no means wealthy, had six servants; two bearers, a sweeper, a cook, a gardener (mali) and a nursemaid or ayah. On the other hand the expats had no understanding of national political aspirations and genuinely believed that India could not manage without them.

British soldiers got on well with – and greatly admired – the Gurkha soldiers from Nepal and enjoyed the company of warriors like the head–hunting Dyaks or Ibans of Borneo who served with the British Army as trackers. British soldiers were always keen to stay in Dyak or Iban 'longhouses' and would go there on leave, many returning to their battalions covered in exotic Iban tattoos.

There is some substance to the charge of racism, and it would be idle to pretend otherwise but the scales must be weighted by the great love that most of Britain's colonial servants had for the local people they were anxious to serve and happy to live among. In many cases these strong bonds of friendship have survived the ending of the Empire and continue to this day.

This then is the story of some troubled parts of the British Empire in the closing decades of the twentieth century, as the Empire came to an end. The accounts this book contains are roughly divided into three parts.

The first part explains how the colony or protectorate or territory was acquired, and describes the country and the local population. The second part explains the growth of the independence movement and the problems affecting the granting of independence by the British. The final part details the struggles around the independence period and each accounts concludes when the struggle is over and the British leave.

This is the general picture but it does vary. For example, the British Army stayed in Malaya after 'Merdeka' to help the new nation fight the Communist bandits and went on to fight for Malaysia during the Confrontation with Indonesia.

There will also be chapters on the issues of Empires and three short resumé chapters of which this introduction is the first. The second, 'Interval', in the middle of the book, covers the state of the Empire in 1968, roughly half-way through the End of Empire period and the only year since the Second World War when no British soldier was killed in action anywhere in the World. The book concludes with an 'Epilogue' chapter, which covers the post-Independence fate of the colonies covered in the previous pages, and the Commonwealth today.

One final point must be covered. This book is largely composed of accounts drawn from people who served in the Empire. Some, perhaps two or three, have objected to the title 'A Fighting Retreat', and especially to the word 'retreat', which they say does not accurately describe what happened. The best and shortest answer to that charge is that 'A Fighting Retreat' is a good title and good titles are hard to come by. 'A Fighting Withdrawal' does not have the same ring to it.

A more reasoned reply is that the British Army has a long and honourable tradition of fighting retreats; one thinks of the retreat from Kabul in the First Afghan War and the retreat to Dunkirk or from Mons in the Second World War or the Great War.

Retreats test an Army's discipline severely but the British Army is a fine, well-trained and disciplined institution. In half a century of conflict the discipline of the Army and the common sense and good humour of the British soldier has rarely faltered.

A final reason is to avoid bandying with words; putting a gloss on the past may be left to those with something to hide. The 'End of Empire' *was* a retreat, forced on the British people by economic weakness, the mood of the times and American pressure; that fact must be faced and not fudged. The politicians may have tried to convince themselves that the Empire has been simply and happily transformed into a Commonwealth but that is claptrap.

The Commonwealth, whatever its merits might be, ceased to be the 'British' Commonwealth in the 1970s and cannot be compared in any way with the might and majesty of the old British Empire. The Empire went for reasons which were considered good and sufficient at the time and not one of the hundreds of contributors to this book regrets its passing in any way; their only regret is that it went too soon for the good of the majority of the local people.

The politicians ordered the retreat from the Empire for reasons which this book will explain, and the British Army carried out those orders. This book tells how it was done and it makes a story of which the British Army – and the British people – have every reason to be proud.

1

Imperial Sunset: 1918–1945

'The day of small nations has long since passed away;
the Day of Empires has come.

Joseph Chamberlain, 1904.

If there were ever any truth in Mr Chamberlain's confident assertion, time was soon to prove him wrong. Within fifteen years of that ringing statement, the Great War had cut a swathe through the ancient empires of Europe. The Prussian, the Russian, the Austro-Hungarian and the Turkish Empires all perished as a direct result of that unnecessary war and others were to follow. Within fifty years of the Armistice in 1918, the Belgian, the Dutch, the French and the British Empire had followed the rest into oblivion.

Before India became independent in 1947, the British Empire covered a quarter of the globe and contained a population of some 500,000,000 people. With Hong Kong gone, the overseas possessions of the British Crown will soon amount to a few scattered islands, and the total population of these remaining territories will be counted in thousands. An adventure that begun over two hundred years ago will have finally come to an end. It was, perhaps, inevitable.

Empires have gone out of fashion. Whether any other Empire will replace the British Empire as a dominant world power is debatable. The making of Empires is not what it was and countries like the United States and the Soviet Union, which put on the British

Imperial mantle after the Second World War, have either found it wise to swiftly drop such pretensions or had that 'Empire' disintegrate, leaving ruin and anarchy behind.

Before describing how the end of the British Empire came about, it might be useful to outline how the Empire was acquired. The short explanation is that the British Empire was put together in the interests of trade, and the wars that were fought in and around the Empire perimeter while the Empire existed were fought to expand or protect that trade.

Lust for conquest was rarely part of the Imperial motivation. The British Empire was, above all, a trading Empire. The British ran it as peacefully as possible because peace is good for trade, and enlarged it either because it was necessary to secure access to raw materials or to create more markets for manufactured goods. Much of the Empire's expansion was made by private, chartered trading companies, not by direct Government intention. Among the first of these was the Virginia Company, set up under a charter issued by King James 1 in 1606, establishing the colony of Virginia. Then came the Hudson's Bay Company, the East India Company, the East Africa Company and the rest, all pioneering the path for Britain's imperial expansion.

This expansion was not always seen as desirable, for Empires were costly. During the American War of Independence, one City trader, Dean Tucker commentated: 'These colonies are a burden; let them go. British commerce does not depend on unenforceable regulations but on the capital and enterprise of British merchants.'

A few decades later the economist Adam Smith took up the same theme: 'If any part of the British Empire cannot be made to contribute towards the support of the whole it is surely time that Britain frees herself from the cost of defending these provinces in war and supporting their civil and military institutions in time of peace.'

This view, that the Empire was not worth the cost of maintaining it, soon crept into political thought. At the end of the nineteenth century the British Prime Minister, Mr Gladstone, opposed any moves to occupy Egypt, on the grounds that the Empire was already too big and too costly and ought to be reduced in size rather than expanded.

Any idea that Britain's politicians or the British people were all committed Imperialists can therefore be refuted. Throughout the life of the British Empire voices were raised, often in the highest places, to declare that the Empire was a dreadful waste of energy and money and best got rid of. However, throughout the nineteenth century most of the major powers, including the United States and Imperial Russian, were busily engaged in expanding their territory and spheres of influence and in this activity Britain could not be left behind.

Empires are not new. The Greeks, the Persians, the Romans, the Mongols, the Spanish, the Austro-Hungarians, all had Empires in their time, but the British Empire was not like any of these. The British Empire created in the years after the victory at Plassey in India in 1757 was a curious, complex, largely maritime creation, containing elements ranging in size from whole continents to small coral islands, from vast, self-governing Dominions to tiny, undeveloped protectorates.

Jake Jacobs, who served as a District Officer (DO) in East Africa in the 1950s when the British Empire was already in terminal decline, gives some examples of this diversity:

When I joined the then Colonial Service after the Second World War, I applied for a posting to Palestine because I spoke Arabic. As a result I found myself, not surprisingly, in Uganda and Uganda was not a Colony at all, but a Protectorate.

To the east of Uganda lay Kenya, which was not a mere Colony, but a Colony *and* a Protectorate. To the south lay Tanganyika, now Tanzania, which was then neither a Colony nor a Protectorate but a Trust Territory. To the North lay the Sudan, which was none of these things but a Condominium. Further north still lay Palestine, which was different again and ruled by Britain under a League of Nations Mandate.

All became part of a 'Colonial' heritage and that heritage covers so enormous an area and so many people, of such ethnic variety, living in areas so far apart and acquired by Britain in such a variety of circumstances as to make nonsense of the suggestion that all inherited the same thing – even if we could accept that Britain had a grand and consistent policy under which these Colonies were acquired and ultimately disposed of – or not disposed of, as is still sometimes alleged.

Another Briton abroad, N. M. Carter who worked in Tanganyika (Tanzania), can describe this Colonial diversity at a local level:

Not being engaged in the Colonial administration, independence and the events leading up to it had little impact on our community. My work gang comprised Africans from Kenya and Uganda and Nyasaland as well as Tanganyika and the Head Boy spoke perfect English in addition to his native Bugandan and Ki-Swahili.

As for Tanganyika, the present Tanzania, Britain only took over Tanganyika from the Germans after the Great War, so we were not there long. It was 'mandated' to us by the League of Nations, and relics of German rule remained. The reason there is a bend in the boundary between Tanganyika and Kenya is that Queen Victoria allowed her grandson, the German Kaiser, to include Mount Kilimanjaro in his territory . . . Kilimanjaro was first named Kaiser Wilhem Spitz. The first leader of Tanganyika, later Tanzania, was Julius Nyerere, a teacher who spent three years at Edinburgh University. He founded TANU, the Tanganyika African National Union, and Tanganyika became the first East African territory to gain independence.

My opinion was – and still is – that the British Empire was a good thing and that it was dismembered too soon. The balance is weighted but it was to be praised for more than blamed . . . the Commonwealth is hardly comparable with the Empire – and is not meant to be.

My three memories of Tanganyika are firstly the ability and dedication of all Government personnel; secondly, the beauty of Kilimanjaro, whenever it could be seen, a sight far more impressive than the Taj Mahal; and thirdly, that my time in Tanganyika was the happiest ten years of my life.

Lt.-Colonel G. P. T. Carpenter, an officer of the 2nd (King Edward VII Own) Gurkha Rifles, looks at the end of Empire from a military point of view:

British forces were not stationed in parts of the Empire to foil the evolution towards self-determination and self-government, but in order to maintain order and prevent or overcome hostile interference with the establishment of democratic governments in the territories about to achieve independence. Borneo and Malaya are just two examples of this.

This was part of British policy, a commitment to independence, a policy proclaimed as a long-term objective at the Westminster Conference in 1926. It became an urgent objective from 1946 under the first post-war Labour Government when it was realised that Britain was 'broke' and no longer had the resources to maintain her Imperial position.

I never saw myself or the forces I commanded, as being in opposition or overlordship to the friendly people in our former Empire or Colonial territories; nor did ordinary people in these places see us as oppressors.

The bonds that held the Empire together and made it work were often personal. Mike Gorrie, who served in the War with the Baluch Regiment of the Indian Army, and now lives in Singapore, recalls his Empire experience:

Some of the happiest and most challenging days of my life resulted from the existence of the Empire. As young men in the Malayan Civil Service we were confronted by responsibilities that the average chap of the same age would never have met elsewhere. In my twenties I was 'father' to some seventy-one thousand people and had the challenges of the Communist terrorist (CT) Emergency as well . . . Which added to the excitement of daily living. I would not change my past career for anything; it was great.

Best of all, in the post-Colonial years I found myself accepted as friend and fellow citizen by our former Colonial people. My wife Joan is English and I am a Scot but I am proud to have been accepted as a Singapore citizen and prouder still when I see how the Singaporean citizens cherish their Colonial history.

Similarly, when Joan, who had never been to Pakistan before, accompanied me to the Baluch Regimental reunion last year, she was astonished at the fantastic reception and hospitality we received. Prime Minister Benazir Bhutto specifically asked to meet the seven British officers and the three wives who had come from overseas to attend her inauguration as Colonel-in-Chief of the Regiment.

These are not the words of dedicated 'Imperialists'. They go some way towards refuting the popular, modern conception of the British Empire, that it was a tyranny imposed on the world by the might of the British Army and the Royal Navy and run by racists who rode about on elephants wearing solar topees and dismounting from time to time to lash a native or commit adultery.

Significantly, the place of the British Empire in world history and its potential for good or ill becomes clearer at the end than during its hey-day, perhaps because only now, fifty years after it ended is there time to evaluate it. Some people claim that it is still too soon to have a clear view of the British Empire but 'oral history' depends on living people. The justification for an 'oral' history' is that the memories, opinions and attitudes of people who worked in the Empire and saw life there at first hand deserve to be put on record, or the revisionists will have a clear field to distort the past and rewrite the history.

This book is about the end of Empire in those places where there was conflict around the time or about the issue of Independence in those countries of the old British Empire, where many British Servicemen spent their youth, and sometimes shed their blood. These countries have passed into the hands of other rulers and the time these young soldiers spent in such places, forty or fifty years ago, now seems as distant and outlandish to the modern generation as those of men who served in the legions of Imperial Rome.

Mal Martin, a soldier of the Suffolk Regiment, who saw the End of Empire in India, is only one of several correspondents who pointed out that parallel:

I suppose the big question today is, should we have been in these places at all? Perhaps not, but then it can be argued that the Roman legions had no business invading Britain two thousand years ago or the Puritan settlers should not have gone to the Americas three hundred years ago. That is the way it was and you can't change it. As to how it ended, don't forget that in 1947, at Partition, the Indians were climbing into British Army compounds seeking protection from the fury of other India mobs. We soldiers had our uses, even for the local people, whatever they say today.

Empires may have been created and maintained by traders and administrators but they were defended by soldiers. Soldiers protected the frontiers or maintained the civil peace and internal security. As this book will reveal they also often bought the time that the politicians needed to find some constitutional basis for independence. The soldiers have had little thanks for their contribution. Most of the battles listed in this book will never be recorded on their Regimental drums or Colours, but that is no reason why they should be forgotten, for little wars, in a score of places, marked out the birth of the new Commonwealth.

War is the great destroyer of Empires. The Great War extinguished the Empires of the defeated powers, Russia, Turkey and Germany, the first through internal revolution, the other two by economic exhaustion us the result of war. After the Second World War it was the Empires of the victorious powers, Great Britain, France, Belgium and Holland, which fell away and perished. Funding the war was the principal cause of their decline, and when the war was over their colonial inheritance was destined to pass to the new imperialists, the United States and the Soviet Union. These nations soon found that filling the imperial role could be a costly and thankless task.

As even a minor British consul could have told the leaders of the American or the Soviet people, running an Empire is not easy. The United States of America and the Soviet Union assumed the imperial role with alacrity and enthusiasm after 1945 and soon ran into trouble. This cannot be because either State lacked experience in extending their hegemony over other nations. Whatever their politicians or historians may claim today, both were imperial and colonial powers and had been since the early years of the nineteenth century.

The United States began extending her influence over the American continent in the early years of the nineteenth century with the proclamation of the Monroe Doctrine in 1832. In that statement President James Monroe declared that the United States would not permit any European Power to meddle in the affairs of the American continent, or set up colonies there. The United States reserved to herself alone the right to meddle in the Americas and has done so whenever she has felt her national interests threatened.

The Monroe Doctrine still holds good and was restated as recently as 1961 in President John F. Kennedy's First Inaugural Address, which contained the following significant passage:

> To our sister republics south of our border, we offer a special pledge – to convert our good words into good deeds – in a new alliance for progress – to assist free men and free governments in casting off the chains of poverty, but this peaceful revolution of hope cannot become the prey of hostile powers.
>
> Let all our neighbours know that we should join with them to oppose aggression or subversion anywhere in the Americas, and let every other power know that this hemisphere intends to remain the master of its own house.

The keys to that house would, of course, remain in the possession of the President of the United States.

By invoking the Monroe Doctrine the United States created an empire in all but name in the Americas, an empire driven by the energy of her traders, the avarice of her financiers and the willingness of her politicians to embark on military adventures; motives not a great deal different from those of the nineteenth-century British imperialists. Hence those frequent American military incursions into sovereign states like Grenada, Haiti, Panama, Santo Domingo, across the Mexican border and into Vera Cruz, and constant political interference in Chile, Nicaragua, Salvador and various other Latin American countries, not to mention the nineteenth-century seizures of Texas and California, two vast regions of North America which clearly belonged to the people of Mexico.

Nor was American imperialism restricted to the American continent. Rudyard Kipling's oft-quoted exhortation to 'Take up the White Man's Burden' which is usually assumed to be an encouragement to British imperialists, was actually addressed to the American people following the United States takeover of the Philippines.

As for the Soviet Union, the main state of that unholy alliance, Russia, had been advancing resolutely across the nation states of Asia throughout the nineteenth century. By the fifth decade of the twentieth century, the Soviet Red Armies had swept West over Europe in the 'Great Patriotic War' of 1941–5 – a conflict known elsewhere as the Second World War – in which from 1939 to 1941 Soviet Russia was the ally of Nazi Germany.

As her share of the spoils, Soviet Russia consumed Estonia, Latvia and Lithuania and extended her Communist hegemony over the states of Poland, Hungary and Czechoslovakia, creating an 'evil Empire' that lasted for fifty years until economic forces – again – forced a collapse in 1990–1.

It can be claimed that these Russian and American advances, annexations, subjugations and subversions do not mean that the United States and the Soviet Union were 'empires', because they had cast off their Kings and Czars and reconstituted their countries as Republics. The fact remains that, by simple definition, those nations who exercise power and control over other nations and keep their people in more or less willing subjection are in fact 'empires', whatever title they choose to bestow on their national constitution.

That said, words do have a power. The fact that the British 'Empire' called itself an 'Empire' gave the anti-imperialists a hard stick to beat the British with, but it does not change the facts. Adopting the imperial role, even without the imperial title, creates problems and incurs responsibilities that the 'imperial' power may never have intended or anticipated or wished. The point being made here is that such problems and responsibilities affect all imperial powers, not just the British, and those who single out the British and their Empire for condemnation over the exercise of such responsibilities need to take a wider view.

These points are not made to cast blame on the United States of America, or on that recently fragmented superpower, the Soviet Union. They are made to point out the fact that empires, whether acquired by accident or with the best of intentions, bring with them certain seemingly unavoidable problems. If that point is clear, then a lot of what follows becomes less contentious and more understandable.

It is not the intention to avoid all references to moral lapses in British Imperial history but they have to be kept in context. The context of this book is Britain's fifty-year retreat from Empire, a retreat that left in its wake a Commonwealth of fifty-two free and independent nations. Each of these nations inherited a viable country with a workable constitution from that departing power, the British Empire. Few empires of the past can claim as much.

The British, or at least the English, have had three Empires in their history. The first, which we may call the English, or more correctly the Angevin Empire, began in 1162 when Henry II of England married Eleanor of Aquitaine and so acquired lands stretching from the Scottish Border to the Pyrenees. This was a long-lasting Empire which endured until 1453, when the army of John Talbot, 'Great Marshal to our Lord King Henry VI for all his wars within the realm of the French', was destroyed by the French at the battle of Castillon.

The second, which we can call the New World Empire, began in 1620 when the Pilgrim Fathers landed on Plymouth Rock, and ended in 1776 with the American Declaration of Independence. During this period other Western European powers, the Spanish, the Dutch, the Portuguese and the French were also acquiring colonies and extending their empires across the globe.

This book is concerned with the last fifty years of the third British Empire. That 'Empire' began in India in 1757, when Robert Clive beat the French at the Battle of Plassey and so ensured that Britain and not France would take over the Mughal Empire in India. That third Empire began to unravel in August 1947 when, after one hundred and ninety years of the Raj, the British hauled down their flag and withdrew from the Indian sub-continent. It is at that point that this story begins and it ends in July 1997 with the British departure from Hong-Kong.

A great deal has changed in the world since the end of the Second World War, not least for the British people and their island nation. In 1945 Britain was the head of a vast Empire and Commonwealth that had proved loyal to the Crown in two World Wars. The Commonwealth contained fifteen member states, the rest of the Empire being colonies or protectorates. South Africa was still in the Commonwealth and Britain governed the Indian sub-continent as a colony advancing towards constitutional independence and self-rule. Britain was the dominant political power in the Middle East, the protector – and very often the proprietor – of the Arab oilfields.

To the majority of the British people the British Empire was something to be proud of. The British had strong family links with the peoples of Australian, Canada, New Zealand and South Africa, and their Empire had stood intact against German and Japanese aggression for six long years, ensuring the salvation of the free world.

Michael Pocock, now a professional historian, recalls some views of the Empire from the ranks of the rifle Company he served in during the Second World War:

> When War broke out in 1939 I was at the end of my first year at Oxford. It was thought that anyone who had been at public school and Oxford was fully capable of leading men in battle, but fortunately for the men concerned, the instructors at 164 OCTU thought this did not apply in my case and threw me out. I therefore spent the war with the 'Odds and Sods' holding such responsible positions as the Sergeant Major's 'char-wallah', or tea boy.
>
> In July 1941 my battalion, the 11th Lancashire Fusiliers, arrived in Malta, where shortly after arrival we were given a lecture by the Provost Marshal. He divided the islanders into two groups, the men and the women. We were not to get into fights with the men, as no matter who started it, the British soldier would get the blame. As for the women, he came straight to the point. 'Do without 'em if you can, sleep with 'em if you must, but for Gawd's sake don't marry 'em.'
>
> The reverse of this was put to me by a Maltese nurse as a reason for giving the brush-off to an RAF Flight Sergeant, 'Any Maltese girl of good family seen on the streets with someone in British uniform would be ruined socially.'
>
> On the way to the Middle East we got a day ashore in Capetown, where the British authorities were very anxious that we should not offend the South Africans over the matter of race. We were told before we left the ship that the penalty for shagging a black woman was seven years in a civvie clink and no one in the Top Brass would lift a finger to get us out. It probably wasn't true but no one took any chances.
>
> Most of this advice was based on colour, on which point the lads were at one with the Nazis. There was a great row and a formal protest by the troops to the Commanding Officer when a Maltese odd-job man was found using the ORs' (Other Ranks)

showers. I remember my friend Jack Hallows telling me that when his battalion in India had to have what was then called a 'short arm inspection', checking the lads' penises for signs of VD, there was an outcry when the doctor who arrived to inspect them turned out to be Indian. I don't suppose he enjoyed a morning looking at a lot of pale cocks either, but no one thought of that.

On the other hand, in Egypt, after an outbreak of petty theft blamed on the son of one of the Egyptian barbers, our MP Corporal went to great lengths to prove the lad innocent. 'I wasn't going to see the kid punished for something he had not done,' he told me, and he meant it. Not much of the Master Race in that, just a decent English working man who thought it would matter if a little native boy was wrongly accused or badly treated.

As for the Empire, I was one of a platoon of soldiers ordered to attend a 'Civil Affairs' lecture about the Empire which was given by a bored Lieutenant, only marginally less ignorant than we were. The issues he raised were well summed up by a Fusilier when we got back to our billets – 'To 'ell with bleedin' Empire – we're fighting for us own.'

This confirms my own opinion as a professional historian. The American Secretary-of-State, Dean Acheson, was talking through his hat when he made that remark about Britain 'losing an Empire and not finding a role'. The average British citizen did not care about the Empire. When I was growing up in the twenties and thirties the Empire never touched the lives of the working-class people in my father's parish or the middle-class business people whose sons I met at Liverpool College.

My studies reveal that the landowning class who ran the show from 1688 to 1945 regarded the Empire as a damned nuisance, which is why they got rid of it as quickly as possible after the War, without any regard to the losers, the sahibs and settlers, the Indian princes . . . and if General Galtieri had been a bit more tactful or Maggie Thatcher a bit less courageous in 1982, the Falkland Islands would now be part of the Republic of Argentina.

Reality will eventually intrude, even on imperial dreams. In 1945 the United Kingdom seemed to be among the most powerful industrial economies in the world, second only to the United States. The pound was a major reserve currency and one pound sterling would buy four

American dollars. Britain had more than a million men under arms and the British Empire covered a quarter of the globe. To the ordinary people who had fought and won the recent war, Britain was one of the great powers which had overcome Fascism, a country with immense military, economic and political resources, the pride and pinnacle of an Empire.

All this may have seemed true as the nation danced in the streets to celebrate VJ Day, but on the day after the Second World War ended, the British awoke to find themselves ruined. Their financial reserves had been paid over to the United States to buy arms and munitions, and those funds had not proved suffcient to prevent a steady slide into debt. Britain owed money everywhere and the means to repay it were simply not adequate. Britain's industrial base had been eroded in the war and the first charge on the national exchequer should have been a massive programme of industrial regeneration.

The national infrastructure was in tatters, roads and railways worn out, manufacturing plant obsolete, the workforce tired and discontented. The people were eager to obtain the fruits of the victory and unwilling to accept that the peace had brought with it only an extension of hard times. Moreover, they could remember the hungry Thirties and the promises of 'a land fit for heroes' broken after the Great War. This time the people would permit no backsliding from the politicians.

The new Labour Government of 1945 promised a new deal for the working class, free education, nationalisation of the major industries, a free Health Service, improved pensions for the old, a massive housing programme. This is what the people had fought for, this is what they had been promised and to their credit the Labour Government attempted to deliver on that promise.

However, the Government of the day also decided on the need to maintain the Empire and the Sterling Area and play a major part in foreign affairs and in the work of the United Nations. Britain did not then realise, and perhaps has not yet realised, that her days as a world power were over.

Plans for sweeping change at home, the desire to maintain an Imperial role and match the power of the United States, all had to be paid for, and the money was just not there. Moreover, the politicians missed the vital point that power and influence in the modern world depends on economic strength.

The most essential post-War task was to revive the nation economically, establish modern methods in the running of industry and create an efficient up-to-date industrial infrastructure that would pay for all the rest. This part, the creation of a modern, thriving, well-managed industrial state, was the part that the first post-War Government and most successive governments chose to sacrifice in the interests of maintaining the Welfare State and a world-wide power position structured around the Empire and the Commonwealth. To this day, Britain lives with the effects of that decision.

Even the tasks that were undertaken proved more than the nation could support in the grim fifteen years after the war. Existing assets were squandered and neither the generous Marshall Plan Aid provided by the United States nor the writing-off of most of Britain's debts could stop the slide into permanent economic weakness.

Where other countries used Marshall Aid to rebuilt their factories and industries, Britain spent it on current expenditure, to stave off financial collapse, all with strictly limited effect. The pound sterling slid and the Sterling Area had to be abandoned. Meanwhile the Defence budget, strained by the costs of maintaining the Empire, was twice that needed for the defence of the British Isles against the Communist threat, and industrial problems, from obsolescent plants to poor industrial relations, went unchanged or were ignored.

Quite apart from the long-standing ideal of changing the Empire into a Commonwealth of sovereign states, and the current Labour Government's wish to grant freedom to the colonies as soon as possible, the Empire was swiftly revealed as an expensive commitment for which Britain no longer had the men, the money, the energy or the will to sustain.

Other imperial powers, the Dutch and the French and eventually the Portuguese, had even worse problems in the post-War period. They wished to regain or retain their empires, an ambition that involved the Netherlands in a war in Indonesia, the Portuguese in struggles against the nationalists of Mozambique and Angola, and the French in successive wars in Indo-China (Vietnam) and Algeria. These were massive wars, bitterly fought, lasting years, and causing great loss of life. These wars also sowed great dissension at home, especially in France and Portugal.

The wars Britain fought around the Empire were not of such

magnitude and had less effect at home. Britain was spared such trials and trauma but the British Empire – and thereby the British people – had another, more subtle burden to bear in the hard years after the Second World War, the hostility to the Empire of their friend and former ally, the United States of America.

2

The Beginning
of the End: 1941–1947

'We mean to hold our own; I have not become the King's First Minister to preside over the break-up of the British Empire.'

Winston S. Churchill, Prime Minister of Great Britain, 1942.

By the end of the Second World War in 1945 the Americans, both Government and people, had acquired mixed opinions about the British and their Empire. Towards the British people they felt strong bonds of respect and affection, based on a common heritage, shared ideals and comradeship in war. Towards the British Empire, of which the early American colonies had once been a major part, the American Government exhibited unremitting intolerance and hostility. When the Second World War ended the Americans concluded that the British Empire and all the other 'colonial empires' must be abolished as quickly as possible.

For the next twenty years successive US Presidents, abetted by Congress and the powerful American media, devoted a great deal of time and energy towards the achievement of that ambition. To this end they aided liberation or anti-colonial movements in all parts of the world whatever their actions or political complexion. Even before the War ended the Dutch were told that there would be no support in the United States if they tried to return to their colony in Indonesia. The Dutch still tried to retain their Far East possessions but were obliged to give up the struggle east of Suez within a few years. The French managed to hang on to their Far East empire in Indo-China until their army was defeated by the Viet Minh at Dien Bien Phu in 1954. In this the French were assisted by the United States and by the end of the Indo-China struggle the USA was paying nearly 80 per cent of the French costs of the war.

This was not for any love of French colonialism. By the early 1950s the USA had finally woken up to the threat of Communism. After the Soviet blockade of Berlin, various spy scandals and the theft of nuclear intelligence and the Korean War of 1950–3, the Americans realised that there were worse things than benign imperialism and became almost paranoid about the worldwide Communist threat. This had dire effects in the USA, where the Eisenhower Presidency was stained by the McCarthy anti-Communist witch-hunts but did not change American attitudes towards the colonial empires. They still had to go, if only to prevent the spread of Communism.

American anti-colonial attitudes have various roots. In the 1950s and 1960s the struggle against Communism in the Third World fuelled this feeling that the colonies must go, and as a strategy it had certain merits but those colonies struggling against the Imperial powers needed aid and were able to play off the Soviet Union against the United States, who began to compete in their support for the various 'liberation struggles'.

The Americans regarded colonialism as a doctrine that supplied nations with a reason to support Communism. Therefore, or so ran the thinking, if colonialism was removed and a democratic government put in its place, many fertile fields for Communist expansion would become barren ground. This is probably true but there were two hard facts that combined to militate against these democratic benefits coming to fruition in most of the newly liberated nations.

The first is the matter of timing. Most of the colonial territories were simply not ready for independence by the time they got it. The bulk of the populations did not understand what democracy entails. Even today, people in many Third World countries believe that if they have 'democracy' then good things will automatically follow.

Democracy is a hard doctrine, requiring a sophisticated electorate and was a new, even fantastic concept in many Third World countries in the heady days after the end of the Second World War. One part of the concept that proved very hard to put over was the notion that one's political enemies should be allowed a say in public affairs and a seat in Parliament.

The second difficulty lay in the matter of to whom power should be handed over when the imperialists withdrew. Clearly, it must go to someone or some party with a grasp of administration and affairs. This usually meant military officers or the political, foreign-educated élite. As a result, most of the 'liberated nations' rapidly became either military dictatorships or one-party states. In either case the losers were the ordinary people.

The US Government was not overly concerned with that in the late 1940s. Colonialism was wrong and created a breeding ground for Communism and America had not poured out blood and treasure in the Second World War in order to hand the people for whom they had fought back to their imperial masters.

Their solution was to work for the destruction of the colonial empires and obtain freedom for the people; this was not done with any evil intent but it might have helped if the US Government had known or remembered a proverb from the Kikuyu tribe in Kenya. 'If you throw away your old ways and familiar customs you must first make sure you have something of value to put in their place.'

If the need to stem the advance of Communism was the main consideration for the United States Goverment, some of the others were more high-minded. Many of the reasons for this anti-colonial enthusiasm can be traced to the foundation of the United States and the deep feelings for the concept of liberty cherished by the American people. Field Marshal Bramall a former Chief of the Defence Staff, touched on this point when interviewed in 1995:

> The Americans detested the British Empire; it was an obsession with people like Roosevelt but I don't think it was motivated by any desire to do us down in particular or take over British trade with the Empire. That may have been the effect but that was not the principle. The Americans genuinely believed that the British Empire was wrong and they wanted it done away with.
>
> They were quite blind to the good things about it, certainly

until Vietnam taught them a hard lesson. They got another one in Central America with their support for terrible right-wing regimes in Salvador and the rising in Nicaragua, but their views were based on principles, not profit or even politics. It was a simple matter of believing that colonialism was wrong.

The Americans have always – or at least until recently – cherished an almost Puritan view about their country and there is nothing base or mean-minded about that. The United States was founded on high ideals and – at least until recently – has generally tried to live up to them and be an example to the world. A year after the Massachusetts Bay Company was founded in 1629, John Winthrop, the leader of the company and the first Governor of the colony, enshrined this belief in a memorable phrase:

> We shall be as a city on a hill. The eyes of all people are upon us. So that if we shall deal falsely with our God in this work we have undertaken, and so cause Him to withdraw his present help, we shall be sorry and a by-word throughout the world.

That phrase, about 'the city on the hill', has been frequently quoted by American Presidents, and this notion that the United States must set an example to the world is not ignoble. The problem is that not all the problems of the world can be solved by example.

Reactions to America's anti-colonial stance varied. The French largely ignored it and went their own way. As a result, since pressure did no good and produced an alarming anti-American reaction in Paris, the Americans soon gave up and either left the French alone, or solicited their aid carefully. The French withdrew from the military side of NATO – but continued to be involved in the political part – sent the Foreign Legion to crush rebellions in their former African colonies, supported bloodstained tyrants like Bokassa, fought the long and bitter Algerian War, defied the United States whenever the mood took them and paid very little attention to the wishes and dictates of Washington. Had Britain done even half of these things in her territories, the Americans would have had a fit and brought the matter to the attention of the United Nations. The

British case was different and the main reason for that difference was economic.

Britain was heavily in debt to the United States in 1945 and needed American support to prop up the pound. That, however, was only one lever and as Britain recovered from the war that excuse for appeasement fell away. On the colonial empire issue there was little need for argument because Britain had always intended to give up her Empire at some date in the future. When it came to granting independence to the colonies, the Americans were pushing at an open door.

The only real argument was over the timing but carping about 'British Imperialism' made America look good at the UN and in the Third World and gave American politicians a warm virtuous feeling. The major reason for Britain's failure to profit from Anglo-American relations in the post-war years was, however, entirely Britain's fault

The final, fatal and most enduring lever deployed against British interests – was – and is – the conviction of successive British Governments that they enjoyed some form of favoured status with the United States. They also believe, some of the Prime Ministers excessively so, that this status – this 'Special Relationship' – gave the British influence in Washington which they were anxious, even excessively anxious, to retain. One cost of staying friendly with the United States was the rapid winding up of the British Empire.

The first step towards this end came even before the United States entered the war. In August 1941, Winston Churchill and the American President, Franklin D. Roosevelt, met and drew up a declaration of their shared political views, a declaration which came to be called the Atlantic Charter. This Charter contained clauses 'ending discrimination by all States, large or small, against access to the trade and raw materials of the world'.

These clauses struck at directly Imperial Preference, the trade links that bound the British Empire together, and were designed to permit US access to Britain's worldwide markets. This would ensure that the United States did not plunge back into another Depression when the war boom ended. Other clauses in the Charter covered freedom 'for all the countries of the world' and the Americans soon made it clear that these clauses applied as much to the colonies of their allies, the Colonial Powers, as they did to the Nazi-dominated states of Europe.

When Churchill realised that the Americans were making this claim he strongly rejected that conclusion, but within months of the Atlantic Charter meeting, Roosevelt was declaring that 'The British have signed the Atlantic Charter and the United States Government means to make them live up to it.' In his speech at the Mansion House Dinner in November 1942, Churchill replied bluntly to this statement: 'We mean to hold our own,' he growled. 'I have not become the King's First Minister to preside over the break-up of the British Empire.' Fine words indeed but by the time War ended the world was no longer listening to Winston Churchill.

At Yalta, in 1945, President Roosevelt took the side of the Soviet dictator Joseph Stalin, since Stalin, whatever his faults – and murdering millions of Soviet and Polish citizens was not the least of them – was not tainted with the evil of imperialism. Stalin replied to this American naivity by seizing half of Western Europe at the War's end, and but for the atomic bomb would have seized the other half.

After the War this anti-colonial inspired American meddling continued – in Palestine, in Africa, over the Egyptian Canal Zone, in Cyprus and, most fatally, over the Suez operation of 1956. An emerging state or colony had only to display anti-colonial colours to attract American support for any suggestion, however unreasonable, and however much this support worked against the interests of her former ally and democratic partner, Great Britain. Towards Great Britain itself the United States remained benign, writing off most of the war debt and giving Britain vital economic aid under the Marshall Plan. Without such American generosity, Britain would have foundered, but this generosity did not extend to Britain's colonial Empire.

Britain's general acquiescence to this continual badgering was undoubtly caused by her weak economic position, but, as with all appeasement, bowing to America's wishes did Britain little good. Claims of a 'Special Relationship' or that 'the British will be the Greeks in America's Roman Empire' should have been seen for what they were, pathetic attempts to claim or retain a place at the top table when world affairs came to be discussed. This was always an unlikely outcome, given the relative strengths of the two nations as the decades passed.

The British Government should have realised that the 'Special Relationship' – a phrase rarely heard in the United States, even inside the Washington Beltway – in so far as it ever existed, was strictly a one-way affair. Britain supported the United States in every issue – Vietnam being one notable exception – and the United States did whatever she thought her national interests demanded, whether the British liked it or not. This meddling began in 1942 and has continued ever since, even into the 1990s when the United States became increasingly involved in the troubles of Northern Ireland.

There is, of course, a reason for such meddling, and altruism is only part of it. Another reason for exerting pressure on Britain over her imperial or colonial affairs is to gain votes and popularity with that new and ever-expanding universe, America's large ethnic minorities.

At the turn of the century, US President Theodore Roosevelt deplored the existence of 'hyphenated-Americans' and in an address to the Republican Convention he declared, 'There can be no fifty-fifty Americanism in this country. There is room here for only one hundred per cent Americanism, for those who are Americans and nothing else.'

That is not the way it is today. The American President supported unrestricted Jewish immigration into Palestine in 1947, whatever effect it had on the Arabs or the British Mandate, to ensure the support of the American-Jewish lobby. To placate the Irish-Americans he supports Irish nationalism and by extension IRA terrorism within the United Kingdom. This is not how the subject is viewed in America but that is what it comes down to in practice. If that means the British must always be in the wrong, so be it. Getting elected, or re-elected, is all that matters.

The United States cannot be blamed for this. The American Government had their policies over the Empire and the means to pursue them and if exercising those policies went down well with the home electorate so much the better. The real fault lies with successive British Governments and especially with the majority of Britain's post-War Prime Ministers, who should have charged a stiff price over the years for their political, diplomatic and military support.

Few people value that which they get for nothing. Britain too has leverage and her leaders should have used it. Without British support the United States would be fully exposed to the chill winds of international criticism. Without Britain's uncritical support America's problems with the Soviet Union, Red China, in the Gulf War, in Bosnia, with the Arabs and in Latin America would have been far worse. If that support had been more critical, or less reliable, the USA might not be so inclined to take it for granted. This support has not gained the British people any visible advantage with the United States Government. None of this would have altered the outcome but United States involvement in the End of Empire story is significant and continuous and needs to be understood. In spite of Churchill's ringing declarations in 1942, the British Empire of his childhood was doomed. Over the next twenty years the British Empire would be transformed into a Commomweath of Nations, perhaps as a face-saving political gesture, perhaps from a sincere desire to retain the best of the old in the face of the new. Opinions seem to be divided on this point.

With some of the general background covered and the two main parameters defined – the nature of Empire and the limits of this book – it is time to consider the British Empire in general, how it was acquired, organised and administered, scotching in the process a number of popular misconceptions – the first of which is that the 'British Empire' as a uniform, centrally – controlled 'Empire' ever really existed.

There is a widely held belief that the British Empire was much like the Roman Empire, a unified state, run from a power-base in the United Kingdom and ruled locally by proconsuls, Governors or Viceroys, who reported to the seat of imperial power and took every opportunity to oppress the local people and line their own pockets.

The British Empire was not like that at all. The British Empire was nothing if not varied, and those who worked in it regarded their responsibilities to the people under their charge as far more important than their duty to the 'powers-that-be' at the Colonial Office in London.

William Broadway served in the Survey Directorate of the Royal Engineers in West Africa, Kenya and Tanganyika and can enlarge on this point:

Before World War II, Britain was a great power. Well, the War drained the British Lion of its strength and left it on its knees. Besides, Britain and the colonies were changing rapidly; it would be true to say that after the war no Colonial Power, not the Dutch, not the French, certainly not the British, was in any position to pay for the changes that the Colonial people expected, though Britain tried harder than France or Holland. Nevertheless, we should have brought the local administrations up to date to allow for change. In fact, the local administration appeared to do the opposite, widening the gap between the Colonial Administration and the local people.

As early as 1947 it was very obvious to me that this was happening in Kenya. There was unrest among the Kikuyu, which eventually led to the Mau-Mau problem in the 1950s. Many thousands of African and Asian and West Indian servicemen came from the Colonies to fight, and die, for the Allied cause during the War; I met a number of them during my service and like the British servicemen of World War I they dreamed of returning home to a better world, one fit for heroes. Like the British soldiers after World War I they were to be disillusioned.

I believe that the British left their colonies too soon. We should have stayed another ten years, more or less, depending on the particular country. This could only have been achieved by modernising the administrations and introducing more democratic institutions to stave off unrest. It was necessary to understand the local politicians and involve them in negotiations and decision-making. As it is, by going too early we allowed an autocratic and undemocratic class of people to gain power, which has made the vast majority of our former Colonial people poorer, particularly those in the rural areas.

Matthew Nash, who served with The Black Watch during the Borneo 'Confrontation' with Indonesia in the 1960s, reports similar opinions from Sarawak:

During my service we visited many longhouses of the Sea Dyaks or the Iban in Sarawak or North Borneo, sometimes alone, sometimes with a British political officer. The locals were very friendly and very pro-British and there were pictures of the Royal Family everywhere; we always had a good time.

I once asked a village chief: 'What do you want?' and he replied, 'We would like our independence eventually, but we are not ready for it yet, so for now we would like to stay with you . . . so why is The Queen leaving us?'

The political officer was close to tears as he tried to explain why the British Government wanted nothing more to do with them and that they would have to become Malaysian. He didn't say it quite like that, of course. Once we had an American TV crew filming a piece on the 'reluctant' British handing over their Empire and they got a real surprise when the Ibans said they did not want the British to go – absolutely not.

Yet another view comes from Christopher Blake who served throughout the Second World War in the Somerset Light Infantry and as an officer in the Dogra Regiment of the Indian Army. After the war he joined the Civil Service in Malaya where he remained until independence.

I believe that one of the reasons for the Empire's rapid decline was the sheer exhaustion of the British people. Two World Wars, won by the skin of her teeth, had left Britain tired, impoverished and disillusioned. Another element was the advent of a Labour Party Government in 1945, to whose adherents the word 'Empire' had always been anathema. These factors, along with political demands from within and without, especially from that former colony, the United States, made the 'End of Empire' inevitable.

Most people have heard that statement, that the British Empire was created in a fit of absence of mind. In the political sense that is quite right, for there were no deliberate attempts to take over countries, either peacefully or by force . . . the British Government never made a conscious decision to acquire a particular colony; even Sind, now part of Pakistan, was acquired by General Charles Napier without the wish or blessing of the British Government.

That is not a fashionable view today. From what has been written by some twentieth-century critics, a man from Mars might get the impression that the British Empire was acquired by force and ruled by vain, corrupt autocrats, addicted to alcohol and women. As with other things British, the worst denigrators are the British themselves, an ailment described as 'post-colonial guilt'. Even the BBC is not free from this affliction. I can recall a BBC reporter interviewing a Minister in the Malaysian Government, and when the Minister spoke with approval of the British influence, the reporter looked puzzled because praise for the Empire was 'not what the BBC wanted'.

For the last forty years British schoolchildren have been told, among other untruths, that the Empire was ruled in the interests of Great Britain and that the local people always took second place. That is sheer bias. Force was used in the Empire, of course, for example to suppress communal riots between Hindus and Muslims in India, but the events at Amritsar in 1919 are always quoted by our denigrators as if they were an everyday occurrence.

This sort of sniping has to be refuted by the facts. The British Empire was not held by force. How could a few thousand British troops have contained the four hundred million of the Indian population against their will?

The Empire's transition into a Commonwealth was conducted peacefully and by mutual agreement in all but a handful of countries. In Malaya, for example, force was used to prevent a Communist takeover, not to delay independence. In my opinion, wherever it took root, the British way of life can claim to be the the most powerful influence for good that the world his yet seen.

It had its faults, certainly; there were those who made little attempt to disguise their contempt for local practices or the local people, or were reluctant to accept the friendship of local people, but there were many more who worked in the fields to improve the crops or tried to improve the lot of the local people, men who commanded respect. Above all they were honest, in countries where corruption is a part of daily life.

Over the centuries, hundreds of thousands of British people, civil and military, gave their lives to upholding the British Empire, but let a Spaniard turned American, George Santayana, have the last word on the Empire. 'Never,' he wrote, 'since the heroic days of Greece has the world had such a sweet, just, boyish master.

The British Empire was not built to endure or created by a desire for permanent conquest. It was always the intention of the British

Government that the territories of the Empire should advance to freedom on a steady path from dependent colonies through internal self-government to Dominion status and eventual independence. The hope was that these countries would then remain prosperous, democratic countries, able to trade successfully and profitably with the 'Mother Country' while linked to her by the loose ties of Crown and Commonwealth. Even if the reality turned out to be somewhat different, this was the fundamental, high-minded idea.

It has already been pointed out – but it will bear repeating – that the real argument was over the time this process from dependent colony to independence should take, but one of the problems in winding up the Empire was the sheer diversity of the component parts. The situation in the various countries covered in this book will be described in detail in the relevant chapters but to illustrate this diversity some attention should be paid to how large parts of the Empire came into existence in the first place.

By 1945, the older countries of the British Empire, the so-called 'Old', Dominions, Australia, Canada, New Zealand and South Africa were all self-governing, independent states and had been for many years, but they still displayed considerable diversity. For example, Australia, though a Dominion, was also a 'Commonwealth', one nation created from a number of former colonies.

New South Wales gained its Civil Constitution as long ago as 1823 and the Colony of New South Wales became self-governing in 1842. Tasmania had been established as a colony in 1817 and Victoria and South Australia soon followed. These four Colonies were all self-governing by 1855. By the end of the nineteenth century, Australia contained six Colonies; a Federal Constitution which established the 'Commonwealth of Australia' was drawn up in 1900 and accepted by the British Parliament in 1901, since when Australia has been independent.

The first British settlers to arrive on the two islands which became New Zealand found an established, intelligent, native civilisation, the Maoris. The British annexed the islands in 1840, having acquired much Maori land by the Treaty of Waitangi. This treaty had recently been called into question and the Maoris have been compensated for the loss of their lands with a grant of £500 million but arguments over the Treaty are not new. This Treaty and the land issue led to the first Maori War in 1843 and conflict between the settlers and the Maoris continued until the 1870s, though New Zealand became self-governing in 1856 and a Dominion in 1907. During this time six New Zealand provinces were established, each with an elected Council with Maori delegates sitting in the House of Representatives.

In Canada, the third of the Old Dominions, there was, and is, another complication, the simmering dispute between Anglophone and Francophone Canada, essentially between the Catholic French-speaking province of Quebec and the rest of the country which had been settled by the British. After the defeat of the French General Montcalm by General Wolfe on the Plains of Abraham in 1759, Canada was first divided into two colonies, Upper or English Canada and Lower or French Canada. This attempt to satisfy the two main national groups did not endure.

The first step towards modern Canada came with the Durham Report of 1839, which proposed merging these two colonies and then granting full self-government to the entire country. Self-Government was established by Act of Parliament in 1841, but only affected the eastern parts of the country. Problems arose as the Dominion expanded and more colonies or 'Provinces' were created in the West. The answer was to federate, and the Dominion of Canada was duly created by the British North America Act of 1867, the first Act to employ the word 'Dominion'. The first act of this new 'Dominion of Canada' was to purchase most of Western Canada from the Hudson's Bay Company, which had held land in Canada since the seventeenth century.

In 1867, British Columbia, separated from the rest of Canada by vast prairies and the hard terrain of the Rocky Mountains, was not a Canadian province but a British colony and only entered the Canadian Confederation in 1871, after having obtained the assurance that the Canadian Pacific Railway would be extended over the mountains to Vancouver. Other parts of Canada were even more reluctant to sign up with this new Dominion; Newfoundland, an island discovered by Henry VII's navigator, John Cabot, in 1497, refused to join the new Dominion and only became part of Canada in 1949.

South Africa, divided between the native Bantu, the Boers and the British, was the scene of frequent disturbances and at least three major wars in the latter days of the Victorian Empire, the Zulu War, the Boer War and the South African War of 1894–1902. After this last war was over, the British Government, with rare foresight, gave immediate internal self-government to the two Boer Republics, the Transvaal and the Orange Free State, and in 1908 these two Boer 'Republics' joined with the British Colonies in Natal and the Cape to form the Union of South Africa, which came into existence in 1910.

This 'Union' was neither a Federation nor a Dominion. The Union of South Africa was rather like the United Kingdom of Great Britain and Northern Ireland, where one Parliament makes laws for all the states or provinces in that Union, though – just to make it confusing – the 'States' of that Union may retain laws and powers of their own.

The laws of the Union of South Africa and the Republic of South Africa which followed it gave little attention to the interests and aspirations of the Bantu people, but the resulting apartheid policy was ended by the overthrow of the Nationalist Government and the election of President Nelson Mandela in 1993. Apartheid was the reason South Africa left the Commonwealth, and now that it has ended South Africa has hastened to return.

Turning to Asia, the differences continue. In India in 1858 the British Government took over only 'British India', that part of the country ruled by that juggernaut of trade, the East India Company, before the Indian Mutiny.

The rulers of British India had to contend with the beliefs and customs of the three main religious groups, Hindus, Muslims and Sikhs, who were frequently at odds with one another. The British also had border problems in the North West and fought many wars and campaigns against Afghanistan or against Pathan tribesmen raiding across the North-West Frontier. An additional problem was that the British never ruled directly in every corner of the sub-continent. India also contained hundreds of semi-Independent or 'Princely States', ruled by Nawabs, Rajahs or Maharajahs, all of whom had direct treaty links with the British Crown.

The territory occupied by the 'Princely States' amounted to about half the Indian land mass and contained about a quarter of the population. Some of these states, like Kashmir, Hyderabad and Mysore, were of considerable size, while others were little larger than an English park. The Indian Princes paid allegiance to the Viceroy of India as the representative of the British Crown. This was but one of his duties for the Viceroy was also responsible to the British Government for the affairs of 'British India' – the Raj – in his role as Governor-General of India.

In British India his rule was total but the Princes retained control of local affairs in their States, though all were advised by a 'British Resident', an official appointed by the Viceroy, who could recommend that the ruler be deposed if he acted unwisely. Many of the princes maintained armies but matters of defence and foreign affairs were delegated to the Viceroy. There were also anomalies within the States, as in Kashmir, where a Hindu ruler ruled over a mostly Muslim population, a potential source of trouble and a circumstance which would cause great unrest between India and Pakistan in the decades after Independence.

The smaller colonies in Asia, Malaya, Singapore, Sabah, Sarawak, the 'settler colonies' in East Africa and the islands of the Caribbean, presented a similar hodge-podge of political and administrative arrangements and these will be explored when the conflicts in those places come under discussion in later chapters.

The British Empire was therefore not a homogenous creation but exceedingly complex, and these complexities were compounded by the various situations within the various colonies. When the British came to give up a colony, they could not simply hand over power to anyone who wanted it and take the next boat home. While the Empire flourished the British attempted to cater in a wide variety of ways for the different situations, peoples, religions and customs which they inherited in assuming their Imperial responsibility, and they could not abandon this responsibility at the first demand for independence.

So, if the countries were so diverse and the desire for independence so strong, what were the chains that bound these disparate countries together into one worldwide Empire? The writer Jan Morris has given a few answers to that question:

> Those verses about 'Britannia ruling the waves' were not a jingoistic shout of self-satisfaction but an injunction to greatness. The Empire itself was not simply a display of power, or an opportunity to profit, but an impulse to achievement.
>
> To the British of the Imperial era, anything was possible, nothing was beyond their strength or their ambition, and what ambition it was; a few million inhabitants of an offshore island exerting their

will upon time! They made their language the *lingua franca* of half the world. They shifted peoples, animals, flora, from one continent to another. From soccer to Parliamentary democracy, they left behind a legacy of Britishness that was permanently to change the face of nations.

These were some of the Imperial motivations and achievements and these created the strongest Imperial links. In the great days of the Empire, there were other bonds, some no less strong for being less tangible. The first of these was loyalty to the Crown and the 'Mother Country'.

Today, at the end of the twentieth century, it is hard to realise the enthusiasm and affection that once existed throughout the Empire for those two bastions of the Imperial ideal. This was not a worldwide delusion, cherished in 'pukka' clubs and Colonial institutions, but a fact of life in every corner of the Empire.

Even those people who had never been to Britain and whose families had been settled for generations in some well-established corner of the Empire, in the savannahs of Kenya or the red deserts of Australia, would refer to Great Britain as 'Home' and the great rite of passage for Antipodean youth was a year or two living and working in Britain.

Many students from both the old and new countries and colonies of the Empire came to Britain to attend university and a great number stayed on to make their home in the Old Country. Although Britain is not often referred to as 'Home' these days, that visiting tradition continues. It even operates in reverse today when many young British people spend their 'Gap Year' before university travelling and working in the Commonwealth.

This loyalty to the Crown and the 'British connection' is understandable in those countries which were largely created and colonised by people from the British Islands, but it extended far beyond those limitations and found its strongest expression in the hard days of war.

On 3 September 1939, when Britain declared war on Nazi Germany, the first message of support came from the tiny West Indian island of Barbados. Thousands of West Indians came to serve in the British Army and the Royal Air Force and many remained to make their homes in the British islands after the war was over.

Robert Menzies, the Prime Minister of Australia declared: 'Where Britain stands, stands the people of the Empire and the British world', and thousands of Australian servicemen promptly joined the fight against the Axis powers.

Times change; when Britain took up the Argentine challenge over the Falkland Islands in 1982, the first action of the Australian Government was to order those Australian soldiers and airmen serving with British Forces to return home immediately. Home they went, but with great reluctance. New Zealand, on the other hand, instantly deployed a destroyer to the Persian Gulf in order to free a British ship for the Falklands Task Force.

From the Old Dominions in 1940 came such forces as the first-class 2nd New Zealand Division, a force which contained many hard fighting Maori battalions, which fought in the Western Desert and at the Battle of Cassino in Italy. From Canada came seamen to man the corvettes and fight the Atlantic convoys through to Britain, airmen to serve in the bomber crews of the Royal Canadian Air Force and the superb Canadian infantry which stormed the beaches of Dieppe and Normandy before sweeping on to the frontiers of the Reich.

To the war in Europe and North Africa came thousands of Australians to serve in the Royal Air Force, or in the crack Australian infantry divisions which fought Field Marshal Rommel's doughty Afrika Korps all the way from Alamein to Tunisia. From Kenya and Uganda came the men of the King's African Rifles, to fight in Somalia and in the jungles of Burma.

Every country in the Empire sent men and women to the fray but the largest contribution of all came from India. The Viceroy of India declared war on behalf of Britain without consulting his Indian ministers, but more than a million Indians came to fight for the King-Emperor in North Africa and Burma and all of them were volunteers; there was no 'draft' or conscription in India.

So they came, in their tens of thousands, from every corner of the world to help the 'Mother Country' and the Empire. They came for a great many reasons. Some came from a sense of loyalty and duty, others from a desire for travel and adventure, some because their friends were going and they did not wish to stay behind. Most of them came because they felt it was the right thing to do.

The British Empire had its faults but an Empire which could command such a following was never a despotism. The British wanted trade but they never demanded tribute from the colonies. Quite the contrary; all the money raised by taxation within a colony was spent within the colony and the sums required were frequently topped up by contributions from the British Government and the British taxpayer. The Empire was a family; in 1887 the Queen Victoria India Famine Relief Fund raised the sum of £2 million in Britain, equivalent to over £20 million today, and that without the aid of television or the mass media.

Britain was also responsible for Imperial Defence. Although the contribution of the Empire soldiers, sailors and airmen to the defence of Great Britain must never be overlooked and has already been acknowledged, the main burden of Imperial Defence at any time, and especially in time of war, fell on the British taxpayer and the British serviceman. Since Britain was the largest country in terms of wealth this was only fair but it should not for that reason be forgotten.

It has been maintained that when the time came to wind up the Empire the British either stayed too long or left too soon. That depends on the situation in each country but in many cases the British seem to have left at the right time, even if matters went awry later.

Field Marshal Lord Carver, a former Chief of the Defence Staff, has firm opinions on this point: 'Once you have decided to go, then frankly, the sooner you go the better, and that works for nations as well as people. Besides, once everyone knows you are leaving, your power base has gone and with it all your influence; no one is interested in your views or opinions. They have to butter up the new administration or get jobs with the new rulers. Far better to go and let them get on with it. Aden was a mess, but otherwise I think we got it about right.'

H.E. Maude, a British Administrator and historian of the South Pacific, saw independence come to his corner of the Empire:

I was at one time or another Administrator of Pitcairn, Consul to the Kingdom of Tonga, Chief Assistant Secretary to the Western Pacific High Commission and Administrator (or Resident) of the Gilbert and Ellice Islands Colony. I could see the end of the Colonial time looming and joined the International South Pacific Commission, first as Assistant Secretary-General and then in charge of Social Development Research.

In the Gilbert and Ellice islands, I think we left at just about the right time, at least for the educated élite among the islanders. For the ordinary villagers it was different and I doubt if they are as well off now. I remember an old man getting up after I had given a pep talk on the virtues of independence.

'Of course,' he said, nodding at me, 'this man thinks it a good thing for us to be without the Europeans who have lived with us since the Flag [1882]. They can all go home to their own country and their own *utu* [extended families] and be happy. But as for me, I think it is a lousy idea. We trust the Europeans, for they have nothing to gain from us and can take important decisions. But as for us . . .' (and he gave a searching look at the hundreds seated around him), 'I don't trust any of you and you don't trust me. Why should we shout for joy?'

Ten years later I went to receive a Doctorate at the University of the South Pacific in Fuji. The other recipient of a Doctorate that day was the President of the Republic which followed us in the Gilberts. Where else would the President of a free Republic walk hand in hand with the symbol of the oppressing 'Imperialist' power he had supplanted?

D.J. Sparrow soldiered with the Royal Marine Commandos in the 1960s:

There will always be comments, good and bad, about the British Empire. Our forefathers were no different from those men who went to the Moon. Some of us will always want to see what's on the other side of the hill and that's the way we were.

We don't have anything to be ashamed of. Our country has done more to help those countries marked red on the old maps than any other Colonial power, and we helped them even after they got their independence. Some countries who wanted to go it alone, like Tanganyika in 1964, or Malaysia during Confrontation, soon came back asking for our help . . . and they got it. The list is long and a word of thanks from one or two of them would not go amiss. As for those in Britain who say we did more harm than good, they are commenting from their armchairs. Those of us who were out there in the old days know different and I am glad our story is finally being told.

Apart from a shared history and trade and self-interest, two other powerful bonds holding the Empire together were those of law and language. Of these the latter is arguably the most important. If the British brought more than one long-lasting benefit to the countries they occupied, the English language must rank among the most important. In India, though Hindi is the the main language, some two hundred other languages are in common use; as a result the language mainly used for communication and business is, and probably always will be, English.

The other bond, the rule of law, has been much reduced in many countries of the Commonwealth in the decades since independence. While the Empire endured, every subject of the Empire was equal under the law and that tradition may be revived some day. This principle may have been overlooked at times and repressive laws were certainly enacted and enforced in various colonies, especially during times of war or civil strife, but during the days of Empire the people of many countries generally enjoyed a better system of justice than they had known before – or since – and most of them were aware of that fact.

The British Parliamentary system is not necessarily suitable for every newly formed country, especially for those with an unsophisticated electorate. The British system of Parliamentary government has often been changed and adapted even in those countries which employ it but the majority of the countries of the former Empire still follow a legal and constitutional system which is recognisably based on the British model.

It certainly varies, and to quote Jake Jacobs again, 'The role of a "loyal Opposition" in particular, is one which many African and Asian countries find hard to grasp', but as a system to aspire to, the British model remains intact.

A final bond – though the list is endless – must be the British educational system and to a lesser degree, the Anglican Church and the Christian religion. Opinions vary on whether the actions of the Christian missionaries were entirely beneficial in every corner of the Empire but their intentions were good. The missionaries gave many of the colonial people their first taste of education and provided essential medical care in places where no Government facilities existed. In many parts of Asia and Africa the education of the ordinary people was largely in the hands of the missionaries and their influence in creating an educated class was vital.

In more sophisticated communities, like India and parts of Asia, private schools were set up for the children of the local élite, often on the lines of British public schools. The buttress of this educational platform was the role of the British universities, which not only sent lecturers and professors to teach in overseas institutions, but also welcomed tens of thousands of scholars from all over the Empire. These came to Britain to finish their studies in law and medicine, science and engineering, and all the elements required of the modern, independent and democratic state they hoped and intended to create on their return home. Indeed, it is among these professional people that the Commonwealth bonds are strongest today.

Clearly, opinions will vary on whether the British Empire was a force for good or ill but while the final judgement may be deferred the good work done should not be forgotten. History will make many judgements as the British Empire fades from living memory. The history of the independence period has already been rewritten in many of those countries which once paid allegiance to the King-Emperor and the versions vary. Perhaps such revisionism is inevitable but those soldiers and civilians who served in the Empire have a right to state their case and put their evidence forward on how it really was as the Empire ended.

It might be said that none of this really matters now. Old wounds have healed, old enmities have been forgotten or forgiven, fresh alliances forged. The decline of Empires is a fact of history and in fading away the British Empire is simply following a path that other Empires have taken before it.

The 'End of Empire' was inevitable but how it ended, the story of that 'Fighting Retreat', is still a complex, fascinating, and entertaining tale which begins in India, in the troubled years shortly after the end of the Second World War.

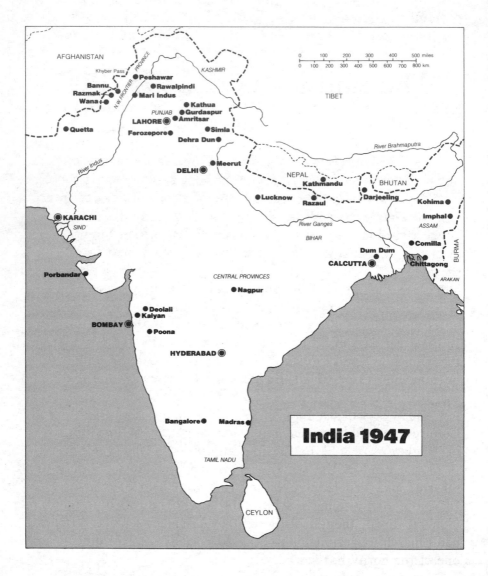

India 1947

AFGHANISTAN

Khyber Pass

N.W. FRONTIER PROVINCE

KASHMIR

TIBET

Bannu
Razmak
Wana
Quetta

Peshawar
Rawalpindi
Mari Indus

Kathua
Gurdaspur
PUNJAB
LAHORE Amritsar
Ferozepore
Simla
Dehra Dun

River Indus

DELHI Meerut

NEPAL
Kathmandu

River Brahmaputra

BHUTAN
Darjeeling

Kohima

KARACHI
SIND

Lucknow
Razaul

River Ganges

BIHAR

Imphal
ASSAM

Comilla

BURMA

Porbandar

CENTRAL PROVINCES
Nagpur

Dum Dum
CALCUTTA

Chittagong

ARAKAN

Deolali
Kalyan
BOMBAY
Poona

HYDERABAD

Bangalore Madras

TAMIL NADU

CEYLON

0   100   200   300   400   500 miles
0   100 200 300 400 500 600 700 800 km.

3

The End in India: 1945–1947

They say there's a troopship just leaving Bombay,
Bound for Old Blighty's shore,
Heavily ladened with time-expired men,
Bound for the land they adore . . .

Bless 'em All

In the great days of Empire, and for a good many years afterwards, British soldiers and civilians posted abroad travelled to their duties on ocean liners or troopships. A trip on a troopship was part of the Imperial experience, a way of learning, in the space of a few short weeks, just how things stood in the far corners of the Empire where the pecking order was far different from that back in 'Blighty'.

At the head of the social order stood the senior colonial civil servants and their lady-wives, together with their daughters. Then came the Army, King's Service, of course, ranged by rank from General down, though below that of Brigadier an officer from a good marching regiment stood ahead socially over an officer from one of the horny-handed Service Corps.

Then came the businessman, the 'box-wallah', who might, just, be worthy of notice if he had contacts or had been to a very good school. Otherwise he was 'in trade', a form of social death, and could not be invited to regimental messes or the more splendid functions. Finally, at the very bottom of the heap, was the British private soldier, the 'squaddie'. All these people came together briefly when the trooper sailed for the East.

Troopships were not the most comfortable way to travel, especially for the Other Ranks, as Marine Terry Brown of 42 Commando recalls from his voyage to the Far East in 1950:

> Our troopship was run in the usual democratic fashion. A few dozen officers had about two-thirds of the ship to swan about in and the men, a thousand of them, were crammed into what was left, living like pigs. We crossed the Bay of Biscay in a howling gale and if I could have found my way to the upper deck I would cheerfully have flung myself overboard. We went through the Suez Canal, exchanging ribald shouts with the British troops stationed in that hell-hole, and stopped in Aden for a run ashore, where I bought a watch from a trader. The watch stopped as the trooper sailed out past Steamer Point and never went again . . . and so we went to Malaya, to fight the Communist bandits.

Even as the British Raj was ending, the 'troopers' were still taking men to India. Michael Wood, a young second–lieutenant in the Royal Artillery, was on the last British troopship to leave Bombay in 1948:

> My first recollection of India was when we arrived, also on a troopship, looking down from the deck of the M.V. *Georgic* on a dockside teeming with barefoot, turbanned, dark-skinned dockers, many bearded, in their startling white garments gathered up between their thin, bowed legs. I don't think any Indians wore trousers in those days.
>
> This was in mid-1946. We were officer cadets aged eighteen or nineteen, having joined up too late to take part in the War, most of us taking only our second look at a foreign shore (the first being Cairo on our way out), so we looked on the Indians with curiosity and they looked at us with . . . what? In retrospect I suppose some sort of distaste or even hatred, but it didn't show at the time, if it existed at all.
>
> My second recollection was the realisation that three and a half thousand miles and twenty-one days sailing was not that far after all. On disembarking we were marched on to a real train with a huge steam engine about twice the size of any we had seen in

England. At the first junction outside Bombay the train stopped and we got talking to a British military policeman standing in the sidings. I asked him where he came from as he had a Yorkshire accent and it turned out he lived only a hundred yards from my home! It was like that in the Old Empire.

The train took us to Kalyan, a transit camp for troops arriving in India. I don't remember too much about Kalyan but I do remember the char-wallah who came round each day at four in the afternoon, dispensing strong sweet tea out of a huge copper urn and selling delicious, very sweet, oily cakes.

On to the Officers' Cadet Training Unit (OCTU) in Bangalore, South India via Poona. Bangalore was like a Colonial version of Cheltenham or Harrogate, but the climate was better. We didn't see much of India in Bangalore as we were too busy learning to be officers in the Indian Army. We were taught by British officers and Sikh NCOs who shouted at us and served courteously in the Mess by white-coated Indian waiters.

After a few months of this India was granted independence and we were told that the Indian Army didn't want us. The British infantry had too many officers, so we were wooed by the Royal Signals, the Royal Engineers and Royal Artillery. I chose the latter and was transferred to the RA Depot in Deolali, a hundred miles north-east of Bombay. Deolali (the origin of 'Deolali Tap', a state of temporary madness induced by service in India . . . people who had it were said to be 'a bit Deolali') was a revelation after the bullshit and stiffness of Bangalore. We also got out and about more and saw something of rural India.

I had a bearer in Deolali called Tukram, who told me he had once been Winston Churchill's bearer. I was suitably impressed with that reference until I heard from my colleagues that all their bearers had been Churchill's bearer too. The closing months of the British rule in India passed reasonably uneventfully as far as we were concerned. We did have some action, in that we had to supplement the dwindling British forces in Bombay during some of the riots in the few months before the Brits finally left. The Indian police, however, needed little help from us; a handful of them could put more fear into the rioters than a whole battalion of British troops.

India was a way of life. We stayed at gentlemen's clubs which would not have been out of place in London's St James's, the porters and waiters in fine white uniforms treated us exactly as they would treat a general. I understand that not much has changed in these establishments; a friend from Hong Kong, an ex-Brigadier and General Manager of the Royal Hong Kong Yacht Club, stayed at the Bombay Yacht Club in 1994 and said it was like stepping back in time.

In Deolali we detected no feeling of hostility from the local people. The locals' main concern was how they were going to get on without the trade the British troops had brought them. The few British civilians we met intended to stay and thought life would go on as before, '. . . for how could the Indians possibly manage without them?'

The last battalion to leave was the Somerset Light Infantry, in about February 1948, but there were still plenty of British troops in India and Pakistan after that, trying to sort things out. Lord Mountbatten, who became the first Governor-General of India – and Pakistan – after Independence, gave a formal send-off to the 'last British troops to leave India' in August 1948, but *we* were really the last, following two or three weeks later on the SS *Otranto*, upper deck this time as we had been commissioned by the time we left. The ship was carrying a motley bunch of people from all three Services, the ones who 'switched off the lights' of the Indian Empire . . . The Raj.

Apart from our cadre of newly-commissioned officers, the officers seemed to be seasoned Captains and Majors who were returning to be demobbed and were pretty uninterested in India's fate or future; their principal preoccupation was what they were going to do with themselves in 'Civvy Street'.

For the bulk of the British people in India at this time, the end of the Raj was often like this, a quiet, personal affair without much drama or any sense that an era was ending, just a question of packing up, getting on the the trooper and going home. Only later did the full significance of leaving India become apparent.

India was the lynchpin of the British Empire. The undivided Indian sub–continent was the largest single territory of the Empire, the 'Jewel in the Crown'. Without India the British Empire was visibly in decline.

The British came to India in the seventeenth century and acquired their first major foothold from the Portuguese. This was the city of Bombay, the dowry of Princess Catherine of Braganza when she married King Charles II. Bombay then became the capital of the Bombay Presidency and a major trading centre for the East India Company.

The Indian *Empire* – the Raj – came into existence on 1 January 1877, when Queen Victoria became Empress of India and ascended the throne of the Mughals. To acknowledge her accession, her Viceroy in Delhi, Lord Lytton, received the homage of some sixty Indian princes. Most of India had become a direct possession of the British Crown in 1858, after the Indian Mutiny revealed that the East India Company, which had governed or controlled large parts of India since Clive's victory at Plassey in 1757, could no longer rule the sub-continent unaided.

The majority of the people in the British Empire were Indians. By 1945 there were some four hundred million Indians and about a quarter of them were Muslims. Most of the rest were Hindus and in that mix lay the source of India's great problem, for the two religions were irreconcilable. Keeping the peace between the Muslim and Hindu communities had been a major preoccupation of the British during the Raj, and political and religious differences between Hindu and Muslim politicians bedevilled the process leading to independence.

The ending of the Raj was the decisive step for once India went the extinction of the Empire would surely follow and as the War ended in August 1945 the end of British rule in India was already in sight. Exactly two years later, on 15 August, 1947, the Raj ended but in place of the old India stood two separate and hostile nations, largely Hindu India and largely Muslim Pakistan.

India has always been a divided land, containing many races and religions, a country held together by the grip of conquerors. Before the British came, the Mogul Emperors ruled most of the country from their forts and palaces in Delhi and the north, exercising dominion over nearly a thousand semi-independent Princes. After the victory at Plassey in 1757 it was the East India Company which controlled and contained the conflicting factions of Indian life and held the rugged frontiers of the North. After the Mutiny power passed to the British – the Raj – and when Queen Victoria became 'Express of

India' on 1 January 1877, the British Empire at last had an Imperial ruler. This Empire in India was to last just seventy years.

While the Empire endured and provided stability, the teeming millions of India's vast population mixed and mingled, though the Hindus were more numerous in the South and the Muslims more common in the North. There was one more major group, smaller than the Hindus and Muslims but important because of where they lived, and because of their abilities as warriors. These were the Sikhs, who lived in the Punjab and Kashmir

By the time the binding force of the Raj was removed, this intermingling had created large pockets of one race or religion in territory largely occupied by one of the others. Even before independence racial trouble was simmering in towns across India, from the Khyber Pass to Tamil Nadu and once the control exercised by the British was removed these groupings turned their attention to settling some long suppressed scores.

The largest single grouping in India were the Hindus, whose political representatives were the All-India Congress Party led by Pundit Nehru but inspired by Mahatma Gandhi who had once been the Party leader. The Muslims were aspiring either for self-governing Muslim provinces in an independent India or a separate state – Pakistan. The Muslim leaders were Mohammed Ali Jinnah and Liaquat Ali Khan who dominated the Muslim League, the political voice of Muslim aspirations.

There were also the warlike Sikhs, whose religion was akin to that of the Hindus but who had their own aspirations to statehood and were an important element in Indian society, because a high proportion of native Indian Army officers were Sikhs.

The final major elements in this volatile brew were the Princely States, of which there were several hundred. Some, like Hyderabad, were as large as Wales; others were little bigger than Hyde Park. All the Princely rulers, the Rajahs, Nawabs and Maharajahs, were linked by treaty to the British Crown and feared for their future in an independent India – and by 1945 it was clear to all that an independent India was coming.

To trace the course of the independence struggle in India there is no need to go back to the Indian Mutiny of 1857–8, even though Indian history now chooses to present that local rising as the first step towards national independence.

In fact, the Indian Mutiny affected only part of the Bengal Army and a few native principalities. A more likely date for the start of the independence struggle is 1876, when a young Indian, Surendranath Banerji, formed an organisation, the Indian Association, with the specific aims of campaigning for Press freedom and a lowering of entry requirements for the Indian Civil Service. His aim was not to end the Raj but for Indians to play a greater part in running it.

A more significant step came in 1885 with the foundations of the All-India Congress Party, one of whose founders was an English civil servant, A.O. Hume. The Congress Party provided a focus for the aspirations of the growing and better-educated Indian middle class, and its advent was given a cautious welcome by the Viceroy, Lord Ripon, who felt that educated Indians should have a voice in the affairs of their own country.

By 1900, the Congress Party was seeking direct involvement in Government and here began the problem that was to lead to partition less than fifty years later. Most of the Congress members were Hindu and the aim of their policies was to achieve independence for a Hindu state. This prospect did not appeal to the large Muslim minority. One result of Congress agitation was the formation of the Muslim League in 1906, and India was already simmering with political discontent when the Great War broke out in 1914.

During this time the three great leaders in the independence struggle, Mohandas Gandhi, Pandit Nehru and Muhammed Ali Jinnah, came to the forefront of Indian affairs. The last two were politicians; the first was widely thought to be a saint. All three were lawyers and members of the English Bar.

Thanks to a great deal of media attention, Mohandas Gandhi, the 'Mahatma' or 'Great Soul', has come to be regarded as the liberator of India. There is a great deal of truth in this belief but three other facets of the 'liberation struggle' should not be omitted. The first is that the British intended to leave India anyway; like the Americans later, the Indians and their Mahatma were pushing at an unlocked door. The second is that most of the practical work needed to create an independent India and Pakistan fell on the shoulders of the British Viceroy and the principal Hindu and Muslim leaders, Nehru and Jinnah.

The third facet is that the religious and racial divisions between the Muslim and Hindu communities, and the difficulties of creating either a united India acceptable to both parties or two separate states, were the main reasons for the delay in achieving independence. These were practical issues that Mahatma Gandhi chose to ignore. Perhaps saints can do this; politicians and administrators have to be more pragmatic.

Mohandas Gandhi was born in 1869. His father had been Prime Minister of Porbandar, a Princely State, though the family trade was in the grocery business; the word 'gandhi' means grocer. Gandhi married at the age of thirteen, and in 1888 he sailed from India to enrol at the Inns of Court. Gandhi spent three years in England and they seem to have been happy ones. He read widely, became a vegetarian, took up ballroom dancing and was called to the Bar in 1891.

Two days later he sailed for South Africa where he remained for five years. During that time he took his first steps into politics, founding the Natal Indian Congress. That apart, Gandhi had his first encounter with British soldiers when serving as a Red Cross orderly in the South Africa War.

He also encountered naked racism and fought many court cases in South Africa on behalf of Indian litigants. His efforts to obtain justice for his clients usually met with little success but some time during this South African period he began to develop his own theories on ways to obtain justice under oppression. When forces too strong to be fought had to be overcome, another method had to be found. Eventually Gandhi found it. He called it 'satyagraha', non-violent resistance, and in the end 'satyagraha' toppled the British Empire in India.

Gandhi returned to India in July 1914, just before the outbreak of the Great War, and was soon involved in Indian politics. The Great War saw the watershed in Indian politics but the future was shaped by two events, one political, one military. The political one came in 1917 with the announcement of the American President Woodrow Wilson's 'Fourteen Points', which contained a declarations on self-determination for subject nations, the first signal that the United States was taking up the anti-colonial cause.

The second came in the Punjab on 13 April 1919 when, after days of rioting and many deaths, a force of Gurkhas under Brigadier General Reginald 'Rex' Dyer opened fire on a mob in the Jallianwala

Bagh, an enclosed square in Amritsar, the capital of the Punjab, killing three hundred and seventy-nine people and injuring more than twelve hundred. For many Indians, especially Mohandas Gandhi, that act exhausted the national patience with British rule.

British rule in India was already faltering and had weakened anyway in recent years. In 1916 'Home Rule Leagues' had been formed in India under the influence of an English woman, Annie Besant, who became President of the Congress Party in 1918.

In 1917 the path to independence was temporarily smoothed by the 'Lucknow Pact' an agreement between Hindus and Muslims which ensured Muslim support for independence, provided that the Hindus recognised the Muslim demand for separate Muslim constituencies. The pressure for independence, and distrust between the two communities, led to rioting and widespread civil unrest. Caught in the middle of a World War the British Government wanted no trouble in India and thought to diffuse the situation with a declaration of post-War intentions, which was read out in Parliament in August 1917:

> The policy of H.M. Government, with which the Government of India is in complete accord, is that of the increasing association of Indians in every branch of the administration, and the gradual development of self-governing institutions with a view to the progressive realisation of responsible government in India, as an integral part of the Empire.

Reduced to simple terms, this envisaged India progressing to the independent Dominion status under the Crown already enjoyed by Canada, Australia, New Zealand and South Africa. The devil, as ever, was in the detail, lurking in words like 'increasing', 'gradual' and 'progressive', and hung on the length of time this process would take, far more than on what the eventual outcome might be. Then came Amritsar and the end of any notion that the Indians would always tolerate the British veto in Indian affairs.

Having obtained this declaration in the years between the wars, the Congress Party campaigned for an even larger share of power after Amritsar and duly achieved it. In 1935 Congress achieved a degree of national political power with the passing of the Government of India Act. This offered internal self-government for the provinces and the appointment of Indian governors. Nehru's Congress Party welcomed this move which would, it believed, make Congress the heir to the Raj and the succeeding power when the British finally left. One of the most vocal supporters was a rising young Hindu politician, Suhbas Chandra Bose. Unfortunately for Gandhi, Nehru and Bose, Jinnah and his Muslim League had other ideas.

One of the most curious facts about Muhammed Ali Jinnah was that he could not speak Urdu, the language of the Muslim community. When he wished to make a speech or write a letter or talk with Nehru he had to speak English. Like Gandhi, Jinnah was a lawyer, a product of the English Bar. Jinnah had started his political career in the Congress Party, supporting Nehru and the Party demand for 'swaraj', or self-government, before detecting Congress aspirations for a Hindu state and defecting to the Muslim League in 1913. Once there he become a bitter enemy of the Hindus' spokesman, Jawaharlal Nehru.

Jawaharlal Nehru was a product of the Raj he hoped to destroy. Born into a wealthy Hindu family in 1889 he had been educated at home by an English tutor and at Harrow, an English public school. Nehru was a disciple of Gandhi, the political voice of the Mahatma, the man who translated all Gandhi's dreams – save one – into reality. That unrealised dream was for a United India but as the prospect of independence drew closer, so the two communities, Hindu and Muslim, drew apart. Eventually the spectre of partition took on a visible form.

By the time the Second World War broke out in September 1939, the British Viceroy in Delhi was talking to Congress and the Muslim League, attempting to reconcile their differences. The Viceroy was also concerned by the five million Sikhs who, under their religious leader, Tara Singh, wanted their own State in the 'new' India, in the important region of the Punjab.

In 1940, Jinnah tabled his claim for a part of India, demanding a Muslim state in the North West and North East – the latter to include the Ganges Delta and the vital port of Calcutta. This would give the Muslims two blocks of territory in the sub-continent but – speaking for Congress and the Hindus – Nehru rejected this claim, not least because Calcutta was predominantly a Hindu-populated city.

In 1942, with the triumphant Japanese closing on India's frontiers around Manipur the British Government sent a mission to India led by a senior Labour Party politician, Sir Stafford Cripps. Cripps was empowered to offer the Indian politicians a three-part plan, linked with a firm commitment to self-government *once the War was over*.

Immediately after the war, elections would be held to establish a Constitutional Assembly in India. A Constitution would be prepared and issued by this Assembly and Britain would abide by its terms, provided any Princely State or Indian Province which wished to remain directly linked to Britain was allowed to do so. An Anglo–Indian Treaty would then be negotiated giving self-government to the rest of the country. Meanwhile, in 1942, an Interim Governmnet of India would be established, with Indian politicians holding all the national portfolios except Foreign Affairs and Defence.

The suggestion that the Princely States and some Provinces could opt out of the independence ticket proved anathema to Gandhi, who described acceptance of the Cripps proposals as 'drawing a cheque on a failing bank'. He also stated that the only reason India was under threat from the Japanese was because of the British presence. 'Let the British leave at once,' he declared, 'and the Japanese would desist from invading.'

Since the Japanese had been rampaging across Asia for the last nine years and in 1937 had killed one hundred thousand Chinese citizens in the city of Nanking in a three-day orgy of violence, this statement by the apostle of 'satyagraha' was too naive, and after days of fruitless discussion the Cripps Mission went home in disgust. The Congress Party then began a 'Quit India' campaign which only ended after considerable bloodshed (in one incident two Canadian Air Force officers were literally torn to pieces by a Hindu mob), and the detention of all the National leaders. These leaders were kept in detention until the end of the war.

One leader who was not detained was Subhas Chandra Bose. Bose was another Indian with experience of British life, born into a wealthy Indian family and educated at Cambridge University, where, as he said in letters home, 'the sight of white waiter and porters serving his meals and cleaning [his] shoes gave [him] considerable satisfaction'. On his return to India he became a disciple of Gandhi and a leading figure in the Congress Party, rated as highly as Nehru among the Hindu people. By 1930 he was President of the All-India Congress and Mayor of Calcutta. During the 1930s Bose's political activity led to several terms of imprisonment but by 1939 he was again President of Congress.

In 1940, after another spell in prison, he fled to Afghanistan and eventually to Germany where he met Hitler and attempted to raise an Indian Legion from the ranks of Indian Army POWs in German prison camps. When this failed the Germans sent him by submarine to Japan.

The Japanese Far Eastern Army had a large number of Indian prisoners captured in Malaya or Burma. Some of these had already been formed into a fighting force mustered in Malaya under the leadership of a Sikh Captain, Mohan Singh, and a Punjabi Captain, Shah Nawaz Khan. The arrival of Bose, a substantial political figure, gave new impetus to these officers and Bose managed to recruit a substantial number of Indian prisoners into his 'Indian National Army' or INA.

A far larger number of Indians stayed 'true to their salt', and refused either to join Bose's regiments or fight against their former comrades in the Indian Army. Many suffered great brutality for refusing to join the INA and some were put to death by the Japanese. Bose himself bore down hard on Indian soldiers who refused to join the INA. One officer, Captain Mahmood Khan Durrani, was singled out for torture, first brutally treated by the Kempetai, the Japanese Gestapo, and then tortured and degraded by Indians of the INA under Bose's personal direction. For his courage under this treatment, Mahmood Khan Durrani was later awarded the George Cross by the Viceroy of India, Lord Wavell. Bose was killed in an air crash in 1945 but his influence was to live on and bedevil relations with the Indians when the war was over.

In spite of Congress's 'Quit India' campaign, attacks on British Servicemen or civilians were rare. Maurice Leng was serving with the Royal Air Force in Madras during the 'Quit India' campaign:

We had a very pleasant life at Madras. We worked mornings only, so the rest of the day was free. Dressed in civilian clothes, I took the electric train into Madras and browsed in the bookshops along Mount Road, or wandered around the markets and shops, eating in good Chinese cafés, followed by a visit to the cinema or the YMCA to pick up the Anglo-Indian girls, finishing at Spencer's Hotel for a few drinks.

Although the Congress Party frequently held 'Quit India' demonstrations in the streets, at no time, even when alone, did I experience any hassle or even verbal abuse. A number of times I was stopped by English-speaking natives who implored me to write home to King George or the Prime Minister, requesting that we do NOT quit India. At the Queen Victoria statues – there were quite a few of these back then – low caste and Untouchables prayed for her help, and again, not to quit India.

June Powell's family had been in India for several generations:

The Viceroy and State Governors in India had their own orchestras comprising hand-picked army bandsmen from various regiments with a Director of Music who was a trained army band-master. In the early days these were fully-fledged symphony orchestras but by the start of World War II they were reduced to about ten members, some of whom had been with the orchestras for up to twenty years.

After a particularly bad time with his cavalry regiment during the First World War, in the early twenties my father, a very good flautist, was head-hunted by the Director of Music to the Governor of Bengal. My father joined the band and became Director of Music just before the last war. He was still in that position when power was handed over in 1947.

The Governor had two official residences, the main one in Calcutta and a hot weather one in Darjeeling. I was born in Darjeeling in 1926 and went to boarding school there until I left and joined the Women's Army Corps (India) – the WACI – in 1943 and was posted to a military hospital in Comilla, where the 14th Army Headquarters was based.

In 1944 I met and married my husband, a Staff Captain (Movements) in Comilla and Chittagong, dealing with the troops and supplies pouring into the Arakam. We followed one another around the Arakam until I left the Army to have our first baby in October 1945. By the middle of 1946 my husband was due to be repatriated but volunteered to stay on as we were expecting another baby. He was welcomed with open arms, not only because of the troops returning from Burma but also because of the eventual handing over of all military stations to the Indians and the repatriation of all personnel to England. So we came to be in Calcutta in 1946 during the dreadful riots and killings leading up to Partition.

In spite of the 'Quit India' campaign of 1942 and the detention of the Congress leaders, the offer of independence was still on the table in 1945 and would not be retracted. When the Second World War ended, the Nationalist leaders were promptly released and negotiations for independence began again.

This time the Indians were offered all the portfolios with the exception of that of Commander-in-Chief (C-in-C) of the Indian Army, which would remain in British hands with the C-in-C having a seat in Government. In June 1945, two months before the Japanese surrender, the Viceroy of India, General Wavell, called a conference at Simla to debate these proposals.

Archibald Wavell was a fighting soldier. He had commanded the British Army in the early campaigns against Rommel in the Western Desert before falling out with Churchill and being sent to India. Wavell was a dour, highly intelligent man with a great deal of well-hidden sensitivity. He had astonished Churchill at a Cairo conference by telling the Prime Minister that he found relief from the stresses of command by compiling an anthology of poetry; this collection of verse, *Other Men's Flowers*, is still in print sixty years later.

Wavell was well aware of the simmering animosities among the Indian leaders but quite unable to keep them in check. As Gandhi himself told the Viceroy, 'Either you must accept the Hindu point of view or the Muslim point of view. The two are irreconcilable.' Gandhi himself deplored the very idea of a partitioned India, but Wavell had to press on – somehow – down the path to independence. At the Simla Conference in 1945 all the problems of India burst into the open.

Put simply, the Congress Party – a Hindu-dominated body – wanted all of British India, at once, and on their own terms. The Muslim League, while equally hot for independence, wanted a share of British India for their Muslim state, Pakistan. Nor was this all: the Indian Princes preferred the status quo and the Sikhs were anxious over the future of the Punjab. The British – not for the last time in the End of Empire period – were caught in the middle.

With a rising political clamour round the conference table and growing violence in the streets, the Simla Conference failed. In July 1945 the Labour Party took over in Britain and in August 1945 the Second World War ended. The matter of Indian independence was resting on the Cabinet table in Downing Street the day after peace was declared.

The Labour Party was fully committed to Indian independence; the problem was how to achieve it. In September Wavell declared: 'His Majesty's Government is determined to promote the early realisation of full Government for India . . . with elections during the coming 1945–6 cold season.'

This did nothing to stop the violence and in October 1945 there were bloody intercommunal riots in Calcutta followed by problems with the hitherto loyal Indian Army and Navy, problems exacerbated by the difficulty of what to do about the 'Jifs' (Japanese – Indian Forces), the former soldiers of Subhas Chandra Bose's Indian National Army.

Put simply, these soldiers were traitors. The loyal soldiers, the sepoys of the Indian Army, certainly felt that way, and Jifs taken prisoner in Burma were often shot out of hand. Many of the Jifs were anxious to surrender and many had indeed only joined Bose's force to get back to the front line, desert the Japanese and rejoin their old units. More than half the INA soldiers sent to Burma crossed over to the Indian Army lines within the first few weeks.

The INA was not a happy, united or effective fighting force. Distrusted and neglected by the Japanese, the Jifs surrendered in droves and there were thousands of them in Indian Army prison camps when the war ended. The problem now was what to do about them.

To the Indian politicians the Jifs were a propaganda godsend, and the leaders, Nehru and the rest, chose to regard the Jifs as heroes of the independence struggle and martyrs to British Imperialism. Now that the full horrors of imprisonment under the Japanese had been fully revealed, there was some sympathy for the Jifs even among soldiers, for who can say what they would have done if offered relief from similar conditions?

In the end the British decided to divide the Jif prisoners into three categories, white, grey and black. Those graded 'white' were allowed to return to their units and make what peace they could with their former comrades in arms. Those graded 'grey', as fairly willing INA volunteers, were dismissed from the service and sent home. Only those listed as 'black', where there was evidence of coercion or brutality on their part against fellow prisoners, were reserved for court martial. Even that produced a howl of outrage from the Indian politicians.

Most of the INA were simply discharged, but it was decided to try three leading INA officers for treason against the King-Emperor and the murder of fellow prisoners. To avoid accusations of racial bias those chosen were a Hindu, a Muslim and a Sikh. The inevitable result was to infuriate all three communities. Indian nationalists also resented the fact that the trials took place in the Red Fort in Delhi, once the palace of the Mughal Emperors. The Victory Parade in New Delhi was boycotted by the Congress Party and political dissension spread to the Indian Army.

The trial of the three INA leaders on counts of treason and murder, began on 5 November 1945 with Jawaharlal Nehru among the defending counsel. The trial lasted two months, with riots outside the courthouse and in towns across the country. All three were found guilty, cashiered from the army and sentenced to terms of imprisonment but the Raj had no heart to pursue the issue and in the end all three went free.

The new leaders of India had little thought for the hundreds of thousands of loyal Indian soldiers who had fought for their country against the Japanese or indeed for the bulk of the Jifs. Once they had served their turn as political pawns the Jifs were dropped by the politicians.

Nehru, the first leader of independent India, later agreed that former INA officers could return to the Army but only in their former rank, the one held before joining the INA. Other Indian soldiers would not serve with them, though, and most of them soon left the service. The Jifs remained useful as an anti-imperial tool. As late as 1974, the then Prime Minister of India, Mrs Indira Gandhi, never one to miss a chance of denigrating the British, awarded pensions to the surviving Jifs.

In the Indian Navy a series of Congress-inspired strikes in 1945–6 led to mutinies in ships anchored in Bombay and Karachi; these mutinies were put down without difficulty by the Indian Army. All these risings were part of an attempt by Congress to make

India ungovernable and force the British to leave before granting any concessions to Jinnah and the Muslims.

The elections promised in 1942 were duly held in February 1946. The result was a clear division of seats between the Congress Party and the Muslim League. The voting, however, was not clear-cut. Enough Muslims voted for the Congress Party in the North-West Frontier Province and Assam to give Congress a majority in both those Muslim-dominated places, while in the Punjab the Sikhs flung their votes behind Congress to deny power to the Muslim majority. However, if the elections were confirmed by a similar vote at a national level there could be no doubt that Congress would hold all the Hindu seats and stand out for an All-India solution, without partition. Equally clearly, the League would hold all the Muslim seats, and Jinnah therefore demanded Pakistan.

The next step, as agreed in 1942, was to draw up a Constitution and the British delegation arrived in Delhi in March 1946 charged with that specific task. They sat round a table with Jinnah, Nehru and Gandhi for two solid months and went back to London empty-handed.

Britain was still clinging – just – to the All-India solution, but in the light of Hindu demands and Muslim intransigence, the British now put forward a plan, 'The Cabinet Mission Plan', which proposed grouping the provinces into three parts under a National Governmental umbrella, responsible for the major portfolios.

The major, Hindu, block of provinces roughly coincide with the frontiers of the present India. The second group, the Punjab, North-West Frontier Province and Sind would be Muslim; this group is roughly similar to the present Pakistan, and the Eastern Group, Bengal and Assam, also Muslim, is similar to the present Bangladesh. As for the Princes, they would be free to join the group of their choice but were advised to join a group contiguous with their own territory.

This was an archetypal British compromise and had the usual effect of satisfying no one. At first both the League and Congress saw some merit in the Cabinet Plan Mission, not least because it would get the British out and leave the Indians – Hindu and Muslim – to settle their own affairs. However, on 27 July 1946, the League withdrew their support from the Cabinet Mission Plan and in August, not knowing what else to do, the Viceroy, Viscount Wavell, asked Pandit Nehru to form an Indian Government, without the League. Jinnah then declared that his Party 'would bid farewell to conventional politics' – and all hell broke loose in cities right across India, culminating in Direct Action Day, 16 August 1946, when the gutters of Calcutta ran with blood.

Mal Martin was serving in India as a Private in the Suffolk Regiment when the trouble spread to the Punjab:

I left England on 16 October 1946 on board the troopship *Mooltan*. Four days later I had my eighteenth birthday off Cape St Vincent, Portugal. I was one of a draft bound for the 2nd Battalion, The Suffolk Regiment. We landed at Bombay in November and started a three-day journey by train to Ferozepore.

The battalion moved to a training area called Dina for Brigade exercises. We had only been there a few hours when our company commander was approached by an ancient Indian who handed him a tattered piece of paper to the effect that we had frightened the animals, damaged the crops and abused the women. Compensation was demanded.

Our Company Commander was of the opinion that the paper was older than its bearer and came out every time troops were in the vicinity. As we were so far from base we did not have our own char-wallahs, fruit-wallahs etc., but a new lot of camp followers materialised from nowhere, which was the incredible thing about soldiering in India. Our lads maintained they had no money and asked for their purchases to be entered into a book or 'kitab' as it was known. The vendors were reluctant but agreed in order to make a sale.

Weeks later those very same vendors materialised in Ferozepore to claim their money as all troops had to leave Dina suddenly because of rioting elsewhere. I was asked by one vendor to identify the names in his 'kitab' book. I read out such names as Donald Duck. Mickey Mouse and so on. 'Who is this man, Donald Duck?' I was asked. Higher authority finally sorted things out.

We had received some training in Internal Security with the battalion. This involved ways to combat rioting with the aim of dispersal rather than bloodshed. An Indian magistrate or official was to accompany each patrol and only if he considered the situation out of control could we to resort to firearms.

We arrived in Lahore to find the rioting had subsided but we set up road blocks to disarm anyone moving about. Sikhs were allowed to carry one weapon, probably a dagger, but we had to disarm any Sikh who was also carrying a sword. They were quite reluctant to give up the extra weapons, but we retrieved them without violence. As things quietened down we returned to our base at Ferozepore, which was about forty miles away, and before long we were on the move again, this time to Amritsar. As we approached the city we could see the situation was serious. The sky glowed with numerous fires from within the walls of the city and an unusual smell, in a land of smells, was apparent. It was the smell of burning flesh.

We entered the old city by various gates, each Company separating and patrolling a different area. As 'D' Company prepared to go in I noted one of our platoon, an ex-Airborne man, go visibly pale. I probably did as well and not surprisingly; we stumbled on scenes of massacre in the narrow streets. Dead, dying and partly-burned bodies were everywhere.

Bodies had been piled on burning belongings and the Golden Temple was surrounded by such funeral pyres. A curfew had been imposed and we were ordered to roll down our sleeves and don gas goggles as sulphuric acid was being thrown down on us from the rooftops. We often had to threaten with rifles to get people off the roofs, but I saw no one actually shot.

We had a short rest and some Sikhs, breaking the curfew, offered us tea and, of all unlikely things, crystallised carrots. We accepted, only to learn later that bodies had been thrown down the various wells, fouling the only water supply within the city.

Rioting broke out again and a whole Gurkha Brigade had to go to the assistance of the police. Because of the general unrest we began long-range patrols from Ferozepore which could be dicy. 'D' Company was 'Showing the Flag' in the town of Gurdaspur when an angry mob ran slap into us. Our Company was little more than platoon strength, about fifty strong, and we just managed to extend across the main road in single rank – so much for I.S. riot drill and its concept of the all-round square.

I wasn't armed for close-quarter combat, so my Platoon commander thrust his Thompson sub-machine-gun with a full magazine into my hands and took out his revolver. We held the mob off but they would not disperse. Their spokesman claimed that people of their religion were being slaughtered in a nearby village and they were going there to sort things out in their own way. Our Company Commander handled things very well and persuaded the ringleaders of the mob to accompany a squad of us to the village to see what had actually happened. We held the remainder at gunpoint for about two hours until they returned with the news that there had been no massacre, at least on that particular occasion.

The mob eventually dispersed and no one was injured. I have often thought, later in life, how other armies would have dealt with that situation. Shoot first and ask questions afterwards, perhaps. I sometimes think of the Indian who had my gun barrel pointed at his chest for a couple of hours – we were near enough to shake hands. Perhaps, if the mob had surged forward I would have had to squeeze the trigger. Maybe his son now runs a grocery shop in Ipswich – who knows?

Situations like those in Amritsar and Lahore were taking place all over India but the worst riots were in the Hindu city of Calcutta. In Calcutta the intercommunal rioting in 1946 lasted three days and cost some five thousands lives, with thousands more, Muslims and Hindus, being injured and often mutilated. For the moment though, the Raj still existed and the rioters were soon curbed by the soldiers of the British Army. In the end some forty-five thousand British and Gurkha soldiers were deployed in the streets of the major Indian cities.

June Powell, the Army wife, was now living in Calcutta:

Why the Indians didn't turn on us, I don't know. It could be due to the fact that Sir Frederick Burrows delayed so long in calling out the military or because the Indians knew that we were actually leaving, or maybe they were too busy killing each other.

In Calcutta, gangs of 'Congress wallahs', in their white 'Pandit Nehru' caps, roamed the streets looking for Muslims to attack. Cars were overturned and all the shop fronts smashed. If you met up with one of these crowds there was much posturing, yelling and shouting and even some pushing and shoving, but at no time was I afraid to go out. The police were armed and went out in small groups of four or six.

The riots in Calcutta in 1946 were stamped out by British troops and Gurkhas, but rioting then spread to other cities. In September Bombay went up in flames; in October rioting spread to Bihar and the Central Provinces, then, as already related, to Lahore and the Sikh holy city of Amritsar. By March 1947, when Rawalpindi went up in flames, the death toll in intercommunal rioting ran into tens of thousands and the country was clearly becoming ungovernable. This rioting was not anti–British or indeed anti–Government, but between Hindus and Sikhs on the one hand and Muslims on the other.

Mal Martin continues his story:

At that time the British Army was contracting as many long-serving soldiers were demobbed after the War. Infantry regiments began to lose their 2nd battalion; this happened to the 2nd Suffolks in May 1947. The regulars were posted to 1st Suffolks in Palestine and the rest of us had the choice of either the Essex Regiment or 2nd Royal Norfolks. We had been on exercises with the Royal Norfolks and their reveille was half an hour earlier than ours, so several lads opted for the Essex. On such things are great decisions made. Some of us felt a greater affinity to the Royal Norfolks, so we found ourselves in hill stations above Rawalpindi, with magnificent views of the Himalayas, Kashmir and the North West Frontier.

We were withdrawn from the hills as Independence Day in 1947 approached and entrained for a transit camp near Bombay three days journey away. Two trains took the battalion to Kalyan. One was attacked on the journey but the mob backed a loser when armed British troops appeared instead of the expected civilians. This was after independence and it was then all too frequent for train to arrive at its destination in India or Pakistan with all passengers slaughtered. That happened at Ferozepore after our departure.

We boarded the troopship *Georgic*. As the ship moved away, the Indian forces lined up on the quay gave us three rousing cheers; as our Colonel asked us to respond, the Tannoy loudspeakers broke down and only a handful of troops cheered. A group of Indians then jeered and threw stones at the departing ship, but the vast majority of Indians didn't want us to go. We were one stable faction in a country divided by religious strife and the caste system.

I often wonder what became of all those char-wallahs, fruit-wallahs, sweet-wallahs, knapi wallahs, dhurzi wallahs and the

Untouchables, plus the other camp followers who eked out some sort of existence because we were there. Perhaps they were among the unfortunate quarter million or more Indians who were slaughtered by their fellow countrymen in the days after Independence as we sailed home.

Alan Crocker was in Calcutta with the Royal Engineers during the 1946 riots:

During the horse-racing season the riots used to stop from about half an hour before the first race until about half an hour after the last race. This was because the people of Calcutta, both Indian and European (the full-time expatriates, not temps such as myself) had a passion for horse-racing.

During the riots, British troops travelling by motor vehicle did so with an armed escort of soldiers. Motor cyclists, like me, were instructed to carry their weapons in an inconspicuous manner. Mine was a Colt .45 revolver, not easy to conceal wearing jungle battle dress. Furthermore, the rioters had a habit of stretching piano wire across streets used by British troops, at about the height of a motor cyclist's neck. This made riding a slightly difficult operation, requiring excellent eyesight and exceptional reflexes.

During the riots it was commonplace to see dead bodies lying on the pavements, even in the main thoroughfares. Requests for removal made to the police usually brought forth the response that this was the job of the hospital. The hospital replied that it was the job of the police. Attempts by individuals or small groups to give food to the starving met with no success. Whatever their hunger, people would not touch European food.

The riots of 1946 should have given the Congress politicians clear warning of what might happen later, but the lesson was not learned. In Calcutta, the main offenders against the Muslims were the Sikhs who, aided by members of the local criminal fraternity, killed and looted until the British Army came on to the streets and restored order. This was in the last days of the Raj; only the British could stop the Indian communities tearing out each others throats . . . and the British were leaving.

*   *   *

Wavell's decision to transfer power to the Constituent Assembly did have some effect, especially on the leaders of the Muslim League. In October 1946 Jinnah decided to participate in the Assembly and in December 1946 five Muslims joined Nehru's Government. This Government met for the first time in December 1946, when the Congress Party rammed through a resolution claiming British India for an independent sovereign Indian Republic. At this the Muslims again took to the streets and Jinnah renewed his calls for a Muslim Pakistan.

The British wanted out of India. They also wanted to leave a stable country behind, firmly set on the road to prosperous independence but this was now seen to be in impossible. Independence had been on the table for five years and British patience with Indian politicians was exhausted.

The Indians had wanted independence and demanded independence and fought for independence; now they had it on the table they were too busy arguing and fighting among themselves to grasp it. The British Government was only interested in withdrawal, as fast and as cleanly as possible, but Wavell was unwell and exhausted and unpopular with Attlee.

A new man was needed, one last Viceroy who could be charged with the task of winding up Britain's rule in India and overseeing the end of the Raj. The Prime Minister's choice fell on a public figure and war hero, a member of the British Royal Family, that charismatic personality, Admiral Lord Louis Mountbatten.

4

The End of the Raj: 1947–1948

'I would rather have every village in India go up in flames than keep a single British soldier in India a moment longer than necessary.'

Jawaharlal Nehru, President of India, 1947.

Mountbatten remains the enigmatic figure of Indian Independence. Did he, as some claim, grasp the nettle and bring independence successfully to the sub-continent with the minimum of delay, or was he the architect of precipitate withdrawal which led to the massacres that followed independence, and therefore indirectly responsible for the death of at least half a million people? Was he motivated by the desire to leave India in as good a state as circumstances might permit, or simply in a hurry to get back to Britain and resume his career in the Royal Navy? Fifty years after independence came to India, opinions are still divided on this point.

In 1947, Admiral Louis Francis Albert Victor Nicolas Mountbatten, Viscount Mountbatten of Burma, a man known to his intimates as 'Dickie', was 46 years old and at the height of his powers. He was also not without influence. He was the King's cousin, had a rich and charismatic wife and was an international celebrity, popular with rich and poor at home and abroad. Mountbatten had had a 'good war', returning home laden with honours and without a scratch, after serving at the sharp end in destroyers, then as Chief of Combined Operations and finally as Supreme Allied Commander, South-East Asia.

Mountbatten was certainly a hero. Under air attack off Crete in 1941 he had fought his destroyer, HMS *Kelly*, until she sank under him, hanging on to the bridge telegraph as she turned over, determined to be the last man off the ship. He had made a fair fist of Combined Operations, apart from the tragic fiasco of the Dieppe Raid in 1942, and done good work in Burma, reviving the flagging fortunes of the 14th Army and sending it under General William 'Bill' Slim to final victory over the Japanese. Having accepted the surrender of the Japanese in Malaya he was home again, rested from the wars, and in need of a new assignment.

To the Prime Minister Clement Attlee, Mountbatten was a gift. Attlee had already decided that Viscount Wavell, the current Viceroy of India, was a spent force, tired and short of ideas. A new broom was needed, to force through independence, bang a few heads together, placate the Princes and get Britain free of this Hindu–Muslim wrangle. Mountbatten was also popular with Churchill and Churchill was dead set against Indian Independence and prepared to make trouble in the House of Commons. If anyone could talk Churchill round, or at least persuade him not to make too much public fuss over Indian Independence, that man was Dickie Mountbatten.

Mountbatten's vanity was attracted to the role of Viceroy, with all the Imperial trappings that went with it. His Royal connections would also go down well with the Indian Princes, many of whom he knew from the polo field. It was a task of immense difficulty but difficulties had never deterred Mountbatten. Indeed, that was one of the doubts most often expressed about him; his courage was undoubted but his judgement was less certain. Some felt that he ignored the difficulties inherent in a task and went for hard and direct solutions, leaving a mess behind for others to clear up.

His command of a destroyer flotilla in 1941–2 had not been without controversy and the matter of the disastrous Dieppe Raid in 1942 was still unresolved, but none of this bothered Prime Minister Clement Attlee. He needed a new broom in India and Mountbatten was his man. The two men met to discuss the problem on New Year's Day 1947 and hammered out a deal.

Mountbatten was well aware of the problems in India and accepted Attlee's assignment on two conditions. First, that he would have full powers to negotiate whatever terms he could with the Indian politicians. Secondly, to concentrate minds and put a stop to the wrangling, a firm date should be fixed for Indian independence and arranged *before* he took up his post in Delhi. Both demands were met. The date for Indian independence was fixed for 'not later than July 1948'.

Accompanied by his wife Edwina and daughter Pamela, Lord Mountbatten arrived in India in March 1947. He was installed in office with considerable splendour and spent the first few weeks travelling about the country, meeting the various leaders and hearing their views. It was finally dawning on Congress that partition was the only practical solution to the Hindu–Muslim dilemma and they reluctantly agreed to the principle. Only Gandhi refused to accept partition, but events in India had run away from any solution that 'satyagraha' could provide.

On 2 June 1947, Mountbatten announced that the British Government accepted partition as the solution to the independence dilemma and that since this fact was now accepted by the Hindu and Muslim leaders, the transfer of power from Britain to the two new countries, India and Pakistan, could take place 'immediately'.

Pressed by a journalist to explain this term, he announced that 15 August 1947 would be the the the date for Indian independence and the ending of the Raj. India had been dominated by the British for nearly two hundred years; now it was to be divided into two independent, sovereign states . . . in just ten weeks. India reeled.

Over the decades since 1947, one of the recurring questions about the independence of India is: 'Was Mountbatten wrong to leave so quickly, but had he really any option?'

Field Marshal Lord Carver, who represented the British Government in Rhodesia when independence came to that troubled country, was consulted on this point:

I don't know; I wasn't there. You have to leave that sort of thing to the judgement of the man on the spot. He had *carte blanche* to do what he thought best and that is what he did. Mountbatten was a very able man, very intelligent, pragmatic. On the other hand he was extremely vain and a born intriguer.

I can recall feeling that his Staff were called on only to put the rubber stamp on something Mountbatten had fixed up behind the scenes and I remember Field Marshal Freddie Festing saying, 'If the front door was wide open, Dickie would still prefer to come down the chimney.'

With hindsight? Well, on balance, yes, he was probably right to go for it and leave India when he did. There comes a time in these affairs when everything is on the move, and nothing can stop it. We were leaving India and everyone knew it, so the best thing was to get on with it and pull out as soon as possible.

The task of pulling out certainly concentrated minds, for everything the Raj contained had to be divided between India and Pakistan: territory, the contents of the Treasury vaults in Delhi, the administrative equipment, civil and military aircraft, Naval ships, dockyard equipment and – above all – the Indian Army. The Indian Army was the heart and soul of the old Indian Empire and now that too had to be divided between the two national armies. Depots, tanks, guns, fuel, ammunition, forms and typewriters, uniforms, regimental silver, sporting trophies, everything had to go. It says a great deal for the discipline of the old Indian Army and goodwill that existed between the regiments that this difficult and often emotional task was carried out swiftly and with so little rancour. Eventually the men and the regiments had to be divided. The main division was fairly simple, Sikhs and Hindus to India, Muslim troops to Pakistan, but many regiments contained a mixture of religions and there the situation was more complicated. Above all, there were the Gurkhas.

Here Britain, too, wanted a share of the spoils and had her eyes an those famous fighting hillmen from Nepal. There were twenty-seven Gurkha battalions in the Indian Army, all of which the Indians wanted to retain, but eight battalions of Gurkhas, from the 2nd, 6th, 7th and 10th Gurkha Rifles were transferred from the Indian to the British Army and shipped at once to Malaya. The other Gurkha battalions were transferred to the Indian Army where they still remain, and flourish.

One of the officers serving in India at that was Lt.-Colonel Anthony 'Titch' Harvey, then a Captain in the 5th Royal Gurkha Rifles, a regiment destined to stay with the Indian Army after Independence:

I joined the Army in 1940, my bid to save the nation. I was eventually commissioned into the 9th Devons, but nothing much seemed to be happening so I volunteered for the Parachute Regiment. My application was accepted but then I was told that I had to go to the Indian Army. I didn't volunteer, I was simply sent. This was mid-1942, after the disaster in Burma and Singapore, and the Indian Army badly needed officers.

I only knew about two kinds of Indian soldier; the first lot were big chaps with beards and turbans and I found out they were Sikhs. The second lot were small and carried big knives and were always laughing. Well, I am not very big, so I thought the second lot would suit me better, and I made my way to the Gurkhas. It was the best decision I ever made.

I went first to the 1st Gurkha Depot and spent three months there learning Gurkhali and Urdu. Gurkhas could speak Urdu but very few spoke English. You have to remember that the Gurkhas were part of the *Indian* Army, not the British Army; that will be important later on.

Well, getting into action was a bit of a problem; I got shunted about a bit but finally ended up in Italy where I saw a truck in Bari with the 8th India Division sign on it and hitched a ride to the front. I eventually found my battalion, the 1st/5th Royal Gurkha Rifles on the Garigliano and joined them in time for the third battle of Cassino.

I loved the 1st/5th; I got my first MC with them, at Lanciano on the Rapido river and saw the Gurkhas in action for the first time. They are . . . well, you know . . . the Gurkhas will never let you down. I took a Company of 95 Gurkhas into action at Cassino and inside half an hour there were only forty-seven left but they were still full of fight . . . so yes, I loved them, and I still do.

The Gurkhas made soldiering fun. I remember an officer of the 10th Gurkhas in Borneo, years later, during Confrontation, saying, 'In time the officers measure up to the men,' and I agree with that.

Anyway, you don't want to hear about all that, you want to hear about India in 1947. I was an ECO, Emergency Commissioned Officer, but I had always wanted to be a soldier and now I wanted a Regular commission and a posting with the Gurkhas . . . and then came independence.

I spent 1946 with the battalion; the 1st/5th was a marvellous battalion, but I could notice the growing anti-British feeling in India and the steady Indianisation of the Indian Army, though many of the young Indian officers, and especially those coming to the Gurkha regiments were very good, the pick of the crop. Then came 1947 and Mountbatten and the break up of the Indian Army . . . and one of the saddest days of my life.

I told you that the Gurkha battalions served in the Indian Army – they had British officers, but were in the Indian Army – so there was the problem. As I said, many of the Gurkha soldiers spoke Urdu and had families in India but few of them spoke English. Their home-from-home was the Indian Army, not the British Army; well, it was a hard choice when the time came to split up the Gurkha regiments, and most of them never had a choice. In the end four regiments of Gurkhas came to the British Army and went to Malaya. There was some movement of men between the regiments but the move was by regiment. The first to go was the 2nd Gurkha Rifles which has a strong affinity with the 60th Rifles, the King's Royal Rifle Corps, and that's why they were chosen.

The 1st/6th were in Burma so they were swiftly shipped to Malaya, and then the 7th and 10th Gurkhas were sent to join them. There was then an attempt to make the 7th Gurkhas into gunners, a bloody silly idea, but we all became part of the 17th Gurkha Division.

I went to the 2nd/6th and I am glad about that; it was a fine battalion but the 1st/5th were special to me and Nehru grabbed it . . . maybe because they were the 'Royal' Gurkhas. We won four VCs in the War and they are still the best regiment in the Indian Army; don't let anyone tell you different . . . the 5th Gurkhas are bloody marvellous.

Anyway, in August 1947 we were at Nagpur, in the Central Provinces, south of the Punjab. We then had to relieve the 2nd/6th Gurkhas who were in Army Reserve and go to Delhi as the Viceroy's Bodyguard. Mountbatten was one of those people who loved ceremony. Delhi was in a bit of a state; there was a huge Muslim refugee camp outside the Red Fort and we spent a lot of our time on Internal Security, patrolling the Chandri Chowk, trying to keep the mobs apart. I can't say I ever felt in personal danger but later on, when we took over the railway station, we saw a lot of death. The railways were deathtraps for travellers. I remember an old blind beggar who was beaten to death by the Sikhs.

One of our tasks at this time was to take a trainload of Muslims to Ferozepore, about fifteen hundred of them. We were attacked by the Sikhs but us soon as the train stopped for any reason, we deployed soldiers along the track. The Sikhs tried to lure the British officers away but we twigged that and told the driver to get in the cab and take the train on, and the Sikhs fled. We got the train up to the frontier and sent these Muslims to safety and I said to them, 'Tell Mr Jinnah that the 5th Gurkha Rifles have delivered his people safely home.'

Trouble started up all the time, often for no reason. Muslims would attack Hindus, the Hindus would retaliate and, of course, they were all living together, with their communities side by side. Under the Raj they either lived together peacefully enough or we went in and sorted them out, but once we left there was nothing to stop them killing each other, which they did, in quantity.

In my opinion the men'sahibs ruined India. I loved it there, even the food; you can't beat boily-roast chicken and caramel custard. There was a lot of sadness at the end, especially among the Anglo-Indians. The Indians did not want them and the British had no time for them. If you want to know about that time you can't do better than read *Bohwani Junction*, the book by John Masters.

John Masters was an officer in the 4th Gurkhas, 2nd Battalion I think it was, and a great man for the women, but when I read that book I can almost smell India and see that station. The Anglo-Indians ran the railroads but otherwise there was no place for them. Anyway, that's how India ended for me. My wonderful battalion went off to the Indian Army and I went to Malaya to join the 2nd/6th, arriving there just in time for the Emergency.

In 1947 the Gurkha battalions were stationed all over India and Lieutenant J.P. Cross was with the 1st/1st Gurkha Rifles on the North West Frontier as the Raj there came to an end there, with the creation of Pakistan:

The North-West Frontier of India has never been tamed. It is a wild, barren and hilly tract of land lying alongside Afghanistan. Its inhabitants, the Pathans, are subdivided into many families, most of whom seem to be in a state of perpetual feud with each other and it is a sign of manhood to carry a rifle.

In January 1947 the resident Gurkha battalion at Razmak was the

1st/1st Gurkha Rifles. It was an old and well-established battalion, raised in 1815 and allowed to incorporate 'King George V's Own' in its title. Pre-war it had done a number of tours up among these barren mountains, the peaks of which are some twelve thousand feet above sea level. It had recently come up from the sweltering plains of central India and six thousand feet up in Razmak the difference in climate was very marked. Most of the senior ranks had cut their teeth on Pathan bullets and after a war that took them to Africa, Burma and French Indo-China, here they were, back again. They knew what to expect when the road to the plains had to be opened.

At that time all was rumour; rumours of partition, rumours of leaving British India, rumours of transfers to the British Army, rumours of officers' postings – nothing but rumours. All we could do was to carry on as though we had implicit faith in the future. None of us for a moment ever imagined we would have to join in the pell-mell rush to coincide with the politicians' countdown.

Indianisation of Indian units meant their British officers pulling out, but not us. We had no Indian officers to hand over to in Gurkha units and we could not just leave the battalion and shove off. Abandoning the men was something we never envisaged, but that is what was to happen. Luckily for our peace of mind, this dreadful occurrence could not be foreseen.

During the spring of 1947 large masses of Pathans moved eastwards. They caused no trouble but precautions were as stringent as ever. Then just as suddenly, this mass movement ceased. News was hard to come by so rumours proliferated. It took six weeks for urgent signals to reach Razmak from Delhi and mail from home also took six weeks. The local cinema showed the latest available newsreel, British and American troops crossing the Rhine during the last winter of the war, two years before.

Later in the summer we heard news of fighting in Kashmir, which explained the influx of Pathans through our territory. It was decided to have a 'Flag march', a practice column comprising most of the Brigade Group, possibly three thousand men. Razmak was left in the hands of a rear party and the column reached Damdil, two days walk to the east. On Sunday, 15 June 1947, the battalion moved up a valley called the Mami Roga Algad and hilltops piquets had to be established. One, too weak by Frontier standards, endured intermittent sniping from a position on a further ridge. Unbeknown to the troops, a band of Pathans in greater strength were in hiding twenty yards from the piquet.

Some time after noon the sniping Pathans noticed the waving of red flags which heralded the piquet withdrawal. Their sniping became heavier. At a pre-arranged signal they stopped firing and those in hiding ran up the hill, overcame the Gurkhas and threw them downhill, snatching two rifles and a Bren gun. One wounded man was left behind but rescued by Lieutenant Peter Davis, who braved the Pathan covering fire to do so. Davis carried the man to safety and then dashed back to get his rifle and was only nicked on the top of one finger.

We watched as first we saw the Pathans, mere dots on the hilltop, close and grapple with the smaller soldiers, then as we tried to make out what was happening, the soldiers rolled downhill. When later Davis made his lone counter-attack, with 'D' Company giving covering fire, the excitement was intense.

It was good to see that Davis was awarded the Military Cross in 1950, three years later, the only case of a gallantry award being allowed without a supporting campaign medal.

Communal violence was growing. A neighbouring Gurkha battalion had to evacuate its camp at Wana to go to Chaklala and the few remaining Sikh workers of the Military Engineering Services had to be smuggled out of the camp in the same convoy. Riding openly in trucks was impossible as the Sikhs and Pathans loathed each other. Unfortunately, a Pathan naik, the driver of one of the RIASC lorries, had knowledge of the Sikhs and had liaison with the tribesmen so the convoy was ambushed by over a thousand Pathans. The naik got out of his vehicle and showed the ambushers where the Sikhs were hidden. They and the three Gurkhas with them were overpowered and shot in cold blood. Although the naik was subsequently identified, no action was taken.

On 9 August the long awaited details of our future were made known. As we were the 1st Gurkhas we all thought we would be chosen for transfer to the British Army. Not only were we not chosen as a regiment, but the men had neither the right to opt for British Service, despite previous promises, nor to go on discharge.

The Gurkhas could not understand it; nor could we for that matter.

We were left without positive directions and could therefore give none. Pressure of events obscured the heartbreak. Nor was there any properly planned handover to Indian officers. They never came till after the bitter end, and the end was bitter.

Within a week of hearing this sad and sombre news, we gathered in the Mess on the evening of 14 August, the eve of Independence. We dined together and at the end of the meal, Mr President rose, and tapping his request for silence said, 'Mr Vice, for the last time, the King-Emperor.'

A toast must be given by Mr Vice in the same way he receives it, so he rose, gripped his glass, lifted it for the loyal toast, 'Gentlemen, for the last time, the King-Emperor.'

We all rose, and lifting our glasses, intoned, 'For the last time, the King-Emperor.'

Pakistan Independence was celebrated next day. In Razmak a Church service was held and as the minister prayed for the peace of the two new Dominions, Pathans were sniping the camp from a neighbouring hill, and the Rajputs, clad in dhotis, were pelting them with three-inch mortar bombs. It was a bad omen.

A parade was held and for the first time ever the Pakistani flag was unfurled over tribal territory. The local Brigadier, the local Political Adviser and the Parade Commander gave three cheers and the troops jubilantly responded. After the parade had marched off, they all danced around and chanted. 'We are no longer slaves, we are no longer slaves.' Wherever an 'I' (India) appeared in the soldiers' cloth shoulder-titles, it was inked round to make a 'P' (Pakistan).

We were now in charge of Hindu soldiers in a Muslim country. There was nothing we could do except take all possible precautions when out of camp, on the range or opening the road. The men looked to us for guidance about the future and we could give them none.

We were all warned to return home. I was having my tin trunk painted and just starting a letter home, 'Dear Parents, I should be home by Christmas . . .' when the bugle blew the Officers' Call, 'At the Double'. I put my pen down and ran to the Adjutant's office. There, (having taken weeks to filter through from Delhi) news greeted us. We were 'frozen' and ten out of the fifteen officers were posted to 1st/7th Gurkha Rifles as part of the British Army in Rangoon. Of the remaining five, three were to go to the

7th Gurkha Rifles Regimental Centre and two to remain to hand over the battalion to the Indians, who were not scheduled to arrive until after we had left. We would leave in December. I went back to my room dismissed the painter and then remembered my letter. I continued '. . . but not this year.'

The Rajputs left for India soon after that but the 1st/1st Gurkhas stayed in Pakistan until early November. The comparative seclusion of the Frontier had left us uninvolved in the horrible massacres sparked off by Partition. Down in Punjab, however, grim evidence of the unbelievable turmoil, the heartlessness and the senselessness of it all hit us hard.

Men, women and children, tens of thousands of them, who were of the wrong faith, in the wrong country, their homes broken, impoverished and utterly without hope, made their forlorn journey from the Land of Penance to the Land of Promises. Millions never saw the end of their journey. Each morning, thousands would refuse to get up from the side of the road. It was a heartbreaking task for those involved; we passed it by on the sidelines but even so were sickened by it. On one road, one hundred and twenty miles of bullock-carts were moving, nose to tail, with death smelling sickly sweet the whole while. We saw lorries mow down whole families and the drivers press recklessly on. When millions die, what are a few more deaths?

The Pakistan politicians had set 31 December 1947 as our deadline to be out of the country. I now commanded 'C' Company, which was stationed five miles over the Jammu province border in a village called Kathuwa. Prime Minister Attlee had forbidden British officers of India and Pakistan to go into Jammu or Kashmir because there was a danger of their fighting each other. Even so I had to go, to prepare what I could for a new company commander when he came. I trudged the dusty five miles morning and evening. Folk had the jitters. Latrines had to be dug around our temporary camp, and this was reported within twenty-four hours by Radio Pakistan as 'Indian troops are digging defensive positions at Kathuwa.'

The end was not far off. Garbled orders and incomplete messages about us leaving and Indian officers taking over never made proper sense. However fine the motive behind the act of pulling out, where men meant more than cyphers and numbers, it hurt. Those who have never served in a tight-knit community like a Gurkha battalion can have little idea of the wealth of camaraderie and the warmth of human relationship that exists between officers and men. Nothing really made sense and it was a heartless and painful experience.

Thus the end came. I spent the last two nights in Jammu territory with my Company. There was no relief to hand over to and I hoped that by talking with the men informally I could tell them a little of what they wanted to know without my being disloyal to my own side.

On parting, tears were shed and the sorrow was genuine and hard to bear. My last view of my men (mine by proxy and mine no more) was moving out on foot and by camel on a patrol looking for Pakistani infiltrators. I walked back over the border into India, indignant at the unseemly haste of having to meet an unrealistic political deadline. We were abandoning our men, we had broken trust and, by God, it hurt.

The Gurkhas had never been subjects of the King-Emperor. They have King of their own, the King of Nepal, but as this account reveals the affection and respect that existed between the Gurkha soldiers and their British officers transcended national loyalties. Even the British private soldier, usually no great lover of native troops, kept a special place in his heart for the sturdy Gurkhas. This respect and affection was never better expressed than in the tribute paid to his Gurkha soldiers by Sir Ralph Turner, who gained the Military Cross while serving with the 2/3rd Gurkhas in the Great War.

My thoughts return to you who were my comrades, the stubborn and indomitable peasants of Nepal. Once more I see you in your bivouacs or about your fires, on forced marches or in trenches, now shivering with wet and cold, now scorched by a pitiless and burning sun. Uncomplaining you endure hunger and thirst and wounds; and at the last your unwavering lines disappear into the smoke and wrath of battle.

The love of Indian regiments and Indian soldiers was not restricted to the Gurkhas. Other British officers, serving with the Dogras or the Rajputs, the Jats or the Baluch, wrote singing the praises of their regiments and the gallant sepoys, anxious that in any account of the end of Empire their men should have a place.

In Delhi, meanwhile, life was proceeding in vice-regal fashion, as Reg Jinks recalls from his time on the GHQ Signals staff:

Two weddings took place which I recall because they touched us at least peripherally. These were the weddings of Princess Elizabeth, our present Queen, and the Viceroy's daughter, Pamela Mountbatten. Princess Elizabeth was married in 1947 and we were all asked to contribute for the unit wedding present and donate a personal sum at the weekly pay parade. The total collected from the entire Unit was just eight annas.

It wasn't, I think, so much antipathy to the Monarchy, just dispassionate indifference. It couldn't be left like that, of course, and some expensive gift was purchased from Unit funds and sent to England with all good wishes from GHQ Signals. Pamela Mountbatten got married in Delhi with a great deal of pomp, including a guard of Indian cavalry. Our Captain McCluskie ran across a troop of slow-moving cavalry rehearsing for this event and was annoyed by an officer of HM Forces being refused right of way by what he described as a bunch of carnival-wallahs out on a spree.

Jim O'Sullivan was also in Delhi at this time, and has a slightly different view of Mountbatten's activities:

The presence of the Mountbattens in India while we were there should not be forgotten. After Independence Lord Louis stayed on as Governor General and he and Edwina did a tremendous public relations job with the new nations. There has sometimes been criticism of them in recent years but very few ordinary people in India at that time would say a bad word against them.

Aristocrats they may have been but they possessed a 'common touch' when dealing with ordinary people. Lady Edwina tirelessly attended functions; our Anglo-Indian friends proudly showed us photos of her handing out trophies at a hockey tournament. We rarely saw him in Delhi but felt his presence there. One morning one of the lads snapped him going for a morning drive in his natty little white sports car – protected by two armoured cars, fore and aft.

Mountbatten and his family may have enjoyed the fading splendours of the Raj, but the soldiers of the British Army were simply anxious to get home and let the Indians and Pakistanis get on with the independence they had sought for so long. Sergeant James 'Ted' Relph of the Border Regiment recalls the last days of the Raj for his battalion in Calcutta:

On Tuesday 19 August, I wrote home as follows: 'We had a holiday on Friday and Saturday but could not go out till noon on Saturday and then only in parties of four, so I didn't go. We saw most of the celebrations from the roof. You will have heard of the happy way in which Calcutta celebrated its Independence Day. No riots of any kind; on the contrary Hindus and Muslims joined forces and rode round on every imaginable vehicle with cries of '*Jai Hind*' (may India flourish) and '*Hindu Muslim ek tio*' (Hindus and Muslims are one), laughing, cheering, flag-waving and setting off fireworks off till far into the night.

'There was a lot of cheering during the evening of the 14th, and at midnight it became louder and lustier. Next morning the flag of India was broken over Government House to the tune of a salute of guns fired from the Fort here by a detachment of 91st Field Artillery. Then I am told that a mixed and happy crowd decided that as Government House was theirs, they must inspect it and thousands are said to have surged round during the day and bathed in the private swimming pool. Also there was a crowd who decided that as Fort William was theirs, they must have a look inside. However, they were tactfully turned away. There was no Union Jack flying on the Fort, only a huge Indian Flag on the water tower, the highest point.

'Yesterday was a Muslim festival and we all expected trouble, but no: the Hindus joined the celebrations and distributed cigarettes and sweets to the Muslims. Even Gandhi came and wished them a 'Happy Id'. Some shops which have been closed for months are open again. One wonders how long this idyllic state of affairs will last. The chaps who did go out (in civilian clothes, not in uniform) were greeted by all and joined in the celebrations.

'I was Battalion Orderly Sergeant on Sunday. All went according to plan. Since then I've been checking the library in the mornings. We have all our packing boxes ready now; the library is going home with us. Today we were issued with the first part of our Blighty kit – serge blouse and slacks, angora shirt, gloves, woollen underpants and balaclva helmets – greatcoats to follow.'

Lieutenant D.J. McCaskill of the Lancashire Fusiliers had a slightly more alarming experience when his battalion came to leave Deolali:

One of the signallers, let's call him Fosdyke, was plagued by a terrible stammer. He had always suffered from this impediment, and as such, had been removed from normal duties and made responsible for battery charging and maintenance. To use him in any other work was impossible, and I have no idea how he came to be in the Army, let alone in the Signals.

Now we were getting ready to return home, moving to Deolali seemed to offer the prospect of doing something about his impediment, for apart from the military camp, the town also contained the main Army mental hospital – the only one in India. Being Deolali – 'doo-lally' – is a term used even now to denote being mentally unstable, though I expect the origin of the phrase has long since been forgotten.

The mental hospital was proud of its successes which included curing speech impediments, with a special mention of stuttering, and I urged Fosdyke to take advantage of its services before he left. He thought it would be worth a try. I got him an explanatory note from the battalion M.O. and off he went.

Three days later, the Signal Sergeant came running into my office. He was usually quiet and studious but on this occasion he was quite unlike his normal self.

'Fosdyke's back, Sir,' he panted.

'Oh, good,' I said, rather startled. 'Is he any better?'

'I don't know about that. He says he's going to kill you – and he's on his way here now.'

There was barely time to get the Sergeant, Corporal Brown and the storeman to stand beside me before Fosdyke burst in. No knock, no thank you, not even a salute. He appeared distressed, so I decided this was not the time to start quoting King's Regulations.

'Glad to see you back,' I said; 'How did you get on?'

'Get on?' he shouted, 'Get on? I've been locked up with the criminally insane for two whole days.'

Some reaction seemed required. 'Well, I'll tell you one thing,' I said cheerfully, 'you've lost your stutter.'

Fosdyke seemed taken aback: 'I suppose I have,' he admitted.

I sat him down, got the storeman to make us all a cup of tea, and asked him to tell us what happened. I felt that it would be more difficult to kill a person if you'd shared a cup of tea first, and in any case, we were all agog to know what had disturbed him.

It emerged that Fosdyke had appeared at the Deolali Psychiatry Clinic and produced the M.O's note. The trouble was that no one could decipher the doctor-like scrawl on the letter. Poor Fosdyke tried to explain, but his stammer made it difficult and the authorities decided to err on the side of caution. His kit was taken away, he was put in pyjamas, shown into a ward and left there.

All the nurses were hefty-looking men, and the fact that they locked the door of the ward when they left didn't help matters. Fosdyke was further alarmed when one of the other men in the ward said that he – the speaker – was the Pope, and would see that no harm came to him.

This set Fosdyke battering on the door immediately, but the very muscular male nurse who arrived had heard all this before and went away again. At mealtimes, Fosdyke was only given a spoon – to stop him harming himself, he was told – and it was made clear that if he didn't stop complaining he would be put under restraint. It was two days before the hospital were able to contact the battalion M.O. and find out what it was all about. Only then did Fosdyke see the hospital doctor.

'I only came in to have my stammer cured,' Fosdyke protested.

'It doesn't seem too bad to me,' said the doctor; 'I'm returning you to your battalion.' And so he did.

As you can guess, the story went round the camp like wildfire, and poor Fusilier Fosdyke couldn't show his face without being greeted by guffaws of laughter. Perhaps most important, he never again betrayed the slightest sign of a stammer – but he never thanked me, either.

The C-in-C India, General Sir Claude Auchinleck, himself an officer of the Indian Army, was appointed Head of the Armed Forces Reconstruction Committee, responsible to the Indian and Pakistan Defence Ministers for the fair division of the Indian Army. With a small Staff, Auchinleck set about the task of dismembering an Army he had loved and served all his life.

A quarter of a million Hindu and Sikh troops went to India, one hundred and forty thousand Muslim troops formed the Army of

Pakistan. The thirty British battalions of the 'British Army in India' began to withdraw soon after independence, first to their bases at Deolali and Dum Dum, then to the embarkation ports at Bombay and Karachi. While they were heading home, all the latent troubles of partition broke out across the sub-continent.

The task of territorial partition, the fixing of the boundaries between India and the two wings of Pakistan, was given to a British civil servant, Sir Cyril Radcliffe. His team was faced with a terrible task, for every village along the proposed borderline had a reason – usually water and grazing rights – for having a little more territory on the other side of the line. Radcliffe had poor maps, few assistants for reasons of security, and no personal knowledge of the territory.

Worst of all, he had no time. Radcliffe had just a few short weeks to carve out two countries from this vast and violent continent, an enormous task, not least in the Punjab where the farms and towns were variously occupied by Sikhs, Hindus and Muslims, all dependent on irrigation and uncertain water supplies. One of the strangest images of the entire independence period is that of Sir Cyril and his team, labouring through the days and nights in their bungalows, the floors and tables littered with paper, slowly drawing lines on maps to create the new frontiers of India and Pakistan.

The announcement of the final frontiers – the 'Award' – was delayed, perhaps wisely, until after independence. The Viceroy, Mountbatten, concealed the outcome of Radcliffe's work until 17 August, two days after independence, knowing that whatever Radcliffe proposed the Indians and – as they must now be called – the Pakistanis, would find fault with it.

In fact, along most of the frontier the two nations agreed to the line without fuss. The big problem was in the Punjab. The partition of the Punjab had been one of the stumbling blocks to independence and independence would not end the trouble here. Whatever Radcliffe suggested was sure to cause trouble in the Punjab because any boundary line would carve right through the land of the warlike Sikhs, who wasted barely an hour before taking up the sword and attacking their Muslim neighbours, hoping to solve the boundary question with a slash of their tulwars. A dead man and his dead family had no claim to anything but each attack provoked a reprisal. To escape these massacres the people living along the border, Sikh, Muslim, Hindu, were soon on the move.

As a result of the Partition Award millions of people, Muslims and Hindus, were forced to leave their homes. The best estimate has about five and a half million people travelling in each direction, Muslims trekking north to Pakistan, Hindus heading south for the elusive safety of the new India. Within days of Radcliffe's decision being announced the Muslims, Sikhs and Hindus were attacking each other's refugee columns and trains, massacring their former fellow citizens by the thousand and tens of thousand.

The massacres were at their worst in the Punjab where trains were soon pulling across the border into India filled with dead bodies, the carriages marked 'A Present from Pakistan' and carrying as heavy a load of Muslims in the other direction as 'Presents to Pakistan'. While this was going on, the British Army, with no role left to play and forbidden to interfere, stood by and watched the bitter fruits of independence.

Len Lambert was a sergeant in the Royal Scots Fusiliers at this time:

From 1945 to 1947, until we left India, we were turning out to quell riots. We faced mobs of up to two thousand people and to confront a chanting mob of that size is quite an ordeal. As time went on, the Indians got quite vicious against British troops and as we travelled around in trucks which were protected by wire mesh, we were stoned and spat upon.

I was a young sergeant, just twenty years old, and had been a sergeant for about six months. I was given the job of escorting an ammunition train from Meerut City to Jubbulpore – and I was in charge. I can tell you it was a tricky job. All kinds of gangs were on the loose trying to blow up anything or steal ammunition and arms. However, I got it to its destination with little trouble. A huge portion of this ammo was brought out of Burma when the war finished.

In one of the towns we arrived at, fierce rioting had taken place the night before. Some people had their heads chopped off by an ordinary wood axe. The journey was very trying and full of incidents and at one point we travelled with fixed bayonets.

On leaving New Delhi we saw mile after mile of bullock carts on their way to Pakistan and others coming the other way – mile after mile – the bullock carts causing havoc with the dust they were creating. Fights took place and hundreds were killed on both sides.

All they did was cover the bodies with sand, but as the wind blew the sand off the bodies, the vultures had a field day; no one seemed to be upset about this, neither the Indians nor us troops, but by this time I had served nearly three years out there and some of the lads had served longer, so we were not unused to many of the sights we came across, having become very hardened to all this.

Counting the dead bodies and the skeletons was impossible, there were too many. The dead must have run into thousands . . . it was a sight, which unless you had witnessed it yourself, it would be hard to believe.

After the second and last convoy returned to New Delhi airport, all the troops involved were very relieved that it was all over . . . the heat, the dusty roads made worse by the bullock carts . . . sometimes our transport was down to walking pace because we could not see through the dust. Even though there were thousands of corpses, there did not seem to be any smell of death. I think this was because of the vultures. There were black clouds of the birds, dropping from the sky at will to feed. We completed two convoys and that was the end of that.

Not only Indian and Pakistani citizens were on the move. The diary of J.T. 'Ted' Relph of the East Lancashire Regiment recalls the evacuation of British civilians:

On the morning of Wednesday, 29 October, I ended up as part of a reception committee to pick up Europeans from Simla, Dehra Dun, and bring them into Delhi in convoys of anything up to fifty vehicles. The convoy set out while we set to and prepared the beds, mattresses, blankets, plates, mugs, whatever, for the people they collected.

At about 15.30 they arrived, hundreds of them, gouty old colonels, mothers with small children, one old lady of eighty-nine who had been in India for fifty years, and young women of Anglo-Indian descent; all were now en-route for England. The CO gave me charge of two little girls unaccompanied, whose parents lived in Delhi but who had been at school in Mussoorie. I took them home and was given a cup of tea and came back to write this in bed.

I have finished guarding the railway station, which is quite filthy with the large number of refugees who have arrived from the Punjab. This seems to be the cause of much congestion in Delhi, but of course the railway staff rightly refuse to go north if they are liable to be cut to pieces.

One refugee went up to the Sergeant Major and asked if he could send a telegram? 'Certainly, but who to?' 'To Winston Churchill,' came the reply. 'Ask him to come and see what quitting India has done and maybe he will send the British back.' Some of the Sikh police are beating up the Muslims with their lathis, others are charging the refugees up to Rs 5 for a chaggle of water . . . if the Scots of the Royal Scots Fusiliers don't catch them at it and throw them out of the station.

Massacres were not only taking place in India and the Punjab. There was plenty of bloodshed in Pakistan, with the Pathan tribesmen swarming out of the hills to attack the Sikhs and Hindus. The *Red Hackle* journal of The Black Watch contains several accounts of the end in India and the birthpangs of Pakistan in 1947 from members of the 2nd Battalion:

Hopes of a continued peaceful existence in the N.W.F.P. had gradually been lessening during the last few weeks of the Battalion's stay in Peshawar, and it was therefore with some misgivings as to how long it would be before we saw them again, that the rear party watched the second train carrying the last half of the Battalion steam out of the cantonment section.

After the hand-over was completed – a process which dragged on interminably due to the fact that nearly all the local civil employees were Sikhs or Hindus and they were far more interested in making plans, should the necessity arise, for preserving their own skins.

All went normally until Sunday, 7 September, when the plans of the Sikhs and Hindus were suddenly put to the test. At about 0930 hrs, a fusillade was heard, and thereafter a certain amount of intermittent firing. Major Irwin went at once from the Mess to the barrack block and ordered all men inside in order to ensure that no one should be involved in any incident. An extra armed guard was posted at each end of the building.

He then went down to the Orderly Room of the 3/8 Punjab Regiment (Muslims, who had moved into the other half of the

Roberts Barracks about a week before) and there learnt that there had been 'an unfortunate misunderstanding' between a standing patrol of the 3/8 Punjab and a patrol of the 19th Lancers (Sikhs and Hindus) in which two members of the 3/8 had been killed – the Lancers also suffered casualties. The situation was, however, reported to be calm and no more trouble was expected.

However, the news – distorted by its verbal passage from place to place, spread through the countryside like lightning – so that by 1200 hrs some two thousand Pathan tribesmen and villagers had collected outside the North-West end of the cantonment. The whole Rear Party was reminded once again that we were strictly forbidden to take part in any trouble, unless, of course, we ourselves were threatened. Suitable precautions were taken and the men were once again told to remain under cover until further notice.

Firing commenced at about 1230 and by 1300 hrs the cantonment was swarming with tribesmen in lorries, tongas and on foot, intent on the murder of all Sikhs (in particular) and Hindus (as a sideline) and the looting of all shops owned by them.

Having taken all the necessary precautions, the officers returned by various covered routes to the Mess, over which bullets were passing almost continuously. The meal (and most other meals for the next three days) was consumed with a loaded pistol ready to the hand of each officer.

During the afternoon, further tribesmen entered the city, and by evening the Sikh quarter was burning furiously – the whole of the night sky glowing crimson. The authorities considered that it would never be known how many perished in the flames, for we were told that the tribesmen not only surrounded the burning area and prevented anyone from leaving but they even drove people from other quarters into the area.

On Monday morning, Major Irwin was called away and given the job of helping to organise the refugee problem, so that the command of the Rear Party fell upon Captain Lindsay. During Monday six Tonga loads of tribesmen galloped up the road through the barracks and attacked the canteen (owned by a Hindu). They did a certain amount of damage, but failed to find the Hindu staff, most of whom were concealed in barrels in the godown (warehouse). During the day looting continued unabated along the Mall and in the Saddar Bazaar area. By this time nearly all Sikhs and Hindus who had not been murdered were concentrated in various large buildings and were temporarily safe.

There still remained a few isolated persons, including the Canteen Manager. He, disguised as a Muslim, decided to make for safety in a building in the Saddar Bazaar. He got as far as the gate of the Officers' Mess, where a passing band of tribesmen recognised and murdered him – a particularly messy proceeding during which he was shot seven times and then finished off with a meat cleaver.

This sort of thing went on until Wednesday afternoon, by which time the Military and Police had got themselves organised and speedily drove the tribesmen off. After Wednesday afternoon there was no more organised trouble, but there were continual isolated incidents all over the cantonment and the city. The cantonment presented a dismal spectacle – all Hindu shops burst open and looted – bodies still lying about, and scattered parties still intent on looting.

Lieutenant D.J. McCaskill, saw the end in Lucknow:

It could be said that the task of the Regiment in Lucknow at the end was not so much holding the Empire together as keeping the Muslims and Hindus apart. I know it is an unfashionable opinion today but I don't feel that Britain has too much to be ashamed of. There were so many different cultures and religions in India that only a third party could keep any peace between them.

The British have their faults – who hasn't – but we must have had something going for us since the huge sub-continent remained a single unit while we were there, and only splintered into fragments of its once glorious self after we left. Even after all the recriminations and arguments of the past there still seems to be a friendliness between the Indians and the British, especially with so many now making their homes among us. So don't believe all you hear of the evils of the British Empire – there was a lot of good in it too.

Mrs June Powell was still living in Calcutta when India was partitioned:

The Hindu–Muslim clashes over Partition in 1947 were much worse than we had seen in 1946 . . . this was when the real violence started.

All the Indian shops and the bazaar closed. The roads out of Calcutta were full of bicycles, rickshaws, bullock carts and people on foot, leaving the city, and when the killing started the bodies were left in the streets. That is when His Excellency, the Provincial Governor, brought in the Army. For a few days I did not leave the flat because of the dead bodies lying around, but once they were cleared I went out again, mainly to find food.

Naturally, I would not allow the children out, although my *ayah* and her husband wanted to take them to the park. One day her husband did go out and came back with a chicken. We let the servants bring their families and friends to shelter under our roof and the top of the house was absolutely packed with Gurkha families.

With the streets being patrolled by troops on foot and in armoured cars and tanks, a brooding calm settled on the city. People and traders who had left, returned and shops opened again, but things were never quite the same again; the atmosphere was different. When I walked through the bazaar the shopkeepers no longer came running out after me, shouting and laughing and trying to get me into their shops with rolls of coloured silks, jewellery, carvings, or even Indian sweets, as they had always done. I was buying things to take back to England, but it was no fun any more.

In actual fact I was totally petrified of going to England. I only knew what I had read in books and I was always being told by older women that I would never cope. I was twenty-one, with a toddler and a baby in arms. I had never cleaned a house, cooked a meal, or done any washing and ironing. I packed my home but didn't really know what I would want. I had all the wrong clothes and the first thing I did when we docked in Liverpool in November was to buy a pair of walking shoes and a warm coat. I was completely heartbroken on leaving India. One of the worst moments of my life was standing on deck as we left Bombay and watching the Gateway of India slowly disappear.

Sapper Colin Bean has other memories of the last few days in India.

In Nicol Road we were in what was still British India – one of the reasons why, early in 1946, the lower ranks of The Royal Indian Navy mutinied. Going around in Bombay at that time one could not be unaware of the – up to then – reasonably peaceful activities and posters in the city. Our job in the R.E's. was to expedite the evacuation of Army stores and personnel.

To help us with the acres and acres of paperwork, members of the 'Wasbees' and 'Fannies' were drafted into our offices. Young ladies, Indian, Burmese and British, who had enrolled in either the Women's Auxiliary Service, Burma (W.A.S.B.) or the Women's Transport Service (F.A.N.Y. – First Aid Nursing Yeomanry). One evening, after a particularly street-noisy day, the last copy of that day's quota of movement and Embarkation Orders had been finished. My superior officer put it to me that I should accompany the young ladies back to their billets, just in case. Furthermore, the gallant Lieutenant insisted that Corporal Bean should take his officer's pistol and sit next to the Indian driver, also just in case. One of the young W.A.S.B. ladies was L/Cpl. Cowan, daughter of Major General D.T. 'Punch' Cowan. A precious cargo, so wasn't I lucky?

The Indian Army driver was about as keen as I was at the prospect of driving through the streets of Bombay at this time of night, after a riotous day. He spoke no English and understood only enough to recognise 'Turn left' or 'Turn right' accompanied by suitable gestures. We broke the city speed limit, and the pistol became more insecure in my perspiring hand, but nothing happened until we drove in front of the Town Hall, when behind us we heard a metallic 'ping' and in the side mirror I saw the tarmac behind us spurt up from the roadway, closely followed by two more 'pinging' noises. One of the young ladies, very calmly leaned over my shoulder and said, 'Excuse me, Corporal, but I think we're being fired at.' The Indian driver had already yelled '*Tik hai Sahib*,' and increased speed.

Eventually, the ladies having been safely delivered, the driver and I got back to Nicol Road by a different route. As I was about to return to my own camp, the officer said, 'Oh Corporal, my jolly old shooter please. Don't have to use it, did you?' 'No Sir,' I replied. 'Thank God for that,' he said. 'I'd forgotten to load it.'

Not everyone who wanted to leave could leave and the large Anglo-Indian community had nowhere to go. Alan Crocker again:

One of the most pathetic things about India, apart from the terrible poverty of the majority contrasting with the lifestyle of the wealthy, was the talk of Anglo-Indians. Listening to people who were despised by the Indians, and at best tolerated by the British, talking about 'Home', was heartbreaking. It is not a myth that this section of the community, most of whom had never been out of India, would talk of 'Dear old Leicester Square' and wonder 'When will I see Piccadilly again?'

So, in various ways, independence came to India and Pakistan. A few small details had to be tidied up from the days of the Raj, including one task at Lucknow. On the evening before independence, as soon as it got dark, a small party of British soldiers went quietly to the ruins of the Residency in Lucknow, the place held by a small British garrison against all odds during the Indian Mutiny ninety years before. To commemorate that famous stand, the ruined Residency was the one place in the British Empire where the Union Flag flew day and night, and was not pulled down at sunset.

Now the Raj was over and the British flag would finally have to come down, but the British soldiers preferred to do that themselves. The flag duly came down, but that was still not enough. The flagpole was dismantled and sawn off close to the ground and the hollow where it had stood for nearly one hundred years filled in with concrete. When a jubilant crowd of Indians came next morning to haul down the Union Flag, they found that it had already gone and all traces of where it had once been flown had vanished.

The Raj was over, but the role of the British soldiers in India still had a few months to run. In the newly divided Punjab, the most sensitive part of the entire sub-continent, the warlike Sikhs were up in arms, raping and killing, kidnapping children, burning Muslim shops and looting Muslim farms while from the mountains to the north Muslim Pathan and Afridi tribesmen came across the frontier to fight them, turning the region into a battlefield.

Murder and massacre was now taking place all over the sub-continent, escalating and spreading during the weeks immediately before and after independence. Nowhere did the troubles reach the scale of violence achieved in the Punjab and just before independence, after weeks of violence, the Partition Command finally asked General Auchinleck to send troops to the Punjab.

This force, the Punjab Boundary Force or PFB, chiefly consisting of the 4th Indian Division of the old Indian Army under Major General

T.W. Rees, arrived in the Punjab at the end of July 1947 ready for the anticipated outbreak of violence following independence. The PBF eventually reached a strength of fifty-five thousand men and needed every one of them for on 17 August 1947, while the citizens of Delhi celebrated independence, the news broke of the Radcliffe Award, and the Punjab exploded.

Patrick Carpenter, an officer with the 2/2nd Gurkhas, records his views of that time:

> For better or worse, independence came to India in August 1947, with the creation of India and Pakistan. I use the phrase for better or worse though it is doubtful if there was anything good about it. Partition sowed the seeds of war between the two countries, and money that should have been spent on development went on maintaining large armed forces, mainly because of mutual distrust and suspicion, which broke out in armed conflict from time to time.
>
> Estimates vary but probably a million peoples lost their lives in the immediate aftermath of independence, especially during the migrations, I recall a British officer in the 9th Gurkhas telling me that his company had been rushed to sort out the consequences of a massacre in the Punjab; they found nothing but the mutilated corpses of men, women and children, massacred in totality. A trainload of people, about two thousand in all, had been halted by placing rocks on the line, and a horde of Sikhs, concealed in the ripening grain, had swarmed onto the train and slaughtered everyone on board with their tulwars.

The inter-communal massacres went on for weeks, in some cases to months. Among the casualties of this violence was the PBF which was too small to contain the violence and blamed by both sides for either attempting to do so, or failing to do so. Both communities accused the PBF of being partial to the other side and after two weeks, at the end of August 1947, the Force was split up and sent to its respective territories, where the battalions continued to do what they could to stem the flood of violence. They could do very little; two centuries of suppressed violence and hostility had burst into life.

Mountbatten was asked to stay on by Nehru and Jinnah, to act as Head of State while the new nations found their feet, but Nehru would not let him employ British troops, though these were recognised as on impartial force. Nor was Clement Attlee willing to let British soldiers become involved in this business; the Raj was over.

Eventually, either from a lack of victims or exhaustion with the slaughter, the killing ceased. Gandhi was active in the Punjab and Bengal, preaching against communal violence, and gradually the massacres petered out. One of the last victims of the violence was the Mahatma himself, shot to death on 30 January 1948 by a young Hindu fanatic.

Jinnah and Nehru now had their independence; the frontiers of India and Pakistan had been set down on maps and marked out with blood. Kashmir and the larger of the Princely States were still causing problems and would do so for decades to come, but the Raj was over and the time had come for the last British regiments to leave. British troops had been departing for months from Karachi and Bombay and Madras and remnants would remain here and there for the next couple of years but the last full battalion to leave, marching through the India Gate at Bombay on 28 February 1948, was the 1st Bn. The Somerset Light Infantry. This event was seized on to mark the departure of the British and their Army and it turned into a memorable scene.

Major Freddie de Butts was in charge of the Guard of Honour for that last parade:

By the time we came to leave there were only about two hundred men in the battalion. This meant that the majority of the Battalion was the 'Escort to the Colours' and we held practices daily, under RSM Ken Batlett's tuition, until the drill was of a very high standard. We were all looking forward to the final ceremony, hoping that friends at home would be able to see it on the cinema news, and there is a very good account in the Regimental Journal.

Our last week in Bombay was a hectic one. Packing, handing over barracks, giving and attending farewell parties, and practices for our final parade left little time for ruminating on the fact that a whole chapter, indeed a whole volume, of the history of the British Army was drawing to a close. At last, on 27 February 1948 we completed our embarkation of stores on the *Express of Australia* and prepared for the final Parade.

Hundreds of spectators arrived to occupy the five hundred seats in front of the 'Gateway of India' on either side of the archway, and thousands without tickets were crowding the square and the streets. All the Guards of Honour were arriving on Parade with bands playing and Colours flying.

Looking back from the Gateway, on the right were Guards of Honour from the Bombay Grenadiers, the 2nd Sikhs, and the Royal Indian Navy, while on the left were those from the 3/5th Gurkhas, the Mahratta Light Infantry, and a second Guard from the Royal Indian Navy.

The 'Escort to the Colours', provided by the Battalion, consisted of six officers and fifty Other Ranks. As soon as the Governor was seated they marched on to the parade to the Regimental March, though without the assistance of buglers, who could not be provided for the occasion. Major-General Batemen presented us with a beautiful silver model of the 'Gateway of Indian' and a National Flag of India. The model is exact in every detail, stands about a foot high, and is mounted on a black plinth which bears the following inscription:

28th February, 1948

To commemorate the comradeship of the soldiers of the British and Indian armies, this model of the 'Gateway of India' is presented by the soldiers of the Army of India serving in Bombay Area to 1st Bn. The Somerset Light Infantry (P.A.) on the occasion of the departure of the last British unit to have served in India.

– September 1745 to August 1947 –

Ultimus in Indis.

Now the time for departure had arrived. First, the Indian Guards of Honour gave a Royal Salute and 'God Save the King' was played. To this the Somerset Light Infantry replied with a Royal Salute and the Indian National Anthem, 'Vande Mattaram'. Then the Escort Trooped the Colours to the tune of 'Auld Lang Syne' down the centre of the parade and out through the Gateway of India. The whole manoeuvre was carried out with the utmost precision, providing an inspiring and most moving sight.

Finally, the C.O. Lt.-Colonel Platt and General Whistler said their goodbyes and passed through the Gateway to a launch on which the Colours had already embarked. As the launch pulled away, the Colours flying in the breeze, the crowds were shouting, waving, and in some cases weeping.

Now it is all over, but the significance of those moments at the Gateway of India remains with us, and always will. They are not remarkable just for the fact that they terminate a chapter of British history but because they symbolise in a unique way the affection and admiration of India, not only for the British soldier, but for the whole British race and the tradition of Empire. Never can an occupying Army have such a send-off.'

The views of the Somerset's Regimental correspondent seem to have been shared by Sir Maharaj Singh, the Governor of Bombay province, as expressed in his farewell speech:

In the past we have had our differences with Great Britain, but this is not the occasion to recall them. Rather, I think today of the finest act in the long and historic connection between the United Kingdom and by India; that is the grant of freedom last August by your country. That act of courage and wisdom, which will stand the test of time, carries with it, I am confident, the full sympathy of the British soldier of all ranks, as well as the British civilians.

Now you are going home. All of us, whether Indian or British or representatives of other nations, wish you well on your journey and in the life that awaits you in your country. We earnestly hope and believe that friendly relations will continue to exist between our countries and that India and England will play their part in the preservation of the peace of the world which is so essential for the welfare and progress of mankind.

I have read to you messages from His Excellency The Governor-General, and the Prime Minister of India. It remains for me, on behalf of my Government, the people of the Province, the City of Bombay and myself, to bid you Farewell . . . and Godspeed.

5

The Palestine Mandate: 1947–1948

'When Arthur Balfour launched his scheme for peopling Palestine with Jewish immigrants, I am credibly informed that he did not know there were Arabs in that country.'

W.R. Inge, Dean of St Paul's, London, 1939.

If the problems in India come into sharp focus immediately after the end of the Second World War, the problems of Palestine had begun decades before – and Palestine was not really part of the British Empire at all. Palestine had been taken on in 1923 under a 'Mandate' from the League of Nations, an international body formed after the Great War to resolve the problems of that war and lay the foundations for world peace.

The British Mandate in Palestine was for a fixed period of twenty-five years and was to terminate in 1948 but the years of the Mandate were never less than difficult, trapping the British between the vested interests of two conflicting groups, the local Arabs and a large, rapidly expanding Jewish minority. To trace the origins of that entanglement we must go back to the Great War of 1914–18 and the long-cherished aspirations of the Jewish people for their own national home.

Until 1917 Palestine had been a province of the Turkish Empire.

The Great War finished off the 'Sick Man of Europe' which had allied itself with Germany during that conflict. After the war was over the victorious powers carved up the Turkish Empire, granting independence to certain parts, annexing others, and declaring 'Zones of Influence' in various parts of the Middle East. Under the latter heading France became influential in Syria and the Lebanon while Britain remained in effective control of Egypt and became powerful in Iraq, Trans-Jordan and Palestine, the parts occupied by her armies at the end of the War.

Britain did not take on the Palestine Mandate from altruistic motives; the first reason for accepting the responsibility for creating a Jewish home in Palestine was that peace in the area was judged crucial to the security of Britain's imperial lifeline, the Suez Canal. For the same reason Britain annexed the island of Cyprus, which the British had occupied, with Turkish permission, since the 1870s. The second reason was that some years previously the British Prime Minister, Arthur Balfour, had committed his country to a policy outlined in a letter which came to be called the Balfour Declaration.

To the Jews of the Diaspora, Palestine – Zion – Israel – was the Promised Land, pledged to their people by Jehovah, a gift from the Lord to Isaac and Jacob and Moses. Demands for a return to the Land became louder during the nineteenth century, when the Jewish communities in Russia and Poland were persecuted by anti-Semitic authorities. A steady stream of Jewish refugees flowed into Palestine throughout the latter half of the nineteenth century but by the start of the Great War they still numbered less than 10 per cent of the population. The rest were Bedouin or Hashamite Arabs or Palestinians, loyal to their tribal chiefs. Then came the Balfour Declaration.

Britain had supported the idea that the Jews should have their own homeland for many years. At one time it had even been suggested that Uganda, a fertile but under-developed British territory in Central Africa, might make a national home for the Jews, but for the Jews of the Diaspora there was only one land they wanted, Zion, or Israel, from which they had been expelled by the Romans nearly two thousand years ago. Unfortunately, in the intervening centuries this land had been occupied by the Arabs.

With the collapse of the Turkish Empire, Balfour felt that the Arabs 'would not grudge that small niche (Palestine) being given back to the people who, for all these hundreds of years, had been separated from it' and the worldwide Jewish community – the Zionists – certainly wanted it back. The Arabs, and in particular the Palestinians, were equally determined that they should not have it.

The Hashemite Arabs of Palestine and Jordan had fought against the Turks for a homeland, and various people, including T.E. Lawrence – Lawrence of Arabia – had said they should have it. This already had the makings of a pretty mess and so, thanks to Balfour's Declaration, the British ended up in the middle of a bitter fracas.

Arthur Balfour involved Britain in the affairs of Palestine in 1919, when, in a letter to the Zionist financier, Lord Rothschild, he declared his support for the establishment of 'a national home for the Jewish people' in Palestine. Lord Rothschild passed on this offer of support to Chaim Weizmann, the 'Father of Israel', who promptly took him up on the offer, but Weizmann wanted more than Balfour had actually suggested. Balfour was proposing a Jewish home; Weizmann wanted a Jewish state.

Balfour was well aware that Palestine contained seven hundred thousand Arabs and said as much in a note to the Cabinet, adding that since the Four Powers who had won the war were totally committed to Zionism and the setting up of a Jewish home in Palestine, the Palestinians were not to be consulted since they were certain to disagree. It was decreed that the interests of the Palestinians were not to be damaged by the entry of the Zionists into their country but how this trick was to be managed was not made clear. This pious hope, like much else in that unhappy land, was doomed from the start.

Balfour's Declaration was given fresh impetus and official sanction in 1922 by the League of Nations, a forerunner of the marginally more successful United Nations. Taking up the proposal enshrined in Balfour's Declaration, the League charged Britain with a 'Mandate' – to establish in Palestine a 'national home for the Jewish people'. A later generation of British 'squaddies', spat at, stoned and shot at in Palestine, while being vilified in the Press around the world, wished that Balfour had kept his mouth shut and spared them a thankless and impossible task.

Following the terms of the Declaration, the Mandate added that this was to be done 'while respecting the rights of the existing population', but again there were no suggestions as to how this could be achieved. Jewish immigration increased, as did Arab resistance, culminating in a massacre of Jewish immigrants in Hebron in 1929. In repelling the Arab attacks on Jewish settlements the British killed over a hundred Palestinian Arabs.

By 1935 the British had had to deploy two full divisions in Palestine to keep the hostile communities apart. With the advent of Adolf Hitler in Germany in 1933, Jewish immigration increased and the Arab people of Palestine began to feel increasingly threatened. This was hardly surprising as by the end of 1934 new Jewish settlers were arriving in Palestine at the rate of a thousand a week.

In 1939, with ten years of Mandate still to run and war on the horizon, the British Government issued a White Paper, a discussion document, on the Palestine problem. In it they restricted Jewish immigration to seventy-five thousand over the next five-year period and set up internal self-governing institutions which would – it was hoped – encourage the leaders of the two communities to work together in forging a unified state in the territory of Palestine.

This White Paper pleased no one and almost provoked a breach with the President of the United States, Franklin D. Roosevelt. The Americans had long taken an interest in the affairs of Palestine and Roosevelt saw no reason why the Jews should not be allowed unrestricted immigration into Palestine, whatever the resident Arabs felt. He also felt, and made that feeling public, that the British were dragging their feet in the creation of the Jewish homeland offered under the Mandate.

This attitude was not entirely unconnected with the need to mobilise the support of the powerful and wealthy US Jewish community in Roosevelt's re-election bid for a third term in office. One lesson the British still had to learn was that trouble must be avoided in an American election year. 1940 was such a year and the difficulties for the British administrating the Mandate in Palestine and the views of a million Palestinian Arabs, who saw their rights to the territory threatened, interested the President and the Jewish community in America not at all.

They could claim the credit for establishing Israel and saving some Jews from Nazi Germany; any failing or shortfall could be blamed on the British. The British could also be blamed for letting down the Arabs by failing to 'respect the rights of the resident population'; that thought comforted the American oil lobby.

All politicians like to be popular and among American politicians,

Democratic and Republican, there was a great desire to be seen as the honest broker over the Palestine question, the vessel of decency, the supporter of every side. Understandable though this was, in the end someone had to take the hard decisions over the situation and bear the consequences.

As long as that someone was not the President of the USA, the Americans felt good about all they were doing. They made no effort to study the situation objectively or mediate between the warring parties. They had chosen the good guys – the Jews – and the bad guys – the British – so there was nothing to talk about. As for the Palestine Arabs their 'dog-in-the-manger' attitude to the territory was not worth consideration.

The President of the United States – and most people who had no direct contact with the situation – felt that the old Turkish Empire was so vast that there should have been no difficulty in carving out a slice of territory for the Jews that would not – or at least should not – upset the Arabs. There is a certain amount of truth in this, but the size of territory was not the issue. This was a question of place and the particular place was Jerusalem.

Jerusalem is a Holy City to three religions – Christian, Jew and Muslim – but especially to the last two. There is no need to labour this point; the bloodshed and intransigence involved in this Arab–Israeli issue since the end of the Second World War has made the extent of the problem plain.

Two groups, Arabs and Jews, were determined to possess the Holy City and the land around it. Each side had its backers and neither side was prepared to compromise. In 1947–8 the problem of satisfying these incompatible demands was in the hands of the British, and the world at large – and the Americans in particular – expected them to solve it.

During the war the Jews of Palestine supported the Allied cause and many Palestinian Jews served in the British Army. Sending their young men to fight in the British Army was one way of providing the hoped-for Jewish state with a supply of trained and experienced soldiers, and the Jewish Agency, a body set up to advise the Mandatory authorities on Jewish affairs, was active throughout the war, buying arms, setting up a defence force, 'Haganah', and establishing defensive positions around Jewish settlements. The Agency also encouraged immigration, which went on throughout the war years, and continued to build up strong links with Zionist groups in the USA.

When the Second World War ended, the Jews of Palestine were in a stronger position. Their numbers were now approaching half a million, while the Palestinian Arabs mustered three times that amount, but in some towns the Jews outnumbered the Arabs. In addition the great wave of sympathy for the Jewish people caused by the events of the Nazi Holocaust added to the apparent justice of their claim.

The Arabs could point out that attempting to soothe European guilt by giving away Arab land was hardly just or fair, but their voice was drowned by the cries demanding justice for the Jews and urging that they should have some part of the world as their own national homeland.

The British supported this view but they still had to keep the peace in Palestine and maintain a balance between the Arab and Jewish communities. This inevitably led to conflict, for the Mandate was due to expire in 1948. When it did the Jews of Palestine knew that they would need to fight for their new state, Israel, against the massed might of the Arab world.

To do so the Jews needed weapons, especially tanks and artillery, and a vastly increased Jewish population. The best way to achieve those aims was by destabilising the mandatory authority, Great Britain, which was controlling the import of arms and restricting Jewish immigration. The first step to that end was anti-British propaganda, claiming that the British were pro-Arab and anti-Semitic. Before long Jewish groups in the USA were comparing the British actions aimed at containing intercommunal violence in Palestine with those of the SS in Nazi Germany.

Jewish resistance to the British Mandate had begun before the Second World War when an extremist Zionist sect set up an organisation called Irgun Zvai Leumi – IZL or Irgun – to campaign for the establishment of Israel. On the outbreak of war most of Irgun elected to support the Allied cause but a splinter group led by Abraham Stern decided to continue the fight against the British. This group, better known as the 'Stern Gang' was responsible for many terrorist atrocities and murders in the following decade, though Stern himself was killed in a gunfight with the Palestine Police in 1942.

In 1944, with the end of the war in sight, Irgun, now under the leadership of Menachem Begin, a future Prime Minister of Israel, began to attack the sinews of British administration, starting with bomb attacks on the immigration offices, tax offices and police stations. Since the war was not yet over these activities met with general condemnation, even from the Jewish Agency and Haganah, the main Jewish defence force, the forerunner of the Israeli Army.

This disapproval did not deter Irgun or the Stern Gang; in 1944 the Stern Gang murdered Lord Moyne, the British Resident in Cairo, and started a series of bomb attacks on British installations. The British were now considering various options in Palestine, one of which was partition, the territorial division of the country between the two communities. This was certainly an option but the stumbling block was Jerusalem.

John Loxton was working on the Palestine Survey at this time and his diary records the mounting violence:

On 31 October 1944, Lord Gort, a military man, succeeded Sir Harold MacMichael as High Commissioner. One of his main concerns was the resurgence of terrorism, this time by Zionists. On 16 November, Lord Moyne, the British Government's Resident Minister in the Middle East, had been shot dead in Cairo. His killers were arrested and one was identified as Eliahu Bet Zuri, a former employee of our department.

At his trial by a Military Court in Cairo, it was said that he was aged twenty-three and had been influenced by the Stern Gang for six years, unknown to his father, who was a respectable postmaster. Ballistics experts established that his Nagat pistol was the one used to kill police in five shootings earlier in 1944. He may not have been the user every time but he did testify that it was 'reliable'.

He was also thought to have been the author of an ambush on the Jaffa road just below Jerusalem when the High Commissioner's car was stopped by a survey tape across the road and fired on. His Excellency was saved by his bullet-proof windows but one of his aides was hit; the attackers escaped. Bet Zuri was hanged in Cairo on 23 March 1945 but his body was returned to Israel in 1982 and he was reburied as a national hero.

On 8 May 1945 flags were hoisted to mark VE Day. On 15 August the District Commissioner took the salute at a VJ Day march past. The war was over but there was no peace in Palestine.

As a result of the deteriorating security situation, an Army Brigade Headquarters was set up in Nazareth on 21 October 1945, so we had many military visitors; one evening we happily defeated the Brigadier and Brigade Major at the bridge table. One of the visiting officers gave me a 9mm Beretta and fifty-six rounds, taken from an Italian soldier. 2 November was the anniversary of the Balfour Declaration, marked by an Arab general strike. I spent Christmas in Jerusalem and while at a cinema on 27 December, the nearby Police Headquarters was demolished by a large bomb. The cinema shook and showers of dust fell, but the film went on. So did the violence.

In March 1946 a Partition Commission came to Palestine and we saw a lot of their map expert, Willatts. He had to prepare detailed maps of the proposed boundaries and the department had to do a lot of drawing and printing.

On 19 June there was a curfew in Tel Aviv after five British officers had been kidnapped by the Jews. On 29 June troops occupied the Jewish Agency in Jerusalem. On 22 July 1946 the south wing of the King David Hotel in Jerusalem, leased for the Secretariat, was blown up. Among the hundred dead I lost four friends. This was the worst of many such incidents.

In spite of the increase in violence, much of it directed against the British Army and British civilians, normal life somehow went on. In the summer of 1946 a British schoolboy, Michael Shaw, was on holiday in Jerusalem:

The bombing of the King David Hotel in Jerusalem, which housed the British Secretariat, occurred a fortnight before I flew out with a party of British schoolboys. My father was in the building at the time but uninjured. He was the Colonial Secretary, and due to death threats by the gang led by Israel's future Prime Minister, Menachem Begin, we moved into the fortified Government House, where General Sir Alan Cunningham, the High Commissioner, had his headquarters.

I remember travelling to the airport in a convoy of British armoured cars escorting my father, who was sent back to the U.K. by the High Commissioner. My mother, my brother and I went home a week later. I remember a farewell party for my father in the undamaged part of the King David Hotel when my mother was less than polite to the High Commissioner because of my father's hasty and unnecessary departure.

While we were waiting for my mother outside the badly damaged Hotel, I recall looking at the bloody marks on the wall of the YMCA opposite; the Postmaster-General's body had been blown across the road when the bomb went off and splattered onto the YMCA. My mother used to visit the widows of the men killed in the Secretariat and I usually accompanied her on these trips. I remember many weeping ladies so it was a sad family holiday in the summer of 1946.

The bombing of the King David Hotel by Irgun was the most terrible and memorable atrocity of the entire end-of-Mandate period. It was an act of pure terrorism; the explosives had been smuggled into the kitchens of the hotel in milk churns, no warning was given and the loss of life was terrible; ninety-one people were killed and forty-five injured, many losing limbs. These totals included a large number of Jews, staying or working in the hotel at the time.

John Burra was working with the Forestry Service at the time of the King David Hotel bombing:

In mid-1946 the Conservator was stabbed by a 'nut-case' Arab and I was propelled into the post of Acting Conservator of Forests, Palestine. I came up to Jerusalem and settled into the Scots Hospice, a pension owned by the church of Scotland as a place for young ordinants to spend time in the Holy Land prior to taking up a parish in Scotland. Then I went down with fever and had to cancel a meeting to hammer out the next year's budget, held at the King David Hotel.

On the morning in question I was sitting up in bed, feeling better, looking out towards Jerusalem and the King David Hotel – when my vision seemed to become blurred. I lay back and decided that a further day of recuperation was needed. Then the sound of the detonation arrived; I sat up again and saw that the blurring had been clouds of dust caused by a heavy explosion. I spent the next couple of days attending the funerals of friends who had perished.

The attack on the King David Hotel was a reprisal by the Jews against the actions of the British Army, which was now deployed in

Palestine assisting the police to contain the growing violence. These Jewish strikes against the Mandatory Authorities had begun on 31 October 1945, just two months after the War ended, with a series of attacks on transport facilities and immigration control offices.

In November 1945 there were serious Arab–Jew riots in Jerusalem and Tel Aviv, sparked by the British Foreign Secretary, Ernest Bevin, pointing out that the Mandate was pledged to establish a Jewish home, not a Jewish state. These riots were put down by the 3rd Parachute Brigade, part of the newly arrived 6th Airborne Division. The riots lasted a full week and there was some loss of life.

During December 1945, the focus of Jewish attacks shifted to RAF airfields, police stations and armouries; there were frequent exchanges of fire and some loss of life on both sides. The High Commissioner, Lord Gort, left Palestine in November 1945 and was replaced by another British general, Sir Alan Cunningham. Cunningham decided to mount a major blow against the terrorists of the IZL and on 28 June 1946, seventeen thousand British troops flooded into Jerusalem and other cities on Operation Agatha. The Jewish Agency offices were raided, arms were found and the Agency shut down, with a large number of Jews suspected of terrorism being arrested. The resulting reprisal was the bomb attack on the King David Hotel.

The British response to the King David bombing was another four-day cordon and search operation, code-named Operation Shark, again mounted by the men of the 6th Airborne Division. This removed a few hard-core terrorists from the scene but the violence, which aimed to destabilise the British position, was starting to have some effect, especially in the UK and the USA, although in Palestine life still went on.

John Loxton continues his story of Palestine at the end of the Mandate:

On 13 November 1946 a train was blown up in Tel Aviv, and on the 17th another bomb exploded nearby, breaking windows in the Department. On 27 January 1947 Judge Windham was kidnapped while in court in Tel Aviv, so next day there was a curfew; our office stayed closed that day and again on 1 February. Four days later a detachment of the Coldstream Guards Anti-Tank Company moved in to guard the Department.

Following the kidnappings, Government ordered the evacuation of all British women and children; under Operation Polly they were concentrated at Sarafand on 4 February and flown to Maadi Camp in Cairo until they could be dispersed to various destinations. Those of us remaining in Jaffa and Tel Aviv were moved to Sarona, which was surrounded by barbed wire and guards.

Windham was released after Government gave in to his kidnappers' demands (release of some detainees) and he was playing bridge with us again on 16 February. On 2 March 1947 martial law was imposed on Tel Aviv, but in spite of the disruption the Jaffa-Tel Aviv Rotary Club, with members from both communities, continued to meet on Thursdays at a restaurant in Eilat Street.

At the end of March I flew to Cyprus. Flying back to Haifa on 31 March we saw oil tanks blazing after a bomb. I took some photographs from the plane, whereupon my camera was confiscated; however, after the film had been developed and security checked, it was returned to me.

On the 18th our post truck was shot at in Allenby Street, but without casualties. A week later, in spite of the security defences, the Sarona police station was wrecked by a bomb, leaving six people dead. I rushed out of our house, helped to search the wreckage and took some photos.

The beginning of the end came when the map of the proposed Partition was published on 25 November 1947. The Zionist extremists had been fighting the Government for three years because of restrictions on immigration; now the Arabs resumed their attacks against the proposal to take part of their homeland.

We now had to try to partition the staff of the Department. In the afternoon a truckload of survey plans of Arab lands was hijacked by the Zionists. Three days later a further attack was made on the Department for the same purpose. On 3 February local Arabs moved in on the RAF buildings that we were not using and started looting doors, windows, roof cladding and so on. The police were called out and two looters were shot dead.

A department truck was held up in Tel Aviv on 8 February 1948 and driven away. Thereafter I tried to run the Department from our new Ramle office to which we commuted in a police armoured car. Iraqi irregulars were now taking control of Jaffa and Ramle towns.

On 10 March a nine-thousand-gallon petrol tank was blown up at Lydda station. Trains were being blown up and stations looted. The Jewish Agency in Jerusalem was bombed . . . and so it went on.

On 9 April my possessions in six crates left Lydda on an open railway truck for Haifa. When the train arrived there, the station was a no-man's-land between battling Arab and Zionist forces. I feared the worst, but a week later a friend phoned to say my boxes were now safe in the port.

Instructions arrived for me to fly out on 21 April but no plane arrived that day; someone had forgotten to charter it. It arrived at Lydda two days later; the departing passengers included the British airport staff. We later heard that the Arabs looted the airport buildings that night and the Hagana took control the following day.

Palestine was in every way a fascinating country; the focal point of three continents and three major religions and cultures – cosmopolitan – steeped in thousands of years of history, littered with interesting historical sites. The people of all races, as individuals, were friendly and I never encountered personal hostility.

Bombings, shootings, sabotage, riots, kidnappings, pitched battles between the two communities, attacks on British soldiers and the police, that was daily life in Palestine at the end of the Mandate. Clearly, the Palestine situation was difficult enough for the people on the spot but the British Government also had to cope with carping from American politicians, Press and people, and the hostility of the Arab world, which was openly on the side of the Palestinians.

The Americans were strongly pro–Jewish and very anti–British, some violently so; one Hollywood motion–picture mogul made it into the British Press by declaring that 'he had a holiday in his heart every time a British soldier was killed in Israel'. Large sections of the American media echoed this sentiment and they were not above staging incidents which put the British Army in a bad light.

Denis Edwards of the Parachute Regiment recalls one such stage-managed event:

Somewhere in the world there is a picture of me which was used by the Jews for propaganda. When the King David Hotel was bombed, every available Airborne soldier was trucked into Jerusalem and we cordoned off the Jewish quarter while a massive search was made for terrorists, arms and explosives.

I was on the flat roof of a tall building, prodding with my bayonet at a large bundle of sacks and rags conveniently left in one corner. Suddenly the door behind me, at the top of the staircase, was flung violently open and I swung round - expecting to see an armed Jewish terrorist - and found myself face to face with a very attractive young woman.

At that moment a photographer - an American, I think from *Time Life* Magazine - leapt past her onto the roof and took a picture of me, with my bayonet just inches from the young woman's stomach which - contrived or genuine - showed signs of being in the last stages of pregnancy.

It was a 'set-up'. I was a bit taken aback when I realised that. I jumped past the young woman and tried to get hold of the camera but the photographer shot back down the stairs and disappeared before I could catch him.

American opinion was not undivided over the Palestine question; the Pentagon and the American oil interests were anxious not to be too vocal in supporting the Jews for fear of upsetting the Arab oil sheiks but they had an excuse; the only point on which all sides, Arab, American and Jew, were agreed was that the British were to blame for everything and must be ejected from Palestine as quickly as possible. After that, peace and justice would surely reign.

At one point early in 1945, Winston Churchill became so irritated at the continual American carping over Palestine that he suggested that since the Americans were so unhappy about the way Britain was handling Palestine, the best solution would be for them to take it over themselves. 'I am not aware that any advantage has ever accrued to Britain from this painful and thankless task,' he said, 'and someone else should have their turn now.'

There was no rush of American or UN volunteers to pick up the British burden. As 1945 merged into 1946, Britain was left to battle on alone, shot at by both sides, accused and sneered at by the organs of world opinion, pressured by the US President and Congress.

Ian Wilson of the Royal Engineers – a Platoon Commander in 23 Field Company – arrived in Palestine at this time:

Soon after my twenty-first birthday, in July 1945, I found myself on a draft to the Far East together with some fifty of the younger men from my Company. We reached Ostend when the atom bombs were dropped on Japan, the War in the Far East ended and we were sent instead to the Middle East. I was posted as a lieutenant to 23 Field Company RE supporting 1st Guards Brigade in 1st Infantry Division in Palestine in December 1945. Many in 1st Division had served in the Italian campaign and were due to return home on either demobilisation or repatriation in the following several months.

The insurgency was very low key when I arrived in Palestine. Some targets had been attacked with explosives, but the aim seemed to be to cause nuisance, not to hurt people. Relations with both Jews and Arabs were generally good. I remember being invited to a Jewish 'kibbutz' and to take coffee in Bedouin encampments. Many civilians, both Jew and Arab, were employed by the Army and they worked conscientiously and kept the peace during working hours, even though some undoubtedly kept their eyes open for advantages to be gained. Some Arabs were expert at silent pilferage; Jews were less adept at direct theft but there were proven incidents of the diversion of consignments of stores by Jewish clerks.

GHQ, British Forces Palestine and Trans-Jordan, were in Jerusalem. 1st Infantry Division had arrived in the spring of 1945, 6th Airborne Division came in the autumn and 3rd Infantry Division deployed two brigades by the end of the year. 1st Division HQ was in Haifa, my Company was in a large tented camp some fifteen miles south of Haifa. The main preoccupation of the Army was military training, not internal security, and I soon came to admire the enterprise, industry and contentment in the Jewish settlements.

Apart from periodic bomb patrols along the Haifa railways, our programme included military training and improving the camps of 1st Division. As time went by, the triggering for the bombs grew more sophisticated and casualties began to grow among the Sapper officers called out to deal with them. A number of Jews who had served in Special Operations Groups during the war were active in the Jewish underground and were very good at mines and booby traps.

The successful destruction of all the bridges across the River Jordan in June 1946 was an illustration of the Jewish underground's capability. 23 Company RE replaced the crossing at Jisr Bana' at

Jacub, with a Bailey bridge which I saw on television years later, as the Israeli Army crossed to capture the Golan Heights.

There was little Arab insurgency at this stage, though an Arab was caught in July with a load of mines which he had contracted to carry for the Jews; another Arab was trying to buy the consignment with counterfeit notes.

Then, from about mid-1946, a stream of dilapidated, often unseaworthy vessels, loaded to the gunwales with refugees from Europe, arrived offshore, aimed at flooding the country with illegal immigrants. The conditions on board these ships were appalling; the latrines were half-moons cut in the scuppers, filth and lack of sanitation scoured the pathetic passengers, many of whom were in no state to travel in the first place. A number of births were recorded. These ships were intercepted by the Royal Navy and the passengers off-loaded and transhipped to camps in Cyprus. I took part in a number of these transhipments in Haifa harbour, some peaceful, but on at least one, the *Lohita*, we met with considerable violence.

It was a distasteful task to greet people similar to those we had helped to liberate from Belsen in 1945 and send them off to other camps. It was moving to see the fanaticism shown and the hardship endured. On one occasion we built aerial ropeways to rescue the passengers from a ship which had evaded the blockade and beached near Tel Aviv. On another occasion no transports were available and I had to organise the conversion of two cargo ships into prisons. It was ironical that these were 'Liberty' ships. We were angry at the organisers of this trade in human misery, the real value of which was publicity.

In October I received a bomb call from Haifa East railway station and despatched a subaltern and section of men. They found an oil drum in the booking hall, and a warning notice. They were preparing to rope it clear of the building when a noise was heard in the drum. The officer just managed to get his men clear before the entire centre of the station was blown up. This officer was killed by another device in May 1947.

Relations with the Jews were turning sour. We were now stationed in the RE Depot at Beit Nabala and new explosive devices were appearing all the time. I had to dismantle a device made from tin packed with explosive and camouflaged to look exactly like a roadside milestone. It had been detected by a weary Guardsman on patrol who sat on it and noticed it was loose; fortunately for him, the electric firing mechanism malfunctioned.

Sapper casualties from attempting to neutralise devices were such that the order was given to blow in-situ from early 1947. By then I had taken apart seven homemade devices and I was lucky; eight Sapper officers were killed in Palestine trying to do the same thing.

The rules for repatriation had changed by 1947 and the completion of three years overseas service allowed one to go home. I boarded a troopship in Suez but hardly had it sailed when the officer I handed over to was wounded by a booby-trap when cutting down the bodies of Sergeants Martin and Pain, the two British soldiers kidnapped and hanged by the Jews in July 1947.

I believe that Britain has nothing to be ashamed of in Palestine. The Colonial Government did its very best to be fair and keep a balance between Arab and Jew. There may have been some animosity but Jewish excesses did little to calm the anger of rather inexperienced troops in a post-war situation. Perhaps the final act, walking out of an almost impossible situation, could have been better handled but it was really a UN problem which they could not solve either when the time came.

Lieutenant Wilson's time in Palestine covered some of the main events at the end of the British Mandate. The beginning of the end came in May 1946 with pressure from the US President, Harry Truman, for the immediate issue of one hundred thousand visas to Jewish immigrants. To have complied with this demand would have caused the Arabs to rise up in revolt, and the British Government wisely refused. As a result, as soon as ships could be found and the traffic organised, Jewish chartered ships began to appear off the coast, bringing swarms of illegal immigrants to bolster the Jews of Palestine.

When they could be found these ships were intercepted and turned back by the Royal Navy. One of the officers in charge of the boarding parties was Captain Michael Reynolds of the Royal Marines:

I was appointed Captain of Marines HMS *Phoebe*, a cruiser, in 1946, and left at the end of the commission in 1949. *Phoebe* was normally the flagship of the Rear-Admiral, Destroyers, but operated on occasions as a private ship. She operated for two years in the Mediterranean based on Malta but on several occasions we were in Haifa, for much of the time at the end of the Mandate, and at the actual end when we embarked Lt.-General Macmillan, the GOC Palestine, and his staff.

During our time in Haifa, the situation was always a bit uneasy. We carried on with our normal activities but there was always the lurking danger of being shot at by Jews or Arabs. However, we played football or hockey and went shooting on Lake Galilee. On one occasion we were challenged to a hockey match by the Ladies of Haifa team; in vain we suggested that we should make up mixed teams but they would not hear of it. We returned to the ship after the match, bruised and battered by the ladies, having won the match by just one goal.

We normally accepted the veiled hostility we encountered without bothering to find out why; after all, the Mandate was ending and we would be leaving anyway. Meanwhile the busy destroyers went out to capture the vessels arriving offshore with illegal immigrants but eventually it was decided that we in *Phoebe* should take a hand and become the 'receiving ship' for these immigrant ships when they were brought into Haifa. The routine was that these ships came alongside us and the immigrants were processed on board before being allowed ashore, either for shipment back to Cyprus or into camps in Palestine.

The processing was largely for health reasons, for the people were in quite a poor state when they came ashore. We set up two canvas screams, one for men and one for women, and all who passed between them were drenched with DDT to kill the lice. They were then passed on to the Parachute Regiment who took care of them ashore.

We all felt very sorry for these people and secretly admired them; I remember one old lady dressed in a beautiful coat, the wife of a distinguished brain surgeon whom I carried off a boat in my arms. The boats and ships they travelled in were often in a terrible state, overcrowded and uncomfortable, some far from seaworthy; it must have been almost unbearable to be caught and turned back in sight of the Palestine shore.

Soon afterwards we had news that two large immigrant ships had been sighted and HMS *Phoebe* and HMS *Liverpool* were ordered to intercept them. We sailed back for Malta, and were told to 'train for boarding operations'. It was a bit difficult to know how to train because we had to consider the worst situation, where our boarding would be opposed; then we would have to force our way on and work the ship back to Cyprus, our eventual destination. We decided that the rig of the day would be battledress, steel helmets, side arms and cudgels . . . and eventually we sailed and had a contact.

The ship we were set to board was the *Pan Crescent* . . . I forget the other one. The Admiral negotiated with the two ships and all the problems were apparently solved before we went on board. The only thing overlooked was that some of the passengers decided to demonstrate their hostility by emptying a bucket of piss and shit over me as I climbed up the ladder.

Otherwise the trip to Cyprus went without a hitch. The engine room was run by American engineers who even sent me up a bottle of booze to celebrate the New Year. The only unusual incident was a man who told me that if I declined to take the ship to Cyprus I could enjoy the services of his daughter. I don't think the daughter was over-keen, probably because of the smell; I like to think that was the reason anyway.

Captain Reynolds was lucky; other British boarding parties were met with scalding steam from hoses, fire bombs, pistol shots, and attacks by groups of men wielding axes and crowbars. A number of British sailors and immigrants were killed in these high seas encounters and relations between the British and the Jews and the British and the Americans continued to deteriorate.

The struggles during the Mandate became a media battle. The Jewish leaders in Palestine decided to make the British position untenable by a concentrated series of terrorist acts and sabotage, while their friends in the media, and especially in the United States media, continued to vilify the efforts of the British Army, the Royal Navy and the British administration to control the violence and partition the land on some equitable basis.

The forces at the disposal of the Administration in 1946 were not large. They consisted of the Palestine Police, a mixed force of British, Jews and Arabs, numbering around five thousand men, two infantry divisions, the 1st and 6th Airborne, and elements of the 3rd Commando Brigade, Royal Marines, and the 7th Infantry Brigade. These were barely enough to keep the two communities apart and when the publicity generated by attacking police stations and immigration offices had died down, the Jewish underground started a fresh campaign with attacks British soldiers.

Peter Faggetter was a soldier in the Parachute Regiment at Tel Litwinski:

> There was a steady stream of incidents from 1946 on. At Tel Litwinski I undertook my first solo guard as there were only about six or seven of us to defend the camp, the rest being away on Cordon and Search. We had a searchlight on a tower, seventy feet or so above the compound and used that to sweep around the camp, while waiting for a sniper to pick us off.
>
> The roads of Palestine proved the last for a lot of British soldiers in the two years my feet were treading the Promised Land. At the beginning of November one of our three tonners containing a patrol from our battalion was mined just down the road from the camp; thirteen chaps were wounded, three seriously. From Litwinski we moved to Lydda airfield, now Lodd Airport, where we shared the camp with some RAF people. I was not very enamoured of that place and believe it or not, one day it snowed.

On 25 April 1946 the Stern Gang attacked an unarmed bathing party of British troops and murdered seven soldiers in cold blood. This attack had a serious effect on the British Army, which had previously been sympathetic to Jewish aims. The 6th Airborne Division had seen a lot of fighting in north-western Europe and had first-hand experience of liberating the Nazi concentration camps. As a result, the airborne soldiers had arrived in Palestine fully prepared to like and support the Jewish community, but the Stern Gang attack and murders of 25 August 1946 changed all that. The Army were soon taking a firmer line and reacting swiftly to all attacks.

However, normal life went on, as Robin McGarel Groves, an officer of 42 Commando, Royal Marines, remembers:

> There was sniping and shooting every night and our road blocks were passing through a constant stream of dead and wounded Jews

and Arabs. Our diary for 10 May 1948, just before the end of the Mandate, will give an idea of what went on, though the early days were worse:

0700: Road block opened.

0730: Jewish lorry from hospital with six men and furniture.

0745: Armoured ambulance to hospital with one corpse and two wounded men.

0810: Brother of Mufti of Jerusalem and five Arabs pass through.

0940: Two British three tonners for hospital, turned back by Jewish road block.

1000: Heavy explosion in area M 904557.

1600: Second and third Arab defence line observed in area.

1715: One Jewish lorry with three bodies, eight wounded men and six nurses.

1730: Explosions and heavy machine gun fire from Old City.

While we were in Jerusalem 42 Commando came under command of 1st Guards Para, commanded by Colonel John Nelson, a dashing and most impressive soldier who took a dim view of all this shooting and decided that the way to eliminate it would be by mounting an attack on the Hadassar Hill with 1st Guards Para and 42 Commando. It was a great relief when this scheme was abandoned because we were pulling out, we did not have much in the way of support and the Jews were well dug in.

Life still went on, though. We played games, saw the sights, organised bathing parties to Athlit, where the Irish Guards had a camp. Prossi's restaurant in Mount Carmel Avenue was a popular spot for Sunday lunch, with good cooking and superb brandy sauce. There was also the Piccadilly Bar, a night club on Mount Carmel, popular with the younger officers in 42, at least until some members of Haganah entered one night carrying Sten guns and festooned with grenades. They had just captured Acre (Acco) and were looking for trouble, so being heavily outnumbered and unarmed, we left.

John Burra, working with the Forestry Service, continues his story:

When I arrived in Palestine in late 1945, I sensed the tensions resulting from the Balfour Declaration – on the Arab side but more so on the Jewish side. Working in Palestine had its problems – with Friday the Muslim Holy Day, and Saturday the Jewish Sabbath, while on Sunday, as a Christian, I expected to rest. Thus a full staff was on duty only for a four-day week – not a lot of time to get things done.

In the field the Staff was evenly divided between Arab and Jew. The general attitude was one of guarded tolerance but at times an expatriate such as myself had to intervene to 'keep the peace'. I had a driver, but the Conservator (Head of Department) pointed out that we were liable to attack by either side and it was wise to be free to act without having to control the vehicle. I was issued with a revolver which was kept under the back seat of the car. For most of the time I was based in Haifa. No quarters were provided; some of us felt safer in a Jewish home, others in an Arab house.

I opted for a very nice room overlooking Haifa Bay in a large block of Jewish-occupied flats. I had one room with a bed-settee in one corner, a packing case with cooking utensils and necessary food in another, my library and gramophone in the third; the fourth corner was occupied by the door. As I was out in the field for at least half the month, I didn't find the quarters cramped, but it does show that the alleged Imperialists didn't live in remote splendour with lashings of servants and concubines whom they thrashed daily with a horsewhip!

It might be as well to restate the causes of this shambles. The Arab side is easy to understand. The Arabs had lived in Palestine, the ancient Philistia – home of the Philistines – for twenty centuries. Now their homeland was being given away by the British to create a state for people that the Europeans – at least the Germans, the Russians, the Poles – had been murdering in millions until just a few years ago. If the Americans and British and the rest felt guilty about their neglect of the Jews, why did they not find a home for them in their own country? The British and Americans did not welcome Jews in their golf clubs so why should the Arabs welcome them in Palestine?

The British side is also easy to understand. They had taken on the Mandate in 1922 for reasons already described, and been caught up in the wave of guilt and sympathy that had engulfed the Jews after the Holocaust. They could see no solution that would satisfy everyone and only wanted the Mandate to expire so they could pull out. They had done their bit and their best and if the world was not satisfied, someone else could have a go.

The Jewish situation is more complex. Their desire for a Jewish homeland, for a place they could call their own is easy to comprehend and was given great impetus, firstly by the Balfour Declaration and then by the Holocaust. If any group of people, any race, any nation, was entitled to such a homeland and such security, that group was the Jews. The problem was – and remains – that the land wanted, the 'Promised Land' of Israel, was inhabited and owned by the Palestinian Arabs. If the Jews got their homeland, the Arabs of Palestine would become homeless in their place.

What is harder to understand, even after fifty years, is why the Jews thought that murdering British soldiers would help their cause. The only logical answer is that they hoped to destabilise the Mandate and force the British to leave before the country could be partitioned. Then, with American help, they would take over the entire country.

This they succeeded in doing by force of arms, but the price of that takeover was fifty years of strife and terrorism. In 1994–5 the Israelis accepted that the price of peace involved granting land on the West Bank and Gaza as a homeland for the Palestinians. This amounts to partition and if that fact had been conceded fifty years ago, Israel, and the world at large, would have been spared a great deal of hardship and bloodshed.

In May 1946, with two years of the Mandate left to run, the search for a political solution was getting nowhere. The British Foreign Secretary, Ernest Bevin, then attempted to heal the widening breech with America over Palestine by proposing an Anglo–American Committee which would investigate the problem and suggest acceptable solutions. President Truman accepted this proposal and in May 1946 the Anglo–American Committee duly presented their report. The main proposals were that the one hundred thousand entry visas should indeed be issued, but there was no enthusiasm in the report for the creation of a Jewish State.

President Truman – his eyes on the Jewish lobby – chose to endorse the former proposal and avoid comment on the last one. This was no assistance to Great Britain, but having agreed to accept the report the British decided to issue the visas. Bevin also told Truman bluntly that unless America did less carping and took a more positive role in finding a solution, Britain would give up the Mandate, withdraw from the country at the earliest possible date and let the Jews and Arabs fight it out.

At this time, Captain J. Masters was with the Royal Engineers, serving in Palestine as part of 6 Airborne Division:

As the Division was being steadily reduced by post-war demobili-sation, I was transferred to 1 Airborne Field Company, who were stationed just south of Haifa, the last Sapper Field Troop left in the country. We finally departed from Haifa on the last ship to sail. That boat was named the *Ocean Vigour* and she had been one of the boats which carried illegal immigrants over to Cyprus. To be accurate I was about the third last Sapper to step off the jetty and leave Palestine; there was an unseemly scramble to be the last!

I visited Palestine (Israel) last year, 1994, returning to the scene of our adventures. Amazingly, when listening to our tour guide, an ex-Hagana man, I was intrigued to hear him talking about two ex-British Army tanks which were taken over to them in 1948 by a couple of British deserters. I knew part of the story because at the time they were spirited away, my Troop was building a pier into the bay at Haifa where our ships could be loaded with vehicles and armour.

Two Comet tanks did not arrive. Much to our amusement, we were told that they had 'gone missing with their drivers'. It tran-spired that the drivers were courting two Israeli girls and decided to stay with them. By some means unknown they had managed to slip away from their tank convoy and link up with Hagana.

The two men were later involved in fighting against the Jordanian Arab Legion and during one battle were the sole armoured support to an Israeli infantry attack. At a critical point one of the tanks broke down and the British driver called his mate on the radio to tell him that he would have to withdraw. That call was picked up by a British officer serving with the Jordanians and this news allowed them to sit tight in their positions.

The story did not end there. It seems that the two lads married their Israeli girlfriends and died years later of natural causes. They are buried in a Christian cemetery somewhere near Tel Aviv. Again, quite by chance, one of our number visited a friend in the same town while we were there and met the wife of one of our deserters. So the story was rounded off nicely.

I have to tell you that there was a large measure of respect for

Hagana among the soldiery in those days; I think we understood their desire for freedom better than the politicians. However, that did not prevent us from reacting with considerable vigour if we were shot at by either side. One incident I well remember was the ambushing of a Parachute Regiment patrol. The Arabs were given a set time to hand over the culprits but without result and we were then told to blow up the house which had been used by the ambushers.

I have to admit that we were not too careful about calculating a precise charge to simply bring down one building. We put in a little extra for luck and took out the houses on either side too. Towards the end my Troop was stationed in the police station on Kingsway in Haifa, which had been damaged earlier by a bomb. As Sappers we were also tasked with blowing up whatever could not be shipped away and this included tanks and armoured cars plus several hundred radio sets.

Before leaving we witnessed the battles between the Arab armies and the Hagana as they fought over the ground we were giving up. We were part of a body which was known as 'Cray Force' and our task was to form a screen to cover other units who were moving out through the docks at Haifa. From time to time it was necessary to fire on whoever got too close for our comfort and the results were always very satisfactory.

We finally left Haifa on 30 June 1948, leaving the town firmly in the hands of Hagana. A few days before we left, a United Nations peacekeeping force arrived. My troop was in support of 40 Commando, Royal Marines for a short time near the end, and I remember the outcry when we read the headlines in the National press, 'Guards Last Out'. The Guards were not the last out; they were sitting out in the bay days before we left with the Commandos.

The story of the two missing tanks is backed up by an account from Robin McGarel Groves of 42 Commando:

One of the problems at the end was the security of our weapons and equipment which the Jews in particular were keen to get hold of. There was a semi-official price list, ranging from £20 for a pistol to about £20,000 for a Comet tank. This last prize is what may have motivated two tank drivers who drove their tanks through the wire at Ramat David by the airport and defected to the Israelis. The two tanks were used in various battles with the Arabs before being blown up by a British 17-pounder anti-tank gun which the Arabs had acquired by equally dubious means.

I myself acquired a brace of Deerhound armoured cars and two ex-Palestine Police armoured cars which had been declared surplus to requirements at the end. The price was a bottle of whisky and I felt very proud as I drove our new possessions up to Commando HQ. The C.O., Ian Riches, took a different view; I think he was horrified but after explaining how useful they would be on patrols and as road blocks, we were allowed to keep our armour to the end, when they were set on fire and destroyed with explosives.

While the military were coping with the day-to-day problems of internal security, the politicians were still attempting to find a peaceful settlement − but to trace developments on that front we must go back to 1946.

In September 1946 the British Prime Minister, Clement Attlee, called a conference of Jewish and Arab leaders in London. This conference sat throughout the autumn and well into the early months of 1947, without coming to any mutually acceptable conclusion. Meanwhile, in Palestine, Irgun and Hagana continued to attack British facilities and shoot at British Army and police patrols. Relations between the British authorities and the Jews were reaching a new low, and worse was to follow when the Jews added kidnapping to their list of terrorist activities.

In December 1946, a court sentenced two Irgun youths to a term in prison and eighteen strokes of the birch for taking part in a bank robbery. In reprisal, Irgun kidnapped four British soldiers and flogged them. The British then granted an amnesty to some other Jewish and Arab criminals and a fatal pattern was set.

If any Jew was sentenced by a British court, kidnappings of British servicemen followed, to force the reprieve or release of Jewish prisoners sentenced to death for murder or terrorist operations. These men were sentenced for murder or bombings, not for their religious or political beliefs, but the Jews refused to accept that; in their eyes, these men were martyrs.

In February 1947, the London Conference ended, with the delegations quite unable to agree to any course of action. Britain then went to the United Nations and while not yet ready to give up the Mandate, stated that the problem was beyond British resources and other powers should now bring their influence to bear.

The Irgun response to this proposal was to blow up the British Officers' Club in Haifa, killing and injuring more than thirty people. Then followed another wave of intercommunal violence and the British were forced to impose martial law and a curfew on Tel Aviv and the Jewish quarter of Jerusalem.

Dennis Edwards was in Palestine with 6th Airborne Div HQ:

I was a corporal at the time. I had served with 6th Airborne in the Ox and Bucks Light Infantry, part of the Air Landing Brigade, since it was formed in 1942 and was in the first Horsa glider to land at Pegasus Bridge on D-Day.

I stayed with the battalion as a sniper all the way through to the end of the War at Wismar. Then we were sent to India and finally we ended up in Palestine. I had now done the Para course and since I was a Regular soldier on a seven-year hitch, I was due to leave the Army in March 1948, just before the end of the Mandate. Anyway, Palestine . . . there was trouble every day from one side or another. Take my diary for December 1947:

1st: Clashes and bloodshed between Jews and Arabs.

2nd: Clashes continue. Arabs stone and fire on British troops.

3rd: Jewish timber yard set on fire in Haifa. Arabs fire on investigating patrol of troops.

4th: Tip-and-run raids from Jews and Arabs, firing or throwing grenades from cars in Haifa.

5th: Eight incidents involving Jews or Arabs and security forces in Haifa. Troops fighting with Arabs one moment and Jews the next. Patrol from 7 Para involved in battle at Wadi Rushmiya bridge; Arab attack repulsed, six armed Jews who had taken part arrested.

7th: 7 Para move out en route to UK.

8th: Arabs attack armoured car in Stanton St, Haifa, killing the British driver.

9th: Stern Gang attack 6th Airborne military police jeep outside Eldorado cafe in Pine Road. One NCO killed.

That is just one week in one small town, Haifa, so you can imagine what it was like in other parts of the country. We left on 1 January 1948 on the SS *Orduna*. It was a big ship but the usual treatment applied. The first and second-class passengers were given the two upper decks and we – the third class – had the lower deck. This allowed about a hundred and fifty officers to have two decks while the troops – about fifteen hundred of us – had a whole deck to ourselves, but never mind, we were on our way HOME!

Dennis Williams was in Palestine with the 17th Field Squadron, Royal Engineers:

Our duties consisted of searching convoys coming into the city, filling craters in the roads and, of course, guard duties. Anyway, we were returning to camp after making a mine safe at a monastery, and were about five kilometres outside Jerusalem on the Jaffa Road when we came under mortar fire. The two-ton tipper I was travelling in was hit, killing a mate either side of me, and I was wounded in the arms. After walking what seemed like miles, we were picked up by a Jewish ambulance and taken to the Hadassah hospital, where I was given some morphine and then passed on to a B.M.H. as they were not allowed to operate on British soldiers.

Matters in Palestine were now moving to their inevitable conclusion; the British had had enough of Palestine and the Jews and Arabs were preparing for war when the British left. In February 1947 the British Government decided to hand the problem over to the United Nations, where the members of the General Assembly had been whinging about British policy in Palestine for the last two years.

A United Nations Special Committee duly arrived in Jerusalem in June 1947 and set about yet another investigation into the causes of and solutions to the Palestine problem. To aid them in their deliberations, Irgun set light to the oil refinery in Haifa, which blazed for three weeks. Irgun also attacked the prison at Acre, releasing a number of Jewish terrorists, though five Irgan terrorists were captured in the fight, three of them being tried and sentenced to death.

Then, in July 1947, came the famous incident of the *President Warfield*, a Great Lakes steamer converted into the immigrant ship *Exodus*. Crammed with four thousand refugees, this ship soiled from the French port of Séte and attempted to land this large cargo of illegal immigrants on beaches near Haifa.

The Royal Navy became involved in a vicious fight on board the *Exodus* as they attempted to take control of the ship and the incident was widely reported in the Press, especially in the USA. The *Exodus* returned to France, where the French authorities refused the refugees permission to land and the *Exodus* eventually took her wretched Jewish passengers, many of them concentration camp survivors to – of all places – Germany. After this well-publicised incident – and publicity was one of the objects of these immigrant sailings – yet more abuse was hurled at Britain's weary head.

The *Exodus* affair was the best known event in the summer of 1947, while another incident, equally shocking, passed almost unnoticed outside the Army and the UK. On 29 July 29 1947, the day the *Exodus* docked in France, Irgun kidnapped two British Army NCOs, Sergeant Matin and Sergeant Pain, and hanged them, later suspending their bodies from trees in an orange grove.

Dennis Edwards saw the end of this affair:

We all saw the bodies. They were hanging from trees in the orange grove just across the road from our camp, Camp 21. They must have been put there overnight, for when it got light there they were. Quite a lot of people went across and looked at them but were kept back until the RE's arrived, but as you will have heard, they were booby trapped and the officer who cut them down was badly injured. There was a lot of bad feeling about that. The soldiers were very angry and you cannot blame them.

When this story came out there was great public revulsion in Britain and brawls took place, both in Britain and in Jerusalem, between British troops and Jewish civilians. British Army discipline, sorely tried in the last few years, still held firm but the British public and their leaders had already had more than enough of this pointless, thankless task.

The matter of Palestine was handed over to the UN Special Commission and they presented their proposals to the General Assembly in September 1947. These were that Palestine would be partitioned between Israel and Jordan. Israel would have about five and a half thousand square miles – about two-thirds of the land – and Jerusalem and the land around it would be an international zone. In addition, one hundred and fifty thousand Jewish immigrants would be granted immediate entry visas. Finally, the League of Nations Mandate would end when Britain had implemented these proposals, a process which the UN considered would last another two years.

The British Government flatly refused to have anything to do with this scheme. Instead the British Government declared its intention of withdrawing all British troops to fortified camps and leaving Palestine at the earliest possible moment.

The Jews refused to accept partition and the Arabs were furious at the UN award, which gave about two-thirds of the land – their land – to one-third of the population and were arming afresh and mustering 'volunteers' from Jordan and Iraq to correct this situation when the British pulled out.

The UN blustered but the British were adamant. The final date for the British departure changed several times but the end came and the Mandate ended on 24 May 1948. No one, least of all the USA, came forward to fill the UN requirement for a two-year extension of the Mandate; 1948 was another US election year.

The last British unit to leave was 40 Commando, Royal Marines, commanded by Lt.-Colonel R.D. (Titch) Houghton, which left on 27 May 1948 embarked on the LST's *Striker* and *Reggio*. By the time the last of the Royal Marines left Haifa, the first Arab–Israeli war had already started. It has been claimed that the British were the root cause of all subsequent problems in the region for failing to achieve a working agreement between the two warring parties before they left.

These accounts of life in Palestine at the end of the Mandate give the lie to that claim. There was no possibility of peace. The two parties with the greatest interest in peace were the Arabs and the Jews but it would be another forty-five years before they even attempted to find a solution to their problems off the battlefield.

For the British politicians and the British soldiers there was one small consolation at the end of the Mandate; at least one unhappy chapter in Britain's Imperial history had been brought to a conclusion. The struggle for Malaya, which had already begun, took a good deal longer to resolve.

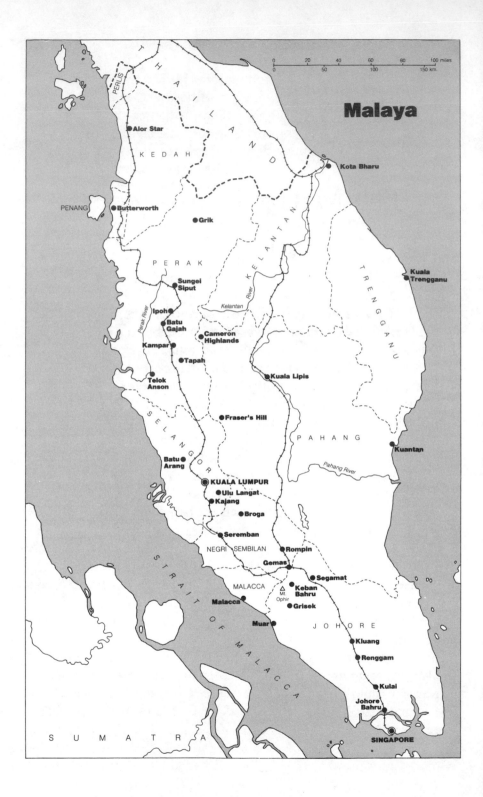

6

The Malayan Emergency: 1948–1952

'The first lesson of guerilla warfare is that success goes to the side that has the initiative.'

Lt.-Colonel R.C. Leathes, 45 Commando R.M.,
Malaya, 1950.

The fall of Singapore to the Japanese on 15 February 1942 sent a tremor through the Western Empires. Photographs of General Percival, the British commander of Singapore, advancing with his Staff to surrender and the spectacle of British troops sweeping the streets under the bayonets of Japanese soldiers, dented the long-cherished legend of Western superiority and paved the path for Asian nationalism.

It is therefore hardy surprising that when the European colonial powers, the French, the British and the Dutch, returned to reclaim their possessions in the Far East three years later, they received a very mixed reception from their former subjects.

The French plunged into a war with the Communist Viet Minh which culminated in their disastrous defeat at Dien Bien Phu in 1954 and the expulsion of the French from Indo-China. This defeat, and the American-brokered peace which followed, led to the partition of Indo-China into North and South Vietnam. This partition, never accepted by the Communist North, led the United States to support South Vietnam and so into the long and disastrous Vietnam War.

The Dutch attempt to re-establish their rule in Indonesia met with an even more abrupt rebuttal. British, and even Japanese, troops were in action there by the end of 1945, trying to protect Dutch civilians from their vengeful colonial subjects, and following violent insurrection in Java the Dutch were eventually forced to withdraw. The British, on the other hand, returned to Singapore and Malaya in September 1945 and received a fairly warm welcome from the majority of the local inhabitants.

The main reasons for this cheery reception were that the population of Singapore and the Malaya peninsula came from a varied racial stock; Malay, Chinese and Indian. All three communities regarded the British presence as insurance against racial conflict and the best guarantee of eventual independence. In addition, having endured a great deal of brutality, exploitation and destruction during the recent Japanese occupation, they needed a period of calm to rebuild the country and its institutions before they could start on the path to independence.

It also helped that on returning to Malaya in 1945 the British declared their firm intention of granting the country independence at the earliest possible date. The local people trusted Britain's word and were not to be disappointed. They also trusted the British not to leave until the country was safe from civil war.

The main obstacle to that end in the immediate aftermath of the War was the growing influence of Communist China on the large Chinese communities in Malaya and Singapore, and the lurking presence of a large, well-armed and formidable Communist guerrilla force, the Malayan People's Anti-Japanese Army or MPAJA, which had just completed a long campaign against the Japanese. This force was preparing to seize Malaya for the Communist Party and the British had hardly arrived back in Malaya before the troubles began.

John Loch, then an officer in the Parachute Regiment, arrived in Malaya as part of Operation Zipper, the Allied invasion of Malaya, which was called off after the dropping of the atomic bomb brought an end to the war:

> The invasion still went ahead as it was considered the easiest
> way to transport troops to Malaya in order to re-establish the

45 Commando arrive by helicopter at the de Lesseps Statue, Port Said, November 1956.

Paratroopers 1 of 3 Para land on Gamil Airfield, Port Said, November 1956.

Evacuating the wounded, King David Hotel, Tel Aviv, Palestine.

Jewish immigrants under escort from 6th Airborne Division soldiers, Palestine 1947.

Captured Communist bandit, Malaya 1950.

Train ambush, Perak, Malaya 1953.

Captain Peter de la Billière (second left) with SAS patrol in Malaya.

Jungle patrol, Malaya 1950.

1st Battalion, Green Howards. British mortars pound a communist camp, Malaya 1951.

Road patrol, Malaya 1954.

British gunner, Mau-Mau dead, Kenya 1953.

Lt David Evans and KAR Patrol prepare to hunt Mau-Mau, Kenya 1955.

Lt David Evans and KAR NCOs. On the left is WO/PC Sawe, now (1995)
GOC of the Kenya Army.

Patrol of King's African Rifles, Kenya 1954.

Royal Ulster Rifles patrol searching villagers, Cyprus 1956.

Helicopters and assault craft take 45, 42 and 40 Commando Royal Marines in to land at Port Said, November 1956.

British presence and round-up the surrendering Japanese. We disembarked in Singapore and marched through welcoming crowds to the Chinese High School for Girls, where we were billeted.

The battalion then spent three idle months in Singapore but fortunately three days after our arrival the Military Administration found that they lacked police officers and called for volunteers, and I found myself on the night train for Kuala Lumpur. I was then sent to Ipoh where I was to command a police district; my instructions were that I must be firm, fair, and show the flag. I was then sent to Kampar and left at the Police Station, knowing nothing about the politics of surrender and less than nothing about being a police officer.

There were no Japanese in Kampar. I had a large police station, about one hundred constables, two inspectors and a lock-up full of prisoners. What was odd, at least to me, was the presence of bad-tempered Chinese soldiers with their belts full of grenades, hands full of automatic weapons and red Communist stars on their caps. They turned out to be members of the MPAJA and clearly resented my presence. They had emerged from the jungle expecting to find themselves the masters, and were resentful that the country was once again under colonial rule.

The station was soon surrounded by a large mob of Chinese, all mustered by the Communists, all shouting and obviously angry. Apparently, just before the Japanese surrender, the Malay Police had rounded up and shot some twenty Chinese, and the locals wanted these Malays handed over. They said the bodies had been buried behind the station and when we dug up the kitchen garden, sure enough we found corpses. What was I to do?

In the end I rang my superior and he sent a lorry load of Indian gunners who restored peace; the crowd was furious but I never did discover who shot the men in the garden. There was more trouble with the Communists over the next few days but more of our troops were arriving and in the end the Communists took themselves sullenly back into the jungle or went off to march in the Victory Parade in London.

Trade, not a lust for conquest, brought the British to Malaya. The original lure was spices, but in the nineteenth century this trade was surpassed by the mining of tin and the development of rubber plantations for the new automobile industry. These were new reasons but British military and political involvement in Malaya began to 1782, when the East India Company sent an expedition to occupy the port of Penang and secure access to the spice trade.

During the Napoleonic Wars the Company took the Dutch-held port of Malacca but the major step to colonialisation came in 1819, when a British trader, Sir Stamford Raffles, acted on his own initiative and seized the island of Singapore at the tip of the Peninsula. Around this tiny but strategically-sited trading outpost grew a thriving port. Other small ports and trading stations in the various Malay Sultanates along the coast of Malaya then developed and came under British protection as the 'Straits Settlements', a territory chiefly remembered by several generations of British schoolboys for the production of colourful stamps.

These Settlements needed protection, not least from Chinese and Indonesian pirates who swarmed around the islands of Indonesia and in the South China Sea. The pirates could be curbed by the Royal Navy but a far more insidious threat to the native Malays of the peninsula was the ever-expanding Chinese community. Chinese traders, under the protection of the British, began to settle along the shores of the Malayan Peninsula in the 1850s and were soon displacing the native Malays, especially on the island of Singapore.

The Chinese are the Jews of Asia, clannish, industrious, successful in their commercial undertakings, culturally sophisticated and politically astute. The Chinese thrived wherever they settled and were soon established as the mercantile middle class of Singapore and Malava, with large communities in the towns and cities of the Peninsula.

The native Malays are a country people. They prefer to live in their villages or 'kampongs', growing rice in the surrounding paddy fields, herding their water buffalo and living a gentle, pastoral existence. The Malays are Muslims and an artistic people but their gentle way of life left their country wide open to exploitation and takeover by the thrusting, mercantile Chinese.

The Malays however, are not entirely quiescent and when they revolt or 'run amok', even the Chinese take cover. Maurice Winter, who went to Malaya after the War as a planter, remembers Malay anger during the Bertha Hertog riots in Singapore during the 1950s:

The Hertogs were a Dutch couple, living in Java before the war. Their baby, Bertha, was looked after by an *ayah*, a nanny, and when the Japanese arrived the family was split up. The Hertogs eventually got back to Holland but the baby stayed with the *ayah*, who looked after the child throughout the war. The Hertogs came back to find her in 1950. Why the Hertogs waited so long to recover the child is not clear but Bertha was then about fourteen or fifteen years of age and in the meantime the *ayah* had moved to Singapore. When the Hertogs found her, she refused to give up Bertha, who had been brought up as a Muslim.

The Hertogs started legal proceedings to recover their daughter who, it was alleged, had fallen madly in love with a Malay gentlemen in his twenties or maybe older, by the name of Mansoor Adabi. The next thing reported in the papers was that Bertha had been recovered, made a ward of court and placed in a Roman Catholic convent.

The Muslim population of Singapore then began to get very restive. The Press referred to Bertha as 'a poor Muslim girl, unable to read her Koran, in the keeping of a hostile religion', and so on, and crowds began to gather. Before long there were full-scale riots, mostly directed against the Europeans. Cars were upset and burned, Europeans chased in the streets, beaten and stoned.

I was in Singapore on Monday, 11 December 1950, getting my car fixed, and I found the city eerily quiet. I hailed a trishaw and the Chinese driver told me the Malays were angry, and that mobs were charging about all over the city, stopping cars and beating or lynching the drivers. I made my way to an hotel called the Cockpit and found that I had got off the streets just in time as the Malays were on the rampage.

I was pinned in the Cockpit all day Tuesday with nothing to do but drink beer and loaf about until the fury of the mob blew itself out. By Wednesday morning things were quiet again and I gather that Bertha was eventually restored to her parents and returned to Holland.

Frank Groves of the Royal Engineers also saw another side of the Malay character when he encountered an 'amok':

This was on the train from Singapore to Penang in 1948. On the way I met up with three Royal Signals and joined them for a game of Solo. They were going up to KL and then back to the UK, and after a bit they went off to purchase a banjo [a sandwich] for lunch. Shortly after they went off I heard a banging on the door of the carriage. When I opened it one of the three – Driver Ralson – staggered in backwards, holding his chest, with blood pouring from him.

We sat him down and opened his shirt and could see that he was bleeding from the chest and back. The lads attempted to stem the flow and virtually plugged the holes with towels from their packs.

Sensing that something serious had happened, another Sergeant and I went into next carriage – a native carriage – and found another Royal Signals man, Sergeant Marston, lying in the aisle, quite still and discharging blood. Lying on the seat next to him was the third soldier, holding his lower abdomen, where his intestines were exposed; he was bleeding from the mouth but was still alive.

All the natives were at the far end of the carriage, jabbering in Malay. We pulled the communication cord and the train stopped and then we learned from one of the Malays that when the three soldiers had entered the carriage one of the Malays had pulled out a 'kris' – a wavy-bladed knife – and gone 'amok', or crazy, stabbing the Sergeant in the heart and slashing the second soldier across the stomach. He was heading out when the third soldier walked in. This was Driver Ralston who, in spite of being stabbed in the chest, managed to kick the 'amok' off the train.

We asked the guard to reverse the train so we could look for the killer but although we had rifles we had no ammunition and two wounded men to look after; eventually reason prevailed and we went on to Kajang. I read in the paper the next day that the 'amok' had killed thirteen people on this rampage before he walked into a police station and gave himself up.

During the nineteenth century there was frequent war between the Chinese settlers and the native Malays and eventually the Malay rulers, the various Sultans of the Peninsula, appealed to the British for advice and protection. In return they accepted the appointment of a British Resident in every Sultanate, who offered advice, which the Sultans were usually well advised to take.

So the British came to Malaya, to ensure intercommunal peace and protect their valuable trade in tin, rubber and spices. In their wake came tens of thousands of Indians, first as labourers, eventually to make up the third element in this volatile ethnic mix. By the end of the Second World War the population of the Malay archipelago mustered some two and a half million Malays, two million Chinese, about six hundred thousand Indians, and about thirty thousand British. This latter element were largely traders, planters, managers of commercial enterprises or members of the colonial administration, many accompanied by their families.

There were other elements, like the timid Sakai forest people who lived in the depths of the jungle, and the Dyaks, Ibans and Sea-Dyaks of Borneo, who came to the Peninsula in the 1950s to serve as trackers with the British Army, but these three main groups, the Malays, Chinese, and Indians, were to become the chief contenders for political power in Malaya when the British kept their promise and left. Before that could happen there were problems to solve.

The native Malays were unhappy that the Chinese had taken over the commerce of their country. The Chinese, on the other hand, were anxious to add political weight to their commercial success. The Indians were simply anxious, for whatever race succeeded in controlling Malaya, they would be the minority community. There was no obvious way for the British to frame an independence constitution that would be fair to all parties and ensure a sound, post-independence democracy. While this issue was being debated, the Chinese Communist Party of Malaya decided to stage a military uprising and drive out the British 'imperialists'.

This they were well placed to do. During the Second World War the Communist guerrilla bands in the jungle had provided the only effective resistance to the Japanese invader. This Chinese Communist formation – the Malayan Peoples' Anti-Japanese Army (MPAJA) – had been supported and supplied by a British Special Operations unit, Force 136, and commanded by a dedicated Vietnamese Communist, Loi Tak, and his Chinese deputy Chin Peng.

In 1947, Loi Tak, who had had enough of jungle warfare, absconded with the Communist Party funds. The Party eventually hunted him down and killed him, but in 1948 the Malayan Communist Party, an entirely Chinese organisation, realised that there would be no popular national rising in Malaya as there had been in Indonesia and Vietnam.

They therefore directed Chin Peng to reform the MPAJA as the Malayan Peoples' Anti-British Army – MPABA – destabilise the country and drive the imperialists – the Running Dogs – out of Malaya and Singapore. Since the British had already left India and been jarred out of Palestine, the prospects for a similar result in Malaya were viewed as favourable. In Malaya, however, the British elected to stay and fight.

Chin Peng was an experienced guerrilla leader, well used to jungle warfare. He had fought against the Japanese for several years and in return for his efforts a grateful British Government had awarded him the OBE and invited him to march in the Victory Parade through London in 1946. The irony of this was not yet evident when the Communist insurrection broke out in 1948.

The Malayan Peninsula is well suited to guerrilla warfare. It is some seven hundred miles long and about two hundred miles wide at the widest point, running from the tip at Jahore up to the Thai border. The island of Singapore, on the southern tip, lies within two degrees of the Equator and the entire Peninsula is cloaked in thick jungle, although by the middle of the twentieth century commercial exploitation had replaced a certain amount of primary jungle with thick secondary jungle – 'lalang' – rubber plantations and 'tin-tailings', the excavated debris of tin mines.

Around the jungle fringe were the kampongs of the Malays and a number of settlements occupied by the Chinese, who either ran local shops and small industries or worked as labourers on the rubber plantations or in the tin mines. Controlling these Chinese settlers was to prove the key to the success or failure of the Malaya campaign.

A mountain range runs down much of the Peninsula in a great arc from the Thai border to the east coast. The land below those cloud-capped mountains is a patchwork of jungle, swamp, rice paddy and rubber plantations, dotted with small villages, plantation compounds and a few small towns. The climate is tropical and humid, the rainfall heavy, the terrain never less than challenging. All this makes Malaya a hard country to soldier in.

Terry Brown came to Malaya in 1950 as a nineteen-year-old National Serviceman serving in Perak with 42 Commando, Royal Marines. He says:

What the movies never show you is the sheer, knackering effect of heat and humidity. Any prolonged movement was exhausting and we sweated constantly. Only high in the mountains was the heat bearable. If you were in 'lalang' or secondary jungle, or tall grass, or in rubber plantations, it was stifling, almost unbearable. Bashing the 'ulu' was very hard work.

Mostly we were hacking our way through thick jungle with parangs or machetes, or flogging up steep, muddy jungle trails weighed down with packs and weapons and ammunition, or up to our hocks in swamps, from which we emerged well covered with leeches. It rained nearly every day in head-aching deluges and we were never dry. In addition, many of the plants had thorns which dug into our skin and clothing. One could always tell the jungle soldiers; they were the pale, thin ones ... the ones with the suntans stayed at base, and all this for twenty-eight shillings a week – about £1.40.

Chin Peng had no trouble reviving the former wartime MAPAJA organisation. The Communist set-up in Malaya at the start of the trouble is described by a Commando officer, Captain Anthony Crockett of 42 Commando:

By the time we arrived, in 1950, the MPABA had become the Malayan Races Liberation Army (MRLA) in an attempt to broaden their appeal to races other than the Chinese. The MRLA was a loose military force and its tactics were based on fear; intimidation, terror, murder, arson, abduction threats and blackmail.

Their efforts were mainly directed at the Asiatic population, principally the Chinese, and aimed to disrupt the machinery of Government, public services and the operation of large European concerns, such as tin mines and rubber estates. Their organisation was split into three more or less independent bodies, the MRLA proper, who lived in the jungle, the Min Yuen, the plain clothes workers who supplied the MRLA with men, food and information, and the Lie Ton Ten or Killer Squads who were the gangsters, the strong-arm thugs, charged with rubbing out people opposed to the Communist takeover.

Maurice Weaver, a planter, remembers how it all started:

The first hint of trouble that I can recollect was the report of a pot-shot taken at a 'kepala', a contractor's headman, in April or May 1948. He was riding his bicycle home and the shot hit him in the jaw. Everyone thought how queer that was, and wondered at the motive. Then in May a gang raided Kim Foh's house in Layang 2.

Luckily for Kim Foh he was in the latrine when they called and was able to make his escape but they shot his sister in the leg and extorted money from her. Various other reports about attacks on Chinese personnel then came trickling in; we thought it might be a private war between supporters of Mao and Chiang Kai-seck, the Chinese Nationalist leader, but before long reports came in of attacks on European planters and by June things were turning nasty.

We needed guards and I was issued with a revolver. Shortly after that a Chinese in Layang 2 and two Chinese in Rengam were murdered. Young Malays were recruited as Special Constables and by August we were all armed and I had joined the Police as an Honorary Inspector. At the end of August there was the Sembrong affair.

The bandit attack on the Sembrong estate, adjacent to Ulu Remis, came at about first light. They first attacked the manager's house and broke in. Luckily the manager was able to hide or they would have killed him. The assistant manager called John Boden, the manager at Chemara, knowing that John was a tough, reliable guy. John called Larry Watkins, the Security Officer for Ulu Remis. Larry grabbed one of the guards, drove up as fast as his car would take him to pick up John and another guard at Chemare. Then the four of them, in John's jeep, hurtled off to Sembrong.

What they did next was very courageous, but not altogether wise, at least from the point of view of guerrilla fighters. However, neither John nor Larry were guerrilla fighters; they had both held commissions in the war but that was no preparation for what was to follow. The bandits had now occupied the Sembrong Estate HQ, a cluster of wooden houses, sheds and warehouses.

The jeep approached the HQ by road, in full view of the bandits in the buildings and was a sitting duck. The bandits opened fire with rifles and two Brens and the Chemara guard was killed outright. The others leapt out and Larry and his guard made it to the shelter of a monsoon drain. John Boden ran for the office door, found it locked, ran for the drain, took a burst in the stomach and was killed instantly.

Larry and the surviving guard, with about ten Sembrong special constables, then battled very bravely with the bandits, killing three and wounding several more before reinforcements arrived and the bandits melted away into the rubber.

The bandits were about a hundred in number, well armed and in uniform. They killed five people at Sembrong, burned all three smoke houses, rubber stocks and the Estate office, and damaged the manager's bungalow.

Now this little battle is small beer compared with what went on in the war and indeed compared to some of the things going on in the world today, but Larry told me afterwards that it was worse than anything he had experienced in the war and he was a gung-ho, fearless sort of chap.

Next day I had the job of sorting out John Boden's personal effects. To this day I don't know why I did it, but I drove up to Sembrong, to the scene of the action. There, soaked into the gravel road, was a dense purplish patch of blood. That was the last I ever saw of John Boden.

To fight any guerrilla campaign, and especially one against a well organised, aggressive foe, takes a great deal of skill. It also requires a high level of cooperation between the Police and the Army, to ensure coordination of activities and policy between the military and civil powers. When the Malayan Emergency began in April 1948 this essential coordination was lacking.

The administration of the country and all matters concerning defence and foreign affairs were handled by the High Commissioner for Malaya, Sir Edward Gent. Military matters were in the hands of the General Officer Commanding Malaya, (GOC Malaya), a post held by Major General Galloway from his HQ in the capital, Kuala Lumpur. General Galloway had inadequate forces at his disposal and a whole country to protect. The Police force was undermanned and poorly trained and commanded by a Civil Commissioner. These gentlemen tended to go their own ways and although they all had the same aim, the security and stability of the country, they had different ways of achieving it. Such a division of command did not exist in the ranks of the Communist forces.

Chin Peng could muster about ten thousand men in the MRLA but at first these could not all be armed or fed. He therefore left the older men to form active Communist cells in the towns and kampongs and took some three thousand fighting men into the jungle, moving his headquarters to Johore, the southern State of the Malay Peninsula, just across the causeway from Singapore. Those left in the towns began work at once, formenting a series of riots and strikes across the Peninsula, backed by strident Communist propaganda, the Lie Ten Ton murdering anyone unwilling to take part in this activity or openly opposing Communist actions.

Maurice Weaver continues his account of a planter's life in the early days of the Emergency:

Naturally, the Sembrong affair left us all very shaken. There were a number of planters' wives living on the estates and these were sent to Singapore. Then a battalion of the Devons arrived, and a detachment of Gurkhas who were based at Sembrong. Various little battles took place in the surrounding jungle but after a while things began to settle down. More arms turned up and were distributed among the planters, though they were not always suited to the circumstances.

I was issued with a single-barrelled shotgun – single barrel if you please – which was the best they could find, and a few months later with a Sten-gun, a 9mm, 28-round magazine, sub-machine-gun. I carried that blasted gun everywhere, even into the bog when I went in there. At night it lay on the floor beside my bed so I only had to put out my hand. When we went into Singapore the weapons were left at the police station at Jahore Bahru.

There were outrages in other parts of Malaya, especially around Penang, but we were left in peace for a while, perhaps because we were too well armed – which is doubtful – perhaps because there were softer targets elsewhere. There was the odd incident from time to time, such as when three bandits armed with pistols attempted to attack the 'Monkey Shooter'; his job was to see off the monkeys that fed on the palm fruit and he was armed with an automatic shotgun. They must have been barmy to attack him as his was the more powerful weapon and he was a good shot; he promptly killed one bandit and the other two fled.

In January 1950 I was sent to Seremban, travelling on the night train from Layang 2, booked into a first-class sleeper at the rear of the train. I was sleeping peacefully when I was awoken by a popping noise. The Emergency was into its stride by then and I had become a very light sleeper. I knew at once that the train was being shot at and immediately rolled onto the floor, strapping on my pistol and putting a magazine into the Sten.

The popping became louder and bullets came through the carriage wall, just where I had been lying. A Malay lady on the bunk opposite did not hear the shooting and was hit by a bullet which came through the window and caught her in the thigh, the impact knocking her out of bed. Later on, the bandits took to derailing the night train instead of just shooting it up. Eventually the Railway Company got fed up with the night mail never arriving on time and cancelled the service.

In April 1950 the administrative officer of Kluang was killed in an ambush while on his way to an incident. On another occasion the manager of Chemara met a bandit patrol when on his rounds with his special constables, one of whom was killed. From marks on his body and the bullet holes, they reckon he was first wounded and then killed in cold blood. The manager was hit in the arm and ended up in hospital. Alan Serfent met a bandit patrol while walking around his rubber plantation and he was shot dead.

In November 1950 I was finishing my tea in my bungalow when I saw two columns of dense black smoke rising above the trees on the far side of the estate. A party of us, led by a former Palestine Police Sergeant, went to see what was happening. A bandit patrol had stopped two estate buses, ordered the occupants to get out, robbed them and took their identity papers, then set the buses alight. Burning buses and robbing the passengers did not seem the best way to win over the locals to their cause. In any case, they were trying to break an unlocked door, for Malaya was already on track for independence and there was no need for all this banditry. I think they were a bit thick, being basically thugs without much intelligence.

By January 1951 I had been provided with an armoured car, an old Ford V-8 which had armour plate built around the front seat. Then my employers found me a Reising sub-machine gun, much better than the old Sten. My contract ended in March 1952; my company wanted to extend it by six months but I said no. I was feeling exhausted and run down by then and wanted to get home. They flew me back to London and it was just like when I had departed four years previously, cold, dull and drizzly, like walking into a refrigerator.

All-out terrorist operations by the Communist bandits began in June 1948 with a series of attacks on rubber plantations, tin mines and police stations. These attacks were carried out by groups of up to a hundred well-armed terrorists and caused considerable destruction and loss of life.

The outbreak of terrorism did not take the British administration entirely by surprise but the Government was woefully unprepared for the sheer scale of the violence. In any terrorist campaign, the advantage of surprise always lies with the terrorist, and within weeks attacks and atrocities had multiplied in number and spread right across the country.

Frank Groves remembers the early days of the Emergency:

I served in the Far East and was a Sergeant in the Engineer Training Centre at Kluang when the Emergency was declared. Although I was an Engineer NCO, I was also a qualified weapons training instructor.

The first acts of terrorism in the Johore State took place at a small town called Layang Layang, close to where we were stationed at Kluang. Some local leaders had been executed by three armed terrorists who each had Thompson sub-machine-guns, relics of our arming of the natives against the Japanese during the war.

As we were the nearest military unit I was ordered out of the Sergeants' Mess at 10.00pm to organise a patrol of locally enlisted Malay soldiers and then to find and eliminate the villains. We were dressed in full battle order with steel helmets, boots, gaiters or puttees and assembled at the local Police Station in Layang Layang to listen to the Malay Police Corporal as he described how he had wounded one terrorist with a twelve-bore shotgun. At daybreak we set off to search for the three bandits, one of whom was wounded.

We struggled through ten miles of jungle and were soon completely exhausted by the heat and the way we were dressed. We carried out wartime street fighting drills on all the small villages and huts but found no sign of a bandit. Many lessons were learned from this first patrol and in later months we became much more sophisticated.

One offshoot of this first engagement was the need to arm the Malay police force and equip the police stations for defense. I had two roles to play here. I was given two Malay-speaking corporals and a 15-cwt truck plus the necessary weapons, to instruct the local police in the use of the rifle, Sten-gun and grenade.

The other offshoot was the defence of the police stations. Here we developed a system of placing cigarette-tin charges, full of plastic explosive and nails, at numerous points around the wire perimeter. These were wired to No. 33 electric detonators and controlled by a board wired with contacts for each charge. By using a single probe wired into the circuit, the police could detonate a charge in the area where an attack was coming from. It was an early-day system in an emergency but better than nothing.

European planters and managers also came under attack, especially in the State of Perak, where three British planters were murdered in cold blood in the first week. On 18 June 1948, a State of Emergency was declared in Malaya and remained in place for the next twelve years.

The Communist rising and the State of Emergency which followed found GOC Malaya in a difficult position. He had under command eleven infantry battalions, three British, six Gurkha – those battalions recently transferred from the Indian Army – and two Malay, but this force was barely sufficient for the country-wide task. When 45 Commando were deployed in South Perak they had six hundred men to cover an area of nineteen hundred square miles, about as big as Northumberland, much of it swamp, mountain and jungle.

Neither was the military in entirely good order in the first few years. The Gurkhas were the cream of this force, but their battalions were under strength. It was some time before the Gurkhas could be provided with a proper range of logistical support and formed into a new formation, the 17th Gurkha Division, which was to serve with distinction throughout the Malayan Emergency and in the Borneo Confrontation which followed.

The British battalions were also in a state of flux, as long-serving, war-experienced soldiers went home and were replaced by young, eighteen- and nineteen-year-old National Servicemen. These National Servicemen were called up for a two-year stint and, after training, would serve for little more than a year in the jungle. The locally raised Malay battalions, while up to strength, were not trained in jungle operations at all and the whole force was short of transport and logistical facilities.

Even worse was the lack of good intelligence. Brigadier Joe Starling was then a Company commander in the 1 Bn., The Suffolk Regiment, the battalion which was to kill more Communist terrorists during its three-and-a-half-year jungle tour than any other British unit in Malaya:

> 1 Suffolk was ordered from the Middle East in 1949 to reinforce 2nd Guards Brigade, based in Central Malaya. On the day we arrived in Malaya, Chin Peng judged it the right moment to implement Stage 3 of his takeover plan and 'liberate' substantial tracts of country. A Gurkha battalion re-liberated it and the Communists went back into the jungle.
>
> In this sort of situation there is no substitute for getting to know your area well, and this includes getting on good terms with the police and the civilians. 1 Suffolk were fortunate in that we spent most of our time in South Selangor, apart from a short spell in Jahore, and got to know every track and ridge on our patch like the back of our hands. We also made a point of getting on well with the police who had 'enjoyed' the worst of relations with our predecessors.
>
> Intelligence was much more difficult at that time. The Special Branch, the police intelligence arm, was in ruins. Some men had defected to the Communists, some had been murdered. Those who remained were of dubious quality and at odds with the uniformed

branch and with each other. Reinforcements were arriving, mostly from the Palestine Police, but they knew as little of the country and its problems as we did. The build-up of Intelligence took years rather than months, though sometimes a lucky break gave us some good kills.

At first we conducted a series of section-sized training patrols before taking on any larger operations. Such was the arrogance of the enemy at that time, that they were based on the jungle fringes and we could hardly help bumping into them; after three weeks of operations we were averaging a kill rate of half a bandit a day.

There were not many helicopters, though we did use artillery air strikes but in the main it depended on the infantry soldier. It was a very personal kind of war. The British soldier, Regular or National Service, soon became very good at it and in a peculiar way even enjoyed it.

The security forces, police, military and auxiliary did what they could, but between 1948 and 1950 the advantage lay with the Communist terrorists, the 'CTs', or 'bandits' as the soldiers called them, and the CTs took that advantage with both hands. One of the main political problems was that the Colonial Administration was in disarray. On re-entering the Colony in 1945 the original British intention was to set up a 'Malay Union'. After writing a Constitution and holding elections this 'Union' would form a Government to which the British would eventually hand over power. This was a workable plan but there was, inevitably, a snag.

This 'Malay Union' should have included Singapore as well as the Malay States. Had this intention come to pass, the large and rapidly expanding Chinese population of Singapore would have given the Chinese a preponderance in the Malay Union. The Sultans of the Malay States therefore proposed setting up a 'Federation of Malaya' excluding Singapore, which would, at least for a time, remain a British colony.

Sensing that this offered them the prospect of power in Singapore, the local Chinese agreed, and the Federation of Malaya was duly established in January 1948. Unfortunately, the infrastructure for running this new Federation had not been established when the Emergency broke out and many problems followed which were to bedevil the anti-terrorist campaign later. Then, in July 1948, the first High Commissioner of the Federation, Sir Edward Gent, was killed in an crash; he was not replaced by Sir Henry Gurney until October and in the intervening months the security situation went from bad to worse.

Sir Henry had been Chief Secretary to the Mandate in Palestine. In his train as Police Commissioner came another officer with Palestine experience, Colonel Nicol Grey, a Royal Marine officer and formerly Inspector General of the Palestine Police. Grey was not by temperament or experience a police officer but he was followed in turn by several hundred former officers of the Palestine Police, who came to serve in Malaya and stiffen the local police forces.

Other changes followed when General Galloway's time expired. He was replaced as GOC Malaya by a Gurkha officer, Major General C.H. Boucher. All these gentlemen were highly experienced officers but all were new to Malaya, and that coordination and cooperation so necessary for the successful mounting of an anti–terrorist campaign was still lacking.

John Anderson was planting rubber in Malaya during the Emergency and remembers the routine in the early days:

I arrived in Malaya on 1 April 1951, landing at Penang from a Blue Funnel ship, *Ulysses* some twenty-eight days after leaving Liverpool. The Malaya to which I arrived was very different from the pre-war Malaya known to many of my immediate mentors. The local population had seen the British ignominiously swept from the Peninsula and Singapore by a numerically inferior Japanese army and this event was still referred to by them as 'The Time of Running'.

Any belief in the omnipotence of Imperial Britain was now heavily qualified by the experience of this retreat and only the brutality of the years of Japanese occupation made the British re-occupation a welcome relief.

Nevertheless, political activity with independence as the main aim was in progress, but the rate of progress was severely hampered by the ongoing Communist-led insurrection, euphemistically called 'The Emergency'. The Emergency lasted twelve years, being declared over in 1960. Planters suffered ninety-nine fatal casualties, about 10 per cent of their complement, and a window in the west end of St Mary's Church in Kuala Lumpur commemorates this fact.

I write as a planter, but there were heavy civilian casualties in the tin mining industry and in Government service. Nor were the killings confined to expatriate and Malayan management personnel. Terrible atrocities were carried out against the labour forces of the estates and mines, particularly against those Chinese who were seen by the Communists as collaborating with the 'Imperial Power'.

I was involved in an alarm on my very first day, when the planter with whom I was lodging was reported killed. This arose from a deaf tapper seeing seven CTs passing by shortly after the planter went out on his rounds. The Tamil tapper raised the alarm – a procedure not without risk as estate workers seen to be supporting the 'running dogs' were executed by the CTs.

A police unit arrived on the estate in their 'soft' vehicles and moved off into the rubber – just as the planter reported shot came in from the opposite direction. I then learned that I was the replacement for his assistant who had been killed the previous year. On the following weekend the folly of security forces being moved in 'soft' vehicles was demonstrated by the sight of two police Landrovers in the compound of the District Police HQ.

There were neat holes through the aluminium backs of the driver's and passenger's seats – holes through which a cricket ball could comfortably pass. The policeman was able to tell me that this was the effect of a Bren-gun and was even able to suggest the name of the CT gunner. The weapons and training had been provided by the British during the war, and the CT unit responsible was operating south of Kajang.

The general feeling was that to avoid an ambush, routine should be avoided and routes varied. The day started with muster at 0545 hrs, when the Tamil labourers, the 'tappers', reported for work and were allocated their tasks. We assistants were expected to be present but it was found that unexpected appearances in various areas of the estate were effective in maintaining the necessary level of discipline.

As far as possible no appointments were to be made, and I never made up my mind where to go until I actually set out. It was safest to walk, but constraints of time and distance often required that a car had to be used. Wise, security-conscious parking, could minimise the danger on the return. In this way the normal working day was not severely disrupted by the Emergency.

There were curfews in operation from 1500 hrs to 0600 hrs in the areas away from main roads and from 1900 hrs to 0600 hrs overall. Workers' housing areas, manufacturing plants and the planters' bungalows were all eventually surrounded by perimeter fences. In some cases these were floodlit. Planters were issued with curfew passes, which meant that it was possible to travel in the evenings but this could be a pain if a journey involved getting through wired-in villages. As the years went on, an increasing number of armoured cars were used. The fact was that security for the individual planter was minimal and we could have been picked off very easily; I am still wondering why we weren't.

Once the Emergency had been declared, military reinforcements began to arrive, and there was no shortage of local volunteers, Chinese or Malay, to serve as guards, if only to protect their village and families. Former officers of Force 136 also came back and formed a Special Operations Unit – Ferret Force – which provided over twenty jungle patrol units; other patrol forces were raised from Malay and Gurkha units already in the country.

To these were added a new element, Iban trackers from Borneo, many of them former headhunters, who were attached as trackers to front line battalions and proved an invaluable aid to British units operating in the jungle. Marine Terry Brown again:

> Our Troop Iban was Tan Yan. These trackers from Borneo were a fearful sight, short brown bodies, all heavily tattooed, with long black hair reaching down to their waists in camp, though they tucked it up in their jungle hats when on patrol. They carried rifles and a parang with which, given the chance, they would lop off CT heads. Tan Yan's 'going ashore' dress was a jungle green shirt and shorts, black and green football socks, plimsolls, and a green Commando beret. As we proceeded down the street in Kajang, the pavement ahead of us cleared magically.

Apart from the British and Gurkha battalions already in Malaya, other units to arrive from Britain in 1949 included the 4th Hussars with their armoured cars, the 2nd Guards Brigade and 26th Field Regiment, Royal Artillery. As CT activity increased these were followed in 1950 by the Suffolk Regiment, the Somerset Light Infantry and the Royal Marines of the 3rd Commando Brigade from Hong Kong. Many of the men in these units had served in Palestine; they were used to anti-terrorist work but not to jungle warfare.

'We did not have much in the way of jungle training,' says Terry Brown of 42 Commando, 'though a Jungle Warfare School was set up later in Jahore. In fact, when we got up to the unit at Kajang all we had was a talk in the dining room from an officer who said, "It's quite simple, lads: if we get shot at, we go straight at them." I remember thinking, "Blimey, what manner of men are these?"'

These new units arrived by troop ship and had to be transported upcountry from Singapore. The train journey through the Peninsula was not without risk, as Percy Dee of the Coldstream Guards remembers:

Some of my mates and I were returning to our unit at Tapah, and on the way I was to come just half-an-inch from being another occupant of Bath Gajah Military Cemetery, where a few of my old colleagues still lie.

We left Singapore for Kuala Lumpur on the night mail train. It was generally accepted that the troops on the train formed the train's guard, but it was a shambles that night, with at least two hundred men on board, all from different units, and no one in charge. Everyone got down to sleep for the carriages had bunks, one up and one down, on either side of the corridor. Most of the windows had roller blinds but mine was missing. The train lights were on but I occupied a bottom bunk and dozed off. After crossing the causeway at Johore Baru we had reached somewhere between Kulai and Sedenak when I was awakened by one hell of a commotion. The train was going slowly but men were falling down from the top bunks and diving for the floor.

I rolled off the bunk as well and felt what I thought was a handful of stones hitting me behind the head. We were under fire. I was conscious of the noise the bullets were making as they went straight through the carriage. The lights were still on and a chorus of voices shouted and yelled, 'Put the . . . lights out!'

Before I reached the floor the lights went out and I could tell that someone was underneath me. Then all went quiet except for the slow clickety-click of the train wheels.

I felt sure that a few of us had been hit but thankfully everybody got up. Before I got up from the floor I felt something running down my neck; it was a mixture of sweat and blood and I could feel chunks of glass sticking in the back of my head. Then the lights came back on and people started moving about. My mates, who were uninjured, started to remove some glass and produced a towel to mop up the blood. We could see that the bullets had come from right to left of the train, and gone straight through the glass and woodwork. My window was shattered and there was a round hole about four inches in diameter very close to where my head had been. A burst of automatic fire had come through, aimed at me laying there with no blind at the window.

The train stopped at Sedenak station where it was said that some soldiers and civilians were dead. The train moved off for Kluang and I was taken to the BMH where I stayed two nights before returning to my regiment at Tapah. I have the scar of the bullet wound to the back of my neck to this day but I also received a nice letter of apology from General Manager of Malayan Railways!

In 1949 the CTs attempted to establish 'no-go' zones, so called 'liberated' areas, where police and army patrols were routinely attacked and the European planters and village headmen were murdered. This scheme met with an immediate response from the Army and swiftly collapsed. A sweep through the 'liberated area' at Bali Arang, north of Kuala Lumpur, by the Gurkhas and men of the Royal Artillery serving as infantry, dislodged the CTs in that area and drove them into the jungle with the loss of twenty-six dead.

Further attempts at establishing 'no-go' areas in Kajang and Kelantar were also defeated but the CTs were now operating in considerable numbers – some of their gangs were three hundred strong – so apart from the advantage of surprise, they usually outnumbered the guards or garrisons of the villages and plantations selected for attack.

In an attempt to break the power of the CT gangs, General Boucher ordered a series of Brigade-sized sweeps, from south to north starting in the State of Jahore. Five battalions with air support swept across the state but the results were meagre. The CT gangs simply slipped away into the deeper jungle and when similar 'big–battalion' sweeps were tried out in Selangor and Perak a few months later they proved equally ineffective.

General Sir William Jackson has described this first year of the Malayan Emergency as the 'big battalions on both sides' period, when the advantages seemed to lie with the Communists. In fact, though the number of successful 'contacts' with CT gangs were few in relation to the large numbers of soldiers deployed, the Security Forces were getting results; in the first six months of the Emergency over five hundred CTs were killed, and the Communists were denied an early victory.

In December 1948, the Central Committee of the Malayan Communist Party therefore issued their 2nd Operational Directive. This ordered the CT 'battalions' to break off the fight and withdraw into deep jungle to rethink their tactics, retrain their men and prepare for a future offensive. A small force of CTs was to remain on the jungle fringe, to carry on the attacks and keep contact with the Min Yuen.

This pause in terrorist activity had an unfortunate effect on the British administration. As a result of the Communist withdrawal, the number of terrorist incidents fell from over two hundred a month to fewer than one hundred and the British attributed this, wrongly, to the success of the 'big battalion' sweeps.

The local administration foresaw a swift end to the Emergency and Sir Henry Gurney even claimed that the Emergency would end 'within the year'. Among a number of premature moves Ferret Force was disbanded and the officers returned to civilian life. The 'big battalion' sweeps went on, and the number of CT attacks fell still further which seemed to confirm Sir Henry's claims. Hopes began to grow that the CTs had actually been defeated.

Joe Starling continues his tale of life with the 1st Bn., The Suffolk Regiment:

'D' Company, was based in a former Chinese school at Kajang, a small town on the main Kuala Lumpur-to-Singapore road. This was bounded on one side by the jungle-covered hills of the main range which bisected the Malayan Peninsula from North to South and on the other by the vast Kuala Langat block of jungle marked on somewhat unreliable maps as 'unexplored – probably swamp'.

The Company Commander was a man of action who had fought the Japanese in Burma and regarded chasing Communist terrorists as scarcely worthy of the term 'military operation'. None the less, he quickly set about dominating that part of his operational area which bounded the rubber estates on either side of the main road and from whose numerous kampongs (villages), largely inhabited by rubber tappers, terrorists drew their principal support.

The first operation we attempted was a small-scale ambush based on information from the Special Branch, which resulted in two dead terrorists. It might have been more had not the Special Branch guide become over-excited in the heat of the moment and rushed off in pursuit of the remainder, getting himself shot dead in the process by the flanking Bren gun group who were unaware that he had left his position. By the time the confusion was sorted out (of the ten soldiers involved only the Sergeant had ever been in action before) the three surviving terrorists were long gone – but a valuable lesson was learned (or perhaps relearned) on the necessity for absolute control when in ambush positions, which paid dividends in later operations.

The Company Commander decided that the five terrorists engaged by the ambush party must form part of a larger group. He and his Platoon Commanders spent a tense evening poring over maps and trying to out-think the local terrorist commander.

It was finally decided that the terrorists were intending to raid the two European-run rubber estates surrounding the village of Broga, high in the mountains at the end of a one-track road. Accordingly, the Company deployed at first light next morning – trying to move through jungle by night is not a productive activity – with one platoon sweeping to the north and one to the south, while Company HQ controlled progress from the axis of the road. 10 Platoon, much to their chagrin, were left behind, partly to secure the base against attack and partly to provide a mobile reserve which could be moved, in vehicles, to blocking positions if required. This was in the days before helicopter mobility changed the face of minor tactics, although the helicopter was occasionally used for VIP visits and evacuating casualties.

During the day it transpired that 'O' Group had guessed wrongly.

The terrorists hadn't gone on to Broga but had turned off, possibly as a result of the previous day's ambush, to attack the hydro-electric power station which supplied current to the local area. This was an unguarded facility – there just weren't enough troops to guard everything – and it was burned to the ground following the murder of the duty crew of four Indian workers.

This news reached the Company Base from the Malayan Police in the late morning and the Commander of 10 Platoon, having failed to make contact with the rest of the Company on the radio, decided to take a patrol to make physical contact with the Company HQ near Broga. Leaving his Sergeant to guard the base with the bulk of the Platoon, he set off with six men in two jeeps up a former logging track, which was just passable for some miles by vehicles with four-wheeled drive. When the track ran out, the vehicles were concealed and the radio operator and the two drivers were left to guard them, while the other four set off across a jungle ridge from where it was fondly expected they would soon be able to locate Company HQ. Just over the crest of the ridge was an old logging camp, and there, much to their surprise, the little group came upon the terrorist gang, clearly taking a rest after distancing themselves from the power station they had destroyed that morning.

There was no way of determining how many terrorists there were at the time, although Intelligence later set it at around thirty. The Platoon Commander and three men were virtually on top of the camp before they realised quite what they had blundered into. Happily, having their weapons ready, they were able to get off the first shots which killed two of the terrorists. At this point the Platoon Commander's Sten gun – a notoriously unreliable weapon – jammed with an empty case in the chamber. His instructor at the Small Arms School would have been proud of the speed with which immediate action drill was carried out to clear the stoppage. Meanwhile, in view of the disparity in numbers, an element of bluff was called for and the Platoon Commander started exhorting 'B' Company to 'get up on the right flank and "C" Company on the left,' at the top of his lungs.

Having lost another man, the terrorists' leader decided to call it a day, at which the terrorists literally melted into the jungle. The Platoon Commander decided not to chance his luck much further and, having secured the weapons of the three dead terrorists, returned to the rest of his group by the jeeps, where, by some fluke of weather conditions, the radio operator had made contact with the rest of the Company. Unhappily, they were too far from the contact to do more than send out follow-up patrols. These later accounted for another terrorist who had been so badly wounded he was unable to keep up with his comrades.

This chance contact with the terrorists so soon after their attack on the power station established a degree of moral ascendancy by 'D' Company, which the Company Commander took considerable pains to maintain. The overall effect was to make the terrorists more cautious, more suspicious of informers and to base themselves deeper in the jungle.

The Platoon Commander and his team of three came to realise that they had been lucky to see off several times their own number in their first contact of the campaign, but they did what they had been trained to do – engage the enemy – and made use of a simple deception to disguise their lack of strength. Risky, but it worked on this occasion.

With a military solution apparently in sight, the High Commissioner turned his attention to the political situation, which proved far more tricky. However necessary they might be for the protection of life and property, the implementation of Emergency Regulations alienated the local population, whose goodwill was essential. The Government was also anxious to placate the Chinese, on whom these regulations bore most severely. Since the insurgents enjoyed considerable popular support from the Chinese community, this was understandable but the Chinese felt aggrieved. On the other hand, any overt attempt to please the Chinese aroused resentment among the Malays, who did not want the Chinese in their country anyway.

To provide those in the Chinese community who did not support the Communists with an alternative political voice, Sir Henry Gurney encouraged the setting up of the Malayan–Chinese Association, or MCA. This failed to flourish, not least because the CTs were in a position to intimidate or kill anyone who supported it.

Gurney was equally unsuccessful in his attempts to resettle the Chinese squatter community from around the jungle fringe and so sever their connection with the Min Yuen. Fresh powers were invoked to arrest and remove known Communist agitators or sympathisers from the villages and ship them back to the Chinese mainland, but such collective punishments and military sweeps through the squatter villages were not always well handled and caused great resentment.

Even so, in September 1949, a year after Gurney arrived in Malaya, the Government felt able to suspend the death penalty for terrorism and offer an amnesty to all CTs willing to surrender. Scarcely a hundred bandits took advantage of this offer, and within weeks Peng's retrained and remotivated CT gangs returned to the attack in force.

From September 1949 the number of attacks doubled and redoubled to top four hundred a month, mostly in the form of ambushes or attacks on road and rail transport. Communist confidence in eventual victory in Malaya was enhanced by the victory of Mao Tse Tung in China and in October 1949, by the establishment of the People's Republic of China, a nation swiftly recognised by the British Government.

These Communist successes in mainland China led to an inevitable rise in support for the CT gangs in Malaya. If the Communists *were* going to drive the British out of Malaya, then it was only common sense to support the Communist insurrection now, when such help was needed, rather than wait for some eerie vengeance at the hands of the CTs when the revolution was finally accomplished. The British Government was losing the battle for 'hearts and minds' and fresh methods would have to be introduced. The first requirement, however, was more troops.

Two more Gurkha battalions arrived from Hong Kong in April 1950 and in May the crack 3rd Commando Brigade, Royal Marines was deployed in Perak and Selangor. Among them was Corporal Victor Peglar of 42 Commando:

A junior NCO involved in jungle warfare in Malaya did not have an easy existence. The physical discomfort was considerable; one lost weight and acquired a pale complexion. The tanned, fit-looking chaps were people serving in the support arms who never ventured into the 'ulu'. Very little sunlight penetrates to the jungle floor.

Spencer Chapman, the author of *The Jungle is Neutral* who served with Force 136 had, during the Japanese occupation, operated in the state of Perak where my Commando was stationed.

Several people carried that volume in their packs for use as a guide book. Chapman's thesis was that the jungle provides a level playing field, it favours neither the attacker nor the defender. He also propounded the theory that if you abandoned an officer, an NCO and a private soldier in the jungle, the private soldier would die first, the NCO next and the officer last. I doubt that Spencer Chapman had any experience of Royal Marines; my experience of young Marines blows that theory out of the water.

As a young man in my early twenties, the justification for my being personally involved in jungle warfare was not something that concerned me. There had been a certain amount of political indoctrination during the troopship journey from Hong Kong to Singapore but this was of superficial influence. I did not need motivating, my unit was going into action and my main concerns were that I should perform well and earn the respect of my peers.

The incident that might have led to a wider consideration of the global significance of the Malayan conflict, involved being ambushed in an open area of tall 'lalang' south of Sungei Siput in Perak. There was a general fire fight with the normal confusion and noise. The Troop Commander threw phosphorous smoke grenades which set the grass alight, and the EY rifle man fired a 36 grenade from his launcher which landed in a large pot of rice cooking on the terrorists' camp fire. When we finally charged through their camp there was rice everywhere.

One of the weapons from which we were under effective fire was a Japanese copy of the German Spandau. This machine gun has a phenomenally high rate of fire which gives it a quite unique sound that has been likened to the sound of tearing rough calico; not a pleasant noise when you are on the receiving end. The other machine gun turned out to be a standard British Bren gun.

I noticed a particular area of foliage shaking in unison with the sound of bursts of machinegun fire coming in my direction and I fired six or seven aimed shots back. Subsequent investigation revealed that a terrorist had been firing the Bren around the right-hand side of a tree trunk and that my aimed shots had all gone into the tree trunk itself. I found a neat pile of cartridge cases at the base of the tree. They were standard British .303 cartridges and all bore the mark of the rectangular Bren firing pin. I collected a few and put them in my pocket.

The point of the story is that the cartridge cases that I collected turned out to have been of quite recent manufacture, much more recent than the ammunition issued to British troops in Malaya. This made me ponder on how an enemy of my country came to be trying to kill me with ammunition made in my country more recently than the ammunition with which I had been supplied.

The use of armoured cars to keep the roads open had proved invaluable and the 13th/18th Hussars arrived to join the 4th Hussars in this testing and dangerous duty. By the end of 1950 there were no fewer than twenty-five infantry battalions in Malaya, and this number remained constant until the Emergency ended ten years later. This was now a Commonwealth war, with contingents from Britain, Australia. New Zealand, Fuji and East Africa taking part, as well as Malay battalions and those of the four Gurkha regiments which were now part of the British Army.

In spite of this vast increase in numbers the struggle against the CTs was not going well. The Security Forces were simply flailing at the jungle, spending countless man-hours on fruitless patrols. Most of their successes were due to chance contacts rather than any clear plan.

The overall Commander of the Malaya Forces was Lt.-General Sir John Harding, GOC Far East Land Forces, based in Hong Kong. General Harding was a thinking soldier. Although he had many other problems within his bailiwick, not least the advent of Communist China and the Korean War, he devoted a considerable amount of thought to the problems of Malaya.

Harding knew that troop reinforcements alone could never win the Emergency; a coordinated political and administrative solution was necessary. Harding was supported in this view by the current Chief of the Imperial General Staff (CIGS), Field Marshal Sir William (Bill) Slim, wartime Commander of the 14th Army, victor of the Burma campaign, and no stranger to the jungle.

Harding and Slim felt that the current approach to the Malayan problem was piecemeal and therefore ineffective. In their view what was needed was one man – a Director of Operations – who could oversee all the elements available for curbing the CTs, police, civil and military, and report directly to the High Commissioner who would remain solely responsible for devising and implementing a long-term political solution. At the moment the task of coordination largely fell on Colonel Nicol Grey, who had enough on his hands running a rapidly expanding national Police Force.

Harding and Slim envisaged a much larger role for the Director of Operations, and the man finally selected to fill the post was Lt.-General Sir Harold Briggs, who arrived in Malaya in April 1950. Briggs was an old friend of Slim and had served on his Staff in Burma. Briggs had experience in the jungles of the Far East and, though now retired, he agreed to put on his uniform again and take up this new challenge in Malaya.

Briggs's role was not advisory. He could and did devise plans and issue orders, though the Commissioner of Police, Colonel Grey, could appeal to the High Commissioner and the various Brigadiers could appeal to the GOC Malaya if they felt the need.

Briggs devised a long-term plan – the Briggs Plan – which aimed at combining civil, police and military activity into one coordinated effort aimed at stamping out Communist insurgency, holding free elections and leading the country to independence. His first step was to form a Civil–Military Command, made up of the Director of Operations, the Commissioner of Police, the Commanders of the Army and Air Force, and, filling a most vital role in any counter-terrorist group, the Director of Intelligence. This national body delegated some of its powers to similar bodies at State level.

The Briggs Plan contained two main elements to tackle the fundamental problem of terrorism and insurgency. According to Mao Tse Tung, the terrorist moves among the population 'as the fish swims in the sea', so the first step was to remove from the CTs their main source of support and food supply, the Chinese rural population. If the Chinese squatters could be moved away from the jungle edge and resettled in areas where they could be protected from Communist intimidation, the level of support they could give to the CTs would be much reduced.

Moreover, to maintain the 'hearts and minds' element, the resettled villages would not be squatter camps but good places in which to live, with piped water, schools and health clinics, far better than their old kampongs. From these villages they would be convoyed in guarded trucks and buses to their work on the plantations. This project cost a vast amount of money and took several years to complete, but eventually seven hundred and fifty thousand Chinese and Malays were living contentedly in secure, well-found settlements.

The second plank of the plan was a coordinated military set-up, based on a network of company-sized garrisons in the villages and fortified police stations. From these garrisons and police stations the security forces would sweep out and gradually eliminate the CTs in the immediate area and sweep the country clean.

The Briggs Plan was always envisaged as a long-term solution, and there were complaints when the initial results were less than impressive. Soon after it was implemented the number of terrorist incidents actually rose; the CT gangs seemed able to slip away easily from military sweeps and several Army patrols and security force bases were ambushed or attacked.

The Briggs Plan therefore came under attack, not least from the planters and settlers who preferred immediate protection for their homes and businesses rather than any vague, theoretical solution. Given the situation their attitude was not unreasonable. In the first two years of the Malayan Emergency nearly nine hundred civilians, over three hundred policemen and one hundred and fifty soldiers had been killed by the CTs. The CTs had lost twice that number, over two thousand killed, wounded or captured, but their losses were made up by recruitment from the Min Yeun.

During the Emergency the British made every effort to take CTs alive, not least because if well treated they were a useful source of information. Captured CTs could often be 'turned' and persuaded to lead Army patrols to the camps of their former comrades. The CTs were far less benign; in the twelve years of the Emergency, no British soldier or civilian captured by the CTs was returned alive.

The CTs took no prisoners, killed the wounded, tortured, burned and bayoneted those they found alive in their ambushes, cut up pregnant women and murdered small children to terrorise their parents and relatives. They massacred the garrisons of police stations and the anti-Communist inhabitants of small villages. They bombed houses, burned rubber trees, blew up tin mines, threw grenades into cafés, shot up trains and ambushed roads. The Malayan Emergency was a vicious little war which went on in all parts of the peninsula and lasted for years.

Before long the Briggs strategy began to take effect but there were still problems. The police force had expanded rapidly from about ten thousand to over sixty thousand in less than two years; Colonel Grey had difficulty in finding good officers to command the force, and as more pressure came upon it so both morale and efficiency began to decline. The outbreak of the Korean War in June 1950 meant that no further troops could be sent to Malaya just as the jungle war was reaching a climax.

Meanwhile the number of CTs in the jungle actually increased, rising from about three thousand in 1948 to over seven thousand two years later. The worst blow came on 7 October 1951, when the CTs ambushed and killed the High Commissioner, Sir Henry Gurney.

Sir Henry had forgotten the fundamental need to vary his routine and had taken to spending most weekends at Fraser Hill, a resort in the Cameron Highlands some fifty miles north of Kuala Lumpur. He went there quite openly, his Rolls Royce flying the Union Flag pennant on the bonnet and accompanied by a small escort. Eventually the CTs struck.

A force of thirty-five well-armed bandits came out of the jungle one Friday to ambush the Fraser Hill road. The Governor's car was stopped on a bend by a felled tree and met by a storm of automatic fire as it came around the corner and his escort, a truckload of armed police, were shot down or dispersed into the jungle fringe. When the bandits began to hose the wrecked Rolls with machinegun fire, Sir Henry calmly got out and walked away from the car, deliberately drawing the fire away from his wife.

Gurney was shot down and killed before going more than a few paces. With his death a great gloom and sadness descended on the country, together with a growing desire to get to grips with the Communists and put a stop to their activities once and for all. This would call for tough measures. A new Governor would be needed, and the man selected was not a diplomat but a famous fighting soldier, Lt.-General Sir Gerald Templer . . . The Tiger of Malaya.

Templer's arrival marked a watershed in the Malayan Emergency but there was still a long way to go before the Communnist threat was eliminated. Nor was Malaya the only problem facing the British Government at this time. The Egyptians were becoming restive over the Canal Zone and a full scale tribal insurrection had broken out in Africa, in the Crown Colony of Kenya – Mau-Mau.

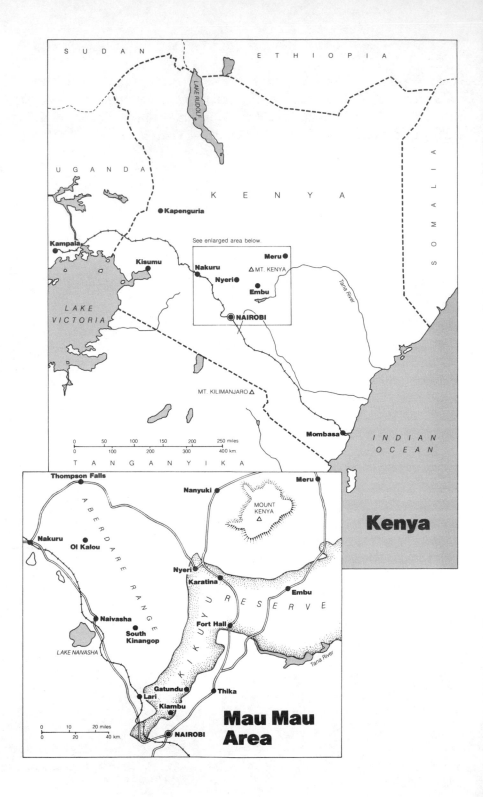

Kenya

Mau Mau Area

7

Mau-Mau: 1952–1956

'Many have suffered from the attempts of Mau-Mau to gain their aims by widespread violence and intimidation; most of the sufferers are peaceful, law-abiding Africans. This action – the State of Emergency – has been taken to stop the spread of violence, not against men who hold particular political views.'

Sir Evelyn Baring, Governor of Kenya, Declaration of a
State of Emergency, October 1952.

The problem in Kenya was, if anything, more complicated than the one in Malaya, for in Kenya there was no nationwide demand for independence. The small but all-powerful group of white settlers were determined to forestall it, the large Asian community viewed the prospect with unease, the majority of the Africans had yet to consider the matter.

The British had acquired Kenya almost by accident. In the last decade of the nineteenth century, after ending Dervish rule in the Sudan at the battle of Omdurman in 1898, the British became interested in establishing a line of colonies and protectorates north to south through Africa, from Cairo to the Cape.

By the early 1900s the British colonies stretched from Egypt, which was run, if not ruled, by the British Resident, Lord Cromer, down the Nile through the new condominium territory of the Anglo-Egyptian

Sudan and on to Uganda. It was the construction of a railroad to Uganda from the East African coast at Mombasa, that first brought the British to the rolling upland plains and jungle-clad mountains of Kenya, not a desire to take on another vast area of the Dark Continent. The country that became Kenya was then a fief of a trading corporation, the British East African Company.

The British Government only took on Kenya to protect the railway and warn off the active German settlers in Tanganyika. The railway brought with it thousands of Indian labourers who were eventually to settle in considerable numbers in all the colonies of East Africa and add another element to a simmering racial mix. This British advance brought benefits to the local people, stamping out the slave trade, a major industry for the Arabs of the coast, and protecting the agricultural tribes against raids from the warlike Masai.

Following the completion of the railroad and the acquisition of the Tanganyika territory from Germany after the Great War, thousands of British settlers arrived in East Africa. Their aim was to farm, especially in the rich lands north of Nairobi, in what became known as the White Highlands, much of which lay in the territory of the Kikuyu tribe between the Rift Valley and Mount Kenya.

Unlike the British in India and Malaya, the people who came to Kenya were not transients, who intended to return to home after their working lives were over. They came to stay, and having made a productive country out of what they saw as a tribal wilderness, regarded Kenya as their home, a country they had created.

Increased farming activity between the wars, and the introduction of cattle ranches and coffee plantations, led to an increased demand for land. This land was taken from the resident Africans and brought the settlers into conflict with the pastoral tribes. By the 1950s there were about thirty thousand British or South African settlers in Kenya, plus about eighty thousand Indians and some five hundred thousand Africans, mustered in numerous tribes.

Tribalism is the curse of Africa and Kenya – or the territory which became Kenya – was, and still is, occupied by a number of African tribes. The main groups in Kenya are the pastoral, cattle-rearing tribes, the Masai and their northern relatives, the Samburu, and the agricultural tribes, the Luo, Embu, Meru, Kamba and Kipsigis and, the largest tribe of all, the Kikuyu. The Masai and the Samburu wanted as little contact as possible with the Europeans, and the Masai in particular have managed to maintain much of their traditional cattle-based lifestyle, driving their herds across the savanna, disregarding frontiers and most of the trappings of Western civilisation.

This disdainful attitude to Western ways met with the approval of the European settlers while the unwarlike Kikuyu were regarded with distaste and suspicion. This did not prevent the settlers hiring the Kikuyu as servants or employing them in large numbers on their farms. The Kikuyu were more intelligent and sophisticated than the other tribes and, as a result, more resentful of the white occupation of the finest farming land in Kenya, territory which they had long regarded as their own.

This resentment over land seizure was compounded in the early years of the twentieth century by further discontent among the Kikuyu at attempts to interfere with their culture and religion. Behind the settler came the missionary, and the missionaries not only attempted to educate and convert the tribes, they also took steps to eradicate certain native customs which they found repugnant, most especially female circumcision. More than the other tribes, the Kikuyu felt that their customs, traditions, the very soul of their tribe was at risk from these white intruders, who hid behind a cloak of moral superiority while plotting to seize more Kikuyu land.

Another, less sophisticated people might have taken up the spear and war club and engaged the invaders in a bloody insurrection but in the 1920s the Kikuyu took the political path by forming the Kikuyu Association, though one of the declared aims of the Association was 'to stimulate enmity between black and white'.

The Kenya Association achieved little success in this ambition. Most of the Kikuyu and the other tribespeople wanted no more than peaceful change and natural justice, and in these aims they enjoyed some support from the British Government, which declared in 1923 that 'The interests of the African native must be paramount and when those interests and those of the immigrant races, Asiatic and European should conflict, the interests of the former should prevail.'

Whether the ruling white settlers and the Asian traders followed this hopeful injunction is doubtful. The settlers had no intention of relaxing their grip on the country and were frequently at odds with the Governor and the District Officers (DOs) of the Colonial Office, who were in charge of African affairs and often regarded by the settlers as too much in favour of the natives.

In 1927 the Hilton Young Commission was sent out to examine affairs in the colony. The Commission came out against the white settlers achieving their aim of self-government, on the grounds that their small numbers did not give them a mandate for power over the resident Asian and African people.

The white settlers deeply resented this rebuttal. They felt that they had civilised the country, built up its economy and created a nation in the wilderness, and that these undoubted achievements entitled them to rule in Kenya, if not for ever, then at least for the foreseeable future.

This view was shared much later by some members of the Colonial Service, as David Evans recalls. Like a number of new recruits to the Colonial Service, David Evans first went to Kenya as a National Serviceman, seconded from his own regiment, the Royal Welch Fusiliers to the King's African Rifles during the Mau-Mau Emergency.

After my National Service I took the Devonshire Course, a one year course of training for the Colonial Service. Much of the training was very practical, and at the end of it I was posted to the Kapenguria district in the northern part of the Rift Valley province. The senior District Commissioner asked me when I thought independence would come to Kenya.

I replied. 'Within about five years.' At this he became scornful and almost angry. 'Impossible!' he said. 'My son,' (the boy was then about four years old) 'will be a District Commissioner in Kenya. If you, David, wish to continue in the Colonial Administration, you should change your trendy-lefty ideas.' This was in 1959, after Mau-Mau, but I doubt if he realised that the Colonial Service had already been renamed the Overseas Civil Service.

The Hilton Young Commission had posed other questions: how long could the franchise be denied to the intelligent, educated Indians who handled a great deal of the colony's trade, and what should happen when the African majority expressed a wish for independence, the declared goal of Britain's Empire and Colonial policy? These questions were asked but not answered and the Kenya Colony prospered peacefully for several decades under Britain's colonial rule.

During the 1930s the Kikuyu Association splintered into two separate associations, the Kikuyu Provincial Association, which aimed to obtain self-government within the Kikuyu Reserve and follow a democratic, peaceful route to independence, and the more militant Kikuyu Central Association (KCA) which had as its gathering cry, 'Get Back Our Land'.

The General Secretary of the KCA was a Kikuyu, Jomo Kenyetta, who usually lived in Britain – where he had a white wife – and spent his time fostering left-wing contacts in London and pressing the Kikuyu claims on anyone in Britain who would listen. Kenyetta spent fifteen years in England, from 1931 to 1946. During that time he joined the Communist Party and was twice invited to visit the Soviet Union.

Kenyetta returned to Kenya in 1946 and found the climate right for a further advance towards African independence. During the war, large numbers of native Kenyan soldiers had seen service abroad with the King's African Rifles. When they returned home they were no longer content with their former lowly status under white colonial domination. They had seen the world and widened their horizons. They were well aware that the British grip on the Empire was by no means as firm as they had formerly supposed. Given a little push, the white settlers of Kenya might be prepared to leave or at least share power with the African majority. The settlers, whose numbers had increased after the Second World War, did not see it like that at all.

The return of Jomo Kenyetta breathed fresh life into the KCA but political activity and agitation was only one plank in the independence platform. Behind that facade of unrest and political action a more sinister activity was afoot, the formation of a clandestine terrorist organisation – Mau-Mau.

The origins of the name Mau-Mau remain obscure. According to Sir William Jackson, a literal translation of these Kikuyu words simply means 'greedy eating', but the name caught on, not least among the white settlers who heard it, and may have referred indirectly to the more disgusting elements in the powerful Mau-Mau oaths, the binding element of the movement.

Oath-taking is a normal part of Kikuyu tribal life. Even in a simple dispute over a field or a cow, the parties to the dispute will bind themselves by oaths. The influence of witch-doctors and the power of oaths is undisputed by the tribespeople and accepted as a normal part of life. To a Kikuyu, breaking an oath is a terrible thing.

Mau-Mau was built on this belief. The Mau-Mau recruit was bound to the organisation by a series of oaths which not only ensured his obedience to the organisation but also, by their obscenity, separated the Mau-Mau activist from the normal restraints of tribal behaviour. A Kikuyu who progressed to the rank of Mau-Mau fighter took a series of ever more vile yet powerful oaths and so became a virtual outcast from the body of the tribe, with nothing to hope for but the success of Mau-Mau. These oaths and the rituals which went with them had a dire effect on those who took part. Some of the oathing ceremonies went as follows:

> The fifth ceremony of the first oath: The recruit is put into a circle and made to take off all his clothes. A ram is killed and its whole breast is cut off, including the penis. The recruit is made to squat on the ground within the circle. The meat is placed on his penis and chest. It is held in position and one end of the meat is eaten by the man. A menstruating woman stands on one side and the meat and penis of the ram are then placed in her vagina. The combination of meat and penis is then returned to the man who is made to eat parts of it, including portions of the penis and testicles.
>
> The fourth oath: A ram is killed and the penis is cut off. A ewe is killed and the vagina is cut off. The penis is then inserted in the vagina. The penis and vagina are then inserted into the vagina of menstruating Kikuyu prostitute. This combination is removed from the vagina of the prostitute and is licked seven times by the man receiving the oath. Then every man who has taken the fourth oath that night lies with the prostitute.

The effects of such oathing ceremonies can be imagined. Many oaths were even worse, involving parts cut or gouged from the bodies of Mau-Mau victims.

Oaths alone would not have made Mau-Mau effective. The real danger arose because the intelligent Kikuyu people had no difficulty setting up a clandestine organisation, founded on the cell-like basis suggested by Kenyetta's Communist contracts. Mau-Mau cells were set up in Nairobi where tens of thousands of Kikuyu worked, and in the Kikuyu Reserve, a vest tract of territory running north-east from Nairobi, skirting the southern tip of the Aberdare Mountains and terminating on the slopes of Mount Kenya and by the western edges of the Embu and Meru reserves.

Almost all the Mau-Mau activity between 1952 and 1954 took place in this area. The rest of Kenya was undisturbed and it should not be assumed that the majority of the Kikuyu supported Mau-Mau: far from it. The bulk of the tribe favoured a peaceful democratic route to majority rule and during the Mau-Mau uprising most of the victims were Kikuyu, loyal to the Government and the decent principles of their tribe.

The Mau-Mau military organisation followed the path of that established by the CTs in Malaya, in that there was a military wing and a much larger passive wing in the villages and townships on which the Mau-Mau gangs relied for supply and intelligence.

The build-up of Mau-Mau was well in hand when Kenyetta set up his own political party, the Kenya African Union, for Kenyetta intended to support the armed struggle with overt political activity. His KAU party had three aims, firstly, to disguise the activities of Mau-Mau until they were considered strong enough to take the field; secondly to press the British colonial administration for constitutional change and political power; finally to provide the native African with an alternative source of power to that provided by the colonial administration.

Kenyetta handled this phase of his political life with considerable skill. He certainty hoodwinked the Governor of Kenya. Sir Philip Mitchell, and his use of moderate diplomatic language engaged the support of the flourishing anti-colonial elements in Britain and the United States. His speeches also went down well with those in the settler community who knew that in the long-term at least, African independence was inevitable.

Kenyetta also managed to conceal his involvement with Mau-Mau. The existence of this organisation had been detected by the government in 1947 soon after it had been established, and Mau-Mau was declared an illegal organisation in August 1950. Looking back on the whole independence decade in Kenya, it is hard to understand why an intelligent, politically astute man like Jomo Kenyetta did not put his whole weight behind the political process and seek independence by constitutional means. The decision to expel the whites by terrorist means led to years of bloodshed and a great loss of African lives and proved totally ineffective, while the political route paid almost instant dividends.

The Mau–Mau 'revolt' broke out in May 1952, with attacks on white farms and the murder of loyal Kikuyu. Between May and October fifty–nine Africans had been murdered and mutilated, including a loyal Kikuyu headman. Chief Waruhiu. It was the murder of Chief Waruhiu that spurred Sir Evelyn Baring to declare a State of Emergency on 21 October. A week later, on 28 October, the first white settler was murdered, Mr E.T. Bowyer of South Kinangop. Mr Bowyer was in his bath when his servant admitted a Mau–Mau gang to the house. The gang hacked Mr Bowyer to pieces.

Ben Moger was in Kenya throughout the Emergency and saw some of the worst Mau–Mau incidents at first hand.

The Governor at the time I arrived was Sir Philip Mitchell, who had been in Kenya since the war. He said he would never marry a woman who couldn't beat him at golf and a South African lady did finally beat him, so he had to marry her. Kenya was very formal in those days. On arrival you had to sign the Embassy book and you would eventually be invited to lunch; the day I went we got one lamb cutlet apiece, so the hospitality was not lavish.

The next Governor was Sir Evelyn Baring, son of Lord Cromer, the chap who ran Egypt in the 1880s. I met him socially several times and liked him, but he was terribly unpopular with the settlers. They saw him as a representative of the British Government and thought he would sell them down the river to the Africans.

The settlers were a mixed bunch. They used to say that Kenya was 'A Sunny place for Shady people', talking about the 'Happy Valley' set and Lord Errol and all that business. I suppose there were a lot of ne'er-do-wells, and a few remittance men, and people drank too much but a lot of them had fought in the war and only wanted to farm their land and have a quiet life . . . to most of the settlers Mau-Mau came as a terrible shock.

We trusted the Africans and liked them too, mostly, and we thought they liked and trusted us. That was the worst of it really, the betrayal of trust, the servants setting on their employers or opening up the house to let a gang rush in when they were at dinner or asleep ... I saw the results of the Ruck murder ... which was absolutely terrible. This happened in January 1953, three months after the State of Emergency was declared, but it will show you what we were up against.

The Rucks lived at Kinankop in the foothills of the Aberdares, where they had a farm. Roger Ruck was very keen on horses and one night in 1953, when Mau-Mau had been going on for quite a few months, they had locked themselves into the house for the night when the syce – the groom – knocked on the door and said, 'Bwana, come quick, your horse is sick.'

Roger's wife was seven or eight months pregnant and she told him not to go out but Roger, the bloody fool, got his revolver or a shotgun, locked his wife in and went out towards the stables. He hadn't gone a few yards before he was rushed from behind and pinioned. Then they dragged him out on to the lawn and started slashing at him with pangas.

His wife must have seen this from the window. She was a brave girl for she got a .410 shotgun and went out to help him – the syce cut her down and hacked her open and they took out the baby (sorry about this) and killed it. Well ... then they went into the house, where the Ruck's other child, a boy of five or six was asleep in bed upstairs. I can't understand it but the syce – who had played with this child since he was born – took the gang upstairs to the child's bedroom, and they cut off the little boy's head.

I went up there next day and it was absolutely terrible – there was blood all over the place. What happened there came out at the trial of the syce. The wife used to run a clinic for the local Africans and they were in a terrible state about it as well ... the Mau-Mau blood oath killed her, for Africans are kindly people who love children.

These atrocities, terrible as they were, were still on a small-scale and the greatest number of attacks were made, not against the settlers, but against those Kikuyu who were not supporters of Mau-Mau. Even so, the settlers were becoming thoroughly alarmed and thoroughly impatient with the colonial administration which seemed to be in no hurry to grasp the problem.

Geraldine Hagan, whose husband was in Government service, lived in Kenya through the years of Mau-Mau:

My first impression on landing in Mombasa was being surrounded by black faces and thinking that I would never be able to tell one from the other. Around Nairobi the country was different; the 'Highlands' was the European farming land, large green pastures, well-tended and organised like the farms in Britain. We were between five and seven thousand feet above sea level, and the altitude certainly affected the Europeans physically and mentally. Women did not have the energy to scrub and wash clothes as they had in England, and all Europeans had servants working in the house and garden.

The African has a great sense of humour, and in their way were nature's gentlefolk. I was always greeted courteously and I found them likeable people, but the attitude of the Africans towards the Europeans in general was mixed, laughing at them and making rather crude jokes. They always said the Europeans had a bad smell and that they were not white but red men! To know and understand the Africans better, it was essential to learn and speak Swahili, but very few Europeans bothered to learn much of it.

Many missionaries spoke a tribal language and ran hospitals and schools, teaching useful skills like carpentry, but many Africans were amused by the behaviour of the Europeans and found their ways strange, particularly the European justice system. They could not understand that a man had to be proved guilty before being convicted. They would say, 'Well, we all know he must have stolen, he's always been a bad lot.' They didn't think going to jail was a punishment, and called it 'King George's Hotel'.

The idea of the Mau-Mau was to get the Europeans off the land and it was quite frightening to be left in a bungalow, with two small boys, in a very isolated area. My husband had been recruited for the KPR, the Kenya Police Reserve, so I was often alone at night for weeks on end, with the thought that a gang of up to thirty drugged Africans could smash the door down and cut us to pieces . . . it was very worrying.

When Sir Philip Mitchell left office in June 1952, a month after the first killings, he warned the British Government that more trouble was brewing, but his replacement, Sir Evelyn Baring, did not arrive for another three months. This vacuum at the top gave Mau–Mau a chance to expand.

When Sir Evelyn finally arrived, in September 1952, he found a full-scale terrorist campaign raging around the Kikuyu reserve and in the Aberdare Mountains, where some sixty Kikuyu, men, women and children, had been murdered or mutilated – or murdered *and* mutilated – by Mau-Mau in the first weeks of the rising.

Baring took a firm grip on the situation and applied at once to the Colonial Office for more British troops. The only military resources available within the colony were two battalions of the King's African Rifles, the 23rd and 26th, native troops recruited from the martial tribes and commanded by British officers, and the local Territorial Unit, the Kenya Regiment, raised from the white settlers.

The KAR battalions had already been deployed and since there were very few Kikuyu in the regiment, the loyalty of the 'askaris', the private soldiers, was not in doubt. The Kenya Regiment was a settler force, organised as an officer training unit. As more of the British military arrived, soldiers of the Kenya Regiment, most of whom spoke Swahili or other tribal languages, were attached to the British units as guides, interpreters and intelligence officers. A further supply of European officers came from the Kenya Police Reserve and a great many Africans and Kikuyu joined auxilary units, to guard their own villages and herds.

Sir Evelyn requested the immediate assistance of British troops and the first reinforcements, the 1st Bn., The Lancashire Fusiliers, were sent from the Canal Zone on 20/21 October 1952.

On 21 October, Baring declared a State of Emergency and ordered the arrest of those African leaders known or suspected of involvement in Mau-Mau. More than one hundred and eighty Mau-Mau activists were arrested, including Jomo Kenyetta, but this action came too late to stop the spread of trouble. On the same day the Lancashire Fusiliers arrived. One of the Fusilier NCOs was Sergeant Harry Whitehead, of the Mortar Platoon:

We flew down from Egypt in four-engined Hastings and went from Nairobi to Fort Hall, where we arrived looking like Red Indians as we were coated with road dust. Fort Hall lies in a hilly area and the town had broad walks and lean-to's which, with the pistols and rifles carried by the settlers in their wide-brimmed hats, made it seem like the Wild West.

We were quickly out on patrol and it was not long before we saw signs of Mau-Mau handiwork. We were sent out to find a missing

Kikuyu chief who had vanished together with his two askari guards. On the way back, having found nothing, we were stopped by an excited African who pointed out a small shop, or 'duka', indicating we should look inside.

Fearing an ambush we went in with weapons cocked. It was a small groom, roughly ten feet square. It was a shop and a bar and the chief and the two askari must have stopped for a drink and been surprised in there. The walls had been whitewashed but congealed blood lay everywhere, on the floor, splashed on the walls . . . it was like an abattoir and stank to high heaven. We found the bodies, bloated and mutilated, in a nearby ditch.

As we were taking this in, the natives pointed out a group running out of the village and told us 'Mau-Mau'. Pointing at this group and down at the bodies. We were too far away to catch these people but we yelled 'Halt!' and then opened fire. Two of the group fell but were helped up and fled into the trees.

The outbreak of Mau-Mau proved a gift to anti-British and anti-colonial forces all over the world, who saw the British reaction to the outbreak as another manifestation of British Imperialism. Mau-Mau activists became adept at exploiting this anti-British feeling and were aided in their actions by left-wing politicians like the Labour MP Fenner Brockway, who was invited to Kenya by the KAU, arrived on 28 October, a week after the declaration of the State of Emergency, stayed ten days and returned to Britain, where he wrote pamphlets and made speeches decrying the colonial presence and the actions of the administration, demanding an immediate end to colonial rule.

Word of the Mau-Mau atrocities at the Ruck's farm or against the Kikuvu loyalists did not stem this flood of discouraging propaganda. There was great concern in left-wing circles that the British troops or the white settlers were taking a strong or even brutal line with the Africans. Accusations of brutality were very common, though they rarely withstood close inspection. Such accusations were frequently made against those who were most active, or most successful, in stemming Mau-Mau activity. That said, there was a reluctance to take prisoners in the early days, especially after the massacres and murder, the local Africans taking a particularly hard line against any Mau-Mau who surrendered or was wounded. Any Mau-Mau caught in the act by their African neighbours were certainly given short shrift, and the gangs that were surrounded and caught were often wiped out to the last man. The Mau-Mau Emergency was a very vicious war, with little quarter given on either side.

During the Mau-Mau time a great deal of pressure and danger fell on the women, planters' wives who were often left to run their farms and look after their families while their menfolk were off chasing Mau-Mau gangs. Many women did much more than this and took their part in defending their homes and isolated farms against Mau-Mau attack.

After her husband has been slashed to death during a gang attack on their farm at Thomson's Falls, Dr Dorothy Meiklejohn, though herself gravely wounded and bleeding from a dozen panga slashes, drove herself seven miles to the nearest police post to raise the alarm. After prolonged surgical treatment in London, she eventually returned to her farm at Thomson's Falls, because, she said, 'Kenya is my home.'

Mrs Grimwood stood beside her husband with a rifle and fought off a sixty strong gang which attacked their farm at Kingangop. Mrs Ghislade Lusso did the same when her home was attacked, taking her small son up in her arms before running to fight beside her husband.

The terrible and tragic history of Mau-Mau is illuminated by tales like these. Mrs Phillipa Jolly picked up the pistol from beside her plate and shot down a panga-swinging terrorist who broke into her dining room during dinner. Miss Barbara Barclay was in bed when a gang burst into her house near Menengai. Taking her pistol from under the pillow, Miss Barclay left her room and ran at them driving the gang out of the house and back into the forest. She too, refused to leave her home and stayed on after the attack.

One gallant lady who beat off two Mau-Mau attacks on her farm near Nanyuki was Miss Joan Scott.

The farm was at Kangaita, about 150 miles from Nairobi and had belonged to the Rucks – the family murdered by Mau-Mau at Kingacop; Roger Ruck was a splendid chap, and his wife was a doctor, who did a lot of good work for the Africans.

Anyway, Roger sold the farm at Kangaita to an older couple and I ran it for them. When the trouble started I told my labour that if they stood by me, I would stand by them, whatever happened and they were all right. Most of them were in Mau-Mau but had only taken the first oath and only that because they had to. We still took full precautions, and locked ourselves in the house at dusk and did not let any of the staff in; that is how most of the people who were killed got chopped, when their staff let a Mau-Mau gang into the house through the kitchens.

We were attacked twice in April 1953, the first time by a gang dressed in police uniforms, who ransacked the house when we were out and made off with everything; all I had left to wear was a pair of khaki shorts and a ballgown; not very practical for running a farm near Mount Kenya. They tied up the staff but did not set the house alight or kill anyone and they fled into the forest when we came haring up the hill in my old van.

Our boys were wonderful and stood by us as they had promised. Every man, woman and child on the farm turned out to chase the gang away, armed with sticks and knives or whatever implement they were using at the time. The sight of this mob coming scared the gang off which was probably a good thing; there were about forty of them and my pistol might not have been much use. Troops arrived later and took up the chase but a heavy rainstorm soon obliterated the gang's tracks

The second attack came in the middle of the night when Mrs Oulton and I were alone in the house as Mr Oulton had gone to Nairobi. We were woken about 3am by shooting and yelling and bugle calls from the labour lines and the banging on petrol drums. For some extraordinary reason the gang had not cut the farm telephone and while we were sitting up in bed wondering what to do, it started to ring and a very hysterical African said that the camp was full of Mau-Mau and they were shooting everybody.

We called out to the house staff and let them in from their quarters, telling them that we were going to go down to the camp and see what was happening. Apart from our pistols we had a Mauser rifle that belonged to Mr Oulton, a brute of a gun. I can see Mrs Oulton now, dithering about the rifle, saying to me 'Do you want it or shall I take it?'

Before leaving the house we discovered that the line to the police station at Nanyuki had been cut so we let off the emergency rockets which we hoped would attract the patrols from the KAR camp nearby. Then we undid the bolts to the front door.

As far as we were concerned the most frightening moment was leaving the house because we did not know if the gang were waiting in the dark outside. It was a nasty moment opening that door; I can remember the feeling now. A frightful row was going on, everyone beating on tins, a lot of shouting, shots and bugle calls.

We got into the Chev truck, piled the boys in behind and went on the outer, KAR road, so that we could call on a neighbour, Peter Clarke and enlist his support. Though we did not know it at the time, the Mau-Mau were just ahead of us, running across the back of the camp. When we got to the camp, lights on horn blaring, we found the gang had gone, but they had taken two of our boys with them. One escaped and came back, the other stayed and became a Mau-Mau 'brigadier'. The one who deserves real credit is Mukira, our nightwatchman who had been caught in the hut by the gang and refused to come out for oathing. When he refused a number of shots were fired into his hut but fortunately, they missed him . . . and that's about it really.

Fusilier Sergeant Harry Whitehead soon saw another Mau-Mau atrocity:

This was in early January 1953, three months after we got there, just before the Ruck family were murdered. Support Company was at 'Ol Kalou' when we got a call for assistance from a settler who was worried about two of his neighbours, a Mr Ferguson and a Mr Bingley. This gentleman had heard Ferguson's dog barking and howling as if hurt, so he had gone out – a brave thing to do, since the Ferguson home was just inside the Aberdare forest but he wanted to see what was going on. He found the Ferguson house dark and apparently deserted, but the dog was still howling. He went back home and sent for us.

We sent up two sections in two 15-cwt trucks. At the house all was dark and silent now. Sergeant Connelly and I each tried the door and finding it locked, knocked and shouted a number of times. Eventually Sergeant Connelly kicked the door open, and with weapons at the ready we entered.

The air inside stank with the smell of blood and death. It was a sight that will stay with me for the rest of my life. In the living room we found the bodies of Mr Ferguson and Mr Bingley and they had not just been killed, they had been butchered . . . in both senses of the word.

Later we found out what had happened. The gentlemen had gone into the room for dinner and had seated themselves at the table when the cook had unlocked the outer door and let in Mau-Mau. He had then gone into the dining room carrying a tureen of hot soup which he then threw over the two gentlemen . . . as the two leapt to their feet, shocked, forgetting their weapons, the gang rushed through the door with their pangas and slashed them to pieces. They had no chance to defend themselves.

On the following days we were kept busy hunting for the gang and clearing all the Africans away from the forest edge, forcibly if need be, to create a totally empty zone for our patrols. In these areas we could shoot on sight.

These sudden and terrible Mau-Mau attacks did not always succeed. On the night after Ferguson and Bingley were killed, a gang attacked a farmhouse occupied by Mrs Hessleburger and Mrs Simpson, only to be driven off by their rifle and pistol fire. For their gallantry on this occasion both ladies were later awarded the MBE.

While the military attempted to contain the violence, the British Government found itself caught between those who said Britain should give way to this 'liberation struggle' and grant immediate independence to the Africans, and those white settlers who felt that Sir Evelyn Baring and his administration were already far too soft with the Africans and their independence demands.

The settlers were a vocal and powerful minority and in January 1953, following the Bingley, Ruck and Ferguson murders and a further series of attacks and atrocities against the Africans, a large crowd of settlers staged a march on Government House and were only dispersed with some difficulty after appeals from two settler representatives, Michael Blundell and Humphrey Slade. The Mau-Mau rebellion actually ensured that British rule would continue, for there could be no question of leaving the country and handing the people over to the tender mercies of Mau-Mau.

The British do learn from their mistakes and took a lesson from current events in Malaya, where the Briggs Plan was taking effect. General Sir John Harding, who had taken over from Field Marshal

Slim as Chief of the Imperial General Staff (CIGS), arrived in Kenya in February 1953, detected familiar signs of confusion and recommended the appointment at once of a Director of Operations, responsible to the Governor. This appointment was approved by the British Government and General Sir George Erskine arrived in Nairobi in June 1953 as C-in-C and Director of Operations, with Brigadier R.W. (Loony) Hinde, as his deputy.

General Erskine and Brigadier Hinde drew up a list of operational priorities for the long and short term. Their first priority was to break the power of the gangs in the Reserves and the Aberdares and ease the pressure on – and from – the vociferous white settlers. The next major task, which would take careful planning and much secrecy, was 'Operation Anvil', a cordon-and-search of the city of Nairobi, to flush out and capture those many terrorists and their supporters who were known to be sheltering in the city and supplying the gangs. This would necessarily involve a large number of troops and was not immediately possible. Finally, they wanted more engineers, to drive tracks up into the forests of the Aberdares and Mount Kenya, and so deny Mau-Mau any place of refuge.

The first requirement, however, was for more troops, and more battalions duly arrived, including the 1st Bn., The Devonshire Regiment, the 1st Bn., The Buffs and the 1st Bn., The Black Watch. John Rankin came out to the Black Watch in 1954 as a National Service 2nd Lieutenant:

On arrival I was sent up to Battalion HQ at Nanyuki, and was sent from there to join C Company at Thompson Falls. The Pipes and Drums were beating retreat there on the evening I arrived and that gave me a chance to meet some of the settlers. On the whole they were kind and hospitable to the Forces, but some of the farmers were resentful that we were not successful in preventing stock thefts by the gangs, who drove the cattle into the forest for food. This would have been a difficult, task, partly because of the huge areas involved, partly because the gangs received considerable help from the Kikuyu farm labourers, who turned the stock loose and warned the gangs of any military presence.

We maintained a pretty full programme of patrols and ambushes, albeit with scant reward. We inflicted few casualties but at least we managed to keep the gangs on the move and this made them easier to track. To assist us we had native trackers but few of them were any good. In the beginning there was the assumption that any African would be a natural tracker, even if he had spent his whole life in the back streets of Nairobi. Eventually a school for trackers was set up in Nanyuki where it was discovered that 90 per cent of them were quite useless and incapable of being trained.

Another problem was the frequent encounters with wild animals, principally rhino and elephant. Rhino tend to sleep during the day but when disturbed in the high grass would announce their presence with a series of terrifying snorts followed by a high speed charge at close quarters. The received doctrine for anticipating the arrival of a ton and a half of enraged rhino was to wait stoically until it was upon one, and step aside at the last second. The more natural reaction was to run and climb the nearest tree. Elephants were less dangerous and would rarely press home a charge; they were only interested in scaring us away from their herd. Fortunately, there were very few buffalo, the most dangerous animal of all.

Light aircraft were of tremendous service in Kenya, where the roads were unsurfaced and impassable in the rains. Rations and mail were dropped in and they were a useful means of communications. Our '88' wireless sets were relatively inefficient but the aircraft radio could be picked up at any distance, and used to relay messages.

The monotony of life was relieved when I was sent on the trackers' course at Nanyuki. The course lasted a week and was run by Don Bousefield, a Kenya Police Reserve officer who was a big game hunter in civilian life. We spent the days tracking animals, and each other, through the forest, and by the end of the week I suppose we were about as proficient as the average native tracker.

The course was interrupted when we came upon and followed the tracks of a Mau-Mau gang, by whom we were shortly ambushed. This was my first time under fire and my reactions were, firstly, considerable fright, and secondly, an irrational indignation that some idiots were using firearms in an extremely dangerous manner. However, we returned the fire and advanced into the ambush position from which the gang soon scattered.

Don Bousefield, a brilliant shot, had sprinted to the top of a large anthill, from which he was able to fire three shots from his .276 Mauser rifle, all fatal, at the retreating gang. The rest of us managed to account for one terrorist and wounded another, who crawled off into the undergrowth and was flushed out by a tracker dog: he died of his wound later. Our only casualty was a man who had the tip of his nose shot off. We captured an assortment of weapons, including a very handsome Holland & Holland double barrelled rifle.

While the British battalions were getting used to the country the number of KAR battalions had been increased to six, by withdrawing KAR battalions from Uganda and Tanganyika.

David Evans, who later became a District Officer, was a National Service subaltern in the 23rd (K) Bn. of the King's African Rifles:

By the time I arrived in Kenya, in mid-1954, the Emergency had been going on for about twenty months and the security forces were on the offensive. Most of the gangs had been driven into hiding places in the reserves but some gangs were operating in the Rift Valley province. The big gangs were in the forests of Mount Kenya and the Aberdares, where we had deployed three of our companies.

One of the first incidents I remember came not long after I joined C Company at Karatina, when we heard that the battalion NAAFI truck, a three-tonner, with three armed askari in the back and an African WOPC (Warrant Officer–Platoon Commander) in charge to guard the goodies, the unit beer and cigarettes, had been ambushed on Pole Pole Hill when coming up from Nairobi. 'Pole Pole' in Swahili means slowly slowly.

Our CO. Lt.-Colonel Joe Bartlett, reacted with unparalleled activity. Two heavily armed platoons, some sixty men, were assembled and about to depart for the scene of the ambush when the NAAFI truck came in through the camp gates. The WOPC was slumped in the front seat, an arm hanging limply out of the window, the three askaris were lying stiffly in the rear, and bullet holes were visible in the back of the truck. The driver brought the truck to a halt, almost in front of the CO and, on opening the door, promptly fell to the ground in a heap.

I heard the CO mutter. 'My God, they made it! What a damned good show! There'll be a gong for someone in this!'

As we all gathered round it became apparent that not only had no one been wounded, but all of them were blind drunk.

It transpired that they had been fired on, receiving a volley of shots in the rear. They returned fire, the driver urging the vehicle up Pole Pole hill and then they discovered that some of the shots had shattered bottles of booze in the back. Led by the WOPC, the askaris decided to sample the spilled liquor. Unfortunately they did not stop there and soon moved on to the undamaged supplies . . . which proved their undoing. This attack on the NAAFI truck was considered by the 23 KAR as the worst outrage in the Emergency.

Military action alone would not solve the problems in Kenya. Although the rising was centred on the Kikuyu and had no general support, Kenya could not be separated from the rest of the colonies and here as elsewhere sooner or later, independence was coming. The settlers were determined that the reins of power should be passed to them, as the creators of modern Kenya and the ones most capable of running a modern state. Their 'kith-and-kin' card was a strong one but the British Government did not share this opinion, and in February 1954, the Colonial Secretary, Oliver Lyttleton, arrived in Nairobi with the outline of a draft Constitution. When it was revealed the settlers did not like it.

Lyttleton's plan called for a local Administrative Council to run the colony, consisting of six locally elected Ministers, three European, two Asian and one Arab, plus five nominated Africans who would serve as Under-Secretaries in the new administration. This left the settlers without a clear majority. They now saw that whatever their wishes might be, the end of white rule in Kenya was bound to come and would probably be granted as soon as the current troubles were over. Settler resentment against this proposed Constitution was fuelled by the fact that the forces of law and order appeared to be winning the struggle against Mau-Mau.

One of the terrorist leaders, 'General' China, was captured in March 1954. To save his neck he offered to arrange the surrender of the many gangs formerly under his command. General China was unable to deliver on this promise but with the Mau-Mau in obvious disarray and Kenyetta in prison, the settlers saw no need to hand over political power to the Africans. What, after all, had they been fighting for?

More moderate minds accepted the inevitable and outside the Mau-Mau areas, political activity of a more normal kind began to occupy the minds of the population, but the fighting in the forests went on.

The area most concerned with Mau-Mau covered Mount Kenya and the Aberdares, some five thousand square miles of jungle and mountain, the peaks rising to more than three thousand metres, where the jungle and rain forest gave way to open moorland. The Kikuyu settlements, their small farms or 'shambas', lay around the lower slopes of the mountains, on the forest fringe, and were surrounded in their turn by the much larger white farms and coffee plantations.

The Mau-Mau gangs, their total strength amounting to some ten or twelve thousand men, soon withdrew into the jungle, from where they would emerge in gangs one hundred to three hundred strong, to raid the villages on the Kikuyu reserve and attack the white farms beyond. Mau-Mau were not well armed; most of them had only simis or pangas, sharp-edged weapons like cutlasses, or primitive homemade guns, more dangerous to the user than the target, though as time went by they acquired modern weapons from the farms and police stations they raided. Even so, the odds were weighted against the gangs and the odds increased as more British battalions arrived.

As soon as sufficient troops were available. General Erskine ordered the execution of Operation Anvil, the search of Nairobi. On the morning of 24 April 1954, the citizens of Nairobi woke up to find the city ringed by troops. Once the town was sealed, the police and the Special Branch began to sweep through the African settlements. The first phase of 'Anvil' took two full days, during which more than eleven thousand Africans were detained for questioning and about eight thousand taken into custody for further screening. More than sixteen thousand were put through the net in the end and some three thousand were ordered out of the city and sent back to the Reserve.

Lieutenant John Rankin of the Black Watch was involved in Operation Anvil:

The whole operation was supposed to be top secret, but I dare say the grapevine had been at work. 'Anvil' involved police and several battalions of troops. The object of the latter was to cordon off Nairobi while the police screened all members of the Kikuyu, Embu and Meru tribes for Mau-Mau. The first cut was into two groups; those suspected of Mau-Mau and the non-suspects. The latter were released, the former divided into three groups: 'whites', with little involvement, and these, too, were released: 'greys', more heavily involved but who could be rehabilitated; and 'blacks', the hard core, who were imprisoned and in some cases executed, if found guilty of murder.

The operation began at 4am and went on for days, a thankless and boring task as far as the troops were concerned. The Jocks did their work well and treated the locals with courtesy. I remember seeing one particularly filthy old Kikuyu woman who had tried to break through the cordon being led gently back by a Jock who saluted her and said. 'I'm afraid you cannot cross the road at this time, ma'am.'

This contrasted with the behaviour of a native policeman whom I observed throwing a stone at a tiny toddler who had wandered out of his parents' shack towards the cordon. I cannot remember being angrier at anything, before or since, and had the child been hit. I genuinely believe I would have shot the man.

During the day we were treated to a pretty hostile demonstration by a few hundred women singing Mau-Mau songs. These ladies were dispersed by the RSM and his pace stick. Sorting out the Mau-Mau was pretty arbitrary but their love of show was remarkable. Forest gangs often took photographs of themselves, which we eventually got hold of, and these proved of great use in picking out suspects. The pattern of the first day was repeated in the ensuing weeks with little variation in the monotony.

'Anvil' had two immediate benefits. Firstly, the incidents of violence and crime in the city fell remarkably, dropping by 90 per cent. Secondly, 'Anvil' cut the supply lines sending food, arms and money to the gangs in the reserves and the Aberdares. Hundreds of Mau-Mau supporters or activists were detained or imprisoned and a new passbook was issued to the city workers to prevent further infiltration by gang members tired of fighting in the forest.

The downside of the operation was that thousands of unemployed Kikuyu on the reserves were open for recruitment into Mau-Mau gangs, whose numbers already contained a large number of workers sacked from the settler farms as untrustworthy. These men provided the Mau-Mau leaders with much useful information about the farms for planning effective raids.

The six KAR battlions were busy hunting Mau–Mau around the Reserve and in the forest. David Evans of the 23 KAR again:

We were sleeping rough in the rain forest when I was ordered to take two sections of my Platoon up Tumu Tumu hill, which was near the Scottish Presbyterian Mission Hospital. It was pretty steep and we got to the top at dusk to find an abandoned Mau-Mau camp. We had only been up there a few minutes when all hell broke loose below at the hospital. A Mau-Mau gang had come out of the forest and were firing shots into the wards which contained a number of children and elderly Kikuvu from the surrounding district.

We rushed back down the hill and arrived at a vantage point from where I saw the last terrorist entering the fort of the Kikuyu Home Guard across the drawbridge. It was getting dark so I fired a 2-inch mortar parachute flare to light the place up, and we saw the Mau-Mau running off through the camp into a large banana plantation at the rear. We sprayed the area with Bren gun fire and put down a mortar 'stonk' with high explosives. Our I0, Alan Liddle, then led a sweep through the area next day and found various human remains, including limbs, so at least one of our bombs took effect.

On another occasion we were led on a patrol by a surrendered Mau-Mau in search of a series of hiding places said to have been used by a Mau-Mau leader, 'General Tanganyika'. We found several camps but no General, though we recovered a panga and a pair of shoes that had once belonged to Mr Leakey. Mr Leakey was a white Kenyan and anthropologist who had recently been captured by Mau-Mau near Nyeri. They sacrificed him to the Mau-Mau gods by burying him alive in an ant hill.

Some time later, A, C and D Companies were in position near Kianjogu in the Kikuyu Reserve where an anti-terrorist sweep was in progress. At 0745 hrs the ever-active Lieutenant Robin Arliss, with 8 Platoon, saw five terrorists and chased them towards the Sagana river where my 7 Platoon was waiting. The first Mau-Mau ran along the skyline, silhouetted against the sky, and we hit him with a burst of tracer. He went into 'dead ground', but left a blood trail.

Then the other four Mau-Mau appeared with Robin and his men in hot pursuit. Robin was chasing one particular terrorist who wore captain's pips on the shoulders of his leather jacket and who was shooting back at him with a Luger pistol which, we later discovered, had also belonged to the late Mr Leakey. Robin ran in towards this fellow and shot him in the head.

We were below and could not shoot up at the three last Mau-Mau because 8 Platoon were right behind them. One of the Mau-Mau rushed down the slope and tried to hide in the river but Private Mukuni went after him and flushed him out with a grenade. Both platoons then went back to the area where the Mau-Mau had first been seen, where we recovered two home-made rifles and a quantity of ammunition. I sat on a rock to take a breather and have a chat with Corporal Kimuilu before going off to speak to Robin. While I was talking to Robin we heard a shout and saw Corporal Kimuilu apparently having a tug of war with his rifle.

Kimuilu had been sitting on the rock when a hand had emerged from a hole and grabbed his rifle. Corporal Kimuilu got it back just as we arrived. We looked around, found the entrance to a very small cave under the rock, sprayed it with Bren fire and then tossed in a grenade – another dead terrorist. For some reason this little operation got a big write-up in the local paper, the *East African Standard*.

David Evans again: 'Mau–Mau relied on hit–and–run tactics, so our method was to patrol by day and ambush the forest edge by night when they came out to get food. There were many skirmishes in the forest and most of them resulted in one or two Mau–Mau killed and a few more wounded and the capture of food and ammunition. For every terrorist killed at least four more were wounded and many of these were to die in the forest later.'

A further two thousand, seven hundred Mau–Mau surrendered, a number of them as a result of the 'pseudo gangs', small groups of Africans and Europeans who disguised themselves as Mau–Mau and entered the jungle to track down, infiltrate and eliminate the terror gangs. These 'pseudo gangs' had been created and organised by an officer of the Rifle Brigade, Captain Frank Kitson, who had been seconded to Kenya for intelligence duties:

The usual method of getting a contact was by patrolling, ambushing or cordon and search. All these methods depended for their success on a large measure of luck and a great deal of persistence. My job was to tour my district – I had two districts, Kiambu and Thika –

find out all I could about terrorist activity and use this information to provide the police and the soldiers with contact tips.

In the course of this work I picked up a number of captured or surrendered Mau-Mau, and we kept them with us, often for days, for questioning. Some of them were more than willing to tell us all about their former comrades and that gave us the pseudo gangs idea. This meant dressing up Europeans as Mau-Mau and one of the best at disguise was my sergeant, Eric Holyoak, a Field Intelligence Assistant (FIA). I had about twenty FIAs in the end and they did most of the work.

Pseudo gangs went into the forest, met Mau-Mau, gained their confidence and led them into error or ambush. It was tricky work, but as we got more prisoners and turned them against their former comrades – and de-oathed them – so we could put more pseudo gangs in the field. By the end of my time – I left Kenya at the end of 1955 – we could put out a lot of gangs, and it worked. In Kiambu we piled up a series of successes in one six-week period: all except one of the main gangs in Kiambu were broken up, their leaders killed or captured.

The business of 'turning' a terrorist against his former comrades had three parts to it. He had to be given a strong incentive to change sides: that part was the carrot. Then he had to realise that failure would lead to something unpleasant happening to him; that was the stick. Some people might think that was enough, but I believe there had to be a third strand. He had to believe that what he was doing was the right thing to do and that there was nothing fundamentally dishonourable about his action.

Captain Kitson and his European settler aides went out on these pseudo gang operations, heavily disguised as Mau-Mau fighters, their skin darkened and their heads covered in Mau-Mau wigs; their courage in doing so is worthy of record, for had they been detected and captured their fate would have been grisly indeed.

Operations against Mau-Mau reached a pitch of intensity in 1954 and 1955, with aircraft and artillery joining in the efforts to flush the gangs out of the forest or make their life there unendurable. The first aircraft used were American Harvard trainers fitted with bomb racks for 20lb fragmentation bombs and these were later joined by RAF Lincoln bombers dropping 1,000-pounders. How effective this air interdiction was is debatable. As far as the troops on the ground were concerned, the main effect of the bombing was to injure or irritate the larger wildlife – buffalo, elephant and rhino.

Patrick Oxonby arrived in Kenya at the height of Mau-Mau:

89 Field Survey Squadron, Royal Engineers was based in Nairobi. Some of us had been posted to Kenya from the UK, others like myself went from Egypt.

We went to Kenya on a troopship, *Charlton Star*. There were eight of us on board, a number of WRACs, whom we never saw, probably being heavily guarded, and eight hundred men of the King's African Rifles. I shall never forget them all singing as we sailed up the channel to Mombasa. They were happy to be away from the Canal Zone and so were we.

The next day we travelled to Nairobi by train, a memorable journey and in those days the locomotives were in steam and very powerful. The power was needed to take the trains from sea level to Nairobi and elevations of more than two thousand metres.

The squadron was based at High Ridge Camp in the Parklands area, a suburb north-east of the city. The squadron's task was to cooperate with the Survey of Kenya in the revision of existing maps at 1:50,000 and on new mapping. There were only forty personnel and we led a life of luxury, having our beds made, rooms cleaned and all laundry done by African 'boys'. When we woke up we found our 'KD' immaculately starched, ironed and folded on our bedside tables and were handed a nice cup of tea. To get this excellent service we each gave the African in charge a little extra money.

One morning we found no pressed KDs, no cups of tea and not an African in sight. It transpired that they had been taken away early by the Kenya Police as Mau-Mau suspects. It turned out later that the man in charge of the room cleaning and laundry was a Mau-Mau treasurer. Our tips had, no doubt, gone to buy arms.

New staff were engaged and care was taken that they were not Kikuyu or Meru tribes, these being the Mau-Mau tribes, but we never again got the same quality of service.

Nairobi was a good town for a night out as long as you stayed in the well-peopled centre. There were three big hotels, the New Stanley – a little too expensive for us – the Torre and the Queen's.

All were Asian owned but neither Asians nor Africans were allowed into them unless they worked there.

Most of the settlers carried sidearms because many lived outside, Nairobi. We heard many stories of attacks at night on lonely houses. Every night in Nairobi itself small-arms fire could be heard, much of it as a result of criminal activities. I experienced one such attempted robbery in a milk bar when two Africans rushed in and tried to rob the till. The owner took out his Beretta pistol and shot at them. One was hit but it didn't stop him escaping; the Beretta is a small-bore weapon.

There were strict social divisions in the colony. At the top were the 'Europeans'. Next came the 'Asians', descendants of those who came from the Indian sub-continent in the early days. They were mostly Moslem but there were also large numbers of Sikhs and Hindus. The Asians controlled most of the commerce in the colony, from small shops, known as 'dukas', to big concerns. From the Asian ranks came the clerks, draftsmen, mechanics, and so on. There were also Asian doctors, dentists and lawyers, and many were in the police force which had been expanded dramatically to cope with the Mau-Mau uprising. In spite of this, Asians were barred from many hotels and clubs.

At the bottom were the Africans, who were used for the menial jobs. They were the waiters, dressed in long white shirts and wearing a red fez. In many of the smaller guest-houses the cooks were also African, mainly from the Luo tribe. They were also the rank and file of the police as well as, of course, being in the King's African Rifles.

Then there were the British forces. The attitude of the Kenya Europeans towards the troops was ambivalent. It did not do to go out in uniform, for we would be politely refused entry to a number of places. In fairness, it must be said that this attitude had been brought about by the behaviour of some of the troops who had come into Nairobi after weeks in the bush. One instance involved the smashing up of the Torre's quartet's musical instruments when they wouldn't play *The Bluebells o' Scotland*. I will not name the regiment involved but they had been called the 'Ladies from Hell' by the Germans in the Great War. In the end they were banned from Nairobi by the military command.

We soon had suitable 'civvies' made, and in January 1954 I became twenty-one years old, which meant I could bring my wife out. The quartermaster sergeant and I rented a bungalow twelve miles out of Nairobi on the road to Kiambu. It was a typical, colonial-style square bungalow, with a verandah all round. The bungalow was on a coffee plantation and bordered on the Kikuyu reserve.

On most days Mount Kenya could be seen and on a clear day even the snow-covered dome of Kilimanjaro . . . a wonderful sight. We bought a 1938 Ford Tudor for £50, or one thousand Kenya shillings. Our wives arrived in May, mine with our first daughter who was then eight months old.

One day, when I was on duty, the man I shared the house with broke our agreement and went out with his family. We had agreed that there would always be one of us present, and his absence left my wife alone with the baby. She noticed a group of African men at the bottom of the garden which bordered on the coffee plantation because they kept looking over the hedge at the bungalow. She assumed they were coffee pickers and went out to hang up the washing. While doing this something made her turn around.

To her surprise, there stood a large group of Africans, dressed in khaki greatcoats and carrying 'pangas' (machetes), spears, and what looked like homemade shotguns. She said the only Swahili she knew, '*Jambo, habari aku?*' which means, 'Hello, how are you?' and smiled. She was only nineteen. The group just stared. The leader of these men, a group of about twenty-five, was a big man with a yellow complexion and rather mongoloid features, probably from the Meru tribe. Looking back afterwards we realised he may have been General 'China', one of the more notorious Mau-Mau leaders.

All the men were unkempt and with long hair and were only about five yards away. They continued staring. Suddenly, from the other side of the bungalow came the sound of vehicles, whistles and general tumult. The men, still staring at my wife, took to their heels and ran through the plantation towards the Kikuyu reserve.

Up the drive raced a Land Rover and an Asian police inspector got out. He asked her if she had seen a group of Africans. When she said 'Yes' and described what they looked like, he was horrified and told her she was lucky to be alive. He asked her if she was alone in the house with the baby, and when she said she was, he said she must never be alone again in the house because it was too dangerous. Meanwhile, the police went off after the fleeing

Mau-Mau gang. The inspector got back in his vehicle and drove off, leaving my wife alone again, apart from the baby! A few weeks later we moved into a guest-house in Nairobi. It became too dangerous in that particular outlying area.

Mrs Oxenby was lucky. The total number of Europeans killed was not large but the killings went on throughout the years of the Emergency. In November 1952, Mr Meiklejohn was killed at Thompson Falls, and his wife seriously wounded. Then came the deaths of Messrs Ferguson and Bingley and the Ruck family, followed by the death of Mr Gibson in Nyeri in February 1953. A month later the Ngare Ndare Police post was overrun and all the Africans in it massacred. Later that month Mau-Mau struck again, this time at the police station in Naivasha, and then came the Lari Massacre. So it went on for years, with a constant need for vigilance by the whites and great loss of life among the loyal Africans.

For the settlers the biggest fear throughout the Emergency was that their staff and servants might have taken the Mau-Mau oath and could be waiting for the chance to admit a gang on to their property, to hamstring cattle or burn crops, or massacre the labour force. A worse nightmare was of the door bursting open and a body of Mau-Mau erupting into the bedroom or dining room, swinging razor-sharp pangas.

In June 1953 a Seychellois mechanic, his wife and five children were chopped to pieces near Nanyuki. A month later Mr MacDougall was murdered, also in Nanyuki, and another murder was committed in Nanyuki in September when Mr Beccaloni was killed. There were attacks on Europeans in Thika, where Major G.L.G. Shaw and Mr Bekker were killed in October and November and in March 1954 Mr and Mrs Ruxner-Randall were killed by a gang at their home near Thika.

Atrocities against the loyal Africans were on an even larger and more constant scale, and taking place almost every night in the villages of the Kikuyu Reserve and along the fringes of the forest. The police and Army also took casualties, among them Major Lord Wavell, son of the late Viceroy of India, who was killed while serving in Kenya with the Black Watch.

During 1955, Erskine concentrated his efforts in the Kikuyu. Meru and Embu reserves, in a successful attempt to reduce the flow of supplies and recruits to the forest gangs. A series of amnesties helped here and brought many weary fighters out of the jungle, where a number were snapped up and 'turned' on their former comrades by Captain Kitson. By April 1955 more than five hundred hard-core Mau-Mau terrorists had been killed since the start of the year and the number of terrorist attacks showed a steady decline.

In early 1955, Brigadier Hinde ordered the Army to start a series of sweeps into the main Mau-Mau strongholds, Operation Hammer in the Aberdares and Operation First Flute around Mount Kenya. Operation Hammer was a reasonable success, dispersing the gangs and killing around one hundred and sixty Mau-Mau. Lieutenant David Evans took part in the next phase, 'First Flute':

D Company was based at Chehe, on the edge of Mount Kenya. Within days we were going up this massive mountain, with its deep ravines, endless rivers and streams and very dense undergrowth, on Operation First Flute. Each platoon, in full musketry order, was to camp on the very edge of the very tall, dense bamboo part of the rain forest. We were to make camp – basically sleeping under our poncho capes on bamboo leaves – about one map square away from each other and maintain radio contact at specified times.

In addition to weapons, ammunition and rations, each platoon carried one '88' radio set with wire aerial and short rod aerial, one '46' set with similar aerials and three sections of short rod aerial, five '88' batteries, six '46' batteries, one ground spike and wire for a 'Nanyuki' aerial, one shovel, one stretcher, two camp kettles, one canvas bucket and other minor items. Changes of clothing were in each man's 50lb 'Bergen' pack. Later, captured Mau-Mau were used as porters, once they had been 'de-oathed' and screened. This was to give us greater range on mountain patrols but presented security problems, especially at night – a two-edged sword.

For the next three weeks Platoon Commanders were to keep moving forest camps, liaising with Company HQ, in order to winkle out the forest terrorists from their large and well-hidden camps.

Within twenty-four hours one of my sections, led by a Mkamba Sergeant, came across a well-armed and well-equipped camp which, we later discovered, contained two hundred Mau-Mau.

The Mau-Mau guard – up a tree as usual – set off the alarm by firing at our patrol first and then running off (always away from the camp) to confuse us and to give more time for the Mau-Mau to get away. The section met with a fusillade of shots. As the rest of the platoon closed in we saw the shots ricochetting from the very thick, tall bamboo. Above the noise, the Mkamba sergeant shouted (as if we didn't know), '*Watu wengi!*' ('Many men!'). Carefully the three sections fixed bayonets, spread out and in what we hoped was an extended line in that thick vegetation, let fire with everything we had. In front of us, Mau-Mau firing stopped.

We had heard that they had a Bren gun, one of the two captured from the Kenya Police, the other presumably a Sten, and a number of good rifles. Just as we entered the camp we threw in two hand grenades: the only effect of that was to disturb a colony of colobus monkeys in the tall trees above. More shots rang out as the Mau-Mau tried to cover their retreat, splitting up and disappearing in different directions. The Platoon stayed together, entering a very well disguised camp which was about two hundred yards in diameter – about the biggest I had yet seen. We kept on returning fire.

At the first lull in the firing I called up 11 Platoon on the radio. They were searching map square 6962: we were in 6861, telling the seconded Kenya Regiment Platoon Commander, Billy Matheson, the direction where most of the gang seemed to be running. Actually they were running in all directions *away* from us.

It transpired that 11 Platoon had met a large number of the gang in flight and killed two of them which, added to the three we, in 10 platoon, had just killed, made a total of five, in about fifteen minutes. I also alerted 12 Platoon, which was in map squares 7062 and 7063 – just too far away and in the wrong direction to be of immediate assistance. It must be emphasised that the Mount Kenya rain forest was so dense that one frequently could not see one's enemy, nor one's friends.

Mau-Mau camps had a diversity of small tracks in order to enter and make a quick exit. Game tracks were also used to help disguise Mau-Mau footprints. This Mau-Mau camp had no less than nineteen kitchen fires burning when we entered. From the number of lean-to bamboo huts and sleeping arrangements we estimated that the gang had numbered about two hundred. Each kitchen had army mess tins, tin mugs, frying pans, large and medium cooking pots, aluminium dishes, large tins for storing food, pangas, mirrors and so on. We found thirty large sacks of maize, two sacks of rice, ample supplies of tea and sugar, and by almost each fire hundreds of bananas and plenty of sweet potatoes. This was the first hide in which I had not seen meat of any form. There were not even animal skins, which was unusual.

An immense supply of clothing of all kinds was left behind and we burned everything in the existing kitchen fires. Unfortunately, there were no prisoners. We found only one good home-made rifle, a few rounds of .303 and a World War I bayonet. It was clear that although the gang had been taken completely by surprise, it had managed to get away with its weapons. Documents captured showed that this had been the camp of a General Kanji.

General Kanji's camp was well laid out on a slope going down to a river, and although immense by most standards, was well hidden from the air. Tall trees and thick bamboo were a natural defence. By the time we had thoroughly destroyed the camp, the safari ants had entered the eyes, nose, ears and mouth of all the dead terrorists. Fortunately I had photographed and fingerprinted them earlier.

There is a sequel to this. Six years later, in May 1961, long after the Emergency was over, I was approached by a well-dressed young Kikuyu who said that he recognised me as the 'Effendi' in the KAR who had sat listing all the captured supplies in General Kanji's camp in 1955. He had been a 'moto' (small boy) with the gang and had squeezed into the centre of a dense clump of bamboo and stayed there for hours.

He told me that since leaving the forest he had been learning English and studying hard; he hoped to go to university soon. We went to a small bar nearby and split a large 'Tusker' beer to 'old times' and toasted Kenya's future.

General Erskine decided that the time was right to pull his troops out of the settled areas and mount a major all-out push into the forests. This was well under way when General Erskine left Kenya in May 1955 and was replaced by General Sir Gerald Lathbury. Lathbury continued these operations and had rounded up the last of the effective gangs by the end of 1956.

Operations continued from mid-1955, but declined steadily as more British battalions were withdrawn. Military operations finally stopped in October 1956 when the last of the major Mau-Mau leaders, Dedan Kimathi, was wounded, captured, tried and executed. Mau-Mau fighters continued to lurk in the forest, coming in and surrendering from time to time over the next ten years, but by the New Year of 1957, the Mau–Mau revolt, which had claimed so many lives in a pointless struggle, was effectively over.

The fact that the worst effects of Mau Mau terrorism fell on the Africans and not on the white settlers is demonstrated by the final casualty figures. In the four years of Mau–Mau, from June 1952 to October 1956, two thousand, four hundred and sixty five people were killed by Mau–Mau. Just thirty-two of these were Europeans. Nearly two thousand were loyal Africans, mostly Kikuyu. Mau–Mau casualties were much higher. By the time the Emergency ended, some ten thousand Mau–Mau had been killed and two thousand, six hundred and thirty three had been captured, some of them to face trial and, if found guilty of a capital charge, executed.

After the end of the Emergency the British Government promptly moved on, as promised, to the next phase, the granting of independence. On 1 June 1963 a new internal self-government Constitution for Kenya came into force, with Jomo Kenyetta named as Kenya's first Prime Minister. A few months later, on 12 December 1964, Kenya became a republic within the Commonwealth, with Mr Kenyetta as President.

David Evans, who served in Kenya first as an infantry officer and then as a colonial official, has some views on this rapid change: 'Naturally, all of us, not only those involved in the Kenya Administration, thought that this advance to independence – UHURU – was too fast for the good of the Africans. African "equality" did not last long. Some soon turned out to be "more equal than others" and they and their families proceeded to plunder the kitty in style.'

David Nicoll-Griffith was another Colonial Administrative Officer, who spent ten years in Kenya, from the start of Mau–Mau in 1952 to the start of independence:

The ending of the Mau–Mau Emergency heralded the start of more acceptable expressions of political aims. As far as my district of Fort Hall was concerned, this meant activity by KANU, the Kenya African National Union, which, at least to begin with, was exclusively Kikuyu. There were huge political meetings and what was said at those meetings was distressing for the simple people were being duped with false promises. "You see those nice houses over there? If you vote for us you will all get to live in nice houses after independence."

There were cases of tribesmen from the Reserve being stopped in the street and asked to choose a car from those parked nearby. The number of the car was then written on a piece of paper and given to the man in exchange for a ten shilling note, with the promise that he could claim the car after independence.

Anything we might have said would have fallen on deaf ears and anyway we were being labelled as the cause of all life's woes and our position was not improved or helped by 'fact finding' visits from British politicians. These rarely lasted more than a week or ten days, and that was not long enough to get the feel of the country: I did not get the feel of Kenya until I had been there several years. Yet on the basis of such visits articles appeared in the British Press entitled 'Kenya under the Iron heel' and suchlike, with an illustration of a jackboot.

All of us had spent our working lives trying to help the indigenous people to a better and fuller life, to educate them to the point where they could safely manage their own affairs in the face of the complicated world outside. It was therefore depressing to realise that the 'facts' these politicians discovered were not designed to present a balanced view of the country and its problems, but only to make political capital. When you worked there it was different.

I can remember visits to my office by local politicians, anxious to try their hand at this new game, gentlemen in dark glasses, all carrying briefcases. They would walk in unannounced and lean across my desk to tell me of the wonders that would come after independence. One of them informed me that they would do away with 'restrictive laws which hampered the freedom of the people'. I asked him to give me an example and he said, 'Why, for instance, do you insist on vehicles keeping to only one side of the road? We will allow them to use as much of the road as they want.'

When I pointed out the folly of such a move he retorted that it was only an example and stalked out of my office. Most of the local people were apprehensive at the prospect of a post-independence Government dominated by one tribe, and that tribe the one responsible for Mau-Mau.

It was a depressing time, a time of winding down, not by our wish but by political pressure from Britain and the United States.

In talking of independence, most of us looked forward to our own UHURU and the compensation we hoped to receive for the loss of our careers. When the time came to leave though, I felt only sadness.

8

The Fight for Malaya: 1952–1960

'The shooting side of the business is only twenty-five per cent of the trouble; the other seventy-five per cent depends on getting the bulk of the people behind us.'

General Sir Gerald Templer, 1 November 1952.

After the death of Sir Henry Gurney, the team he had led against the Communists began to break up. Sir Harold Briggs gave up his appointment as Director of Operations through ill health and died soon afterwards. The Conservative Party won the British General Election of 1951 and the new Colonial Secretary, Oliver Lyttelton, arrived in Malaya on a tour of the Far East, listened to loudly-voiced complaints of the expatriate community and elected to sack Colonel Grey, the Commissioner of Police.

Lyttelton also examined the triumvirate command structure in Malaya and decided that it would not do. What was needed, he told the British Cabinet, was one man, a strong man who could hold all the reins in his hands and combine the three roles of High Commissioner, Director of Operations and Commissioner of Police. Such a man was not easy to find but 'come the hour, comes the man', and the man chosen for this task was a British Army officer, Lt.-General Sir Gerald Templer.

Gerald Templer was born in Colchester in 1898 but the Templer family had long connections with Ulster, a province which, according to the military historian Corelli Barnett, has produced 'the closest thing Britain has to a Junker caste'. Gerald Templer's father came from Armagh and became an officer in the Royal Irish Fusiliers, a regiment Templer joined in August 1916.

He went to France in October 1917 and served in the trenches for the rest of the War, fighting in the Battle of Cambrai, when his battalion suffered over 50 per cent casualties on the first day. In the battles around St Quintain in March 1918 his eight-hundred-strong battalion was rapidly reduced to three officers and twenty-eight men. Although Templer came through the war without a scratch, the experiences of those days on the Western Front stayed with him throughout his life.

When the Second World War broke out in September 1939 Templer was a Lt.-Colonel in Military Intelligence, serving on the staff of General Gort, the Commander of the British Expeditionary Force, with whom he went to France shortly after war broke out. When the Germans attacked in June 1940 Templer survived the subsequent shambles and arrived back in Britain before Dunkirk but in time to deliver a stiff rebuke to the American Ambassador, Joseph Kennedy, father of President John R. Kennedy. The Ambassador had been declaring that Britain's defeat was inevitable as the British had lost the will to fight. Tired of this denigration, the War Office selected Templer to tell Kennedy about the fighting in France.

'At the interview,' Templer recalls in his diary, 'Kennedy told me that "England will be invaded in a few weeks and your country will have it's neck wrung by Hitler like a chicken."

'I got up and told him exactly what I thought of him in the most undiplomatic language . . . I was quivering with fury.' Diplomacy was never Templer's forte.

Templer was then sent to raise and command the 9th Bn., The Royal Sussex Regiment before being given command of a Brigade in a Home Defence Division under an up-and-coming general officer. Bernard Law Montgomery.

From then on Templer's rise was rapid. In 1942 he was a Major General commanding the 47th (London) Divisoin and a few months later was appointed Lt.-General commanding 11 Corps and became the youngest Lt.-General in the British Army. He held this appointment for a further year until 1943 when he requested a field command, reverted to Major General and went to North Africa to command the 1st Division in First Army, part of the force under the command of the American General, Dwight Eisenhower.

When the Allies invaded Italy, Templer was sent to command the 56th (Black Cat) Division in Fifth Army and led the division in the fighting around the Volturno river and the Gustav Line. His division fought in the Anzio beachhead and after suffering heavy losses went to rest and reform in Egypt. In July 1944 Templer took his Division back to Italy to join the 8th Army in the push north of Rome. On arrival he was given a new command, the 6th Armoured Division, but a few days later he was injured by a mine and spent the rest of the war in Intelligence and at Montgomery's HQ in Belgium and Germany. When the war ended he was a Major General, and earmarked for higher things.

A man does not become a General in the British Army if he suffers fools gladly. Major-General Gerald Templer did not suffer fools at all. A slim, alert man, the archetypal British soldier, he first came to public notice in 1945 when, as Director of Civil Affairs at 21 Army Group HQ, he sacked Dr Konrad Adenauer, then the Mayor of Cologne, 'for laziness and inefficiency'. Since Dr Adenauer later became Chancellor of West Germany and architect of the *Wirtschaftswunder* which dragged Germany from the ruins of war to the economic domination of Europe, it will be seen that General Templer set very high standards indeed.

Templer progressed steadily in the post-war years, earning credit wherever he went by his good sense and efficiency. Above all Templer was a leader, and after Gurney's murder, when it was decided that Malaya needed one man to take complete charge of all the country's affairs, civil and military, the name of Templer soon came to mind. The Foreign Secretary, Oliver Lyttelton, met Templer and was impressed and recommended him to Churchill. Churchill met Templer in Ottawa in January 1952 and offered him the post of High Commissioner with 'absolute power . . . civil and military power . . . and I shall see that you get it'. With that understood, Templer left for Malaya.

Templer fell on Malaya like a thunderbolt: in the words of one Colonial officer, 'he really made things hum'. Commanding both the military and the civil powers, he accepted no excuses for delay or failure. His first step was to amalgamate the War Council with the Executive Council and charge this new body with the active prosecution of the war against the CTs. He also decided to improve the intelligence gathering element and reformed this department under the leadership of another efficient officer, Jack Morton.

On the political front he pushed through a measure giving the vote to nearly half a million Malayan-born Chinese who had hitherto been denied the franchise and pressed forward with the creation of a Malavan Army, raising more battalions of the Malay Regiment. Learning the lessons of India, although this force had British officers on secondment, Malay officers were commissioned from the start and were soon commanding companies and battalions.

General Templer was forever on the move, visiting most parts of the country, even small villages where the population would assemble a round his helicopter or staff car to hear a speech. These speeches did not always come out as the General intended. Visiting one kampong where the inhabitants had been supplying food to the CTs, the General attempted to deliver a full-blooded ticking off, through his interpreter.

'You are a bunch of useless bastards . . .' he told the villagers.

'His Excellency wishes to tell you that your mothers and fathers were not married,' said the interpreter.

'. . . and you had better know that I am a bit of a bastard myself . . .' went on Templer.

'His Excellency wishes to add that his mother and father were not married either . . .'

Some words do suffer in translation.

Templer realised that the strongest political card the British had to play was their commitment to independence once the Communist threat had been reduced. This commitment had been made in 1946 and Templer repeated it in his first speech to the Legislative Council in Kuala Lumpur in March 1952. Apart from beating the bandits he intended to press on at once with arrangements for a fully self-governing Malaya, and he took immediate steps to bring more Malays into Government, setting up Chief Executives in every State, meeting political leaders and handing over the Speaker's chair in the Council to a Malay. His aim was to give the Malays practical political experience before independence came.

This move met with a warm response from the leading local politician, Tunku Abdul Rahman, who asked for immediate internal self-government, a move that Templer and the British Government were happy to support. The Tunku's party swept the board at the subsequent elections and Malaya was set on the road to independence far sooner than anyone had anticipated. All this cut the ground from under the Communists and their supporters.

In spite of his close attention to the broad picture and his wide range of duties. Templer never forgot that the war would be won in the jungle. He visited units all over Malaya, sent more men into the jungle, and to improve mobility in that ever difficult terrain he demanded and got an increasing number of helicopters, which now began to make their appearance on the battlefields. In general, though, the campaign in Malaya was fought on foot and the man at the sharp end was the infantry soldier.

Captain R.A. Puddy, then a Senior NCO in the 1st Battalion, The Somerset Light infantry, arrived in Malaya in 1952:

I was stationed at Kajang, about sixteen miles south-east of Kuala Lumpur, as Platoon Sergeant of 11 platoon, 'D' Company. Our area of responsibility was very hilly and steep-sided river valleys abounded, so we were either scrambling up or sliding down jungle-covered ridges as the grain of the land always seemed to run across the line of travel. The jungle, however, was primary jungle and movement through it was reasonably easy once you had cleared the secondary jungle between the rubber, plantations and the jungle proper.

A patrol usually lasted four or five days, as that was about the limit of what could be carried in the form of rations, ammunition, radio batteries and so on. If the patrol was to last for more than five days an airdrop would be taken. In order to take an airdrop, a Dropping Zane would be cut using the issued machete or more likely locally made parangs which could be honed to a very fine edge – I could shave with mine. Sometimes it was necessary to cut a Landing Zone for a helicopter, in which case an airdrop of explosives would be taken. One thing we found out was that plastic explosive makes excellent fuel for our tommy-cookers.

The first day of a patrol was usually spent moving several thousand yards into the jungle, then establishing and securing a patrol base. On succeeding days the area would be patrolled by small patrols going out on compass bearings like the spokes of a wheel. On arrival at the patrol base the patrol would split up into pairs, each pair erecting a crude shelter using one poncho for the roof and one to lie on. A water point was established, a latrine dug and a small patrol ensured the local area was clear of Communist terrorists. A vine was pulled down from the trees and erected at chest height around the base to prevent patrol members straying in the darkness – very easily done. At stand-to at last light the patrol commander issued anti-malaria paladrin tablets and rum and the medical orderly took care of any small injuries.

On my first patrol, while issuing rum and paladrin, I was quietly telling each man that if he strayed outside the vine he was liable to be shot, when one rather cocky lad said, 'You wouldn't shoot me,' and ducked under the vine. I promptly fired two shots into the ground between his feet. I think he and the rest of the patrol got the message. One thing we had to do before settling down for the night was to change from our soaking wet (water and sweat), smelly clothes into a dry set which we carried. It wasn't so pleasant changing back again in the morning as the clothes would still be wet, cold, and covered in ants or small flies.

Wild animals did not bother us at all. We once had a tiger cub come into our patrol base and after foraging around it left, watched all the time by his mother who was only a few yards away. On another occasion I sat on a stream bank for half an hour watching two tigers playing in the stream at the base of a waterfall. They were no more than twenty-five yards away but they ignored me completely. Two things that did bother us, however, were hornets, which were very aggressive, and leeches which could only be knocked off by touching with a lighted cigarette. Once I counted over forty leeches on me. It was important not to just pull the leech off, as it could leave its head embedded in you, and this usually turned septic.

On completion of the patrol all signs of our presence would, as far as possible, be eliminated, and with lighter packs and lighter hearts we would set off to the vehicle rendez-vous which, provided timing and navigation were correct, would see us back to the relative comforts of Kajang camp. It was also good to be able to talk normally again, as we maintained silence in the jungle.

My patrol once took part in an ambush that almost went 'by the book' on the jungle rubber trees edge, to the north of the Ulu Langat road. I knew it would be difficult to get into the area undetected as there was a certain amount of ribbon development along this road, so I decided to camp at 11pm and ordered the driver to drive slowly while we jumped off the moving vehicle. He was then to carry on to Ulu Langat and wait thirty minutes before returning. This was in the hope that it would be thought we were picking up a patrol, not dropping off one.

All went well, with no sprained ankles, and we set off through a rubber estate on a compass bearing. At about 11pm we arrived at what we hoped was the right place. We rolled up in our ponchos and grabbed a few hours sleep. At first light I was able to confirm we were in the right place, so I moved the patrol several hundred yards into the jungle, left our heavy kit with two men to guard it and moved back to the ambush site. On inspection of the ambush site I found it to be on a spur in the shape of the letter 'U', three sides of the 'U' being scrappy jungle while the open end led to the rubber estate.

As it was not possible to see from one side of the 'U' to the other. I placed three men on one side while I took the other side with the Bren gunner (I only had five men to cover the ambush). We had barely settled down when I heard a slight noise off to our right. I thought this must have been made by an animal as all was quiet for the next forty-five minutes. By this time the rubber tappers had arrived and, as usual, were making quite a din, shouting and singing in Chinese. I think one of the tappers must have given a signal that all was clear because two CTs appeared from out of the jungle and started moving down the jungle-rubber edge. I indicated to my Bren gunner to take the leading man while I took number two.

When I opened fire I saw my target drop, but the Bren gunner said he had missed. I swung round, saw undergrowth moving and emptied my magazine in the general direction. On investigation we found one dead CT and a blood trail left by the second. We followed this for several hundred yards before losing it. I then called for a tracker dog which duly arrived with an Iban patrol who were expert trackers. They followed the track most of the day but eventually lost it. One Iban tracker said he must have been lifted out by helicopter as the track just stopped dead. It was unfortunate that one of the CTs was hidden by rubber trees when I opened fire and, of course, a Bren gun is rather unwieldly in close country, but we almost pulled off the perfect ambush, by 7am of the first day.

I was ordered to take my patrol deeper into the jungle to where an unoccupied CT camp existed, as it was thought the injured CT may have headed there. In order to avoid any accidental shooting I was ordered to crawl into this camp at midnight, alone. I crawled in, which I admit was a bit spooky, to find the camp empty. Several months later this CT surrendered. I had hit him five times and he still had two bullets near his spine. He died when an attempt was made to remove these bullets at the local hospital.

Another rather scary job I undertook was when a police patrol in an armoured car reported that they had been fired at on the Kajang to Broga road. I was asked if I would travel the same road alone except for the driver in an open one-ton Dodge truck in the hope that I would be fired upon! I was assured there would be a full patrol following at a discreet distance who would deal with any situation that arose. Luckily I was not fired on, so all was well.

In 1954 I was promoted WOII and this finished my jungle bashing. I had by this time worn out forty-eight pairs of jungle boots and at least as many suits of OG (olive green). I still, however, had my original jungle hat: no old sweat would be seen wearing a new jungle hat.

I was awarded the Military Medal in the 1955 Queen's Birthday Honours List, but by this time my patrol had all been demobbed, and though I was very proud of the award I felt a little sad, as it was as much their medal as mine. My main memories of the three years I spent in Malaya are of the loyalty of the National Servicemen, the patience and dedication of the pilots who gave us our airdrops – most of whom were Australian – and the vastness of the jungle which, as Spencer Chapman said, 'I found to be neutral'.

3 Commando Brigade were operating in Perak, where a young officer in 40 Commando, Lieutenant Jeremy Moore, had his first taste of combat:

When we arrived in Malaya our CO was Bertie Lumsden, a very flamboyant character, who got in some good successes against the bandits. Then 45 Commando started to get more kills. People were very 'kill-conscious' in those days and one day we received a surrendered terrorist who told us of a bandit camp, probably occupied. I took out a small patrol to ambush one of the tracks leading to it where, according to our terrorist, the CTs had a post box. We took the surrendered terrorist with us but it soon became obvious we were on the wrong track.

When this became clear we were on the edge of the rubber and I felt exceedingly exposed, so I led the patrol up a bank which overlooked the track and we were just getting into position – I was just briefing the Bren group, when 'lo and behold' there they were, a bunch of CTs coming down the track from the jungle, three scouts in front, a bigger group still in the trees behind. We just froze.

They were opposite us when one of them saw our Bren gunner, who was still squatting over his gun. He realised he'd been seen, flung himself behind the gun, cocked it and opened fire, shooting the CT in the groin. We killed two of them and tackled the party but they got away. Our CO was cock-a-hoop that his Commando had got a kill – well, two kills – and after that I could do no wrong.

3 Commando Brigade killed or captured two hundred and twenty-one terrorists during their two-year stint in Malaya, for the cost of thirty Royal Marines killed.

Military operations continued and intensified in all parts of the Peninsula. Helicopters began to arrive in 1953 and gave the jungle soldiers greatly added mobility on operations, apart from their role in evacuating the wounded. Another useful addition was the creation of the Malaya Scouts, an SAS-style body, raised by an experienced jungle soldier, Mike Calvert. This unit eventually became the 22 SAS Regiment and played an important part both in deep-penetration operations and in winning the most important part of this – and all other – colonial struggles, the battle for hearts and minds.

George Butler who served with the Parachute Regiment in the Second World War, served in Malaya with 22 SAS:

My best soldiering took place in Malaya with 22 SAS, with plenty of scope for initiative and self-sufficiency. Decision making was less impersonal, and by following the basic rules of diet, taking the tablets and so on, I lasted every operation and didn't miss a single day in the jungle throughout the tour.

Patrolling was hard work in jungle conditions but after training we found no difficulty in doing the job, and life among the tall trees became second nature. The first time I saw the tin mines and the huge rubber plantations, I realised the importance of the Far East to our economy. Whether the tea planters, tin miners and rubber plantation owners thought the same about us, I was never certain.

Though my Troop, under Lieutenant Glynn Williams, covered many hundreds of gruelling miles, we didn't have a great deal to show for it. After many months of fruitless patrolling our first contact resulted in Private Dougan being hit in the shoulder and neck by a CT shotgun as he followed a line of new traps laid on a steep slope. As he spotted the camp, the sentry fired, then ran. As there were only four men on the patrol there was no chance of an organised follow-up. Dougan had to be treated and base camp had to be warned. By the time we got there all signs had gone. Dougan was evacuated by Royal Navy helicopter and recovered.

In the same area later, Private Dougan, with Corporal Finn and Private Gerry, spotted a CT by a water point. As the CT raised his weapon, Dougan fired his shotgun and killed him stone dead. The body was evacuated by air but we didn't find out who he was in the CT hierarchy. I always believed the Chinese to be a small race, but this man weighed about twelve and a half stone and was nearly six feet tall.

Malaya was an example of enlightened colonial rule. The system of employing local workers in all posts held by Europeans paid dividends when they received Home Rule shortly after we left. Though there were many different races, religions and factions in Malaya, it was as peaceful, well run a country as I have ever seen: a credit to all its administrators, past and present.

Of all the units committed to the jungle war in Malaya, none stayed so long or did so well as the Gurkhas. They were there from the beginning to the end and by 3 December 1952, four years into the Emergency, they had killed more than a thousand terrorists, that figure being reached when a patrol of the 1/6 Gurkhas killed a terrorist on 3 December 1952. This was three times as many as the best British battalion. No one in the British Army grudged the Gurkhas their success and these splendid troops were universally

popular, though when they arrived in Malaya they were not in good
order. Lt.-Colonel 'Titch' Harvey again:

Leaving India was depressing and there was a lot of sorting out
to do. Fortunately we had some good officers and the men were
superb, as usual, so our Colonel in the 2/6th soon had us in good
shape. In fact the Emergency did us a power of good, gave us a
purpose and a reason to work hard and you had to work hard
if you wanted to kill the enemy. I forget the precise figure but I
think the best estimate is that you had to put in seven hundred
hours on patrol before you saw a CT. Then you got one chance
for a snap shot and he was away: unless he turned the tables and
ambushed you first, of course.

The first Gurkha battalion to arrive in Malaya, the 1/6th, sailed into
Penang from Burma in February 1948 and was later commanded by
the formidable Lt.-Colonel Walter Walker, who was to command
all the British forces in the later Confrontation with Indonesia. Five
more Gurkha battalions arrived later, and were in position when
the Emergency broke out in June, based all over the country but
commanded by Gurkha Brigade HQ in Seremban. The last two
Gurkha battalions arrived from Hong Kong in 1950 to join the
newly formed 17th Gurkha Division.

In October 1949, a Gurkha patrol from the 1/10th came across a
hut in which they found Naik Nakun Gurung of the 1st Gurkhas.
He had fought against the Japanese in Malaya in 1942 and had been
living in the jungle ever since; he did not know that the Second
World War was over.

The Gurkha battalions were all composed of regular troops but
they did contain a few British National Service officers. One of
these was Michael Wasiliewski who joined the 1/7 Gurkha Rifles
in Segamat, Jahore, in April 1955:

I was at Mons Officer Cadet School when I saw a notice on
Company Orders that NS officers could apply for commissions
with the Brigade of Gurkhas. I knew that the Gurkhas were
splendid troops and were in the Far East and since I wanted to
see a little of the world at Her Majesty's expense, I applied and
was accepted. On arrival at Segamat I was met by the Adjutant,

Major O'Leary, and I heard later that his first comment after my arrival was, 'Well, at least he speaks English.'

'I was the first NS officer to join the 1/7th – and I believe only the second to join the Brigade of Gurkhas – so the novelty might have accounted for the warm way in which I was greeted but I was soon to find that this warmth was typical of the 1/7th and no doubt of other Gurkha regiments as well.

The British officers felt the bond of being an élite, stemming I think from the Indian Army origin of the Brigade, but also referring to its superb men. It took very little time for it to dawn on me that until I learned Gurkhali I would be of no use, since very few Gurkhas knew English. It was decided that I would spend an initial period at HQ on attachment to the Intelligence Officer.

By 1955 the CTs were on the defensive and the roads were fairly safe. Nevertheless, it was prudent to take precautions, so many of our lorries were armoured and wherever possible escorted by an armoured car. By May I was with 'A' Company, which was based on a rubber plantation in Bandan. This company was commanded by Major John Cross, a very lively, cheerful thirty-year old. Even by Gurkha regiment standards he was exceptional in his devotion to the men and his excellent knowledge of Gurkhali.

The routine was six days on patrol followed by three days rest, but there were constant variations to this: some patrols were as long as three weeks. My main task was to learn the language but an ambush was the task of the first patrol I went on. We made our way to the ambush site through smallish swamps and lallang and spent two days lying still from dawn to dusk in the ambush position. It was stiflingly hot and keeping still for hours is very uncomfortable. The CTs did not come and we had to abandon that ambush to take part in a battalion operation.

This time the target was a group of twenty-five or more CTs and 'A' Company were to attack the group's camp while the other companies encircled it. The plan did not work out as intended but many of the CTs walked into 'C' Company's ambush, two being killed and one captured. This ambush was written up in the *Straits Times* on 12 May 1955.

I served a year with the Gurkhas and it was a great wrench to leave the regiment and the exciting life of a soldier during the Emergency. Later I was to think that I should have applied for a regular commission but in my heart of hearts I knew that that I would have found prolonged service in the Army hard to bear.

All the Gurkha battalions did well in Malaya and recording Gurkha 'kills' became a feature of daily life at GHQ. In October 1952 a Gurkha battalion put up the top monthly target to seventeen terrorists killed. In April and May of 1955 the Support and Rifle companies of the 2/10th killed five terrorists. The 2/6th managed to kill six CTs while the battalion officers were at a cocktail party. The eight Gurkha battalions were the backbone of the fight against the CTs and by the time they had killed their thousandth CT in 1952, they felt they had the situation well in hand.

Matters were also improving for the civilian planters. John Anderson again:

In 1952 King George VI died and was succeeded by the present Queen, who was crowned in 1953. Both events were properly acknowledged in Malaya, the Coronation being marked by a holiday on the estates. In the morning I paraded with the estate school children and the subordinate staff – all of South Indian descent – for a group photograph against a suitable banner expressing loyal sentiments. In the afternoon there were sports for the staff and labour force, including families. I managed to win 'putting the shot' and was rewarded with a Coronation souvenir Thermos flask.

The estate to which I was transferred in Kedah was more remote and isolated, bordering on the forests that extended northwards into southern Thailand, where it was considered that the leader of the Malayan Communist Party, Chin Peng, had his base. The working day was much the same and considering that there was only one way in and out, and that this road passed through some forest, remarkably quiet from the CT point of view.

An incident arose when an Assistant on the neighbouring estate wandered along a well-known path in the forest and came upon a small group of CT couriers, possibly taking information, food, medicine and so on to and from south Kedah – where there was considerable activity – to Thailand. He received a charge of buck-shot in the leg for his trouble and that stirred things up. Hornet aircraft from the RAF base at Butterworth strafed the forest, and boundary fields of my estate were patrolled by a unit of Surrendered Enemy Personnel (SEPs). These ex-CTs were commanded by a British police officer, and were a particularly nasty looking bunch, but effective, as they were essentially hoping to keep their skins preserved from puncturing by their old pals. I was glad when they left.

The story began to circulate that there was an unofficial non-aggression pact operating, with the forest path being an acknowledged CT route, the labourers' quarters on the estate a safe overnight stop, and nobody saying anything. This may well have been the case. The SOs, about ten in all, only had rifles and two Sten guns. We were some five or six miles off the main road, with no telephone or radio communication. There was no way in which we could have survived a sustained attack.

Kedah was a State of considerable political influence in the movement towards independence. The leader of the United Malay National Organisation (UMNO) and first Prime Minister of Malaya was a member of the Kedah Royal house, Tunku Abdul Rahman. It is surprising that very little political feeling was ever experienced on the estate.

The only incidence arose from an SC, a Kedah Malay, who asked me if I believed that the whole world would soon speak Malay. This was at a time when the Malay language was being promoted as the Bahasa Kebangsaan, loosely translated as the National Language, but more accurately as the 'language of all races'. This was seen to be the way forward to unity among the three major races in Malaya, as the majority of the older members of the Chinese and Indian races spoke no Malay.

1955 saw me in the Rompin area of Negri Sembilan, very active Emergency-wise and very much involved in food denial. All rice was cooked centrally on the estate, within the wired compounds, and under the armed presence of a Company of The Royal Welch Fusiliers. This unit was based on the estate in the ex-group hospital buildings. Armoured vehicles were provided by a squadron of Hussars. A few miles down the road was a Gurkha unit on Henrietta Estate. I was on this estate for just a few months but had very little contact with the British Army units. Moving to north Johore, in an area looked after by the South Wales Borderers, this remained the case.

So we moved towards Independence. There had been great

efforts with 'Bahasa Kebangsaan', with days, weeks and months during which all official correspondence was to be in Bahasa, to which it came to be referred, and the telephonists at the exchanges were only to speak Malay. There had been the appropriate conferences and visits, but this made very little impact on the estate, even though on the particular estate in North Johore, of which I was then Manager, there was a reasonable racial mix in the labour force. One significant administrative change had occurred in that a Malay civil servant had been appointed to be our District Officer and a number of Malay District Officers were guided by an Administrative Officer, a British civil servant of vast experience.

The date for independence, 'Merdeka Day', was set for 31 August 1957. A few weeks prior to this I had an unexpected visit from the AO suggesting that I select a suitable site for helicopter landings in the event of a need for emergency evacuation. This was to be advised to him in confidence.

Advice was also given for a plan of withdrawal on to a strong point, suitably stocked with food and water and a means of defence, and to agree this with my European staff. At that time we numbered five, all bachelors. Our oldest member had fought in the Malayan campaign of World War II and had spent some terrible years on the Japanese railway in Thailand. Another was an ex-soldier with considerable service in the Emergency and two CT kills to his credit, plus another ex-soldier and two ex-RNs.

We agreed to withdraw to my bungalow, it being the only brick building and situated on a hilltop with good fields of fire. We had a considerable armoury of semi-automatic weapons and an enormous stack or ammunition and two armoured Landrovers at our disposal. Having said that, it was a considerable surprise to be advised about such precautions. At no time did I hear of any tension of an anti-British or inter-racial nature; when questioned, the AO only made mention of vague rumours.

Just before 'Merdeka' Day it was announced that while there would be suitable ceremonies and celebrations in Kuala Lampur, celebrations in other parts of the country would be restricted to a reading of a proclamation by District Officers and a flag raising ceremony at District Offices. Other celebrations would follow, area by area, in a sequence defined by the availability of security forces to provide adequate cover. Thus the day itself was to be a normal working day on the estate.

My bungalow was well stocked with food and water stored in containers within the house, but apart from that the European staff went about their work as usual, though carrying arms in view of the Emergency. Not a shot nor a shout, but quiet satisfaction of a good day's work done . . . so ended British rule in Malaya.

Looking back, was it a good thing that we were there all those years and ruled as we did? Unhesitatingly I would say, yes. We could point with some degree of pride to the British-built infrastructure that we left and be told how insignificant that was compared with the massive development in the country today, but in my view the strength that we left was our reputation for fair dealing.

The first Prime Minister, Tunku Abdul Rhaman, was equally even-handed and moderate in all things, and that carried the country smoothly forward into the first decade of independence.

The credit for ending the Malayan Emergency must largely go to Sir Gerald Templer, who saw that whatever steps taken to improve security must be seen as a movement towards eventual independence.

'The answer lies not in pouring more soldiers into the jungle but in the hearts and minds of the Malayan people,' said Templer in 1952, shortly after taking up his appointment.

This precept was born in mind in everything he did throughout his time in office, especially in the social and political arena. As one step in this direction, to improve the morale, but also the public image of the police, currently a para–military force, Templer recruited Sir Arthur Young, formerly Commissioner of Police in the City of London, and charged him with creating a force which the public could like and trust. Under Sir Arthur, the Malayan Police Force became a friend to the local people, not an arm of a repressive government.

Templer could be ruthless; villages that were not supporting the struggle against the CTs could find themselves under curfew or facing fines, but his aim was to stamp out terrorism as a step to independence and he was determined to carry that aim through, not least by winning the respect, the 'hearts and minds', of the ordinary citizen.

Templer was not engaged in a public relations exercise: he saw where resentment could fester and took steps to eliminate it. When he first arrived at Government House and met the servants he was quietly informed that 'The British in this country do not shake the hands of Asian servants.'

'Don't they?' said Templer. 'Well, they do from this moment on.' Then he sent for the servants and shook hands with them all. Templer had no time for snobbery or pomposity, and neither did his wife Peggie. The first thing she did on arriving at Government House was to inspect the servants' quarters and, appalled at what she found, ordered immediate improvements and redecoration: when the Public Works Department seemed reluctant to oblige she told Templer, he breathed fire on the Department and the work was done.

Such actions did not make the High Commissioner and his wife universally popular. The High Commissioner for South East Asia, Malcolm Macdonald, resented the wide-ranging powers given to a mere soldier and many of the settlers and planters felt that Templer was too friendly with the natives and not paying enough attention to their own interests and security. Others, perhaps the majority, saw what he was trying to do and gave him their full support. Under Templer Malaya changed, permanently and for the better.

With Malaya well on the way to peace and independence, General Sir Gerald Templer and his wife Peggie left Malaya in May 1954, driving to the airport in an open unprotected car, through streets lined with cheering, waving people. Waiting at the airport was a great crowd of dignitaries from all the local communities, many of them in tears. A phial of water from the Sultan's Well in Malacca was handed to Sir Gerald with the advice that anyone who drank it would return to Malaya: the General took half, and gave the rest to his wife.

When Malaya became independent three years later, the Guests of Honour at the 'Merdeka' ceremony were General and Lady Gerald Templer.

Independence – Merdeka – had come but the Emergency was not over and the British troops remained under the Anglo-Malayan Defence Agreement. Finding a terrorist in the jungle was never easy and only came after long and relentless patrolling, an activity that became even more relentless as the terrorist threat declined.

E. V. Berriman was in Malaya with the Green Howards and recalls his one contact:

I had not met the Platoon Commander, Lieutenant J. V. Nicholl, or the Platoon Sergeant before the morning when we mustered at the start of the patrol. While we were climbing the first hill, Lieutenant Nicholl remarked that his hobby was mountaineering. Most of the men in the battalion also had a climbing hobby – mainly on to a bar stool, staying there until the money ran out, in female company if possible.

Late one afternoon our searchers returned and the Forestry guide was bursting with excitement. He had found a really big, well-used track and the guide was positive that the bandits using it would all be drunk. Nicholl said, 'No, it's too late in the day to go off now.' So the plan was that at first light we would all move off on this track, find the bandit camp and attack it.

We moved off next morning and came to the track. The ground round about was very damp and in trying not to step on the track we tip-toed forward. About a quarter of a mile further on we came to a very slow, stagnant stream with a tree trunk felled across it as a footbridge. In the water at the right-hand side of the trunk was a pair of white plimsolls. Everybody was looking about them, thinking that the first man on to the trunk bridge would be fired at by the bandit sentry hidden across the stream.

Then the Forest guide jumped up and ran over the tree trunk so we leapt up and ran after him. On the far bank we stopped and knelt in the firing position, staring into the undergrowth, listening intently. Not a sound . . . none. The track went uphill through very thick undergrowth. We got organised into our usual march order, then forward, up the hill from the stream, expecting to come upon a bandit sentry post concealed just off the track. Suddenly, a sharp burst of automatic fire and some single shots.

Everyone dropped flat behind the nearest tree. Sharp orders from Lieutenant Nicholl, 'Everybody up, packs off, get forward!' I was feeling a wee bit scared but as soon as I stood up all fear vanished.

Behind me I heard Lance-Corporal Laurie giving orders to his Bren group: 'Follow me Bren group. Right! Right! Right!' This 'Right' wasn't just an order, it was also to let the Platoon's Commander know where the Bren group had gone, a very necessary order in such thick country.

The rest of us spread out in line, on either side of the track. I was on the left-hand side of the track with Lieutenant Nicholl on the right. I could see two riflemen on my left, but no one else was visible. 'Push on, push on!' A waving of arms as a signal and about another twenty yards further forward we heard a burst of Bren gun fire. It sounded as though half a magazine, twelve to fifteen rounds, had been fired. We all dropped or crouched down to the ground and I could see Lieutenant Nicholl and the man on my left both kneeling on one knee, looking hard forward.

The rifleman stoop upright very slowly, then slowly knelt again. Lieutenant Nicholl gave the order 'Forward' with a wave of his arm. 'Got one, he's behind that big log,' someone said to the Platoon Commander. We went forward to the top of the hill but there was not a sound or a sign of anyone.

So now we had a dead bandit who we covered with branches. I saw no sign of any weapon, but he may not have been carrying one, or his companions may have picked it up before they ran off. The patrol's front scouts, who had fired first, said they saw three men in khaki uniforms walking towards them. The second burst of firing had been Private Owens, the front Bren gunner, shooting at the bandit as he tried to run away.

What happened was this: our leading scout, a Lance-Corporal, armed with a Sten gun, saw the bandits and fired at them, wounding one. The wounded bandit crawled off the track into the undergrowth. We formed a line, and advanced, the bandit heard us coming and tried to get away by climbing over the big tree trunk. Owens saw him and shot him. The bandit was about ten yards or so off the track when that happened.

The patrol carried on up and over the hill, searching for the bandit camp which we were sure was somewhere near, but we found nothing. Lieutenant Nicholl decided to turn about, retracing our steps, and go back down the track to where he had first picked up the signs of men walking through the mud. After a while we stopped for a brew-up. Several of the men ate nothing, or very little, still too tense and wound up from our first real meeting with the Communist bandits.

I shared a tin of Huntley & Palmer's fruit cake with Corporal

Ken Barritt. No one else wanted any but I remember Ken Barritt saying, 'Well, I can go home a satisfied bloke now. I was thinking I would never get to hear a shot fired in anger.'

Another tale of jungle soldiering comes from Sergeant David Cridge of the 1st Bn., Somerset Light Infantry:

I still vividly remember the Malayan Emergency, though it's over forty years since the Advance Party of the Somerset Light Infantry, about thirty strong, boarded a troop ship at Liverpool and steamed off to Singapore.

We had a lot to learn, but there were a few basics, such as how and where to build your night shelter, the layout of a base camp, toilet and water point, sentry positioning, and quick meal preparation, taking into consideration the sudden nightfall in Malaya.

The battalion was based at Kuala Lumpur, and the four rifle companies were given areas directly around the capital, but all were based far enough away from each other to be completely independent. We learned jungle warfare mainly by experience, in my case by getting lost for thirty-six hours in the swamps, trying to work out why I couldn't find the river clearly marked on my map.

Shortly after we had settled into our area, the whole company went into the jungle on a sort of 'see how it goes' basis. The Major took the lead, with his three Platoon Leaders, all 2nd Lieutenants, close by. The three platoons stretched out over two hundred yards at times. A company patrol isn't very practical, and after a few hours a good dry base area was found and a camp made. An initial immediate area search patrol ensured that no terrorists were in the area, although I felt sure every living thing within half a mile would have been aware that a large force was present.

The following morning I was ordered on patrol with six men of my platoon. At briefing I was shown exactly where we were on the map, exactly where I had to patrol, including the one obvious turning point, the branch of a small river. The advice I had been given about the unreliability of the maps was completely overridden by the authority of the Briefing Officer who made it sound so easy. In fact, there are two types of jungle in which navigation can be done only by compass: swamp or secondary jungle, and I was heading into swamp.

Close on noon, we were still travelling north, and there hadn't been any sign of running water, let alone a stream. We stopped for a break, then we turned due east, relying solely on compass and distance estimates. At 2pm I decided to turn south and hoped that if we pushed on a bit, by 5pm we would be level with or slightly north of base, but the going was hard and it became too late and too dangerous to head in towards the camp after dark. So we had to make the best of things and hunch against the trees that had roots above the water level.

We were all fit and young and a night out, soaking wet, hungry, being attacked by mosquitoes, would do us no harm, and one of the lads had decided to bring along a chocolate bar and a tin of fish, just in case. In the morning we discovered the leeches had found us, dropping off inside our jackets, trousers and boots, after bloating their bodies with our blood.

We got going again and after about one and a half hours. When we should have been getting close to base, we slowed, looking and listening for signs. In mid-afternoon, travelling slowly west, the leading scout heard English voices. It was a patrol heading out and although it was dangerous we stopped them. I never got lost again. In fact I developed an almost native sense of direction over the next three years.

Late one night a Tamil rubber tapper called at the local police station and said he was going to meet two CTs just after dawn, taking them food. He was to meet them in the middle of a rubber plantation, and the Lieutenant picked eight from the platoon, with me as the NCO. We were to go in with the Tamil guide before first light and form an ambush covering the meeting area. 'Don't get too excited lads,' said the officer, 'and don't kill the informer.' We had two Bren guns, one to be sited at either end of the ambush.

Our officer made one thing clear: he would open the firing. The idea was to give the Tamil a chance to get clear before we shot the CTs, but what we hadn't taken into account was that when resting or talking it is customary for Chinese and Indians to adopt a squatting position. Sure enough, our man was tapping the rubber tree within fifty yards of us just after dawn when two Chinese men approached him. They squatted on the main track, and although almost in the centre of the 'killing zone', they could not be seen.

The officer was next to me and he kept popping up and down to try and get a view. After what seemed ages the Tamil walked away from the CTs, who quickly started back the way they came. I felt there was not much chance of their escape but I was still a little concerned. The Tamil hadn't got too far away when the officer made the first shot. Now, unless you hit a vital spot with a shot from a carbine you don't stop anything, and he didn't; the CTs started running but they were heading towards a Bren gun position which opened up 'on auto', firing bursts.

Now the CTs were screaming and changing direction away towards the other Bren, which also opened fire. They were now at right angles to the killing zone and running away. We all gave chase except for the Bren gunners who shut down. One CT dropped to the ground and the other collapsed, riddled but still alive. He asked for water and our Officer gave him some before the man died. It seems cruel now but it was our job.

Shortly after one successful operation we suffered two setbacks. The first involved a young and likeable corporal, who had joined the Army from a Boys' Home and made it his life. He made one mistake. His briefing was 'A straightforward patrol through light jungle and rubber plantation, with no other friendly forces in the area.' He knew the Malay Police were wearing jungle hats with a blue band. He led his patrol quietly and professionally with an Iban as his guide. The sudden appearance of another patrol in his area only led him to believe it was Malays off course, and the wearing of blue bands on their hats confirmed his suspicions.

I had always been suspicious of meeting 'Friendly' forces by accident, but the corporal shouted, 'Halt!' The other patrol (believed to be CTs) promptly opened fire and ran. The corporal lay dead, shot in the head, and in the total confusion the assailants got away.

The second setback took me right back to where I started my story – getting lost over two years previously. The Platoon was always receiving new men to replace those who had done their time and gone home. I was the only original now, and my new officer, a smashing fellow, would, I thought, see us through to the end of our tour. He immediately blended into the Platoon, turned a blind eye to my complete disregard of bullshit, and we were getting on fine until a mistake was made.

The Platoon, minus me – I was on educational training – had gone out for a three-day patrol. On stopping to prepare their first base camp the officer decided it would be quicker to conduct the usual area search with two patrols instead of the normal one. He left an experienced corporal with the remainder of the Platoon, while he led out one small patrol. A very inexperienced corporal led the other.

Not only did the two patrols stray, but on their return towards base they ran into each other. Apparently the corporal's patrol became aware of the approach of the officer's patrol and immediately opened fire. Because the return of fire was so fierce the two patrols soon realised a mistake had been made, but not before our officer was a fatal casualty; before he died, he said, 'Tell the Sergeant it was my fault.'

We didn't get a replacement officer. There were only a few months left to our tour and I readily accepted the responsibility of running the platoon for the remaining time. I felt it was the least I could do, and a few months later I was proud to lead my platoon as the Battalion marched through our county town of Taunton.

A large number of the soldiers serving in Malaya were National Servicemen, two year draftees, conscripts. One on them was Walter Gregory, now a Canadian, then a signaller in the Coldstream Guards of the 2nd Guards Brigade. Walter Gregory has some comments about relations between the planters and the private soldiers:

There were very few National Servicemen in the Guards. The Guards didn't want them so they treated them just like Regulars; if you know the Guards that was bad enough. In fact, there were so few National Servicemen in the Guards that when my two years was up it took an extra three months before I could convince anyone that I should be released. My National Service colleagues and I had volunteered for the Guards and for Malaya. Soon after reaching the 2nd Bn. I became attached to the Signals Platoon, and was on patrol most of the time.

There is a photograph somewhere of Coldstreamers carrying a CT body out of the jungle, tied to a pole; the path beneath their feet indicates they were near a village and it was usual for bodies to be laid out in the village market place for a while as a hint or a warning. The first body I saw on base was a young woman with her breast shot off.

Later on, when we were in deep jungle it became easier to have the Iban lop off CT heads or hands rather than bring out the whole body. A Labour MP, Bessie Braddock, made a terrible fuss about that; there was one newspaper article with headlines yelling something like 'Mothers of England, do you know what your sons are doing?'

Bessie Braddock did not like prisoners being transported by truck with their hands handcuffed to the overhead bars. At least we took prisoners; the bandits didn't.

There was also the feeling that the British planters had little respect for ordinary soldiers; we felt we were doing all the dirty work and protecting their way of life.

For example, most patrols started or finished at a tin mine, rubber or tea plantation; rarely did we see a white face. The British officer would disappear into the office or bungalow on his own, while the men were left to hang about outside. This is the sort of treatment the British soldier has put up with for centuries from his own people. A nod, a wave of the hand, would have been nice and worked wonders. On places run by the Chinese or Malays at least they would send us out an urn of tea or cool drinks.

The expatriate community had a lot to put up with in Malaya but most of the hard, dirty work was done by young soldiers, British, Gurkha or Malay, who got little thanks for it, either from politicians at home or from the expatriate community in Malaya. Many of the latter had served in the Army and should have known better. Shrugging their shoulders, the 'squaddies' simply got on with the job, ticking off the days until the flight home.

While the soldiers combed the jungle much work was being done to improve anti-Communist propaganda, with messages aimed at the CTs still in the jungle and at their Min Yeun and Communist party supporters in the cities and settlements. This, together with improved intelligence by the Security Forces, led to a steady decline in support for the CT gangs, an increase in surrenders and a rise in the number of successful contacts. The power and effectiveness of the Communist campaign began to ebb away, and with the prospect of national elections and an independent Malaya, the Communists decided to give up the 'armed struggle' and take part in the normal political process, at least until the British had left.

This decision led to a meeting in the jungle between Chin Peng and Tunku Abdul Rahman, leader of the main Malayan political group, the multi-racial Alliance Party, in December 1955. Since the Tunku insisted that only those parties loyal to the idea of a free and democratic Malay Government could share in the political process, this meeting ended in failure. The Communists were not allowed to interrupt the process of independence, which came eighteen months later, in August 1957, and Tunku Abdul Rahman's Alliance Party remained in power for the next fifteen years.

While the High Commissioner and the Malay politicians were planning the future, the war in the jungle went on, with a rising number of successful operations. One of the most successful units at about the time of independence was the 1st Battalion, The Rifle Brigade, in which Captain Frank Kitson was commanding 'S' Company.

Kitson was a far-sighted officer with firm views on how anti-terrorist operations should be conducted and especially on the use of intelligence to provide the fighting units with contacts and kills.

Others will have told you what the jungle was like, how many hours had to be put in before you had hope of a contact. In Malaya a battalion might hope to kill one terrorist a month, if they were hard working and lucky. The basic method was either 'cordon and search' or relentless patrolling, but I have always believed that intelligence – information – is the key.

It was also clear to me that such information would never be available in a terrorist situation unless we prepared for it in advance. Fortunately, there was a lot of background information available and all it needed was for someone to put it into shape, apply it to the information we had from our people on the ground and work out likely points of contact.

The police and Special Branch will often know a lot about a terrorist or a terrorist group: who leads it, their background, where they live, what else they have got up to and so on. The troops on the ground tend to neglect or ignore this, because what they want is not 'background' information but 'contact' information that will put a terrorist in front of their rifle sights.

My theory was that with the right background information we would know who we were up against and could make a reasonable guess about what they would do and where they might go. Exploiting *background* information will give you *contact* information. I had tried it out with pseudo gangs in Kenya and now I wanted to try it out with ordinary soldiers in Malaya.

What Kitson and his soldiers did in Malaya was remarkable, a model of what a crack Army unit can achieve if supplied with good intelligence.

The Battalion was based in North Jahore and 'S' Company found itself responsible for an area of about five hundred square miles of jungle, swamp and rubber plantation containing a number of CT gangs. By the time Kitson and 'S' Company moved to North Jahore, the battalion had about four months left to serve in Malaya before they left for home.

Frank Kitson continues:

I arrived in Malaya in January 1957, the year of independence, but there were still plenty of CTs about. The Special Branch in Maur and Segamat had given me lots of details on Communist organisation and the lives and personalities of the leaders in my area: I knew that the senior terrorist leader was Ah Chien. I knew how many branches they had, who the Branch leaders were, and where they had been operating until quite recently. Most of this came from informers or the interrogation of surrendered terrorists. The sum of it was that there were six gangs in my area and a total of thirty-six active CTs. Our aim was to get the lot.

They did not live in deep jungle; they had to come out from time to time into the rubber plantations, to spread the doctrine and gather food. It seemed that the best hope of contact was when they came out, so we needed to work out when and where, taking each group in turn. The first two were the eight-strong Grisek Branch and the ten-strong Kebun Bahru branch. I spent a lot of time at the Special Branch offices and we went through the background of every one of the thirty-six terrorists in our area, who their friends and relations were, their methods of work . . . everything. Special Branch also came up with two surrendered terrorists, ex-members of the Keban Behur Branch who had been operating in the area for years. By the time the troops arrived I had a plan.

For the Keban Bahur Branch we settled on Mount Ophir as a likely area for their base. We elected to patrol two likely areas in the rubber where they might come out to make contact, and to ambush the most likely routes which they might chose on the way in and out of the jungle. They had to cross the main Segamat-to-Muar road, and after a certain amount of calculation we settled on four areas to ambush.

Although there is more to Captain Kitson's methods than there is space to describe here, the elements of this procedure are now evident: know your enemy, study his ways, examine his operational area and narrow down the areas to patrol and ambush. The effect of this is to increase the likelihood of contact: after that it depends on the skill and tenacity of the individual soldier and Kitson's soldiers did not let him down.

Captain Kitson again: 'We laid our ambushes and settled down to wait, which is the worst part, and after six days and no contacts my faith in the idea began to waver. It was a terrible night of wind and rain. I had gone to bed and fallen asleep when – it seemed only seconds later – I woke up to find someone looming over me, dripping wet . . . one of the ambushes had made contact and a terrorist had been killed.'

After that, Kitson's men had contact after contact. The first man they killed was Leong Tek Chai, the District Committee Secretary. Soon afterwards a member of the Keban Bahur Branch surrendered after having killed another member of the gang, and this surrendered terrorist agreed to lead a patrol to the terrorists' camp on Mount Ophir. There they found a body in an advanced state of decomposition, ambushed the camp, and after a three-day wait killed yet another terrorist.

This confirmed Kitson's theory that the Keban Bahur Branch was based on Mount Ophir and patrol activity intensified, with gratifying results. A patrol under Sergeant Cassidy bumped into a group of three terrorists and killed them all. In less than a month the Company had killed five terrorists and caused two more to surrender, one of whom had killed his commander before coming in. Eight down out of thirty-six in such a short time was well above average. Kitson now began to apply his Intelligence information and methods against the other terrorist groups in his area.

The Grisik Branch now came in for close attention and results were not long in coming. A patrol under Sergeant Bagley went out to look for a terrorist camp and came under fire in thick jungle; Bagley and his men charged the camp and killed one terrorist as the rest fled. Leaving two men to guard the body and ambush the camp, Sergeant Bagley set off in pursuit. Two days later, word arrived that he had overtaken the terrorists and killed two more.

Ambushes and standing patrols were also successful. Two men, Corporal Bunny Brian and Rifleman Egbert Henry, a West Indian, set up an ambush near a rubber plantation and soon after dawn, when the workers arrived, a terrorist appeared on the scene and was shot down by Rifleman Henry; this turned out to be one of Ah Chien's personal followers. Another was killed in an ambush laid for Ah Chien himself: as a result of these losses other terrorists became disheartened and surrendered.

The result of Kitson's four-month campaign in North Jahore was the elimination of all terrorist activity in his operational area. By the time the Rifle Brigade left, more than half the terrorists there had been killed or captured; within days of the battalion leaving, ten more, including Ah Chien, came out of the jungle and surrendered, followed a few weeks later by all the rest.

By the time of Independence the British and their Commonwealth allies were clearly winning the war against the terrorists. Templer's two-and-a-half year rule was the watershed of the Emergency and by the time Templer left Malaya in 1954, his health affected by years of overwork, the back of the terrorist problem had been broken and the country marched on steadily to independence.

Templer's role was then divided, with General Sir Geoffrey Bourne taking over as Director of Operations, and Sir Donald Macgillary becoming High Commissioner. By early 1956 they were able to grade the country, the 'black' areas being those where the CT threat was still strong, the 'grey' areas where it was in decline, the 'white' areas where CT attacks were few and far between and the Emergency regulations could be relaxed.

The last sixty terrorists in the southern state of Jahore were eliminated by the end of 1959 but as early as mid-1956 a 'white' area had been established in the north, so cutting Chin Peng off from his safe areas in Thailand, isolating the gangs in Perak, Pehang and Selangor.

Each of these areas was then swept by constant patrols and combined Army–Police operations, giving the terrorists no time to rest or regroup. After independence which came on 31 August 1957, the British stayed on under the terms of the Anglo–Malayan Defence Agreement, fighting on in Malaya, and then during the 'Confrontation' with Indonesia in Borneo.

The last major operation of the Emergency came in January 1958 when seven battalions, British, Gurkha and Malay, began Operation Ginger in Perak. This went on for no less than fifteen months, and the meagre results, fifty terrorists killed, one hundred and twelve surrendered, indicate how few terrorists were left. Just over a year later, on 31 July 1960, the Malayan Emergency ended.

The war against the Communists in Malaya lasted twelve years and took a great toll of property and lives. Over ten thousand CTs were killed or captured before the Emergency ended. By then the CTs had killed over five thousand people – servicemen, policemen and civilians. Over five hundred of the dead were British soldiers.

Malaya was a great success on the political as well as the military front. The early commitment to independence was the key to internal stability which the Communists were never able to seriously disrupt, and in spite of the cost in money and lives of the jungle war, once the Briggs Plan was seen to work the Communist terrorists were on the road to defeat and a successful conclusion was never in doubt.

This winning combination of political astuteness and a willingness to use Britain's military strength was sadly lacking in some other parts of the Empire at this time. While Malaya was being brought to independence, the Empire in the Middle East was going through a very bad time indeed.

9

The Canal Zone: 1952–1956

*'The British had always opposed this enterprise but on
the day the Canal opened the British said to themselves,
"Il doit être à moi" – We have got to have it.'*

Monsieur Lemoinne, Address to the French Senate, 1884.

The story of Britain's involvement in Egypt is both long and
complicated and the events leading up to Operation Musketeer,
the Suez landings of November 1956, have certain similarities with
the Wolseley campaign of 1882, which first brought the British into
Egypt. The most striking similarity lies in the fact that both invasions
were triggered by arguments over external loans. The most striking
difference is that the Wolseley landings of 1882 were a military success
and the Suez landings of 1956 were a political disaster.

In the nineteenth century Egypt was a province of the Turkish
Empire, though ruled – or rather misruled – as an independent
state by a series of Viceroys or Khedives. All the Khedives had
larger ambitions. In 1831, the first Viceroy, Mehemet Ali, annexed
the Sudan, that great expanse of sand and swamp that lies to the
immediate south of Egypt, and his immediate successors, especially
the Khedive Ismail, ruined themselves in attempting to achieve the
twin ambitions of conquering the Sudan and modernising Egypt.

When the national resources proved unequal to the task, the
Egyptian rulers resorted to raising massive foreign loans which
they were unable to repay. Eventually two countries, Britain

and France, took over the management of Egypt's affairs. They appointed commissioners and imposed a system of government known as 'Dual Control', in which the Commissioners controlled the national revenues and shared the responsibility for Egypt's domestic and foreign affairs.

This foreign, Christian interference, upset the nationalists in Egypt, especially in the Army. In 1880 an Army Colonel, Ahmed Arabi, led a revolt against Dual Control which led to the Anglo-Egyptian War of 1882. The French declined to get involved in this conflict, having their own problems at other points along the North African shore, but a British fleet bombarded Alexandria, and a British Army under Lieutenant General Sir Garnet Wolseley landed at Ismailia and defeated Arabi at the Battle of Tel-el-Kebir. Arabi was exiled to Ceylon, the Egyptian ruler, the Khedive Tewfik, was totally discredited and the British ruled Egypt for the next seventy years.

Following the death of General Gordon at Khartoum in 1885 and the defeat of the Dervishes at Omdurman in 1889, the British also took over the Sudan. The British ran the Sudan as a 'condominium', the Anglo-Egyptian Sudan. This was nominally an Egyptian province, but actually a British colony and the Egyptians were barred by the British from any say in Sudanese affairs. The Sudanese people were quite happy about this, having no wish to fall again under Egyptian domination.

Apart from the desire to obtain repayment of massive loans and stamp out the endemic Sudanese slave trade, the chief reason for the Anglo-French interest in Egypt was the existence of the Suez Canal. The Suez Canal opened in 1869 and was at first owned partly by the Egyptian ruler, the Khedive Ismail, and partly by the Suez Canal Company, a French concern set up by the man who built the Suez Canal, Ferdinand de Lesseps. In 1875, attempting to stave off financial disaster by selling the last of his assets, the Khedive Ismail sold his shares in the Canal to the British Government for the bargain price of £4 million sterling and the Suez Canal Company became an Anglo-French concern.

In these late twentieth-century days the importance of the Suez Canal to Britain's imperial strategy in the post-Second World War period is hard to realise. The British Government had not yet given up its Imperial pretensions and the Suez Canal was seen as a vital link on the sea route to the Far East and Australasia, along a string of colonies that held the Empire together. This route ran from Britain to Gibraltar and then via Malta to the Canal. Around the Canal lay other bastions of the Empire trade route, Cyprus at the northern end, Aden to the south, while in the middle, along the west bank of the Canal lay the Canal Zone, a vast British military base with gun parks and airfields and a garrison of some eighty thousand men.

Britain's politicians and generals considered the Canal vital to Britain's commercial connections and Imperial military strategy. Troopers were still the main way of getting troops about and using the Suez Canal halved the time it might take to ship troops round the Cape to India and the Far East. More than two-thirds of the traffic through the Canal came from Britain's merchant fleet, trading with Australasia, the Far East and the oil states of the Gulf. The British campaigns against the Turks in the Great War and against Rommel in the Second World War had been fought to retain possession of that vital waterway and the British were still very anxious to hang on to it.

Before they took possession of the Canal Zone in the period just before the Second World War the British had effectively ruled Egypt, and it is fair to say they ruled it well. The first British Resident, Sir Evelyn Baring, later Lord Cromer, has been credited with the creation of modern Egypt and this claim withstands inspection. Baring took over Egypt in 1882 and by the time he left in 1907, Egypt had been transformed from a Levantine shambles to a prosperous, well-run, modern state.

Nevertheless, the Egyptian people were not happy. They might grudgingly concede that the British had acted fairly and administered the country well and without lining their own pockets, but the very presence of the British in their country, running the Army and public affairs, was an insult to their national pride, a daily reminder of the arrogant Western view that the Egyptians were incapable of running their own affairs. The British habit of referring to the Egyptians as 'Wogs' did not help either. The British Army, aware that this term did not endear the soldiers to the locals, made various attempts to stamp it out, not always successfully as Sergeant Chas Golder of the Royal Engineers relates:

> Glubb Pasha, the man who commanded the Arab Legion in Jordan, contended that the British officers and soldiers continually insulted

their Arab colleagues and that this should be stamped out. I think he was trying to hang on to his job after the Arabs were trounced by the Israelis in 1948–49, by blaming our general unpopularity on the uncouthness of the British squaddie.

Anyway, he was a Great Man and his word was law throughout the Zone so we had to attend lectures given by people who had met Glubb and could pass on his message. Our mentor was Major Muir, a no-nonsense Scot who usually called a spade a bloody shovel. He gave a lecture in the dining room where he laid out the new rules for the benefit of our simple soldier minds.

Rule 1: Only return fire if your head has been blown off and only then if in the camp area.

Rule 2: If being beaten up, lie down and cover your head with your hands. Never retaliate.

Rule 3: Do not haggle over prices in the bazaar. This is provocative behaviour.

Rule 4: Do not swear or call anyone a 'Wog'. Calling anyone a Wog is now a chargeable offence.

The Major then invited questions but his lecture was interrupted by a loud banging and yelling at the cookhouse door where a ghaffir was running up and down waving his arms, obviously with some urgent news to impart. Hostile questions from the squaddies and the banging on the door finally got to him . . . 'For Christ's sake!' he shouted. 'Will someone let that bloody Wog in?'

Soon afterwards I got to my office and found a traffic accident report on my desk. It concerned one of our vehicles which had collided with a Rolls-Royce near Cairo. Part of the driver's report read 'two Wogs were inside and their names were King Farouk and Ali Ismael'. I immediately summoned the driver and took him to task, telling him that he should not call King Farouk a wog, and he must rewrite the report.

Back it came; 'I asked them their names . . . they were King Farouk and another wog called Ali Ismael.'

E. V. Berriman was another British soldier who served in the Sudan and in the Canal Zone:

I spent almost the whole of 1948 in Khartoum, Sudan. There was very little unrest and what trouble there was took place between the Sudanese political parties and between the Sudanese and the Egyptians. The British, and especially the soldiers, were treated very courteously. I was then in Egypt on and off from 1949 until April 1953.

Basically, the Egyptians did not want us in their country and they made that quite plain. The big problem for the Army was the constant thieving; nothing was safe from the Egyptians, telephone cables, ammo, laundry. Half the Army was on guard in the Zone, or so it seemed.

As in other parts of the Empire, the British knew that sooner or later they would have to leave the Canal Zone. The question was when, and what sort of system would they leave behind? The Egyptians were constantly pointing out that they had a culture and were building temples and pyramids when the British were painting themselves blue and running around naked. The fact that their country was now a bankrupt, over-populated, feudal shambles was not considered relevant for it was, after all, their country.

The post-war period has provided countless examples of people who prefer to be ruled badly by their own kind than ruled well by foreigners and so it was in Egypt. Gradually, over the opening decades of the twentieth century, the Egyptians began to re-assert themselves. Though the process was interrupted by the two World Wars, Egypt gradually won back full independence from the British, and until 1952 did so without bloodshed.

The Turkish claims to Egypt were finally eliminated when Turkey sided with Germany during the Great War. In 1922 Egypt was declared an independent state and the first national elections were held. Following these events King Fuad was elected to head a constitutional government, on the British pattern. The British, however, did not go away. Britain refused to leave the country or hand the Sudan, that former Egyptian province, back to Egyptian control. This caused considerable resentment and in 1924 the Sirdar or C-in-C of the Egyptian Army, General Sir Lee Stack, was shot dead in the streets of Cairo. After that the gradual British withdrawal came to a stop for another twelve years.

In 1936, following the Italian invasion of Abyssinia and Libya, Egypt felt rather better about the British presence. The British Army was seen as a guarantee of national security and in 1936 the two countries negotiated an Anglo-Egyptian Treaty which put their relationships on a more even footing. British troops were to be withdrawn to the Canal Zone, which was to remain in British hands for twenty years, until 1956. The Anglo-Egyptian condominium over the Sudan was confirmed and the two countries agreed to cooperate in case of war. When the war came in 1939 the British Army re-entered Egypt, fought the Western Desert campaign, won the great battle at Alamein and saved Egypt – and the Suez Canal – from seizure by the German Afrika Korps.

Soon after the War was over, in 1946, the Egyptians asked for a revision of the 1936 Treaty. Their principal demands were for the immediate elimination of two main irritants to Egyptian self-esteem, the British presence in the Canal Zone and the continuation of the Anglo-Egyptian condominium – in reality British control – in the Sudan.

The British were not prepared to concede either point. The security of the Canal Zone was considered vital to Britain's strategic interests and if the Anglo-Egyptian condominium in the Sudan was to be wound up, the British, and more importantly the Sudanese, preferred that the Sudan should become an independent country. Indeed, Britain had already offered the Sudanese internal self-government as a prelude to independence.

When the British declined to comply with their demands, the Egyptians appealed to the newly established United Nations but anti-colonial attitudes were not yet flourishing at the UN and the Organisation declined to intervene.

The Egyptian Government then unilaterally declared that the 1936 Treaty was void and ordered her police and troops to start harassing British troops in the Canal Zone. By doing so Egypt put herself outside international law, for treaties freely entered into can only be changed or broken by agreement between the parties. Besides, the British were not likely to be forced out of the Zone by any army, let alone that of Egypt.

Egypt had felt able to make these moves because the Western Powers, especially the USA, were worried about the Russian threat to the Gulf oilfields and had declared at the United Nations that a vital waterway such as the Suez Canal should be an international responsibility. This declaration seemed to offer Egypt a way of levering the British out of the Canal Zone.

Matters were at an impasse when, in 1952, there was a revolt in Egypt and King Fuad's successor, King Farouk, was forced into exile. Egypt became a republic and Colonel Neguib took over. Neguib enjoyed only a brief hold on Egyptian affairs until he was deposed by a far more effective figure, Colonel Gamal Abdul Nasser.

Colonel Nasser was and is regarded by many Egyptians as a modern reincarnation of Colonel Ahmed Arabi, the man who had led the revolt against the Anglo–French control of his country in 1881–2. Again there are certain similarities though Colonel Nasser was no great soldier. His military adventures usually ended in disaster and the Israelis and the British, even the Yemenis, swiftly defeated any forces he deployed against them, however large.

On the other hand, Nasser was a politician of genius. By enlisting the support of a large number of small, Third World nations in the United Nations General Assembly and the growing, worldwide sentiment against imperialism and colonialism which was rife in the 1950s, he ran rings around the British and French in the Middle East. Following this success he remained a thorn in the side of Western politicians and a hero to those of the Third World until his death in 1970.

The story of the events which led up to the Anglo–French landings at Port Said in November 1956 is a complicated one, but two enduring factors influence the situation and should be borne in mind.

The first is Arab nationalism, which was then in full flood along the North African shore and in the Middle and Near East. The Arabs' usual state of chronic division, previously so useful to Western politicians, was not in evidence here for the Arabs were united by their hostility to the State of Israel which had humiliated the Arab armies in the war of 1948–9.

The Arabs could not accept that this defeat had been inflicted on their forces by Israel's tiny but highly motivated Army. The Arabs concluded that the Israelis had only managed to defeat them with aid provided secretly by Britain, France and the United States. In the early 1950s trouble was brewing for the Western Powers in Algeria, Egypt, Iraq, Jordan and Persia, and those Arab rulers still loyal to their Western Allies found their positions in peril.

The second strand in this tale was the growing competition between the United States and the Soviet Union for the goodwill of the 'Unaligned Nations' – now best imagined as the Third World

– and in particular for that of the oil-rich states of the Persian Gulf. To fend off Soviet intervention and ensure the support of the Unaligned Nations, the USA was more than ready to conspire against her Western allies, the colonial powers Britain and France.

Little benefit accrued from this action. The term 'Unaligned Nations' did not accurately describe the attitude of most Third World politicians – Nehru of India, Sukarno of Indonesia, Nkruma of Ghana and most of the other African and Asian leaders. Their policies were generally committed or aligned to those of Communist China and Soviet Russia. They could be relied upon to support the Soviet line at the UN and were vociferous in condemning the actions of the colonial, imperial, Western powers, though they were not unwilling to accept Western money, or even the help of Western troops, when their domestic policies failed and their people rose against them.

Britain, France and America had few friends in the Third World but their politicians seemed unwilling to face that fact. There was also a reluctance to face the fact that without the political will to enforce their policies, by force if need be, they would be increasingly sidelined by the Soviet Union and ignored by Third World politicians who, where they did not actually admire force, tended to be impressed by it. For the Western Powers, the advocates of freedom and democracy, force was not an option.

It had once been possible to control large areas of the world by the threat or use of military force – the so-called 'gunboat diplomacy' of the Victorian era – but the United Nations had been created to put an end to such solutions. It had also been possible to control or at least strongly influence the Arab nations by running their oil industries and playing on the inherent Arab tendency for dissension.

Now things were changing. The Arabs had learned that those who controlled the bulk of the world's oil supplies could command respect and attention simply by threatening to turn off the well taps. In 1952 the Prime Minister of Iran, Doctor Mossadeq, went a stage further and nationalised the Anglo–Iranian Oil Company. The British were duly outraged and sent a cruiser to the Gulf, but nothing came of it; the days of gunboat diplomacy were over and the Iranians kept control of their oil.

The Suez landings of 1956 – which actually took place at Port Said – were the most significant event in Britain's post-war Imperial history, but to set the scene for the Suez landings we must go back to the Canal Zone in 1952.

After the British refused to leave the Canal Zone, the Egyptians laid the Zone under siege. There was sniping at British sentries and grenade attacks on army convoys, most of them orchestrated or carried out by the Egyptian Police, who had been allowed to remain in the Zone to control the civilian population. Though these attacks had no great military significance they did lead to a number of British soldiers being killed and many others were wounded.

W. English went to the Canal Zone in 1954 with the 33rd Parachute Light Regiment RA, part of the 16th Parachute Brigade:

Our camp was at Geneifa, in the south of the Zone, the last camp before Suez. This was before the Suez landings in 1956 but a couple of years after the Canal Zone trouble had started. The Canal Zone was a dump. Where 'Geneifa' was we never found out. The camp was a tented one and the only amenities were a tent for a Naafi canteen, and up the road, at a place called Fayid, a cinema and the local bazaar. We were not allowed to go to any of the towns or cities outside the Zone, and if we went out in the Zone we had to go in groups or pairs.

We had to carry our weapons everywhere we went. We firmly believed the story that if you fired a round of ammunition, you had to produce a body and evidence of attack. We swam in the Canal but it was rather annoying to have to race for the bank when a cargo ship passed through, as they did constantly. We were prohibited from landing on the far side of the Canal and Egyptian police patrolled the streets of the local towns.

On guard we sat in slit trenches facing the desert. At night, when a cloud passed over the moon, you could swear that men were coming over the sand dunes. We were connected to the next trench by a piece of rope to which a can with a stone inside was attached. If you saw anything, you pulled on this rope to warn the next trench. If you had a nervous friend in the next trench, the can would rattle every time a cloud passed over the face of the moon.

When it was our turn to go to the docks to help unload the ships, we would leave camp early in the morning and travel by truck to Suez. The supplies were taken off the ship and loaded into lighters, which came alongside the docks for us to unload and stack in the godowns or warehouses. Heavy, hot work indeed. One day the Egyptians decided to give us a surprise and planted a time bomb in one of the culverts under the road. Happy to report, they got their timing wrong and it went off an hour before we reached the spot.

One day I went to Ismailia with one of the officers to re-stock the Officers' Mess bar. I was left outside the shops to guard the jeep while the officer went in to haggle with the Westernised Oriental Gentleman. I looked up to find an extremely large and hostile crowd gathering about thirty yards away. I already had a magazine fitted on my Sten, so I openly cocked the gun so that they could see me do it. Then came the stones.

I ducked inside the jeep and looked hopefully at the shop but there was no sign of the Captain, despite my silent pleas for him to put some '*jaldi*' in it. At long last he came out and loaded the booze in the back of the jeep. He saw me aiming my Sten at the crowd and asked what I thought I was doing. A large stone then hit the jeep and saved me the trouble of answering. He then asked, 'How long have they been here?' I told him ever since he had gone into the shop, adding, 'Shall I give 'em a burst?' 'Good God, no,' he said, 'We'll have the whole town on to us.' With some of the fastest gear changes I have ever seen, he got the jeep up to a very fast speed and drove straight at the crowd, and though we were hit with a few stones we got away without serious injury.

After what seemed like an eternity, my time was up, including the extra year that I had to serve because of the 'State of Emergency'. The boat rolled up and I said farewell to the land of sand and flies. I had been there for fourteen months and never got a chance to see any of the ancient sights. The Canal Zone was, for some unknown reason, the only place where British Servicemen had been on active service with over fifty killed and hundreds wounded and were not awarded a GSM – and no one will tell us why.

Julian Thompson, who was to command the British forces landing in the Falkland Islands in 1982, was then a nineteen-year-old 2nd Lieutenant in 40 Commando, Royal Marines:

I was in 'A' Troop under the old Commando organisation but 'A' had gone off to Malta on some swan, leaving me behind with 'S'

Troop. It will give you some idea of how ghastly the Canal Zone
was that the thought of 'A' Troop living it up in Malta made us all
envious. However, I remember the Canal Zone as the place where
I first fired a shot in anger.

The unit were at El Ballah and one of the tricks the locals got
up to was to drive us off the road, nudging our trucks and jeeps
into the Sweetwater Canal. There was no 'Yellow Card' in those
days and we were allowed to open fire if we considered ourselves
threatened.

So, we were in a big QL truck driving along by the Canal when
this huge truck came up alongside. I was riding in the cab and I
saw the Egyptian driver give an evil grin, pull ahead and start to
come over. He kept on coming and caught our truck one hell of
a bang, but fortunately our driver managed to keep control.

I thought this was a bloody dangerous practice that ought to be
discouraged but I only had a pistol and the Egyptian truck had
pulled ahead out of range. A QL had a port above the passenger
seat so I grabbed the driver's rifle, stood up and was ready to fire
when I discovered the rifle was not loaded.

I gave the driver a good cursing, got a clip from his linen bandolier,
loaded up and fired a few shots at the truck ahead, aiming at the
tyres. We were hurtling through a village at the time and I recall
seeing the locals leaping for shelter as we sped by. I don't think I
hit the truck but it put on speed and vanished up the road. When
we got back to camp I told the Colonel what I had done but I was
well within the rules and he was quite pleased.

One of our tasks at El Ballah was to guard a big ordnance depot.
By big I mean big, about five or six miles round the perimeter. At
first we used to patrol within the wire, to stop the locals coming
in and pinching watches and other goodies, but then the Troop
Commander decreed that we should go outside the wire and lay
ambushes.

I was not very keen on this because the depot was surrounded
by a minefield. This had been laid during the Second World War,
most of the markers were gone and the sand had drifted in, covering
some mines and exposing others. I thought this a bit dicey and I
said so but the Troop Commander told me to get on with it.

I then told my Section Sergeant, a Southern Irishman called Oliver,
and he said it was a bloody daft idea, but I had the answer and told

him we had to get on with it. So out we went at night, tiptoe-ing very carefully across the sand, hoping not to tread on something.

We got away with it but there were mines there because one morning just as we were coming back in some foolhardy person drove a jeep into the minefield and there was the most Almighty bang. The jeep drove over an anti-personnel mine and the rear wheel was blown off; had it driven over an anti-tank mine the jeep would have been blown to smithereens.

Service families were also affected by the situation, as Doris Golder relates:

In 1951 I was a young Army wife living in a privately rented flat near Moascar, not far from the railway. My anxieties started in about May, but my husband still had to leave me on my own at night at least every ten days to do camp duties at GHQ Fayid. I was pregnant at the time but that did not allow any privileges and none was expected; this was seen as Army life.

Convoys carrying personnel from GHQ Fayid to Ismailia were frequently stoned or fired upon but there were few casualties. Other terrorist activities included stretching wires across the road at neck height to decapitate despatch riders or people in jeeps, or setting up road blocks to get the soldiers out of their vehicles where they could be attacked, beaten up, even killed.

In the October of 1951 several hundred 'students' got off a train at the railway bridge and scrambled down the embankment to run amok in the flats occupied by Service families. The Egyptian authorities must have known what was intended as the train should not have stopped until it reached Ismailia. The rioters broke into the flats, looting and destroying. My block of flats was set on fire, but the Egyptian police who soon arrived did nothing to control the crowd.

However, two points do stick in my mind. This rabble, though insulting and frightening a lot of women and children, did not otherwise molest us in any way. The second is that although we were only four miles from the Moascar garrison, no troops came to our aid. This event happened after our husbands had gone to work and when they got back that evening they were all armed.

From then on all Servicemen carried arms as a matter of course.

Shopping became very difficult as the local traders were intimidated by Cairo's bully boys and forced to close down. Those who tried to resist were burned out or simply disappeared. The NAAFI store was also burned but they managed to continue trading from a trailer brought over from Cyprus.

Odd shots rang out through the day and night, and eventually it was decided that the families should go home. A couple of lads from the Lancashire Fusiliers came to help us pack and could not do enough for us, especially after my husband invited them to help finish off his booze. We lost a lot of our furniture including all my wedding presents, and I think the lads who served in the Zone deserve a medal. Those two Lancashire Fusiliers were so cheerful and brimming with confidence . . . they took all the tension out of the situation.

Soldiering in the Suez Canal zone certainly merited a campaign medal, for the fighting there went on for years and sometimes burst out into full-scale warfare.

In 1951 the military commander in the Zone was General Sir George Erskine, the officer who was later to take command in Kenya. After some months of harassment, ambushes and bombings he decided to make a few pre-emptive strikes against the Egyptian 'fedayeen' – or 'freedom fighters' – actually the Egyptian Police, who were harassing his depots and killing his men. At the end of January 1952 Erskine sent troops of the 1st Bn., The Lancashire Fusiliers to disarm the Egyptian police in Ismailia.

The Egyptians put up a fight, the 'cordon and search' operation escalated into a battle, more troops and even tanks had to be called in, and when the dust settled, fourteen Fusiliers had been killed or wounded. Egyptian police losses, killed and wounded, exceeded one hundred and fifty.

Harry Whitehead was serving in the Mortar Platoon of the 1st Bn., The Lancashire Fusiliers during this battle:

The sudden ear-splitting crash of a Centurion tank's gun shattered the dawn silence on Friday 25 January 1952. We had taken up position in French Square, Ismailia, around the police station and the Bureau Sanitaire. Our task was to disarm the Egyptian police and auxiliaries who had been carrying out acts of terrorism in the

Zone. Shortly after we had moved into position the Commander of our 3rd Infantry Brigade, Brigadier Exham, drove up to the police station in an armoured car and instructed the Police commander to have his men lay down their arms and come into the street.

There was then a long wait and eventually the Commander came out and said his men were unwilling to give up their arms. The Brigadier repeated his order and a loudspeaker then repeated the command in Arabic. Then a Centurion fired a 'blank' round, as a final warning. The Egyptians responded to this with a hail of fire from sandbagged positions on the roof and at the windows. This fire was promptly returned by the British troops supported by machine-guns on the tanks and armoured cars.

The Mortar Platoon carriers had been placed along the road by the police station and immediately came under fire from the defenders. A head appeared above the parapet, followed by the muzzle of a 50-calibre machine-gun which began to rake the carriers. My instant reaction was to do a back flip out of the carrier and we ran back to take cover in the block of flats used by RAF families. From there we joined in the fighting and could bring fire to bear on both buildings.

Meanwhile our RSM, 'Kitna' Price, was pacing about in the square, as calmly as if taking a Battalion parade, directing operations, keeping the men in order. The Bren gunner protecting our rear then drew my attention to a number of armed Egyptians who were running towards us down the street. On my command we opened fire on them and drove them to take cover in the nearby cemetery, from where they opened fire on us. One shot struck close to my head, so close I felt it pass, but you know the saying about a miss being as good as a mile.

Soon after that the RSM ordered me to take my men on to the roof and give covering fire as the lads stormed the police station with fixed bayonets. A brief but furious battle raged in the courtyard as the lads went in. Sergeant Haslam, a friend in another Company, told me that they had to fight their way in, clearing each area in turn, before the RSM forced the Egyptians to surrender and come out with their hands up.

The first lot packed it in about 11.40, two or three hundred police auxilaries surrendering to the battalions. An hour later the rest of them gave up and came out, carrying their wounded comrades.

We took about a thousand prisoners, many of them stating that they did not wish to fight but had been forced to do so by their officers.

The town was a mess, with burning buildings and walls reduced to rubble. We spent the rest of the day clearing up, removing the bodies and lining them up on the pavement. Ismailia was never the same again and the road along the Sweetwater Canal could not be travelled without attracting a burst of gunfire . . . we came to call it Sten Gun Alley.

During the final attack Sergeant Harry Foster, despite being wounded three times, led his platoon into the station under heavy rifle fire and continued to lead them until the position was taken. For this action Sergeant Foster was later awarded the George Medal.

Gallantry medals are not usually given without a campaign medal and the soldiers who served in the Canal Zone are still rightly aggrieved that their service has not been recognised with such a medal. The Lancashire Fusiliers lost five men killed and nine wounded in the fight at the police station.

On the following day, 26 January 1952, in reprisal for the battle at the police station in Ismailia, the Cairo mob took to the streets, looting British homes, attacking the offices of British companies and burning down such famous Anglo–Egyptian landmarks as Shepherd's Hotel and the Gazeira Club.

Alarmed for British lives, the Conservative Foreign Secretary, Sir Anthony Eden, authorised Erskine and the GOC British Forces in Libya to march on Cairo if need be, but the Cairo rioters were subdued by the Egyptian Army and the threat of invasion faded – for the moment. Trouble in the Canal Zone continued; between October 1951 and March 1952 fifty-four British servicemen were killed in the Canal Zone and sixty-nine more were seriously wounded.

The morale of the soldiers in the Zone was not affected by this trouble but the lack of support from politicians at home was more disturbing, as Sergeant Chas Golder recalls:

There was no general uprising against us in the Zone, in spite of constant exhortations on the radio from the 'Voice of the Arabs' in Cairo. This only led to stone throwing, though there were plenty of attacks on, and indeed killings of, British soldiers, but there was no popular support from the local people. They regarded the Muslim Brotherhood terrorists as criminals and would have nothing to do with them. My Egyptian friends voiced the main opinion: 'Who will give us work and feed us when the British are gone? Not those loud-mouths in Cairo.'

The propaganda war conducted by Radio Cairo had almost petered out when help came from an unexpected source. Dr Edith Summerskill, a Labour Government Minister, came out to the Middle East on a 'fact finding' mission. She must have been the only person in the Middle East to believe the newspaper and radio reports and accused the soldiers of stirring up trouble by being insensitive and ill-disciplined.

She then used the Egyptian radio and press to spread this message; the Egyptian politicians could not believe their luck and we could not understand why the British Labour Party should send such a daft bugger out on a delicate mission. Whether or not the GOC stood up to her, we never knew; what we did know was that she had the verbal dexterity and political clout to be taken seriously.

Dr Summerskill was not the first and by no means the last British politician to roam the world during the 'End of Empire' period, castigating the efforts of the British Government and the British Army. Further aid and comfort to their country's enemies came from certain sections of the Press and especially from the BBC. People from every corner of the Empire, from India in the 1940s to the South Atlantic campaign in the 1980s, remember instances where certain politicians and some elements in the media did their utmost to do down their country or their long–suffering servicemen.

July 1952 saw the military coup against King Farouk and by March 1953 Colonel Nasser was the leader of Egypt. Farouk's overthrow put a brief stop to the trouble in the Canal Zone and talks on a peaceful solution were resumed. The Egyptian aim was still to get the British out of the Canal Zone without delay and when negotiations broke down in October 1952 the Egyptian blockade of the Zone was resumed. It was about this time that the Americans entered the scene.

The main aim of British and United States policy at this time was to keep Russia out of the Middle East and away from those vital oilfields. In this they had more allies than they knew. The Kings and oil sheiks of Arabia were well aware of the threat to their rule posed by the Communist philosophy and would have come down on the side of the West in time of difficulty, if only for self-preservation. The Western Allies seemed unaware of the strength of their position and were impaled on the horns of the other Middle Eastern dilemma, Israel.

The Americans needed to placate both the Arab oil sheiks and the powerful Jewish-Zionist lobby in Washington and New York. One way to do that to the satisfaction of both parties was to play the anti-colonialist card and refuse to offer aid or comfort to Britain and France in their problems with the Arab nations, which would counterbalance United States' support for Israel. In Egypt the British had another problem, for the American Ambassador in Cairo at this time. Jefferson Caffrey, was an Irish-American and needed no encouragement from Washington to support the Egyptians in their struggle against the British.

Britain's economic position was still perilous. The pound had been devalued in 1949, strikes were damaging industry and rationing was still in force for some commodities, seven years after the end of the war. American economic assistance was vital and this gave Washington the necessary leverage. The American Government and the newly elected President Eisenhower, who took office in 1952, put pressure on the British to evacuate the Canal Zone and this pressure soon took effect.

By mid-1954 the British were actively considering a move to sovereign base areas in Cyprus, though here, too, there were rumblings of discontent against British colonial rule. The soldiers in the Zone knew little of this background but they knew that the Egyptians were still fighting against them.

Derek Duncan was in the Canal Zone with 33 Parachute Light Regiment and recalls daily life at this time for a soldier in the Zone:

The night before I arrived at El Ballah, on the Suez Canal, the Second-in-Command of my new regiment was shot. It was 1954 and the Egyptians, while not openly at war with the British, had the habit of firing off a few rounds into the camp from the surrounding darkness and then disappearing. On this occasion, one bullet found its mark.

In the previous months I had gone through basic training with the

Royal Artillery at Oswestry, then to Mons Officer Cadet School and finally the dreaded 'P' Company at Aldershot. With my wings came my posting to 33rd Parachute Light Regiment, Royal Artillery. I had wanted to serve in Airborne Forces since my school days. Gordon Grieve, who married one of my cousins, had fought at Arnhem, and two other cousins had been in XXX Corps trying to reach him, so I felt duty called me to the Airborne.

From a cold English summer I flew out via Malta, landing at Cairo airport in the heat of the Mediterranean sun. Cairo itself was out of bounds to off-duty soldiers, the ban having, I think, only just been imposed after the British had withdrawn into the Canal Zone.

A battered, sand-coloured jeep arrived in a swirl of dust, and I was greeted by Lieutenant Neville Morris, who threw my case into the back of the jeep and off we went to El Ballah. The roads were strips of black in the wastes of sand and approaching vehicles appeared to swim towards us in the shimmering haze. El Ballah was to the north of the Brigade's main camps. It was dusty and hot, but there were some shrubs as well as trees which looked a bit like birches. The few buildings were painted a blinding white. In a camp nearby were the Marines of 40 Commando.

I don't remember my first meeting with the CO or the others, though I came to know them all well. I was allotted a tent, a bed, a desk, a very English wardrobe and a chair or two were organised from somewhere, placed on the sand and moved about a bit so that they were more or less upright. Finally, Norman Lamont, like myself a National Service subaltern, who had arrived a few months earlier, pointed out that a mosquito net was more important than all the rest.

I remember the darkness of the night, the suddenness of the dawn, the sight of the sun as it broke into the sky, and the early arrival of the flies. Within a few minutes, the grinding heat of the day replaced the cool of the early morning. I kept out of the sun as much as I could, especially when we went into the desert on exercise, somewhere south of Suez. We fired our 75mm howitzers, hitched up, moved off, stopped, unhitched and fired again. The explosions and the clanging of the shell cases deafened me, the air was so dusty and the ground so harsh and rocky that I suffered on that first day. I got used to it, though, and came to appreciate just how professional our gun crews were. They had months and years of experience and I was just a new boy, finding that the theoretical gunnery I had learned at Mons really did work in practice.

Opposite the camp at El Ballah was one of the forts belonging to the Anglo-French company that ran the Suez Canal in those pre-Nasser days. At night, a small detachment would occupy the fort to prevent sabotage by the locals and because I was at a loose end I was often put in charge of the detachment. We all began the evening by swimming in the Canal to cool off. Then it was a question of a couple of men being on guard, with the rest ready to join them should anything happen.

One night, finding sleep impossible, I slid into the Canal again, without telling anyone. The sky was black, the stars incredibly bright and any movement threw up a marvellous phosphorescence in the water. The next thing I knew I was being challenged and I then came under fire from a couple of Stens. A hasty, terrified cry stopped the shooting and I was all right. Fortunately for me, Gunners are not at their most accurate with infantry weapons, but the expended ammunition had to be explained the next morning and I got a real dressing down from my Battery Commander.

My boots, 'bulled' to perfection at Mons, the National Service Officer Cadet School, suffered from exposure to the sand. Nevertheless, I repolished them every night. We also washed the previous day's clothes during the long lunchtime break and hung them on the guy-ropes of our tents; they dried in minutes. My father, who had served with some distinction in Mesopotamia in the First World War and had then been a civil engineer in the Sudan, was anxious because the Army no longer wore pith helmets – he said it was essential to keep the sun off the back of the neck. This was a fallacy because the Airborne beret was quite adequate and no one ever got sunstroke.

I was issued with a 9mm Browning automatic pistol and vaguely instructed in its use but I only drew it in anger once. There had been a spate of bombings and I was in a jeep going through the outskirts of Moascar on some mission or other, when an ancient Egyptian made as if to throw a paint tin into the vehicle. We screeched to a halt. Three hefty Gunners leapt out and politely remonstrated with the old man; in other words, they knocked him to the ground and grabbed the tin. It proved to be full of – yes – paint. I put my pistol back and we fled rather sheepishly into the town.

I think I did a couple of parachute jumps from a Valetta, but am not sure. I remember being on a dropping zone – the surface was soft sand – but I may have just been watching or keeping watchers at bay. Certainly, jumps were few and far between. Presumably, aircraft were mainly used for other purposes and no doubt fuel was expensive; things were as austere abroad as at home in the 1950s. As if to mock us, Egyptian paratroops in their dark brown uniforms, were jumping nearby.

These are my recollections of forty years ago but I have forgotten so much in the intervening years.

Early in 1954 pressure from Washington and the new American Ambassador in Cairo, Henry Byroade, led to a resumption of talks between the British and Colonel Nasser. Mr Byroade shared the anti-British, anti-colonial attitudes of his predecessor and the Anglo-Egyptian talks made little progress, not least because the Canal Zone lease was due to expire in two years anyway and the British needed that time to set up an alternative base in Cyprus.

The talks were also jeopardised by other talks between Britain, Iran, Iraq and Turkey, aimed at setting up a Middle East alliance called the Baghdad Pact. The sole aim of the Pact was to contain Soviet expansion towards the Gulf oilfields but Nasser chose to regard the Pact as a threat to his claim for leadership of the Arab world. The Americans, afraid of upsetting Nasser, refused to join, though the Baghdad Pact was the brainchild of the American Secretary-of-State, John Foster Dulles.

By 1954 the British Chiefs of Staff had come to the conclusion that the Canal could be adequately protected by maintaining troops in Aden, Cyprus and Kenya, provided they retained the right to re-occupy the Canal Zone in time of war or regional unrest.

To guard against 'regional unrest', which presumably meant trouble in Egypt or the Gulf oil states which looked to Britain for protection, the Chiefs of Staff wished to store a large amount of military hardware in the Zone and leave a number of troops behind to maintain it. The talks nearly broke down again when the British Prime Minister, Winston Churchill, wanted these maintenance detachments to be in uniform and Nasser wanted them in civilian clothes, but this point, too, was finally settled.

The Anglo-Egyptian agreement ending British occupation of the

Canal Zone was finally signed in October 1954. The terms included a clause confirming the rights of all nations to use the Suez Canal in times of peace, though the Egyptians promptly refused to let ships from Israel or bound for Israel use the Suez Canal at any time. The Egyptians then mounted coastal guns at Sharm-el-Shcik on the Red Sea coast to deny Israeli shipping access to the port of Eilat.

By the time this agreement was signed a number of British units, including the 3rd Commando Brigade, Royal Marines, had already been collected from Port Said by the cruisers HMS *Glasgow* and *Sheffield* and conveyed back to Malta, where the C-in-C HAFMED (Headquarters, Allied Forces, Mediterranean), Admiral Lord Louis Mountbatten, wished to keep his amphibious forces on hand for any urgent deployment.

British withdrawals continued over the next two years and the last British unit to leave, the 2nd Bn., The Grenadier Guards, sailed from Egypt in June 1956. Just six weeks later, on 26 July 1956, Nasser tore up the 1954 Anglo-Egyptian Agreement and nationalised the Suez Canal.

Under the Anglo-Egyptian agreement, Britain could return to the Zone if the Canal were ever threatened. Since they now considered that the Canal was threatened and because the nationalisation of the Canal was seen as a calculated slap in the face, the British and French now intended either to regain the Canal by political pressure or re-occupy the Canal Zone by force. The big question was, why had Nasser done this? The answer, put simply, was money.

Since coming to power in 1954 Nasser had been intent on re-arming and retraining the Egyptian Army – the largest in the Arab world – in order to assume the leadership of the Arab nations and lead a *jihad* against Israel. The stumbling block to that ambition was a Treaty, the 'Tripartite Declaration' of 1950, in which Britain, France and the United States had agreed to prevent another Arab–Israeli war by maintaining a balance of power in the region and restricting the sale of arms. Nasser could get economic aid in the West but his appeals for ships, heavy artillery, radar equipment and modern jet aircraft went unanswered. Then, in 1955, on a visit to the Conference of Non-Aligned Nations in Indonesia, he found a fresh source of supply – the Soviet Union.

In May 1955, the Soviet Ambassador in Cairo, Daniel Solod, offered Nasser unlimited quantities of modern military equipment, including MiG 15 fighters, T34 tanks and Ilyushin bombers, with lavish amounts of spares and training teams, the price to be paid by credits charged against the Egyptian cotton crop. On the surface, at least, this was a straight commercial transaction with no political strings attached.

It would take time to re-equip the Egyptian Army and retrain the Egyptians in the use of Soviet equipment; only when that had been done could Nasser launch an attack on Israel. In the meantime Nasser moved on to his second ambition, to build a great High Dam at Aswan. The Aswan High Dam was an economic undertaking of great importance to Egypt, for by controlling the Nile floods and generating hydro-electricity it would greatly increase the agricultural area in the Lower Nile Valley and give Egyptian industry a massive boost by supplying cheap hydro-electric power.

Nasser's Ministers looked to the West for the necessary finance and in December 1955 the American Secretary of State, John Foster Dulles, announced that the United States, Britain and the World Bank would jointly finance the Aswan High Dam. Then matters began to go wrong.

The Americans had been grievously upset by the Soviet-Egyptian arms deal. This not only removed a strong lever of American influence in the Middle East but also raised the possibility of another Arab-Israeli war as soon as the Egyptians were ready. The powerful Jewish Zionist lobby became most unhappy about this and took their complaints to Washington. US–Egyptian relations deteriorated still further when the Egyptians recognised Red China in May 1956.

The Egyptians were also upset. The World Bank, in negotiating terms for the loan, insisted on imposing certain financial conditions which reminded the touchy General Nasser of those attached to the Anglo-French loans made to the Khedive Ismail back in the 1870s. He regarded these perfectly normal banking conditions as implying that Egypt either could not manage her own economic affairs or intended to welsh on the debt. Fresh doubts arose in Cairo when the Egyptians heard that the Zionist lobby in Washington had put pressure on President Eisenhower's Administration to withdraw the loan offer entirely.

Nasser then over-reached himself. The Egyptian Ambassador in Washington was ordered to seek an interview with Secretary of State Dulles and demand immediate confirmation of the loan – with the threat that if the Western offer was withdrawn or even delayed, Nasser would accept a Soviet loan, which was already on the table. This threat proved a fatal error. Dulles heard the Ambassador out and then retorted that if the Egyptians had already negotiated a deal with the Russians, the Western offer would be withdrawn. The Ambassador withdrew discomforted, and the fat was in the fire.

Dulles had not consulted either the British Prime Minister, Anthony Eden, or the World Bank about this action, but neither of America's partners had any great objection. The Arabs, on the other hand, were outraged. Following their deeply felt suspicions that the Americans and British were secretly supporting Israel – though in fact the nation offering most support to Israel at this time was France – this welshing on the Aswan dam deal was the last straw.

The Arab nations promptly took reprisals. In Jordan King Hussein sacked the British commander of the Arab Legion, the British General, Glubb Pasha, and ordered him to leave the country within twenty-four hours. The 'Voice of the Arabs' radio in Cairo was soon pumping out Nasser's version of events to the Arab world, castigating the Americans and the British for their anti-Arab, pro-Zionist actions. When Nasser retaliated by nationalising the Suez Canal, his countrymen were jubilant and the Arab world in general crowed with satisfaction.

The nationalisation of the Suez Canal Company had been anticipated but informed opinion had it that the Egyptians would wait until the Canal Treaty expired in 1968. The first action of the British and French was to cut off funds to the nationalised company by directing the shipping companies to pay their Canal transit dues into an outside bank. They also ordered the British and French Canal pilots to withdraw from Egypt, declaring that the Egyptians lacked the competence to maintain the Canal or pilot ships through that narrow, hundred-mile-long waterway.

The second of these beliefs was soon found to be false; when the British and French pilots withdrew their services, Egyptian pilots took over and managed the transits perfectly well. The attempt to divert the Canal dues into a holding account in Switzerland was undermined when the American Secretary of State, John Foster Dulles, the man who had precipitated this crisis, refused to direct the American shipping companies to pay their dues outside Egypt. He also declined to discourage American seamen from accepting pilotage posts with the nationalised Canal Company.

Having observed the disastrous results of his recent dealings with Colonel Nasser, John Foster Dulles was now inclined to wait on events and apply diplomatic pressure over the matter of the Canal. His reluctance to support the Anglo–French position was also influenced by the fact that the other great international waterway, the Panama Canal, ran through another nation state – Panama – and was protected by another Canal Zone which was occupied in force by American troops.

The British had kept their part of the bargain and left their Canal Zone and Colonel Nasser had then welshed on the deal. Dulles had no wish to put ideas into Panamanian heads and elected to tread lightly over the Suez Canal question.

There was also a domestic reason; 1956 was an election year in the USA and President Eisenhower's re-election ticket presented him as a man of peace. If he was seen to be supporting the imperial colonial oppressors in their invasion of another country, the ghosts of Concord, Lexington and Bunker Hill would rise from their graves and blow his campaign to pieces. The Suez Canal was not vital to America's strategic interests, and if the British and French were humiliated by Nasser, that was not America's problem.

The Anglo-French regarded Nasser not as a reincarnated Arabi but as a tin-pot Hitler, whose ambitions had to be curbed as soon as possible. The British – and in particular the new Prime Minister, Anthony Eden – were quite determined not to let this affront pass by, regarding it as another Munich, a bitter reminder of that pre-war humiliation when a British Prime Minister accepted the word of Adolf Hitler, an act of weakness which led to the Second World War.

Eden had resigned from the pre-war British Government over the policy of appeasing Hitler and he was not going to appease Colonel Nasser. For their part, the French were already keen to topple Nasser, whom they suspected – correctly – of sending arms to the Muslims fighting French rule in Algeria.

The Anglo-French were therefore determined not to compromise with Nasser in any way. He must hand back the Suez Canal – or face the consequences. In this view the British Conservative Government under Anthony Eden at first enjoyed the support of the Labour Opposition. However, as positions hardened and the countries involved moved towards war, the face of unity at home and abroad began to crack.

Britain could have done without the Suez Canal crisis at this time, for her troops were still engaged in Malaya and Kenya and were facing a new terrorist challenge just to the north of Egypt, on the beautiful island of Cyprus.

10

The Troubles of
Cyprus: 1955–1959

*'When sorrows come, they come not single spies, but in
battalions.'*

Hamlet, IV, William Shakespeare.

By the middle of the 1950s, the intention of successive post-war
British Governments to turn the colonial Empire into a democratic
Commonwealth of free and independent states was running into
difficulty. By 1955 trouble was either brewing or already in place
in various parts of the Empire and Britain's military resources were
at full stretch.

In Africa the Mau-Mau trouble still gripped large areas of Kenya.
In Malaya a countrywide Emergency continued. In the Middle East
there were uncertainties over the wisdom of British withdrawal from
the Canal Zone in Egypt, and Aden was starting to simmer at the
foot of the Gulf. With all this going on, Britain did not need more
problems in the Crown Colony of Cyprus.

Nor were other parts of the Empire entirely quiescent. The British
colonies in West Africa, Central Africa and the Caribbean had found
leaders who were demanding independence from Britain with the
least possible delay, and the anti-colonial voices at the UN and in
the UK, supporting these demands, were becoming more strident
by the day.

To compound these problems there were strikes at home, problems with the economy and political uncertainty, for Winston Churchill had finally resigned from the office of Prime Minister and handed over to Anthony Eden. The old order was changing and the future looked uncertain.

There was one bright spot in the prevailing gloom. On 2 June 1953, Queen Elizabeth II came to the throne of her ancestors among scenes of almost medieval splendour. Her Coronation in June was a dazzling event when thousands of troops, from the two score countries and colonies of the Commonwealth and Empire, marched through the streets of London between cheering crowds in a display of pageantry, affection, loyalty and enthusiasm which even the dreary English weather could not dampen.

The newspapers and the programmes on the television sets, which were just coming into general use, were full of predictions hailing the dawn of a 'New Elizabethan Age', where prosperity and glory would return to gild the drab shores of Albion. For a moment everything seemed new and bright and hopeful. Only time – a relatively short time – would reveal just how hollow whose forecasts were to prove.

The flags and bunting came down, the troops went home, the politicians returned to dealing with their problems around the world and within two years they had a new one. In April 1955, to compound the problems in Africa and Asia, trouble broke out on the Mediterranean island of Cyprus.

Cyprus is a mountainous and very beautiful island on the western flank of the Middle East, a country with great commercial promise, a long and chequered history and one deep-rooted problem; the population of Cyprus mainly consists of two distinct communities, the Greeks and the Turks, and the two communities detested each other.

Cyprus has had a long and chequered history; ruled over down the centuries by the Lusignans, the Venetian Republic, the Ottoman Turks, and from the 1880s by the British, who acquired a lease on the island from the Sultan of Turkey after the Crimean War and annexed the island during the Great War of 1914–18 when Turkey joined forces with Germany.

Since that time Cyprus had served as the northern gatekeeper for the Suez Canal, but until the end of the Second World War Cyprus played no major part in Britain's strategic plans. Cyprus lacked a deep water port so the Royal Navy remained in Malta. The only airport was mainly used for civil aviation and the Army garrison remained small. Only in the 1950s did Cyprus start to figure in Cold War calculations as the Russian threat to the Middle East became clear and pressure mounted against the British in the Suez Canal Zone. Cyprus became important to Britain just at the moment the Greek Cypriots began their bid for independence and 'enosis' – union with Greece.

The important point to make now is that in all her long history, Cyprus has never belonged to the Greeks, though Greece may have had trading ports there during the pre-Christian era. However, during the late nineteenth and early twentieth centuries, the Greek proportion of the island's population gradually increased until they outnumbered the resident Turks, the descendants of families who had lived on Cyprus since the days of the Ottoman Empire.

The number of Greeks in Cyprus increased significantly in the 1920s when, following the Turkish–Greek War of 1920–1, the British offered sanctuary to Greeks driven out of Smyrna and other places on the Turkish mainland. This action, and what stemmed from it later, gives weight to the old saying that a good deed never goes unpunished.

During the 1950s, as the British gradually began to divest themselves of their Empire, the Greeks of Cyprus began to agitate for independence. In this aim they were at first joined by the minority Turkish community who also wanted independence. Then it became apparent to the British and Turks that the Greek Cypriots had not one aim but two.

First, they wished Cyprus to become independent from Britain. With that achieved, the Greek majority, backed by the Greek Church in Cyprus, intended to introduce enosis, and integrate Cyprus with their motherland of Greece. This Greek Cypriot intention dismayed the British and met with total opposition from the Turkish Cypriots. Once again, as in India and Palestine, the British found themselves in the middle of a national and religious conflict.

The Turkish resistance to enosis was supported by two factors, one historic, the other geographic. Turkey had ruled much of Greece and kept the Greeks in subjection from the fall of Constantinople in 1493 until the Greeks gained their freedom from the Turkish Empire in the early years of the nineteenth century. Since that time there had been abundant warfare and racial strife between the two countries and in those places where Greeks and Turks lived together, as in Cyprus, peace between the two communities was only maintained by the presence of the imperial power. There was no love lost between Greeks and Turks at any level and the idea of handing the large Turkish minority in Cyprus over to the Greeks was anathema to the Turkish people and the Turkish Government.

For the second factor it is only necessary to look at a map. Cyprus lies about fifty miles from the south coast of Turkey. From the top of the mountains above Kyrenia, on the north coast of Cyprus, it is possible to see the Turkish mainland quite clearly. Given the ever-delicate state of relations between the Greek and Turkish states, the Turks had no wish to find a large, Greek-held island just off their southern shore.

The British Government, and more to the point, the British Governor of Cyprus and the British troops of the small island garrison, found themselves caught between the warring communities, with both the Greek and Turkish Governments demanding justice – or compliance with the wishes of their respective nationals, which was not usually the same thing.

Such considerations apart, in 1954–5 when this problem came to a head, Britain had no particular wish to leave Cyprus. Since the Canal Zone was even then being evacuated, Cyprus was the only place from where Britain's strategic bombers could reach into Russia, or fly troops to the Gulf States. Kenya was too far away and gripped by rebellion, and Aden was regarded as one of the worst postings in the British service. Even the Royal Navy needed Cyprus as a base for the Eastern Mediterranean, for though the island lacked a deep water port it had sheltered bays and anchorages, and from the airfield at Nicosia the RAF could provide the Fleet with air cover. Cyprus also had an agreeable climate and good training facilities; the British intended to keep it and develop it into a major strategic base. The local Greeks had other ideas.

Geoffrey Plummer recalls Cyprus before the troubles began:

In 1951 I was asked to go to Cyprus to build, commission and manage a new cigarette factory. I can remember that when I

Assault ships closing in on the Suez Canal while more troops go ashore by helicopter.

3 Commando Brigade Sniper looking down Rue Mahrousa, Port Said.

Marines of 45 Commando waiting to embark, Malta 1956.

Marines of 45 Commando Rifle Troop in Port Said, November 1956.

Commando carrier HMS *Bulwark* on exercise in the Mediterranean.

Patrol of 45 Commando in the Radfan, Aden 1964.

Machine gun platoon of the Seaforth Highlanders on the Dhala Road, Aden 1965.

Soldier of First Battalion Parachute Regiment house-searching in Aden Colony.

Soldiers of the Argyll and Sutherland Highlanders in Crater, 1967.

Gurkhas of the 2nd/2nd Gurkha Rifles board a Whirlwind helicopter, Borneo 1965.

Gurkhas awaiting helicopters, Sarawak, November 1965.

Transport One, Borneo. Gurkhas and a Whirlwind helicopter, 1966.

Transport Two, Borneo. River patrol, 10th Gurkhas, 1965.

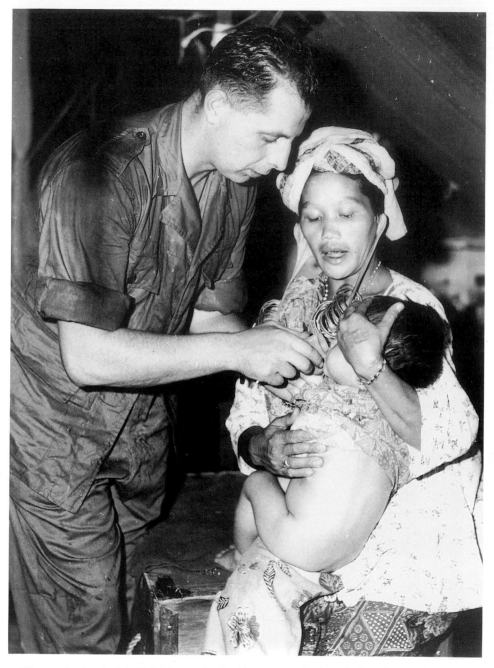

'Hearts and minds'. British medical officer attends Iban baby, Sarawak 1964.

told my friends where I was going, many of them said, 'Cyprus? Where's that?' How times change!

I was twenty-four years old and considered it a great opportunity to go into the big wide world and make a success of my first overseas posting. It was also the first time I had travelled by air, so the seventeen-hour flight from London via Nice, Rome and Athens was very exciting for me.

On landing at Nicosia airport I was surprised to see our agent standing at the bottom of the aircraft steps with a glass of beer in his hand. We walked straight through the Customs with no formalities and my luggage was waiting for me. Arrangements had been made for me to stay with an elderly English gentleman and his wife who took lodgers. I was charged £32 per month for the accommodation, including three meals each day. Many people used to think that those working overseas were always very well off, but I had great difficulty making ends meet on my £600 per year.

Life in Cyprus was very Colonial. I found it easy to settle in and I quickly made many friends. The Government staff were very nice and the centre of social life was the Nicosia Club. Practically all the 'expats' were members as were a lot of Greek and Turkish men from the business community. Most evenings and weekends members would gather at the club to talk, play snooker, tennis or swim, have a meal or just socialise. The club also kept in touch with clubs in other towns on the island, where we were always welcome. Drinking was the usual pastime, but not to excess.

I found Cyprus a wonderful place for my first overseas assignment. At that time Greeks and Turks lived together in harmony and we were able to move anywhere in complete safety by day or night. For eight months of the year much of our leisure time was spent on the beaches, enjoying the swimming and the warm climate.

Although my working life was hard it was very satisfying. I had a new factory to build and equip and a new labour force to train; all this in my early twenties. The local labour force was very adaptable and quick to learn. I was found a good foreman and forewoman who spoke English, and they quickly engaged our labour force. It should be remembered that although many people in Cyprus spoke English, by far the majority spoke only their own language.

We employed staff in the same ethnic ratio as the population,

70 per cent Greek and 30 per cent Turkish. Although the factory was built in the Turkish quarter of Nicosia, this did not cause any problems. At that time Greeks and Turks worked well together. I started to learn Greek but found all my employees were speaking good English before I was very proficient. Working hours were fairly long, forty-eight hours per week starting at 7.30 am each day. Air conditioning was not common, so by law all factories had to close for a two-hour lunch break during the hot summer weather.

Life continued pleasantly for some time. It was the time of ballroom dancing and evenings were spent at the Ledra Palace Hotel which had a very nice ballroom. The hotel is now (1996) on the border between Greek and Turkish areas and is occupied by the UN forces keeping the two sides apart.

Life changed in 1955 when EOKA started to carry out bombings and shootings. Large numbers of British troops arrived on the island and life, although still pleasant, was never the same again. As time went on, expatriate civilians became targets of the terrorists, and a number of my friends were killed. For two or three years we stopped going into the centre of Nicosia, to reduce the risk of becoming EOKA targets. As soon as I got to the factory each morning I would ring my wife to let her know I had arrived safely.

From about August 1955 the shooting of Service personnel became a regular occurrence, so the troops had to be careful and carry arms. We civilians used to travel about without much fear, by day and night, and visit the beaches and places of entertainment. The Turkish minority were pro-British and dead set against EOKA. Many of the Greeks were also against EOKA because they thought they were better off as they were. The police force, which was mainly controlled by British officers, soon became mostly a Turkish force as the Greek members were afraid to serve.

The problems caused by the Greek Cypriot bid for *enosis* affected everyone on the island, but Britain retained a strategic interest in Cyprus and was in no hurry to leave. This desire to hang on was intensified by the Anglo–Egyptian accord of 1954, by which the British agreed to leave the Suez Canal Zone. By doing so they lost control of that vital waterway and the means of access to the even more vital oilfields of the Middle East.

To protect her interests in the Middle East Britain therefore wished to retain a base in Cyprus and another in Aden, at the bottom of the Gulf of Suez, to protect the Canal and provide facilities from which to mount military operations in the Near and Middle East if need be.

The Greek Government, anxious to gain control of Cyprus, offered not only to grant Britain sovereign bases on the island but also to offer bases on the Greek islands or mainland if required. Britain, Greece and Turkey were all members of NATO and it was considered desirable to avoid conflict between the NATO powers. There was another, rather more fundamental reason why the British could not simply accept the Greek suggestion and walk away from the Cyprus situation: they had to consider the interests of the Turkish Cypriot minority.

The issue of independence was not in itself the problem between Britain and her former colonies. Britain had always intended to grant independence to the countries of the Empire, via a series of steps; internal self-government and dominion status leading to full independence. The usual arguments were over the time this process would take and the question of who would take up the reins of power and Government when the British left but it was also important to protect the interests of minority communities.

Empires bring together people who, in the non-imperial state, might either be mutually hostile or prefer to live apart. Under the protection of the imperial power these people mix and intermingle more or less peacefully but when the imperial power leaves and that restraint is removed, old enmities can emerge and fresh conflicts begin.

By 1955 this had happened in India and Palestine and Malaya and was to happen again in Northern Ireland, but it is a product of the Imperial situation and not confined to the British Empire alone. There are enough recent examples from the former Soviet Union, the former Yugoslavia, in the former Belgian Congo and in Rwanda and Zaire to prove that point.

The British aim was not simply to grant independence and depart but to leave behind a peaceful, economically viable, democratic state, friendly to the West in general and Britain in particular. That the British largely failed in this aim, at least in the short term, is not entirely their fault and no reason why the attempt should not have been made. Given the antipathy between various sections of the population and the inexperience of the local politicians in most of the former colonies, it is not hard to see, with hindsight, that civil war or civil unrest was almost inevitable after the British left.

In Cyprus, Britain could have accepted the Greek suggestion, built her military bases and radar stations, handed over power to Athens and departed, leaving the Greek Cypriots to deal with the Turkish Cypriots. Given the situation typified by the account above, it is not hard to imagine what the outcome would have been.

Apart from the fundamental fact that this scuttle would have been grossly unfair to the Turks and therefore not acceptable to the British Government or people, there was another reason. The mainland Turks would not have accepted the abandonment of their nationals to Greek control, and the Turkish mainland and the formidable Turkish Army lay just fifty miles from the north coast of Cyprus.

The Greek Cypriot desire for *enosis* found expression from 1952 in two men, the Archbishop of the Greek Orthdox Church in Cyprus, Archbishop Makarios III, and a Cypriot former soldier in the Greek Army, Colonel George Grivas. Though their aims were the same, independence followed by *enosis*, their methods were different.

Makarios was more than a religious leader. He was also the Ethnarch, the leader of the Greek community in Cyprus, the spokesman for their political ambitions. In 1955 Makarios was still a young man, just 42 years of age, an imposing figure and an astute politician.

Makarios believed that he could bounce the British out of Cyprus by applying diplomatic and political pressure and inciting the anti-colonial lobby in London, the United Nations, the Non-Aligned Nations, and in Washington. Anti-colonialism was the big issue of the 1950s and one which produced an instinctive reaction against the Imperial powers whenever it was raised, whatever the facts or the particular issue. It would remain this way until the Vietnam War distracted the attention of the media, the politicians, the United Nations and, above all, the United States.

As far as Makarios could judge, just playing the anti-colonial card and fudging the reality of the situation with the Turks and Turkey would be enough to get the British out of Cyprus. Colonel Grivas, his ally, believed in a more direct approach.

Grivas had spent most of the Second World War heading a guerrilla organisation in the Greek Islands. When the war was over he took part in the struggle against the Greek Communist Party, and by 1950 he was looking for a fresh cause. He found it in *enosis* and spent the years from 1951 to 1955 setting up a clandestine, terrorist organisation, EOKA, a Greek acronym for the 'National Organisation of the Cyprus Struggle'. Grivas's intentions were well known to the Greek Government and to Archbishop Makarios. Eventually they became known to the British.

Grivas made reconnaissance visits to Cyprus quite openly in 1951 and 1952 but when he returned again in early 1954 he was refused entry. He therefore returned secretly in November 1954 in a small sailing caique, the *Siren*, filled with arms and explosives. A second caique, the *St George*, also carrying arms and munitions, was intercepted off the north coast of Cyprus by the Royal Navy. It was this capture which alerted the British to the imminent start of a terrorist campaign.

Grivas believed that *enosis* needed publicity. The best way to attract the attention of the media was by creating incidents which would place the British Government and Army in a bad light. If he could provoke a reaction that could be used to present the British as oppressors, the true facts of the Cyprus situation and the interests of the Turks would all be drowned in a chorus of anti-British outrage.

His intention was to run a short terrorist campaign from bases in the Kyrenia and Troodos Mountains and he set up five gangs to carry out the task. The original aim was not to cause much loss of life or drive out the British by military means; that was seen to be impossible. Grivas thought that terrorism would draw attention to the Greek Cypriot cause and that the inevitable response of the security forces would help the Archbishop to present Britain's rule in Cyprus as despotic. Grivas also set up killer squads in the main towns. Their task was to kill any Greek Cypriot who found his actions distasteful or who declared *enosis* unwanted or unnecessary.

Makarios was well aware of Grivas's plans and was not greatly concerned about the bloodshed that might follow; his concern was whether Grivas's campaign would prove counter-productive politically, not least in Athens where the Greek Prime Minister had already refused to support anything other than peaceful pressure for *enosis*. Makarios did not see the shootings and bombings as morally wrong. He refused to condemn terrorist violence – though he complained loudly about the actions of the security forces – and for years gave his full support to Grivas's terrorist campaign.

Grivas's campaign began on 1 April 1955, with a series of bomb attacks throughout the island and the littering of streets with leaflets demanding *enosis* and signed 'Dighenis', his codename. These attacks did little damage, caused no injuries, and were soon discontinued, but tension mounted throughout the summer of 1955 and there was a great deal of unrest, especially in the Greek schools.

This pause in attacks allowed time for Makarios and Grivas to assess the reaction in Cyprus, Athens and at the UN. The general reaction was shock and horror; Cyprus was not some half-civilised, far-off country but a part of Europe, British rule was not tyrannical and the Greek and British people had been friends and allies for centuries. Few people could see any need for violence.

Violence, however, was Grivas's chosen path to *enosis* and his men were soon back on the attack. The main gangs were commanded by two men who were to become notorious, George Afxentiou and Markos Drakos. One of Drakos's first actions was an attempt on the life of the Governor, Sir Robert Armitage, by placing a bomb near his seat in a cinema in Nicosia. Fortunately the film ended early and the bomb exploded in an empty auditorium.

In June 1955 the island erupted again, with intercommunal rioting in Nicosia, Larnaca and Limassol and attacks on British troops by the EOKA mountain gangs, who set ambushes on roads and attacked police stations, to steal arms and ammunition.

Grivas did not have many fighting men. He relied for the bulk of his support on civil unrest and riot, for which the Greek Cypriot students and schoolchildren proved apt for his purpose. The sight of British troops and Cypriot police officers brawling with schoolchildren in the streets provided good sympathetic footage for the television screens in Athens and in the world press. Riots were easy to film or report and tended to make the headlines. The growing number of murders, of men and women shot in the back by EOKA, did not attract nearly so much attention and publicity.

Colonel Ian Wilson was in Cyprus with the Royal Engineers as the situation deteriorated:

One of the aspects of living in a potentially hostile environment is an increased sense of danger. I lived for two years with my family in a rented civilian house in the Greek Cypriot area of Limassol. Although the danger remained only potential, the precautions became second nature.

It became automatic to pick up and check a pistol when leaving my house: even my three-year-old daughter found nothing unusual in remarking, 'Got your gun, Daddy?' before I left the house, as if it were a natural dress accessory. It became normal to avoid routine, to vary timings and routes. Whenever I watered the garden I did so with my back to the house. My wife would always look up and down the road before I drove the car out and we all had a heightened sense of awareness for anything out of the ordinary, like someone loitering on the streets.

When the trouble began in April 1955, the British garrison on Cyprus consisted of just two infantry battalions, a regiment of the Royal Artillery and some squadrons of the Royal Engineers working on the new British base at Episkopi. Grivas was able to strike at will against the police and from early June his gangs were ambushing police and Army vehicles and attacking police stations.

The first death came on 19 June when an EOKA terrorist threw a grenade into the central police station in Nicosia. The explosion, perhaps inevitably, killed an innocent Greek bystander. It also injured a dozen Turks and infuriated the Turkish community. EOKA terrorism brought the Turks squarely behind the British Administration and there they remained until the Emergency was over.

Grivas did not confine himself to random attacks. A Greek Cypriot policeman, Constable Pullanis, was murdered for allegedly being too eager to do his duty against terrorism, a grenade thrown into a bar injured a British soldier in Famagusta and a bomb wrecked the home of the Commander-in-Chief Middle East, General Keightley. In July 1955, a sweep among known or suspected EOKA supporters picked up a number of gang leaders, including Drakos and Afxentiou, and they were imprisoned in Kyrenia Castle. A few days later a grenade attack killed a soldier of the Royal Scots. The first British soldier had died in Cyprus – but worse was to follow.

Two weeks after this killing, the British Prime Minister, Anthony Eden, called for a Tripartite Conference in London between the

Turkish, Greek and British Governments to consider the Cyprus issue. This announcement seemed to confuse Archbishop Makarios, who first told Grivas to stop the terror campaign and then flew to London to declare that the Conference was a snare for Greek Cypriot ambitions and that the Turkish Government had no right to be consulted about Cypriot affairs at all.

In spite of Makarios's objections the Conference went ahead on 29 August, 1955, with the Foreign Secretary, Harold Macmillan, in the chair. Macmillan offered the islanders a new constitution, granting internal self-government, with the participation of both Greece and Turkey in the island's affairs as interested parties.

The Conference promptly collapsed. The Greek Cypriots were only interested if the constitution paved the way for a Greek takeover and *enosis* while the Turks would only agree to internal self-government if the Greeks stopped demanding self-determination which, given the Greek majority among the population, would lead to *enosis*. Eden's initiative had been well meant but proved fruitless. The politicians had failed; it was time for the military to take over.

The first result of the failure of the Conference was violent intercommunal rioting in Nicosia. This culminated in the burning of the British Institute by students from the High School in September, followed a few nights later by the escape of sixteen EOKA prisoners from Kyrenia Castle. On that day the first troops of the crack 3rd Commando Brigade, Royal Marines arrived from Malta for deployment in Limassol and the Kyrenia Mountains.

'It was all go,' recalls an NCO of 'Sp' Troop 45 Commando:

We came from Malta in an aircraft carrier and had to trans-ship onto lighters at Famagusta as there were no quays. There I saw my seabag slip from an unloading net and plummet into the sea, taking with it my civvies and my best Blues. Fortunately we had no formal parades or much time off in Cyprus, so that hardly mattered.

Then we got into trucks and went off to a camp site on the south side of the Kyrenia Mountains and started to put up tents. We were still doing that at dusk when I was told to take my section and go up the mountain as an outlying piquet.

Off we went and it got dark, and then an Army Kinema Corporation truck arrived in the camp – just what we needed – and started to show the lads a film, a musical '*Seven Brides for Seven Brothers'*. We were watching it, taking turns with my field glasses, when there was another commotion and the entire unit rushed off into the night. Not having the faintest idea what was happening, we stayed up on the mountain till dawn and came down to discover they had gone to chase the EOKA prisoners who had escaped from Kyrenia Castle. We caught most of them but it was another twenty years before I saw the rest of *'Seven Brides for Seven Brothers'*.

Among those who escaped from Kyrenia Castle that night were Markos Drakos and George Afxeniou. The murderer of Constable Pullanis, Michael Caraolis, did not escape, was tried for the crime, found guilty and hanged.

Derek Lucas, a Marine in 40 Commando, arrived a few weeks later: 'I had been cruising on HMS *Surprise*, the Med Fleet despatch vessel – also the Admiral's yacht – when we were called back to our units. We went ashore in Kyrenia, twelve of us in the ship's motor launch, towing the ship's whaler filled with our kit. We were not expected and sat on the jetty, with not so much as a catapult between us, night coming on and nasty people in the hills. Then came the happy sound, the distant whine of a TCV engine and a burst of activity: '40 Commando . . . scurry . . . scurry, Lucas, you are "A" Troop, right? . . . Draw a rifle and fifty rounds . . . and so it started.'

Two weeks after the Commandos came ashore, Field Marshal Sir John Harding, recently retired as Chief of the Imperial General Staff, arrived as Governor and Commander-in-Chief. This followed the successful Malaya precedent of combining these two roles. Brigadier George Baker became Director of Operations, and the former Chief Constable of Warwickshire, Colonel Geoffrey White, became Commissioner of Police. Colonel White's first task was to send for three hundred British 'bobbies', who were deployed about the island and guaranteed both communities impartial policing.

Fresh drafts of police continued to arrive in Cyprus throughout the Emergency, among them Derek Snape from the Lancashire Constabulary:

I was born in 1933 and served my time in the 2nd Bn., The Parachute Regiment before coming out and joining the police. In 1958 I went to Cyprus and was deployed to a local police station to help the police contain the intercommunal trouble and deal with EOKA. I have to say that some of the Security people were right bastards to the local people.

I remember one time, at about four o'clock in the morning, a young Parachute officer came in with a Greek lorry driver in tow and ordered me to put the man under arrest for breaking curfew. I thought this was despicable as the man had just given him a lift, so when the officer had gone I gave the man a ticking off for being out during curfew and let him go.

I have to add that the local people were always trying it on with the troops, especially during searches, when they would come up and accuse the troops of deliberately breaking things or stealing. We then had to search the troops but we never found any evidence that they had taken anything.

I went back to Cyprus recently and it has changed so much . . . you wouldn't know the place. I took my daughter with me and she was amazed at the warm welcome I got in the villages and at the old police stations. I even met some former EOKA fighters, and like me, they're old men now, and there was no hostility at all.

In the autumn and winter of 1955–6 the security situation continued to deteriorate. Grivas now had a dozen well-equipped gangs operating in the Troodos and Kyrenia Mountains and plenty of Greek Cypriot informers in the Civil Service to keep him abreast of security measures. This leakage of information led to the failure of a massive December sweep of the island's many monasteries, where the monks were storing arms and giving food and shelter to the terrorists.

Not all the terrorist activity was in the towns or directed against the troops, though at the end of October a British sergeant was shot in the back and killed while walking through Nicosia. The main Post Office in Nicosia was blown up in November 1955 and a week later a grenade was thrown on to the floor during the Caledonian Society's annual dance at the Ledra Palace Hotel. Five People were seriously wounded, including the daughter of the Director of Intelligence.

The terrorist campaign in Cyprus was conducted on a stop and start basis. Just when the troops felt they had a grip on the situation, Makarios would call for more discussions or Grivas would announce a cease-fire. With the world's media everywhere and world opinion waiting to brand the British as aggressors, the troops had no option but to relax their grip and the terrorists duly slipped away to regroup. A few weeks later Grivas would strike again; this on-off action was to bedevil security force operations throughout the entire Emergency.

Harding declared a State of Emergency on the island in November 1955 and terrorist attacks continued throughout the winter, even while diplomatic activity continued in London, Athens, Ankara and Washington in the search for a peaceful solution. All attempts failed in the face of intransigence from Makarios who flatly refused to condemn terrorist activity or the taking of lives or to recognise the existence of the Turkish interest.

The taking of lives came to involve the Archbishop's own family. In the early winter months of 1956 an EOKA gang ambushed a Champ containing a lance-corporal and Captain Brian Coombe of the Royal Engineers. Captain Coombe's detachment of Sappers had been working with the Royal Marines of 45 Commando in the Troodos Mountains and had already lost two men in terrorist incidents. Now Captain Coombe was to level the score.

Captain Coombe was driving the Champ when the first burst of fire hit the vehicle, killing Lance-Corporal Morum. The Champ ran into the ditch where Coombe abandoned it and, taking his Sten gun, climbed up the slope to find himself overlooking a group of terrorists in the ambush position. He cocked his weapon, opened fire and for a few minutes shot it out with the group below.

Having fired off both his magazines and tried a few shots with his service revolver, Coombe went back to the crashed vehicle and retrieved the dead corporal's weapon, returning to his position on the ridge to renew his private fight with the terrorists. After a few more bursts there came shouts of 'Don't shoot, Don't shoot,' and three men came out of the gully below with their hands up.

This turned out to be a trap. As Coombe stood up to take their surrender, a fourth man fired at him from cover with a machine-gun. Coombe promptly shot down the three men in the open and then concentrated all his remaining ammunition on the machine-gunner. After a few moments he, too, gave up and shouting 'Don't shoot!' came out with his hands up, before making a run for it and vanishing over the rim of the gully, sped on his way by a further couple of shots from Coombe's revolver.

Coombe was now out of ammunition but the three wounded

terrorists on the slope did not know that. He kept them covered and engaged them in conversation, asking why they were doing this. One man replied that he was fighting to free Cyprus from the 'Hitlerite and Nazi British', a slogan apparently gleaned from Athens Radio. After about half an hour the high-pitched engine whine from the road below announced the arrival of a three-tonner, full of British infantry from the Gordon Highlanders who took charge of the prisoners and conveyed them to hospital and prison.

It transpired that the man who had fired on Coombe from cover and then fled across the ridge was their leader, Markos Drakos. One of the wounded terrorists, who later died from his injuries, turned out to be Haralambos Mouskos, a cousin of Archbishop Makarios. His funeral procession stretched for thirty miles and was attended by thousands of people. Lance-Corporal Morum was buried quietly by his regiment in the British Military Cemetery outside Nicosia.

During February there were constant bomb attacks on British troops and military installations. In March 1956 a major tragedy was narrowly averted when a bomb was discovered on a civil airliner about to take off for Britain full of British women and children. What such an action would have achieved is hard to understand but that narrowly prevented atrocity proved the last straw for Harding.

The Governor had made every attempt to find a solution to the situation and had held many meetings with Archbishop Makarios but to no avail. Every time a solution seemed in reach the Archbishop came up with fresh demands – an amnesty for EOKA killers or Greek control of internal security.

A week after the bomb was discovered on the aircraft, Archbishop Makarios and his henchman, the Bishop of Kyrenia, were arrested at Nicosia Airport as they were about to fly to Athens, and flown instead to exile in the Seychelles. A few weeks later Harding himself had a narrow escape from death when a bomb placed under his bed by a Greek Cypriot servant at Government House failed to explode.

The arrest of Makarios provoked riots in Cyprus and protests elsewhere, not least at the UN, protests which the British countered by releasing intelligence data showing the full extent of the Archbishop's involvement with the terrorist campaign. Inevitably, attempts were made to prove that the evidence of his terrorist involvement was forged but these attempts failed; the Archbishop's deportation was generally seen as completely justified. The British had silenced Makarios; now they turned their full attention to Colonel Grivas.

During the winter of 1955–6 more British units arrived, including the 16 Independent Parachute Brigade under Brigadier 'Tubby' Butler and the armoured cars of the Royal Horse Guards. Harding and Brigadier Baker now had fifteen battalions on the island, enough troops to control the towns and mount major sweeps in the Troodos Mountains. Within weeks, as the winter snows melted, the Army began to put relentless pressure on the mountain gangs.

Among the troops arriving was Corporal Tom Godwin of the 1st Bn., The Parachute Regiment:

The move out was by Shackelton aircraft and never have I been so cold and miserable for so long. Thirty-four of us were shoe-horned into the fuselage and the unlucky ones had to go into the observation turrets where they spent most of the flight blocking up airholes. We were part of the plan to keep Nasser in his place over the Suez Canal, but in the interim we were kept fit by 'tabbing' all over the Kyrenia and Troodos Mountains chasing EOKA. Early morning cordons and searches were often the order of the day in the villages.

Soldiers were allowed out into Nicosia in the evening, in uniform, in groups of no less than four, one armed, usually with a sub-machine-gun.

The Battalion was blessed with a superb Padre, called 'Horace', a large man who would storm through the Company lines on a Sunday morning, belting the tent canvas with a heavy blackthorn stick, shouting, 'Come on, you heathens, let's have you in Church.'

Another young soldier was Spike Hughes, who arrived in Cyprus in early 1956 to join 45 Commando in the Troodos Mountains, and who gives an account of soldiering in the winter-gripped hills:

About twenty NS Marines from 881 Squad, having completed Commando training at Bickleigh in Devon, left the slush and fog of Stanstead to sunbathe at Nicosia Airport, awaiting transport to Platres, then on to Troodos which was in deep snow at 6,000ft. This journey was the only occasion I ever wore my greatcoat. It did further service on my bed where in spite of six blankets I was still cold. I got frostbite on both feet but was not excused guard duties. Canvas 'mukluk' boots were worn but were the only white clothing we had so our winter camouflage was nil.

Fortunately the terrorists suffered from the cold as well, and the biggest threat was the Orderly Officer seeking out sentries hiding from the weather. Our contact instructions were a bit brief. 'On finding a possible terrorist you will say, HALT, STAMATA, DUR three times. If he hasn't fired at you by then you may fire one round. The punishment for firing a round unnecessarily or by accident is six months in the glass house.'

One or two donkeys wandering about at night were therefore shot by Marines reduced to gibbering insanity by a lack of response to their challenge. Everything froze and the cooks melted snow and decreed half a mug of tea was the ration. Most of us used this to shave in; we found it was better not to add sugar as this made it sticky and more likely to cause cuts.

When the weather broke we did a lot of village searches. These usually started in the middle of the night, with us being transported to some remote place, crossing the mountains in the dark in single file and surrounding the village. The searchers would go in at dawn, and were always greeted by the church bell ringing the alarm, to find nothing but blue and white EOKA flags flying from the Town Hall and church. We all wanted one for a souvenir but looting was strictly forbidden.

We nearly always worked with the 1st Bn. Gordon Highlanders and we got on very well together. They chalked their motto 'By Dand' on houses they searched, we chalked '45'. The Cypriots soon got the idea and did their own chalking, so we started using red paint, red being 45's colour. One day a local goat decided to drink the paint and there it stood wearing 'lipstick' with the owner going potty.

My favourite duty was vehicle guard, or 'riding shotgun', as we called it; sitting on the spare wheel behind the cab of a three-ton QL with a Bren gun, hoping that some bastard would try and ambush you, but also praying that they wouldn't. I also enjoyed the scenery a lot more up there while careering around the mountain roads – at least I had the chance to jump if the truck went over the edge. Looking back, our drivers were really good. Other units were always going off the road. Several times we were sent out to guard an army truck until the LAD could get out to recover it.

'Another duty was to guard the police stations. Some, like the one at Amiandos, were always being attacked, rocks, bombs thrown at it, all sorts. Others were uneventful. I spent a good month in the police station at Lania sunbathing between watches.'

The British Army also suffered a number of casualties from shoot-outs between their own patrols. This situation was not always easy to avoid, as one Parachute Regiment officer recalls:

When we went out we were given an area password and on this particular night it was 'Diana Dors', after a popular well-endowed film star of the day; challenge 'Diana', reply 'Dors', okay?

So, my patrol of 3 Para were ambling along in the dark, quiet in our rubber-soled boots, when we saw ahead the sparks from boot-studs and heard the 'effing and blinding that denoted the approach of a non-Para patrol.

As we got closer I gave them a cheery hail but their response was alarming; a shout, the rattle of rifle bolts and a swift leap into the ditch. Thinking they were about to open fire, we all leapt into the opposite ditch.

While I was wondering what to do next, they challenged us, and it went like this:

Voice: 'Oo goes there?'

Me: 'Diana.'

Voice: ''Oo?'

Me (again): 'Diana . . . DI-ANA.'

Voice (rising): ''Ooo?'

Me: 'Di-ana DORS'.

Voice (annoyed): 'Stop fucking about or I'll shoot you!'

Cyprus was a 'Corporal's War', a place where a great deal of the responsibility rested on the junior and senior NCOs, often quite young men, in their late teens or early twenties. They led patrols, guarded police stations, laid ambushes, countered riots and demonstrations, and put up with a great deal of hard work, discomfort and certainly in the towns, a lot of verbal abuse and stone throwing. To this can be added long hours, little sleep and the constant possibility of ambush or bomb attacks. Derek Lucas of 40 Commando recalls one painful incident:

I was standing in front of the mob, doing my bit for Queen and Country, when I saw this brick sailing through the air towards me – it had my name on it in flashing lights, honest! Being a bright young Marine, I bent down to avoid it hitting me in the chest, and caught it full in the face.

Now when you run your tongue over loose broken teeth, they feel like piano keys; my first thought was 'Will the ladies still go for a toothless hero?' My next thought was to get very Angry, with a capital 'A' so I spat out a mouthful of teeth and blood, picked up the brick and heaved it back. For this I got a ticking-off because throwing bricks back at the crowd is not fair . . . all this for twenty-eight shillings a week – about £1.40.

In May 1956, after the snows had melted. Brigadier Baker began a series of cordon and search sweeps in the Troodos Mountains and the Paphos forest in an attempt to eliminate the terrorist gangs. In the first operation, codenamed Operation Pepperpot, the Troodos hills around the Kykko Monastery were to be searched and cleared. The monks of Kykko Monastery were fervent supporters of *enosis* and Colonel Grivas, so a good haul was anticipated.

That done, the troops would move on to Operation Lucky Alphonse, in the Paphos Forest. The troops involved came from 40 and 45 Commando, Royal Marines, the 1st and 3rd Bns., The Parachute Regiment, the King's Own Yorkshire Light Infantry, the Gordon Highlanders and the Royal Norfolk Regiment, under the tactical command of Brigadier 'Tubby' Butler of the 16 Independent Parachute Brigade.

Spike Hughes of Sp (Support) Troop, 45 Commando remembers these operations:

In June we went on the ill-fated Operation Lucky Alphonse, the largest anti-terrorist operation ever undertaken in Cyprus. Troops included 40 and 45 Commandos, the Paras, the KOYLIs, the Gordons and the Norfolks. The plan was to surround a large area of the Paphos forest in sub-areas, like petals of a flower. The central area was called the 'magic circle' and Grivas and his merry men were supposed to be in there.

To make it more dramatic, and to get rid of unwanted ammunition, Vickers machine guns and three-inch mortars would fire on selected targets which were too difficult to search on foot. Good fun for us: at last a chance to fire our three-inch mortars! 'A' Troop were firing two-inch mortars at the same time.

We were firing away when suddenly we got the order. 'Cease Firing! Christ! We've dropped a bomb on "A" Troop! Check ranges and bearings.' The radios were red hot. We were nearest to 'A' Troop so we went to their aid. By the time we got there the medics had treated the wounded and there were four or five lads on stretchers. One Sergeant of 'A' Troop was roundly cursing us and accusing 'Sp' Troop of causing the accident.

Our Sergeant, Vic Pegler, was adamant we had not caused it. Whether a two-inch mortar bomb had hit an overhead branch or had exploded as it left the barrel . . . it was all speculation. Vic Pegler showed how upset he was by hurling a two-inch mortar on the ground and calling it an 'effing bastard toy', the only time I ever saw him lose his rag.

We manhandled the stretchers up to the top of the mountain, where the casualties were picked up by helicopter and taken to hospital. We were left to pick up the unused bombs and dismantle the mortars. We immediately noted that the bombs were well out of date. We also noted that the opposite hillside was alight. 'I suppose it will burn itself out,' someone said, but I was not so sure. The following day the fire had spread, the operation began to collapse and some nineteen British troops perished in the flames. Grivas and his men, if they were ever there, had all escaped.

We were often very tired, having spent long hours climbing over the mountains, day and night. One thing we found particularly irksome was returning to Platres and having to blanco white belt and gaiters for guard duty. I don't know whose idea it was that we should wear white gear, but it was a source of high amusement to 40 Commando and a great nuisance to us.

Apart from searching villages, we also searched areas of mountains and forests, looking for caves, caches of arms, chasing shadows. To manage these sweeps we were spaced out along a road about twenty-five yards apart and would then sweep up the hill with an officer or NCO keeping us in line and moving by compass direction. Our Troop Commander had an amazing compass: it always led him between mountain tops, resulting in the line being closed up on one side and extended on the other. In one fairly dense forest, my line was so extended that I lost touch with both sides and was obliged to guess my own direction for a good hour or so. I was convinced that this would be the time I should find a cave full of guns, or even worse, a cave full of terrorists.

The reaction of the locals as we passed through their towns varied. Most ignored us. Some threw bricks and bottles. Some threw us fruit. Some, usually older men, even saluted.

Operation 'Pepperpot', the first of these major sweeps, lasted for eleven days in May and was highly successful. The troops made dozens of 'contacts', four gangs were dispersed and seventeen terrorists captured, most of them at once turning Queen's Evidence to save their skins, and a large quantity of arms and ammunition was recovered.

The second major operation, 'Lucky Alphonse', began on 7 June. The troops broke up more gangs and scattered the terrorists across the mountains but lost the chance for major success when poor shooting enabled Colonel Grivas and a group of terrorists to escape unharmed from contact with a patrol of 3 Para near the village of Aya Arka.

The patrol did find Grivas's personal diary which gave full details of his meetings with Makarios and confirmed the Archbishop's involvement in the terror campaign. Then came tragedy when, as Spike Hughes has described, mortar fire set light to the tinder-dry forest and started a fire which killed more than twenty soldiers, most of them from the Gordon Highlanders.

Kykko Monastery was revealed as a major centre for EOKA activity, and carefully searched. This search was made under the supervision of British regimental padres who found a quantity of incriminating materiel, but was still condemned as desecration of a holy shrine by Athens Radio. One long-lasting effect of these two major sweeps was to flush Grivas and his main lieutenants out of the mountains: he withdrew to a safe house in Limassol and left the mountain fighting to other men.

The riots and patrol encounters went on throughout the summer as the attention of the world turned to the developing trouble with Egypt over the Suez Canal. The possibility of intervention there had its effect on the troops in Cyprus. In July 1956 the 3rd Commando Brigade was withdrawn to Malta for amphibious training and the 16th Independent Parachute Brigade began parachute training.

One year into the Emergency and with no solution in sight, the British Government decided to ignore Makarios and proceed with plans for internal self-government in Cyprus, the first step towards independence. In July 1956 Lord Radcliffe, the man who had drawn up the partition plans for India and Pakistan, was again called into service, this time to draw up a provisional constitution for Cyprus. This task had hardly begun when the Suez operation diverted higher minds to other tasks.

There were still plenty of troops on the island and in August 1956 Grivas called another of his 'cease-fires'. His forces had been badly disorganised by 'Pepperpot' and 'Lucky Alphonse' and he needed time to regroup. This the British were ill-advised enough to give him.

The civil population, most of whom only wanted to lead peaceful lives, were caught between the terrorists and the security forces and also needed a rest from tension. Apart from the EOKA killings that were taking place daily in the main towns of Nicosia, Limassol and Famagusta, where those reluctant to support Grivas were routinely murdered, they had to endure curfews, house-to-house searches and communal fines and there was growing unrest between the Greek and Turkish communities.

Grivas revoked his 'cease-fire' after two weeks and the violence continued as more and more British – and French – troops arrived on the island in the build-up for the Suez operation. Markos Drakos was now leading a killer squad in Nicosia where a grenade thrown into a restaurant killed the American Vice-Consul, William Boteler.

Grivas apologised for this attack, calling it 'a tragic error', and was very careful not to involve French troops in terrorist outrages, but in November alone his men mounted more than four hundred attacks – ambushes, shootings and bombings – against the British garrison. The casualty figures soared; in that month alone forty people were killed, half of them British soldiers.

After Suez, however, the odds again turned against him. By January 1957 Harding had eighteen infantry battalions on the island and these were turned loose on the EOKA gangs.

By the Spring of 1957 even Grivas had to admit that his forces were seriously depleted. Most of the EOKA leaders had either been killed or captured and the time seemed right for another 'cease-fire' and a further peace initiative. The Radcliffe proposals for a self-governing constitution met with approval in London and Ankara but the Greeks refused to discuss them as long as Makarios was detained in the Seychelles.

In a bid to force the British hand, Grivas offered yet another 'cease-fire' if his political leader was released. Once again, ever-anxious to be seen as conciliatory, the British agreed and Makarios was allowed back into Cyprus in the Spring of 1957, moving on almost at once to Athens where he renewed his campaign for *enosis*. The appeal of this dream was, however, fading among the Cypriot population.

By April 1957 the EOKA campaign had lasted two full years. The terrorists had set off more than thirteen hundred bombs, and killed seventy-eight British soldiers and nine British policemen, as well as sixteen British civilians, twelve Cypriot policemen and four Turks, a total of one hundred and nineteen people.

In return the British had killed fifty-one EOKA terrorists and imprisoned a further twenty-seven; some fifteen hundred had been detained on suspicion of terrorist activity. The terrorists were now taking casualties and among those killed were Markos Drakos and George Afxentiou, the latter trapped in a mountain cave by British troops.

What these statistics do not reveal is the daily horror of the Cyprus Emergency and the vicious nature of the numerous murders. In April 1956 a Greek Cypriot police superintendent, Kyriakos Sristotelos, was killed when visiting his wife and new-born child in a maternity hospital.

In May 1956, in response to the execution of two terrorists in Nicosia Gaol, Grivas hanged two captured British soldiers, Corporals Hill and Shilton. A young English couple, Mr and Mrs Patrick Karberry, were ambushed in their car, dragged from the vehicle and murdered when returning to Nicosia from the beach at Kyrenia. Mrs Karberry was heavily pregnant when she was shot down.

Such actions disgusted the British troops but although there were certainly incidents when rifle butts and entrenching tool handles were freely used, their discipline held. This was true even in the village of Lefkoniko in October 1956 when a bomb hidden under a water tap exploded when soldiers from the Highland Light Infantry had gathered around it for a drink.

There were a great many Highland soldiers in the village when the bomb went off and their subsequent search for the bomber did a lot of damage, but no villager was killed or even seriously injured. This did not prevent the usual visit from a British politician, in this case Barbara Castle, who arrived on the island in 1957 and returned home to condemn the brutality of British troops.

Tom Godwin of 1 Para, recalls some happenings during his time in Cyprus:

The battalion had its share of casualties, borne out by some of those carefully tended graves in the War Graves Cemetery in the buffer zone of now-divided Cyprus. I recall a certain Lance-corporal machine-gunner, who put a bullet between his feet, having forgotten to take the magazine out before cleaning his pistol. That might not be worth mentioning but he had just survived a month in hospital and in detention for having fired a bullet through his hand. He was a good machine-gunner but should never have been given a personal weapon.

Sod's Law also applied to civilians. During a cordon-and-seach we did on the village of Agios Avbrosios, we were part of the cordon and in position before first light. It is difficult to set up an effective cordon in the dark and at first light there is a bit of movement as you shift about to plug the gaps.

During this phase a guy broke cover and legged it through a gap in the cordon and down the mountain. Those who could see him were all yelling 'Halt . . . *Stammata-Dur*,' telling him to stop, but he sprinted on, and appeared to be carrying a rucksack and a weapon.

The Platoon Sergeant, who was no mean shot, dropped him with a shot through the head at two hundred yards; at the subsequent enquiry it turned out that the running man was a deaf-mute shepherd who was probably frightned, and the sergeant's back-sight had been set at 400 yards; such is Sod's Law.

Alan Staff, of C Company, 2 Para, remembers another incident:

This was in 1956, during a sweep called 'Sparrowhawk One'. We were at a farmhouse near Trapeza, using that as our base while we searched the area, when one of the lads poking about in the barn saw a face looking at him through a hole in the wall.

It must have given him a real turn because he fired a 9mm pistol at it. Five terrorists came out from a hide under the floor and we found a lot of arms and equipment; shotguns, bombs made of gas piping, ammo, even a watch, which I pinched but was ordered to give back. These blokes had prices on their heads, £5,000 apiece; I expect they have streets in Nicosia named after them today.

Well, we just guarded these blokes and were getting quite matey when the police arrived, Special Branch, and they were bastards. They really knocked these blokes about; I could hear them crying.

None of us liked this but I have to admit that the terrorists talked. One of them told us there was another weapons hide nearby and we went off and found it, a big steel drum in a gully, packed with arms and explosives; I have been back to Cyprus often since, even to the farmhouse, and that steel drum, rusty now, is still lying in the gully, forty years later.

By the late summer of 1957 Field Marshal Sir John Harding had been Governor for two very active years and was in failing health. In November 1957 he left the island and was replaced by Sir Hugh Foot, who brought with him high hopes for a diplomatic solution. At least the British need to retain Cyprus had been removed from the board, for it had now been decided that Britain's strategic interests could be served in Cyprus by no more than a good airfield and a couple of Army bases. If a workable constitution could be agreed by both communities, the British could leave.

Hopes of a constitutional settlement acceptable to Greeks and Turks were swiftly dashed. Colonel Grivas was still anxious for *enosis* and there was rising concern among the Turkish community, which began to express itself in demonstrations and intercommunal violence and the setting up of their own terrorist organisation, TMT, the Turkish Defence Organisation. Grivas considered the best way to demonstrate that any compromise on sovereignty was impossible was to carry on attacking the British and stir up trouble between the Greek and Turkish communities. This was never hard to do though there had, as yet, been comparatively little intercommunal violence.

Grivas set out to change all that. He began by declaring a boycott of British goods but since this did the Greek traders more harm than their British customers or Turkish competitors, he had to terrorise the shopkeepers to make the boycott work. This move was followed by a series of bomb attacks on servicemen but the British were well used to these by now and they did little harm. Grivas then called yet another 'cease-fire', which was accepted by Sir Hugh Foot in anticipation of a meeting with Grivas. Grivas had no intention of meeting the Governor and turned his attention to the Turks. A number of Turks were murdered by the EOKA and several Greeks were murdered in reprisal by the TMT. On 17 July 1958, five Turks were murdered by EOKA and there was more intercommunal violence.

On 3 October 1958, Grivas demonstrated the impartiality of the struggle by sending his killers to shoot down two women, both wives of British servicemen. These two housewives were shopping with their children at a supermarket near Famagusta when the gunmen moved in. Both women were shot in the back, one dying at once while her child stood by, the other being seriously injured.

This atrocity almost gave Grivas what he had been seeking for so long; an outbreak of violence by the British soldiers. Hundreds of British servicemen left camp and descended on Famagusta to beat up any Greek they could find, but the officers and NCOs were soon on hand to urge the troops back to barracks and no Greek lives were lost: most other armies in the world would have burned Famagusta to the ground.

Athens Radio made a great play of the riot in Famagusta but most people on the island, including the Greek community, were disgusted at these senseless and brutal murders.

Makarios had now begun to realise that *enosis* was not an option while the Turks were so set against it. If this demand were not renounced and the EOKA campaign against the Turks continued there was a likelihood that sooner or later the mainland Turks would invade Cyprus and enforce partition. Makarios therefore announced that he would accept the original British offer of an independent republic. In this he had the support of the Greek Government, but not of Colonel Grivas.

The EOKA campaign was clearly counterproductive but Grivas could not be stopped. His next step was to place bombs in British military aircraft at Nicosia airport. The bombers were suspected to be Greek Cypriots working for NAAFI, the servicemen's canteen organisation. These Cypriots were dismissed and the NAAFI canteens closed. It is some measure of the support enjoyed by the troops that no fewer than twenty thousand British civilians promptly offered to come out from Britain and replace the canteen staff so that the troops would not go without their tea and buns.

Jerry Bastin, who served with 1 Para in Cyprus recalls his time there:

> I was young and it was an adventure. I remember we used to keep the fuel for our lamps in a fire bucket, with the inevitable result that one day there was a tent fire and some bright spark threw our paraffin onto the blaze.
>
> I remember our Section sergeant shooting at a fox and just as he stopped firing a very upper-class voice shouted from the opposite hill, 'I say, you there, would you kindly stop shooting; this is a patrol of the ---- Regiment!' We had no idea any other troops were in the area. I was more miffed because the sergeant had used my rifle and he handed it back saying, 'Don't forget to clean it.' Anyway, we saw the funny side of the incident and went on our way laughing.
>
> Less funny was the time I was sent to fill up the Section's water bottles at a village we were in. After dark there was a curfew and we had just got back to the billet with the water when I realised – horrors – that I had left my rifle leaning against the well-head.
>
> Thoughts of a year in the glasshouse danced before my eyes and I dare not report the loss to the Sergeant or any NCO. I whispered to a couple of mates and asked them to come back with me but no takers, so I had to go on my own. The village was full of trigger-happy soldiers after curfew and I thought my best bet was to whistle *Rule, Britannia* as I went back. On the way I met a sentry who said, 'Keep whistling, mate' . . . and there, just where I had left it, was the rifle. Nothing can describe the relief I felt when I had it back in my hands.
>
> I am sure many ex-servicemen, NS or Regular, have similar tales to tell. I have shared accommodation with a pig, slept in a chicken house and in a vineyard on an incline of about 45 degrees, even in a dried-up river bed that turned out to be infested with snakes.
>
> I have never regretted my National Service, though I know that a lot of people hated every second of it. It was a great adventure, a time when I grew up and it gave me good friends I still have forty

years later. I enjoyed my time in Cyprus, but looking back on it now, with the island divided, it seems that we wasted our time.

At the end of 1958 a solution – the Zurich Agreement – was finally reached between the parties. Cyprus was to become independent in 1959 with a Greek Cypriot President and a Turkish Cypriot Vice President. The Government and Administration was split on a 70:30. Greek–Turk basis, and Greece and Turkey were entitled to intervene in Cyprus on behalf of their nationals if these terms were violated. Britain was to have her two sovereign base areas but otherwise take no part in island affairs.

Colonel Grivas left the island in March 1959, after EOKA had handed in a token quantity of arms to indicate their surrender. Archbishop Makarios became the first President of an independent Cyprus, which was declared as a state within the Commonwealth on 16 August 1960, just over five years after the troubles began.

The Cyprus Emergency cost the lives of one hundred and fifty-six British soldiers. A further two hundred and thirty-eight civilians, mostly Greeks, were murdered by EOKA. Fifty-one EOKA terrorists were killed and some fifteen hundred imprisoned or detained. All this pain and bloodshed was for nothing since the agreement Makarios settled for in 1959 had been on the table since he and his henchmen began the terror campaign in 1955.

As for the promises and resolutions that ended this violence, time was to show just how well they would be kept. Within a few years George Grivas, now a Greek Army General, was back on the island. Trouble between the Greek and Turkish communities began again, leading eventually to civil war, a Turkish invasion and the de-facto partition of the island. Inevitably, the Greek Cypriots blamed the British for this but by then the British had been gone for over a decade. Cyprus was now an independent state and the problem was passed to the United Nations, where it still remains, unresolved, twenty-five years later.

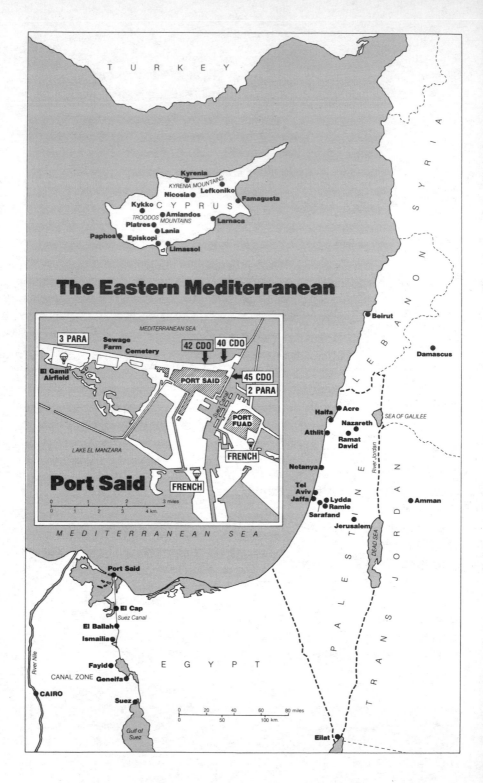

The Eastern Mediterranean

TURKEY

Kyrenia
KYRENIA MOUNTAINS
Nicosia **Lefkoniko**
Famagusta
Kykko C Y P R U S
TROODOS **Amiandos**
MOUNTAINS
Platres **Larnaca**
Paphos **Lania**
Episkopi
Limassol

SYRIA

Beirut

Damascus

LEBANON

Haifa **Acre**
Nazareth *SEA OF GALILEE*
Athlit **Ramat**
David

Netanya

River Jordan

Tel
Aviv
Jaffa **Lydda**
Ramle
Sarafand
Jerusalem

Amman

P A L E S T I N E

J O R D A N

DEAD SEA

Port Said

El Cap
Suez Canal
El Ballah
Ismailia

Fayid
CANAL ZONE **Geneifa**

CAIRO

Suez

E G Y P T

River Nile

Gulf of
Suez

T R A N S

Eilat

| 0 | 20 | 40 | 60 | 80 miles |
| 0 | 50 | 100 km. |

Port Said

MEDITERRANEAN SEA

3 PARA **Sewage**
Farm **Cemetery**
42 CDO **40 CDO**
El Gamil
Airfield
PORT SAID
45 CDO
2 PARA
PORT
FUAD
LAKE EL MANZARA
FRENCH
FRENCH

| 0 | 1 | 2 | 3 miles |
| 0 | 2 | 3 | 4 km. |

M E D I T E R R A N E A N   S E A

11

Port Said and Suez: 1956

'The Suez crisis was a Greek tragedy, entirely of American making from start to finish, written by two men, President Eisenhower and John Foster Dulles.'

General William Jackson, 1986.

One lesson learned from the Suez crisis of 1956 was that delay breeds dissension. Act swiftly in a crisis and the world will go along with the action: give the world time to think and reasons will be found for the injured party to negotiate a settlement or simply accept the new situation.

This rule, which was to guide the actions of Britain's leaders in the Falklands crisis of 1982, was fatally neglected in the Suez affair of 1956. Although Nasser's nationalisation of the Suez Canal was not a complete surprise, the Western nations involved, Britain and France, were not at all sure how to respond to this action. As a result, Nasser had time to muster support in the Third World and at the UN, the Americans declined to act, the British and French leaders prevaricated and were dragged into disaster.

The Canal Company lease on the Suez Canal was due to run out in 1958, and since the Egyptian Government was in no position to pay compensation for such an expensive asset, the assumption was that they would wait until then before taking over the Canal; but for the matter of American refusing to fund the Aswan Dam and taking Britain and the World Bank with them in that refusal, that may have happened.

The fundamental problem facing Britain and France in 1956 was not the Egyptian takeover of the Canal but the message this action sent around the world; that the former colonial powers no longer had the means or the will to protect their assets and that their great ally, the United States of America, would not support them in a crisis.

If the first part of this view were allowed to prevail it would be open season on the colonial territories of the French and British Empires, but the second part was crucial. America buttressed the Western nations economically and American financial support was vital. Although the Canal belonged to Britain and France, America had initiated the crisis with the withdrawal of the Aswan loan and was by far the most powerful nation involved in this subsequent débâcle.

The British and French therefore looked to the United States for leadership and support in resolving this problem as quickly as possible. Mr Dulles duly came to London on 1 August, four days after Nasser's announcement, and met Selwyn Lloyd and Monsieur Pineau, the Foreign Secretaries of Britain and France. The three men drew up a five-point statement of their negotiating position, deploring the Egyptian seizure of a foreign asset and insisting on its return. What this statement did not cover was what they would do if negotiations failed. Neither did they decide how long they were prepared to negotiate before taking more decisive action. In short, they failed to concentrate minds.

Secretary of State Dulles's first step was to call a Conference of Canal Users to discuss the situation. More than twenty maritime nations were involved in this conference, which met in London on 14 August 1956, just two weeks after Nasser had confiscated the Canal. Dulles set up a body, the Suez Canal Users Association (SCUA). The SCUA position, though confused, was broadly that they wanted the Canal to be an international waterway outside local politics and free from military threat. The majority of the SCUA were not prepared to press home these wishes to the point of war, not least because the Canal might be seriously damaged in the process.

The British and French, though willing to find a diplomatic solution, were also preparing for an invasion; they did not simply use the Canal, they owned it, and they wanted it back. The Acting

Chairman of the Chiefs of Staff at this time was the First Sea Lord, Admiral Lord Louis Mountbatten, standing in for the current Chairman, Marshal of the Royal Air Force, Sir William Dickson, who was on sick leave.

Mountbatten had an ambivalent attitude towards the Suez situation, an attitude which stresses the point about immediate action being preferable to delay. His first suggestion, put to Prime Minister Anthony Eden on the evening Nasser nationalised the Canal, was to send the Amphibious Warfare Squadron from Malta to pick up 3 Commando Brigade in Cyprus. They would then land the Marines at Port Said to seize the Canal installations and as much of the Canal as lay within reach of naval guns and carrier aircraft. All this could be done inside a week.

This was a bold plan, and given support from Royal Navy guns and RAF bombers in Cyprus it might – just – have succeeded in bringing Nasser to his senses, or at least to the conference table. On the other hand, the Commando Brigade had only two Commandos in Cyprus and no supporting artillery or armour; if Nasser should send his army, newly equipped with modern Soviet weapons operated by Eastern bloc 'volunteers', to oppose the landing, the twelve hundred Marines of 40 and 45 Commando would be hard pressed.

Besides, a landing alone was only the start of it. Sir Gerald Templer, one of the hawks over the Suez seizure, saw the long-term problem. 'We could probably beat the Egyptian Army with one good brigade,' he said, 'but it would take eight divisions and hundreds of military governors to hold the country thereafter.' After brief consideration Mountbatten's proposal was rejected in favour of a more substantial plan, drawn up in conjunction with the French.

By the end of the month, as plans for an Anglo–French landing were being prepared, Mountbatten had begun to have grave doubts about the entire operation. His first point was crucial, a reminder of a question asked but not answered about the Dieppe Raid of 1942. If the Anglo-French forces did seize Port Said, what were they to do with it? Was it the intention of the British Government to take back a part of Egypt and hold it against all comers? If so, for how long, and what might the rest of the Arab nations, the United Nations, the Soviet Union – and the Americans – choose to do about it?

His second point was equally well made. The Middle East conflict, he said, was about ideas, emotions and loyalties. Such things could not be fought with ships and tanks and aircraft. Britain professed to support the idea of self-determination for all nations: how then could she impose her will on Egypt and invade her territory? Mountbatten felt so strongly that the Suez operation was wrong that he was prepared to resign his command if it went ahead. He was only dissuaded from this step when it was pointed out that a military commander could not leave his post when the servicemen he commanded were about to go into action.

In his assessment of the Suez operation Mountbatten undoubtedly got it right, at least in the short term. If the Anglo-French went for a military solution but failed to gain a lodgement in Egypt the results would be unfortunate to say the least, but military failure was not anticipated. The real risks were political. In the event, the Anglo-French operation proved catastrophic with both Governments criticised, at home and abroad, for launching the attack in the first place and then for failing to carry it through.

The first objection was valid but could have been overcome: everyone loves a winner. The second point had a more devastating effect. The Anglo-French failure to press home their attack in the face of American pressure exposed to the gaze of friend and enemy the fact that Britain's Imperial role and her World-Power pretensions were without substance. Her economic position, unwisely neglected after the end of the War made independent action impossible: America held the purse strings and had wound them round Britain's throat. By late summer of 1956 this hard fact was not yet apparent and plans to retake the Canal went ahead.

Various plans were prepared and abandoned, including one to land at Alexandria and advance directly on Cairo, with support from the British armoured division based in Libya. The politicians then felt that a landing at Alexandria and an attack on Cairo would be difficult to justify in the United Nations which was now becoming seriously concerned with the Anglo-French build-up. The attention then switched to the less debatable ground of the former Canal Zone and Port Said, where the treaty rights of the British and the economic interests of France had certainly been violated.

The final Anglo-French plan called for airborne and seaborne assaults on Port Said and the Canal, followed by a rapid build-up from British troops mustered in Malta, Cyprus and – if possible – Libya, where the British 10th Armoured Division was currently on exercise. This was to be no small amphibious affair: Britain had a large Navy in 1956. The ships involved included the French battleship *Jean Bart* and seven carriers, the British HMS *Eagle*, *Albion*, *Bulwark*, *Thesus* and *Ocean*, these last two carrying 45 Commando which would be the assault reserve and eventually go ashore to make the first helicopter assault in military history, and two French carriers, the *Arromanches* and the *Layfayette*.

These seven carriers could put up more than two hundred aircraft. In all the British supplied one hundred warships, three hundred aircraft, twelve thousand vehicles and forty-five thousand men. The French supplied thirty warships, two hundred aircraft, nine thousand vehicles and thirty-four thousand men from the Foreign Legion and their parachute corps.

By later standards the Suez operation of 1956 was a large-scale amphibious operation. It was mounted in the face of great technical difficulty because the great fleets of landing craft used at Normandy eleven years before had long since gone to the breaker's yard. The tanks, guns, food, ammunition and equipment had to be shoehorned into the available craft, and 'combat loading', by which tanks and guns go on to ships in the order they are to be used, had to go by the board.

'Well, that's the best we can do,' said one RASC (Royal Army Service Corps) officer, as the ramp of an LST closed on a troop of tanks in Malta. 'We've got the bloody things on; some other poor devil can try to get them off.' Malta was the embarkation point for the Naval part of the operation, and as summer drifted into autumn Grand Harbour and the creeks around it filled up with shippings, while the air was rent with the sound of range practices as the troops prepared for battle.

Spike Hughes of 'Sp' Troop 45 Commando remembers Malta before Suez:

The Brigade had been stationed on Malta for years but since the 'Riot in Straight Street' in 1954 the Brigade had not been made welcome by the local populace. This worried us very little. Our thoughts were centred on 'runs ashore', Hop Leaf beer, bottles of 'Screech', the local wine, which cost a shilling (5p) a bottle and the girls in Straight Street.

We also put our mortars on manpacks and ran the assault course. We did tank recognition and were introduced to our support, the 6th RTR (Royal Tank Regiment). According to them the Russian T34 could knock out a Centurion tank from the front at a thousand yards and our anti-tank weapon, the 3.5 rocket launcher, was a joke. We practised with and against them anyway. We also made many practice landings all around the island. Rocky landings, sandy landings, even landings on quaysides using aluminium ladders.

Because of the serious worry over Russian tanks we were joined by an anti-tank platoon of the Duke of Wellington's Regiment. Despite making them cut their hair short and improve their drill times, they thought life with the Commando was great. We said our food was bad and there was little of it – our victualling was done by the Army at this time. They said it was better than in their camp. One Army lad put in the cells commented. 'Here I get a broom to scrub out the cell with – our lot gave me a toothbrush!'

Just a few days before we sailed for Suez, the 'Dukes' were returned to their own unit. They were gutted not to be coming with us and we had grown used to their one size KD uniforms and bright-red hose tops which made them look like a 1940s football team on parade. 45 had now formed its own anti-tank platoon with a new weapon, the 105mm Recoilless Rifle.

On 27 September, 45 Commando was visited by General Sir Hugh Stockwell, the Force Commander for the Suez operation, who hinted at the use of helicopters and said it would be a race between us and the Paras, but he thought the Paras would get to Cairo first.

On 28 October, despite the urgency of training we still celebrated the Corps' birthday in 1664 by Trooping the Colour in KD and white caps. Then came our helicopter training.

This one day of helicopter assault training took place on Ghajn Tuffeiha parade ground. Doors and seats had been removed to allow a greater payload. Our mortar crew, a corporal and three with manpacked mortar, tried various ways of getting in and out quickly. I got the impression that they were more worried about the mortar barrel damaging the rotor blades than they were about possible damage to my head. Our reward was a quick flight around the camp; that was it and our training was over.

The British assault forces tasked to take Gamil airfield and Port Said consisted of the 3rd Commando Brigade, Royal Marines, three Commando units totalling around fifteen hundred men under Brigadier Rex Madoc, RM, supported by tanks and anti-tank guns from various Army units, and two battalions of the Parachute Regiment.

The 3rd Battalion (3 Para), would parachute on to Gamil Airfield just west of Port Said on the day before the seaborne landings at the same time as the French paras landed east of the Canal around Port Fuad. 2 Para would come in by sea, landing behind the Royal Marines, and then push south down the Canal to re-occupy as much as possible of the Zone. This initial landing would be supported by the guns of the Mediterranean fleet, carrier-borne fighters of the Fleet Air Arm and Canberra bombers based on Cyprus and Malta, and once ashore by Centurion tanks of the 6th Royal Tank Regiment. Once the Marines and paratroops had seized a bridgehead, the 3rd Infantry Division would come ashore and take the rest of the Canal. The French would land on the east bank of the Canal, around Port Fuad, and push south from there.

The Egyptian Air Force had over two hundred combat aircraft, including the latest Soviet fighters, Russian MiG 15s and 19s as well as seventy Iluyshin bombers. Their army mustered eighteen armoured or infantry brigades and included artillery regiments armed with British 25-pounders looted from the Canal Zone depots as well as modern Soviet 122mm cannon.

To beef up the Commandos' firepower, anti-tank guns were provided and manned by British Army units. Lieutenant Tim Beath was with the Somerset Light Infantry Anti-Tank Platoon, which found itself attached to 42 Commando:

When the Anti-Tank Platoon dismounted, somewhat wearily, in Malta on 17 August, we were promptly told to re-mount and go and join the 1st Bn., Royal Berkshire Regiment, further down the coast. Here we were to spend two hectic weeks together with the Anti-Tank Platoons of 3rd Grenadier Guards, 1st Duke of Wellington's and 1st Royal Berkshires – learning all about the 17-pounder anti-tank gun and how to drive the Stuart tracked gun-towers, while sorting ourselves into gun-crews.

There were only three 17-pounder guns available in Malta, and by the time we had finished they closely resembled ancient, smooth-bore cannon. Day after day, the sea was churned up from dawn to dusk as we pounded away at firing practice and ships of the Royal Navy were seen to execute smart ninety-degree turns to starboard as they appeared round the point to our front.

By early September we had worn out all three guns and collected six new 17-pounders. Then with six guns, six Stuarts, various 3-ton trucks and a jeep, we motored up the hill to Imtarfa to join 42 RM Commando as their Anti-Tank Platoon. We stayed with these excellent people for some little time.

Joining a Royal Marine Commando presents certain difficulties for a 'Pongo'. To start with, the Marines are embarrassingly nautical; the average soldier is apt to become confused when attempting to differentiate between being 'ashore' or 'afloat'. It should be straightforward enough, but in the Royal Marines either state can apply even when you are on dry land, depending if you are in or out of camp. Scorn is heaped upon the luckless soldier whose only method of telling whether he is 'ashore' or 'afloat' is to see if his feet are wet.

Commandos are also brisk and hearty. They train hard, double everywhere, have tremendous spirit, and are great fun to work with. We were soon practising on- and off-loading our guns and towers in landing craft. The Platoon also did some terrifying cliff scaling training during the Platoon Commander's absence in England, during which Mr Baddeley, who took over for a month as *locum tenens*, greatly surprised the Royal Marines by conducting strictly Light Infantry drill parades on their square. Interest in these performances was considerable.

On 31 October we were ordered to load all vehicles, ammunition and guns on to landing craft for, we were glibly told, 'a one-day test load exercise'. We had practised considerably for just this task and our particular LCT was loaded within forty minutes of the first vehicle being run down the ramp. We put out to sea that evening, and were told, in due course, that we were to sail east for an unspecified destination – and that censorship was in force. Two and two were rapidly put together; it came as no surprise five days later when we were briefed for an assault landing on Port Said.

42 Commando, with the Somerset Light Infantry anti-tank gunners under command, was to land from the sea but 45 Commando was to initiate a new form of warfare by going ashore in helicopters. One of the officers involved in this new venture was Lt.-Colonel Francis Graham Bell of the Army Air Corps:

This year, 1956, was a fateful year, and the Suez Canal which Lady Eden, wife of the then Prime Minister, claimed flowed through her drawing room in 1956, was to affect the lives and destinies of many people, including those in the 'Joint Experimental Helicopter Unit' (JEHU).

JEHU had been formed at Middle Wallop in 1955 to examine the uses of helicopters in an operational role. It was the first joint service Army/RAF unit to be formed since the Second World War, the CO being an Army Lt.-Colonel with an RAF Squadron Leader as his 2.I.C., and the two flights being commanded by a Major and a Squadron Leader – a soldier and an airman – respectively. It all seemed to work, and inter-service rivalries were swamped by a common interest and the camaraderie of the air.

I was the Flight Commander of the Sycamore Helicopter Flight. At that time helicopters had never been used in battle and the task of the Unit was to examine all possible uses, both in battle and in support of the ground forces.

It was decided that if JEHU was going to be used in any intended operation, the Unit would have to be based on an aircraft carrier. Therefore carrier landings and carrier operating techniques would have to be practised. The first step was to mark out the dimensions of a carrier flight deck on the airfield at Middle Wallop. Practice landings were made on this space and the ground crews pushed and sweated as they attempted to fit twelve helicopters into what seemed an impossibly small space.

The next stage was to graduate to the real thing and on 1 October JEHU flew out to the Solent where a Light Fleet Carrier. HMS *Theseus*, was steaming up and down.

A carrier deck laid out on an airfield looks small enough, even surrounded by acres of green grass. When that same area is a carrier deck surrounded by the sea, it looks minute. To this is added the factor of movement, movement of the ship as well as movement of the helicopter. The pilot's first impression is that the whole thing is quite impossible and should be attempted by someone else while he flies back to base.

However, no such option was open and the only thing to do was to get on with it and make the first landing. As we dropped down to three hundred feet above the water and flew along the starboard side of the carrier, it did not look quite so small and at least we could see that there was very little pitching or rolling movement of the deck. We carried out a normal circuit of the carrier and lined up for our final approach.

The Batsman indicated the spot on which we should touch down and, shutting out all thoughts of falling into a remarkably cold sea, I carried out a perfectly normal landing. The only real difference between landing on an aircraft carrier and landing on an airfield seemed to be the amount of adrenalin used.

JEHU spent twelve days on board the carrier practising deck landings; individually at first and then working up to Flight operations, finally operating as an entire Unit with both Flights lifting off the deck and wheeling in formation over the Solent before returning to the carrier.

On 12 October we flew off HMS *Theseus* and returned to Middle Wallop. We had made six hundred and eleven deck landings and completed one hundred and sixty-three flying hours. When we heard that HMS *Theseus* had embarked 845 Squadron, a Fleet Air Arm squadron equipped with ten Whirlwind helicopters and set sail for Malta, we felt sad to be left behind.

Thoughts of Suez receded and the CO decided that a three-day stand-down would do us all a lot of good. Unfortunately, the War Office informed him that we were now on forty-eight hours stand-by to embark on HMS *Ocean*.

We sailed past Gibraltar on 30 October and carried out our first deck landing in the Mediterranean. Everything was perfect and as we luxuriated in the sunshine, we thought of the delightful prospect in front of us. This peace was shattered when a signal was received, ordering the Admiral to make all speed to Malta, there to embark troops. The Port Said landings were 'on'.

There is one final story. Came the day of the landing, Danny Kearns, the 2I/C, was going in the leading Whirlwind with the Flight Commander, while I, the Sycamore Flight Commander, would lead the second flight. With everything ready to go, Danny and I stood on HMS *Ocean*'s flight deck, looking at Port Said and speculating about where, exactly, we would land.

We did not have long to wait before the CO rushed up and said, 'You are to land in De Lesseps Square.' We looked at each other and then at the Colonel and I asked, 'Where is de Lesseps Square? Do we have a street map of Port Said?' 'I don't know – and no,' replied our Colonel abruptly and went off.

I looked at Danny and thought deeply. Then I remembered something. 'My mother sailed out to Malaya a few years ago,' I told Danny, 'and she sent me a picture postcard from Port Said, saying that as you enter the Suez Canal there is a magnificent statue of Ferdinand de Lesseps on the right-hand side. I wouldn't mind betting that is where we are supposed to land.'

So, equipped with this priceless piece of information, we launched the first ever heliborne assault landing in history, guided to the landing zone by my mother's picture postcard.

While the British and French troops were training for the assault, the politicians were equally hard at work attempting to find a more peaceful solution or a reason to blame each other should anything go wrong.

By now the Soviets had become involved, partly to support their new ally Egypt and impress the Arab world, partly to divert attention from problems in their own Empire. On 23 October the people of Hungary had risen in revolt against their Communist overlords and a bloody battle was even now being waged in the streets of Budapest, between local citizens and students and the tanks and infantry of the Red Army.

The Suez affair proved a godsend to the Soviet leaders. While their tanks and troops slaughtered the stubborn citizens of Budapest, they and their Third World allies could rave at the United Nations about the imperialist aggression of the colonial powers at Port Said.

If this alone were not enough, the Israelis were also in the field, partly because they were anxious to make a pre-emptive strike against the Egyptians, partly because they had been put up to it by the French.

The Israelis were not going to wait until Nasser's army had been re-equipped and retrained by the Russians. Israel is a small country without the territory to absorb an assault; to survive, Israel must fight her battles beyond her own boundaries. As soon as Nasser seized the Canal and provided the British and French with a *causus belli*, the Israelis prepared to get involved and were soon in deep and secret discussions with the French.

Meanwhile, John Foster Dulles, the American Secretary of State, was prevaricating. He was particularly anxious not to be seen offering support for any direct Anglo–French action over the Canal. Apart from his personal reluctance to aid the 'colonial powers', there was a pressing political reason for his silence. As often happens in the United States, that most insular of superpowers, foreign policy had become inhibited by domestic political considerations, for 1956 was an election year. Dulles's chief, President Eisenhower, was facing re-election is November and presenting himself to the American people as a 'man of peace'. How then could his Administration support an Anglo–French attack on Egypt?

Dulles therefore pressed the benefits of negotiation on the Anglo–French but declined to put any pressure, economic or political, on Egypt. Without such pressure there was no reason for Nasser to compromise over the Canal. As the weeks passed and the Anglo–French frustration grew, this trend was to continue and even intensify.

Dulles refused to put pressure on the Egyptians but was more than ready to increase the pressure for compromise – or capitulation – on the British. His first action was a refusal to direct American shipowners to pay their transit dues to a holding account of the SCUA or discourage American pilots from going to Egypt where they were soon steering ships down the disputed Canal.

The Canal Users Conference in London ended on 23 August with the decision to send a delegation to Cairo for talks with Colonel Nasser. Dulles had played a major part in setting up and chairing this Conference but he declined to lead the delegation to Cairo, stating that he was needed in Washington. The Third World, led by Nehru's India, was now openly behind Nasser and Dulles had no wish to be seen as a spokesman for Western colonial interests. The delegation to Cairo was therefore headed by Sir Robert Menzies, the Prime Minister of Australia.

The Menzies mission failed because at a Press Conference in Washington the day before Menzies met Nasser, Eisenhower declared that on the matter of the Canal seizure he would 'support a peaceful solution, nothing more'. This gave Menzies nothing to negotiate with, and his delegation promptly withdrew.

Trouble was also brewing for the British Government at home. The political concensus was now leaning towards United Nations involvement, or at least that Britain should take no action without consulting the Security Council. Dulles advised Eden and Selwyn Lloyd not to appeal to the Security Council because any appeal for action there would be promptly vetoed by Soviet Russia. Such a veto would stop any Anglo-French military action in its tracks, for in those heady days the views of the UN tended to be heeded, especially in the West.

There is a kind of breathless naivety in all this; the Second World War had only been over for ten years and yet again the dictators were on the march, breaking treaties, seizing assets, making fools of democratically elected governments, preparing to make war on weaker neighbours . . . and yet again the democratic powers, strangled by a faith in their own institutions and philosophies were making the old mistakes, treating groaning tyrannies like Soviet Russia or arrogant dictators like Nasser as if they were democratic states or freely elected leaders, unable to agree on what action to take and quarrelling among themselves.

Eden was not the only one who muttered about the dangers of another Munich and compared the United Nations to the League of Nations. However, the UN was there, and as members Britain and France were obliged to obey its rulings and seek its approval.

The result of all this prevarication in Washington and the UN was to bewilder the British and infuriate the French. The French were also worried that the ever-perfidious *Anglais* would eventually succumb to the growing pressure from Washington and do nothing. The French were determined to topple Nasser and they therefore concocted a secret plan with the Israelis.

There is no longer any need to doubt that the French and British colluded with the Israelis to invade Egypt in 1956. Government papers released years later have made it perfectly clear that the French and the Israelis were planning a joint assault on Egypt as early as mid-September 1956 and that the British Government – though not consulted beforehand and vehemently denying it afterwards – were subsequently made aware of this intention and went along with it.

This plan was put into effect after the Security Council had debated the Suez seizure on 5 October and refused either to strongly condemn the Egyptian action or permit the Anglo-French to go ahead with any direct attack under the UN banner. This meant that Nasser had got away with seizing the Canal, and his allies in Washington and the Third World were jubilant. This also meant that some excuse had to be found which would permit the Franco-British to go ahead and invade. The best excuse was the protection of the Canal; the French had already prepared such a plan and the Israelis were part of it.

The basic Franco-Israeli plan was for the Israelis to launch an attack across the Sinai desert towards the Suez Canal, two days before the French launched naval and parachute landings at Port Fuad and Port Said. After the Israeli attack – but before the French assault – the French Government would issue an ultimatum to Israel and Egypt, ordering them to cease fighting and stay away from the Canal.

Failing Egyptian compliance the French would land forces in Egypt, to 'protect' the Canal and save it for the international maritime community. This cover plan may have seemed crafty at the time, at least to the French, but it fooled no one. The word 'collusion' was soon to be used and it stayed in use for years.

The French were far less subservient than Britain to American and Third World opinion and were determined to go ahead anyway. If the British went along with the plan, so much the better. If they elected to stay out of military involvement they could serve a useful purpose by using their fragile political influence to keep the Americans from interfering until the Egyptian army had been shattered and the Canal secured.

In the event, when the British Ministers were informed of this plan at a highly secret meeting in Paris, they chose to support it. Matters then escalated rapidly when Colonel Nasser, convinced that the UN General Assembly was on his side and the Western Powers impotent, overplayed his hand by preparing an attack on Israel.

On 24 October Nasser announced a military alliance with Syria, to box in Israel between their armies. In response to this, on 26 October, Israel mobilised her reserves. Three days later Israeli forces entered Sinai. On the following day the British Fleet sailed from Malta and joined the French at sea. France and Britain then issued their joint ultimatum to Egypt and Israel, requiring them to withdraw all troops within ten miles of the

Canal. As previously arranged, Israel agreed. As expected, Nasser refused.

Britain and France waited twelve hours for his compliance: then they went to war. At 16.15 hrs on 31 October 1956, British Canberra bombers took off from Cyprus to attack Egyptian airfields around Cairo, Alexandria and Port Said; at least one British pilot refused to take part in the attack and was removed from his aircraft to a military prison.

Five days of aerial interdiction then followed, resulting in the complete destruction of the Egyptian airforce. This action did not force Colonel Nasser to the conference table but it caused outrage at the United Nations, in Washington, in the British Parliament and in the streets of London, where there were demonstrations against the morality of the Suez operation.

British public and political opinion was totally split by the Suez operation. A large and vocal minority was completely opposed to the landings and expressed their outrage in the Press and in Parliament. An equally large, though less strident minority could see good reasons for the action and gave it their full support. The majority of the nation had no wish to go to war with Egypt but felt that once the decision to attack had been taken, then their troops should be supported.

That said, as the bombing went on, public reaction in Washington, London, even in Paris became generally unfavourable. There were demonstrations, letters in the Press, hostile editorials and political pressure. Most of the real pressure came from Washington where the American Government, especially John Foster Dulles and President Eisenhower, seemed absolutely outraged.

Their hostility was a surprise and a great blow to the British Prime Minister, Anthony Eden. He had assumed that while the US Government might make some public protest, in private they would see the problems – and dangers – of giving in to dictators, and if not offering support, would at least stay neutral and let the Anglo-French deal with the situation. If this was his hope, Prime Minister Anthony Eden was to be bitterly disappointed.

Eisehower and Foster Dulles pursued the British Government with every political and economic weapon at their disposal, joining the Soviets in condemnation of the Suez attack. The Russians, delighted at this unexpected support, and at the smokescreen Suez threw over the butchery then taking place in Budapest, offered military aid to Egypt and threatened to attack London and Paris with nuclear weapons. Matters were clearly getting out of control.

Meanwhile, somewhere east of Malta, a Fleet was on the sea and among the men of 45 Commando embarked on HMS *Theseus* was a young Royal Marine officer, Lieutenant Michael Marchant:

> I had just got back from my honeymoon when I was sent to Malta. I fetched up in 45, in charge of the snipers. In the weeks before we sailed we did a lot of training with the 6 Royal Tank Regiment and the Anti-Tank Platoon of the Duke of Wellington's Regiment. I also carried the Regimental Colour when we 'Trooped the Colour' just before we sailed for Port Said . . . and then I nearly missed the boat.
>
> My wife had arrived and we had taken a small flat in St Paul's Bay; the unit was just up the road at Ghain Tuffeiha. I was standing at the bus stop on this Monday morning in October when Major Ian De'ath came along in his Volkswagen. He stopped, beckoned me over and said, 'Don't you know the Brigade are embarking and ready to sail?'
>
> No one had told me. There was then some frantic packing before I boarded HMS *Theseus*. She was carrying half the unit and some helicopters . . . and and a week later we went ashore in Egypt.

W.H. Cameron was an engineer on a Royal Fleet Auxiliary in 1956:

> I was a junior engineer serving on the RFA *Retainer*, an ammunition ship supporting the Royal Navy. I was called back from leave in August 1956 to join the ship in Southampton. From there we proceeded to load ammunition prior to sailing for Malta.
>
> We sailed through the Bay of Biscay close to a destroyer the British Government had just sold to the Egyptians; we thought it funny that they had no ammunition and we had thousands of tons of it. We heard later that this destroyer had gone up the Gulf of Aquaba to shell the Israelis but had broken down and was sunk by the Israeli Navy.
>
> They kept saying on the BBC news that there was no interference from the Americans but there was and I saw it. On one occasion

we were replenishing HMS *Eagle* when an American helicopter hovered above the deck of *Eagle*. I watched the signal lamps flashing at it but it did not move away until a petty officer rushed to a multiple Bofors gun and swung the barrels directly on to the helicopter which was only a few feet above it. The US helicopter got the message and flew away.

On another occasion we were in convoy line abreast with RFA *Olna* (a tanker), RFA *Fort* and our escort, an anti-submarine frigate, when an American naval ship sailed right through the convoy. Other ships I can remember were the French battleship *Georges Lecques* and the New Zealand cruiser HMNZS *Black Swan*. We did not see any action at Suez but we were issued with tin helmets and told that the Egyptians could not fly over the sea. This was just as well, as our anti-submarine frigate escort did not seem to have much in the way of guns on it, although we were told that there were Russian submarines in the area.

Spike Hughes of 45 Commando again:

We boarded HMS *Ocean* on 2 November. My Troop was billeted in the Boy Seamen's Mess Deck, which was soon covered with three-inch mortars, Vickers MMGs and an amazing assortment of gun cotton, primers and fuses, belonging to the Assault Engineer Platoon. Most of us crashed out on the deck but some old hands slung hammocks. We rigged and de-rigged our manpacks time and time again to get them as manageable as possible.

Everyone had a different load; mine was the mortar barrel, four bombs, tool kit, small pack, and so on. The weight came to 100 lbs and more. Every now and again the ship's Tannoy would pipe 'No smoking on this deck . . . that deck' . . . and so on. We didn't know where we were but figured that as we couldn't smell any Avgas it was all right to smoke. Then the ship's RSM came in, went a funny colour as he saw the fags and explosives, and ran away. One of our Sergeants later ordered us not to smoke at any time on this deck.

Nobody seemed to know where we were going to land but there were 'buzzes' in abundance . . . Port Said, Ismalia, or even Cairo. There were large numbers of 'Rock Apes' (RAF Regiment) on board who were sure they were going to Cyprus for exercises.

When details of the Operation were piped they allowed us to jump the queue for showers and kept wishing us good luck. This was a bit disconcerting as they were the back-up troops to JEHU and clearly felt that we had no chance of surviving any opposed landing. I don't recall being aware of any anti-Suez feelings in the UK. We weren't 'Gung ho!' about going but it was 'Our Canal' and we were going to get it back.

The news that the Paras had dropped on Gamil Airfield a day before we went ashore was received with disbelief. Surely it would have been better for the air and sea assault to take place at the same time in order to stretch and confuse the defenders? Or was this our Force Commander, Sir Hugh Stockwell, giving the Paras a twenty-four hour start on the mythical race to Cairo?

Mike Jones was a National Service Marine in a rifle troop of 40 Commando:

I was then nineteen and in 'Y' Troop of 40 with Captain Morgan as OC. We formed up at St Andrew's Barracks in Malta and sailed in LSTs (Landing Ship, Tank) living on the tank deck among the vehicles.

We spent most of our time queuing for meals – which took hours – but we test fired our weapons and the crew got their hands in firing the anti-aircraft Oerlikons, which made the whole ship vibrate: it was like being in a biscuit tin. No one knew what was going on, of course, but as we sailed along more ships came up, including a French battleship, the *Jean Bart*, but I heard later that an instruction had been issued that no support gun bigger than a six-inch could be used, which put the *Jean Bart*'s main artillery out of use.

While the Marines were sailing east, the Parachute troops in Cyprus were preparing for the attack. The following account is taken from the records of 33rd Parachute Light Regiment which went to Port Said by sea:

On Monday 29 October, the regiment was in the Troodos Mountains on an operation against terrorists when we were ordered to return to Nicosia. It was said that the Corps Commander was arriving and wanted to see some loading trials. We were therefore to do a dress rehearsal loading all guns, vehicles and equipment and on Tuesday we were given our tables showing how many vehicles and men were allotted to each ship.

By this time Israel had attacked Egypt; no one in the Brigade believed that this was an exercise, and they were right. The following day the first battery of guns was loaded on the ships.

It was a very sad blow to the regiment to hear that no aircraft were available to take our guns and that all of them would go by sea. However, one Forward Observer party was to drop with 3 Bn., The Parachute Regiment on Gamil Airfield on the 5th. There were enough vacancies to enable this party to go with one hundred per cent reserves. It consisted of two officers, ten men and four No. 62 wireless sets.

The regimental party jumped on Gamil Airfield with 3 Para. No one from the Regiment was injured or wounded. Three of the four No. 62 wireless sets carried down with the men landed undamaged but no contact could be made with the bombarding ships. A message from Tac Bde HQ said none was available and as the parachute landings took place a day before the amphibious landings, the bombarding ships were out of range. This was a great disappointment as on the next day when they were available the battalion had cleared its area and no fire was required.

During 5 November 3 Para had magnificent air support from a continuous cab-rank of ground attack fighters but there were times when they did require close artillery support.

3 Para landed on Gamil airfield at 0700hrs on 5 November, parachuting from Valetta and Hastings aircraft. They were met with heavy rifle and machine-gun fire and each man was carrying 150lb of equipment. It therefore took time for the battalion to form up on the ground and take their first objectives east of the airfield, a sewage farm which bred vicious mosquitoes, and a walled cemetery that the Egyptians turned into a strong point.

One of the men who jumped that morning was Corporal John Morrison of 'A' Company, 3 Para:

We got our briefing on the Sunday, 4 November, about midday. The battalion task was to take and hold the right flank of the proposed beach-head for the assault landing; the French Paras were to land on the left flank at Port Fuad and the Marines were to come in the middle.

The snag was that we had to go in a day early and hold out – one parachute battalion – for twenty-four hours.

We had a meal at about 11pm, got our kit and went in lorries to the airfield at Nicosia. That was very busy, lots going on, aircraft taking off and taxiing about; we had to stay in our 'sticks' and pay attention.

We jumped at about 7.30am so we must have taken off at about 4am. We were in Hastings and I remember that we had a BBC correspondent called Wood in the aircraft.

We flew on, nobody saying much and then it got light. As we stood up and hooked up, I looked out of one of the windows and saw a Naval fighter diving across the bay with its guns going. Then the usual: RED on. Stand in the Door. GREEN on. GO! GO! GO! GO! . . . and out I went.

The battalion jumped in three waves, the first at 500ft, the next at 800ft and the last at 1000ft. I was in the last wave and, of course, we spent longer in the air. There was shooting going on and just after my chute opened a large piece of flak or something went through my canopy and tore a great big hole in it. Well, what with getting rid of my weapons' container and all, I was a bit busy and the upshot was that I hit the deck with a hell of a bang and broke my shoulder.

There was a fair to-do on the ground with mortaring and machine gunning and a bit of an assault, especially around a cemetery but nothing came down the road towards Port Said. We did as ordered, dug in and held on until the landings next morning. One of our blokes, Corporal Woods, was hit and died later of wounds. Around 3pm on the Tuesday afternoon I was helicoptered out to *Theseus* and eventually back to Malta where my shoulder was set . . . and that was that

During 5 November, 3 Para was attacked and raked with cannon and machine-gun fire by a brace of French jet fighters but the cemetery was taken without loss. The battalion held its ground throughout the day and night waiting for the arrival of the seaborne troops before pushing on into Port Said and suffered some forty casualties in the two–day action. The Parachute Field Regiment account continues:

At about 0900 hrs on 6 November, wireless contact was made with the assault part of the regiment still fifteen miles out to sea. Information was received that the guns of the cruiser HMS *Ceylon* were allotted to support 3 Para. The forward observer party with 3 Para on the airfield, and one in the LST waiting to support 2 Para when they landed, both established communications with HMS *Ceylon*, but neither had any targets.

Even if 3 Para had required Naval gunfire support, HMS *Ceylon* could not have provided it for indecision was spreading in the ranks of the British Government. Among a constant stream of directions now reaching the Force Commanders was a refusal of close air support from bombers and then a ban on Naval gunfire support from gun calibres larger than 4.5 inch. Air support was soon restored but Brigadier Rex Madoc, commanding 3 Commando Brigade, only obtained a promise of Naval gunfire support one hour before his Marines were due to land.

The troops had also noticed that certain elements of the Press were not on their side and were publishing full reports of the forthcoming landings in their newspapers. A delegation from 40 Commando called on one correspondent and informed him that if there were any more leaks of information in his journal they would take him with them into their landing craft and put him out through the bow door first.

Colonel Graham Bell again:

Aboard HMS *Ocean* was the Joint Helicopter Unit comprising six Sycamore 14s and six Whirlwinds HAR2, with twenty-one officers and one hundred and three other ranks, together with seventeen officers and one hundred and three other ranks of 45 Commando, Royal Marines.

Aboard HMS *Theseus* was 845 Squadron Royal Navy with ten Whirlwinds (eight HAR22 and two HA2) and twenty-three officers and one hundred and five ratings, together with twenty-three officers and two hundred and eighty-six other ranks of 45 Commando.

Our task was to lift the whole of 45 Commando into Port Said.

This was to be the first time helicopters were employed in an operational assault and the future of the helicopter as a military vehicle depended on its success.

Two operational orders were prepared. The first covered a landing on the beaches and the second a landing on the golf course: both these orders were issued at 0730 hrs 'Zulu' on 4 November. (Timings throughout were given as ZULU time, this being Greenwich Mean Time, instead of using local time.) There was a great deal of speculation as to which plan would be adopted when the time came since the final decision would be left until the last moment.

Unknown to us, the Egyptians had just deployed an infantry battalion on the golf course, complete with anti-aircraft guns, and any landing there would have been hazardous in the extreme. In the planning, Jock Scott, our CO, had accepted a fifty per cent casualty rate, a fact which he managed to keep from us until after the shooting was over. If we had attempted to land on the golf course, I consider that the first wave would have been pretty well annihilated – when a helicopter hovers to debouch its troops it really is a sitting duck.

As we steamed our zig-zag course through the night in company with other darkened ships, we listened to the speech made by Hugh Gaitskell, then Leader of the Opposition.

We were not impressed. As a speech to troops on the eve of battle, it was bound to lower morale, for he made it clear that the Country was not wholeheartedly behind us. In the past it was the custom to present a united front and to back up the troops going into battle until the objective had been achieved.

Now those troops were being vilified by one of the leaders of the country, in the defence of whose honour they were at that moment prepared to die. Shortly afterwards, the Padre came on the ship's Tannoy system and gave us a very uplifting address. We continued through the night with the feeling that God was on our side even if the Labour Party was not.

At 0356 hrs on 6 November, both carriers dropped anchor some nine miles off Port Said, about five cables apart. As dawn broke we could see Port Said immediately in front of us, a great pall of black smoke rising into the sky above it. The helicopters were ranged on the flight deck and a signal was received informing us that the first wave was required ashore at 0610 hrs. We still did not know where we were to land but we got ready, manning the helicopters with the pilots and the first load of Marines.

The Whirlwinds took off first and then the Sycamores moved up to their take-off positions. Within five minutes all the helicopters were airborne and we shook out into four 'vics' of three aircraft. 845 Squadron then joined up for the combined run-in and we formed up into four waves with the six Whirlwinds of JHU leading. They were followed by five Whirlwinds of 845 Squadron, the six Sycamores of JHU and then the four Whirlwinds of 845 Squadron.

We flew in low at seventy knots and because the landing area was confined and partly obscured by smoke blowing across from the town, the Sycamores had to keep close to the Whirlwinds in order to give a rapid back-up but not too close so that we would have to come to the hover and wait while they moved away.

As we reached the entrance to the Suez Canal we could see the statue of Ferdinand de Lesseps on the starboard bow. The Whirlwinds in front of me turned to starboard to drop their troops and I followed at a safe distance. The dust and the smoke swirled across the landing area and there seemed to be complete confusion. Helicopters at the hover, to allow their troops to disembark, put up an enormous amount of dust and the whole area was obscured. I felt my way into the Square and wondered what was in store for me.

As I came to the hover, my Marines fell out of the aircraft, and with their weapons at the ready, rushed forward to join their comrades. I took off again at once, flying through the smog of battle back to the ship to collect the next load. We had been incredibly lucky with our initial fly-in and we continued to ferry the troops to and fro from HMS *Ocean* to Port Said.

There had been problems at the start of the day. We had loaned two of our pilots to the Royal Navy because they were short of aircrew. One of these, John Shaw, was the second pilot of the first helicopter to enter into the shore area to see where it was possible to land. The area he and his pilot chose was the football stadium, and as they landed they came under fire from Egyptians in the stands. In the end they flew straight up and, avoiding more bullets, returned safely to the ship. On landing it was discovered that the aircraft had some twenty bullet holes in it.

All the troops of 45 Commando were ashore in one hour and

twenty-five minutes. The total lift by the helicopter squadrons was four hundred and fifteen men and twenty-five tons of equipment. Everything went remarkably smoothly and our only setback was when a Sycamore had engine failure on its second lift off from the deck. Bryan Shaw, the pilot, was slightly shattered to discover that a large anti-tank missile had been resting just behind his head when they thumped back onto the deck.

Anyway, no damage was done and the Sycamore was pushed out of the way and the operation continued. This helicopter survived the operation and after many years' service with the RAF, following the disbandment of JEHU in 1959, it became 'Gate Guard' at Middle Wallop and now resides in honourable retirement in the Museum of Army Flying at Middle Wallop.

Apart from carrying out the actual assault, a major task for the Flight was the ferrying of casualties back to the ships. I think the record was held by a young Marine who was back in the ship's sick bay twenty minutes after leaving the ship to go ashore.

There were also moments of drama – Jimmy Stuart from JEHU, flying as a relief pilot with 845 Squadron, just managed to get on to the deck before his fuel tanks ran dry. In another incident, a Whirlwind from 845 Squadron, with wounded on board, did run out of fuel and had to ditch, but the pilot saved his casualties.

Spike Hughes of 45 Commando, was one of the Royal Marines in this first–ever helicopter assault:

As we came up onto the flight deck, loaded like beasts of burden, we could see the great pall of black smoke over the coast, all seemed to be happening with quiet efficiency. We were soon aboard the 'chopper' and on our way. Sitting with my legs apart, facing the open doorway, I saw first sky and then sea. It looked extremely uninviting but as we levelled off I actually began to enjoy the ride until an aircraft appeared and headed straight for us – ours or theirs? Then it was gone and it hadn't fired. Then we were over the breakwater and being directed to our landing area by the hand of a great statue – Ferdinand de Lesseps was pointing the way.

As we touched down in blinding, swirling dust, my mortar barrel and I were forcefully assisted out. 'Run ten yards, drop to the ground, take up firing positions,' were the orders. The weight on my back and the dust storm convinced me that to kneel would be better. When the chopper took off, our Corporal called us to move to him. I couldn't move my leg – it was as if stuck to the deck. I thought I had been hit, but had no pain. I was kneeling in a patch of tar . . . someone pulled me up and we moved on.

We set up our mortars but either our ranging shots could not be spotted or there was no suitable target, I forget which. Then we witnessed the incident when a Royal Navy Wyvern swept in firing rockets on our troops a couple of hundred yards away. An anti-tank gun disappeared in a flash as a doll-like figure tumbled through the air. Then there were figures rushing to make a cross with orange and pink silks, which were supposed to be our ground markers. Our CO's HQ Group had been hit and they were putting out indentifying panels. Who needs enemy aircraft with the Royal Navy around?

At one point in our travels a Centurion tank stopped close by. 'Are you all sure it's one of ours?' asked the Sergeant. Before anyone could reply it had fired an ear-bursting shot down the street and ejected a large brass shellcase. This was none too friendly, so it must have been ours.

The first night we slept in a large apartment block. Looting was forbidden although the French troops in Fuad appeared to be liberating everything they could lay their hands on. There were some ducks in a pen nearby and 40 Commando had found some Scotch in the Customs Houses. Due to the expertise of our platoon storeman, we dined on boiled duck with whisky sauce that night, although we were obliged to sit on the floor so as not to expose ourselves to sniper fire.

By midnight the 'war' was over. During the next week we patrolled the town, gathered in all manner of arms, enforced a curfew and tried to control refugees and escaping enemy soldiers.

3 Commando Brigade got ashore and had secured all its objectives by mid-day, although fighting went on in the town centre and at the Canal Company offices for much of the day. 40 Commando overran the Canal offices and the Navy House which X Troop of 40 took with the support of tanks at around 1500hrs. The only major setback was caused by a Fleet Air Arm Wyvern fighter which straffed the

advancing column of 45 Commando as it moved into the town and severely injured the CO, Lt.-Colonel Tailyour, and several of his officers and men.

With the town taken the Commandos moved on to clear the houses of snipers and machine-gun posts. One of the officers involved here was Captain Derek Oakley of 'B' Troop, 42 Commando:

We came ashore in armoured tracked vehicles called Buffaloes and trundled into the centre of town. Some of the men seemed unaware there was a war on. The man driving our Buffalo wanted to stop at the traffic lights and wait till they changed to green and some of the lads on house clearing were ringing the doorbells to flats and waiting for people to answer . . . so much for the brutal soldiery, but one way or another we got the job done.

Helping 42 get the job done was the Anti-Tank Platoon of the 1st Bn., The Somerset Light Infantry, and Tim Beath takes up the story:

Port Said was under a pall of smoke and there were fires along the sea front, into which rocket-carrying fighters of the Fleet Air Arm were continually dipping; some mild Naval gunfire was being directed at selected targets. At H-hour the assault troops landed and disappeared into the town and at H+15 our landing craft disgorged my Platoon onto dry land.

We rumbled away to meet our six Corporals, Rose, Tilley, Barker, Crawford, Bradley and Dando, who had landed, amidst considerable excitement, with the assault troops and found 42 Commando engaged in clearing houses on the foreshore. They were meeting with annoying resistance, necessitating very thorough searching and house clearing. All six guns were immediately positioned in the area to cover tank approaches, but our own Centurions were the only tanks active in Port Said. They were invaluable – sitting astride roads and methodically discouraging Egyptian resistance – firing with very great accuracy.

Our detachments used small arms fire against groups of Egyptians, but only Corporal Barker's crew found a target for the big gun. They engaged a group of approximately twelve men with remarkable effect. It was during this that the Platoon suffered a tragic blow when Corporal Crawford was killed and Private Penny, a member of the same gun crew, was wounded. These losses set us all back and it became a sad day for the Platoon.

By nightfall 42, 40 and 45 Commandos had taken the town and except for intermittent sniping all was quiet. 42 Commandos' casualties amounted to six killed and twenty or so wounded. We slept under beach huts that night, to the sound of explosions and whinings overhead from a burning ammunition dump. By the following day it was obvious that our 17-pounders were not the ideal weapon for built-up area work. After the 'Cease Fire' we lined up our guns in a row and virtually forgot about them. The six crews thundered about in their Stuart tow'ers, doing riot control duties here, searching for arms dumps there and guarding our dumps from looting Egyptians.

To a man, Regulars, National Servicemen and Reservists, we were proud and as pleased as punch to have gone into action with 42 Commando, a unit for whom we had the highest regard.

While the Marines and their allies were fighting their way through the streets of Port Said, more troops came ashore, among them 2 Para, which had the task of advancing down the Canal and pegging out claims as far south as possible.

Les Lambert was a Reservist, recalled to the Parachute Regiment for Suez:

The 2nd Bn., The Parachute Regiment, came ashore under sniper fire. The RAF or the Fleet Air Arm were knocking out Russian-built T.34 tanks only two hundred yards in front of us, helicopters were busy ferrying in stores and the Naval fighters screamed overhead, wheeling and darting in and out of the smoke. The whole town echoed to the sound of machine-gun fire and the dull 'crump' of mortars. The whole of Port Said appeared to be on fire.

My platoon eventually got to the road junction which joined the main road running south along the Suez Canal. There we were met by two tanks which were to be our support. I split the platoon and put half on each tank and went up on the first tank and we discussed tactics. The sergeant shouted something down into the tank and out popped a lad with a bottle of whisky which he opened and handed to me to take a couple of swigs before handing it round to the others. That whisky gave me a real warm feeling, as the night had become very cold. I gave the order to roll, but we had to keep stopping to clear positions and some old shacks on the way . . . and take some prisoners.

We were halted at El-Cap and told by our commander that America had 'stopped the advance'. We began to dig-in and I sent our prisoners back down the line. At one of our road blocks a jeep, with what we thought was a French paratrooper and two reporters, crashed through and made very high speed to the Egyptian lines, which were only about five hundred yards away. We heard a few bursts of machine-gun fire and saw the jeep crash; they were all killed.

America had indeed 'stopped' the Suez operation. As soon as Eisenhower and Dulles realised that the British and French were going ahead with the invasion, the US Ambassador was instructed to go to the Security Council, demand a withdrawal and impose severe and immediate sanctions if the British and French refused to comply.

Without waiting for a response, the US Federal Reserve began selling pounds to drive down the value of sterling and put pressure on the International Monetary Fund to withdraw any support for the pound. Oil sanctions were introduced, with an instruction that American companies were not to make up any shortfall in Britain's oil supplies from the Middle East, which had already dried up.

On the morning of 6 November, as the British troops went ashore, President Eisenhower telephoned Prime Minister Eden with a stark ultimatum; a cease-fire by midnight and the subsequent withdrawal of British troops, or face complete economic isolation and the forfeiture of America's friendship. What such friendship was worth in such circumstances is debatable but Eden had no option but to comply.

Britain was in an impossible position. The Commonweath was divided, the old Dominions largely supporting Britain, the New Commonwealth solidly behind Nasser. At the United Nations, Russia and the United States were in rare alliance, condemning the British, French and Israelis as aggressors, ignoring Nasser's violation of an international treaty and the Soviet build-up of Egyptian arms that had led Israel to launch her strike in the first place.

Worst of all was the lack of support at home, where the Labour and

Liberal elements were loud in condemnation and the oil embargo in the Middle East and the USA had deprived the country of fuel. With anti-war demonstrations in Trafalgar Square and long queues at the petrol stations, the country seemed to be slipping out of Government control.

The final straw was that the Prime Minister, Anthony Eden, was ill and mightily disillusioned with his American friends. He resigned in January 1957, two months after the landings, was taken into hospital and then departed for a long convalescence. Harold Macmillan became Prime Minister and set about the painful but necessary task of rebuilding relations with the USA.

Meanwhile, even during the landing phase, work had begun on clearing the Suez Canal of the blockships sunk in the Channel by the fleeing Egyptians, and restoring public services in Port Said. One of the officers thus engaged was a Major Harry Klein:

On 6 November our task was to head for the waterworks. Fighting was still going on and as we drove up to the gates of the plant, my driver, Jock Swann, was shot in the stomach. He was evacuated and before long I had men deployed at the Sewage Farm, the waterworks and the electricity station, busy restoring services.

There was a lot of concern about water as the French were using the reservoirs for washing and lavatories. I got on very well with the people in the Mayor's office but about the time the UN troops arrived a British officer, Lieutenant Moorhouse, was kidnapped. The Mayor asked if I could get some Egyptian police sent from Cairo to take over when we left. I said I would try if he would use his good offices to find the young officer; the end result was that the police did arrive but the officer was found dead.

Another Sapper officer helping to clear up Port Said was John Arnold:

We flew to Malta and boarded the aircraft carrier *Theseus* for the landing. Along with my revolver I had been issued with five rounds of ammunition and a helicopter pilot insisted on giving me a box of twenty-five rounds from his survival kit. I am glad to say that none of it was used.

We sailed eastward behind the aircraft-carrier HMS, *Eagle*, which was zig-zagging as an anti-submarine precaution. Once on board we were issued with a voluminous set of orders, setting out our duties in Port Said. Apart from maps we were given our tasks, which were to restore the water and electricity systems.

At daybreak we were manoeuvring off Port Said where the assault force was going ashore in landing craft after a Naval bombardment. Our OC was keen for some of our unit to be flown ashore to secure the public services like water supply and sewage works but this was not allowed.

As evening approached, *Theseus* moved slowly into Port Said harbour and anchored with a small boat circling about, dropping small charges into the water to deter frogmen. It was after midnight when we were finally allowed onto Z-craft to be ferried across to the quayside. It was completely dark apart from a fireworks display of tracer from further west where Egyptian troops were getting rid of ammunition.

It was impossible for us to leave the quayside so we set sentries and slept where we were. At dawn we moved on to a grassy patch on the esplanade and brewed up for breakfast with our twenty-four hour ration packs. It was a rude awakening to the realities of war to see a Coca-Cola truck going around the town picking up bodies.

The Squadron HQ was based in ex-Customs officers' accommodation, which had clearly been evacuated in a panic, since we found food on a table, a loaded automatic pistol in a bedroom and a small amount of Egyptian currency. This enabled us to employ Egyptian civilians who had, prior to the invasion, been working for the municipal authority. It was some two weeks later that Egyptian currency was made available officially for this purpose and it came as a surprise to the higher command that we had got in first.

The Municipal Depot lay alongside the Arab quarter. Our forces made very few incursions into the Arab quarter; one was to attempt the rescue of Lieutenant Moorhouse who had been kidnapped by the Egyptians; he was later found dead.

Just before Christmas we learned that UN forces were to relieve us. Our final task was the least pleasant. This was to solder up the metal linings of the coffins of the casualties we had suffered for shipment back to Britain. We sailed back to Southampton in troopships, leaving behind the statue of de Lesseps at the entrance to the Canal, wearing a green Commando beret which the Royal

Marines had placed there. Legend has it that the Egyptians were forced to demolish the statue to get the beret down.

So the Suez affair ended, with a small defiant gesture to cover a major political defeat. When the Egyptian army re-entered Port Said, their first action was to destroy the statue of Ferdinand de Lesseps. The British assault troops, the Marines and Paratroopers, had left on 12 November and all the British and French troops were out by 3 December. Their losses had not been high; twenty-two British soldiers had been killed, ten French, two hundred Israeli and about two thousand Egyptian. The UN troops arrived on 19 November. The Royal Engineers stayed on to clear the Canal and left just before Christmas. The Israelis withdrew across Sinai in early March and the Canal re-opened on 25 March.

In Port Said all was soon much as it was before that day of violence in November 1956, but for the British and French Governments it would never be the same again. Their politicians had learned a harsh lesson about where the real power lay in the post-war world and although their empires still had a few years to run, any use of their imperial power was clearly subject to sanction.

Meantime there were other battles and fresh campaigns for the fighting men. The French soldiers returned to Algeria to find a full-scale rebellion on their hands, while the Royal Marines, paratroopers, tank men and light infantry so recently engaged at Suez were soon back in Cyprus, taking up the struggle with EOKA.

As for 45 Commando, their successful helicopter assault at Port Said was the opening of another era. In Cyprus they formed a new arm, 45 Heliforce, to chase EOKA across the hills. Then the Marines embarked on one of the new Commando carriers to cruise the fringes of the Empire until at the end of the decade, as Port Said slipped into memory, 45 Commando took on a new commitment south of Suez, in the troubled Crown colony of Aden.

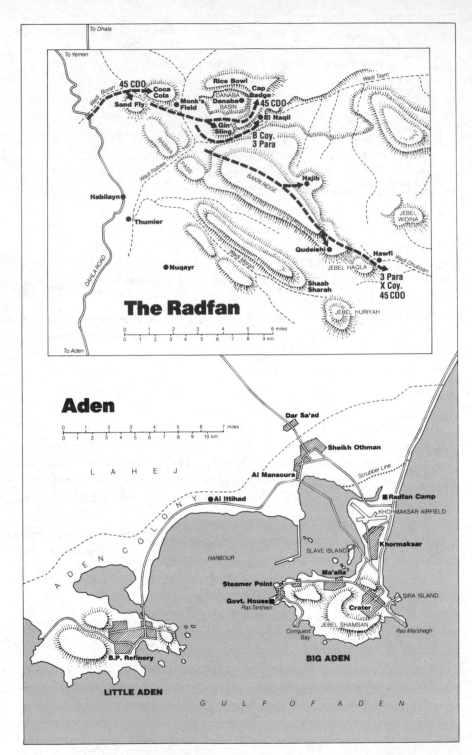

The Radfan

To Dhala
To Yemen
Wadi Boran
45 CDO
Coca Cola
Sand Fly
Monk's Field
Rice Bowl
DANABA
Cap Badge
DANABA BASIN
45 CDO
El Naqil
Gin Sling
B Coy. 3 Para
RABWA
Wadi Rabwa
PASS
Wadi Taym
Habilayn
Thumier
BAKRI RIDGE
Hajib
JEBEL WIDINA
Wadi Metan
Nuqayr
Qudeishi
Hawfi
Wadi Dhubsan
JEBEL HAQLA
Shaab Sharah
3 Para X Coy. 45 CDO
DAHLA ROAD
JEBEL HURIYAH
To Aden

0 1 2 3 4 5 6 miles
0 1 2 3 4 5 6 7 8 9 km.

Aden

0 1 2 3 4 5 6 7 miles
0 1 2 3 4 5 6 7 8 9 10 km.

L A H E J

Dar Sa'ad
Sheikh Othman
Al Mansoura
Scrubber Line
Radfan Camp
Al Ittihad
KHORMAKSAR AIRFIELD
A D E N   C O L O N Y
SLAVE ISLAND
Khormaksar
HARBOUR
Ma'alla
Steamer Point
Govt. House
Ras Tarshein
SIRA ISLAND
Crater
Conquest Bay
JEBEL SHAMSAN
Ras Marshagh
B.P. Refinery
BIG ADEN
LITTLE ADEN
G U L F   O F   A D E N

12

Aden and the Radfan: 1960–1964

'Being in Aden was like stepping back into Biblical times, only all the natives were armed.'

Bryan Ricketts, 'C' Troop, 33 Parachute Light Regt., RA.

The Suez fiasco of 1956 sent shock waves through Britain and the Empire, accelerating the movement towards colonial independence. Suez had demonstrated, beyond any possibility of doubt, that Britain was no longer a world power but a country constrained by economic weakness, and the force of political opinion at home and abroad. Some cartoonists chose to present the new British position in an allegorical light, showing the British Lion as toothless and mangy, surrounded by jackals waiting to snap up the the scraps on the imperial table, while on a nearby tree perched the American Eagle, looking suspiciously like a vulture.

The British needed to reappraise their role and only maintain responsibilities they could actually afford, having finally grasped the words of the economist Maynard Keynes, who in 1946 pointed out that 'Britain cannot police half the world while we are in debt to the other half.'

The first effect of Suez in Britain was the resignation of the Prime Minister, Anthony Eden, and his replacement by Harold Macmillan. Macmillan saw his first task as restoring good relations with Washington, and by March 1957, five months after Suez,

Washington and London were again on speaking terms. This achieved, there followed a complete reappraisal of Britain's economic and political position, especially with regard to her remaining colonial and Empire responsibilities.

These responsibilities were already declining as more and more colonies became independent. Macmillan was determined to reduce Britain's imperial role as quickly as possible and those tentative Independence dates already tabled were gradually reviewed and brought forward. Nationalism and self–determination were the new watchwords and the movement for colonial independence was therefore picking up speed, a fact summed up by Macmillan in a speech in Capetown, South Africa, in February 1960:

> Ever since the break-up of the Roman Empire, one of the constant factors of political life has been the emergence of independent nations. The wind of change is blowing through this Continent and whether we like it or not this growth of national consciousness is a political fact. We must all accept this fact and our national policies must take account of it.

Macmillan had made this speech some weeks before in Accra, but it was this second delivery that caught the attention of the world. His 'Wind of Change' speech became a landmark in the march to colonial independence, a public statement by the British Prime Minister that the Empire had to go and with the greatest possible despatch.

The 'Wind of Change' speech gave great encouragement to nationalists in every part of the Empire. It did not address the fact that while the intention to go might be there, the actual leaving might be difficult. Of nowhere was this more true than in the Crown Colony of Aden, one corner of the old Empire that the British were at first most anxious to retain.

The British acquired the colony and protectorate of Aden almost by accident. It came into British hands in 1839 through the initiative of Captain Haines, an officer of the East India Company, who landed Marines in this dusty little seaport at the foot of the Red Sea to curb Adeni pirates who had been harassing merchant ships on passage from India.

The short sea route to India via the Sinai Desert and the Red Sea was already becoming important and Aden was developed as a naval base for the protection of India-bound shipping. For the next half-century Aden was ruled from the Bombay Presidency and became noted as one of the least desirable postings in the Empire service. In that at least, nothing much changed during the one hundred and thirty years of British occupation.

With the opening of the Suez Canal in 1869, Aden became a coal bunkering station on the India seaway, and a garrison for British troops protecting the southern approaches to the Canal. As oil replaced coal, Aden became even more important, due to the proximity of the Gulf oilfields.

An oil refinery was built at Little Aden in the 1950s, harbour facilities were improved, a modern airfield constructed and a small British garrison established. Aden became an important link on the sea route to Australasia and an important military base. As a glance at the map will reveal, Aden is a strategic spot, close to the oilfields of Arabia, within easy steaming distance of East Africa and the Gulf of Suez, and no great distance from India.

After the loss of the Canal Zone and the Suez débâcle, Aden became the vital link holding Britain's Far and Middle East interests together. Aden was also the base that supported Britain's friends among the sheiks of the Trucial States. The Aden airfields came to contain squadrons of bombers which were employed against dissident tribes in Oman and used to protect British interests and allies in the Persian Gulf.

This last role was still important in the 1960s and the need for such a base was underlined on 25 June 1961, when General Kassim, the new President of Iraq, announced the annexation of Kuwait. Kuwait had been a British protectorate since 1899 and this protectorate had only been terminated on 19 June 1961, six days before General Kassim announced his annexation.

The Amir of Kuwait promptly called for British assistance and within days 42 and 45 Commando, with tanks and artillery were deployed along the Iraqi frontier. Further troops and aircraft poured in from Aden and Kenya and the Iraqis eventually dropped their claim – at least until 1991 when an actual Iraqi invasion provoked the Gulf War.

The 1961 threat was provoked by the widely held Arab belief that Britain was finished as a nation and lacked both the means and the will to protect her interests and guard her allies. A similar belief imbued the inhabitants of Aden Colony and the Aden Protectorate which surrounded it, and they, too, began to agitate for independence. The catalyst for this demand was the new leader of Egypt, Colonel Gamel Abdul Nasser.

The Aden territory was divided into two parts, the colony and the protectorate. Aden Colony was quite small, just seventy square miles of rock and sand on the shores of the Red Sea. The colony contained the port, the airfield, the BP oil refinery, the British HQ and town and suburb of Aden and Little Aden and Crater, all straggling round the large natural harbour, which occupies the crater of an extinct volcano, the feature which made Aden such a useful naval base.

The Aden Protectorate, which surrounded the colony, was much larger, about the size of England, divided into two parts, the Eastern and Western Protectorates, running inland for about a hundred miles towards the frontiers of the Yemen and Saudi Arabia. The protectorate was crossed by just two major roads – often rather rough tracks – which ran through the tawny, steep-sided mountains, one heading towards the Radfan country on the borders of the Yemen and the outpost of Dhala, the other directly into Yemen and the town of Taiz where it divides, with one branch heading towards the capital of Yemen, San'a, the other to the coastal town of Hodeida.

Yemen occupies most of the country north of the Protectorate and is bordered in its turn by Saudi Arabia. The roads from San'a and Dhala were used by camel trains coming down to the coast from the interior, and the Dhala road in particular was to be the scene of constant bickering between British troops and local tribesmen in the years to come.

One of the first British soldiers to arrive on the frontier at this time was Gunner Bryan Ricketts of 33 Parachute Light Regt., Royal Artillery:

We came out from England in November 1957, having gone home after Suez. We were just in troop strength and split between Dhala and Beihan and equipped with 75mm guns. Aden was and remains the hottest place I ever served in. Down in the town of Aden it was hot and sticky even at night. Up at Dhala it was very hot but the nights could get cold. We went through one period when there was an electrical storm every afternoon with torrential rain, then back to heat and sunshine.

I remember one chilly spell up on the border when our TSM, Stan Barker, and the Troop Sergeant 'Crash' Walker – he got the name as a glider pilot during the War – came round with a rum ration. The snag was that at each tent 'Crash' and Stan stayed 'to just have one with you lads' and they were in a fair old state by the time they had finished the rounds.

The locals had very taking ways; they would take anything we didn't nail down, and the wildlife was an eye-opener. Baboons are nasty so-and-so's and I have seen a fully-armed Company halt to let a pack cross the track. There were extremely large spiders called camel spiders, scorpions, snakes and chameleons. We would place the latter on our red berets to see if they would change colour and they usually obliged. Once we found ourselves in the middle of a locust swarm; it was quite an experience, like being in a very heavy snowstorm.

Being up-country in Aden was a bit like being on the moon, wild and rugged but with wonderful views. More than once I found myself actually looking down on our fighter aircraft as they screamed up the wadis to attack some Arab position. I saw a pair of Meteors attacking a rebel held village and one of them was brought down by ground fire; the pilot had no chance to get out at that height. It was a hard place to soldier in.

The British had set up the protectorate in the nineteenth century by negotiating treaties with the local sheiks, intending to use them as a buffer zone against any ambitious expansionist ruler in Saudi Arabia or the Yemen who might fix greedy eyes on the port of Aden. To keep the sheiks in line the British set up a force of Arab soldiers commanded by British officers, often from the RAF Regiment. This force, the Aden Protectorate Levies, was bolstered in times of trouble with aerial interdiction from aircraft based in Aden.

Soldiering in this part of Arabia was not unlike that experienced by British troops on the North–West Frontier of India during the hey–day of the Raj. Both areas of the protectorate contained a number of warlike mountain tribes who enjoyed raiding the caravans on the Dhala road, shooting at British soldiers and chewing *qat*, a hallucinogenic drug extracted from the leaves of the *qat* bush.

The sheiks of the Aden Protectorate did not relish the British presence but at least the British usually left them alone; not so the Imam, ruler of the Yemen, who had greedy eyes on Aden and the sheikdoms of the protectorate which, he claimed, rightly owed allegiance and tribute to his Court in San'a.

These Yemeni claims to sovereignty over the Protectorate and Aden grew louder and stronger during the late 1950s when British power was seen to be in decline. These demands grew more insistent after the Suez débâcle when any form of British connection was condemned by Colonel Nasser. In 1958 Nasser established the United Arab Republic, pulling together Egypt, Syria and later the Yemen. This 'Republic' eventually came apart, but it took action against those perceived as too openly pro-British. In July 1958 the King of Iraq, his entire family and the Prime Minister, Nuri el Said, were murdered in a Nasser-backed coup. Rioters in Baghdad also sacked and burned the British Embassy.

Similar coups were simmering in Jordan and the Lebanon and were only prevented when the rulers of those countries called for Western assistance; the United States duly landed Marines in the Lebanon and the British sent a Parachute Brigade to Amman. Checked in Jordan and the Lebanon, Nasser turned his attention to British rule south of the Canal, in the Crown Colony of Aden.

The British were not unaware of Nasser's intentions, which were being loudly proclaimed as a liberation movement for the oppressed people of Aden and the protectorate by the 'Voice of the Arabs' radio in Cairo. In 1959, in an attempt to prevent the protectorate being reduced by degrees as one sheik after another was picked off by the Nasser-backed Yemenis, the British encouraged the protectorate sheiks to join together and form a South Arabia Federation.

Since the sheiks enjoyed their independence this proposal met with a lukewarm response, at least until more anti-sheik broadcasts by the 'Voice of the Arabs' radio made them reconsider their position. In 1959 the sheiks of the Western Protectorate, the part closest to Yemen, joined together in the Federation of South Arabia, each sheik nominating members to the Federal Council and taking it in turns to act as Federal Chairman.

The next step in a deteriorating situation took place within Aden Colony. British Petroleum (BP) had built a refinery at Little Aden in 1954. Following the loss of the Anglo–Iranian refinery at Abadan and the problems over Suez, the facilities at Aden expanded, and more labour was required. Before long people from the Yemen were moving into the colony to find work. Once there these workers formed themselves into Trades Unions and quickly outnumbered the native Adeni workers. These Yemeni-dominated Trades Unions eventually formed an association, the Aden Trades Union Council, which became a political force and a front for a Yemeni takeover of the Federation and Aden Colony.

The leader of the ATUC, Abdullah Asnag, made little secret of his aims: to expel the British and take over the colony for the Yemen or, to be exact, for the United Arab Republic – or Colonel Nasser. Asnag was also an extreme left-wing Socialist and his second aim was to overthrow the sheiks of the Protectorate, and establish a 'Democratic People's Republic of Yemen' rather on the lines of the then Soviet satellite, East Germany.

Matters were thus poised, in September 1962, when the Iman of the Yemen died and was replaced by his son, Al-Badr. A week later Al-Badr was overthrown and reportedly killed in another Egyptian-fostered coup led by the leader of the Yemeni Army, General Sallal.

This coup was greeted with glee by Asnag and his supporters who demanded the immediate evacuation of Aden by the British imperialists and the joining of Aden and the Protectorate with the new Yemeni republic. Colonel Nasser was a vociferous supporter of this plan and to give it weight sent two Egyptian divisions, totalling some twenty thousand men, to aid the 'People's Struggle' in South Arabia.

Sallal and Nasser's ambitions then received a check. It transpired that Al-Badr had not been killed in the coup. He resurfaced in Saudi Arabia where the King was thoroughly alarmed by this 'socialist republican' outbreak on the borders of his realm. The sheiks of the protectorate were equally disturbed and when, flush with Saudi money, Al-Badr bought arms and began a guerrilla war against the Sallal forces and the Egyptian Army, the protectorate tribesmen flocked to his banner.

Al-Badr then received another unexpected but very welcome ally in the person of Major John Cooper, one of the original soldiers of the wartime SAS, who had been recruited in London by the founder of the SAS, Colonel David Stirling, and sent to help Al-Badr. Cooper and some 'unofficial volunteers' from 22 SAS Regiment began to make the Yemeni mountains a most uncomfortable place for the soldiers of the Egyptian Army. The Egyptians eventually had to commit some seventy thousand troops to the Yemen and were still unable to defeat Al-Badr's forces.

While this hot little war was simmering in the Yemen, the situation in the Aden Colony and Protectorate was becoming tense, exacerbated by the ranting of the 'Voice of the Arabs' radio, which was urging Arabs everywhere to throw off the colonial yoke. The local situation was complicated enough without such encouragement but the deteriorating political situation in Aden was at least partly the fault of the British themselves as they seemed undecided about the long-term possibilities of maintaining land bases in Africa or Arabia and uncertain about the need to retain troops East of Suez at all.

Defence thinking in the late 1950s and early 1960s tended to favour reliance on the nuclear deterrent rather than large conventional armies for maintaining Britain's strategic clout, and the use of amphibious forces based on Commando carriers or rapid reaction from UK-based forces to provide military assistance to Britain's allies in case of need.

Switching to the nuclear deterrent had several advantages, chiefly that it would enable Britain to end conscription for National Service, which was both expensive and unpopular. The growing size and range of transport aircraft gave small, well-trained regular forces a certain strategic mobility, provided landing fields existed and overflying rights could be negotiated.

It was still necessary to train and base troops abroad for reasons of acclimatisation, for troops dumped in the desert or jungle could not be immediately effective. Aden, therefore, was an anachronism but potentially a useful one, which – if only for reasons of prestige and to keep faith with the protectorate sheiks – Britain could not lightly abandon. As the politicians hesitated, the situation in Aden began to worsen.

Charles Carruthers was stationed in Aden from 1963 to 1965, working as a telegraphist:

I was just nineteen years of age and away from my family for the first time. The transformation shock was tremendous for Aden was noted for the 'Barren Rocks' and lived up to its name. I was on a two-year tour and wondered how I was going to last out, having felt the heat and humidity and seen the squalor of the place.

ADEN AND THE RADFAN 333

Aden was still a British Colony and we were treated as the 'sahibs' then but it was not an attractive posting. I was in a club at Steamer Point the night after I arrived and a Scots lad asked me how long I had to do – he obviously saw I was a 'moonie' fresh out of the UK – and I told him one year and three hundred and sixty-four days. He said he was finished the following day and I really envied him.

I was allocated a billet at Temple Hill which had been put up before World War II, and what with bed-bugs and the noise of dogs howling at night and working split shifts, I was soon run down. Up to December 1963 things were fairly quiet; then a grenade incident at Khormaksar airfield, aimed at the High Commissioner, sparked off the State of Emergency which carried on till the end of our time in Aden in 1967.

The local people were also being stirred up. President Sallal was shouting the odds over Radio Yemen about killing all the British, and President Nasser of Egypt was backing him up. In 1964 the military campaign in the Radfan began, mainly to stop the Yemenis running guns into the colony. The 'Red Wolves of Radfan' were the main contestants fighting the British troops; the Radfan was like the surface of the moon with a terrible heat thrown in. At night it cooled down and you could sometimes see the lights of Aden. The 'Red Wolves' were crack shots, even with antiquated guns, but they soon got modern weapons and land mines. The Dhala road had to be cleared each day and the Red Wolves re-mined it at night.

Things were also hotting up back in Aden. The National Liberation Front (NLF) were not too happy with our future Aden Federal Government set-up using the sheiks, and sporadic terrorist incidents occurred. I was in the Astra cinema at Steamer Point one evening when some NLF Arabs got onto the GPO roof and fired a missile through the wall of the British Forces Broadcasting Service. They also threw a grenade at a sentry on the roof. The cinema cleared out and we stayed behind a barrier while shots were exchanged. The Arabs got off the GPO roof and ran up a side road past ASD Cold Storage, where the Forces medical supplies were held, and machine-gunned a Ministry of Public Buildings worker who came out of his house to look. A taxi driver was also shot in the mêlée.

Another incident happened when I was guarding the Tarshyne Officers' mess. WRAF and WRAC girls would check Arab and Somali 'Bintas' (home-helps), as they came in, while we checked any Arab men. During the evening a steward from the Officers' Mess came out with lemon juice for us and was generally convivial. He was a local Arab and seemed quite happy in his work. I finished at midnight, went down to the armoury to hand in my whistle, rifle and ammunition and was on the way to my billet when there was a tremendous explosion.

The following day I found out that the Arab steward had been wiring up a bomb under the main dining table, timed to explode in the morning, hoping to kill the AOC, Air Vice Marshal Johnnie Johnston and Admiral Le Fanu, when the bomb went off prematurely, blowing him to pieces.

Such incidents continued: one night the Oasis Bar was bombed and the carnage there was terrible, but my tour was up before it got really bad.

Most of the violence in 1963–4 was caused by a newly created, Yemeni-backed political organisation, the NLF, the National Liberation Front, which hoped to take over the colony when the British finally left. It was generally conceded that the British intended to withdraw from Aden fairly soon, as part of a general retrenchment away from South Arabia and back to the newly established British bases in Cyprus.

This intention was thwarted by Government indecision over the 'East of Suez' policy – whether Britain actually needed to maintain troops in Asia or the Indian Ocean area at all. Having lost the Canal Zone, the two most likely places for a strategic base north and south of Suez were Kenya and Cyprus but with independence looming in Kenya and the recent troubles in Cyprus, neither looked a very good long-term bet. If Britain really intended to maintain forces in the Middle East and East of Suez the obvious base was Aden. Now there was trouble there, which British indecision only encouraged.

One answer to the land base problem was to do away with land bases altogether. With this aim in view the early 1960s saw the introduction of the 'Commando carrier' concept. Two aircraft carriers, HMS *Bulwark* and HMS *Albion* were equipped with helicopter squadrons and refitted to carry a Royal Marine Commando as a mobile striking force and centrepiece of a roving amphibious fleet.

These carriers and the newly commissioned assault ships, HMS *Fearless* and HMS *Intrepid*, with support ships of the Royal Navy and the Royal Fleet Auxilary, could roam the oceans at will, stopping to refuel, rest the crews and exercise the Marines at friendly ports allied to Britain through NATO, the Central Power Treaty Organisation, (CENTO) or the South East Asia Treaty Organisation (SEATO). The Commando carrier concept gave the Royal Marines a greatly enhanced amphibious capacity but the new role was not without problems. To begin with, some doubts existed over who actually commanded the embarked Commando, the CO of the unit or the Captain of the ship.

> The problem arose [says one Commando officer] because some ships' Captains regarded the Commando as the ship's armament, like guns or torpedoes, over which he, the Captain, had ultimate control . . . and you can see the similarity. Some Commando COs were disconcerted when ordered to parade the men on the flight deck so that the Captain could inspect 'His' Commando. The snag was that a Royal Navy Captain with sufficient seniority to command a capital ship usually out-ranked a humble Lt.-Colonel of Marines – quite apart from the fact that Royal Navy Captains think they are God anyway. We usually got round it by embarking the Brigadier, and that kept the matelots in their place.

While these delicate problems were being debated out at sea, tensions rose in Aden. The crux of the problem was, if and when the British withdrew, to whom would they hand over power? The British had not yet announced that they intended to leave but the world, and especially the Arab world, believed that Britain was in terminal decline and their retreat or expulsion from Aden could only be a matter of time. Anticipating this moment, Aden had now produced a number of contenders for post–independence control and between them they created a political situation of almost Byzantine complexity.

The sheiks of the former protectorate hoped to maintain the existing Federation, incorporate the colony into it – the colony, then called Aden State, merged with the Federation in January 1963 – and gain UN recognition as an independent republic. This aim was contested by Mr Asnag, who wanted a socialist repblic linked to the Yemen or Egypt. Mr Asnag had the unions on his side and the Adeni workers in general supported his party, the People's Socialist Party or PSP.

There was also the rival and more violent faction, the Marxist National Liberation Front or NLF; both the PSP and the NLF enjoyed Yemeni support at first, though the NLF was not keen on replacing the British with the Egyptians and eventually elected to fight for a South Arabia free of all outside ties. All that was for the future. The current aim of the NLF and PSP in 1963–4 was to foment unrest among the protectorate tribes and get rid of the British and the sheiks.

Asnag was determined that Aden should be handed over to his PSP, the political arm of the Adeni Trades Union movement. Knowing that victory for the Socialists in Aden would mean their extinction, the protectorate sheiks looked to the British to provide protection during the current trouble and to set up a strong, equitable Federal Government before they left. This latter hope was not to be fulfilled.

Aden finally exploded into violence at Khormaksar airfield on the morning of 10 December 1963, when a grenade was thrown at the High Commissioner, Sir Kennedy Trevaskis, who was leaving to attend a conference in London. The High Commissioner escaped unharmed but the grenade killed an Indian lady and mortally injured the High Commissioner's assistant, as well as wounding fifty more people and a State of Emergency was declared the same day. With unrest mounting within the colony and war in the Yemen, it was decided to reinforce the Aden garrison and move troops up to the Radfan in order to stop the traffic of arms and explosives into the colony and protectorate down the Dhala road.

The forces in Aden consisted of the Federal Army of four battalions, formerly the 'Aden Protectorate Levies', now commanded by Brigadier James Lunt. This force still had British officers but Adeni officers were being trained and were replacing the British at a rapid rate. There was also a force of Tribal Guards in the protectorate and a National Guard of police reservists used within the former Aden Colony for public order duties.

The British garrison consisted of two battalions of infantry, some artillery, tanks and armoured cars, a squadron of Royal Engineers largely employed on road building and mine clearing, a squadron of RAF Hunter ground-attack fighters and some Shackleton transports converted into bombers. These operated from the airfield at RAF Khormaksar just north of the Arab suburb of Crater.

This move up-country to Dhala and the Radfan, brought the British Army to the frontier, in particular the 3rd Bn., The Parachute Regiment, and 45 Commando, Royal Marines; 45 Commando had arrived in Aden in April 1960 and were to remain there for the next seven years, until British rule ended in November 1967, spending much of their time around Dhala and in constant contact with hostile tribesmen.

According to the Commanding Officer of 45 Commando, Lt.-Colonel Paddy Stevens, the tribesmen of the Radfan were 'a xenophobic lot, equipped from boyhood with rifles, who regarded the arrival of the British Army in their mountains as the chance for a bit of target practice.' The Radfan tribesmen had made a steady living for centuries, extracting money and goods from caravans using the Dhala road, and resented British attempts to limit their trade.

Aided and inspired by the Yemenis, who were in turn aided and supplied by the Egyptians, the Radfan tribesmen soon had Dhala under daily attack. By mining the road from Aden and ambushing army convoys, they made the position of the British and Federal garrison as difficult as possible. The normal method of discouraging such attacks was air interdiction; dropping leaflets telling the tribesmen to desist and bombing their villages if they didn't. Bombing and napalm attacks had been employed by the Egyptian Air Force against Royalist forces in the Yemen and attracted critical comment around the world, so this deterrent could not be employed by the British in the Federation. The task of countering the attacks was therefore given to the infantry.

By January 1964 the forces deployed against the tribesmen in the Radfan had increased considerably and Brigadier Lunt felt able to plan a campaign, Operation Nutcracker, to penetrate the country east of the Dhala road and quell the more intransigent Radfan tribes. Brigadier Lunt might also have had the fit and experienced 45 Commando but this unit had been called away in January to suppress an Army mutiny in Tanganyika, one of a number of mutinies that took place in Kenya, Uganda and Tanganyika (now Tanzania) shortly after independence.

Brigadier Lunt's main force at Dhala consisted of three battalions of the Federal Army, some light tanks, batteries of field artillery, Wessex troop-carrying helicopters from the Commando carrier HMS *Centaur* and ground-attack Hunter fighters. Within four weeks this force had driven the tribesmen away from the Dhala road and enabled the Royal

Engineers to build another road up into the heart of the Radfan itself. This advance into the centre of the Radfan was greeted with great enthusiasm by the loyal tribes and Brigadier Lunt was presented with an engraved sword by the Emir of Dhala.

The problem was that this effort could not be maintained. When the British and the Federal Army withdrew to Dhala and Aden in March 1964 the tribesmen returned to their old haunts and their old ways. The withdrawal also enabled the Yemeni radio stations to claim that the tribes had in fact defeated the Federal Army and their British allies. Brought under pressure once again, the protectorate sheiks invoked the Defence Treaty and called for the return of British troops. This time it was 45 Commando RM, now back in Aden, that led the advance up the Dhala road.

In 1964, 45 Commando was commanded by Lt.-Colonel T.M.P. (Paddy) Stevens. Colonel Stevens had landed with 41 (Royal Marine) Commando on D-Day and fought on in north-western Europe as a rifle troop commander until victory in 1945. Colonel Stevens had anticipated an early return to the Radfan and had drawn up a plan, as in the days of the North-West Frontier, to pursue the tribesmen to their fastness in the hills, however remote that might be, and demonstrate that there was no peace and security for them if they persisted in attacking the Dhala road.

Colonel Stevens's first task was to get his men fit:

> We were down in Aden where the climate is vile but the men were pretty fit anyway, not least because sport was the only recreation Aden offered. The Radfan assault could only have been carried out by very fit troops, and luckily there was a hill behind our base in Little Aden with a track over the top. I put my kit on and set the 'check-time' which everyone in the Unit had to better. Before long some of the fitter men were putting up some amazing times. By going over this course twice a day, in that heat and humidity, everyone got a lot fitter and of course it was a lot cooler four thousand feet up in the Radfan, where this training paid off.

This second advance into the Radfan was commanded by Brigadier Hardgroves, the Commander of the Aden Garrison. Colonel Stevens's particular task was to penetrate the Radfan and take a hill in the middle of the area, codenamed 'Cap-Badge', from which his force could dominate the principal village, Danaba, which was known to be a tribal stronghold.

To achieve this aim, he had in his command 45 Commando, 'B' Company, 3 Para and 'A' Squadron, 22 SAS Regiment, plus helicopters, Royal Engineers, the guns of 'J' Battery, Royal Horse Artillery, and some Federal units. Colonel Paddy Stevens again:

> The first intention was to move in by helicopter but there were not enough helicopters – there never are enough helicopters – and it was decided that we should go in by night and on foot. Doubts were expressed as to whether we could move our entire Commando through that country in single file at night, but the SAS did it with small parties and I remembered how 1 Commando Brigade had moved out of the Normandy beachhead in 1944 . . . so that's how we did it.

The task of 45 was to seize the 'Cap Badge' feature and dominate Danaba, for 'Cap-Badge' divided the Wadi Taym from the Danaba basin, two fertile and populous areas which the tribesmen would be sure to defend. To the north of the Danaba basin lay another high feature, a long ridge codenamed 'Rice Bowl'. The secret of the Radfan fighting was to hold the high ground, so taking these two features was vital. The snag was to get to them. 45 elected to advance by night from around Thumier, through the rugged terrain of the Wadi Boran, into Danaba and so up 'Cap-Badge'.

This route meant skirting or taking two other hill features, codenamed 'Sand Fly' and 'Coca Cola'. While 45 were marching in, 'B' Company of 3 Para were to parachute on to the Wadi Taym, landing on a DZ held by the SAS and this position was to be held until 45 arrived. The advance from Thumier began on 30 April 1964 and while 45's part went well, the operation soon ran into trouble.

The ten-man SAS patrol under Captain Edwards, tasked with seizing the DZ for 'B' Company of 3 Para had infiltrated towards 'Cap-Badge', but were discovered by a shepherd early on the morning of the 30th; the SAS were then surrounded by armed tribesmen who came swarming up from Danaba. Pinned down and under heavy fire, the SAS lost their commander, Captain Edwards, and their radio operator who were both killed, and the patrol was only saved from complete annihilation by calling RAF Hunters in to to strafe their

position. The SAS eventually withdrew but were forced to leave
the two dead men behind. Since the DZ could not be secured,
the parachute drop was called off but meanwhile 45 Commando
had began their march into the Radfan.

One of the Marines marching on Danaba that night was Sergeant
Eric Blythe of the Mortar Platoon:

> I joined 45 in Aden after they got back from Dar es Salaam. Paddy
> Stevens was the CO and the first operation was the move up to
> 'Cap-Badge'. It was rough country but Aden is a rugged place to
> soldier in and you had to be fit. I didn't like the fact that you
> could be seen for miles and the enemy snipers were excellent.
> The Paras got hit badly in the Radfan, because the enemy were
> waiting for them. They had six killed and we fired over three
> hundred smoke bombs to cover their position. When I was with
> 'X' Troop 45, on Battery Ridge in the Radfan, we had to go down
> into the valley, but the heights had not been properly picketed and
> we got pounced on at once by the snipers; you had to control the
> heights or you got hit.
>
> Some time later a Para officer, Lt.-Colonel Farrar-Hockley, arrived
> by helicopter and landed right in front of us, so we had to go forward
> and various people got hit.

In spite of the going, which was rough, and their loads, which were
heavy, 45 made good time that first night. Radio communication is
always difficult in the mountains but a message got through telling
Paddy Stevens what had happened to the SAS and that the parachute
drop had been cancelled. 'B' Company of 3 Para were now coming
up by lorry to Thumier to join 45, and Colonel Stevens was told to
'go firm' on 'Coca Cola' and 'Sand Fly' and await further orders.

By midnight the leading section of 'X' Company was near 'Coca
Cola', west of Danaba. This feature had to be scaled and Colonel
Stevens held a hasty conference with Major Mike Banks, the OC of
'X' Company, after seeing that the route up 'Coca Cola' would be
very difficult, especially for the Heavy Weapons Troop with their
mortars and machine-guns.

Major Banks was a Himalayan climber of considerable experience
and there were other trained climbers in 45, some fortunately equipped
with ropes. Major Banks assembled his climbing team, established a

route to the top of 'Coca Cola', and laid out a 'rather tatty length of line' up which the ladened men of 45 hauled and panted their way to the top.

By first light the Commandos were on top of both 'Coca Cola' and 'Sand Fly' and overlooking the Danaba basin, much to the consternation of the tribesmen, who had been busy harrying the SAS patrol. The Marines had, however, lost the initial advantage of surprise and from then on would be advancing against stiff opposition when they moved on to take 'Cap Badge'. When that time came Paddy Stevens again elected for a night approach.

'Cap Badge' mountain, the Commando's ultimate objective, lay to the east, rearing up more than 1,000ft (350m) above the plain. After five days on 'Coca Cola' and 'Sand Fly', probing out into the Danaba basin, and having been relieved on those features by the Royal Anglian Regiment, 45 moved to take 'Cap Badge', having been joined meanwhile by 'B' Company, 3 Para. The Commando descended into the Danaba valley, skirted the village and with 'X' Company under Mike Banks leading the way up the rock faces, the Marines and paratroopers were established on 'Cap Badge' by first light.

'B' Company of 3 Para captured the village of El Naquil, losing six men wounded and two killed before they overran the enemy positions, and they had to be reinforced by 'Z' Company of 45, before the Marines and paratroopers were able to consolidate their positions on the mountains. The tribesmen came out to fight occupying stone 'sangars' on the slopes of the hills around Danaba and El Naquil and Paddy Stevens eventually called in Hunter aircraft to dislodge them with rockets.

Having taken Danaba and the surrounding features 45 and the Paras stayed on for another week, patrolling the area, entering all the tribal villages, making their presence felt, before they returned to Dhala to prepare for the next phase of the Radfan operation.

The forces composing 'Radforce' now consisted of 39 Brigade under Brigadier Blacker, a force containing 45 Commando, the 1st East Anglians, the 3rd Bn., the Parachute Regiment, the King's Own Scottish Borderers (KOSBs) and the 1st Bn., The Royal Scots, with the 2nd battalion of the Federal Army, supported by tanks and armoured cars as well as Hunter aircraft. The Radfan campaign was taking on the elements of all-out war.

In mid-May 3 Para and 'X' Company of 45 moved out to scale the

Bakri ridge and after a four-day fight cleared it of dissidents, moving on from there to occupy the Wadi Dhubsan, another tribal stronghold. It was during this operation that Lt.-Colonel Farrar-Hockley, the CO of 3 Para, came under fire in his Scout helicopter, which was forced down by ground fire. The final phase was an advance by the East Anglians and the 2 Bn. FRA into the Wadi Misra in early June. The advance into the Wadi took a week and finished with an all-out, full-day battle around the village of Shaab Sarah, which broke the back of local resistance.

By October most of the Radfan tribes had submitted and the troops, while keeping their guard up, were able to devote themselves to 'hearts and minds' operations, offering medical assistance to the tribespeople, building tracks and airstrips and generally ensuring that any future advance into the Radfan would not be as difficult as the one they had just made. There was, however, one unpleasant aftermath which came to light after the Radfan operation had ended. The bodies of the two SAS men killed at the start had been found where they fell by the tribesmen and decapitated. The heads had been taken to the Yemen and displayed impaled on stakes in the market place of Taiz.

Although the occupation of the Radfan quelled the tribesmen's activities for a while and blunted the NLF–PSP hopes of a swift British defeat, 45 Commando and other British battalions were to be kept busy in the Radfan on and off for the next two years.

Major Tom Godwin was then a platoon sergeant in 'D' Company, 1st Battalion, The Parachute Regiment, and recalls these days in the Radfan:

The Company had flown from Bahrain to Aden to take up position at the 'Beau Geste' fort outside Dhala village, some seven hours' drive from Aden town. The Company was to look after the interests of the Emir of Dhala and, together with the Federal National Guard, to deny the area to the 'Adoo', the tribesmen coming in from North Yemen. This was the second tour of six weeks that the Company had copped, while the other rifle companies had carried out one tour in Aden town.

The Commander of 'D' Company, Major Rick Oddie, was a soldier's soldier. He had boxed for the Battalion as a subaltern and he always led from the front. The Company soon made its mark when the Royal Air Force Regiment requested assistance to site an anti-tank gun on a pimple some three hundred feet high, just outside the camp perimeter. This proved too difficult for the boys in blue – well, we were over five thousand feet. Not to be deterred, half the Company heaved it up there with toggle ropes and the anti-tank gun was in the perfect position to cover the Dhala to Aden road.

That evening the anti-tank crew were given the order to test fire the spotter rounds and main charge at maximum range. They were all delighted and in 'firing for effect' got three HE rounds in the air together before the first round exploded. The explosions were deafening, reverberating around this silent valley.

At the crack of dawn next day, hot foot into our camp came the British Political Agent who forbade the Company to fire this weapon ever again. Apparently the shell explosions had caused the expensive ceiling within the Emir's Palace to detach itself and it had crashed into the harem with a cloud of dust. We were advised to show less initiative and stay where we were.

During the second week we were there, unbeknown to the Agent, a fighting patrol went out, made up of half the Company under the OC, with the CSM and us two platoon sergeants. The OC gave the Company 2/IC a rendezvous for five days hence, naming the spot where the Company was to be picked up by armed convoy, and off went the fighting patrol due north, piqueting the highest ground. The third day was spent on a 'cordon and search' of a village where British troops had never been before.

Each evening before last light, stone sangars were made and the Union Flag was hoisted: the OC said, 'The buggers know that we are here, let them come and take us!' All went well as we dominated the area and no one would have been any the wiser but for the fact that on the return journey to Dhala, a driver cut the corner and by not following the exact track of the vehicle in front, caused the rear offside wheel to run over a Mark VII mine.

The 3-tonner was mineplated and sandbagged, so apart from the immediate loss of the tailboard and rear axle and a certain amount of dignity as one was thrown out of the vehicle, no one was badly injured. The convoy then came under not very effective fire from over six hundred yards away as the soldiers were still diving for cover, except for the OC, of course, who was far too busy walking around taking photographs.

We then had another visit by the Political Agent, who was more than a little peeved not to have known where the half-company had been for the past four days. The Company was promptly relieved from its duties at Dhala and sent to man three outposts at Monks Field, Hotel 10, Cap Badge. There we were to come under command of the Scots Guards.

My platoon position overlooked a crossing point where camel trains and the odd beat-up vehicle used to pass. The point was manned during the day by a Section who used to search the odd baggage animal or vehicle. The Section was usually in position by 0600 hrs. One particular morning, as the Section was on its way down the steep slope, the Platoon Sergeant smelt a rat and told the men to take cover. He had noticed that by first light there were usually Arabs at the crossing point, but there were none that day. The Section duly waited a good twenty minutes, and what happened then was half-expected. The cross-track area where the Section usually stood, disappeared with a mighty explosion.

The Platoon Sergeant, Aussie Fotheringham, was a canny old soldier who had fought with the Canadian Army in the Korean War. After the first explosion he held the Section where it was for another half-an-hour or so and was well rewarded for his patience when the secondary explosion went off.

While the troops were fighting in the Radfan, attempts were being made to find an acceptable, long-term, political solution in Aden. A Conservative Minister, Duncan Sandys, visited Aden in May 1964 and reconvened the Conference that had been stopped by the grenade attack on the High Commissioner the previous December. This Conference took place in London the following month and concluded that the Federation should become independent not later than 1968 but that the British base would remain in place, to protect British interests in the Gulf and assure the survival of the protectorate sheiks.

The British hoped that this announcement of departure would end the uncertainty and concentrate local minds in a bid to find and support a constitutional solution. The actual effect was to produce chaos.

The various political parties began to fight among themselves, sparing time to attack the British and declare that the idea of a British base in Aden after independence was not acceptable. Those who had hitherto been loyal to the British, especially officers in the police and the Federal Army felt themselves exposed for, as in India, once the British had announced the intention to leave, their power and influence began to seep away. Those locals in positions of authority therefore wisely sought some form of accommodation with the potential inheritors of the new country.

The Aden problem was then taken over by the Labour Government of Harold Wilson, which came to power in October 1964. The NLF had switched tactics from inciting the tribes in the Radfan to urban terrorism in Aden Town, and began a sustained campaign just as the new Colonial Secretary, Anthony Greenwood, arrived in Aden on a 'factfinding' mission. The most tragic event of this new terrorist campaign came when a hand grenade was thrown into a children's party at RAF Khormaksar, killing one teenage girl and injuring four others. Grenade attacks had become very common with the NLF targeting the officers of the Aden Special Branch for particular attention.

Ray Ashworth, a teenager, was in Aden at this time:

My father was an Army officer, posted to Aden in 1964. We arrived in August and by then it was getting difficult, the troubles were starting and we were confined to Aden and Crater. Within these towns there was little trouble that first year and we could visit the Officers' Club at Tarshyne every afternoon. We could hear the thud of grenades in the evening and the radio would say 'no casualties or damage'. If there were casualties they were nearly always Arabs. At a guess there were five or ten Arab civilians killed for every Briton or Arab soldier or policeman.

I heard at school that the NLF used to pick up Arabs off the street and give them £5 to throw a grenade. Most of them would take the money and throw the grenade on to waste ground. We also heard stories of a spate of exploding Arabs, who had misread the instructions which said, 'Take out the pin and throw away'. The worst problem was the constant need for security. At the worst times we could not go out at night or even cross the main road. So I was very bored that year.

We had a first-class school at Khormaksar. I had been at school in Germany and Aden, studying for 'O' and 'A' levels and I missed no schooling but others were not so lucky. You could meet twelve-year-olds from Service families who could barely read or write because of being moved so often. There was always a guard on the school, at first an RAF man with a Lee-Enfield and then a Light Infantry man with an SLR (self-loading rifle).

One night I was walking down the road with my father and his boss, Lt.-Colonel Alec Seaton. A car passed and something fell from it, a smoking tube the size of a toilet roll holder. I was grabbed from the rear and swept behind a parked car and there was a loud bang. All the cars were riddled with shrapnel and there was a great smell of petrol. The only one hurt was Mrs Peart, who was walking some way behind us with her husband. Mr Peart pushed her to the ground and fell on top to protect her, but he weighed 18 stone (252lbs) and she got a bit crushed.

Another night, when Dad was Brigade Duty Officer, he got a call from the commander of a Saladin armoured car in Crater, requesting permission to open fire with its main 75mm gun. This was usually forbidden and Dad had difficulty getting hold of the Brigadier or some other senior officer. Eventually he found a senior officer and permission to fire was refused. Later on he was asked, 'What would you have done if you had not found me?' and Dad said that if British soldiers' lives were at risk he would have given them permission to fire – 'and you would then have been court martialled,' was the stern reply.

Matters were also complicated on the civil side. The High Commissioner, Sir Kennedy Trevaskis, did not get on with Anthony Greenwood, the Colonial Secretary, and they disagreed in particular over the correct response to the demands of Asnag's PSP. Trevaskis saw the PSP as the stalking horse for the Yemenis; Greenwood saw it as a decent Trade-Union movement, striving to better the lot of the workers and as such worthy of Labour Government support.

Trevaskis therefore resigned and was replaced by Sir Richard Turnbull who in turn appointed Abdul Makawee, leader of the Opposition in the Legislative Council as Chief Minister after the previous Minister resigned. Constitutionally, Turnbull had no option, other than a return to direct British rule, but it proved a terrible mistake. Since Makawee was an open supporter of Yemeni nationalism and a declared opponent of British rule in Aden, his appointment can only have been occasioned by some form of political death-wish.

From the moment of his appointment Makawee spared no pains

to support the local terrorists and obstruct the actions of the High Commissioner and the police. When members of a Constitutional Commission arrived from Britain to discuss the Federation's future he refused them permission to get off their aircraft at Khormaksar. The High Commissioner's refusal to over-rule Mackawee on this issue was seen as yet another sign of British impotence but eventually, and rather quickly, Makawee overplayed his hand.

The final straw came when a grenade was thrown at a party of British schoolchildren waiting for a flight out at Khormaksar; five of the children were injured. At that point Turnbull had enough of Mackawee, who was dismissed from office and promptly 'fled' to the Yemen and then to Cairo, from where he continued to rail against British rule in 'South Yemen'.

With Makawee removed and direct rule reimposed, the Federal Army, which now took over the responsibility for security, had no difficulty restoring order. The Labour Government had learned that ending colonial rule was not as easy as it looked from the Opposition benches and by the early months of 1965 it seemed as if independence might come peacefully and the British could leave with heads high, their prestige intact and their allies comforted. It was not to work out like that.

13

The End in Aden: 1964–1967

'An Arab is a man who would pull down a whole temple, just to have a stone to sit on.'

John Gunther, 1955.

Although the resumption of direct rule in Aden State – as the colony was now called – brought a brief halt to hostilities, this action did not reverse the British determination to leave as soon as possible. The criteria for leaving required the creation of a stable Government and some guarantee that British forces could use the facilites of Aden if British interests in the Indian Ocean or the Gulf should ever be threatened.

Such a proposal was already on the table. When Duncan Sandys announced in 1964 that the Federation would be granted independence not later than 1968, and added that Britain intended to retain the Aden base and use it to oppose any attacks on the newly independent Federation and to protect British interests in the Indian Ocean and the Gulf, he reassured the protectorate sheiks. The problem now was to draw up a constitution for the newly independent state and leave a workable Government in power. It was already becoming clear that this would not be easy.

While the Royal Marines and the Army had been campaigning in the Radfan, matters had gone from bad to worse in Aden itself. The Yemeni-backed National Liberation Front, or NLF, had entered the fray and was supporting Asnag's Trades Union activists with strikes, riots and grenade attacks on the British garrison and civilians.

To assist in maintaining internal security, in early 1964 fresh troops had been sent in from the Rhine Army and Northern Ireland, and the King's Own Scottish Borderers (KOSBs), who had just left Aden, found themselves back in that undesirable troublespot where they were joined by the 1st Bn., The Royal Scots. Other battalions were to follow as the situation deteriorated.

That battle on the Bakri Ridge in June 1964 had finally broken the back of tribal resistance in the Radfan and was seen in Aden as a defeat for the NLF but final submissions in the Protectorate were not made for another nine months, until March 1965. This enabled the Army to switch troops back to the colony where a busy urban guerrilla war was now being waged against the soldiers and the British expatriate community, with an endless succession of riots, strikes, bombings, grenade attacks and shootings. In spite of all this, here as in other colonial territories life went on almost as usual for at least part of the population.

Linda Wood lived and worked in Aden through most of these troubled years:

I was in my late teens when I arrived in Aden, in the New Year of 1964. My father had taken early retirement and then accepted a two-year contract with the British Government there, and my mother, my younger sister and I flew out from Gatwick just after Christmas 1963. Our first home was in Dolphin Square in Maa'lla. At that time there was no trouble in Aden itself; up-country was where things happened. We had no car yet so we wandered at will, took buses, and went shopping in Crater where the Arab shops had all the best materials. Evenings were spent at the Seamen's Mission at Steamer Point, watching the ships go in and out, at the Union Jack Club or at Gold Mohur, the swimming club at Conquest Bay. These good times were not to last.

My best friend from Scotland, Annelise, had the wanderlust and came to Aden looking for a job. As she was a striking blonde, half Danish, with expensive habits like Campari and French cigarettes, she needed to finance her lifestyle, and her good typing speeds (I think) got her a job at the High Commission. A limousine with a flag fluttering on the bonnet would pick her up each morning and return her at 3.30pm, the hours between apparently spent in an endless social whirl, feeding the peacocks on the lawn of Government House with the Hon. Jeremy Rawlins, Sir Richard Turnbull's ADC.

She had landed one of the best jobs in town, so I decided to join Aden Airways as a stewardess, not least because they lived opposite our house and their life seemed very glamorous. One long-haired brunette drove a red Alfa-Romeo sports car, and had a boyfriend flying Hunter jet fighters for the RAF, and another was engaged to a very grand Army officer from a very post regiment. That seemed the life for me.

Aden Airways, a subsidiary of BOAC – now British Airways – was hard to get into. It took six months to get a work permit and the Aden Government were keen, rightly I suppose, to employ local girls, though serving alcohol and night stop-overs did not sit easily with the Islamic lifestyle. While waiting, I tagged along in Annelise's glory, to the Queen's Birthday Party at Government House in hat and long white gloves, to a party on HMS *Eagle*, an aircraft carrier, and visiting HMS *Albion*, a Commando carrier, on its way to Borneo where there was fighting.

About this time the first bomb went off at a cocktail party, injuring Squadron Leader Lavender, who was standing near the sideboard where the device had been hidden. He was badly wounded but recovered and stayed to finish his tour of duty, and in spite of his badly scarred chest was a beach regular.

Although my memory of events is rusty, from that time on bombs started going off all over the place. My father's new car arrived, a godsend as we could no longer use the buses. He parked it in Maa'lla Strait, near the Service hiring, and lo and behold the car in front was blown up. Our car had only been in Aden two days – they had to be shipped out from the UK – when it was caught in crossfire and sustained bullet holes. Its nickname was Puff (the Tragic Waggon). There was now a growing distrust of the Arabs we lived among. Were they planting these bombs? Civilian groups were formed, like Neighbourhood Watch, to patrol the square, the men carrying sticks, as few civilians were armed.

Then my work permit arrived; hurrah! At the same time – 1966 now – Harold Wilson's Government came to power and declared that Aden's independence was coming, at which all hell broke loose, with various Arab factions slugging it out for power in the streets. FLOSY (The Front for the Liberation of Occupied South Yemen) seemed to be behind all the bombings.

I had other things to think about. My uniform was very sexy and, given the climate, very silly. A tight skirt and jacket, figure-hugging blouse, stockings (tights had not arrived in Aden yet), black high-heeled shoes and a hat worn tilted forward over the nose. The effect was wonderful and instantaneous. My little sister was being picked up for school in a military bus with armed escorts at the same time as the Aden Airways transport collected me for the training course. The 'squaddies' on the bus greeted me with a chorus of wolf whistles and I tilted my nose; wonderful. I still didn't know one end of a pilot from the other but, what the hell, life was just beginning.

After the elections of 1966 the new Labour Government confirmed that the British were to withdraw from Aden, both the former colony and the protectorate, 'not later than 1968'. This confirmation added that the British did not, after all, intend to retain troops in South Arabia after independence. Britain's economic situation would not sustain a presence East of Suez and the ending of National Service meant that troops were no longer available for worldwide commitments. Europe was the place that mattered now and the remnants of the Empire would have to be disposed of. The Labour Government also hoped that with this final thorn removed, Anglo–Arab relations would move on to smoother ground; in practice it had the opposite effect, delighting Britain's enemies, horrifying those in Aden who had trusted Britain's promise. No one was more pleased – or more relieved – at this decision than President Nasser of Egypt.

By 1966 Nasser had committed half his Army to the war in the Yemen. There his troops had received such a drubbing that he was on the point of pulling them out. The British announcement of independence for South Arabia encouraged him to stay, and Cairo Radio promptly claimed that the Egyptian Army would remain until 'final victory' was signalled by a British withdrawal from Aden, an event marking another victory for Nasser and fresh humiliation for the British. This claim was untrue but most Arab nationalists believed it. All the Arab countries took up the cry of victory, and on a local level the Yemeni Government saw the victory they could not win on the battlefield being handed to them on a plate.

On the other hand, those sheiks in the Federation who had supported British rule rightly felt themselves betrayed. The rule and safety of the sheiks was underpinned by the British presence in Aden. Once the British left, their enemies in the Socialist 'liberation' parties in Aden and the Yemen would certainly fall upon them with troops and artillery and aircraft. If, or when, Britain abandoned them, their fate was sealed.

The British declaration also had its inevitable effect inside Aden State itself. Those Adenis who had so far stayed out of the fight were now forced to take sides to ensure their future security, joining either with the NLF or Asnag's and Makawee's Trades Union based party, the PSP. In January 1966 these two parties formed a joint grouping, FLOSY – the Front for the Liberation of Occupied South Yemen, 'Occupied South Yemen' being their term for the territory known otherwise as Aden State.

The supporters of the NLF, mostly Yemeni tribesmen from the hills, soon fell out with the followers of the PSP, most of whom were Aden townsfolk or Yemeni expatriates employed in British installations in Aden. In December 1966 the NLF withdrew from the Front and the two groups, FLOSY and the NLF, began to fight for control of the Federation after the British left. By January 1967 civil war between these factions was added to the problems of the British administration and before long their dispute had spread to the battalions of the Federal Army.

The Federal Army was now known as the South Arabian Army or SAA, a force created by combining the Federal Army with the Federal Guard. The SAA had expanded considerably since that Federal Army involvement in the first Radfan campaign and was now a well-balanced force, with its own artillery, armour and engineers, totalling about fifteen thousand men, mostly mustered in ten infantry battalions. Most of the officers were now Arab but this too was a source of contention, as they came from different tribes. The stabilising British element was being steadily reduced and had fallen from a high of fifty officers and two hundred and fifty NCOs to just four officers and ten NCOs.

The commander of the SAA was a British brigadier, Jack Dye, a fine and resourceful officer, who retained the loyalty of the force in spite of NLF and FLOSY blandishments, and privately made himself responsible for the safety of the protectorate sheiks, helping them to move their families and possessions to Saudi Arabia as the British presence declined.

In June 1967 it was declared time for the British to abandon their positions in the protectorate, hand over the Dhala position to the SAA and withdraw to Aden, there to start the final phase of the withdrawal. 45 Commando, commanded now by Lt.-Colonel John Owen, was still in the Radfan.

When I arrived in 1967, we still had two companies in the Radfan and were running the Dhala road convoys, but our problem during the withdrawal phase was in Aden itself, at Maa'lla. It was the usual 'Corporal's War' of patrols, road blocks, bomb-throwing, sniping . . . the troops were wonderful, as usual, full of good humour.

Higher minds were devoted to keeping the Arabs happy and one of their proposals was that the troops should no longer refer to the locals as 'wogs'. An order to that effect went out and the troops' reaction was almost instantaneous: within days - perhaps hours - the locals were referred to as 'the gollies'.

By 1967 the heart of the problem was in Aden itself, especially in Crater, the old Arab quarter, in Maa'lla, the port area, and in the townships of Sheik Othman and Al Mansoura which lay just to the north of the city. In an attempt to stop arms and ammunition being smuggled into Aden from the Federation, a stop and search line, the 'Scrubber Line', had been established outside Aden, astride the Dhala road, but this failed to stop a steady supply of weapons reaching the dissidents in the city, often with help from the Adeni police.

On 19/20 January 1967 the NLF ran a two-day campaign against the British which was quickly squashed by the deployment of British battalions in the city, after Turnbull had directed the British Army to take over responsibility for internal security from the local police. After the NLF rioters had been dispersed the FLOSY rioters took to the streets with an equal lack of success, but by the time the riots petered out in mid-February, British troops had had to open fire almost forty times and there had been more than sixty shooting or grenade attacks against British servicemen or civilians. These bomb attacks included strikes against civilian aircraft.

Linda Wood again:

Aden Airways operated two Vickers Viscounts for their international routes to Cairo and DC3 Dakotas for upcountry work. The Viscount service was to a very high standard, starched head covers, silver trays, the lot, but the DC3 flights were the best fun in the world, and we all did 'Dak' flights sometimes. As there was only one cabin crew member you were your own boss and responsible for heaving the chocks on board and making sure they came back on departure. I actually had to say, 'Chocks Away'! At take-off you had to scramble up the steeply sloping floor of the DC3 to the cabin crew take-off station, sitting on the floor with your back to the forward bulkhead.

Life in Aden was very good, though we moved to Tarshyne Beach as Dolphin Square was not safe, especially if you worked for the Government. Admiral Sir Michael Le Fanu, C-in-C Middle East, lived just above us. His wife was confined to a wheelchair and every morning he would push her to the beach before it got too hot, and when she was not at school my little sister went with them. The Admiral had red hair and the sailors called him 'Dry Ginger' as he had stopped their 'tot', the Navy's daily rum ration.*

However, the fighting was never far away. Our friends, the Hunter fighter pilots, lost a lot of their 'gung-ho' approach to life when one of them was shot down and killed by tribesmen in the Radfan. Until then they thought that nothing could touch them. Further rumours that the dead pilot's genitals had been removed added a new seriousness to the situation.

My Mum and Dad left Aden in November 1966, very loathe to leave me behind. My friend Tricia had a spare bedroom so I moved in with her, starting a new phase in my life. At this time an Aden Airlines' DC3 was blown up in mid-air, with all the passengers, mostly Arabs, being killed as well as all the crew. This incident brought us into the front line and flights were moved to the RAF base. The pilots were issued with guns and we were called to a meeting by the Chief Stewardess.

* The 'tot' was not stopped until 30 July 1970. Le Fanu was called 'Dry Ginger' long before that because of his red hair and his dry sense of humour, which the sailors appreciated.

If we wanted to leave we would not be held to our contracts. Those who stayed would be paid danger money. We all remained, of course. I can't remember how much the danger money was but it was added to our salary and was worthwhile. Anyway, to keep the Flag flying was the thing and the flights continued, initially with no passengers. On my first trip to the airport after the tragedy I was shepherded away from the hangar area where the coffins of the two dead pilots were awaiting shipment home.

The way to combat urban terrorism is through good intelligence, but with the local police unreliable Army operations in Aden were seriously hampered by a lack of facts. Attempts to extract information from captured dissidents got the soldiers into trouble and led to visits by Amnesty International and eventually to an Army enquiry. This exonerated the troops from the more lurid allegations but there is little doubt that many of the soldiers were taking a hard line with captured terrorists.

Brigadier Joe Starling was in Aden at this time with 1st Bn., The Parachute Regiment, based at the Dhala Camp on the outskirts of the city:

Battalions can be divided into 'Gentlemen' and 'Players' and 1 Para was definitely a 'Player' battalion. Several successful operations in Sheik Othman and Dar Said netted a number of prisoners and their information led to more successful operations, on the snowball principle.

Sadly, those in high places did not approve of 'Player' battalions or vigorous interrogation. Word came down that if any more prisoners were 'shot trying to escape' or 'fell downstairs' there would be a full investigation and dire consequences. Clearly, it was time for a rethink.

The continued flow of intelligence information is essential and was vital to reduce the steady toll of British lives, but how to maintain this was the problem. Fortunately, the Chartered Bank had just taken delivery of a new toy, a main-frame computer, then a vast machine with multi-coloured lights, whirring wheels and grinding noises; twenty minutes of this activity produced a one-page bank statement.

We had access to this gadget and it gave some bright spark an idea. Captured terrorists were introduced to this machine and told that prolonged exposure to its rays would make them sterile. Arabs are very keen on their macho image and this made them gasp. The terrorist was then sat by the machine, the machine was switched on and put through a programme. The statement appeared and was studied and the prisoner informed that he had lost the reproductive power of one ball; would he now care to talk lest the other one suffer the same fate?

It didn't always work and you might not approve of it but it produced information that led to the discovery of several ammo dumps, the foiling of some ambushes and a most satisfactory round-up of terrorist contacts and cut outs. The prisoners, in pristine condition, if a bit pale and shaken, were then safely handed on to the RAF Police.

The Arab terrorists were taking a steady toll of British lives but the death toll was also rising steeply on the Arab side. This was not due to British countermeasures but because the NLF had decided to eliminate their FLOSY rivals while they were distracted by their campaign against the British. Thirty-five leading members of FLOSY were shot or bombed or otherwise murdered in February 1967 alone, including three sons of the self-exiled Mackawee, who were killed by a bomb at the family home. In their spare time both these organisations attacked the British who were beginning to wire themselves into small fortresses about the town.

Tom Godwin again:

In the early Spring of 1967 1 Para was ordered to Aden on a six-month tour. Our base was Radfan Camp, a tented cantonment not far from Khormaksar Airport, the airport we would withdraw from later that year, ending British presence East of Suez. Meanwhile there was work to be done and a nasty little war to fight, rocket attacks at strong points, grenade attacks by the roads, night firing at piquets or patrols. The Sheik Othman area was dominated by 1 Para, from a fortified strong point known to the soldiers as Fort Walsh, after our CO, Colonel Mike Walsh.

The battalion was blooded, so to speak, on 6 June 1967, when all hell let loose on the area with all the piquets being fired on in a coordinated attack. The battalion was very quick to retaliate and the 'addoo', the wogs, did not realise that cover from view is not the same as cover from fire: rattan and old tea chests will not keep out a bullet like a rock sangar will, when it comes to a fire fight. The battalion got off lightly, the one notable casualty being the CSM of a rifle company who got concrete splinters in his backside when a rocket came through a wall. The opposition did not get off so lightly as we killed about eight and wounded a good few more.

After this brisk little skirmish with 1 Para, the dissidents found it better to engage the British infantry with rocket attacks under cover of darkness rather than try open engagements during the day. Joe Starling again:

During mid-1967, 1 Para was responsible for Sheikh Othman, a suburb of Aden. The operational development involved the permanent occupation of a number of OPs on a series of dominant buildings. These provided both observation into most of the potential troublespots and firm bases to support patrols moving through the streets.

The most vulnerable and exposed OP was located in the tower of the Sheikh Othman Police Station. It was surrounded on three sides by high buildings, all of which could be, and frequently were, used as firing points to engage the Police Station and other OPs in the area. Since the Police Station was in the centre of the township, its occupation by Security Forces was a constant reminder to the terrorists that 'Big Brother', in the form of 1 Para, was watching them and their attacks on the tower became more and more vicious.

The Civil Police were powerless in the face of heavily armed terrorists and were convinced that they would be unable to prevent the terrorists from burning the Police Station if its garrison was withdrawn. It thus became a point of high politics that the Police Station must be held at all costs as its sacking by terrorists would demonstrate to the world at large that the British could no longer contain the situation in Aden.

The normal garrison of what was known as OP4 was a half platoon of twelve to fourteen men under an officer. The tower itself was always manned by four men, although this was increased in times of crisis, and the reliefs slept on the first floor of the main building. The Civil Police, with whom relations remained cordial, confined their activities to the ground floor which was surrounded by a high wall and was not vulnerable to small arms fire.

The usual defensive measures were taken to make the position as strong as possible and 60 Fd Sqn RE built the equivalent of a fort on the top of the tower, with two loopholes facing each point of the compass.

While the defence of OP4 against small arms fire was as good as could be devised, the garrison began to suffer casualties from blindicide rockets, a Czech weapon of the bazooka family, of which the terrorists seemed to have plenty. There were several direct hits on the tower, culminating in one particularly unlucky shot which hit a corner post, and all four of the duty watch became casualties. Happily, only one was serious and they all subsequently recovered.

A device which had proved successful elsewhere was a 'blindicide screen' of rigid wire mesh which exploded the rockets on impact. The difficulty at OP4 was to fit such a screen over the fighting floor of the tower. This was difficult enough from the purely engineering aspect but to attempt to carry out the construction work involved, much of it exposed to fire, would have invited an unacceptable number of casualties.

The obvious solution was to construct the screen as a complete unit and lower the whole thing over the tower by helicopter. A representative of 13 Flight, Army Air Corps, had a look at the problem and decided that it was a starter provided the all-up weight was such that it could be lifted by a Scout, i.e., less than 1000 lbs.

Working to these limits, 60 Field Sqn RE quickly produced a birdcage-like structure out of tubular scaffolding and wire mesh. The whole thing was lifted by a Scout of 13 Flight on to a mock-up tower in a safe area by way of a rehearsal. The trial was a success and the operation to install it was arranged for the following morning.

On the principle that helicopters, like armour, must have infantry protection, two companies of 1 Para were deployed one hour before first light on to the rooftops of Sheikh Othman along the route to be flown by the Scout.

Promptly at first light the Scout appeared, flew over the surprised inhabitants of Sheikh Othman, and hovered over the police station. The sapper team caught the trailing guide ropes and after only one false start the Scout got the 'thing' in the right position. The pilot on the ground passed the word to drop and the 'thing' came to rest within a few inches of its designated position – a very skilful piece of flying indeed. Surprise was complete and the Scout and covering troops withdrew without incident while the Sappers carried out a few adjustments.

The 'thing' proved most successful and although many more blindicides were fired at OP4 no further casualties were suffered. It was still intact when 2 Para handed over the Sheikh Othman area to the South Arabian Army a few months later.

Linda Wood was in the middle of all this, with the other stewardesses of Aden Airlines:

Another thing I remember about this time was being stuck somewhere when a bomb went off. Tricia and I had gone with her boyfriend (now husband) to a party at a flat in Maa'lla. The flat was a bachelor pad jammed with booze, and no sooner had we arrived than there was the most almighty blast; the whole building shook. Then all hell broke loose in the street outside, machine-gun bursts, rifle fire, grenades: very unwisely we all went out on to the balcony and sat there, slowly getting plastered, watching the fighting. 'There goes another one!' we yelled at every blast. It seems incredibly stupid now, but that was the way it was then.

Curfews were now imposed on a regular basis and one day our

'ayah', or cleaning lady, did not turn up. When she arrived next day we asked her what had happened. 'My brother shot dead,' she replied over the ironing. 'Oh no!' we cried. 'Who by?' 'By the Brit-eesh,' she spat out, without lifting her head. Now the animosity had arrived inside our house.

In May 1967 George Thomson, the Commonwealth Secretary, announced a decision to pull out of Aden by January 1968, just six months away. Thomson sweetened this bitter pill for the sheiks by promising to leave a carrier force offshore to protect the new 'Federation of South Arabia' from attack or invasion and grant the new country lavish amounts of aid. The Federal Government protested that they were not yet ready to take over the defence of their country or cope with the internal security problem and, after a good deal of heated debate, the British withdrawal date was put back to early 1968, before being reversed yet again and fixed at 29 November 1967.

It was now a matter of deciding who would take over the reins of power, the current, British–backed Federal Government, or the two terrorist parties, NLF or FLOSY, who were now battling it out in the streets. Aden had inevitably attracted the attention of the Third World lobby at the UN and this point was taken up by three delegates sent to Aden from the United Nations in New York. Their brief was to 'find an internationally acceptable political solution to the problems of South Arabia'. This visit became a mixture of farce and tragedy.

What three diplomats, one each from Afghanistan, Mali and Venezuela, could do in five days that British diplomats and ministers had failed to do in seven hectic years, was not immediately apparent and the farce began soon after their arrival. The three UN delegates first refused to talk to the Federal Government on the grounds that it was not recognised by the UN. Neither of the two nationalist parties – FLN nor FLOSY – would talk to the UN delegation until it was first recognised by the delegates as the sole representative of the people.

The unhappy trio then demanded radio time to address the Aden people directly, a request which the Federal Government, whom the delegates refused to recognise, gleefully refused to grant, not least because the script was a blatant attack on the Federal Government.

Thwarted, the delegates then retired to sulk in their hotel while the NLF and FLOSY took to the streets and all hell broke loose. In the five days before the UN delegates finally fled the scene there was constant rioting in which eight rioters were shot dead and eighteen British soldiers injured. The UN Mission left Aden to the jeers of all parties and never returned.

Britain then opted for the 'Indian solution', hoping that a firm date for withdrawal would concentrate everyone's minds. In May 1967 a new High Commissioner, Sir Humphrey Trevelyan, a man with long experience of Arab affairs, arrived to replace Sir Richard Turnbull. On arrival Trevelyan made a conciliatory offer to the NLF and FLOSY, stating that he would end the State of Emergency and release all detainees if they would cease the fighting and join in a Provisional Government.

This offer was rejected by both parties who then came up with a counter-proposal; the British troops were to be withdrawn at once, the Federal rulers were to be removed and all power was to be handed over to the 'Nationalist' representatives. Chaos would follow but the British would be gone. Colonel Nasser then graciously announced that he would not enter Aden after the British left but that he supported FLOSY as the inheritors of British rule.

The British rejected the 'Nationalist' suggestion but began to phase out their forces almost at once. The remaining women and children were evacuated and with the withdrawal of 45 Commando from the Dhala position back to Aden, the sheiks of the former protectorate were left unsupported, many now accepting Brigadier Dye's advice and assistance in fleeing to safety in Saudi Arabia.

In June 1967 the NLF attempted to establish a 'no-go' area in Sheikh Othman which, as already recounted, brought on a fight with the 1st Bn., The Parachute Regiment, which had been sorely baited in recent weeks and were spoiling to take on the NLF. By the end of the day six terrorists had been killed, a score more shot and wounded and five taken prisoner.

In that month the Arab armies in general and Nasser's Egypt in particular took a terrible beating at the hands of the Israeli Army in the Six-Day War. Since the Arabs did not believe that Israel could perform such a feat of arms unaided they declared that Britain and the USA had openly supported the Israeli armies in the field. Within Aden, relations between the departing British and the Federal authorities were strained by efforts to form the Federal Army and the Federal Guard into the South Arabian Army (SAA). On 20 June 1967 there was a mutiny at the SAA barracks near Khormaksar and some of the SAA soldiers fired on the British camp across the road, beginning a process that was to cause one of the most memorable events in the Aden tragedy.

This disturbance was quickly suppressed by the SAA's Arab officers but then further trouble occurred. The shooting at the SAA camp had alarmed the men at the nearby barracks and when they saw a British Army lorry passing by, the soldiers assumed it was taking British troops to attack the SAA camp. In fact the lorry contained men of the Royal Army Service Corps returning to barracks after practice on a nearby rifle range. These RASC soldiers were quite unaware of the disturbance until they came under fire.

The soldiers opened fire on the lorry, killing eight British soldiers and wounding another eight. The police then ran amuck, shooting wildly into the British camp, killing a British officer, two policemen and a public works employee. British troops then arrived and restored order, killing one policeman and wounding thirteen.

Lt.-Colonel Peter Downward was in Aden at this time, in command of the 1st Bn., The Lancashire Regiment:

> The battalion had arrived in Aden in January 1967. After the announcement that the British Government would advance the date for the handover of the Protectorate and Colony, things started to intensify, with hostile actions by the NLF and other factions. On 18 June 1967, the Lancashire Regiment observed its principal Battle Honour celebration, Waterloo Day. This was held in the grounds of Government House by courtesy of the High Commissioner, Sir Humphrey Trevelyan.
>
> On 20 June, while at the airport seeing off the Colonel of the Regiment, I was aware of sporadic firing to the north side of the airfield, in the direction of Radfan Camp. Air Traffic Control in the tower could see the general area of the firing and indicated that it was coming from the SAA Camp, which faced Radfan Camp from the other side of the road. I ordered my driver to 'step on it' and

we raced out of the airfield, with my radio operator filling me in with some startling reports of British casualties.

We were flagged down at the first check point (a tented shelter surrounded by sand-bagged walls), where I was amazed to find the men manning the post all at stand-to positions and a couple of wounded soldiers on the floor. The telephone was still operating but it was obvious that the exchange was working flat out and I could not find anyone on the line who could fill me in on the current situation.

I called up my own control on my vehicle radio and learned that the base was under fire. I was warned not to attempt the remaining two miles in my Land Rover so I asked for my armoured scout car to drive down to the check point to pick me up. He arrived in less than ten minutes and I scrambled aboard, taking up my position in the turret, at the same time checking that the machine-gun was loaded. It wasn't, and the only weapons the driver and I had were a loaded rifle and my Browning pistol, also loaded.

We covered the two miles in record time and shot in through the gates. All my troops in camp at the time were in stand-to positions, wearing steel helmets and fully armed. Once inside my Command Post I was briefed by my Second-in-Command, Major Ken Preston. It seemed that there was shooting going on over the whole of Aden, but of immediate concern was the firing being directed at us from the SAA camp, a few hundred yards away.

Apparently, the first lot of firing started shortly after 10.00 hrs when a Bren opened up from the SAA camp against a British Army 3-tonner on its way back from the rifle range about a mile to the west. As I later saw, the vehicle had been well and truly riddled with automatic fire and the soldiers on board never had a chance. Six died and two were badly wounded. I could see the vehicle and the bodies on the road through my binoculars. Another vehicle, a Land Rover, was stationary not far away and I recognised it as being that of my Battalion's Chaplain, the Reverend Robin Roe, who had driven out of the Camp under fire in order to get to the knocked-out 3-tonner in the hope of picking up the wounded.

His vehicle was knocked out with a burst of LMG fire through the radiator and the front tyres. Even Robin, with his unmechanical eye, realised something was very wrong with his vehicle, and on closer inspection of the damage his escort reported later that Robin's one true remark was, 'My God, they're using live ammunition!' For this action, plus other actions in the camp area where we had casualties that day, the Reverend Roe was awarded the Military Cross.

One disturbing piece of news conveyed to me as I went round the position was that one of my junior officers had been hit and was in a poor way. Before the morning was out I was to learn that he had died – 2nd Lieutenant Angus Young, who had read the Waterloo Citation two days earlier. Another young officer, Lieutenant David Cleary, had shown tremendous initiative in getting his platoon into a defensive position under fire and was also awarded the Military Cross.

Before very long I was able to speak with the Brigade Commander over the air and learned that it was not only Radfan Camp that was under fire but other areas as well. There were more casualties, including the crew of a Sioux helicopter of the Army Air Corps which had been shot down, and by the end of the day there were eighteen soldiers and British civilians dead and about a dozen wounded. The RAF Hospital was working flat out and but for the efforts of the doctors and nurses I believe we would have had many more deaths.

It took some time to discover what caused the panic and deaths in Aden that day but the root of it lay in the uncertain discipline of the South Arabian Army and the local police. The Federal Government had offered a new Arab Commander to the SAA to replace Brigadier Dye. The officer chosen, Colonel Burique, was not notably competent but he belonged to the Aulaqi tribe who made up the bulk of the soldiery in the old Federal Army. Four colonels of the SAA, from a different tribe, resented this appointment and had spread dissension among that part of the SAA recruited from the former Federal Guard.

The panic which caused the shooting from the SAA camp had meanwhile spread to the Armed Police barracks in Crater. For some reason the Armed Police, a paramilitary force, feared that they would suffer retribution for the SAA attack and took to the rooftops. From there they opened fire with automatic weapons and rifles on two Land Rovers containing an eight man patrol of the

Royal Northumberland Fusiliers and the Argyll and Sutherland Highlanders.

This patrol had no hostile intentions towards the Armed Police. The Argylls had just arrived in Aden and were being shown the town before taking over from the Fusiliers. They were also looking for a another Fusilier–Argyll patrol under 2nd Lieutenant Davis of the Fusiliers which was touring another part of Crater and had lost radio contact. This Armed Police fire killed seven of the eight soldiers in the two Army Land Rovers and set both vehicles on fire.

While all this was going on, the Argyll and Fusilier patrol under 2nd Lieutenant Davis had come out of Crater. Hearing the firing, Lieutenant Davis volunteered to lead his patrol back in, taking some armoured cars of the Queen's Dragoon Guards in support. Davis's group entered Crater and soon found the two blazing Land Rovers and the litter of dead soldiers. Then his party, too, was swept by machine-gun fire from the police barracks, fire which also brought down the watching Sioux helicopter.

Their vehicle hit, Lieutenant Davis and three men ran for cover while the armoured cars went back for help. Davis and his men must have been overrun when they ran out of ammunition. They were never seen again and their bodies were never recovered.

During the rest of that day three attempts were made to reach the bodies outside the Armed Police barracks but on each occasion the troops were driven back by heavy fire from the police station. The decision was taken to leave the bodies, pull troops out of Crater and cordon the area off. This decision did not go down at all well with any of the troops but went especially badly with the Argylls and their commanding officer, Lt.-Colonel Colin Mitchell, a robust officer who did not see eye to eye with the garrison GOC, Major-General Philip Tower.

The two men were not likely to agree. Lt.-Colonel Mitchell had spent his life with his regiment, serving from the end of the Second World War in Korea, Palestine and Borneo. Major-General Tower was a staff officer, whose previous appointment had been as Director of Public Relations in Whitehall.

General Tower's uncertain temper was not improved by the fact that the Colonel of the Argylls had a definite flair for publicity and had won the support of the British Press. On the other hand, Colonel

Mitchell was not noted for tact and made statements on television that embarrassed the Government as much as they attracted public support. Tower's decision to hold back from Crater was endorsed by the High Commissioner, Sir Humphrey Trevelyan, but the troops of the garrison were very bitter about it.

Colonel Downward continues:

Within the next three or four days, the situation appeared to stabilise in that there were no more major incidents around Aden. The Arab rebels in Crater were now under constant surveillance from the surrounding heights, manned by riflemen of 45 Commando, Royal Marines. Every entrance and exit was effectively sealed, either by road blocks or the natural features of the steep hills on one side, or the sea to the east.

Shortly before Brigadier Jefferies' return to England I was surprised to be summoned by the GOC, Major-General Philip Tower, who detailed me to take over the Brigade as the senior battalion commander and to plan retaking Crater. The operation was to start three days later and it was impressed on me that it was to be carried out with minimum force and that the Argylls were to be assigned to the task.

On moving into Brigade Headquarters, I quickly learned of other activities going on in the area involving the SAS, the Aden Police Intelligence, and the SAA Liaison Officer, Lt.-Colonel Dick Lawson. It was apparent that the group of NLF rebels who had triggered the mutiny had left the area and the control of Crater was in the hands of a somewhat unco-ordinated group of Armed Police.

One incident which could have had very serious consequences was the attempt to destroy the BP oil tank storage area north of Steamer Point. Although the charges exploded, the tanks did not catch fire, but the whole area, including the main road from Maa'lla to Steamer Point was flooded in oil to a depth of several inches. Had this ignited, the whole town would have burned.

One amazing piece of information revealed to me under Secret Cover was that the Bank of Aden in Crater contained several million pounds-worth of gold. Before any military action was taken it was hoped to remove the gold. A working party of half a dozen soldiers drove a small convoy of Land Rovers through a quiet area of Crater to the bank. There they parked their vehicles out of sight while they loaded up. I believe it took more than one run and there was much nail biting until we got the final message, something like 'Cox and Kings', indicating the mission had been accomplished.

At last the way was clear for us to re-occupy Crater and the GOC summoned me to hear my plan. This was for the Argylls, under Lt.-Colonel Colin Mitchell, to retake the area from the seaward, eastern end in three phases. I explained that once we were certain that the first phase had been safely accomplished we would move into Phases 2 and 3; the last phase being the retaking of the area containing the Armed Police barracks, which could be a hard nut to crack if the rebels were still in charge. The GOC approved the plan but emphasised that minimum force was to be observed at every stage and that the three phases were to be spaced out over successive days. I was also instructed to check with him before moving onto the next phase.

Some time before 'H' hour, a platoon of Argylls was flown into Strah Island by helicopter in order to control the approach to Crater via the South Gate. At 1800 hrs on the Monday evening, the main part of the Battalion moved down the main Khormaksar–Crater Road on the east side, and into the built-up area of Crater, linking up with their platoon on Strah Island, which was connected to the town by a causeway. By midnight the first phase had been completed successfully with a minimum of resistance.

Having watched the Argylls cross the start-line earlier in the evening, I returned again at midnight to find the Argylls CO, Lt.-Colonel Mitchell, in his new Command Post, accompanied not only by his own HQ staff but also by a number of Press reporters. These had caught wind of the action and were keen to get the latest news. The reporters seemed to have a good idea of the next two phases and I knew this was not going to please the GOC, Major-General Tower, or the C-in-C, Admiral Sir Michael Le Fanu.

Around 0600 hrs, after a few hours sleep, I was awakened by Brigadier Charles Dunbar ringing to tell me that the BBC Overseas News from London had announced the re-occupation of Crater and the fact that the Argylls had scored a great victory. 'Had I not emphasised the need for utmost security throughout the operation . . .?'

The second phase of the operation went off successfully on the Tuesday evening, and based on all the available intelligence reports I agreed that the Argylls could take the third and last phase, the Armed Police barracks area, in daylight the next day. This was to be during the afternoon, so if there had to be any use of force in clearing the barracks, it would be much easier to accomplish the task in daylight. On the Wednesday I positioned myself on the high ground to the west of Crater at the Main Pass, which was manned by Royal Marines of 45 Commando, and watched through my binoculars. 'H' hour for the Argylls' advance was 1500 hrs but already, at 1400 hrs, the Press seemed to be aware that something was going to happen.

Looking to my right, at the Armed Police Barracks, I suddenly saw a familiar figure, dressed in South Arabian Army uniform. It was Lt.-Colonel Dicky Lawson, the Liaison Officer attached to the SAA, and it was apparent that he was not under arrest and certainly wasn't under fire. The race to open up Crater was clearly on!

I jumped into my Land Rover, together with driver, radio operator and batman, and having briefed the Royal Marines to keep us covered, we shot off down the road towards the Argylls, who were starting to form up ready for the final advance. We drove into the front of the Argylls, much to the amazement of the Press. Calling up the Argyll CO on the radio, I informed him the route was open and he was free to advance his 'H' hour. To prove the point I drove back up the other main carriageway and thanked the Royal Marines for keeping me covered.

Another account, from Tom Pocock, a British reporter for the London *Evening Standard*, states that he led the final advance into Crater, past the two burned-out Land Rovers outside the Armed Police barracks, driving into Crater 'in a bright blue taxi'. This feat was repeated some years later, in 1982, when another *Evening Standard* reporter, Max Hastings, preceded the British advance into Stanley at the end of the Falklands War.

Press reports of the retaking of Crater attribute the success of the operation to Lt.-Colonel Mitchell's Argyll and Sutherland Highlanders who retook Crater to the skirl of the pipes. That was the impression in Aden itself, as Linda Wood recalls:

When the Arabs took Crater it was a very upsetting time. A young officer I knew well was killed there, just after he had taken me to the cinema. We saw *The Blue Max*, about First World War flyers. Even now when that film is shown on television the tears well up as I think of him still in Aden, buried in Silent Valley. His body came out of Crater in a packing case, having been very badly mutilated.

It was a very low time for the Army, but life went on and it seemed to be accepted that we would let the Arabs hold Crater until we moved out. Then one morning I woke up to hear a loud wailing noise, the bagpipes . . . I am a Scot and there was no mistaking it. Over the radio later that day we heard that the Argyll and Sutherland Highlanders had marched into Crater. 'Mad Mitch' and his men restored our faith in all things British and it did wonders for our morale.

Shown every night on television, reported at length in the newspapers, the débâcle in Aden was not doing much for morale in Britain and here, too, Colonel Mitchell was the 'Man of the Hour'. The Crater action made Mitchell and the Argylls both famous and popular in Britain, at least outside the corridors of the High Command. When the Argylls were later listed for disbandment the threat spurred millions of British people to petition Parliament for their retention and the regiment survived. Lt.-Colonel Mitchell was less fortunate.

Relations between Lt.-Colonel Mitchell and Major-General Tower did not improve after the retaking of Crater. Mitchell was outraged when Tower took the salute at a reconciliation parade of the very Armed Police who had killed British soldiers, and Tower was not impressed when Mitchell's response to an order to 'play it cool' and relax his battalion's grip on the population of Crater was to appear on television and claim, 'They (the Arabs) know that if they start any trouble again with us we will blow their bloody heads off.'

To the Press and Public he was 'Mad Mitch', but Lt.-Colonel Mitchell's skilful use of the media did not improve his prospects of advancement in the Army. The usual award for such a battalion exploit would have been a DSO for the Commanding Officer; Lt.-Colonel Mitchell received no recognition whatsoever for his part in retaking Crater and was not promoted again, leaving the Army some years later, still a Lt.-Colonel.

The end in Aden now came swiftly. The SAA took over from the British outside Aden and Little Aden in July, the watchful British withdrawing slowly to a series of defensive lines. On 3 September 1967, the NLF declared that they would assume power, and three days later street fighting broke out between the NLF and FLOSY. The British troops were happy to see them fight it out and on 24 September all British forces were withdrawn behind a line of Victorian defence works, the 'Scrubber Line', just north of Khormaksar airfield.

Colonel Joe Starling recalls the British withdrawal from Aden:

The first phase of the withdrawal in 1967 was the evacuation of Little Aden, custom built as a British Brigade Base and only completed a few months before we pulled out, no doubt at vast expense. The Headquarters of 24 Infantry Brigade and most of its units returned directly from Little Aden to the UK but the 1st Battalion Irish Guards were transferred to the Aden Brigade to act as a Force Reserve – or, as they put it themselves, as hostages to fortune.

In the early hours of one sultry morning, when all of Sheik Othman, terrorists included, seemed to be fast asleep, the radio net heard one OP, manned by the Irish Guards and clearly bored stiff, whispering to another. 'Hello Oscar Four, this is Oscar One. Do ye come from Dublin? Over.' The reply came, 'Hello Oscar One, this is Oscar Four. Shure oi come from Dublin. Whoi? Over.' 'Hello Oscar Four. This is Oscar One. Well, I come from Belfast. Out.' The night was then rent by a long burst of machine-gun fire from one OP to the other. The Irish always found it difficult to discard their domestic disputes.

Lt.-Colonel Downward again:

On the return of the Brigade Commander some days after Crater was retaken. I was happy to return to my own battalion and to see it into its new operational area to the north of Khormaksar, on what was generally known as the 'Scrubber Line', named after the officer who constructed this defensive line, Major 'Scrubber' Stewart-Richardson, Coldstream Guards. This line ran across the isthmus from west coast to east coast and was an obvious defensive position in the event of any attack towards Aden itself. The line was divided into two sectors; the west sector was the Lancashire's, and the east sector was 1 Para's. Both battalions were based alongside each other in Radfan Camp, and both had Operational HQs in the forward areas.

By August it was obvious that the process towards final evacuation had started and by late September the whole of Aden was becoming a fortress. The families had all gone, shopkeepers were starting to fret over the lack of business, and shooting incidents were on the increase, particularly in the built-up areas near the Port.

To the north, along the 'Scrubber Line', there were numerous incidents, and it was obvious that there were many well-trained snipers. Driving along the main road to the east of Al Mansoura became decidedly hazardous as vehicles came under fire, particularly the larger, slow-moving 3-tonners.

One incident worthy of mention involved the Intelligence Officer, Lieutenant Martin Scrase, and the Intelligence Sergeant, Sergeant Dewhurst, who were driving south from Al Mansoura, destined for Radfan camp when shots rang out from the buildings on the right, about three hundred yards away; it was almost certainly a Kalashnikov. The first shot whistled past Dewhurst and Scrase (Dewhurst was driving), the second shot cut through Dewhurst's sleeve and the front of his shirt and on through Martin Scrase's sleeve and the front of his shirt, causing a slight graze to his chest. The third round passed behind both of them but under the knees of the escort who was sitting in the back with his SLR at the ready. The incident attracted considerable Press attention in the UK, for there was no doubt that they were the luckiest men to be still alive.

The sniper with the Kalashnikov became a menace in that area, particularly after he killed one of my NCOs whose head was protruding from the top of a scout car patrolling the area outside the Al Mansoura Gaol.

Finally, an incident which tested my own skill-at-arms. I was visiting the Company based in the gaol to attend the briefing of a foot patrol due to go out into the desert. All the IAs (instant action drills) were rehearsed, and finally the patrol lined up at the short-range to fire a few rounds into the butt to make sure all weapons were functioning properly. It was obvious that something was wrong with the Bren LMG, and it became apparent that the young soldier in charge of the weapon did not know how to use it. He had come through the Depot training on the GPMG, the weapon which had replaced the old Bren, but the Bren had been retained for use in the internal security role in the belief that it was more in keeping with the principle of minimum force.

It was too late to find another soldier familiar with the Bren, so I took the LMG and joined the patrol, having removed my badges of rank. Within a matter of minutes we came under automatic fire from the direction of some buildings to the north-east of us. We got ourselves into fire positions, and I'm afraid in the excitement I forgot all about the principle of minimum force!

We 'followed through' into the village from where the fire had come, and saw a couple of Arabs being lifted into a battered old van; one was wounded, the other didn't move. I hoped he was the one who had picked off my corporal a few days earlier.

The crux of the problem in Aden now was who would take charge after the British left. The key to the solution was the South Arabian Army and in the end Brigadier Dye summoned his Arab officers, and explained the situation once again before locking them in a room and telling them not to come out until they had chosen who to support, FLOSY or the FLN. After twelve hours of debate and a great quantity of coffee the officers chose the NLF. On 13 November 1967, just two weeks before leaving Aden, the British Government recognised the NLF as their successors.

This was a lamentable if inevitable decision. The political failure in Aden was total; Britain's allies, the protectorate sheiks, had been betrayed and abandoned and the colony handed over to an organisation that had earned the right to rule by a campaign of intimidation and murder, waged mostly against their fellow countrymen and political opponents. The British troops in Aden, who had fought so long and done so well in the Dhala campaign and in the streets of the colony, were rightly disgusted.

The SAA were now assisting the NLF to take over power and eliminate the remnants of FLOSY as Joe Starling recalls:

It is sometimes difficult not to interfere in the affairs of others. After the NLF, the Marxists, achieved their victory over FLOSY, the Egyptian-sponsored fundamentalists, there was an orgy of blood-letting.

It was tragic to see truckloads of ashen-faced FLOSY supporters being taken north into the desert beyond our lines and hence outside the area under British control, and to hear the long bursts of machine-gun fire as they were executed by the NLF. A clandestine patrol from 1 Para at Dar Said, found a mass grave being dug up by wild dogs which were feeding on the corpses.

Our orders were very clear: 'It's not our problem, don't get involved.' Sometimes it is very difficult to obey orders.

The NLF preoccupation with the FLOSY situation led to a dramatic decrease in attacks on the British garrison but the troops kept their guard up. The SAA was a still a considerable force and if it attacked the one or two British battalions left in the final perimeter, the outcome was uncertain. The troops themselves were yet again disgusted to discover that they were to turn their brand new barracks and a great quantity of equipment over to the SAA on leaving. Tom Godwin of 1 Para was only one of the men who saw this as a final humiliation and not one to be endured:

On the phased withdrawal, all the stores were to be handed over to the South Arabian Army. The battalion vehicle fleet, such as it was, was to be handed over on Khormaksar airfield to a Government agent, who would than take it to the wire and flog it for £100 to the nearest wog.

Ah well, orders are orders. Such is the discipline and pride of the British Army that the usual programme of preparation for a handover was undertaken. Every vehicle was fully serviced, worn parts exchanged, the cab cleaned and swept, windscreens polished, even though the vehicles were going for a song and to the enemy at that. All the vehicles made it to the wire but not

much further. It is amazing what a little sand in the engine oil
will do . . .

Captain F. C. Townsend RM was the Quartermaster of 45
Commando at this time:

Handing over to the SAA was a headache as there was no let up in
the paperwork. We had to get a signature for everything . . . like
sixteen hundred camp beds, or whatever we handed over to the
SAA. The troops didn't like it and a lot of furniture fell off landings
and ended up as matchwood in the stairwells.

Unless we had to, we intended to leave nothing behind and that
included the C.O.'s desk, a splendid piece of furniture that strictly
speaking did not belong to the unit but somehow symbolises the
strong spirit of 45 Commando. It was taken to pieces carefully by
the unit carpenters, meticulously wrapped and crated and sent up
to RAF Khormaksar from where it was shipped to Blighty to serve
successive COs of 45 Commando. You can see it to this day, in
his office at Arbroath.

Lt.-Colonel John Owen and 45 Commando, Royal Marines, were
in Aden to the end:

As we handed over equipment and buildings to the South Arabian
Army, we could see them flogging anything that wasn't tied down
– fridges, Land Rovers, anything – it was most galling, especially
as we knew the administrative trauma that Freddie Townsend, our
Quartermaster, was going through. All the units vied to be the last
out. 45 Commando were the last of the garrison to leave but 42,
shipped in at the end from the Commando carrier HMS Albion
were disappointingly, but wisely, the very last troops to fly out
– but by helicopter.

However, for the record, the last five into the last Hercules
from Khormaksar were myself, the Brigadier, the RAF station
commander, the Brigadier (General Staff) and the Senior Air Staff
officer. I sometimes wonder if, had we been under fire, this order
might have been reversed.

A naval task force assembled offshore to cover the final evacuation, and that done, there was nothing left to do but leave. 42 Commando came ashore from the Commando carrier HMS Albion to reinforce the garrison and and on 29 November Lt.-Colonel Morgan of 42 Commando had the distinction of being the last man to leave 'the barren rocks of Aden'. As the carrier up-anchored and moved away, gunfire could be heard from the former colony as the conflicting Arab groups fought it out.

In spite of all that had happened there, a number of people left Aden with regret.

Mrs Ella M. Dix-White recalls her departure from Aden:

I always feel homesick when I see a desert scene on television. I had many incidents in my life out there – but it was always interesting even if you always had to keep an eye open.

My children were educated in Egypt and Aden, with short spells in England when we were on leave. My youngest son was born in 1965 and I returned home to have him. When I was fit I went back to Aden and was met at Khormaksar Airport by armoured cars and taken in a convoy to a flat in Maa'lla, with no bearers or cooks or even a nanny as all the locals were in fear of the rebels. We lived there till we had to be evacuated, leaving my husband behind for a while.

I have so many memories of life there, right from the start to the final departure, the near tragedies, the wonderful social life . . . we had to keep the flag flying with correct dress at all times, the tennis tournaments we played despite the heat . . . such glorious times – till the final exit. I found it very embarassing back in the UK when a car backfired and I threw myself to the ground as I had done so often in Aden when the grenades were flying around, but I wouldn't have missed a minute of it.

Linda Wood was another who left Aden sadly:

It was still difficult, right to the end. A friend of my father, Captain Bill Curtis, was killed on a last shopping trip to Steamer Point, shot in the head. His funeral at sea was very moving. A Viscount aircraft was blown up on the ground just before take off, great chunks of it flying through the air.

For the last few days I moved into the Khormaksar Palace Hotel, our flats left to anyone who cared to move in and occupy them. On the way to the airport I remembered all the good times I had had in Aden, all the friends I had made, and the boyfriends, some of whom died and are buried there. Looking out of the window of the aircraft I saw the Seamen's Mission, Conquest Bay, the Rock Hotel, all gone, all just memories.

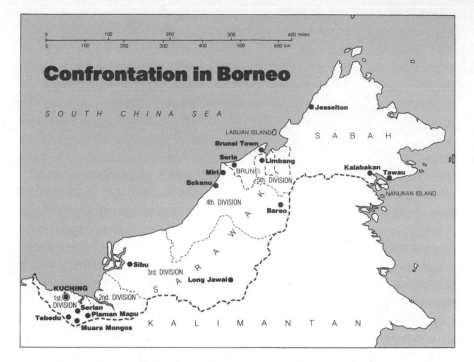

Confrontation in Borneo

SOUTH CHINA SEA

●Jesselton

LABUAN ISLAND

●Brunei Town

●Seria

●Limbang

SABAH

●Miri

BRUNEI

●Kalabakan

●Bekenu

5th. DIVISION

●Tawau

NANUKAN ISLAND

4th. DIVISION

●Bareo

S A R A W A K

●Sibu

3rd. DIVISION

●Long Jawai

KUCHING●

1st.
DIVISION

2nd. DIVISION

S

●Serian

●Plaman Mapu

●Tebedu

●Muara Mongos

K A L I M A N T A N

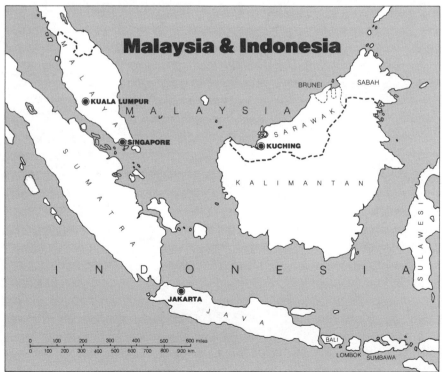

Malaysia & Indonesia

M
A
L
A
Y
A

BRUNEI

SABAH

●KUALA LUMPUR

M A L A Y S I A

S A R A W A K

●SINGAPORE

●KUCHING

S
U
M
A
T
R
A

K A L I M A N T A N

S
U
L
A
W
E
S
I

I N D O N E S I A

●JAKARTA

J A V A

BALI

LOMBOK   SUMBAWA

14

Brunei and Borneo: 1962–63

'All the "new nations" are at grips with the problems of forging a national identity, and employ, with varying degrees of success, the same recipes: education in patriotism, national heroes, national myths and mobilization against a common enemy. In this respect Indonesia is no exception, simply an extreme case.'

Herbert Luethy, *Indonesia Confronted*, 1965.

Imperial responsibilities do not always end when a former colony attains independence. Sometimes the former colony escapes from the grasp of the Imperial power only to come under attack from some other quarter, from some new imperialist in the making. To offer the best example of this situation we must now go back some years to the violent 'Confrontation' with Indonesia which began in Borneo in 1962. Unlike Suez and the Aden débâcle, this campaign, like the Malayan Emergency that preceded it, is one of the success stories of the End of Empire period.

The Indonesian 'Confrontation' began some five years after the British gave up all direct responsibility for Malaya, which became independent in 1957. Some years later the Malayan Government elected to form a 'Federation of Malaysia' by combining with other states containing large Malay populations. The other territories involved in this proposed Federation, those in North Borneo, and the Chinese dominated island of Singapore, were still a British responsibility in 1962, so the British swiftly became involved in this new proposal, and the problems it might cause.

The 'Confrontation' with Indonesia arose gradually, and in two parts, the first an almost Ruritanian and quickly suppressed revolt in Brunei and Sarawak, the second an all-out, three-and-a-half-year attempt by Indonesia to prevent or destroy the Malaysian Federation and overrun the three remaining British colonies and protectorates in the northern quarter of Borneo.

When Confrontation began, Britain had already decided to withdraw her forces from East of Suez but still retained a major base in Singapore. Therefore, when the infant Federation of Malaysia needed help Britain was in a position to offer it, helping to see off the Indonesian challenge and get this new nation off to a good start. So, in attempting to divest herself of the remnants of imperial responsibility East of Suez, Britain was drawn into a new and bitter struggle in the swamps and jungles of Borneo.

Borneo is a much-divided island. The larger, southern part, belongs to Indonesia and is called Kalimantan. The only parts of Borneo outside Kalimantan in 1962 were three British or British-protected territories along the north coast: Sabah or North Borneo, which had come into British hands in 1891 when another of those imperial trading companies, the North Borneo Company, began to extract timber there: Brunei, a Sultanate, which had been a British Protectorate since 1888 and was now oil-rich and the plum of these territories; and finally the much larger Sarawak, a sprawling mass of swamp, river and jungle-clad mountains, now divided into five administrative divisions. Since 1945 both Sabah and Sarawak had been run by the British as colonies.

Sarawak had previously belonged to the Brooke family, the 'White Rajahs of Sarawak', who had wrested control of this country from Indonesian pirates in 1841, and remained in power there until the Japanese Army arrived during the Second World War. After a British Parliamentary Committee under Lord Cobbold had checked that the people wished to do so, these three states were due to join with Malaya and Singapore in a newly-formed entity, the 'Federation of Malaysia'.

The idea of a Federation of Malaysia was the brainchild of the first Prime Minister of Malaya, Tunku Abdul Rahman. The population of these British-controlled Borneo territories were half-Malay, a quarter Chinese, and a quarter Dyak. The Tunku hoped that by linking the North Borneo territories with the Malay Peninsula he could correct the imbalance between the Chinese and Malay populations which would have occurred if Malaya had federated with Chinese-dominated Singapore alone. This seemed like a sensible solution and the Prime Minister of Singapore, Lee Kwan Yew, was also in favour since it got the British out of his territory. The British, being anxious to leave South East Asia entirely, also gave the proposed Federation their blessing. Not so the leader of Indonesia, President Achmed Sukarno.

President Sukarno had ruled Indonesia as a dictatorship since the Dutch had left in 1950. He regarded all the territory of Borneo as part of his 'Greater Indonesia', a complex of islands that swept south and east across the seas from the tip of Singapore and contained all those people who were ethnically linked to Indonesia. To Sukarno, the British colonies in North Borneo were no more than North Kalimantan and when the British left he wanted them to form part of Indonesia and not be federated to the democratically established Malay States. That achieved, Sukarno had even larger ambitions, to create a new state and even larger federation, 'Maphilindo', composed of Malaya, the Philippines and Indonesia, which he would then rule.

If Sukarno's ambitions were the only problem facing the infant Federation, that would have been enough, but other fingers were anxious to dip into this bubbling ethnic and political pot. The Sultan of Brunei, for one, was dead set against Federation. The Sultan had no wish to either share his oil revenues with the Malaysia Federation or install the full trappings of democratic government. He wished either to become an independent state or stay as part of the British Empire, with British troops to guarantee his continued 'independence'. In later years the Sultan was willing to pay for a battalion of Gurkhas to secure Brunei against outside aggression as well as maintaining a private bodyguard of two thousand ex-Gurkha soldiers.

The Sultan was a benign autocrat but when, nudged by the British, he held democratic elections for a local Council, he was surprised and alarmed to discover that his people were not entirely happy with his rule. The big issue of the election was how Brunei should be run after independence, for the British fully intended to leave. .

Many people, including most of the educated classes in North Borneo, felt that they should have their independence first and then decide where their future lay, rather than being simply handed over by the British to the Malaysia Federation. The Party opposed to the Sultan, the Partai Ra' Avat, or People's Party, also wanted the return of Sarawak and Sabah which the Sultans of Brunei had possessed before the coming of James Brooke.

Finally, there was the large Chinese community throughout North Borneo who, as in Malaya, ran most of the commercial enterprises. This community contained a significant Communist minority, with strong links to the Chinese mainland and, having failed in Malaya, the Communists were willing to try again here. As a step to that end they had created the CCO, the 'Chinese Clandestine Organisation', a left-wing body which was said to have over sixty thousand supporters.

All these volatile elements would have a part to play in the explosion that was coming but the detonator was provided by a group of important businessmen and politicians in Brunei, Sheik Azahari and his family.

Sheik Azahari had a three-part plan: he wished to create a 'United States of North Borneo' out of the three former British colonies. He would then put these states under the leadership of the Sultan of Brunei, who would be a Presidential figurehead. With that much achieved the 'United States of North Borneo' would then join up with Indonesia. Neither the Sultan of Brunei nor the British administrators of Sabah and Sarawak were very keen on this idea.

To achieve this end the Azaharis had begun to recruit and train a local and clandestine guerrilla army, the North Kalimantan National Army – TNKU – with arms and help from the Indonesian Army which was poised just across the southern border. TNKU was not a significant military force: by early 1962 TNKU could muster about five thousand ill-armed and untrained men, mostly concentrated in the small towns and villages of Brunei and in the Fifth Division of Sarawak, which lay along the borders of the Sultanate. Local elections, the first steps towards independence had already been held in Brunei and the Azahari Party had done reasonably well but not well enough to ensure their dominance after independence. Their solution to the possibility of political impotence was armed insurrection.

The object was not to beat the British, that was regarded as impossible, but if they could demonstrate opposition to the idea of Federation and the UN took an interest, the Federation would be stalled and the possibilities of creating 'Maphilindo' greatly improved.

The likelihood of a rising was fairly well known to the British Administration by the end of 1962 and in November the British Resident in the Fifth Division of Sarawak, an Australian, Richard Morris, and the Inspector General of the Malaysian Police, were sent to Brunei to report on the situation. The C-in-C Far East, Admiral Sir David Luce, then drew up a contingency plan covering the support available to the Brunei Police in the event of trouble. Various units were earmarked for this task including the 1/2nd Gurkha Rifles, 1st Bn., The Queen's Own Highlanders and two Royal Marine Commando units, 40 and 42 Commando which were either based in Singapore or embarked on one of the new helicopter-equipped Commando carriers.

The reason for this concentration of interest in Brunei, rather than in the other parts of North Borneo, can be summed up in one word – oil – and particular plans were laid to ensure the safety of the oilfields at Miri in the Fourth Division of Sarawak and Seria on the coast of Brunei. These arrangements were made only just in time, for the insurrection began on 8 December 1962 when TNKU forces attacked the police station, the Sultan's Palace and the British Residency in Brunei Town and other places in the territory including the oil town of Seria and the town of Limbang in the Fifth Divison of Sarawak.

The attacks in Brunei Town met with only limited success. The attackers were soon beaten off and chased out of town but TNKU's efforts met with more success elsewhere, notably in the town of Limbang which was in rebel hands by the evening of 8 December, with most of the British residents held hostage by TNKU in the police station. However, the rebels in Brunei had made one fatal error; they had failed to take and block the airfields.

The rising had taken place on a Saturday morning and it took time to round up the British troops and prepare the aircraft in Singapore. However, by that evening two Companies of the 1/2nd Gurkhas had arrived in Brunei town and while the bulk of this force moved to assist the local police, two platoons were rushed towards Seria and the oilfields. These troops were followed early next day by the 1st Bn., Queen's Own Highlanders and men of 42 Commando, Royal Marines.

Brigadier Jack Glennie, who took command of this operation also arrived and sent the Queen's Own Highlanders to clear the rebels out of Seria, and the 1st Bn., the Royal Greenjackets to retake the towns in the Bekanu area in the Fourth Division of Sarawak, and ordered 'L' Company of 42 Commando, Royal Marines, commanded by Captain Jeremy Moore, MC to rescue the British and Australians held hostage at Limbang. Captain Moore, who had won his MC in Malaya, is the officer who was later to command the British Land Forces in the Falklands War of 1982.

I joined 42 Commando in Singapore in 1962. They were on HMS *Bulwark*, off Muscat. Then we went to Aden and up to Dhala for a while, then to Hong Kong. We still had an Empire in those days. It was there that the Commando organisation changed from Troops to Companies – a Commando troop today is like an army platoon. My QMS at the time in 'L' Company, 42 Commando, was Cyril Scoins, a very fine man.

So, Brunei . . . 9 December 1962 was a Sunday. I was in my room at Simbang, doing my Christmas cards, when a Marine came in and said the Colonel would like to see me for an O (Orders) Group. I went to his room and he asked me, 'How quickly can you move the Company?' This 'O' Group was amusing; all the Company Commanders were either on picnics or water-skiing or shopping, and messengers were scurrying everywhere around Singapore island trying to get them back.

We arrived at Brunei airport during the evening of 10 December. 'L' Company was about eighty-seven strong, and we were joined later by a Heavy Weapons section with two Vickers medium machine-guns. The Gurkhas had already retaken Brunei Town from the rebels but the rebels had taken Limbang and were holding a lot of British people there as hostages. Next day, Brigadier Pat Patterson, then commanding the 99th Gurkha Brigade, arrived from Singapore and said to me, 'I want you to think about Limbang and find some transport.'

All I knew about Limbang was that it was a river town in Sarawak, that there were half-a-dozen or so hostages and an unknown number of rebels. A police launch went up there for a look – most movement in Borneo is by river – and got fired on. I got an air photograph of Limbang, enough to identify the main buildings, the police station, the hospital and so on. Then our CO arrived and told me to take 'L' Company up to Limbang and do the job.

I went down to the waterfront at Brunei and met the SNO (Senior Naval Officer), Lt.-Commander Jeremy Black. He had two minesweepers under command and we also found some sampans and a couple of flat craft called 'Z-Lighters' . . . one of them had two yellow bulldozers on board, which we didn't have time to get off.

Jeremy Black came on the trip, with the local Captain of Marine, of Brunei Town, a man called Mouton, who was to help us find the way. Now we knew there were quite a few rebels there and a few hostages, so I didn't want to land outside and make a slow, grinding infantry advance through the town which could put the hostages at risk, and I decided to run ashore in the town and go directly for the police station, which I thought might well be the rebel HQ, and contain at least some of the hostages.

We had my Recce Group, Company HQ and a Troop of Marines in my craft in front and the main company HQ, the MMGs and another Troop and a half on the rear craft. We made good time up the leads into the Limbang river and lay up there for a sleep before setting off again, aiming to arrive at first light. We came to the town quite suddenly when we rounded a bend in the river . . . all the lights were on but they all went out abruptly. We thought we had been spotted but in fact they were putting out the lights because dawn was breaking.

When they finally did see us the place exploded; it was exactly like an ant-heap, with people running everywhere. Our 'I' Sergeant then hailed the town through a loudhailer, and told them the rebellion had failed and to lay down their arms. This request was greeted with a hail of shot.

We drove our landing craft straight at the bank opposite the police station, with the MMG crews on the second craft firing the Vickers in support . . . the enemy had light machine-guns, lots of rifles and shotguns, so the return fire was heavy. A number of people were hit, including the helmsman of the leading craft – lots of bullets were coming aboard and splinters were flying about. Then something hit me in the middle of the back, hard enough to knock me down, and I thought, 'Good grief Moore, you seem to have been hit!'

I put my hand up to feel my back and there was no blood, so I thought, 'Get up, man – there's a battle to be fought.' My

Second-in-Command on the other craft was hit, so Cyril Scoins, the Sergeant Major, took over. He said to the Naval officer on board, 'Move the craft over, please Sir, so I can give fire support to the Company.' The Naval officer shook his head and said. 'Sergeant-Major, Nelson would have bloody loved you,' but he moved the craft over and we got good support.

Two sections were ashore now and doing everything perfectly – observing, firing, checking magazines, moving position – all the things we had practised so many times – it's very exciting to see the blokes doing it just right – you could pick the moment when the Corporal said 'Go!' One of them told me later that he had hated my guts in training when I had them doing these drills day after day, 'but I understood what it was all for in about two-thirds of a second as soon as we came under fire'.

Then I realised that my craft had drifted off the bank – the helmsman had been hit and the Naval officer in charge was currently busy firing a rifle. I wanted to put my third section ashore, so this officer put his rifle down and took the helm and put us back again, about a hundred yards further upstream. Sergeant MacFarlane then took his men over the bow to clear the shoreline from there down to the Police Station.

We found we couldn't get the craft off again, so I went ashore. The main deck of the lighter was pretty chaotic, with lots of packs and cartridge cases littered about, and a couple of bodies. I went up the road past the hospital where Dick Morris, the Resident, and his wife were held hostage. Dick had worked out that the relief would come either from Marines or Paras and to stop us chucking a grenade in, had made up a doggerel verse to the tune of 'She'll be coming round the Mountain' to let us know where they were, and we quickly got them out.

Sergeant MacFarlane and two of his Marines were killed here, shot at very close range. Dick Morris told us there were about three hundred rebels in the town and where the furthest hostages were kept . . . they included a young American from the Peace Corps. We had some resistance from the bazaar, and after Cyril Scoins landed the other two Troops, we set out to do a bit of street clearing.

The two troop subalterns hadn't done this before, so we taught them on the job – a real live firing exercise. The houses were pretty flimsy. One colossal Marine fell through the roof of one house and plummeted all the way down through various floors to the ground floor, landing in a heap beside a bath containing an entire Chinese family, all of them peering at him worriedly over the rim ... The Company performed extremely well and I was very proud of them.

Five Royal Marines of 42 Commando were killed and seven wounded in this operation, with rebel losses estimated at thirty-five killed and many more injured. For this successful assault on Limbang, Captain Jeremy Moore received his second Military Cross.

Meanwhile, on 11 December, the Queen's Own Highlanders under Lt.-Colonel W.G. Hardy had been flown into Seria and retaken the oilfields, rescuing the hostages there, killing a number of rebels at no cost to themselves, and the Royal Greenjackets, having landed at Meri from the cruiser HMS *Tiger*, had embarked on lighters and an assortment of river craft and cleared the rebels from all the surrounding towns and villages. The riflemen suffered no casualties, killed five rebels and captured hundreds more. By 14 December, just six days after the start of the rebellion, all resistance in Brunei and Sarawak had ended. The fighting however, was not yet over.

These initial operations had taught the British one useful and well remembered lesson: that mobility in Borneo would never be easy and cross-country movement must be by river or by air. One memorable statistic is that a patrol of Gurkhas in Borneo once took three days to cover five thousand yards; a helicopter covered the same distance in under three minutes.

Helicopters were to prove the key to mobility in Borneo as Lieutenant Ian Uzzell of 40 Commando – himself a helicopter pilot – recalls:

I joined 40 Commando as a 2nd Lieutenant in November 1962 at Aden, where they were involved in the changeover of HMS *Bulwark* and HMS *Albion* – the second Commando carrier.

40 Commando embarked on HMS *Albion*. En route to Singapore we heard of the trouble in Brunei and that 42 Commando had landed at Limbang with the loss of five men. We increased speed and knew we were heading in the direction of Borneo but we were not allowed to know our destination until after we had paused at Singapore to collect stores. The wives of the married

men had already been told and they informed their husbands of our destination during the four hours they were allowed ashore. It was Kuching, the capital of Sarawak.

We were using the Wessex helicopter for the first time on this tour and on working-up exercises had only worn fighting order. When we went ashore at Kuching, we had to take our full marching order. Being unfamiliar with the new helicopter, my Troop loaded all the weighty stores at the rear. This almost caused the pilot to have a heart attack when the front of the helicopter rose off the ground but not the back! A hasty landing and re-sorting of stores took place and then we were safely taking off for Kuching racecourse. Not knowing what to expect on our arrival. I had briefed my troop of thirty-three men to form an all-round defensive position, but control was lost on landing when it was noticed that a number of ice-cream vendors were plying their trade around the Commando.

My Company was sent to Seria to look after the oilfields there and I went to an outpost called Tebedu, to patrol the border. After a week or so we were withdrawn and flown north by helicopter to Tawau in North Borneo where we carried out river and coastal patrols. We returned to Singapore in January 1963 but were soon back in Borneo as the Confrontation developed.

As in other parts of the Empire, these events in Brunei affected the Civil authorities. Lawrence J. Foster was the Deputy Director of Agriculture in Kuching at the time of the Brunei revolt:

My first experience of unrest in Sarawak came in December 1962, when I was on tour through the Fourth and Fifth Divisions. We had just left Marapit for Bareo when the pilot was told that he had to return to Labaun to pick up troops to quell a revolt! This was a bit of a surprise.

Short of walking out, we had to sit it out, so we elected to carry on with our tour as planned, our baggage carried by women carriers, all of us crossing rivers on tree-trunk bridges perched fifty feet over rushing torrents. Travelling through the Sarawak jungle there is no big game but plenty of monkeys, pigs, snakes and small deer. A local legend says that the tiger would not come to Borneo because when confronted with the bristles of a porcupine he thought they were the bristles of a much larger cat.

Our tour took ten days and when we returned to Bareo we found that Tom Harrison of the Museum had taken charge. He was well known among the natives as he had been parachuted into Borneo during the war and worked against the Japanese, most of whom had lost their heads. These heads were still stored in the village longhouses. Harrison was organising the locals into a kind of Home Guard armed with shotguns, and that was the start of Confrontation.

By mid-December 1962 it appeared that the revolt in Brunei was over and further steps towards Federation and independence could now be taken. However, there were still TNKU elements at large in the kampongs and scattered up the rivers and care had to be taken, especially in Sarawak, in case the Indonesians should attempt to take a hand in the game. British reinforcements continued to arrive and were sent to defend the town of Kuching, the capital of Sarawak.

These included the rest of 42 Commando, all of 40 Commando off HMS *Albion*, a battery of the 20th Field Artillery without their guns and an armoured car squadron of the Queen's Royal Irish Hussars. The most useful addition was the arrival of two helicopter squadrons from the Commando carrier HMS *Albion*, which remained close offshore. This force was placed under the command of Brigadier F.C. Barton, RM, Commander of the 3rd Commando Brigade, who assumed responsibility for defence in the First, Second and Third Divisions of Sarawak.

Forces were also pouring in to the other divisions of Sarawak and Brunei, notably Gurkhas of the 99 Gurkha Brigade, and on 19 December the commander of the 17th Gurkha Division. Major General Walter Walker, arrived post-haste from Nepal to take over as Commander, British Forces Borneo.

Major General Walter Walker was an officer of Gurkhas, a soldier of the old Indian Army. British officers who serve with Gurkha units tend to become passionate about their men and in this Walker was no exception. He had served in Burma during the Second World War and as CO of the 1/6th Gurkhas during the Malayan Emergency, raising that excellent battalion to a new peak of efficiency.

No one who met or knew General Walker was indifferent to him; those men those who served under him came to regard him with respect and affection and their regard is apparent to this day. He was somewhat less successful with his superiors in Whitehall; a fighting soldier, he tended to clash with the Staff on various matters but particularly on anything affecting his beloved Gurkhas.

'Walker thinks that every military problem can be solved with a battalion of Gurkhas', is one typical Whitehall view of General Walker but one which sums up his personal commitment to these first-class troops. Walker considered, with some justification, that the Gurkha soldiers were both the salt of the earth and the finest infantry in the world and he arrived in Borneo after a visit to their homeland where he had had a long discussion on their future with the King of Nepal.

Walker had made this visit in his capacity as Major-General, Brigade of Gurkhas, and had taken the opportunity to brief the King on a still-secret Whitehall proposal that with abandonment of Britain's rule East of Suez, the Gurkha battalions – currently eight – should either be scrapped or greatly reduced and the number of Gurkhas cut from the present sixteen thousand to six thousand men or less.

This Army Council proposal had been revealed in confidence to Walker by General Sir Richard Hull, C-in-C. Far East Land Forces, just before Hull left the Far East to take up his new post as Chief of the Imperial General Staff, the effective head of the British Army.

Hull explained the background to this proposal, the need to reduce commitments, the reliance on the nuclear deterrent and the need to economise. Walter Walker was not interested in any of that. His concern was for his Gurkhas and he had various ideas on how this fate might be averted. While in Kathmandu he discussed these ideas fully with the King of Nepal.

Unfortunately, as General Walker knew full well, these Government proposals were supposed to be Top Secret. For his part, the King of Nepal was furious that he had not been consulted or even informed of these intentions.

Walker also confided details of the problem to the American Ambassador in Kathmandu, Henry Stebbings. Stebbings knew that the employment offered to Nepali men in the Gurkha regiments, and the money they sent home, was a major factor in the country's economy and important to Nepal's political stability. He promised to pass on news of this intention to Washington and get support for the Gurkhas from the White House.

When word of this activity reached Whitehall, those in high command at the War Office and in the Government suspected that General Walker had deliberately broken Hull's confidence, hoping to cause a diplomatic row which, with luck, would lead to the dropping of these proposals and the salvation of the Gurkhas. These indiscreet, though well-meant actions were to get Major-General Walker into serious trouble.

For the moment though, General Walker had other problems. The first requirement was to convince his superiors, especially Vice-Admiral Sir Varyl Begg, C-in-C Far East, that the threat from Indonesia was a real one and that force levels in Borneo must be kept up or even increased. He then followed the example of Templer in Malaya and set up a unified command, involving troops, local Government officers and the police, with himself as C-in C British Forces Borneo and Director of Operations. One of the new Command's first decisions was to disarm the local population, and the police and troops were soon busy collecting thousands of shotguns and rifles from the villages.

The intelligence element, especially along the Kalimantan border, was hastily improved and in this Walker had the help of Tom Harrison, currently the Curator of the Sarawak Museum but formerly an officer in the World War Two Far East guerrilla unit, Force 136. Harrison knew the indigenous people of Borneo well and quickly formed a new unit composed of Iban and Dyak warriors, many of them former headhunters, some of whom had served as trackers with the British Army during the Malayan Emergency.

Harrison sent for his men by the traditional method, the messengers travelling up-river in canoes bearing the red feathers of war. With arms, training and backing from soldiers of the 22 SAS and the Gurkha Parachute Company these men later became the nucleus of the Border Scouts, a war-winning element in the struggle to come. The Border Scouts lived in the longhouses and kampongs along the Kalimantan frontier and supplied accurate intelligence to the British troops positioned in fortified company 'locations' just north of the border.

This influx of British troops led to a swift collapse of the Azahari revolt and the CCO, which might have taken a hand in these troubles, promptly went underground. Many people now believed that the troubles in North Borneo were over and that the Federation of Malaysia could be set up without delay. General Walker thought otherwise. In spite of his looming personal problem with the powers-that-be in Whitehall over the future of the Gurkha battalions, he was certain that Indonesian troops would shortly become involved in this affair and this assumption soon proved correct.

President Sukarno was now playing the anti-colonial card, declaring to the world at large and the UN in particular that the British were up to their old game of divide and rule and that the so-called Federation was simply a puppet of British Imperialism.

In a speech in Jakarta in January 1963 he first used the word 'Confrontation', declaring that confrontation was his only option if Malaya insisted on pursuing a policy of neo-colonialism and hostility to Indonesia. He also claimed that the people of 'North Kalimantan' were opposed to Federation and wished only to join their kin in Indonesia. These claims went down well in the Third World and met with some support in the Philippines, a country which was now sheltering Sheik Azahari, who had fled to Manila after his revolt had collapsed. His two brothers stayed in Borneo until they were tracked down, one being killed and one captured by men of the 2/7th Gurkha Rifles.

So the weeks crawled by, with no movement from the Indonesian Army now mustering across the frontier. Matters were, however, stirring against General Walker in Whitehall. The powers-that-be, problems in Borneo or not, seemed determined to reduce the number of Gurkha battalions and in anticipation of this, following his visit to Kathmandu, Walker had circulated an internal memorandum around the Gurkha units, advising them of the situation.

Walker regarded this as an internal memorandum and had therefore not sent a copy to Far East Land Forces HQ but a copy of the memorandum had somehow reached the office of the Chief of the Imperial General Staff, Field Marshal Sir Richard Hull. Walker had sent a copy of his memorandum to Major-General Lewis Pugh, now retired, but an old friend of Walker's and a former C-in-C, Far East Land Forces, hoping to enlist Pugh's support in his campaign to save the Gurkhas. In March 1963 Walker was summoned to London and his first move on arrival in the UK was to contact Lewis Pugh.

It transpired that General Pugh, equally appalled at the thought of losing the Gurkha battalions, had shown the memorandum to

Field Marshal Sir Gerald Templer. Templer was Colonel of the 7th Gurkhas, an honour and distinction that charged him with protecting the regiment's interests and seeing to their welfare. Pugh assumed that Templer would be be equally concerned at the Whitehall proposals and throw his authority and prestige behind the campaign to save the Gurkhas. Templer, however, saw broader issues and presented them forcefully to General Pugh.

Whatever the strength of Walker's case and however much Templer shared his concern for the Gurkhas, Templer was shocked and furious that any General Officer should be seen as attempting to conspire against the actions or decisions of the British Government, the Army Council and the CIGS. Templer told Pugh that while Walker might well wish to retain the Gurkhas, this was not the way to go about it, and that he regarded General Walker's actions in Kathmandu and the memorandum to the Brigade of Gurkhas as disloyal to his superior officers in London. Pugh's well meant attempt to enlist support from his superiors had got Walker into serious trouble.

It then emerged that the Americans had become involved, sending a plea for the retention of the Gurkhas and the abandonment of the proposed cuts to the British War Minister, John Profumo. When Profumo found out how they came by their information, he was not at all amused.

Templer had decided to show Walker's memorandum to another former CIGS, the Colonel of the 6th Gurkhas, Field Marshal Sir John Harding, and seek his opinion. Harding was not amused either and he sent a copy of the memo to Field Marshal Sir William Slim, the senior soldier in the British Army. Slim shared the views of Templer and Harding and, having marked his copy of Walker's memorandum with words like 'disgraceful', sent it on to the CIGS, Field Marshal Sir Richard Hull. Hence the summons to London.

Pugh told Walker that the Minister for War and the Field Marshals of the British Army clearly did not appreciate such action from a mere Major-General and that real trouble awaited him in Field Marshal Hull's room at the War Office.

So it proved. Hull was furious and Walker only avoided being relieved of his command in Borneo, or even a court martial, by an apology to Hull, first in person, and then in writing. Field Marshal Hull accepted this, telling Walker that but for the apology he would indeed have sacked him from his command in Borneo. He added that he could not let Walker continue as Major-General, Brigade of Gurkhas, and that post would go to Major-General Robertson, who would be recalled from retirement to take up the post.

Somewhat chastened by these events, Walker then returned to his command in Borneo. Walker may have hoped that this was the end of the affair but Field Marshals have long memories and the matter was not yet closed. Fortunately for General Walker, these spats in Whitehall were soon drowned by the sound of gunfire from the Kalimantan frontier and the start of a campaign that would demonstrate, far better than words, the usefulness of the sturdy Gurkha battalions.

Throughout the early months of 1963, Sukarno had kept up the diplomatic activity and continued to press his anti-colonial points on anyone who would listen, biding his time otherwise until his troops were ready to move across the Kalimantan border; then words gave way to armed opposition. The Indonesians who attacked North Borneo were no ragged band of terrorists but a well-trained and well-armed force and when they struck they struck hard.

The first attack of the three-year long Borneo 'Confrontation' took place on Good Friday, 12 April 1963, when a raiding party of Indonesian regular troops attacked the police post at Tebedu, five kilometres inside the Sarawak frontier.

15

Confrontation with Indonesia: 1963–1966

'Wars in those days tended to be classified as general, limited or cold. "Confrontation" was a very limited form of limited war.'

Field Marshal Lord Carver, *War Since 1945*, 1980.

President Sukarno, the Indonesian dictator, saw Britain's 'intervention' in Brunei as a challenge to his plans for 'North Kalimantan' and a setback to his strategy for setting up 'Maphilindo'. He had already declared that the proposal setting up the Federation of Malaysia was no more than a British-inspired plot to maintain a colonial presence in the region and he denounced Tunku Abdul Rahman, the proposed President of the new Federation, as a neo-colonialist and a British puppet. His need now was to prevent the setting up of the Federation, if necessary by military means.

All-out war with Britain was not an option, so Sukarno opted for 'Confrontation' an undeclared border war along the frontiers of Sarawak, Brunei and Sabah. For this Sukarno had one great advantage, an aggressive and well-trained army, one more than a match for the Malay regiments. If properly handled, 'Confrontation' should delay the setting up of the Federation and – with luck – even lead to intervention by the ever active anti-colonial caucus at the United Nations.

To mount a full-scale border war and thwart the British and Malay plans for Federation would take time and Sukarno did not have much time as plans for Federation were already far advanced. A quick, bloody, border strike seemed a good way of attracting attention to the problem and 'Confrontation' began with the attack on Tebedu.

This action killed two policemen but it brought the British Army back into the fray, to support the Federation. Those British troops withdrawn to Singapore after the ending of the Brunei revolt found themselves back in Borneo, manning defence posts on the Kalimantan frontier.

Lieutenant Ian Uzzell was an officer in 40 Commando: 'Tebedu was attacked by regular Indonesian forces and 40 Commando, just back in Singapore, were recalled to Borneo from weekend leave. Once again "C" Company was based at Serian, and I was sent up-river to a village called Muara Mongkos. Here we carried out patrolling and an intensive "hearts and minds" campaign among the Ibans. The Rifle Troops worked very much on their own with radio contact to Company headquarters, twenty miles away. Re-supply was usually by air-drop or the ever-useful helicopter, the key to the whole campaign.'

Len Bishop was a Chief Petty Officer Artificer with the Fleet Air Arm on HMS *Albion* at this time:

HMS *Albion* was a Commando carrier. We sailed from Portsmouth on 3 November 1962 and after various stops along the way met the other Commando carrier, HMS *Bulwark*, at Aden and took over her embarked unit, 40 Commando. We then went to Malindi in Kenya and were there when we were ordered across the Indian Ocean to Singapore and Brunei Town. That was for the Brunei revolt. When Confrontation in 1963 started we went back to Laubaun island and the helicopters were sent ashore.

Albion had had two squadrons of Fleet Air Arm helicopters embarked, 846 Squadron, my squadron, with Whirlwind 7s and 845 Squadron with Wessex. The Whirlwinds were very under-powered and had poor lift. We could carry about three fully armed bootnecks – Marines – or four Gurkhas, and we mostly worked with Marine Commando or Gurkha units, and sometimes with the SAS, flying piquets or patrols up to the border and moving troops about around the jungle bases. The Wessex could carry up to fifteen fully armed troops and they tended to work with Army units like the Leicester Regiment or the Greenjackets but I liked the Whirlwinds and 846 Squadron did good work with them. We got to be called the 'Junglies' and 846 people are called the 'Junglies' to this day.

It was bloody hard work. The weather was hot, the living hard, the life uncomfortable and the insects gigantic, but it's funny, you only remember the good times, and we did have a lot of laughs. The aircraft flew from dawn to dusk, seven days a week, and when they were not up, we were busy on maintenance and repairs. There was no leave and nowhere to go anyway. From December 1962 to April 1964 the two squadrons – and our squadron only had six aircraft – flew over ten thousand sorties.

We CPOs shared a Sergeants' Mess with the Marines from 40 or 42 Commandos when they were not out bashing the jungle. They were bloody good soldiers, I have to admit. We took the piss out of them all the time, but the 'bootnecks' are good: just don't tell them I said so. The Gurkhas were bloody marvellous; when they guarded the camp not a light showed, they moved like shadows.

When the Malay Regiment took over you could hear their sentries' transistor radios, cigarettes glowing in the dark as they wandered about . . . they looked very pretty in their smart jungle uniforms but I don't think they knew much about soldiering.

I think the Indonesians expected to walk all over the Malays, but found themselves fighting the First Team, the Gurkhas and the Royal Marines: bloody hard luck, that. Mostly, though, we had enough to do keeping the helicopters flying.

Don McLean was a trooper in the Army Air Corps:

I was twenty-two when I arrived in Borneo in 1964. In the days of the Rajah Brookes the Ibans were well known for their head-hunting and there had been attempts to stamp out the practice. During the war, when the Japs were in occupation in the 1950s, it is probable that the taking of heads continued. The Ibans were used by the British troops as trackers, and after training by the SAS thy were formed into the Sarawak Rangers.

One story of the Japanese occupation relates to a Japanese Education Major who took it upon himself to visit a longhouse.

I'm told that his head hangs in the same longhouse and his gold-rimmed spectacles are still polished each day!

In the time of the Rajahs, as a test of suitability for marriage, an Iban man had to take a head. When they had done so, they tattooed the fingers of their hands. We saw many of the younger men being tattooed at Tinggan's longhouse . . . neck, face, chest and arms, but never on the hands or fingers. The tattoo was made from the grease obtained from the longhouse pigs mixed with charcoal. Sharpened bamboo needles were used to impregnate the skin. However, all the older men were tattooed on their fingers!

Nanga Gaat was the scene of one of the worst losses – not by enemy action but through the misfortunes of pilot error. Two Wessex helicopters, returning from a border operation and loaded with, it was alleged, a unit of SAS, were returning along the course of the Baleh river. On approaching the junction of Baleh with the Gaat, the outside of the two helicopters banked inwards. Unfortunately the inside pilot had not started his turn and the two crashed into the Baleh, which at that point is around seventy feet deep. All seventeen hands were lost. A small plaque inscribed with their names stood on the bank where the Gaat meets the Baleh, and as a mark of respect the Ibans would not fish there.

Helicopters were to prove a war winner during 'Confrontation' but there were never enough of them. Apart from the insertion of patrols, the movement of men and stores to and between bases and 'casevac' (casualty evacuation), most of the soldiering was done on foot and jungle soldiering is hard work as Marine Dave Lee of 42 Commando can testify:

All the time in the jungle the weather was very humid and our clothes were soaking with sweat, even if we weren't exerting ourselves. The monsoon season was the worst, with heavy rain which sometimes lasted for several days. This, of course, made the going very rough underfoot, swamps rose or became impassable and there was no escaping the mud. Jungle boots were all right for keeping out the leeches but were certainly not waterproof and our feet were constantly wet. It was only when we stopped for the night that it was worth changing our socks and giving the shrivelled-up flesh a respite.

Leeches were a constant menace and a stab with a cigarette end seemed the best solution. After crossing a river, a good search of the body would reveal several of them. When the sun came out, life was a bit more bearable, but our clothes dried on our bodies. Some patrols were easier than others, and if it was near the coast the tracks were easier and the jungle not so dense. Mind you, the mangrove swamps threw up a different problem. They had to be patrolled at low tide and were the perfect place for enemy infiltrators to hide their boats. We learned to keep our feet on the tree roots; if not, it was mud up to our hips. Swarms of mosquitoes made it even worse, the repellent having only a limited effect.

Come early evening and it was time to camp for the night. Chosen carefully, the camp could bring dry clothes – you put the wet ones on again in the morning – a little relaxation and a steaming hot stew. Cooking with the solid fuel tablets was easy and a hot cup of tea at dusk brought thoughts of home.

That first armed infiltration, the attack on Tebedu on Good Friday, 12 April 1963, was only the first of many such raids. The CCO, the Chinese Clandestine Organisation, a Communist body, were at first suspected of this attack, but it soon became clear that it had been carried out by regular Indonesian forces and these forces were soon coming across the frontier in considerable numbers.

Cross-border bickering became common and casualties soon mounted on both sides. The British were now becoming more expert in jungle warfare and, drawing on the lessons of Malaya, great stress was laid on adequate intelligence and mobility, the latter depending on helicopters, the former being aided by the creation of a one-thousand-strong force of Borneo irregulars, the Border Scouts, commanded by Major John Cross, a veteran of the Malayan Emergency: many of the Border Scouts were former members of Harrison's Force or had served in Malaya during the Emergency. Another innovation was the introduction of four-man SAS patrols along, and frequently across, the Kalimantan border.

One of the ironies of the situation was that, in happier times, many Indonesian Army officers had attended jungle warfare courses at the British Jungle Warfare School in Malaya. Brigadier Chris

Bullock was in Borneo at this time, as a Captain with the 2/2nd Gurkhas:

> I suppose you can call it ironic that they had trained at our Jungle School. It means that we knew or could guess what they would do, what their ambush drills would be, and they of course had a fair idea what we might do. The trick was always to do something different, to avoid setting any pattern, but they were good soldiers, though not as good as us.
>
> One of the major hazards of 'Confrontation' was disease. Everyone got fevers and had to be taken out of the jungle for a while, though the Gurkha troops lasted longer than most. The big problems were scrub typhus, which was caused by mites, sleeping sickness, dengue fever and various ailments, like leptospirosis. This was brought on by rats which swarmed in the camps and infected the water.
>
> Patrols or ambushes tended to last about twelve days, and if someone was bitten by mites on the way in and got scrub typhus or dengue a couple of days later, then you had a very sick man on your hands. Helivac was not allowed across the frontier and it would take twelve men to bring him out: four men to clear the way, four men to carry the man and four to carry the kit, weapon and ammunition, food whatever. In the jungle you were doing well if you covered a hundred yards in an hour, so with a casualty you did much less.
>
> The fighting did not all go one way. The Indonesians attacked our camps fairly frequently, so as time went by these company camps became like little fortresses, wired in, claymore mines, mortars . . . but it was essential to dominate the local area and not opt for any kind of static defence.

Life in these jungle forts is also remembered by John 'Patch' Williams, a Sergeant Major of 2 Para:

> The forts were just big dugouts, with plenty of barbed wire and corrugated iron. There were plenty of rats about, coming out of the jungle after food, so you had to watch your hygiene. I remember that in my little dugout – I was a WO11, a Company Sergeant Major – I had decided to tart up the walls with parachute silk: we had plenty of that from the air drops.

Anyway, one day I was living there, having a think, when I saw the silk was moving about, quite actively. After a bit I got up and whipped it aside and there was a bloody great python: it had come in after the rats . . .

Colonel Joe Starling recalls his days in Borneo with 1st Battalion, The Parachute Regiment:

During the Confrontation between Indonesia and Malaysia in the mid-sixties, the SAS Squadrons who kept watch on the Borneo border became over-stretched. You have to remember that the border was a thousand miles long and the terrain was both mountainous, swampy and covered with jungle. Each Parachute battalion therefore formed a Patrol Company to supplement the SAS efforts. Our four-man patrols operated from a firm base well back from the border ridge which was manned by an element of one of the British, Gurkha or Malaysian infantry battalions.

It was hard work but the 'Toms' could always find some humour in it. I remember that the Company Commander of 'D' Company 1 Para was making a whistle-stop tour of all the patrol bases in his operational area on taking over from his predecessor. On arrival at one patrol base manned by a Platoon of the Royal Ulster Rifles, most of them from Belfast, the Company Commander's helicopter was met by the Pengulu (headman) of the local tribe, who had clearly been carefully briefed on how to meet a visiting VIP.

This gentleman, clad only in a loin cloth, stepped forward, banged the butt of his spear on the ground and greeted the Company Commander in very passable English, 'Good morning, Sah! – and fuck the Pope.' The Northern Irish never lose the chance of making their point and must have spent days teaching him that introduction.

The word 'Confrontation' may give rise to the idea that this campaign was more a matter of belligerent statements than actual fighting. This is far from the case. The British, Malayan and Gurkha forces were frequently under attack and often outnumbered by well-trained, regular units of the Indonesian Army operating in company strength of a hundred men or more.

After Tebedu more battalions arrived to join General Walter

Walker's force, including the 2nd/10th Gurkha Rifles who were sent to Sibu in the Second Division of Sarawak and were soon in action on the border, along the steep Kling Klang ridge. It may have been called a 'Confrontation', but to the people at the sharp end it more frequently resembled a small-scale, all-out war. Take, for example, the following action fought by a patrol of the 22 SAS Regiment.

A four-man patrol of 22 SAS was moving carefully up to the border along a track which led towards an Indonesian post which their scouts had spotted the previous day. This post appeared to have been vacated months before, but as the leading SAS trooper approached it and ducked under some bamboo, he spotted an Indonesian soldier a few metres to his flank.

In the first exchange of fire the SAS man was hit in the thigh and fell into a clump of bamboo on top of yet another Indonesian soldier, whom he shot and killed. The SAS had clearly walked into an ambush.

The Indonesian soldiers engaged the SAS from well-concealed positions and the patrol commander, Sergeant Lillico, had been wounded in the first exchange of fire and was unable to move. He could still use his rifle and he therefore returned the enemy fire while the other men in the patrol took cover.

The bullet in the leading trooper's thigh had shattered the bone. Unable to walk, he hopped back to join Lillico, who ordered him to return up the track and bring the rest of the patrol forward. Sergeant Lillico dragged himself back up the ridge and opened a steady fire in the direction of the enemy post. Shortly after this the Indonesians withdrew, possibly under the belief that SAS reinforcements would soon be moving in to surround their position.

The remainder of the patrol had decided to withdraw to the nearest infantry post, pick up reinforcements and return next day to search the area for their wounded colleagues. By the morning of the second day the injured trooper had managed to cover half the distance back to the infantry camp, dragging himself painfully along the ground before he was found by the search party.

Meanwhile, Sergeant Lillico had managed to gain the top of the ridge, some three hundred metres from where he had been hit. The single shots he fired to attract the attention of the search party were answered by bursts of machine-gun fire from the enemy close by, Lillico could hear the noise of a helicopter overhead but dared not risk showing himself while the enemy were still searching for him so he lay up all day and was only finally spotted by the helicopter when it returned during the evening. He was then winched out, a day and a half after he had been injured in that first fierce exchange of fire.

That is a fairly typical Borneo border action. Confrontation was a war of ambush, no prisoners were taken and the fate of the wounded was dire indeed. The fighting took place at close range, in swamp and dense jungle and he who got the first burst of fire in usually won the day. It called for a high level of fieldcraft, accurate shooting and a great deal of guts to fight and win this war of patrol and ambush and it went on for months and years during the period of 'Confrontation'.

President Sukarno did not rely solely on military muscle. He was also active on the diplomatic front. In May 1963, two weeks after the Tebedu raid, he called for a diplomatic Summit with Tunku Abdul Rahman in Tokyo. This meeting went well and was followed by another meeting between Malayan and Indonesian Foreign Ministers in Manila in June after which the Ministers issued a 'Manila Accord'. This accord supported the idea of self-determination for the North Borneo territories, provided that the idea had the support of the local people, a fact that was to be guaged by a UN committee.

Discussions between Britain and Malaya went ahead and in July 1963 the Tunku signed the London Agreement, aiming to set up the Federation of Malaysia at the end of August. This, not surprisingly, enraged President Sukarno and there was yet another meeting between Sukarno, the Tunku and the Philippine Head of State, this time to discuss 'Maphilindo'. At this meeting the Tunku agreed to Sukarno's demand for a referendum on Malaysia in North Borneo, as this only meant putting back the Malaysia 'Founding Day' for two weeks. The test of opinion duly took place and on 13 September 1963 the UN Secretary General, U Thant, announced that the North Borneo States, with the exception of Brunei, had voted for Federation. President Sukarno was furious.

Meanwhile, the border war was hotting up. 'Confrontation' was fought against a well-trained and well-equipped enemy, who usually had the advantage of surprise. These Indonesian companies would fight hard when contacted and when forced to retreat would lay ambushes to trap their pursuers. The SAS therefore adopted a 'Shoot-and-Scoot' policy for their four-man patrols, in which, after making a contact and a brief exchange of fire, the SAS would break off the engagement, radio for reinforcements, often Gurkhas, and then dog the enemy's footsteps until the raiders could be brought to battle. Sometimes, however, there was no time for that.

Lieutenant Skardon, an Australian officer attached to the SAS, had been with his patrol for just four weeks when they first had a contact. Sensing enemy presence in the jungle near their camp, Lieutenant Skardon decided to investigate, taking three men. They found nothing unusual close by and set out next morning to check the main track on the ridge parallel to the creek below their position. The jungle was very quiet as the four men crossed the river and climbed to the track on the ridge, but they sensed that something was not right.

They therefore proceeded with great caution, slipping from one patch of cover to another, until one of the patrol, Trooper White, almost fell over an Indonesian soldier kneeling behind a tree. The Indonesian was killed immediately with one shot but enemy fire now came in on the SAS from every side, as the ambush was sprung. The order was given to get out and clear the area and Lieutenant Skardon moved back with two troopers, while Trooper White stayed behind to cover them, opening fire on a platoon of enemy soldiers who had appeared on the ridge above.

The ground was very open and White was quickly hit and badly wounded. Disregarding the 'Shoot-and-Scoot' policy, Lieutenant Skardon ran back up the slope and dragged White into cover behind a large tree. Still under heavy enemy fire, Skardon then pulled White into a hollow, hoping it would cover them from view, but the enemy were now flooding down the slope to finish the two men off.

Skardon saw that blood had stopped flowing from the gaping wound in White's thigh and feared that White was already dead. Even so, he decided to get White down to the shelter of the river bank. Dragging or carrying White over his shoulder, dashing from hollow to hollow, still pursued by intense but inaccurate fire, Lieutenant Skardon dropped down to the creek.

A group of the enemy now moved in towards the creek from the flank, and had almost cut off Skardon's escape route when he realised that White had indeed died. Leaving the body, Skardon fired a burst at the enemy and made a dash into the creek. Once into the water he was out of view behind the high bank but it was necessary to wade downstream and reach better cover on the far bank before being cut off again. Lieutenant Skardon finally reached some thick undergrowth and hauled himself up the bank into cover and safety.

Next day, SAS troops and Gurkhas swept the area and recovered Trooper White's body. Nearby lay the body of the Indonesian soldier White had shot, and higher on the ridge, the vacated ambush positions of over thirty enemy soldiers, each littered with empty cartridge cases.

The establishment of Federation increased the action on both the military and diplomatic fronts, though Sukarno refused diplomatic recognition to the Federation when it was finally established – without Brunei – on 16 September 1963. Relations with Britain also deteriorated sharply and Indonesian mobs were turned loose against British property in Indonesia, though British expatriates were left unharmed. In December 1963 a mob attacked the British Embassy in Jakarta and after a three-day siege, during which the crowds were restrained – or entertained – by the Military Attache, Major Rory Walker M.C. of the S.A.S. playing the bagpipes, the Embassy was sacked and burned to the ground.

For a while it looked as if all-out war between Britain and Indonesia could hardly be avoided but, on the understanding that compensation would be paid for the damage done to the Embassy and British business property in Jakarta, Britain decided to maintain diplomatic links with Indonesia. Not so the new Federation of Malaysia, which broke off all diplomatic relations with Indonesia on 20 December 1963.

In retaliation, Sukarno severed all commercial links with Malaysia but this move backfired. Indonesia suffered retaliation when all Western aid to Indonesia was suspended in January 1964. This had the unfortunate result of turning Sukarno towards Communist China and gaining him support from the large number of Chinese Communist elements spread throughout the Malaysia Federation.

Sukarno maintained that the fighting on his side in Borneo was being done by TNKU, survivors of the Brunei revolt and this 'war of liberation' took two main forms. The first was a series of cross-border raids in company strength by Indonesian regular forces. The second was the attempt to seize and hold territory within the borders of Sarawak, which could then be declared 'liberated' areas, free of the Federation and 'neo-colonial rule'.

General Walker attempted to counter the former tactic by keeping a close eye on the border, but holding his forces some distance back, in platoon bases, from which forces could be sent out on foot or by helicopter to stem any Indonesian incursion. When the Indonesians began to stay and take territory or spread their attacks to the Malay Peninsula, more sophisticated tactics were called for.

Geordie Mather was in Borneo with 40 Commando:

While in Singapore I was detailed along with other drivers and members of 'S' Company Mobat teams, to form a fighting troop and we became the Tawau Assault Group (TAG). This was made up of Malay Patrol craft and LAABs (Light Aluminium Assault Boats). After many weeks of training in the swamps round Singapore we were ready to go and our move to Borneo proved quite a trip.

On arriving at the docks we were looking for something from the Grey Funnel Line – the Royal Navy – but we boarded the MV *Auby*, a converted cattle boat, a cross between *The Bounty* and an Isle of Wight ferry. I don't think there is a Marine living who will forget a trip on the *Auby* . . . it took a week to get to Sabah, the place that used to be North Borneo.

Being on a rotation basis round the locations, our second stop was on PC3, a patrol craft living off Nanukan Island right on the Kalimantan border. During daylight hours we lay at anchor, watching the island through powerful binoculars. It was a big base for the Indonesian Marine Corps. At night we up-anchored and waited till the fast gunboat came up to do a radar watch.

During my time on PC3 several incidents stand out. The first was when the gunboat got a radar contact and sent our patrol boat to investigate. As we lay there, behind our packs, with weapons cocked, with the Corporal directing the boat out of the darkness floated an almighty big tree. The Marine up front shouted. 'It's a tree!' to which the Corporal shouted, 'What kind of tree?' The reply was, 'A bloody wooden one.'

Indonesian warships were also active. Another incident began when the lookout spotted smoke on the horizon and before long a strange warship appeared and grew nearer. The Corporal asked if anyone was good at knowing the difference between ships and since I knew a bit, I ended up on the binoculars.

It was fast . . . something like a frigate with a big red and white flag – Indonesian – and it had an open gun turret with the gun crew in anti-flash gear. I shouted that it was closed-up for action stations, at which we up-anchored and headed at our flat-out rate of eight knots for the river.

That night, when we went alongside the gunboat. I was sent for by the skipper and asked if I would look through the book of *Jane's Fighting Ships* to see if I could pick out that frigate. It was a Russian built destroyer with a bit more fire power than our rifles, so we kept well hidden until it left the next day.

After that we were sent to the rear for a few days R & R, down near Tawau. We also had camp duties and it was almost like being back in barracks, although we did get a recommendation for getting out of camp in under fifteen minutes to look for an escaped Indonesian. One of our scouts killed him, with a shotgun . . . all this while on R & R. For doing such a good job we were given the task of a fifteen-day patrol into the Gap, an area of No-Man's-Land between the Commando and Gurkha Brigades, to build a forward location base.

The Plan was to build a helicopter pad on top of a hill at the junction of two rivers. It was hell . . . I've never been so knackered in my life. We were taken by river as far as we could go, then by Malayan helicopters, three at a time. Then we bashed it.

It took us a couple of days to get there, crossing rivers by wading or rafting. On one crossing our raft broke up and we were swept down-river. After going under a few times, I swear I saw big words in front of me, 'One more time, Royal.' I came up and struck out and the next thing I knew I was on the bank. One of the lads said, 'You should enter the Olympics,' but it was a long, long time before I went near water again.

Once at the location, we chopped the top off that hill and built a helicopter pad with tree trunks, twenty-five feet by twenty-five feet. An RAF Whirlwind came to take us out, one helicopter taking five at a time, then coming back half-an-hour later for another five. As we got fewer and fewer, we did start to worry, but they got us all out. I still don't know if that heli-pad was ever used.

Our next location was also hell. It was built by the Gurkhas in a mangrove swamp, a hut about twelve feet square and about four feet high inside: Gurkhas are a bit on the small side. There was a gangway of two poles lashed together leading about fifty yards to a tower by the riverside. Food, ammo, everything, was sent in by night. When we relieved the Recce Troop the tide was out and we waded ashore, knee-deep in stinking mud. It was a great start. We only did two weeks there but that was enough . . . we had six-feet long iguana lizards running about, and rats as big as cats, which used to slide down our mosquito nets at night. When the tide was out we had a six-foot drop into the swamp and when it was in the sea came up to the bottom of the hut. We were eaten alive by bugs in that place.

From the end of July to December seemed like a very long time . . . our gear was rotting, the jungle boots were rubbish, our hair was long by Marine standards, and we were knackered. It was nice to get back to Burma Camp and a few pints of Tiger.

I think the physical side of Borneo, with all the diseases took its toll. I know that even today I still suffer from Borneo with arthritis of the spine, which in the end cut short my time in the Corps . . . but look at it another way . . . some of the lads didn't make it at all, so I was lucky.

The first major incursion after Tebedu took place in September 1963 when a reinforced company of Indonesian infantry attacked the village of Long Jawai, fifty kilometres inside the Third Division of Sarawak, killing two men of the 1/2nd Gurkhas, a Border Scout and a policeman. This force was swiftly pursued by the Gurkhas who were flown up in helicopters to block the withdrawal routes to the border. In a series of ambushes the Gurkhas killed twenty-six Indonesians in one ambush and hunted down another dozen who were killed in the swamps. This reverse did not deter the Indonesians for long.

In the early days of 'Confrontation' the Indonesians held the great advantage of surprise and could always take the initiative in cross-border attacks. The next attack came at Tawau in Sabah (formerly North Borneo) on 29 December 1963, when another Indonesian force, mustering about one hundred and twenty men, a third of them from the Indonesian Marine Corps, attacked a Malay Regiment base at Kalabakan, near Tawau. The Malay soldiers were caught unawares, and twenty-seven were either killed or wounded when the Indonesians entered their compound just before midnight and fired machine-guns up into their sleeping quarters through the floorboards of the longhouse.

The manager of the logging company at Tawau, formerly an army officer, tried to organise a counter-attack but the Malays were too shocked to respond and stayed on the defensive until the raiders drew off. This raiding force was pursued by the 1/10th Gurkhas and only about twenty Indonesians got back across the Kalimantan frontier.

Things were clearly hotting up, for in the following month, January 1964, the Indonesians put in three attacks across the Sarawak border, where they were met and fought by the 1 Royal Leicester Regiment, by 40 Commando, who beat off a company-sized attack on the airfield at Kuching, and by the 1/7th Gurkas who intercepted and destroyed a party landing from the sea.

1st Leicesters fought a very good fight against the Indonesian incursions into the Fifth Division. In early January they got the month off to a good start when they found and wiped out an Indonesian machine-gun post on the border. On 21 January, an eighteen-man patrol from the Leicesters found a deserted Indonesian post that could have been occupied by five hundred men. Undeterred, the patrol followed the Indonesian tracks back towards the frontier and, having found another camp still occupied by about sixty men, they attacked it at once, the Leicesters charging into the enemy camp, killing seven Indonesian regulars and capturing a large heap of ammunition.

These reverses encouraged Sukarno to launch a 'peace offensive', a gambit which met with some support in Washington, where the American Administration was becoming worried that this war with a Western country, Great Britain, would drive the Indonesians into the Communist camp. The Vietnam War was now flourishing and America had enough problems in the Far East without further Communist successes in Indonesia. The fact that Malaysia was under attack from Indonesia and asking for Britain's help was somehow overlooked.

President Johnston sent Senator Robert Kennedy, brother of the late President, on a mission to Jakarta, charging him to bring the combatants 'out of the jungle and back to the conference table'. This led to a 'cease-fire' which began on January 23 1964. After five weeks of fruitless talks in Bangkok, the 'cease-fire' broke down on 4 March. During these 'peace negotiations', the Indonesians continued to raid across the frontier, sending parties of between thirty and fifty men into Sarawak, where they were met and beaten back by either 42 Commando or the ever-watchful 1/2nd Gurkhas.

Following the breakdown of the 'peace offensive' Sukarno's generals tried another tactic, sending a large force across the Kling Klang ridge in the Second Division of Sarawak to seize a hilltop position and 'liberate' the surrounding territory. This force was entirely Regular, from the 328th Raider Battalion, and equipped with heavy weapons, including mortars. They were promptly engaged with artillery and attacked by the 2/10th Gurkhas and withdrew after sustaining heavy losses.

Undaunted, the Indonesians came back across the border a few days later to seize and hold the village of Kluah, also within the bailiwick of the 2/10th Gurkhas. Lt.-Colonel Fillingham of the 2nd/10 decided to teach the Indonesian raiders a severe lesson this time and summoned Saladin armoured cars, a battery of 105mm guns and two Royal Navy Wessex helicopters armed with SS11 missiles, to support his attack. Three Indonesian camps were pounded, attacked and cleared, but few enemy soldiers were killed. Skilled soldiers, the Indonesians had disengaged smoothly and withdrawn across the border and the Gurkha attack struck air.

Meanwhile, another thirty-man Indonesian force from the crack 'Black Cobra' battalion had crossed the frontier and attacked the town of Jambu where they were again engaged by 2/10th Gurkhas. This force was cut up by the Gurkhas and in a series of ambushes lost all but one of their men; not one of the 'Black Cobras' made it back into Kalimantan.

These raids, the attempts to hold ground, and the use of heavy weapons marked an escalation in the conflict, and this escalation continued on the political front when President Sukarno declared at the end of May 1964 that he would crush Malaysia 'by dawn on New Year's Day, 1965'. This was fighting talk and Malaysia, with her British allies, braced herself for the encounter.

More British and Gurkha battalions arrived, together with armoured cars, artillery and a few more precious helicopters and General Walker now reorganised his forces into three Brigades. In the West, covering Kuching and Sarawak was 99 Gurkha Brigade, with five battalions. In the centre, holding two divisions of Sarawak and Brunei, was the 51 Brigade of two battalions, while on the extreme east, three battalions of the Malay Regiment held Sabah. The frontier itself, all one thousand miles of it, was covered by the SAS and the Border Scouts.

In view of the increased weight and volume of the Indonesian attacks Walker replaced the old platoon fortified positions with larger Company-sized locations, fortified positions right up on the frontier, all equipped with helicopter pads, light artillery, mortars, a trench network, bunkers, claymore mines, and a maze of 'punjis', or sharp bamboo stakes, spread before the revetments to deter attack. However, Walker had no intention of letting his men become penned up in camps, as the French had been in Indo-China. No more than a third of a company should man the defences: the rest must be out patrolling, or on ambushes and dominating the company area. This 'forward policy' was to pay great dividends in the actions to come.

Once again though, in June 1964, peace was in the air, hopes sent aloft this time by President Macapagal of the Philippines who called a meeting between the contestants in Tokyo. This Tokyo Summit was a farce, and Sukarno only agreed to attend to cover the movements of his forces for a fresh assault on Malaysia. This fresh campaign was aided, quite fortuitously, by an outbreak of intercommunal violence in Singapore between Chinese and Malays. Rioting broke out on 21 July and lasted for four days with more than five hundred people being killed or injured and irreparable damage done to the fabric of the new Federation.

The Indonesian attacks this time took the form of seaborne and parachute raids on the Malay Peninsula. Three small raiding parties landed in Jahore, tasked to move inland and set up bases for an airborne force. The Indonesians expected to be met with open arms but the local Malays reported their arrival to the Security Forces and within days the raiders had been killed or rounded up.

In spite of this the airborne landings went ahead and were equally disastrous. On the night of 1/2 September 1964, Indonesia sent four parachute aircraft full of troops across the water towards Malaya. One aircraft failed to leave the runway. Another crashed into the South China Sea: there were no survivors. The third failed to find the DZ and scattered its men over a hundred miles of jungle and rubber plantation. Only one aircraft found the right DZ and the men who were dropped there were quickly rounded up by 1/10th Gurkhas and infantry of the 1st Royal New Zealand Regiment. The Indonesians continued to send small raiding parties to the Peninsula for the next six months but all two hundred paratroopers sent out on this operation were quickly killed or captured.

Colin Butcher was a corporal in 2 Para at this time:

> We went to Borneo in 1965, starting with a course at the Jungle Warfare School in Jahore, Malaya; days and nights in the jungle, ambush drills, camp drills, patrol drills, all the routines. It is amazing how much kit you can get into a small 44 pattern backpack, once you know how. We were in Malaya when the Indonesians tried out their airborne attacks and that came in handy because we got the Malay Peninsula medal bar for it, much to the disgust of our Patrol Company.
>
> 2 Para had formed the Patrol Company back in 1964, and they went to Borneo to relieve the SAS. They seemed to think they were SAS and went about being all mysterious. You know the SAS, they won't tell you the time, complete delusions of grandeur, and the blokes in Patrol Company were like that, except they got very vocal when we got the Malay medal as well as the Borneo one. I was at Kuching when the wounded came back from Plaman Mapa, where 'Patch' Williams won his gong . . . I saw the GPMG he had been manning and at least four bullets had hit it. I was also at Kuching when the Indonesians attacked the airfield there. Life was lively.

Back in Borneo, the Indonesians had abandoned patrol infiltration in favour of making all-out attacks in considerable numbers against the Company bases on the frontier. In June, one attack on a camp of the 1/6th Gurkhas resulted in the death of five Gurkhas, and similar attacks continued. 'Confrontation' had become a nasty little war and as it teetered on the brink Britain decided to show her teeth.

Vulcan bombers, Javelin jet fighters and more warships were sent into Malaysian waters. By the end of 1964 the British Far East Fleet mustered more than eighty warships, including three aircraft carriers and a missile destroyer, the largest British Fleet seen in these waters since the Korean War of 1950–53. Elements of this Fleet, including the carrier HMS *Victorious*, then sailed through the international waters of the Lombok Straits east of Bali, inviting Sukarno to come out and fight, but his Air Force stayed on the ground and his warships at anchor.

Britain was no longer alone in offering support to Malaysia. The

Australian and New Zealand governments were also sending troops and their artillery units and infantry battalions were soon in the line along the border. Reinforcements also arrived from the UK, including the 2nd Greenjackets, the 1st Bn., The Scots Guards and the 2nd Bn., The Parachute Regiment. By 1955 there were thirteen British, Gurkha or Malay battalions in Borneo, with a further five in Malaya to provide periodic relief. This was not a great number to cover one thousand miles of frontier, but in that terrain the places suitable for campaigning were limited.

Lt.-Colonel Edwin Bramall, arrived in Sarawak as Commanding Officer of the 2nd Greenjackets:

> Our task was to contain the enemy, a task that meant skilled patrolling, good plantoon and section tactics, accurate shooting and a steady nerve. The excellence of the Gurkha soldier for this type of warfare is taken for granted, but once he had time to adjust and given the right training, the British soldier proved himself capable of the same high standards.
>
> The battalion was initially deployed around Kuching, with 2 Para on our left and 2 Royal Australian Regiment on our right. Our task was to take over from the Scots Guards and that was done by early May 1965. By that time we had registered out mortars and the single field gun and were in a position to support the forward platoon in its fortified camp.

The parachute and seaborne raids into the Malay Peninsula forced the Malaysian Government and the British military to review their tactics. So far, in an attempt to contain the political fall-out, they had allowed the Indonesians to remain in peace beyond the Kalimantan frontier, from where the Indonesians could raid almost at will along the thousand-mile border and retreat to safe territory after their incursion was over.

This gave them a great advantage which General Walter Walker now decided to remove. The outcome of that decision was permission from London to start the 'Claret' operations, a series of highly secret raids and ambushes behind the Indonesian lines, which would carry the fighting right into the enemy camp.

One of the officers engaged in these 'Claret' operations was Captain Christopher Bullock of Support Company, 2/2nd Gurkha Rifles:

'Claret' operations were secret at the time and for a long time after 'Confrontation' was over: until just a few years ago I could not talk about them at all and a lot of people have still never heard of them. The object of 'Claret' operations was to carry the war to the enemy and reduce his attacks on us.

The reasons for secrecy are also obvious. We still called it 'Confrontation' because no one wanted an all-out war. We did not want to appear to be escalating the conflict or give the Indonesians a propaganda victory by accusing us of raiding their territory: they were raiding and killing in our territory, or rather in Malay territory, but that was different . . . of course.

One of the great aids to cross-border incursions was that no one was very sure exactly where the border was. The maps were inaccurate and pretty useless and we preferred to rely on air photos, when we could get them; if not we got by with marching on compass bearings. It was very difficult terrain, hilly, swamps, rivers, difficult even without the likelihood of attack or ambush by Indonesians.

One of the rules for 'Claret' operations was that we must not move further across the Border than the range of our supporting artillery, about ten thousand metres for a pack howitzer. A typical 'Claret' operation lasted about a week, maximum. All ambushes were supposed to be covered by our artillery to support us on the way out, and every patrol was accompanied by a Royal Artillery FOO (Forward Observation Officer) who controlled the gunfire. The FOOs could not range the guns, partly because it would give the game away, partly because we rarely knew precisely where we were, but they were very quick to bring down accurate supporting fire.

The Indonesians would come back at us very quickly and try to roll up the ambush position from the flank, so once we had sprung the ambush and got our blow in we had to get out of it quickly and call down artillery to cover our withdrawal.

Our area of operation at this time was across the Kling Klang ridge in the Second Division of Sarawak. The idea was to dominate the ridge: there was no other way to keep those guys out. The ridge was about four thousand feet high and bloody steep. There were only a few possible paths up and across and using known tracks was an invitation to an ambush . . . the 10th Gurkhas had already fought one big battle up there. We nearly got ambushed up there a couple of times but the leading scouts were so good, so alert; they spotted the Indonesian positions and we pulled back out of it.

Unless we could dominate the ridge the Indonesians would have the initiative and there was some doubt on how we should react. You have to remember that 'Confrontation' was a Malay versus Indonesian show, though we actually ran it, and General Walker felt that we had to take the battle to the enemy. That meant crossing the border in strength, finding their camps or lines of communications, usually rivers, and ambushing their patrols . . . so that is what we did.

General Walter Walker started the 'Claret' operations in 1964 but in March 1965 his period as 'ComBritBor' came to an end and he was replaced by Major General George Lea, an officer of the 22nd SAS Regiment. The hard struggle had been fought and won under General Walter Walker's direction and it was generally expected that his efforts would be acknowledged by a knighthood, the usual reward for long, hard and distinguished service.

However, his enemies at the War Office had not forgotten Walker's actions over the Gurkhas and the recommendation from the C-in-C Far East that Walker should have a knighthood was rejected by the Army Board, allegedly at the behest of Field Marshal Sir Richard Hull.

The second proposal, that Walker be awarded the CMG (Commander of St Michael and St George) was also turned down. All that the powers-that-be would agree to was the award of a DSO, the award normally given to a Battalion CO for a successful operation, and Walker already had two of these. The citation for his third DSO claimed that it was for 'the hazards of flying vast distances in light aircraft, over inhospitable country and under threat of anti-aircraft fire'. As Walter Walker himself pointed out, 'Who in Borneo has not done that?'

Major General Walter Walker could at least leave Borneo in the knowledge that the men he had commanded held him in high regard and were well aware what the country owed him. The opinions of Whitehall warriors do not weigh heavily against praise like that.

*   *   *

The Indonesians did not wait long before greeting General Lea's appointment with a burst of activity. On 27 April 1965 a full Indonesian battalion attacked a Company base at Palaman Mapu, in the First Division of Borneo, a position held by 'B' Company of 2 Para. Most of the Company were out on patrol when the attack came in at around 0500 in the morning and the command of the camp effectively fell into the hands of the CSM John 'Patch' Williams:

> The camp at Plaman Mapa was a typical rat-infested border fort, basically a series of concentric trenches dug around a hilltop, with bunkers for the men and stores and the Company HQ and three GPMG positions. The idea was that two platoons would always be out on patrol and one platoon would be in camp. That meant that we were always undermanned and at risk from attack and the garrison at the time was just twenty-seven men, an under-strength platoon, most of them young soldiers just out of training.
>
> In fact, if you had chosen one platoon *not* to have there for an attack, this is the one you would have chosen, but no soldiers could have done better. The border overlooked us and was only a thousand metres away, so the Indonesians could see into the camp quite easily. We were always on the watch, kept our boots and kit on and slept in dugouts just by our stand-to positions, weapons to hand, two mags ready, one round up the spout and safety catches on.
>
> We were pretty well aware that something was up, for in the two or three weeks prior to this our local patrols had found prepared artillery and mortar positions and OPs in the jungle around the camp and it was only a matter of time until the balloon went up, which it finally did at around 0400 hrs when – wallop! – all hell was let loose on the camp.
>
> They kicked off with everything, heavy machine guns, mortars and artillery, small arms fire, all pouring fire into the camp and very accurate. I was in the Company HQ in the middle of the position. Most of the activity and re-supply took place at night, so I slept in the daytime and spent most nights on the radio and had a hammock slung in the HQ, which was handy. The OC got on the radio to battalion and the FCO, Captain Webb from the Royal Artillery, got on to the guns at the next base up the line at Gunan

Gajac, about seven kilometres away, trying to get some fire down outside our wire. While they were doing that the first attack came in on the north sector of our position where a fellow called Kelly was manning the GPMG.

These Indonesians were good soldiers, from one of their TNT Special Force battalions. This was a Company attack, with another Company in reserve and about twenty minutes after the firing started in they came, with three platoons up – about a hundred and fifty men – and they ran up the hill in waves and overran the defences. They got practically to the command post before they were held and we stuck in a counter-attack and drove them out again. This was in the middle of the monsoon, so it was dark as pitch, pouring with rain and a sea of mud underfoot, with us slipping and sliding about in it. We pushed them out but then they came in again.

We had two killed and three badly wounded by this time and were back in our southern sector where Lieutenant Thompson was in command. He was from the Gloucester Regiment, not a Para, had only just arrived in Borneo and had come up to us to learn the form. I think he learned more than he bargained for. Anyway, I told him to take his chaps and counter-attack over the top of the Command post, which he was doing when he was wounded by a mortar bomb.

We were getting good support from Mick Baughan, who was manning a GPMG in another post. He had about twelve blokes in his sector and he sent some of his blokes over to help cover the north section where the Indonesians were trying to break in. The entire attack lasted around one and a half to two hours and they put in three major assaults in that time, plus a lot of mortaring, machine-gunning and shelling.

We were pretty thin on the ground so I got in the forward GPMG post and started to fire on them as they came in. They came up to within about five feet of my position and at least four rounds hit the GPMG; another hit the radio by my head and drove steel splinters and plastic fragments into my left eye – that's why they call me 'Patch', because it blinded me and afterwards I used to wear a patch over the eye.

Anyway, I killed two or three in front of my position and kept on firing. There was a lot of tracer flying around . . . grenades going off . . . a lot of yelling. That went on for quite a while but it gradually quietened down. When I was sure they had gone or pulled back I went back to the command post to give a sitrep [situation report] to the OC. When it got light we decided to send out a clearance patrol to search the area and everyone of the young soldiers volunteered to go on it . . . not bad that. Another good lad was Corporal Collier, who had been badly wounded in the arm but he got a brew on and we broke out the G10 rum. Meanwhile we re-organised, issued more ammo and grenades and got sorted out.

I then took the patrol out and we had a good look round but they were gone. We put a bullet into any bodies round the position and found plenty of blood trails leading off towards the border, so we definitely hurt them more than they hurt us. Later that day the battalion and some Gurkhas arrived and helicopters came in and took out the wounded.

By now I seemed to have lost the sight of both eyes, so I went out first back to the Base Hospital at Kuching and then to Singapore, where they operated on my eyes. They used a sort of giant magnet to draw out the steel splinters but the magnet couldn't pull out the plastic bits from the radio. In the end I had five operations on my eyes. They saved them but the left one does not function . . . and that's about it.

Well, not quite. For his leadership and gallantry in the fight at Plaman Mapu, Patch Williams was awarded the Distinguished Conduct Medal. 2 Para lost two men killed and eight wounded in this fierce little battle; Indonesian casualties were estimated at over thirty.

Later that year, in August 1965, the only VC of the 'Confrontation' was awarded to Corporal Rambadahur Limbu of the 2/10th Gurkas. This award was greeted with acclaim by all the troops in Borneo and rightly went to one of those hard-fighting Gurkhas without whom 'Confrontation' could not have been won.

Tom Bell, serving with the RAF in Kuching remembers the news: 'We had a number of Gurkhas stationed there and the whole camp was delighted that one of them had got the VC. People were stopping each other to pass on the news and clapping our Gurkhas on the back. They had carried the heaviest workload for so long, it was richly deserved and their descendants would never forget it.'

The action for which the Victoria Cross was awarded was a 'Claret' operation, well inside the Indonesian frontier. Corporal Rambadahur's company had stormed an Indonesian position on a sharp ridge, killing twenty–four of the enemy for the loss of three Gurkhas killed in an all–day battle. Corporal Rambadahur fought in the van of the attack, exposing himself to heavy fire, and it was decided that even at the risk of admitting Britain was sending troops into Kalimantan, his bravery should be recognised. Corporal Rambadahur was sent to London to be decorated by Her Majesty the Queen, but it was another three years before the details of his award were made public.

All the battalions engaged along the Border mounted 'Claret' operations but the bulk of them were carried out by the Gurkhas. Christopher Bullock, who took part in a number of cross–border incursions in 1965, describes his last operation:

By the November of 1965 we had put on six 'Claret' operations since August and were pretty tired. We were due to hand over to 42 Commando and I wondered if we would be required to do another one before we pulled out but then I was wanted for a two-Company operation in 'C' Company's area. I then flew to Bokah to meet the 'C' Company Commander, Major Geoffrey Ashley, and he unfolded the plan.

Basically, his recce patrols had discovered two large enemy camps on the Separan river, a tributary of the larger river Khumba. His idea was that we should ambush the river traffic between the two camps. The two camps were sure to use the Separan to support each other and with luck this would enable us to use our classic 'double ambush' technique, first an ambush on the river, then ambush the troops coming to the rescue.

The Separan lies in thick country and my first job on getting back to base was to try and lay my hands on some five-thousand-feet vertical photos of the area; the RAF recce flights were very reluctant to fly that low over the frontier and all I could obtain were ten-thousand-feet ones. Then followed a few days of 'Claret' preparations, rehearsing battle drills, testing weapons on the jungle range, briefing and rebriefing the soldiers until every man knew exactly what he would have to do.

On 14 November 1965 we flew to the 'C' Company base, four

miles north of the border. Once across the jungle we would be five miles or more apart so this was the last chance to co-ordinate our plans. The idea was for one or other of the Companies to spring the ambush while the other ambushed the boatloads of Indonesians coming to deal with the ambush. Geoffrey Ashley warned me that the going would be very tough, with lots of hills and at least two rivers to cross.

Next morning the men set off for the frontier. I had arranged to join them on the border by helicopter and while I was waiting a message came from John Parkes, one of our officers who knew the area, saying that if the Separan was in flood and not in use the Indonesians might use a track behind the river as their communications route. This message added that the flooded river would be a devil to get over and a formidable obstacle on the way back, especially if we had casualties.

We spent the first night on the border ridge and set off early next morning. That day we managed three miles, which was excellent going and I calculated that another half day would bring us to the Separan. We then found the river and Lieutenant Nandaraj and his pioneers put a tree trunk bridge across it. We sent men across and I was just congratulating myself on how well things were going when the leading scout came back to say he had found another river. I went forward and found a much larger river, that did not appear on my aerial photos. At that moment we heard the sound of a motor launch and took cover. This launch appeared to pass down the river we had crossed – we had now removed the bridge – so there must be a river junction a few hundred yards downstream. If so, this did not appear on the photos either.

We therefore established a firm base on a low hill and I sent out three patrols to find the Separan, while Chris Mutton, our artillery FOO, checked communications on his radio, just in case we needed some support. I went out with the Recce Platoon and after about half a mile we came to another, even larger river, which appeared to be the right one. Just as we got there we heard the clatter of a helicopter and it flew right over us.

Under the jungle canopy we could see nothing but a few minutes later we heard a heavy calibre machine-gun open up from distance ahead. I radio'd back to base and was told that they had seen a Whirlwind come over the border into Indonesian territory where it appeared to have been hit by ground fire and gone out of sight, trailing smoke.

We could now hear a lot of excited shouting from across the river ahead and a further long burst of machine-gun fire, so it appeared that an Indonesian base was just opposite us and had been overflown by the unfortunate helicopter. The river was flowing very fast, too fast for boats or a crossing so we turned back for our firm base.

We then had some radio chat with Battalion HQ about the downed helicopter and I had a chat with the returned patrol commanders, one of whom had found a place where a tree across the river seemed to offer a crossing. I felt uneasy perched on such an obvious hill so we packed up and moved down to the river.

The Separan was a formidable obstacle, about eighty feet wide, deep and fast flowing, too fast for boat traffic. I therefore decided that on the following day we would cross and ambush the track in the jungle beyond, which we had been told about. That night two of my officers implored me not to cross as they said it would invite disaster. We were certainly putting ourselves in a very dangerous situation but we could take a number of precautions.

Chris Mutton, our FOO, was an imperturbable chap, confident of giving us artillery support. The Recce Platoon – my company was 'S' Company – were deployed on the south back on a small hill, to cover our withdrawal across the river, and Lieutenant Nandaraj and his pioneers improved the fallen tree bridge with piles and another tree trunk, to aid a swift exit. It was still a tricky bridge to cross fully laden and the thought of crossing back with wounded men was a nightmare.

We crossed anyway, sending the Anti-Tanks ahead, and about a hundred yards from the river we duly found the track, clearly a main lateral route between the two enemy camps. The ground had been churned up by boots and telegraph wire had been strung along on trees above the track in the usual fashion. I now had to set up the ambush.

The Recce Platoon occupied the hill covering the river, with Chris Mutton and his radio to the guns. Four men, including the LMGs, were sent to guard our vital bridge while the pioneers continued work on it. I then went back to the rest of the Company along the track and explained the plan.

We had two GPMGs commanding the killing ground to the north and two LMGs commanding the area from the south, and another in the centre. Eleven claymore mines were then attached in front of trees along the ambush area, covering the path from end to end. I told the men that we would not open fire on a group of less than five men: we had not come all this way for anything less. That done, we settled down to wait and we did not have to wait long.

I had just put a biscuit in my mouth and was handing one to the M79 grenadier at my side when I heard voices followed by the thumbs-down signal for 'Enemy'. Moments later, three Indonesian soldiers, one carrying an Armalite rifle, walked by, chatting. They were so close I could hear the mud sucking on their boots and the M79 grenadier was sitting beside me like a statue, a biscuit between his teeth.

For one ghastly moment I visualised an entire Indonesian company passing by in threes and therefore never being fired at. Well, that was the least of my worries. A minute later six Indonesians came past, followed by a long column of troops, all heavily armed.

This was it . . . and Lieutenant Deoparsad with great presence of mind let them get right into the killing zone before triggering the claymore mines and opening fire with his GPMGs. The rest of us then opened up on anyone we could see.

The Indonesians were always quick to react. Mortar fire came down and, never lacking in courage, they tried to break out to the south, but the river and the LMGs took care of that. We then heard the comforting sound of Chris Mutton's guns dropping shells across the enemy camp.

I then did a remarkably stupid thing. We had been told to verify enemy casualties, so I left cover and crawled out onto the path, followed by my puzzled orderly. I had counted eleven enemy dead, littered along the path, when a shout from my orderly alerted me. Another enemy attack was coming in, this time at the centre of our position, and I was out in the open.

One Indonesian soldier came into a firing position behind a branch directly in front of me and I fired repeatedly at him before I realised he was dead. This counter-attack petered out and our M79 grenadier. Lalbadahur, sped the enemy on their way with his entire allocation of grenades.

I then realised that I must use this lull to break off and get out before a larger and properly co-ordinated attack came in. We had one casualty, a young Lance Corporal, hit in the face by a mortar fragment, and the southern ambush group were already dragging him away. My right hand was also bleeding either from a mortar splinter or back blast from a Claymore mine. Enemy mortars were now thudding away and a 12.7 heavy machine-gun was firing, fortunately over our heads. It was time to go.

It seemed to take ages to get the two flank groups across the river, but then it was our turn and after we were across and had checked that no one had been left behind, a few slashes with a kukri sent the bridge supports crashing into the river.

Chris Mutton's guns were still sending shells across the river but we now had to break off the action and pull clear, choosing a route the Indonesians would not follow. To this end, gathering up our rear parties we headed south, pausing only to send a success signal back to Battalion HQ. We heard rifle shots from the pursuing Indonesians all that afternoon – they used to fire rifle shots to keep in touch – but there was no further contact.

That night we stopped in a secure position and dug in on it. The Lance Corporal hit in the face had lost blood but was otherwise fine and my hand was soon patched up. Our luck had held and the next day we marched fast for the border where we found three helicopters waiting to fly us back to base. This was glory indeed!

Studying the air photos later I realised that our ambush had only been about fifty yards from one of the main enemy bases: no wonder they were surprised. I came to the conclusion that the survivors of the shot-down helicopter, if any, must have been in the column we ambushed. No doubt the Indonesians killed them for they were never seen again.

Taken all in all, 1965 was not a good year for President Sukarno, but in early autumn he got some good news. The strains between the Chinese and Malay elements in the Federation had proved too much, and sadly Tunku Abdul Rahman asked Lee Kwan Yew to withdraw Singapore from the alliance, which Lee duly did in September 1965.

Sukarno did not have long to enjoy this event or to take advantage of it. In September the Indonesian Communist Party staged a coup in

Jakarta. This was quickly put down by the Army and was followed by a general massacre of Communists throughout Indonesia but during the course of these disturbances the Army generals decided that President Sukarno should step down in order to restore normal relations with the West. Sukarno was then replaced by an Army officer, General Suharto.

In May 1966 the Foreign Ministers of Malaysia and Indonesia met to find some way of winding up 'Confrontation', and in 11 August of that year the three-year conflict was brought to an end.

The cost of 'Confrontation', from April 1963 to August 1966, had been considerable. Around three hundred British troops had been killed or wounded, the bulk of them Gurkhas. Some sixteen hundred Indonesian soldiers had also become casualties, of whom some six hundred had been killed. For the British it was a victory, a compensation for the humiliation of Aden, which was being played out as 'Confrontation' ended and still had a year to go.

For the Gurkhas, who had fought so hard and done so well, there was scant reward. Their battalions were soon withdrawn and those plans for a reduction in Gurkha numbers, so stoutly resisted by General Walter Walker, were dusted down and implemented.

Britain could now complete her withdrawal from East of Suez and regard her imperial role as over. By the end of 1967, with the withdrawal from Aden, the overseas Empire had virtually gone, transformed into a Commonwealth. The former colonies were now independent and busy about their own affairs. Britain could relax at last and think about the future, free of such pressing ties – or so it seemed.

Unfortunately, before very long those fading imperial echoes were to cause further troubles in a place rather closer to home, in the streets and fields of Northern Ireland. Before that there was a brief pause for the troops of the British Army, for 1968 was a year of peace.

16

Interval: 1968

'Great Britain has lost an Empire, and not yet found a role.'

Dean Acheson, Speech at West Point Military Academy, 1961.

Twenty-one years after leaving India the British Army took a breather; 1968 is on record as the only year in the fifty years since the end of the Second World War in which a British soldier did not die in action somewhere in the world.

The Borneo Confrontation was over, Aden had departed, Malaya was quiet, in Hong Kong the New Territories lease had twenty-nine more years to run; the Commonwealth was at peace and the problems of Northern Ireland were only a wisp of cloud in an otherwise blue sky. It would not last, but in that brief interval there is time to look around and see what was happening or what had happened in other parts of the old Empire since 1947.

Much of the Empire had already gone by 1961. Burma had followed India and Pakistan to independence in 1948 but declined to join the Commonwealth, unlike Ceylon, which became independent in 1948 and was to become Sri Lanka in 1972. The Anglo-Egyptian Sudan had declined to return to the grasp of Egypt and became the Republic of Sudan, outside the Commonwealth, in 1956.

In the following year, 1957, the Gold Coast became independent and became Ghana in 1960. Malaya become independent in 1957 and part of the Federation of Malaysia in 1963. So the old Empire faded away but not without causing the old imperial power and the British people a considerable number of problems.

British Somalia ceased to be British in 1960. Cyprus went and then Nigeria and then Sierra Leone, but all remaining within the Commonwealth as did the Northern Cameroons which then chose to link up with Nigeria. Then the Southern Cameroons went and Jamaica and Trinidad and Tobago and Uganda, the North Borneo States, Singapore, Zanzibar which joined Tanganyika to become Tanzania, Kenya, Nyasaland which became Malawi, Malta, Northern Rhodesia which became Zambia, followed by the Gambia and the Maldives. So, one by one, the territories of the Empire struck out on their own.

Not all these countries wanted to become independent. Some wished for British national status, rather like the overseas *départements* of France. Malta, and later the Seychelles, both expressed the desire for closer links with Britain, for British citizenship, for the right to vote in British elections and send their MPs to the British Parliament. These requests were turned down, partly from a feeling that the Empire era was over, partly from the fear that the cost of running these places would be a burden on the British taxpayer.

In some parts of the Empire, where the countries seemed too small to survive alone, Britain attempted to form federations, most notably in the Caribbean and in East and Central Africa. These federations soon fell apart, partly through tribalism, partly from a clash of interests, partly because the local politicians found that great personal profit and prestige could go with the title of Prime Minister or President.

In 1965 another imperial link snapped when Sir Winston Churchill died. So the retreat from Empire continued, into the middle years of the 1960s as more and more territories sought their future as independent countries. British Guiana went in 1966 and was soon to become the Republic of Guyana in 1970. In 1966 Bechuanaland became Botswana and later that year Basutoland became Lesotho. In the Caribbean, Barbados opted for independence peacefully in 1966 and in 1967 in the Red Sea gulf, Aden and the surrounding protectorates became the People's Democratic Republic of South Yemen, though the territory was neither a republic nor democratic nor peaceful. In the following year Mauritius went and then there was a pause.

By now most of the large viable territories had gone and troubles were beginning to erupt in some of the new nations, an indication that democracy and freedom are not to be had without strains and stresses. Some countries had hardly become independent when the troubles began.

When the East African territories of Kenya, Uganda and Tanganyika became independent, the various battalions of the King's African Rifles became the backbone of the new republican armies, becoming either the 1st Kenya Rifles, the 1st Uganda Rifles or the 1st Tanganyika Rifles. They retained their British officers for a while but were rapidly becoming Africanised.

Tanganyika became independent in December 1961 and a Republic within the Commonwealth in December 1962. A year later, in December 1963, Tanganyika joined with Zanzibar to form Tanzania. A month after that, the Africans of Zanzibar rose up and massacred their Arab co-nationals, and the Tanzanian Army mutinied.

The African rising against the Sultan of Zanzibar and the local Arabs was a very bloody affair which began on 12 January. The Army mutiny by the 1st Tanganyika Rifles on the mainland began a week later, on Sunday, 18 January, and President Nyerere quickly asked for British help to restore order.

On 21 January, 1964 Mrs Sheila Unwin wrote to her mother about this event:

> You will be wondering what has been happening to us during the 'revolt'. In fact, we have had rather an exciting time. We had gone to bed when the phone rang at about half past one in the morning and Tom was told that the troops at Colito barracks had mutinied. The Rifles have two battalions, one here at Dar, the other at Tabora about six hundred miles up country. Apparently at 0300 hrs the troops had mutinied and captured as many British officers as they could. Pat Douglas, the Brigadier commanding the Rifles, had got away and he turned up here.
>
> Pat collected Colonel Montgomery, who lives in Oyster Bay, and then went from house to house making phone calls to find out what was going on. They ended up at our house so I got up and started making tea; they had all been swigging from the slivovich bottle

which a Czech friend had given us and which came in handy. Pat still had his batman, a corporal, who stood at the gate armed with a panga.

They then left and got to the British High Commission but the other officers caught by the rebels had already been flown out to Kenya. We spent the day sitting about doing a jigsaw, preparing food, or resting. At lunchtime the radio came on with a broadcast from Mr Kabonal in Swahili and English, but we were constantly looking out for the frigate HMS *Rhyll*. We were also wondering what had happened to President Nyerere, who had not been heard of at all. We later heard, on the 21st, that he was alive and well here in town.

Early on the Monday morning, while we were at the Berli's, in walked the American consul from Zanzibar, Fritz Picard. He had a beer bottle in his hand from which he kept swigging and saying, 'Six days ago Zanzibar, and now this.' He got no response from us and eventually wandered off.

That afternoon the *Rhyll* arrived! I was the first to see her offshore and I ran out crying, 'The Navy's here!' with everyone following. Mrs Rosenveld from next door innocently asked, 'Which navy?' and was shouted down with cries of '*The* Navy.' The *Rhyll* was only a frigate with a few troops on board so she could not do much but she looked lovely there, close inshore, flags flying. The Rifles didn't like the look of her and she was ordered by the local Minister for Home Affairs to lie further out.

There were frequent broadcasts on the radio telling people to go back to work, and soldiers went past in cars, bayonets sticking out of the windows. Quite a lot of shop windows have been broken and a lot of poor Asians have lost stock. There was a crowd outside Barclays Bank, wanting to know where 'The Arabs' were. Everything is very disorganised and people panic over nothing.

It seems that there was a lot of dissatisfaction in the Tanganyika Rifles and Mr Kambona, the Minister for External Affairs and Defence, was behind the mutiny. Up to twenty people have been killed and a lot more injured, but things have been far worse in Zanzibar where the poor Arabs and the Indians have been badly hit and the pictures in the papers are pathetic.

While all this was going on in Dar-es-Salaam the aircraft carrier HMS *Centaur* had sailed from Aden with 45 Commando embarked. HMS *Centaur* arrived on the morning of 25 January and the Commando went ashore. Dr Philip Mawhood saw the landings from his house:

> The end came dramatically on Saturday morning. I had begun to listen to the 6 am BBC news when the clatter of gunfire broke out to the north. Throwing on my clothes I drove up to the local peninsula for a view of Colito barracks. The first wave of sixty Marines had been dropped directly on the barracks and had met little resistance. Five hundred more Marines were now being ferried ashore, all by helicopter. The carrier HMS *Centaur* was out in the bay, with helicopters circling the carrier like flies around a honeypot.
>
> The frigate HMS *Rhyll* was steaming close inshore firing anti-aircraft shells over the barracks to intimidate the mutineers – they both had to sail out of Msasani bay later as the tide fell. There were no British casualties and all the mutineers, about nine hundred of them, were disarmed without trouble, except for one group led by corporals who barricaded themselves in the guardhouse. A rocket fired into the roof killed three of them and injured others.

There were a few shots, a 3.5in. rocket fired into the mutineers' guard room, and the Marines of 45 Commando patrolling in the streets and taking over the barracks, where they were replaced a few days later by Marines of 41 Commando. A few hours of decisive action and it was all over . . . at least in Tanzania.

Two days before 45 Commando landed in Dar-es-Salaam, the 1st Uganda Rifles based in the town of Jinja also decided to mutiny and the President of Uganda, Milton Obote, also requested British troops. The mutineers had neglected to seize Entebbe airport and since the British still had forces in Kenya, the 1st Bn., The Staffordshire Regiment, reinforced by a company of the Scots Guards, was flown in from Nairobi. The Staffords commandeered trucks and drove overnight to Jinja where the mutineers surrendered as soon as the British arrived.

Meanwhile, the mutinies had spread to Kenya where the 1st Kenya

Rifles were up in arms at Nanyuki, north of Nairobi. Again, there was a request for British aid, this time from President Kenyatta, and again the aid was forthcoming. An artillery unit, the 3rd Regiment, Royal Horse Artillery, drove up from Gilgil, arriving in the evening to find the mutineers dug in and ready to fight. The mutiny was put down, after a certain amount of firing, on the following day.

This support for the new countries, or rather for the leaders of the new countries, did Britain very little good, even among those people she assisted. Their leaders regularly voted against Britain at the UN and rarely missed a chance to accuse the former imperial power of racism, exploitation and neo-colonialism. The Commonwealth Conference, which was usually held in London at this time, became the stage for an annual anti-British tirade by the delegates from Africa and Asia until the Conference was wisely shifted to other Commonwealth capitals. These violent rants were usually fuelled by independence problems in Britain's remaining colonial territories.

The most long-lasting of these problems was with the white settlers in the colony of Southern Rhodesia, which after years of argument over the independence issue, declared a UDI – Unilateral Declaration of Independence – in November 1965.

UDI had been provoked in part by the problems and disasters that had taken place in other African territories since independence, especially in the former Belgian Congo, which became independent in 1960 and promptly collapsed into a long and bloody civil war, and partly by the break up of the Central African Federation in 1961. This was composed of Northern Rhodesia and Nyasaland – now Zambia and Malawi – as well as Southern Rhodesia and the two former territories soon became independent under African majority rule. Southern Rhodesia was to prove less tractable.

Civil war was already simmering in the Portuguese colonies of Mozambique and Angola, and the two hundred and fifty thousand white settlers of Southern Rhodesia wanted no part of such disasters or any form of African majority rule. Since the British Government was clearly determined to leave and hand over power to an African-dominated assembly, the settlers' solution was UDI. The result of UDI was years of civil war.

UDI lasted until 1980 and will be referred to again. British Forces were only involved at the very end and in the enforcement of sanctions by a royal navy patrol off the Mozambique port of Beira, though after the failure of talks between the British Government under Harold Wilson and that of the UDI Prime Minister, Ian Smith, in 1966, certain Liberal politicians proposed bombing Rhodesia or sending in the British Army to bring the white settlers to heel.

The British people showed no enthusiasm for sending British troops to fight British civilians – their own 'kith and kin' – in Central Africa. This Liberal proposal was considered by the Wilson Government as more likely to cause civil war in Britain than bring independence to Rhodesia–Zimbabwe and was soon refuted. Under an all-white Rhodesian Front Government, Southern Rhodesia faced worldwide hostility and a growing guerrilla war from bases in Zambia and Mozambique but with the support of South Africa, the whites of Southern Rhodesia were able to sustain their independence for many years.

British troops did not get involved in UDI, but the soldiers found themselves involved in protecting several now-independent parts of the old Empire from internal insurrection or foreign attack, or being summoned to assist friendly countries threatened by larger neighbours.

The Iraqis were the major cause of unrest in the late 1950s. Following the overthrow and murder of King Faisel and his family, the new Iraqi junta, largely composed of Army generals, began to plot the overthrow of King Hussain, in the neighbouring state of Jordan. King Hussain had dispensed with the help of his British Commander-in-Chief, Glubb Pasha, in 1956, six months before the Suez operation, but had no hesitation in requesting the aid of British troops. In June 1958 the 16th Parachute Brigade was flown into Amman from Cyprus. Among the soldiers was Lance-Corporal John 'Digger' Grebby of 2 Para:

We arrived in Amman on 18 June and stayed until 31 October 1958. The force was 16 Independent Parachute Brigade Group, less 1 Para, and we were airlifted in from Cyprus to prevent a possible overthrow of King Hussain by the Iraqis, who had already murdered King Faisel of Iraq and set up a military junta.

We were pretty thin on the ground and our support regiment, 33 Regt, Royal Artillery, only had 4.2-inch mortars. We spread out around the city, defending the King's palace and the airfield. There was no tank support unless the Arab Legion or the Jordanian Army were on our side. It occurred to me than that if the Iraqis did come in and the locals joined them, the Parachute Brigade would have a tough time of it.

We could not even dig trenches, the ground was too hard and stony, so we built sangars, stone walls a few feet high, to cover our positions. Later on, in August, the 1 Cameronians and a Field Regiment of 25-pounder guns came in by sea to Aquaba and that stabilised the situation. Our arrival in Amman definitely forestalled a possible coup and another Middle East war, for if the Iraqis had attacked Jordan the Israelis would not have stood by.

The swift arrival of the Parachute Brigade was enough to deter a coup against King Hussain but a few years later the Iraqis tried again, with a probe against the tiny Gulf sheikdom of Kuwait.

In July 1961, the oil-rich state of Kuwait was threatened by Iraq. The Government of Kuwait promptly sent out a call for British assistance and within hours British forces close to the Gulf were on the move. 45 Commando arrived from Aden and two companies of the Coldstream Guards flew in from Bahrain. Bomber and fighter aircraft arrived from Germany and the UK, a parachute battalion flew in from Cyprus and the Commando carrier HMS *Bulwark* arrived from Karachi with 42 Commando and a squadron of helicopters.

Six days after the first sign of an Iraqi threat, there were five British battalions in Kuwait with tanks, artillery and aircraft in support and the Iraqis decided to pull back.

All-out war was a feature of the conflict in the Trucial State of Oman, where the maintenance of stable pro-Western Government was considered important to Britain's strategy in the Gulf. A large number of British troops were attached to the Omani forces, with a major commitment of the SAS Regiment. The SAS become closely involved in fighting Aden-backed rebels in a campaign which began with an SAS assault on rebel strongholds on the heights of the Jebel Akhdar – the Green Mountain.

The Sultanate of Muscat and Oman, with the Trucial States to the north, was an independent state, not a colony, but Oman occupies a strategic position in the Arabian Gulf, overlooking the tanker routes from the Iraq, Kuwait and Iranian oilfields, a region where Britain had clear strategic interests. The aim of the SAS and the other British soldiers and airmen serving in Oman, many as 'contract officers' with the Omani Army, was to keep Oman pro-Western, deter Communist expansion and support the established governments. This task became easier from 1970 when the old and despotic rule of Sultan Sa'id was replaced by that of his Sandhurst-educated son, Quaboos.

'D' Squadron of the SAS arrived from Malaya in November 1958 and began operations with a strike against the romantically named Sultan Suleiman – the 'Lord of the Green Mountain' – a local then in rebellion against Sultan Sa'id. Suleiman's men occupied a stronghold on the Jebel Akhdar massif, a mountain feature in the north of the country. The fighting for control of the Jebel went on for three months and involved RAF bombers and Venom ground-attack fighters as well as infantry, but the massif was finally in SAS hands by the middle of January 1959. After that the focus of dissent switched to the southern province of Dhofar which was still a battleground in the late 1960s.

Dhofar backed on to the now-independent South Yemen, so the rebels had a frontier to retreat behind and a ready supply of weapons. The Dhofar campaign, which lasted until 1972, reached its climax in that year when the SAS beat off a heavy rebel attack on their base at Mirbat. That battle broke the back of the rebel resolve and these attacks slowly petered out.

SAS operations during the early part of this period were supported by RAF Shackleton aircraft serving as bombers and based on islands off the Omani coast. Among the aircrew was Brian Pearce, a navigator with 224 Squadron RAF.

Between 1954 and 1960 I served as a navigator (Flight Lieutenant) in Coastal Command, first in Britain and then in Gibraltar. During this latter period I became involved in Colonial Policing. Essentially this was to provide medium level bombing support to ground force operations in the Oman.

Early in 1959 four aircraft of 224 Squadron were sent to Masirah Island, which then had a primitive desert airstrip. Masirah is located off the Omani coast and prior to this we had carried our practice bombing at RAF Indris in Libya and later at RAF Khormaksar in Aden. We definitely felt resentment from the Aden Arabs but none at all from the Omanis on Masirah. Our task was to support elements of the British Army fighting rebels trying to overthrow the Omani

Sultan. These rebel forces, perhaps a few thousand in all, were led by Taleb, a USSR trained fighter, Ghaleb, the religious leader, and Sheik Suleiman, the Lord of the Green Mountain, whose territory lay west of the port of Muscat.

The Jebal Akhdar rises to about twelve thousand feet and most of the fighting took place on the top or in some passes leading to the crest. To carry the crest the infantry called in Hunter ground attack fighters which used rockets, or bombing support from our squadron, usually in co-ordinated attacks made shortly after dawn. The rebels were equipped with Russian weapons supplied via Aden, the Yemen or Egypt, though it was generally believed that the rebels were in the pay of Saudi Arabia.

There was a lot of activity going on in the region, mostly after oil, in the Rub-el-Qhali, along the Saudi border, or at the Buraimi Oasis, and Britain was in dispute with the Saudis about that. Britain had treaties with the Omani sultan and other Gulf leaders, but it is interesting that Oman was totally underdeveloped at the time and the Sultan was a despot; many on the Squadron thought that Suleiman and Taleb had every right and reason to rebel.

In all, our squadron, or at least my crew, took part in thirteen bombing missions, usually carrying a load of $12 \times 1,000$ bombs. We would bomb from around sixteen thousand feet, working closely with the air liaison officers serving with the ground forces. After bombing we would descend to around two hundred feet above ground level and attack enemy emplacements with our 20mm cannon. This was a bit dangerous but it proved highly effective though the whole idea of bombing these people did concern us.

This rebellion had been going on for some time before the British got involved but the whole situation changed when the SAS arrived in 1959. There were only a few of them, about fifty, but within weeks the rebels had fled from the Jebel Akhdar and the fighting stopped, at least for a while. It goes without saying that the British were involved for economic reasons, to ensure access to the Gulf oilfields.

British involvement in the Central American territory of Belize was without fighting, as post–independence support for a former colony. The former British Honduras became independent as Belize in 1981, after a decade of threats and attempts at intimidation from the government of Guatamala which had long laid claim to the territory.

The threat of invasion – and another Falklands-style conflict – hangs over the new country to this day and may escalate when the British forces are removed. The news that the British intended to leave Belize was taken by Guatamala as the green light for a takeover and the new Government promptly asked for British aid. A garrison of British troops was therefore maintained in Belize even after independence, and the British base was used by the Army to mount patrols along the Guatamalan border, to 'show the flag' and keep the jungle warfare skills of the troops well honed.

Major Tom Godwin of the Parachute Regiment is one of many who have served in Belize over the last thirty years:

> British forces continued to serve in Belize after independence, at the invitation of the Premier, as this helps to maintain the sovereignty of the country against intimidation from Guatamala, though the ostensible reason we go there is for jungle training.
>
> Belize has its own Defence Force but calls upon the visiting British battalion to provide instructors and support. It is fair to say that without British support the local forces would be no match for the much larger Guatamalan Regular army. There is also plenty of scope for adventure training, in the mountains or the offshore cays. It is not a bad posting, with lots of opportunities for leave in Florida or trips to the West Indies. This British support is due to be withdrawn and Belize may yet provide another post-independence flash point.

There were small outbreaks of trouble in a number of colonies around the time of independence, but on balance, and with the exception of the major conflicts covered in this book, Britain managed to divest herself of the Empire without any further problems.

This should not be surprising; the local politicians wanted independence and the British Government was more than happy to hand it over. Only after the British had left did the problems of independence really come to the surface, but post-Independence problems will be considered in the final chapter. In 1968 all was peaceful, but this happy state did not last.

By the New Year of 1969 Britain and her former colonies were able to look back on nearly twenty-two years of progress from

Empire to much expanded Commonwealth. Forty former colonies or dominions from India to Zanzibar, from Barbados to Borneo, were now independent states. Much of the Empire had gone and the rest would soon follow and all was going well. Few of those celebrating the New Year of 1969 could have imagined that the coming year would see fresh and long-lasting troubles arising in the 'Mother Country', actually inside the United Kingdom, in the province of Northern Ireland.

17

Northern Ireland: 1968–1982

'There lay the green coast of Ireland, like some coast of plenty. We could see the towns, towers, churches, houses: but the curse of eight hundred years we could not discern.'

Ralph Waldo Emerson, 1856.

It is open to question whether Northern Ireland has any place in a work designed to cover the final years of the British Colonial Empire. A majority of people in Great Britain and Northern Ireland correctly regard Northern Ireland as an integral part of the United Kingdom – or the 'United Kingdom of Great Britain and Northern Ireland', to give it the full title – and not in any sense a colony, dependency, protectorate, trust territory or mandated possession. Should Northern Ireland therefore feature in this book at all?

Legally, Northern Ireland is as much an integral part of the United Kingdom as Wales, Wiltshire or the Isle of Wight, and is entitled to remain so until the majority of its citizens decide otherwise. That said, for more than a quarter of a century, since 1969, the streets and fields of Northern Ireland have been the scene of a vicious terrorist campaign waged with the aim of severing this connection.

In the process those waging this campaign have caused the death of more than three thousand people, injured, mutilated or beaten thousands more, used torture and brutality on an unprecedented scale and caused terrible damage to the economic and political life of the province.

When those stark facts are taken into account, the actions of the Republican terrorist movement, the Irish Republican Army (IRA), and the bitter struggle to contain it fought by the British Army, simply has to be considered in this book, if only to set the record straight.

It is also a matter of wonder, but a matter of fact, that after more than a quarter-century of conflict, and the relentless attention of the media, large parts of the world still regard Northern Ireland as a British 'colony', where the inhabitants are prevented by force from uniting with the Republic of Ireland to the south.

A majority of people in the United States, for example, see Ulster, or Northern Ireland, or the 'Six Counties' – three names for approximately the same tract of land – as an illegal British outpost on the island of Ireland, where the British Army is an 'Army of Occupation', devoted to terrorising the native population in order to maintain British rule in defiance of world opinion, the Dublin Government and the democratic wishes of the long-suffering local people. This delusion has been skilfully fostered by Sinn Fein, the political wing of the IRA. To justify that statement it is necessary to explain how the British, or more correctly the English – since the people of Northern Ireland are also British – came to be involved in Northern Ireland at all.

Ireland had been constantly attacked and invaded by outsiders from the time of the Dark Ages but the first invader of consequence was a French knight, Strongbow, the Earl of Pembroke, a liegeman of Henry II of England. Leading a contingent of armoured knights, Strongbow arrived in Dublin in 1170 to aid the Irish King of Leinster in his local wars. With Strongbow's aid the King defeated his enemies and Strongbow then married the King's daughter and when the King died in 1171, Strongbow became King of Leinster in his place. From that happy and profitable connection came eight centuries of woe.

Strongbow's liege lord, Henry II, King of England, did not care for his earls becoming kings in nearby countries and sent troops to Ireland to recall Strongbow to his allegiance. Strongbow duly swore fealty to King Henry and the English King thus became overlord of Ireland, though Henry II gave this lordship to his worthless son, John Lackland, Richard Coeur de Lion's brother, later King John.

The English Kings maintained their connection with Ireland throughout the Middle Ages but the next significant step took place in the sixteenth century when, after the Reformation, Ireland became a Catholic back door to the Protestant English kingdom. Queen Elizabeth I, so tolerant in other matters, was very wary of Spanish infiltration and took a very strong line with her Catholic Irish subjects. The Irish wars went on for years and, in the end, having failed to quell her Irish subjects or divert them from the Catholic religion, Elizabeth decided to replace them with Protestant settlers sent from England. It will be seen therefore that the religious divisions that still torment the North of Ireland can also be traced back several centuries and are not a modern phenomenon. Irish folk, however, have long memories.

The soldiers sent to Northern Ireland in 1969 at the start of the present Troubles soon discovered this for themselves. Brigadier Joe Starling of the Parachute Regiment, who has appeared elsewhere in this book, went to Northern Ireland as Deputy Commander of the 3rd Infantry Brigade:

> The Operational situation in Northern Ireland in the early seventies had reached what the politicians called an 'acceptable level of violence' (whatever that means) and some degree of normality was returning to the civic life of the Province.
>
> May is the traditional time for the changeover of Mayors and other civic dignitaries and the local Brigadier was invited to attend the 'Mayor Making' in Lurgan. The Brigadier quickly and legitimately pleaded pressure of work in South Armagh, where the terrorist threat was still temporarily in the ascendant, and detailed me, a Colonel and his Deputy, to attend in his place.
>
> It was a plain clothes affair but, being an old hand in matters terrorist, I took the sensible precaution of slipping a Browning automatic pistol into the waistband of my smart city suit before joining the new Mayor and Corporation at the Cathedral to pray for success during their year of office.
>
> The congregation, like the animals in the Ark, marched up the aisle two by two, and I was paired off with the Bishop. Halfway to our seats the Browning pistol detached itself from my waistband and was working its way down my trouser leg. Begging the Bishop to pause briefly I retrieved it and replaced it in my belt but, sadly, it appeared to the Bishop that, during its short transit, the pistol was pointing straight up his left nostril. Thinking he was about to

be assassinated by the strange person in plain clothes by his side, he threw his episcopal crook to the ground and called upon the Virgin and the Saints for protection.

This contretemps was sorted out relatively quickly and, after a prayer or two, the congregation repaired to the Mayor's Parlour where the serious business of the ceremony – the drinking – was to be conducted.

After the fine Old Bushmills whiskey had circulated quite a few times, one of the Councillors staggered up to me and said in an Irish accent you could cut with a knife. 'Hey, youse. Did youse say y're name was Star-lin?' On receiving an affirmative reply, he went on. 'In that case, ye must be related to the Tim Star-lin of the Province?' Again an affirmative reply as he was a distant cousin. 'In that case vouse must also be related to the John Star-lin that murdered the Roman Catholic Archbishop of Colchester in 1381, the year of the Peasants' Revolt.' This was said as a statement of fact; then, addressing the assembly at large he cried, 'Hey! He's wun of uss. His kinsman killed a Roman Catholic Archbishop; guv 'im another whiskey!'

Memories, or perhaps legends, are the folklore currency in Ulster. No wonder the Irish problem continues to be insoluble.

The Plantations, the 'planting' of Irish lands with Protestant farmers from the mainland of Britain, began under the Tudors and continued into the seventeenth century under the Stuart Kings, when many of the planted settlers came from the fiercely Protestant Lowlands of Scotland.

Then came Cromwell. After winning the Civil War in England, Oliver Cromwell became the scourge of Ireland and the Catholic population, destroying the city of Drogheda, driving the surviving Catholic population west into Connemara, continuing the 'planting' and so laying down another element in that long legacy of bitterness that underpins all the Anglo–Irish difficulties.

Since the majority of these newly 'planted' Protestant landowners came from the lowlands of Scotland they tended to settle in the North of Ireland, in the Province of Ulster, which eventually came to contain a large Protestant majority, as steeped in their religion as the native Irish were in Catholicism. Ireland therefore became an island divided against itself, Catholic against Protestant, North against South. So it has largely remained.

The Protestant landowners in Ireland – the 'Ascendancy' – were not always benign to their tenants. Irish history is studded with stories of neglect, injustice and brutality, culminating in the horrific Potato Famine of the 1840s when a million Irish peasants died of starvation and a million more emigrated to other parts of the Empire and America, taking with them the seeds of that hatred which flourishes against the British to this day. This is not to say that a long succession of British Governments were unaware of Ireland's problems.

Throughout the centuries there have been constant attempts to find a solution that would grant Ireland the independence for which the Catholic majority craved, without providing a base against Britain for the Catholic powers of Europe. When the problem of invasion faded away, after the Napoleonic Wars, another problem arose.

For more than a hundred years, from the middle decades of the nineteenth century when self-government or independence for Ireland was first seriously debated in Parliament, the British Government was pressed to find a solution that would give Catholic Ireland independence without provoking civil war between the majority Catholic population in the South and the majority Protestant population in the North, for the two communities hated each other.

By the 1850s, the issue of Irish independence was top of Britain's political agenda and there it remained for several decades. In the 1880s a Home Rule Bill was introduced in the House of Commons by Charles Stuart Parnell, but the House of Lords, which then had a veto on Commons legislation, swiftly rejected it. In 1893 the Irish Members brought the Bill back, with a similar result; the Protestant vote – the Orange Card – as always large enough to defeat the Nationalists. The Nationalists were not to be denied and they tried again in 1912. Then followed two years of heated debate but the Irish 'Home Rule' Bill was finally passed in 1914. By now, however, there was another snag.

The Great War of 1914–18 had started and the implementation of the Irish 'Home Rule' Bill was therefore deferred until the ending of hostilities. Tens of thousands of Irishmen flocked to the Colours of the British regiments, assured of their own country after the war, but some of their fellow citizens could not wait that long.

The 'Easter Rising' of 1916 was vastly unpopular with the majority of the Irish people, not least because a great number of young Irishmen were serving in the British Army on the Western Front. The insurgents were widely regarded as traitors, at least until the 'Rising' was crushed and the British Government, most unwisely, executed sixteen of the ringleaders. After that, the Irish population turned against the British Government, a Declaration of Independence was prepared without any consultation with Westminster, and the newly formed Irish Parliament, the Dail, held its first sitting in Dublin in January 1919.

Then came the Anglo–Irish War of 1920, a brief but bloody affair, largely between British ex-soldiers recruited into an irregular force, the so-called 'Black and Tans', and a new formation, the Irish Republican Army, an irregular force which was then more or less what the name implied, the Army of the Republic of Ireland. During this period there were violent anti-Catholic demonstrations in Ulster and the IRA gained a great deal of credibility by defending the Catholic populations in Belfast and Londonderry against attacks from Protestant mobs . . . and indeed from the largely Protestant police force.

During this time the leaders of the new Irish Government came to accept that they could not hope to gather the Protestant majority population of the 'Six Counties' in the North into a united, Catholic Ireland. They therefore reluctantly agreed to partition, the legal separation of six Northern counties from the newly established Irish Free State.

No one *forced* the Irish to do this; it was seen as the only way to avoid a civil war between Catholic and Protestant, but things in Ireland are never that easy. Instead of fighting the Protestants, the Southern, Catholic Irish started to fight among themselves.

As other accounts in this book will have revealed, partition has often seemed the only option at the end of colonial rule, when the binding powers of the imperial jurisdiction are torn away from a basically hostile native population. They will also have revealed that partition is rarely successful.

In Ireland, as in India, the main reasons for partition were religious. The cry of the Protestants in the North was that 'Home Rule means Rome Rule', and they would have none of it. Nor were there any means to force the Protestants into a United Ireland. It was very clear that if any such attempt was made, the Protestants would fight and the British voters on the mainland would not support military compulsion. So the sad situation of the present day began to develop, though the intransigence of the north had been already been demonstrated, even before the Great War began.

In 1913 the then leader of the Ulster Protestants, Sir Edward Carson, told the British Government that the Protestants would take up arms if any attempts were made to set up an Irish state at all. To add force to this claim, shiploads of arms were imported from abroad and over a hundred thousand Protestant Ulstermen vowed to use them if any attempt were made to create a Catholic Irish Republic. A year later, in the 'Curragh Mutiny' of 1914, the officers and soldiers of the British Army garrison in Ireland made it abundantly clear that if the British Government attempted to coerce the Protestant population into an Irish Catholic republic, the British Army would refuse to act.

The British Government were therefore in a real dilemma. If they did not grant Home Rule there would be a rebellion in Ireland. If they *did* grant Home Rule to the entire island and withdrew, there would be a Civil War in Ireland between the Catholics and the Protestants. Caught between these two implacable forces, in 1921 the British and Irish Governments opted reluctantly for Partition. At this point the present Troubles of Ireland, South as well as North, really began.

The Government of Ireland Act of 1920, and the subsequent Anglo-Irish Treaty of 1921, created the Six Counties of Northern Ireland: Antrim, Armagh, Down, Fermanagh, Tyrone and Londonderry (or to the Catholics just Derry) as the 'Province of Northern Ireland' and the twenty-six counties as the 'Irish Free State'. The Irish Free State had independent Dominion status within the Commonwealth, rather like Australia and Canada, and retained strong links with the British Crown. This fact alone was enough to infuriate the men of the IRA, who regarded the Treaty and the setting up of the Free State, without the six Ulster counties, as a sell-out to the Protestants and the British Government.

Ireland then had a civil war, between those in favour of the Anglo-Irish Treaty and those against it, which meant in practice between the newly established Irish Government and the IRA. The Irish Civil War of 1922–3 was fought to a very bloody conclusion. The Irish Government of the day had no compunction about shooting members of the IRA, executing thirty-four IRA members by firing squad in the January of 1923 alone.

The British Goverment was not the first to take a firm line with the IRA, and the Irish Government has stoutly opposed the IRA activists ever since, while supporting the idea of eventual Irish unity. Indeed, the Irish Constitution lays territorial claim to '*the whole island of Ireland*' but the bulk of the Government and the Irish people accept that that claim can only be made good when a majority of the Northern Irish people wish it. The Republic of Ireland and the decent people it contains have no wish to coerce the North into union, let alone with bullets and bombs.

On the conclusion of the Civil War, which ended in victory for the Government, the IRA went underground. Those members of its political arm, Sinn Fein, who had won seats in the Irish Parliament, refused to sit in the Dail, regarding it as an unworthy assembly since it only represented a part of the whole island of Ireland. The then leader of Sinn Fein, Eamon de Valera, seeking political office, broke away from the party in 1926 and set up his own party, Fianna Fail.

Eamon de Valera still remained an implacable opponent of Great Britain. When war broke out in 1939 he refused to allow the British Navy to use the 'treaty ports' which reduced the coverage available to Atlantic convoys and certainly contributed to the great losses caused to Allied ships and seamen.

The Irish Free State remained a British dominion until 1937, when it became Eire and fully independent. Eire became the Republic of Ireland in 1949. The IRA, however, remained unsatisfied and were determined to destabilise any long-term prospect of peace over the Northern Ireland issue. It is the IRA that has kept the conflict alive and denied peace to the Irish people and their British neighbours to the north.

From the establishment of the Free State in 1921 there had been periodic terrorist attacks by the IRA on British military installations of personnel in Ulster or on the British mainland. Taking as their motto, '*Britain's difficulty is Ireland's opportunity*', these attacks intensified in 1939–40 in the early years of the Second World War, when the IRA carried out a number of bombings in London. There were further small-scale attacks or even short campaigns in the post-war years, just enough to remind people that the IRA were still in existence, but the Troubles which began

in Belfast and Londonderry in 1968 had nothing to do with the IRA
... at first.

Though religious animosity remains strong, the fundamental cause
of the recent Troubles of Northern Ireland was Civil Rights. Even in
the late 1960s, when the British had largely given up their Empire
or were in the process of doing so, the situation of the Catholic
population of Northern Ireland was far from just or happy. The
treatment of the Catholic population of Ulster by the locally based
Stormont Parliament and local Protestant-dominated Councils was
a disgrace to Great Britain that is quite impossible to excuse.

In Northern Ireland Catholics were, in every sense of the word,
second-class citizens, barred from public office by gerrymandering
in the elections, discriminated against in the job market, in housing,
in education, even when seeking help from the police or justice in the
courts, confronted in their daily lives with the hostility and prejudice
of their Protestant fellow citizens.

They had no redress. The British Government at Westminster
had handed over Northern Ireland to a locally elected, Protestant-
dominated Parliament at Stormont, a Government with its own Prime
Minister and Cabinet. British Governments took little interest in
Northern Irish affairs, but once they had been revealed to a wider
public in Great Britain and beyond, the injustices perpetrated on
the Catholics in the north could not continue; sooner or later change
would have to come. Change, however, is not an easy thing to manage
in Northern Ireland.

Anyone attempting to change this undemocratic state of affairs
would be instantly opposed, threatened and harassed by extreme
elements in the Orange Order, a Protestant organisation set up in the
eighteenth century to resist Home Rule. The influence of the Orange
Order extended to every facet of Northern Ireland's affairs, from the
football clubs on the housing estates to the offices of Government,
where the path to influence and jobs was membership of the Orange
Order. At every level there was prejudice and discrimination and no
apparent wish to end it. In the 1960s, just a few years before the
Troubles began, the Prime Minister of Northern Ireland, Sir Basil
Brooke, an Orangeman, was happy to boast that he did not have a
single Catholic in his employ.

One of his predecessors, Sir James Craig, who was Prime Minister
of Northern Ireland just after the Second World War, told the

Members at Stormont, the Northern Ireland Parliament, that he 'prized his position as Grand Master of the Orange Order in County Down far more than that of Prime Minister of Northern Ireland. I am an Orangeman first and a politician second.'

The result of all this was that the usual democratic ways to ensure justice and political change, through the courts and the law and the ballot-box, were effectively barred to the Catholic population. They therefore cannot be blamed if, in the end, in 1968 and 1969, they took to the streets in a series of Civil Rights marches. In doing so they brought down on their heads the full fury of the Protestant police force, including the largely Protestant 'B Specials' and large sections of the Protestant community. This massive public disorder brought the British Army into Ulster and had one effect that the Protestant politicians in Stormont had not anticipated: publicity.

Television was now starting to shape public opinion, in Great Britain and abroad. The riots in Belfast and Londonderry and the clear brutality of the police against men, women and children making a peaceful protest were brought into British homes night after night by television crews. Before long, questions were being asked about the causes of this uprising and the answers shocked the majority of the British people.

Calls for political and social change were made at Westminster and throughout Great Britain but it was seemingly too late for peaceful solutions. Fury and resentment fostered by generations of discrimination and insult had taken over, the Protestants then took to the streets to fight their Catholic neighbours and the rioting spread across the Province. When it became abundantly clear that the Royal Ulster Constabulary and their part-time colleagues, the 'B' Specials, could not contain the rising flood of Catholic anger and hostility, the time came for the British Army to be committed to the streets.

The most immediate cause of this commitment was the Apprentice Boys' March in Londonderry on 12 August 1969. This annual march commemorates the occasion in 1689 when the apprentice boys shut the gates of the city against the Catholic army of King James II, thus allowing time for William of Orange – 'King Billy' – to arrive, beat King James at the Battle of the Boyne and so claim the British throne. The apprentices of Derry have been celebrating this event for generations and it usually provokes sectarian violence.

So it was this time. The apprentices held their march, Catholics pelted the marchers with bricks, the police baton-charged the stone throwers and chased them into the Catholic Bogside district and a three-day street fight began. Many Catholics, many police and Protestants were injured and British troops were sent in to provide 'aid to the civil power' while the Irish Prime Minister, Jack Lynch, sent ambulance teams to 'Derry' and moved units of the Irish Army up to the border.

The Irish Government also attempted to get the matter raised at the UN, relying on American support for a debate. This support was not forthcoming, after the British pointed out that Civil Rights marches were also taking place at this time in the Southern States of the USA. If Northern Ireland was to be debated in the UN, then the disgraceful, racist treatment meted out to negroes in the USA might also be placed on the agenda. This hint proved sufficient and the US Government stayed out of Northern Ireland's affairs, at least for a while.

Meanwhile, there was trouble in the ranks of the IRA. The current leadership had noted that Civil Rights had proved more effective in arousing interest in Northen Irish affairs than forty years of sporadic terrorism and they now felt the time was right to join the democratic process, allowing their political arm, Sinn Fein, to stand for election and if elected, to take seats at Stormont, the Dail, even at Westminster.

The younger, left-wing element of the IRA, totally disagreed. They felt that the time had come for an all-out renewal of the armed struggle in the north. This dispute widened into a major split between the old Official IRA/Sinn Fein and the New or Provisional IRA/Sinn Fein. Most of the deaths caused in the next twenty-seven years can be laid at the door of the Provisional IRA or PIRA.

The first British Army units to arrive in August 1969 were two battalions of infantry and some men of the RAF Regiment commanded by Flight Lieutenant Philip Neame, who was later to transfer to the Parachute Regiment:

The trouble in the streets had just started but I was not involved in that. The RAF Regiment's prime task is airfield defence and we were sent to guard Aldergrove Airport. The story going around was that a force of three hundred IRA men were going to attack the airfield, but I still did not know exactly what I had to guard.

Well, on arrival, I soon found out. In one of the hangars, crammed in tight, were about a hundred and fifty Phantom fighters, newly purchased from the USA and awaiting conversion to Rolls-Royce engines. Thirty of us, armed with rifles, were to protect the RAF's shiny new fighter force. A Wing Commander appeared as I was taking this in and asked me if there was anything I needed and I said, 'How about some machine-guns?' It all fizzled out, of course, and no IRA appeared but that was my first introduction to the Province. I went back again later when I transferred to 2 Para.

Colin Butcher was a Sergeant when he went to Ulster with 2 Para:

The battalion first went there at the start of the Troubles in 1969. I went there on another tour in 1971 when we were based at Magilligan Camp, up in Antrim, looking across the water to Donegal, which is in the Republic. I was a platoon commander and we did VCPs and mobile patrols, some on foot, some by helicopter.

I remember during one helicopter patrol we saw three men in the middle of a wood and I elected to go down the rope and see what they were up to, since the chopper could not land among the trees. What I hadn't bargained for was that the chopper would then bugger off and leave me.

I landed and went off to talk to these blokes, one with an axe, one with a chain saw, and me with only a pistol. I asked what they were up to and they told me to piss off, and that seemed a good idea so I ambled away, and then the chopper came back, abseil rope trailing, and I was up that rope like a circus monkey. It may seem funny now but it wasn't funny at the time.

Belfast was hard work, lots of problems. We had a map at HQ, coloured for the Protestant (Orange), Catholic (Green) and 'Mixed' areas; in the 'Green' areas you had to be very careful. We then went to Londonderry to relieve the Anglians and were based in the Creggan factory. Colour Sergeant Danny Poynter and I did our recce tours of the Bogside in Land Rovers with the Anglians' driver trying not to go slower than 50mph, but when the battalion arrived we did our patrols on foot.

You really had to watch your step but some amazing things did happen. When we were in Londonderry two of our blokes, the Signals Sergeant and a signaller, came to check our radios and *walked* right across the Catholic Bogside from the Masonic car park to our base; that's a good mile. They were in uniform, red berets, the lot, and when we realised what they had done we were amazed. 'You must be bloody mad,' but all the Sergeant said was that he had thought it a bit funny that no one replied when he said 'Hello' or 'Good Morning'.

I remember Internment starting, on a Monday morning at about 0400hrs. We had as many detachments as possible out, with lists of 'players', and we went from house to house picking them up. They went mad, and so did the whole area, kids throwing stones, women out banging dustbin lids. There was a bit of shooting, but not much. Ballymurphy went wild . . . roads blocked and so on, so we got stuck in and sorted it out, but don't believe all the stories you hear about violence from the troops.

If any soldier got out of order or someone complained about something a soldier had done, the MPs (military police) came to interrogate the troops and had to get a report back within twenty-four hours – all 'hearts and minds' of course. When you got to Ireland you were issued with twenty rounds of 'Front Line' ammo and if you lost a round you couldn't get another one. Mind you, I expect some of the old soldiers had a spare clip or two.

Before we went on a tour we had a training course at a mock-Irish village at Lydd, in Kent; it was just like the real thing, with a pub and a fish and chip shop. We would take it in turns, one lot to be the locals or the IRA, the other Company to be the Army, and we would try to provoke each other. It was all right, but soldiering in Ireland wasn't much fun.

One of the first units to arrive was 41 Commando, Royal Marines, which had been serving as the 'Spearhead Battalion' of the Strategic Reserve when the call came for more troops in Ulster. Lieutenant Ian Uzzell was then Second-in-Command of 'F' Coy.

Everyone will tell you that the early days in Ulster were really rather pleasant and it is quite true. The Catholics had taken a lot of stick from the Protestants, and our job amounted to protecting them from Protestant mobs. They were therefore very glad to see us and have us on their streets. You got cups of tea and slices of cake and warm 'hellos'. It didn't last long, but it was nice while it lasted.

Anyway, we were taking our turn as 'Spearhead Battalion', ready for any emergency, when the call came. It was 41's habit while we were 'Spearhead' to parade one company every morning, fully equipped and ready to move. The latest round of trouble in Belfast erupted on a Saturday night, and on Sunday morning 'F' Company were told that they were not going home but off to Belfast. There were a good many unhappy wives that morning.

Our first tour was quite short, about six weeks. The first time I came under fire was a couple of weeks later in the Divis Flats area. 41 was based in a Catholic area and we were well accepted by the locals, with most of the trouble coming from Protestants in the Shankhill Road. My troop of Marines was responsible for a street on the Peace Line between the two communities, and on Saturday night there was a major riot in the Shankhill; we could hear the noise from streets away.

The order was that we could only open fire if we were first fired upon and after a clear fire order had been given for a specific target. Fire did come down on one of the sentries at the head of the street and my Troop Sergeant gave a clear, concise fire order. . . . 'For Christ's sake, lad, shoot back!'

Fortunately they missed us and we missed them. To make ourselves less conspicuous we had the street lights put out and went dodging down the street from door to door. It was a bit disconcerting to have a door open behind you and a hand come out with a sticky bun and a cup of tea. It was pretty chaotic and the radios were not much use in built-up areas. We soon found that the best way of keeping up to date with the situation was to nip into a house and see what was happening on the TV News.

Good relations between the Army and the Catholic population were not to last. Before moving on to that tragic outcome it might be as well to point out that British soldiers serving in Northern Ireland act 'in aid of the Civil power', not under martial law and the soldiers are bound by a set of instructions known as 'Yellow Card' rules, as well as being subject to the civil law.

The essence of 'Yellow Card Rules' is an insistence on minimum force. The troops are not to open fire unless first fired at or unless they think beyond all possible – or reasonable – doubt that their lives or those of their colleagues are in danger. A warning should also be given before opening fire. These Yellow Card rules, if applied to the letter, would make safe soldiering impossible, but they are designed to protect innocent citizens and bystanders against wild shooting and irresponsible gunplay.

Even so, rules that seem sensible and easy to apply in a warm barrack room take on quite a different meaning when a car is roaring through an ambush position on a dark rainy night, or a man looms up out of the gloom carrying what appears to be a weapon. The soldier who hesitates at such a moment could easily end up dead but the existence of Yellow Card rules should be known and appreciated by the public, since the rules govern Army operations.

The Army was sent in to support the police but the police were unpopular in the Catholic district and this honeymoon between the British Army and the Catholics did not last once the IRA let it be known that social intercourse between soldiers and civilians could lead to a kneecapping or a beating.

The riots of August 1969 brought the IRA back to the housing estates of Belfast and Londonderry and the towns and cities of Northern Ireland became battle grounds for the mobs. One effect of these riots was a form of 'ethnic cleansing' as the two communities attacked each other, the Protestants burning out Catholic families, the Catholics driving out the Protestants and taking over their homes. Meanwhile the police, and especially the private soldier, was caught in the middle, unable to contain the violence and excoriated by both sides and the bulk of the media for attempting or failing to do so.

Before long the need for Catholic–Protestant separation was tacitly accepted by the local town and county councils. Destitute families of either religion were simply rehoused in 'safe' areas, separated from their hostile neighbours by high fences and Peace Lines, patrolled by the Army or the RUC (Royal Ulster Constabulary). Meanwhile more and more troops arrived until there were over fifteen thousand soldiers deployed about the Province.

The IRA were not around when the Troubles began and those IRA men present on the estates during the early days either organised riots or withdrew to the south. Indeed, one of the large signs painted on a Catholic gable end at the time said 'IRA = I Ran Away'.

If so, the IRA were soon back, the slight level of support they enjoyed at first quickly enhanced by heavy-handed policing of Catholic areas. House searches for arms all too often involved a great deal of damage, ripping up floorboards, kicking in doors, smashing partitions. Much of this damage was unnecessary, often involving people unconnected with the IRA and naturally causing great resentment. This sort of action culminated in a three-day search of the Catholic Falls Road in July 1970, an event which has passed into local history as 'The Rape of the Falls', when troops and police clashed violently with the local people.

No one was 'raped' in the Falls Road, but there was widespread violence and a great deal of damage to property. At least three people were killed and over fifty soldiers and civilians treated for injuries. Reports of insults to crucifixes and religious objects kept in Catholic homes added to the injuries, and relations between the communities and between the Catholics and the British Army reached a new low.

The wish to unite Ireland and remove the frontier set up by partition is a legitimate political aim. If the people in the north elected to join the Republic the British Government would not wish to detain them; there are now over fifty, independent, Commonwealth countries, all of them former Dominions or Colonies, who can attest to that fact.

Provisional IRA is a terrorist organisation, with Provisional Sinn Fein as its political arm. To achieve their aims, to make Northern Ireland ungovernable and so sicken the British people with violence that they will opt for a pull out, the 'Provos' act exactly like the Mafia and no prating about the 'armed struggle' should disguise that fact.

Whatever their supporters or apologists maintain, the 'Provos' rob, murder, kidnap, torture and brutalise any who oppose them. They bomb restaurants and bars crammed with innocent people, men, women and children. They kill policemen, shoot teenagers in the legs, or fracture their arms and legs with blows from iron bars. They strip naked, tar and feather young Catholic girls for the 'crime' of smiling at a British soldier. Those who plead the IRA cause cannot deny this.

The IRA also raises funds from gullible members of the Irish-American community in the United States. Most of this money goes to buy arms which are used to kill Irish people, but the fund-raising goes on. The reason why so many US citizens support the IRA is simple. Firstly, the average US citizen has little interest and less knowledge of foreign affairs; the average American citizen might be hard pressed to find Northern Ireland on a map but to most of the American people, the reasons for the Northern Ireland trouble is simple. Quite simply, anything that happens there is Britain's fault.

In the United States, Ulster – Northern Ireland – is a 'colony', like the American colonies were before 1776, oppressed by the British Government, occupied by the British Army. The Irish-American community has strong, nostalgic, if ill-informed opinions about 'The Ould Sod' but all know that in case of doubt it never hurts to blame the British. There is also a more understandable reason: very few people in the USA – and in most other countries including Great Britain – can understand what the Northern Ireland problem is really about, because the true reasons fly in the face of commonsense.

Can a civilised, democratic country and a well-educated European population not find a better way to settle a problem, other than murder and street violence? Talk of the 'Plantings', Cromwell, the Great Hunger, 1916, is no longer relevant. All that is history: you cannot change it so why fight over it?

As for the Catholic–Protestant dispute, surely no one thinks the Inquisition will descend on Ulster and burn Protestant heretics at the stake? In an increasingly secular age, religious conflict seems uncalled for, if not impossible . . . unless you live in Northern Ireland.

The following personal story serves to illustrate the situation in Northern Ireland: the author was sitting in a bar in Coleraine and said to the barman, 'I don't understand fighting over religion, but maybe that's because I'm an agnostic.'

'You couldn't be one of those here, so you couldn't,' said the barman. 'Over here you'd have to be a Catholic agnostic or a

Protestant agnostic.' The barman also said that he could tell a Catholic from a Protestant 'just by looking at him'. This seemed unlikely but the rest of the drinkers confirmed that they could do the same.

Generations of people have tried to make sense of the situation in Northern Ireland but there is no sense to it: it is a state, a situation, a fact of local life. Reason has nothing to do with it. Logic has nothing to do with it; the Troubles continue because the people are not ready to stop it, root out the cancer of the IRA and treat their neighbours as friends.

To most people outside Ireland that simple answer seems impossible; there *must* be a logical reason for a quarter-century of violence and the most simple one is that the British are at fault for not giving the Irish their freedom. That may not be right but it is at least a reason.

American politicians have a more practical reason for playing the Irish card; votes. Some forty million US citizens claim Irish blood and those numbers are worth placating on polling day. American Presidents point out that twelve of their predecessors came from Ireland, many from Ulster. This is quite true; unfortunately, only one, John F. Kennedy, came from a Catholic background. All the rest are descendants of Ulster Protestant families, the sort of people the USA now rushes to condemn. The people of the United States thankfully have little experience of urban terrorism. They tend to accept the IRA at their own valuation, as 'freedom fighters' against the British Army's 'occupation' of Ireland.

People who live in Ireland, north and south, know different. They have to live with the IRA and all that such a connection involves. The IRA demand money from local people for 'protection' or as contributions to the cause. They rob banks and post offices. The IRA are active in the drug trade, though they will beat and kneecap anyone else so involved, not so much to discourage pushers, though that is their claim, but to protect their own trade. Most of all, they stir up trouble between the Catholic and Protestant communities – which admittedly is not difficult to do – and orchestrate attacks on the long-suffering soldiers of the British Army.

After the riots of 1969 the next major clash between the two communities came at the start of the 'marching season' in June 1970, when the Protestants prepared for the July marches to commemorate the deeds of 'King Billy'. On 28 June, eight Protestant Orange Lodges, each with its marching band, set out for the Catholic Ardoyne, followed by a crowd of supporters estimated at over two thousand men and women. Many had been drinking.

This group soon became the target for the stone-throwing of Catholic youths; a riot began, and the two communities were only kept apart by the presence of 45 Commando, the 1st King's Own Scottish Borderers (KOSB) and the 1st Royal Scots. Although the Army was still in favour with the local civilians, both communities turned on the soldiers who were attempting to keep them apart, and the troops became the focus for the crowd's fury.

The soldiers were pelted with catapulted rivets, iron pipes, bricks and glass bottles; nearly every man was injured. One Royal Marine lieutenant was hit full in the mouth by a brick, flung directly and deliberately into his face from five yards range. That night the Royal Ulster Constabulary and four hundred Marines held apart two mobs in the Crumlin Road; one of two thousand Catholics, the other of some three thousand Protestants. The mobs did not disperse until dawn, by which time the troops and police were very weary and often bloody.

On the following day an IRA sniper shot a man dead in the street while he was talking to a Commando patrol. One of 45's Naval medics, PO MacLaughlin, was fired on as he gave first-aid to a riot victim, and was hit in the side as he helped the casualty into an ambulance clearly marked with the Red Cross. PO MacLaughlin was later awarded the George Medal for his courage during this incident.

45 Commando then deployed five rifle companies across the Ardoyne, and subdued the rioters, but another riot began that evening. This was supported by an IRA sniper who opened up on a Marine patrol while a Catholic mob set about burning and looting shops. At one time twenty young Marines from 45 suddenly found themselves surrounded by a shrieking mob of about three hundred people, but managed to extricate themselves without opening fire. Few soldiers in any other army could have done that.

It took days for the Ardoyne area to calm down. All ranks of 45 then set out to restore good relations with the local community, taking on 'hearts and minds' projects, especially among the children, offering entertainment, repairing damaged school buildings and playgrounds. This 'hearts and minds' operation, so successful in other places, and so important if the cancer of intolerance was not to spread to another generation, never stood a chance in Northern Ireland as Brigadier Joe Starling recalls:

> Even if the local people were interested in being friendly with the Army, and some of them probably were, the IRA soon put a stop to it. The children were being educated in prejudice and violence and had nothing else to do but cause trouble, even when they were not put up to it. The troops would put up play areas and organise canoe trips on the Bann but . . . it was heartbreaking. After a bit, just as the troops and the kids were getting to know each other, the IRA would spread the word. Then the canoes would be smashed up and the play area burned, anything to spit in our eye.
>
> The Provos let it be known that it was dangerous to be too friendly with the Brits, beating, tarring and feathering men and women whom they suspected of even smiling at a soldier. The Catholics got the message to 'hate the Brits and be seen to do so'.

These problems were not just found on the streets of the northern towns and cities. The border with the Republic soon became a stalking ground for the 'active service units' – murder gangs – of the IRA, who could withdraw to the safety of the Republic after each attack. In February 1971 the IRA killed their first British soldier, a twenty-year-old member of the Royal Artillery, Gunner Curtis, who was hit by a sniper in Belfast. In August 1971, in response to the rise in violence, the British Government introduced internment: imprisonment without trial.

Inevitably, the introduction of internment caused trouble on the streets of Northern Ireland, protests in Dublin and much heart-searching in Westminster, where the measure, if necessary, was still unwelcome. Internment might have been necessary to remove troublemakers from the scene but it was still seen as in infringement of civil liberties and on that ground alone was most unpopular.

Moreover, the initial sweep to pick up the detainees undoubtedly picked up some innocent people. Though these were quickly screened out and released, internment caused understandable resentment and made Britain more enemies. The internees, all men known to have been involved in IRA activity, were confined in an old Army camp at Long Kesh, later the Maze prison. Internment proved so unpopular in democratic circles and so useful to IRA propaganda that it was eventually abandoned.

The IRA prisoners in the 'H' Blocks of the Maze have been a potent cause of trouble and in the long years of the Troubles Northern Ireland has seen deaths of IRA prisoners on hunger strike, a great many escapes and the long drawn out 'dirty protest' when the IRA prisoners smeared their cells with excrement, and stayed naked, demanding the right to wear civilian clothes as a sign that they were not common criminals but political prisoners. This claim was rejected and after some years the 'dirty protest' was eventually called off.

It would be wrong to assume from all this that Northern Ireland took on the appearance of an armed camp during the long years of the Troubles. Most people living in Northern Ireland throughout this time never heard a shot or a bomb and got on perfectly well with their neighbours.

By the early 1970s violence had spread from Belfast and Londonderry into the countryside, especially to the border area of South Armagh, where the town of Crossmaglen soon became a by-word for IRA activity. The people of Crossmaglen were strongly Republican, flying the flag of the Irish Republic above the Town Hall, stoning British soldiers in the streets and planting bombs on the surrounding roads.

This activity was often sparked off by IRA 'active service units', gangs coming across the border from the Republic, to which they returned when the damage was done. In an attempt to curtail this activity the Army cratered many of the cross-border roads, but to little effect; the local people turned out to fill the craters in again and those who used the roads to get about their farms, many of which straddle the border, were naturally angered.

According to Brigadier Joe Starling, none of this prevented the local people claiming all the British dole money and public benefits they could get their hands on: 'They wanted it both ways. They wanted to be in the Republic but they wanted the higher money available from Britain's Social Security, and 'known players' would come back across the border from some terrorist haven in the Republic to collect it . . . and it would duly be paid over; after all, as British citizens, even reluctant ones, they were entitled to it. People who think the British are bastards should remember that.'

The IRA did not restrict themselves to bombing or shooting. It was equally important to destroy the reputation of the British Army and present the soldiers as aggressive thugs. In this they frequently succeeded. Complaints about the behaviour of the soldiers were made in the Westminster Parliament and the British Press and provided a useful source of propaganda for Sinn Fein and the IRA. Brigadier Starling gives the other side of the story:

> The troops on the streets, most of them young corporals and private soldiers in their late teens or early twenties, always had a hard time. They did not want to be there, they had no axe to grind in this centuries old, mindless, Catholic–Protestant quarrel.
>
> Yet they were under constant verbal abuse, spat at, stoned from men, women and kids, all the time, and at risk from snipers and bombs. They saw their friends killed, shot, blown to pieces . . . and the locals gathering round to sneer or cheer when the British dead were cleared away. This was supposed to be a part of Britain but this was not how decent British people behave . . . or decent Irish people either, come to that.
>
> All they could do, and what they were ordered to do, was to ignore it. Yes, now and then, a few things happened which should not have happened, a fist swung, a rifle butt deployed, but no one is in any position to point the finger at our soldiers and call them brutes. No other Army in the world could have done it. No other soldiers could have resisted the constant provocation to retaliate. We knew, and the troops in the street knew, that retaliation from the troops was just what the Provos wanted.

Philip Neame of the Parachute Regiment recalls his tours in Northern Ireland:

> I transferred to the Army from the RAF Regiment and went to West Belfast with 3 Para. Our patch was the Derrybeg Estate, and when we arrived that was said to be a 'No-Go' area for British troops. We were not having any of that so Support Company took

Jungle fort, Borneo-Kalimantan frontier, 1964.

Gurkhas manning GPMG, Borneo 1965.

Private Smith, Gloucester Regiment, Belfast 1968.

Corporal Les Smart of the 3rd Battalion, Light Infantry on the Peace Line, Belfast 1977.

Riot in Belfast 1970.

2nd Royal Anglians under attack in the Bogside, Londonderry 1981.

San Carlos Water, May 1982. Royal and merchant navy ships under attack from Argentine aircraft.

Paratroopers waiting to go ashore from *Norland*, 21 May 1982.

Argentine prisoners and 2 Para soldiers, Goose Green.

RFA *Galahad* ablaze after Argentine air attack, Fitzroy 1982.

Parachute Regiment soldiers on Sussex Mountain, Falklands 1982.

British forces yomp into Stanley at the end of the Falklands War 1982.

Crowds at Portsmouth welcome the Falklands' Task Force back to Britain.

Marines of 40 Commando hoist the Union flag at San Carlos, May 1982.

Derrybeg on. I suppose we went in with a heavy hand, because if we stood for no trouble at the start we knew we would have less trouble later.

The locals got up to all the usual tricks, plenty of verbal abuse, spitting, stone throwing, even training their dogs to attack us. That last trick stopped when the fiercer dogs unaccountably died. I would deny that the troops were ever undisciplined or out of control.

We set the right message at the start, what was on and what was unacceptable and the troops stood by it. In the Parachute Regiment you get a good type of soldier; if you give them an inch they might take a mile, but if you let them know there is to be no nonsense, they will not let you down. We did the usual things, four-man patrols – known as 'bricks' – around the estate, VCPs at night to keep a check on the known 'players', house searches after tip-offs.

Once we had reached an understanding with the Derrybeg residents it was a low-key tour, quite peaceful. We maintained a presence on the streets, but there was no loss of life and no untoward incidents. We knew the Provos were trying to set us up for a bit of over-reaction and we refused to oblige them.

The 'Provos' got what they wanted on 30 January 1972, a day that has entered local history as 'Bloody Sunday'. During yet another demonstration in Londonderry, matters got out of hand until the police could not cope. Men of the 1st Bn., The Parachute Regiment were sent in as reinforcements and came under fire from a sniper or snipers concealed in the flats behind the crowd. The paratroopers returned fire, killing thirteen people in the crowd, most of whom were unarmed and only running away.

These tragic shootings, the 'Bloody Sunday Massacre' as it came to be called, was a propaganda gift to the IRA. It is only fair to add that although the soldiers were cleared of using excessive force in an enquiry conducted by Lord Widgery in April 1972, many people, and many soldiers, remain unhappy about these shootings.

'Bloody Sunday' has to be put in the context of the times. The stark truth of the matter is that an undeclared war was being fought between the British Army and the IRA, a war fought out in city streets and green fields. In that war many innocent people – innocent in the sense that they had no wish to get directly involved – were inevitably hurt, especially when they attended riots or demonstrations.

The Provos had already declared parts of Northern Ireland – usually Catholic housing estates – as No-Go areas but this pretension was brought to a halt in July 1971 when the British Army launched Operation Motorman in Londonderry, sending in a quantity of troops to saturate the Catholic areas, equipped with bulldozers which swept away the numerous barricades. Operation Motorman did not, however, net a big bag of IRA men; the resistance to Motorman came from local residents throwing stones or petrol bombs, for the IRA had fled.

Following the outcry over 'Bloody Sunday', the British Government now decided to take a direct hand in the affairs of Northern Ireland. They had previously dealt at one remove, through the Northern Ireland Parliament at Stormont, but in March 1972, six weeks after Bloody Sunday, Stormont was suspended and direct rule imposed from Westminster. The ending of Stormont rule was one of the major aims of the IRA campaign. With that achieved, most of the civil rights abuses corrected and steps in hand to end the Protestant domination of Northern Ireland's affairs, the IRA campaign could have been brought to a halt. This did not happen; 1972 became one of the worst years for violence in the long and terrible history of the Troubles.

By 1972 the IRA dominated life in the Catholic areas and by fair means or foul had enlisted the public support of the resident population. Willingly or not, the local Catholics elected to take sides with the IRA. Let a police or army patrol enter the area and the women would arouse the neigbourhood by banging dustbin lids on the pavement, the children would be let out to throw stones and petrol bombs, the IRA would take up ambush and sniping positions and Sinn Fein would telephone the media and invite them to report another example of British aggression.

'Sinn Fein and the PIRA were very good at exploiting the media, far better than the police or the army,' says one BBC-TV reporter who worked in Ulster at that time. 'I remember phoning the Sinn Fein offices and saying, "BBC-TV here ... what time is the demonstration taking place today?" ... "demonstration" being the code word for "riot".

'The reply, after a bit of background discussion was, "What time can you get here?" We eventually got wise to the fact that the trouble often started after we arrived, and was actually arranged for the benefit of the cameras. After that we would keep the cameras in their cases until there was something to film.'

Not all TV crews were so scrupulous, Brigadier Starling again: 'We certainly got the feeling that most of the the media, if not exactly against us, were never willing to give the troops the benefit of the doubt. A young corporal on the streets has a second or two to make a decision: a Press or TV reporter has hours to mull it over and decide he was wrong ... and tell the world so. We also had incidents where French and German photographers and TV crews paid the kids money to start stoning or throwing petrol bombs at the soldiers.'

The suspension of Stormont had no beneficial effect on the Catholic community and greatly angered the Protestants, who saw their domination of the Province's affairs being eroded and a sign that the British were bowing to international pressure and IRA terrorism. The Catholics – or the IRA – also saw the suspension of Stormont as a sign of weakness and their reaction was to step up the violence.

The British tried two initiatives to solve the Catholic–Protestant impasse. The first involved secret consultation with the IRA and public discussions at Sunningdale with locally elected politicians. This led to the Sunningdale Agreement of December 1973 which collapsed after a Protestant general strike in May 1974.

Major operations like Motorman were unusual. Most of the military operations in Ulster were at section or sub-section level, the most common formation being the four-man infantry patrol. This was mainly a 'corporal's war', where the lives of the men depended on the skill, training and patience of the Junior NCOs, who put up with conditions that would dismay a self-respecting vagrant and, apart from the constant threat of attack, endured a steady level of abuse and insult from the local people.

Colonel Michael Marchant was with 42 Commando during Operation Motorman:

I was second-in-command to Jeremy Moore, though we were both 'half-colonels'. 40 Commando were on the streets for 'Motorman' and 42 were to provide assistance as required. We were based in Belfast, billeted in an old mill. A typical day back in the early 1970s might consist of putting a Company or two on the streets by 0600 hrs or maybe before dawn, sending out a few 'bricks' to patrol from a firm base or just sitting in vehicles, waiting. There was little time for leisure, just patrol, eat, sleep, patrol . . . and not much sleep either.

So much depended on the corporal or lance-corporal on the street. He had to get to know his 'patch' and the people in it like the bobby on the beat, and react in whatever way was right when the need arose. The training of Royal Marine junior NCOs is so good, they were able to handle it. The experience trained them in judgement, leadership, observation, so many things.

The biggest single snag in Ulster was that you were not fighting a soldier's war; you were not allowed to take the initiative. It's a sad story, so engrained was the hatred among the locals. I remember driving down one street and my Sergeant said to me. 'You know, Sir, I was born in this street. I remember going down the end as a lad and chucking bricks at the Catholics.' The men had to put up with a lot of stick, take a lot of physical and verbal abuse, but they put up with it wonderfully.

Colour–Sergeant Eric Blyth, another Royal Marine, saw service in Northern Ireland through the eyes of a long-serving professional NCO:

I always found, in any riot, that it was foolish to rush straight in – better wait a bit until they got tired of it. Maybe that was the root of the trouble; we interfered too soon. If we had let them bash each other about for a week or so before we arrived, maybe they would have been ready to pack it in and behave. The daily routine? Well, let's take a police station at, say, Rosslea; we had four posts in the town to cover, plus foot patrols, plus intelligence work, keeping an eye on the 'players', the ones known to be IRA. You noted everything going on in the streets, sixteen to eighteen hours a day.

It was nothing for a patrol to go out at 6am, return at 4pm and go out again at 10pm until 4am or later; it depended on the situation. In the Rosslea area you needed to clear every road, every culvert, every dustbin . . . every time.

When you see a pal go up with a hundred pound bomb, well . . . you get careful. The lads, the young corporals and marines were wonderful, they didn't mind what they did, as long as they did a decent job. Foot patrols were nauseating, with the abuse and name-calling you got from the locals, especially in the city, but in the rural areas it was better.

Lacking a political solution that both communities would accept, the strife in Ulster went on. In March 1973, their activities constrained by army patrols and searches, the IRA introduced 'proxy bombing', forcing a man to drive a car or truck load of explosives to a sensitive site like a city centre, having first kidnapped members of his family and threatening to kill them unless he delivered the bomb. At the end of March a large 'proxy bomb' destroyed a vast area of Central Belfast.

Similar cunning was used to attack soldiers or policemen. Three Army sergeants were lured out of a public house by three young Irish girls and shot down by the IRA in the pub car park. Two RUC policemen were caught in a shop by an 'active service unit', forced to lie on the floor and 'executed' with a shot in the head.

The death toll was rising, and the atrocities mounted, with sectarian killings now adding to the score. In March 1972 a bomb exploded in the Abercorn restaurant, when it was full of women and children, killing two and mutilating – blinding, or blowing off the arms and legs – of nearly a hundred more. The IRA man who planted the bomb must have seen the women and children inside.

The list of civilians killed is studded with the names of the places they died. In the bombing of McGurk's Bar, fifteen Catholics died, including Mrs McGurk and her family, all killed by a Protestant terror group in a mass sectarian killing.

In the Donegal Street bombing on 20 March 1972, the blast was set off by the Provisionals in a street crowded with women and children who had run there after a bomb threat had caused them to flee from another street. Six people died here. So the IRA campaign went on, each killing an IRA battle honour, each one an atrocity.

During the 'Bloody Friday' bombings in Belfast in July 1972, a total of twenty-two bombs left around the streets went off inside an hour and injured over three hundred people. Fleeing from one bomb explosion they ran into another, driven about the streets like birds before the beaters. Unlike 'Bloody Sunday', 'Bloody Friday' is forgotten in Republican and 'liberal' circles.

In 1972, IRA violence also spread to the British mainland. In Febuary 1972 a bomb at the Parachute Regiment HQ at Aldershot killed a number of women cleaners. A few weeks later, in early March, there were bomb explosions at the Old Bailey law courts and in Whitehall. Other, far worse, atrocities were to follow in Northern Ireland and on the mainland of Great Britain. In 1974 a bomb at the Tower of London killed a New Zealand woman and injured forty-one schoolchildren on a school trip.

In February of that year a bomb placed on a coach travelling down the M62 motorway killed nine off-duty soldiers, a woman and her two children. Seven more innocent people died when pubs in Woolwich and Guildford were bombed in October 1974 and the ultimate horror came in a pub in Birmingham where an IRA bomb killed twenty-one young people and injured another one hundred and sixty-eight, none of them connected in any way with the Army or Northern Ireland.

People were arrested, tried and sentenced for the Guildford, Birmingham and M62 bombings but released and compensated years later when the evidence leading to their convictions was held to be fabricated or insufficient. The belief in the honesty and impartiality of British justice was another casualty of the war in Northern Ireland. Someone planted the bombs on that coach and in those pubs and the IRA know who it was, but as ever, the IRA have chosen to remain silent, even when innocent people are sent to jail. It is, after all, good anti-British propaganda.

There is no need to continue with this litany of violence, year after year, atrocity after atrocity. By now the point is surely made and the situation adequately described. What must be told is how the story developed over the next twenty years until a fragile peace came again to Ireland in August 1994.

The 'Troubles' may not be over yet but in the spring of 1982 the problems in Northern Ireland disappeared from the news for a few weeks. Another shorter but even more violent struggle was to capture attention after the Republic of Argentina sent a Task Force to seize a British colony, the Falkland Islands in the South Atlantic.

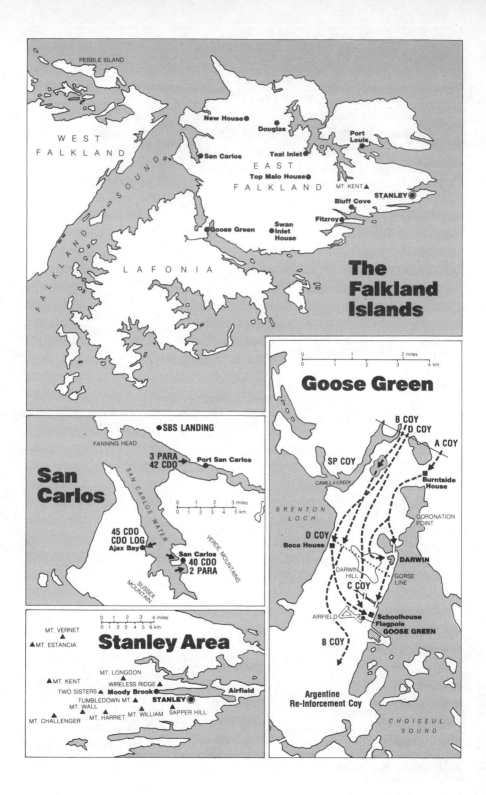

18

The South Atlantic: April–May, 1982

'We never thought you would do it – not for a moment. These are not the gunboat days of Empire and why would you, a European nation, send a whole army, ships and planes, all that way for a few hundred farmers and a lot of sheep?'

Juan-Carlos Garcia to the author in Buenos Aires, 1984.

Operation Corporate, the Falklands War of 1982, was Britain's last colonial foray. The war was provoked in April 1982, when the Argentine Junta, sent a Task Force to invade the Falkland Islands, a British Crown Colony. The Argentine Army attacked and overran the British garrison, evicted the Governor, hauled down the Union flag, absorbed the islands into the Argentine Republic, 'for ever', and renamed the capital, Stanley, as Puerto Argentina. By 1982, the British had left more than forty of their former colonies but never like this.

The Falkands Islands had been a possession of the British Crown for over a hundred and fifty years and the inhabitants showed every sign of wishing to remain in that situation. On the other hand, the Argentines had been attempting to acquire the islands, 'Las Malvinas', by diplomatic means since the 1820s and only when all diplomatic routes failed had they resorted to military action and sent in a Task Force.

Argentina held that the Falkland Islands was a territory they had inherited from the Spanish Empire in the early 1800s and which, in spite of countless appeals, the British had refused to hand over. The British held that one nation should not invade the sovereign territory of another friendly nation and attempt to take that which had been held in peaceful, if not undisputed, possession for well over a century. Besides, sending Task Forces was a game at which two could play. Within days of the Argentine Task Force seizing the Falkland Islands, the British has despatched a Task Force to take them back.

The Prime Minister of Great Britain, Margaret Thatcher, had learned the lessons of Suez 1956 and wasted no time in taking action. The British Ambassador at the UN was instructed to approach the Security Council and obtain a Resolution ordering the Argentine forces to withdraw. Thatcher was a friend of the US President Ronald Reagan and his support was also enlisted. Finally, bearing in mind the basic error of 1956 – delay – she ordered the Chiefs of Staff to get the Argentine Army off the Falkland Islands with the greatest possible despatch. In all this she enjoyed the full support of the Opposition parties, the media and the British people. A rerun of the Suez débâcle was never on the cards.

Britain's claim rested on a principle enshrined in the United Nations Charter – the right to self-determination. This had been included to aid the colonial nations in their fight for independence against the imperial powers. It had never been envisaged that some countries would exercise their 'right to self-determination' by electing to remain colonies, but so it was in the Falkland Islands.

The biggest British mistake in the weeks before the war was a failure to interpret the intelligence data warning of the coming threat. Had this been done in time the Argentine Junta could have been warned off, or the Falklands garrison reinforced. Even so, the Argentine action was a trifle premature; Britain's military forces were small but professional, highly motivated and efficient, but the British Government intended to scale down the Royal Navy surface fleet. Had the Fleet reductions begun, the creation of a Falklands Task Force would have been difficult or impossible.

Fortunately, the reductions had not yet taken place and although the Task Force had to rely on STUFT vessels (Ships Taken Up From Trade – requisitioned merchant shipping), like the liners *Canberra* and *Queen Elizabeth II*, to transport the fighting troops, the dockyards worked day and night to fit these ships for war, and the Falklands Task Force was put together within days of the Argentine landings.

Before we cover the events leading up to the invasion, it would be as well to ventilate the Argentine claim to 'Las Malvinas'. This goes back to 1810, when the Spanish Empire in South America fell apart and the components of that Empire fell into the hands of the various South American republics. Argentina claimed the Spanish colonial possessions in her area including the 'Malvinas' or Falkland Islands which lie four hundred miles east of the mainland, and the outpost of South Georgia.

The Spanish garrison on the islands was withdrawn in 1811 and an Argentine garrison established in 1826 was expelled by a United States warship in 1831 because Argentine troops had interfered with American whaling ships cruising among the islands. The Argentine Government re-established the garrison, but in 1833 a British warship, HMS *Clio*, arrived, evicted the Argentine soldiers, hoisted the British flag and claimed the islands for Great Britain. The British settlement at Stanley, the island's capital and port, was established in that year, 1833, and continues to this day.

HMS *Clio* was asserting a British claim to possession which predated the Spanish and Argentine occupations. The 'Falklands' were so named in 1690 by a Captain John Strong from Plymouth, who named them after Viscount Falkland, the Treasurer of the Navy. Breton seamen hunting seals in the South Atlantic, had already named the islands the 'Isles Malouins' after their home port of St Malo and the Argentine name, Las Malvinas, is a Spanish version of this Breton name, so clearly the Bretons were there before the Spanish.

There have always been two claimants to the Falkland–Malvinas Islands, but by 1982 the British had held them for one hundred and fifty years. To the British, the Falklands were simply a useful piece of territory on the sea route to the Pacific. To the Argentine Government and people, however, the possession of the Malvinas is a highly emotional matter. They feel they have a right to the islands dating back to their struggle for independence in the early years of the nineteenth century, a right which the British have constantly denied them.

The British took the islands as a step on the road to Australasia, a safe port in the wild seas of the South Atlantic, a coal and oil bunkering station and a repair yard for Royal Navy and merchant ships. During the Great War two sea battles were fought off the Falklands and in 1941 the British cruisers which engaged the German battleship *Graf Spee* at the Battle of the River Plate, were refuelled and repaired in the Falklands before returning home.

In 1982 the population of the islands was around eighteen hundred people, all of British stock, mostly engaged in sheep farming. The islanders were determined to stay British and as long as they felt that way the British Government had no intention of handing the islands over to Argentina and maintained a small garrison for their protection. The British garrison in 1982 consisted of sixty Royal Marines, known as Naval Party 8901, based at Moody Brook barracks near Stanley, bolstered by occasional visits from the Royal Navy Antarctic survey ship, HMS *Endurance*.

If the idea of handing the islands over to Argentina had ever been seriously considered by any British Government, it was out of the question in the early 1980s. The Government of Argentina was then in the hands of a military Junta headed by General Galtieri, and the Junta were engaged in a vicious war against those people in Argentine society whom they dubbed Socialists, 'left-wingers' or Communists. These were, in the main, liberal-minded Argentine citizens who simply yearned for a return to democratic rule but they were seen as enemies by the Junta.

Those who attracted the ill-will of the Junta were 'disappeared'; kidnapped in the street, taken to police or army barracks, brutally tortured and murdered, their bodies buried in unmarked graves. Opponents of the Junta simply vanished, but protests against the Junta did not die out. Every week 'las madres de la Vientecinco de Mayo', the mothers of the '*Desparacidos*' – the Disappeared – would parade in the Plaza de Vientecinco de Mayo in Buenos Aires, hoping to shame the Junta into returning their husbands or children, or tell them where their bodies were buried. This was another reason for the Falklands invasion; if the Junta could capture the Malvinas, their local sins would be forgotten or overlooked by the joyful Argentine population and one day in the Argentine autumn of 1982, this seemed to have happened.

On 2 April 1982, a very different crowd filled the Plaza de

Vientecinco de Mayo. The population of the capital was there, waving a sea of blue and white Argentine flags, cheering the generals of the Junta. The excesses and cruelties of the 'Dirty War' were instantly forgotten, for a dream of generations had suddenly been realised. The Junta had sent a Task Force to the 'Malvinas' overrun the British garrison and retaken the islands for Argentina.

The Falklands invasion sent a shock wave through Latin America. Every country except Chile broadly supported Argentina, though many of them were concerned about Britain's reaction to this aggression. Nor was this concern confined to Latin America. The United States swiftly took a hand in the game with the American Secretary of State, Al Haig, a former Army General, shuttling between London, Washington and Buenos Aires seeking a diplomatic solution. So too was the Third World lobby at the UN, where the United States Ambassador was openly siding with Argentina, claiming that American interests in South America would be damaged by any open support for Great Britain. The pressure was on for a compromise.

This, however, was not Suez, 1956. The British had a right to retake the Falklands, the Argentine Junta had acted illegally and was morally distasteful, and everyone knew it. The British Prime Minister, Margaret Thatcher, intended to get the Argentines out of British territory and she had the will and the troops to do it, whatever the United States or the UN said or did. In spite of their wish to placate the countries of Latin America, the United States gave her support to Great Britain.

The US Secretary of State Haig was well aware of the limitations of the Argentine Army and disgusted by the bombast of the Junta generals. He warned the Argentines that the British Army was a formidable fighting force and when one announced that he would be 'proud' if his son died defending the Malvinas, Haig, who had seen war in Vietnam, replied briefly, '*Well, you might feel that now but, believe me, when the body-bags start coming home ... it's different.*'

Haig's hard work had little effect on the progression to war but the Americans were soon giving Britain a good deal of furtive support and openly urging the Junta to pull their troops out of the Malvinas. This the Argentine generals flatly refused to do.

* * *

The Argentine Junta had sent a considerable force to retake the Malvinas. Designated Task Force 40, it consisted of two destroyers and two frigates and the submarine *Santa Fé*, escorting two troopships, the *Isla de los Estados*, and the tank landing ship, *Cabo San Antonio*. This carried nineteen American landing craft and some tracked amphibious armoured vehicles. More Argentine naval vessels covered this troop convoy from the north, a group of warships centred on the aircraft carrier, *Veintecinco de Mayo*.

The landing force consisted of six hundred troops of the 2nd Argentine Marine Infantry and a company of the Argentine Amphibious Commandos, one of the few regular units in the Argentine Army. The Royal Marines of Naval Party 8901 were therefore outnumbered ten to one but these Marines were professional troops who would put up a good fight, whatever the odds.

Rumours of an Argentine invasion had been circulating in the days before the actual landings, too late for re-inforcements from Britain, but in time for the garrison to make certain preparations. In April 1982 the Falkland garrison was unusually large because a handover was taking place, with fresh troops under Major Norman Norman replacing those leaving under Major Gary Noote.

As a result, the Governor of the Falklands, Sir Rex Hunt, could call on some eighty men to defend his territory, sixty-six Marines and three officers of Naval Party 8901, and two officers and nine men from HMS *Endurance*. These Marines were lightly armed with platoon weapons, rifles, Sterling sub-machine-guns, light machine-guns and some rocket-launchers. To these Regulars could be added twenty-three members of the Local Defence Force armed with rifles.

There was also a Canadian civilian, Bill Curtis, who offered to join the fight, and Jim Fairfield, formerly a corporal in the Royal Marines, who had married a local girl and settled on the islands. Claiming that there is 'no such thing as an ex-Marine', Mr Fairfield arrived at the Royal Marine barracks at Moody Brook where he was issued with a 7.62mm rifle and sent to join the men defending Government House. The battle for the Falklands began about 0615 hrs on the morning of 2 April 1982.

The first assault was put in by 92 men of the Amphibious Commandos, who assaulted the barracks at Moody Brook. The Royal Marines had withdrawn from Moody Brook, but the Argentine soldiers sprayed the barracks with machine-gun fire and cleared every room with phosphorous and fragmentation grenades. That done they hurried off towards the sounds of firing around Government House, where the Royal Marines were now in action.

A six-man Argentine 'snatch-squad' had approached the House just before dawn, hoping to seize the Governor. They ran into the Marines, who opened fire at once, killing three Argentines in the Governor's garden. Elements of the Argentine infantry then came up and a fire fight began around Government House lasting about half an hour, dying down around 0700hrs when the Argentines drew off to await the arrival of their Commando Company from Moody Brook.

The bulk of the Argentine forces were now coming ashore in Amtrac amphibious vehicles from the *Cabo San Antonio* and heading in convoy for Stanley. This column came under fire from Royal Marines and was halted on the edge of Stanley by an eight-man party under Lieutenant Bill Trollope, RM. These Marines engaged the Amtracs with machine-gun fire and scored a hit on the leading vehicle with an 84mm Carl Gustav rocket. This drove the Argentines out of their vehicles, and as they began to deploy, the Royal Marines fell back within the town.

Small fire fights and sniping were now taking place all over Stanley but the garrison was heavily outnumbered and the pressure was increasing. Still the Marines fought on and took a toll of the invaders. Corporal Stefan Yorke was commanding a detachment of five Royal Marines at the harbour, and one of his men fired a Carl Gustav rocket and sank an Argentine landing craft as it entered Stanley harbour.

By 0730hrs, most of Stanley had fallen to the Argentine forces but fighting was still going on around Government House, where a number of Argentine soldiers had been killed. However, with the Argentines landing heavy weapons, this position could not be held for long and at 0830 hrs Major Norman proposed to the Governor that his men should break out into the surrounding countryside and fight on from there. This proposal was not taken up and negotiations began with the invaders. At 0925 hrs the Governor ordered the Royal Marines to cease firing and the Argentines came up and entered their positions.

The Royal Marines suffered no casualties defending Stanley. Estimates of Argentine soldiers killed or wounded during the invasion lie between thirty and fifty. The Royal Marines taken prisoner were stripped of their weapons, photographed lying in the road under guard and then flown out to Buenos Aires for shipment back to England but they had put up a good fight and shown their quality. 'Don't get too comfy,' they told their guards as they filed aboard the aircraft. 'We'll be back.'

While these Royal Marines were fighting for Stanley, the Royal Marines at Grytviken on South Georgia had also come under attack. The garrison there consisted of a rifle troop – roughly a platoon – of twenty-two Marines, commanded by Lieutenant Keith Mills, RM, who had been sent from Stanley to evict a party of Argentine scrap-metal merchants who had landed in South Georgia and hoisted the Argentine flag. This party had gone when the Royal Marines arrived but soon after they landed an Argentine Navy frigate appeared offshore and called on them to surrender.

The Royal Marines' heaviest weapon on South Georgia was an 84mm Carl Gustav rocket-launcher, but when the Argentine frigate *Guerrico* entered the bay and called on the garrison to lay down their arms, the Royal Marines promptly opened fire, shooting down an Argentine Puma helicopter from the landing ship *Bahia Paraiso*, and scoring hits on the *Guerrico* with the Carl Gustav and a 66mm rocket. The *Guerrico* then withdrew out of range and began to shell the British positions with her 100mm gun. Having no means of replying to this weapon, Lieutenant Mills wisely decided to surrender, having sustained one casualty, Corporal Nigel Peters, who was hit when firing a 66mm rocket into the Argentine frigate. These Marines were also sent back to Britain and the people of the Falkland Islands settled down under Argentine rule, anxiously awaiting news of their liberation, though the Argentine soldiers insisted that the islands would belong to Argentina 'for ever'.

On 6 April 1982, just four days after the invasion, while the Argentine generals were still celebrating their Malvinas victory, disquieting news came to Buenos Aires. A British Fleet was on the sea, warships, aircraft carriers and troop transports crammed with fighting men, bringing south three thousand Royal Marines from the crack 3 Commando Brigade, and soldiers from the 2nd and 3rd battalions of the Parachute Regiment and the SAS, with artillery and light tanks in support. More men would follow, from the Guards and the Gurkhas, as many as necessary. The man appointed to command this landing force, Major General Jeremy Moore, MC and Bar, an officer of the Royal Marines, says:

> My involvement with the South Atlantic began on 17 October 1981, when the IRA exploded a bomb under Lieutenant General Pringle's car. As the next senior general, I took on part of his work while he recovered from his injuries. Robin Pringle took over command of the Corps again on 31 March 1982, and we had a General Officers' meeting on 1 April, which discussed the alarums around the Falklands and what we ought to do about reinforcing the Falklands garrison.
>
> The snag was, that lacking a long runway on Stanley we would have to fly the troops in via Argentina . . . hardly possible! Anyway, the phone rang at about 3 o'clock on the morning of the 2nd and Michael Wilkins said, 'You had better get up; Argentine forces have invaded the Falkland Islands.' So I got up and we got on with it.

Unlike most of Britain's post-imperial conflicts, the battle for the Falklands was not a 'corporals' war'. It involved aircraft carriers, submarines, frigates and destroyers, thousands of troops, artillery, armoured cars, air strikes, Exocet missiles and bombing missions. It was an all-out war, fought at the end of a long logistical supply chain. In this fight Britain had one clear advantage, a fully trained, professional Army, Navy and Air Force. Though small, the British forces committed to the Falklands were made up of formidable, professional fighting men. The Argentines had the numbers but the quality was lacking.

By the time the British Task Force approached the Falkland Islands, the Argentine forces ashore had been increased to around twelve thousand men. The bulk of these were half-trained conscripts, for Argentina does not have a large standing army. Apart from her officer corps and a cadre of senior NCOs, the bulk of the Argentine Army is made up of one-year conscripts called up at eighteen years of age for one year's National Service and the 'Class of '63', young men born in 1963, had just been called up when the Argentines invaded the Falklands. These young men, '*los chicos de la guerra*', were to bear the brunt of the fighting when the British came ashore and it is no reflection on their courage to say that they were not up to the task.

Britain's ability to retake the Falklands depended in particular on two arms of the Service. The first was the Royal Navy and especially the twenty Harrier fighter aircraft of the Fleet Air Arm, embarked in the two small carriers HMS *Hermes* and HMS *Invincible*. The next vital component, the cutting edge of the Task Force, was 3 Commando Brigade, Royal Marines, the one British formation fully trained in amphibious warfare.

By 1982, 3 Commando Brigade, Royal Marines, which has appeared frequently in this 'End of Empire' story, was much more than a single brigade of highly trained infantry. It was a little Army, an independent, highly mobile Brigade Group. The main component was the three Commando units, 40, 42 and 45, totalling some three thousand men. Of these, 42 and 45 Commandos were specially trained in Mountain and Arctic warfare, and all three units had seen recent service in Northern Ireland.

Their artillery was provided by 29 Commando Regiment, Royal Artillery, their sappers were from 59 Commando Squadron, Royal Engineers. The Brigade also had a special unit, the Commando Logistic Regiment, whose skills were to prove vital. The science of logistics, of keeping a force fed, supplied with the necessities and in fighting trim, is one of the less glamorous sides of the military art, but a vital one in war.

'When you come to write this down, don't forget to stress the role of the "Loggies", the Commando Logistic Regiment,' said Major General Julian Thompson, then the Brigadier commanding 3 Commando Brigade. 'But for the "Loggies" and their logistical support, the Task Force could not have worked. We knew that the Logistic Regiment would work because we had made damn sure it would work and beyond designed capacity. When I needed more troops and we got 2 and 3 Para, the "Loggies" looked after them as well.'

In addition, 3 Commando Brigade had an Air Squadron equipped with Gazelle and Scout helicopters, an Air Defence Troop equipped with Blowpipe missiles, the 1st Raiding Squadron, equipped with assault craft, also manned by Royal Marines and the Mountain and Arctic Warfare Cadre of the Royal Marines, who went on the expedition as a reconnaissance force for the Brigade.

This Brigade was selected as the core of the Task Force, but in view of the strong enemy forces now established on the Falklands, it was soon decided to add another infantry unit, the 3rd Bn., The Parachute Regiment (3 Para), two troops of light tanks from the Blues and Royals, and a battery of the Air Defence Regiment, Royal Artillery, equipped with Rapier anti-aircraft missiles. 2 Para was later added to this force. The two parachute units were taken from 5 Brigade, so when 5 Brigade was sent to the Falklands they received two battalions of the Scots and Welsh Guards which, with the 1/7th Gurkhas, brought it back up to strength. Various other units were added to the landing force, including two Squadrons and the RHQ from the 22 Special Air Service Regiment and some SBS men of the Royal Marines.

Two men had the ultimate responsibility for the conduct of the initial landings: Brigadier Julian Thompson, commanding 3 Commando Brigade, Royal Marines, and Commodore Michael Clapp, the Commodore, Amphibious Warfare. They were fortunate in having the invaluable advice and support of Major Ewen Southby-Tailyour, Royal Marines, who had once commanded the Falklands garrison,

Ewen Southby-Tailyour was a yachtsman and an experienced Commando soldier. During his time in the Falklands he was continually sailing round the shores, probing into remote bays, taking soundings, checking beaches, assessing the potential and the snags for an amphibious landing against just such an eventuality as the one which arose in 1982. All this information went down on a private set of charts which came to contain the most accurate, up-to-date, detailed set of landing instructions for the Falklands Islands group. When Mike Clapp and Julian Thompson sat down to work out where to land their troops, Major Southby-Tailyour's charts and his well-informed opinions were an indispensable source of information.

The three Task Group commanders in the South Atlantic were Rear Admiral J.F. 'Sandy' Woodward, flying his flag in HMS *Hermes*, commanding the Carrier Battlegroup, Commodore Mike Clapp commanding the Amphibious Task Group, and Brigadier Julian Thompson, commanding the Landing Force. Woodward had the additional task of co-ordination but all three reported to Admiral Sir John Fieldhouse, Commander-in-Chief, Fleet, in his headquarters at Northwood near London. Fieldhouse reported in his turn to Admiral of the Fleet, Sir Terence Lewin, Chief of the Defence Staff, who was a member of the War Cabinet headed by the

Prime Minister, Margaret Thatcher. The views of all these people, including Margaret Thatcher, would soon bear down heavily on the shoulders of Brigadier Julian Thompson, commanding the fighting troops from his trench above Ajax Bay.

Brigadier Thompson was asleep on the morning of 2 April 1982 when the call to action came:

> The phone rang and Jeremy Moore's voice said, 'You know those people down South? They're about to be invaded. Your Brigade is to come to seventy-two hours notice to move, with effect from now.'
>
> 3 Commando Brigade is always at seven days' notice to move, but many of my Brigade Staff and the CO of 45 Commando were in Denmark, planning an exercise. 45 Commando were about to go on Easter leave, and one Company of 45 was in Brunei; 42 were already on leave but 40 Commando, were on hand and had just finished a range course at Altcar. Anyway, we summoned the troops back and got on with it.

The officer commanding 45 Commando RM was Lt.-Colonel Andrew Whitehead: 'I was in Denmark when someone came thumping on my door at five o'clock in the morning. I flew back and got up to Arbroath in one of the Air Troop Gazelles. The unit was about to go on leave and "Y" Company were in Brunei so I actually got the Commando together for the first time on Ascension.'

Captain Ian Gardiner was commanding a company in 45 Commando: 'My telephone call came at 0400 hrs. I think my reaction was quite usual, "Pull the other one," I said, "1st April was yesterday." Then I ferreted about in the garden shed for my kit and was in barracks by 0600 hrs. We had an "O" Group at 0630 hrs when, our orders were: "3 Cdo Bde is called to readiness for amphibious operations in the South Atlantic." The bulk of the unit were off within four days.'

Andrew Tubb was a young Marine in 45 Commando: 'I was with the Recce Troop of 45. The unit was about to go on Easter leave when Lance-Corporal Pete McKay, who was killed at Ajax Bay, came into our room about five in the morning and shook everyone awake. "Leave is off," he said. We sailed for Ascension on *Stromness*, a Fleet Auxiliary. We lined ship for leaving harbour – it was raining but there were huge crowds of people to see us go. The dockyard maties even had a whip round to buy us videos! Can you imagine that? On the way south we ran a full training programme, fitness, first-aid, aircraft recognition, weapon training. Everyone "dug-out" on the training and was mad keen.'

Captain Gardiner again: 'Everyone wanted to go. I had men in my office in tears – literally – because they couldn't come with us, men who had finished their time in the Corps and done twelve years, begging to be allowed to stay on and come to the South Atlantic. I didn't think it would be easy. I knew we would have casualties, wounds, deaths. I told the men so and I asked them to think about it . . . but never let it be thought that the Royal Marines didn't want to fight for the Falklands. I was never in any doubt that we had chosen and trained the right kind of people and I was proud of them. If I don't mention that again, you can assume it.'

Not only the Royal Marines wanted to go. The battalions of the Parachute Regiment were frantic not to be left behind. Major Philip Neame was a Company Commander of 'D' Company, 2 Para: 'When the Falklands business blew up I was in Scotland with the kids, doing a bit of climbing. I got myself back to Aldershot in a hurry, though nothing much seemed to be going on. Our CO, Lt.-Colonel 'H' Jones, was skiing in the Alps and came hurtling back from Méribel to pull every string he knew and get 2 Para in the Task Force. Everyone in the battalion felt the same way, even if most of them did not know where the Falkland Islands were.'

At Hereford the CO of the SAS Regiment was equally anxious and got on the phone at once to Brigadier Thompson in Plymouth, offering 'D' Squadron of the Regiment as a raiding and recce force. So, one by one, the units of the Task Force assembled.

Major Neame of 2 Para again: 'I went back to the Falklands in 1989 and had to explain to the local people that we didn't go there to save them or even to fight for the Falklands. We went because Maggie said "Go", and we wanted a good scrap. The islanders were just the excuse. That said, I think we had to do it.'

Field Marshal Lord Bramall is even more certain that the war was necessary:

You can't let people get away with things like that. If the war did nothing else, and I can think of many things, it certainly taught the world that the British mean business. Soldiering is one thing we are very good at, and we sent the 'First Team' down there, the Commandos, the Paras, the Gurkhas and the Guards.

It was a near-run thing. In another year, if the planned Defence cuts had been put into effect, we could not have mounted the operation. There is another reason; if the Government had allowed the Argentines to get away with taking the Falklands, the Government would have fallen. Parliament and the people would not have stood for it.

A considerable fleet was en route for Ascension, and when the first ships of the Task Force sailed out of Devonport the slope of Plymouth Hoe was a solid mass of people, many of them with relatives in the Task Force, waving Union flags and wishing their men God Speed.

Sixty-five ships sailed south, liners, cargo ships, destroyers, frigates, aircraft carriers, landing ships, transports, submarines, carrying seven thousand men to the assault. All these ships were heading for Ascension Island, three thousand miles north of the Falklands, where the hurriedly loaded ships could sort out and 'combat-load' their stores and the men could go ashore to fire and test their weapons. Fresh supplies and more troops arrived by air. The first ships of the Task Force arrived at Ascension Island on 10 April, but the last did not come in until 10 May. While at sea, the troops took a renewed interest in first-aid, practiced weapon drills endlessly, and pounded around the decks in full kit, trying to stay fighting fit.

On 12 April the British Government established a Maritime Exclusion Zone around the Falkland Islands. On the same day a force of three ships, the destroyers HMS *Antrim* and HMS *Plymouth* accompanied by the tanker *Tidespring*, sailed from Ascension. On board were 'M' Company, 42 Commando, and 'D' Squadron, 22 SAS with men from 2 Section SBS and 29 Commando Regiment, Royal Artillery. Their task, Operation Paraquat, was the liberation of South Georgia.

On 14 April the small 'Paraquat' Task Force met HMS *Endurance*, which had been cruising the South Atlantic since the Argentine landings. On 19 April the submarine HMS *Conqueror* put a reconnaissance party of Marines from the Special Boat Squadron ashore on South Georgia. This was followed by a landing force of Marines, SBS and SAS men who went ashore by helicopter at Grytviken, under cover of shell fire from HMSs *Antrim* and *Plymouth* on 21 April. At 1700 hrs on 25 April, the Argentine garrison surrendered, without the invading force firing a shot, although Major Cedric Delves and his SAS had elected to go off on their own, lost two precious Wessex helicopters in crashes on the nearby glacier and were lucky to avoid loss of life.

Operation Paraquat was a useful prelude to the campaign, a hint of things to come. The South Georgia task force had also sunk an Argentine submarine, the *Santa Fé*, and captured a hundred and fifty Argentine troops. Most important of all, they had retaken South Georgia only twenty-two days after the Argentine forces had attacked Lt. Mills's small party – and done so at no cost in lives. This happy situation did not, alas, continue.

On 2 May, the British submarine HMS *Conqueror* sank the Argentine cruiser *Belgrano*, one of the most controversial acts of the Falklands War. It was later claimed that the *Belgrano* was no threat to the Task Force and outside the Exclusion Zone but hostilities were in progress, the *Belgrano* was an enemy warship, and an Argentine Admiral has since publicly admitted that had he been in command of the British submarine, he would have done exactly the same thing.

Sinking the *Belgrano* had the beneficial effect of alerting the Argentine Navy to the probability of attack by British submarines, and from then on their Navy took no part in the war. This is particularly important, because aircraft flown from the carrier *Veintecinco de Mayo* would have severely hampered the Task Force, which had only twenty Harrier fighters to protect the ships and support the troops ashore.

This lack of aircraft was a major concern to the Force commanders, but fortunately the Harriers and their Fleet Air Arm and RAF pilots proved more than a match for the Argentine Dagger and Mirage aircraft. As the carriers sailed within range of the Falklands the Harriers started to bomb the airfield at Stanley and the Argentine Army positions around the capital, aided in this task by Vulcan bombers flying 'Black Buck' single bomber raids from Ascension. While this air activity intensified, the Fleet sailed South from

Ascension and on 21 May 1982, just seven weeks after the Argentine invasion, British troops went ashore at San Carlos bay in the Falkland Islands.

The decision to land at San Carlos on East Falkland, was not taken until 12 May and the decision was a compromise, for San Carlos was not an ideal landing site. It offered a sheltered anchorage, and adequate beaches for a landing, but fifty miles of moor and mountain lay between San Carlos and Stanley, the island's capital. The first task though, was to get ashore and establish a bridgehead. The Falklands War was largely an amphibious operation and it will help if the reader understands the basic elements of 'amphibiosity', and in particular how an amphibious operation is commanded.

Brigadier Julian Thompson again:

> According to 'The Book' – Allied Tactical Publication (ATP 8) – the Commodore (Amphibious Warfare) is in charge of the landing. The British prefer to be more practical and the command is shared co-equally between the Landing Force Commander – me in this case – and the Commodore, Amphibious Warfare (COMAW), Commodore Mike Clapp. The Commodore is responsible for getting the force ashore in accordance with the Brigadier's plan, and the Brigadier commands the land operation which begins the minute the first man steps ashore; but right up to the moment of landing, the Commodore has the right to call the whole thing off.
>
> After the landing, when my brigade was ashore, the Commodore Amphibious Warfare 'chopped' his share in the operations of the Landing Force to me – but still retained control of all amphibious support craft, landing ships and helicopters for the support phase, except the helicopters in my own squadron. As long as we both understood the rules and followed them, it worked splendidly. Mike and I knew each other well and had worked together for years.
>
> After Jeremy Moore arrived and took over from me as Land Force Commander, Mike 'chopped' control of the helicopters to Jeremy's Divisional HQ . . . but all ship movements, the landing of men, stores and equipment, still had to go through COMAW.

Various problems can inhibit amphibious operations. The weather can prevent the best laid plans being carried through while at any time, the sea state, the availability of landing facilities, such as jetties or piers – or suitable landing zones on beaches where landing craft can unload, the tides, the presence of kelp beds or offshore rocks, can all affect the landing, which is another reason why COMAW HQ, which knows all this and the availability of suitable shipping, must have ultimate control. The Royal Navy and the Royal Marines knew this and therefore got on with the job without bickering, for understanding the problems and how to deal with them is all part of 'amphibiosity'.

It would also be as well to describe the various types of landing ship and their capabilities. There were two main types of vessel under COMAW control, the first being the LPD (Landing Platform Dock). Commodore Clapp had two of these, HMS *Intrepid* and HMS *Fearless*, ships of some size, displacing about twelve thousand tons. The LPDs were valuable and the Naval commanders at Northwood, were very determined that they should not be over-exposed to air attack.

LPDs could not run ashore on to beaches or causeways. For landing purposes they carried four smaller vessels called LCUs (Landing Craft, Utility), each capable of carrying about one hundred and fifty troops in full kit, and a certain amount of transport. To launch the LCUs which were carried in the dock, the LPD flooded down, taking on some five thousand tons of water, and the LCUs were duly floated out. The LCUs carried by *Intrepid* were named and numbered Tango 1 to 4, those on *Fearless* were Foxtrot 1 to 4. They were manned by a crew of seven Royal Marines, commanded by a Senior NCO, and were the workhorses of the amphibious fleet, capable of carrying troops or vehicles.

The LPDs also carried LCVPs (Landing Craft, Vehicle and Personnel) which could put troops ashore on open beaches. Smaller craft include Rigid Raiders and Gemini dinghies, which were used for landing small parties or on ship-to-shore errands.

The second major craft was the LSL (Landing Ship Logistic). These were manned by men of the RFA, the Royal Fleet Auxiliary, the support and supply arm of the Royal Navy. Six of these were in commission, all named after Knights of the Round Table, *Sir Galahad, Sir Tristram*, and so on. These had bow and stern doors for Ro-Ro (Roll-on, Roll-off) operation, like a civilian car ferry. Displacing about five and a half thousand tons, they could carry troops, stores or transport. They also had a helicopter pad, and carried two Mexefloat rafts, large platforms propelled by outboard engines, which could carry stores or vehicles ashore if the LSL could not be beached.

Before landing the first task was to eliminate an Argentine artillery and mortar post on Fanning Head, which overlooked the entry to San Carlos Water. This was carried out by an SBS force equipped with GP machine-guns and accompanied by Captain Rod Bell, a Spanish-speaking Royal Marine Officer, equipped with a loudhailer. 'We gave them plenty of chances to surrender,' he said, 'but they wouldn't . . .' The landing forces could see the tracer arcing about Fanning Head as they embarked in their assault craft.

The first landings were made by 40 Commando and 2 Para, who landed under the Verde and Sussex Mountains by San Carlos settlement at 0440 hours local time . . . and an hour late. Delays continued to accumulate as the landing craft returned to the troopships and brought 45 Commando and 3 Para ashore, 45 Commando landing at Ajax Bay, 3 Para a mile west of Port San Carlos. Dawn had broken and helicopters hurried to bring in the Rapier Air Defence missile launchers and the 105mm guns of 29 Commando Regiment RA, while the Marines and paratroopers around the beachhead began to dig in. All eyes were on the sky, waiting for an Argentine reaction; they did not have to wait long.

The first action of the day began when Argentine small-arms fire from Port San Carlos shot down two British Gazelle helicopters and damaged another. 3 Para cleared the Argentines out of Port San Carlos, and with the landing beaches secure, the troop and supply ships came through the narrows into the San Carlos anchorage.

The work of ferrying men and stores ashore got under way in earnest, with the white bulk of the cruise liner *Canberra* looming over the smaller ships. This work was still going on two hours after dawn when an Argentine Pucara aircraft from Goose Green attacked the ships with cannon fire but veered away when faced with a wall of fire from the ships and the troops around the shores of the bay. More serious air attacks on the shipping by mainland-based Skyhawk, Mirage and Dagger aircraft began at 1030 hours and went on at intervals throughout the day.

Lance-Corporal Spiers of Commando Brigade HQ was a machine-gunner on the *Canberra*:

We had built sandbag sangars round the decks, each with a GPMG and a two-man crew, about thirty guns in all. I could see the troops digging in up on the hill ashore and then three Mirages whistled overhead. I clattered away on the GPMG at everything in range – it was frightening at first, but then it was fun. The jets came screaming down the valley, firing cannon, dropping bombs on the ships, and we were firing at them with machine-guns, rifles – everything.

The only snag was that we got a bit over-enthusiastic. Fire from the port side was falling on 45 Commando, and fire off the starboard side was landing around 40 Commando – equally their 'overs' were coming onto the ships, but it didn't seem to hurt anyone.

Four Argentine fighters were shot down during the morning, with Sea Harriers adding six more in the afternoon, although the Argentines had by then succeeded in hitting the Type 21 frigate HMS *Ardent*, which had to be abandoned on fire and later sank. Argentine bombs or cannon fire hit many ships in the anchorage that day, as Julian Thompson remembers: 'I could hear the Naval radio net, and captain after captain was reporting to Mike Clapp, "I can steam and fight but not steer," or "I can fight but I can't steam." I remember that the frigate HMS *Argonaut*, crippled by bombs, had to be towed by three LCUs commanded by Ewen Southby-Tailyour.'

The Argentines should have concentrated more of their air power against the troops dug-in around the Sound. For this they had a useful aircraft, the Pucara, a fast ground–attack fighter, some of which were based on the airfield at Goose Green, the majority on the airstrip on Pebble Island off the coast of West Falkland. Julian Thompson was well aware of the Pucara threat and the Goose Green airfield was targeted for a raid as soon as possible after the troops got ashore. Five days before the main landings took place, on the night of 14/15 May, elements of the SAS had been sent to deal with the aircraft on Pebble Island.

The men selected came from 'D' Squadron, the unit that had had such an unfortunate time on the South Georgia glacier. This time everything went as planned. The men were flown in by helicopters of 846 Squadron and in a five-hour raid supported by gunfire from the frigate HMS *Glamorgan* destroyed most of the Pebble Island facilities, including a radar station and an ammunition dump as well as ten ground–attack fighters and a transport aircraft. This pre–invasion raid was now showing dividends as Argentine aircraft from the mainland harried the shipping in Falkland Sound.

Over the next five days San Carlos Water became known as 'Bomb Alley'. Soon after dawn each morning, wave after wave of Argentine fighter bombers from the mainland came in at low level to attack the shipping. They hit HMS *Argonaut* and *Antrim* on 21 May, the frigate HMS *Antelope* on 23 May and the landing ships *Sir Galahad* and *Sir Lancelot* on 24 May. HMS *Antelope* sank later, as did HMS *Coventry*, sunk on 25 May. Most of the air attacks were against the ships. It was not until 27 May that the Argentine air force turned its attention to the troops on shore, and by then the landing area was secure and enough supplies had been landed for the advance to begin. Then came a setback. 3 Commando Brigade had been waiting for the arrival of 5 Brigade, but as the Navy was suffering considerable losses, it was decided that most of 3 Commando Brigade should move out from the beachhead and invest the Argentine main positions around Stanley, leaving 40 Commando to defend the beachhead. This plan was disrupted on 25 May when an Exocet missile hit the supply ship *Atlantic Conveyor*, which was carrying eight helicopters, including three large Chinooks and a considerable quantity of vital stores.

Julian Thompson again:

> The loss of the *Atlantic Conveyor* was a setback. To shift troops and stores forward and support the advance we needed helicopters and we did not have enough of them. Let us be clear about that. This was not a case of sending troops out to fight with fifty rounds of ball ammunition and a bag ration; this was a war. Helicopters were the key to a rapid advance, and when the *Atlantic Conveyor* was hit, that was a real blow – but even helicopters have their limitations. For example, it took eighty-five Sea King helicopter lifts to move just one battery of 105mm guns up to Mount Kent. So, moving the battery forward out of the beachhead to cover the assaults on Two Sisters and so on, a round trip of over an hour, would take three days – that's to move just one battery of artillery!
>
> Now, about Goose Green. We had planned to raid Goose Green before 5 Brigade arrived – nothing terminal, just a battalion raid by 2 Para, with gunfire support, wellie-in, duff-up the garrison

and bugger off, that's all. Now, after *Atlantic Conveyor* bought it, I couldn't move the guns to support 2 Para because we were short of helicopters, so I called the raid off. Then the people in the UK got impatient and asked me what I was doing.

I replied: 'Recce-ing Mount Kent for the advance.' When Goose Green was mentioned I told them I couldn't move the guns to support 2 Para, so the raid on Goose Green was off.

They said – and I quote – 'You don't need recce for Mount Kent, and you don't need guns to assault Goose Green.'

Well, two comments on that. Firstly, you don't send men forward unless you can support them – that meant with artillery, and war uses up ammo very fast – and artillery ammo weighs one hell of a lot . . . it's not *easy*.

Secondly, the purpose of infantry is to take and hold ground. You can perform both parts more effectively if you know all about that ground and who is on it . . . and that means recce. With my available helicopters I could either occupy Mount Kent, which was the key to the next phase of our advance on Stanley – and a glance at the map will tell any bloody fool that – or assault Goose Green, but not both – and the real aim was to take Stanley, evict the Argentines and end the war.

I was then given a direct order to attack Goose Green. Not just raid it but take it and hold it. So I sent 2 Para against it with as much gunfire support as we could muster and fly down in one night. The main support was from HMS *Arrow*, plus two 105mm guns and two 81mm mortars from 2 Para's Support Company. The big problem was a shortage of ammunition and then *Arrow*'s 4.5in gun developed a fault.

Political considerations prompted the order to attack Goose Green. The Government in London were afraid that if there was any delay now, the UN might impose a cease-fire which would leave Argentine troops holding at least part of the Falklands. They wanted a battle that would render any such compromise impossible, and politically they were right. From the military point of view the attack on Goose Green was unnecessary. The real task was to expand the bridgehead, build up supplies and, when 5 Brigade arrived, thrust hard and directly for Stanley, but the battle fought by the 2nd Battalion, The Parachute Regiment at Goose Green on

28 May 1982 was one of the memorable engagements of the Falklands War.

Major Philip Neame was the OC of 'D' Company, 2 Para at Goose Green:

> The attack on Goose Green originated as a raid, not as an all-out attack to take the place and hold it. The proposal to raid Goose Green was on and off two or three times before we actually went in and in that time the plan seemed to change. We also began to get a better idea of what Argentine forces were there. In the beginning, from SAS patrol reports, we had the idea that the garrison of Goose Green was two or three hundred, a couple of companies, just about right for a good battalion shove. By the time we attacked, this estimate had grown and we thought there were maybe six or seven hundred there, say the best part of a battalion, which was not so good. In the event there were nearly twice that many.

The settlement and airfield at Goose Green lies on a small peninsula, about 2 km wide, and some 8 km long from the battalion 'Start Line'. About half-way to the objective, the airfield at Goose Green, a low rise spanned the peninsula between another settlement, Darwin, and a ruined cottage called Boca House. This feature, known as the Darwin Hill, contained the main Argentine defences. More troops were dug in behind Darwin Hill, defending the airfield, with others billeted in the houses or the schoolhouse. There were also a number of minefields and some outlying defensive positions. Goose Green was defended in depth and the open ground around the airfield gave the defenders a clear field of fire. 2 Para therefore elected for a night attack and Colonel 'H' Jones, 2 Para's CO, allocated six hours for his battalion to advance from the 'Start Line', penetrate the Argentine lines and be inside Goose Green. After six hours it would be broad daylight and unless this aim was achieved his battalion would be fully exposed on open ground.

Major Neame:

> Some people, especially those who were not there or have not seen the ground, have commented that the plan was unimaginative, bashing down the centre of the isthmus into the settlement, but

if you look at the map you will see that the options are limited. There is precious little room for manoeuvre. What we could have done with was some effective artillery support, and the light tanks of the Blues and Royals, which we had later on Wireless Ridge. With that we would have walked it. As it was, well . . .

We had not fought the Argentines and we had no idea what they would do, but the thought was that if we gave them a good clout they would fold. 'H' (Lt.-Colonel H. Jones), our CO, had got the battalion into the frame of mind that they could do anything and the odds did not come into it, so we thought that if we hit the Argies hard they would collapse. 'H' had inspired that battalion; if we had had up to fifty per cent casualties, the rest would still have gone on. It may be that during the battle he got too close to the action to really see what was going on across the entire area, but such was the man.

When 2 Para attacked on 28 May the garrison of Goose Green made up of about five hundred infantry soldiers in three companies from two different Argentine regiments, and about a thousand Argentine Air Force personnel. The airmen took little part in the fighting and stayed under cover while the battle went on. For support the soldiers had three 105mm Italian pack howitzers and a number of 30mm heavy machine-guns, intended for air defence but equally effective against attacking infantry. Even if most of the Argentine forces were not involved in the battle, the advantage still lay with the defenders; the usual attacker-to-defender ratio should be about 3:1 and it was obvious from the start that Goose Green would be a hard nut to crack.

Philip Neame:

D Company was sent to secure Camilla Creek as the assembly area for the attack, and the rest of the battalion joined us there after a 20K bash from our position on Sussex Mountain, near San Carlos. When we went up it was still a 'raid' but when the battalion arrived it had become an attack, to take and hold Goose Green. It was a chilly night and we were on 'light scales', which meant no comforts like sleeping bags. Each man was carrying between 80 and 130lbs when we moved off for the attack.

The plan was for a six-phase attack but since that didn't happen we need not waste too much time on it. H-Hour was at 0330 hrs local time and as we crossed the Start Line, from the left we were 'A', 'C' and 'B' Company, followed by 'H's' Tactical HQ and with my 'D' Company in reserve. 'A' Company attacked Burntside House just beyond the Start Line and then moved up the left flank along the shore towards Darwin. The rest of us came on a bit later and pushed on until we were driven a bit off track by a minefield . . . and that is when things started to go awry. If what happened after that sounds confusing, well, battle, and especially a night battle, is confusing.

'A's' attack went in OK but 'B' met resistance on the right flank. It was very dark and they got scattered as the various Sections found enemy trenches and positions and started to deal with them. We had overshot the Start Line and I found that my Company was actually ahead of Colonel 'H's' Tac-HQ. He took that as a personal insult and went charging off up the track. We seemed to have nothing to our front and I wanted to push on but was told to wait. Then we started getting fire from the right flank, from the 'B' Company area.

Anyway, we attacked this position. We had no idea how big it was, but heavy machine-guns were firing at us from the right flank and it got pretty chaotic. We were concerned that we would hit 'B' if we returned fire; we had a platoon pinned down and another one had vanished into the dark to take on some enemy position. In fact, just like 'B', my Sections were being pulled in all directions, seeking out the enemy. Remember it was very dark, low cloud . . . a nightmare. In the end I put up flares to indicate where I was and we eventually overcame the opposition, but we had lost two men killed and two missing. We now had to reorganise and get on.

It took 'B' about an hour to reorganise and us about the same; round-up the blokes, sort out who was who and where everyone was . . . and I began to realise that 'H's' time-and-space allocation, those precious six hours to get under cover before daylight, was going out the window. We were not doing a 'phased attack', we were doing an 'advance to contact', pushing on in the dark until we bumped something, sorting it out and then sorting ourselves out, and pushing on again. It works but it takes time. We were not getting artillery support and were very much on our own.

'H' told us to move ahead of 'B' Company, but it is fair to say that at about this time, two hours into the advance, chaos was reigning. Most of this was due to the dark and the nature of the ground;

there was no cause for concern over the battle, as the resistance was not excessive but we were beginning to slip behind on the timings which were seen to be hopelessly optimistic. Six phases in six hours was simply not on and it got worse, for dawn and the main Darwin Hill defences arrived at about the same time.

The situation now was that 'B' Company were moving up to attack the Boca House position on the right flank; this was on the crest of the hill, such as it is. Boca House itself is a ruin in the lower ground behind. 'A' Company, with only two platoons up, had run into tough opposition on the left and come to a complete stop. 'H' was now up with 'A' Company on the Darwin Hill, where a number of people had been killed, trying to sort things out. I was listening to all this on the battalion net. Then Argentine artillery started to range on us and I lost another soldier here, Private Meakin, so I moved the Company forward into the lee of the hill.

From this position I could see the coast to my right, and we saw Argentine survivors from the 'B' Company attack on Boca House slipping along the shore. They were in dead ground and getting away, though we fired at them. What they could do, we could do, and outflank Darwin Hill at the same time, so I asked 'H' for permission to move but he was still busy on Darwin Hill and told me to stay put. It was clearly going to be a long day, so I told the 'Toms' to get some food inside them and a brew on. My porridge was just starting to bubble when I heard on the battalion net that 'H' had been killed.

How did we react? Well, I don't think we were surprised. Given the way he was, it was almost to be expected. We certainly were not dismayed. We had now lost five men in 'D' Company, including three killed, so we took it in our stride and got on with it. Tony Rice, of the Royal Artillery, was at 'H's' Tac-HQ and he took over for the brief while it took Major Chris Keeble, the Second-in-Command, to come up and take over. I never got my porridge. We were ordered forward to join 'B' Company and take Boca House, and suddenly we were moving again.

We hit the Boca House position with machine-guns and Milans and suddenly they were putting white flags out. We got there along the shoreline and there was another pause there we used to re-supply with ammo. Then it was time to get up and move on; I was about to be noble and lead the advance on Boca when

Corporal Harley said, 'You are too valuable, Sir. I'll lead the advance . . . from that moment I have always had a soft spot for Corporal Harley. Anyway, we overran the Boca House position. It had been a Company position and there were about forty Argentines still in it when we went in; twelve dead and the rest wounded or dismayed.

From Boca we could see right across the airfield to the Goose Green settlement, and it was an amazing sight. There were about fifty Argentine soldiers running hell-for-leather back towards the settlement, led by an officer riding on a tractor; it was something straight out of *Monty Python*! It was now about mid-day, or late morning and the main Argentine position had collapsed, so 'A' and 'C' Companies were now coming forward from Darwin.

2 Para had done a great deal but they had lost their commanding officer, Lt.-Colonel 'H' Jones, killed attacking a machine-gun post on Darwin Hill. A number of other men had been killed or wounded and there was still a great deal left to do. The Argentine defenders had meanwhile received reinforcements. About the time the Darwin Hill position collapsed, a weak company of infantry in eleven helicopters were flown into the Goose Green settlement. More were to arrive later. In the late afternoon a further one hundred and fifty troops arrived, also by helicopter, having been collected from the Argentine strategic reserve force on Mount Kent. This latter force arrived just in time to be taken prisoner by 2 Para.

Major Philip Neame again:

The trick, now that we had them on the run, was to keep the pressure on, but there was the old problem of reorganising after an attack. I only had two platoons up. I had left 10 Platoon on Darwin Hill to mop up, under the Company 2 I/C, and the machine-guns had not yet arrived from the beach; I had about fifty blokes with me but that would have to do, so we took off across the airfield after the Argentines.

We were about a third of the way across the airfield when we saw some trenches and tentage away to our right. I sent 12 Platoon across to investigate and pressed on with the rest towards the schoolhouse. Then Chris Keeble came on the air and told me to do exactly what I was doing, to press on. There was a minefield to our front, a very obvious one, and that pushed us away to our left, towards the schoolhouse with the last platoon, 11 Platoon. About this time we were joined by the Recce Platoon and the Patrol Platoon from 'C' Company. They had been shelled on Darwin Hill and were a bit shaken and under no particular command. We slammed some 66-rocket rounds into the schoolhouse; or rather we tried to. It took four attempts before we got a hit and by that time we were in hysterics, falling about with laughter after every miss, cheering the eventual hit.

Then I got the bad news and I sent Chris Waddington's 11 Platoon to circle the schoolhouse and take it while I headed back to the centre. The news was that Jim Barry of 12 Platoon had seen white flags at the tentage, the 'Flagpole Position', and had decided to go up and take the surrender. We were busy at the schoolhouse and by the time I got back to tell him not to go, or to be bloody careful, he had taken a section of men and advanced towards the Argentine lines. Well, for some reason, they opened up on him.

Jim and two NCOs were killed and several more men were wounded. I didn't think then – and I don't think now – that it was a false surrender to lure my blokes into the open. There was a lot of firing and machine-gunning going on, and I think the Argentine soldiers got confused. Neither is it true that afterwards the Argentine defenders at the Flagpole or at the schoolhouse were massacred in revenge. In fact, throughout the entire campaign my men were extremely good to Argentine prisoners and the wounded, as front line soldiers usually are.

By the time I got to 12 Platoon, the Platoon Sergeant, Sergeant Meredith, had neutralised the Flagpole Position, by firing into it and setting off a bomb dump inside the Argentine lines. He had also extracted the bodies and the wounded. My reaction was, 'Then why aren't you going forward?' To which Meredith replied, 'I would not go any further forward than this.'

Since heavy small-arms fire was coming towards us from Goose Green, he was probably right. Anyway, we were scattered and I needed to regroup the Company before we went any further but meanwhile Chris Waddington had stormed through the schoolhouse with grenades, setting it alight:

It was now about three o'clock in the afternoon, we had been on the go for twelve solid hours and were feeling pretty tired.

I started mustering the lads and finding out where the rest of the battalion were. They were consolidating on Darwin Hill and 'D' took about an hour to reorganise near the Flagpole position, while being harassed by some 'Triple-A' fire from guns beyond Goose Green. Keeble told me he had ordered in an air strike and we awaited the Harriers blasting the 'Triple-A' before we moved.

We heard the sound of jet engines and were looking up for the Harriers when an Argentine Aeromacchi appeared and came diving in on us. It was like the movies; we were all standing or sitting about in the open, there was no cover, lights were flashing along his wings, cannon fire was stitching up the turf and coming right towards us . . . and somehow he missed the lot of us . . . a bloody miracle.

The next thing was a Pucara aircraft which whistled over us and dropped napalm. We opened up with everything we had and we hit him; the pilot ejected, landed nearby and we picked him up. He looked pretty apprehensive, for troops are always supposed to be eager to meet any ground attack pilot who has dropped napalm on them, but we were not hurt and we sent him back to San Carlos that night, undamaged.

It was getting dark and Chris Keeble came on the air again and told me to go firm where I was as 'other things were afoot'. We spent the night huddled together in a minefield; the mines were poorly laid and you could see them. We were fully exposed to a counter-attack but I was not worried. Somehow I knew that the fight was over.

Word soon came that the formal surrender of Goose Green would be at dawn. So at dawn we were all sitting up on a bit of high ground and we watched the Argentine troops coming out of Goose Green, hundreds and hundreds of them. It is a good job they jacked it in when they did; we were all knackered, down to our last few rounds of ammunition and right out of food.

What do I remember most? I remember that bloke on the tractor . . . hilarious. I also remember that we had fifteen killed and eighteen wounded at Goose Green, and I remember watching one of my men die in front of me. That is a fragile moment that sticks in my mind. I'll always remember that.

Goose Green may have been an unnecessary battle but it was a famous victory and useful politically, which was the object of the attack in the first place. After Goose Green there was no more talk of a negotiated settlement or intervention by the United Nations. The Falklands War would be fought to a finish and no one on the British side had any doubt who would win it.

The Argentines lost around forty dead and one hundred injured at Goose Green and fifteen hundred Argentine soldiers or airmen were taken prisoner. It cost 2 Para fifteen men killed, including their Commanding Officer, Lt.-Colonel H. Jones. About thirty-five parachute soldiers were wounded. Lt.-Colonel Jones was later awarded a posthumous VC and a large number of his soldiers were decorated.

As the dead of Goose Green were being buried on the battlefield, Major General Jeremy Moore arrived to take command of all the landing forces. The other new arrival at San Carlos was Brigadier Tony Wilson's 5 Brigade, consisting of the 1st Battalion Welsh Guards, the 2nd Battalion Scots Guards and the 1/7th Gurkha Rifles. General Moore agreed with Brigadier Thompson's plan for a rapid advance on Stanley via Mount Kent and ordered this advance to begin. 5 Brigade were promptly committed to the advance on Stanley, leaving 40 Commando behind to guard the beachhead. The Marines of 40 Commando were not at all happy about this.

'I was not happy either,' says Brigadier Julian Thompson: '40 Commando was a damned fine unit and I wanted them up front with my Brigade. I had sent them out before the order arrived but was told to bring them back, but if I had known they were to be left behind I would have got them committed somehow. 40 Commando were not left out of the later fighting for two Companies were later attached to the Welsh Guards and the Heavy Weapons platoons went up to support other units in the battles around Stanley.'

Major General Jeremy Moore had always intended to use 5 Brigade in the advance but acknowledges that there were some worries about the fitness and training of the Guards battalions: 'They were short of recent field training but every man wanted to be there at the front, and you cannot imagine the pressure the Brigade of Guards can exert.'

The pressure of the Brigade of Guards must have been considerable, for the fit and formidable 1/7th Gurkhas, whose very presence in the islands worried the Argentine troops, were tasked with garrisoning Goose Green and took little further part in the Falklands War. So began the 'Great Yomp' – the march on Stanley – for the shortage of helicopters meant that if the troops were to reach Stanley they must do it on foot.

45 Commando led the advance from the beachhead, crossing Ajax Bay to Port San Carlos in landing craft, then passing through 3 Para's positions and covering fourteen miles across the boggy, tussocky ground before nightfall. The march went on until the following morning, when 45 marched into Teal Inlet. There they met up with 3 Para, which had arrived by a slightly shorter route.

Colonel Whitehead: 'The word "yomp" is the surviving catchword from the South Atlantic campaign. Each marine was carrying about 120 lbs with all his kit and ammunition and we yomped first to Douglas Settlement over murderous ground. On the first day we stopped an hour before dark and cooked a meal, then marched across country on a compass bearing until 2 am. 45 marched every step of the way from the beachhead to Stanley – about fifty miles . . . and we took Two Sisters Mountain on the way.'

Ahead of the advancing troops lay the first major obstacle, the snugly-entrenched and well defended Argentine positions on the 1,500 foot high slopes of Mount Kent, sixteen miles from Teal Inlet, twelve miles west of Stanley. The task of taking this position was given to 42 Commando on the night of 29 May.

Three Sea Kings collected K Company of 42 from San Carlos and tried to fly them forward the forty miles to Mount Kent, but were forced to turn back by blizzards. On the following night they tried again, taking 'K' Company, Commando TAC-HQ, and the Mortar Troop. 'K' Company advanced on Mount Kent and found it deserted, and so on the following night more of 42 arrived, accompanied by artillery, and dug in on Mount Kent, where they waited for more stores, ammunition and men to join them before the next phase of the advance, on Mount Harriet, Longdon and Two Sisters, the first line of hills surrounding Stanley.

As a prelude to this, 3 Para moved up to two small peaks, Mount Estancia and Mount Vernet, and Julian Thompson moved his Brigade HQ up to Teal Inlet. All was set for the major push on Stanley, but before that could happen, disaster struck the Welsh Guards at Fitzroy.

19

The Battles for Stanley: June, 1982

'A calculated risk, plus luck, is not the same as foolhardiness, plus luck. "Getting away with it", does not validate the original decision, for future strategies could be based on delusions and the second time they may not work.'

Ewen Southby-Tailyour, *Reasons in Writing*, 1993.

The loss of the *Sir Galahad* and the death of many Welsh Guardsmen was one of the most tragic events in the Falklands War, a classic example of how a series of actions, each taken with the best of intentions, can lead to tragedy.

The story of the Fitzroy disaster begins on the afternoon of 2 June, when a small party of 2 Para, now back under command of 5 Brigade, was sent forward by helicopter to Swan Inlet House, a position half-way between Goose Green and Fitzroy. At Swan Inlet Major John Crossland of 'B' Company phoned Fitzroy and was told that the Argentines there and at Bluff Cove had pulled out. That day 5 Brigade happened to have six helicopters available, including a Chinook, and Brigadier Wilson decided to rush 2 Para forward. By the morning of 3 June, this parachute battalion was in position around Fitzroy and Bluff Cove settlement.

Unfortunately, no one had told the Force Commander, Major General Jeremy Moore, about this move. 2 Para's actions therefore caused certain problems, not least that it put 2 Para about thirty miles ahead of the rest of the Force and totally without support or supply unless it was sent up by the ever-scarce helicopters. If the Argentine forces were to turn on 2 Para, their future might become uncertain so moves were rapidly put in hand to send up support from the rest of 5 Brigade.

The balance of 2 Para went up, also by helicopter, but it was decided to send the rest of 5 Brigade, the Welsh and Scots Guards, up to Fitzroy and Bluff Cove by sea. This posed the problem of providing the ships with air cover and adequate anti-aircraft protection during the unloading phase. The big ships, HMSs *Fearless* and *Intrepid* were valuable craft, so it was decided that they would only take the battalions half-way by night, returning to the protection of the San Carlos defences before dawn, while the men were sent on to Bluff Cove, seven hours sailing away, in the smaller LCUs. The LCUs were commanded in this task by Major Ewen Southby-Tailyour.

The Scots Guards went up, half-way on *Intrepid* and then on to Bluff Cove in Southby-Tailyour's four LCUs on the night of 5/6 June, enduring a very rough passage before the men got ashore. With the bedraggled Scots Guards now safely delivered to Bluff Cove, Major Southby-Tailyour turned his attention to the next phase, bringing up the 2nd Bn. Welsh Guards from San Carlos.

The basic problem of shipping the men up in different craft was compounded, as we shall see, by the reluctance of certain Army officers to understand, or at least accept from an informed source, the basics of 'amphibiosity', the gentle art of getting troops ashore. A further problem was a shortage of LCUs. Everyone wanted the LCUs, because apart from helicopters and mexefloat rafts they were the only means of putting troops or heavy stores like ammunition, vehicles and the all important air defence systems ashore over open beaches. With that much established, let us now turn to Bluff Cove on the morning of 6 June.

Before leaving San Carlos with the Scots Guards, Southby-Tailyour had been told that the second phase of the plan would involve bringing his four *Intrepid* LCUs back out to sea on the following night for a rendezvous with the Welsh Guards on *HMS Fearless*. To save time, HMS *Fearless* would have her LCUs preloaded with the Welsh Guardsmen and heavy stores and the craft would, in effect, swap, the *Fearless* LCUs being launched for Bluff Cove, the empty *Intrepid* LCUs from Bluff Cove returning in *Fearless* to San Carlos, where they were sorely needed.

The weather at Bluff Cove and the sea state outside the anchorage was turning ever more foul that morning and Southby-Tailyour decided that he must return to San Carlos and sort matters out for the coming night's operations. He ordered his LCU coxwains to clean up and sit tight and went to find a helicopter. From that moment on it began to get very complicated and what follows should be taken slowly.

Before leaving the settlement he was approached by Major Chris Keeble from 2 Para who requested Southby-Tailyour's permission to use some of the LCUs to shift his troops and stores back to Fitzroy across Bluff Cove creek once the Scots Guards had taken over their positions. Since this was a simple task and kept his LCUs close to the anchorage, Southby-Tailyour agreed. That done, he flew back to San Carlos. At San Carlos, Southby-Tailyour was informed that the movement up of the Welsh Guards would go as planned. The Welsh Guards duly embarked on HMS *Fearless*, being ordered by Divisional HQ to land at Yellow Beach, Bluff Cove.

However, *Fearless* was to sail with only *two* of her four LCUs, the other two being retained at San Carlos to continue loading or unloading ships there. Also in San Carlos at that time was the LSL *Sir Galahad* loading ammunition, a Rapier anti-aircraft battery, and later a Field Ambulance, all urgently needed and bound for the 5 Brigade base at Fitzroy.

The Naval plan now was for HMS *Fearless* to rendezvous at sea with Southby-Tailyour's four *Intrepid* LCUs, put out her own two previously loaded LCUs and load the troops into two *Intrepid* LCUs. These four LCUs would then deliver the Welsh Guards to Bluff Cove and *Fearless* would take the two empty *Intrepid* LCUs back to San Carlos. This was a slight variation on the first plan but it kept things moving and everyone was happy.

It is important to understand this procedure and that, so far, no one had mentioned even the possibility of landing the Guards at Fitzroy. The Commanding Officer of the Welsh Guards – instructed by Divisional HQ – was convinced that their destination was Bluff Cove. So was Ewen Southby-Tailyour. However, Commodore Mike

Clapp, who, it will be recalled, controlled all shipping movements, had told the Captain of HMS *Fearless* that the LCUs' destination was Fitzroy. This variation in orders was to have a dire effect later. The troops were anxious to go by sea to Bluff Cove because they had heard that the bridge linking the two settlements of Bluff Cove and Fitzroy had been destroyed. This bridge had, in fact, been repaired and it was now possible to walk between the two settlements but the troops did not know that.

Southby-Tailyour then flew back in appalling weather to Bluff Cove. There he found one LCU riding out the storm off the entrance to the anchorage, and attempted to winch down on to it. When that proved impossible he had himself put down by the settlement, went to the anchorage . . . and found his other three LCUs were missing.

He sent a message back by helicopter to San Carlos telling COMAW that the weather was bad but that he expected it to moderate. He did not mention the missing craft, assuming that they had simpy gone off to find a sheltered anchorage and would soon be back. Only when it got dark did he began to radio around the Settlement, asking other units if they had seen the landing craft. By midnight, when he should have sailed for the RV, his landing craft were still missing.

This is what had happened. Shortly after Southby-Tailyour had left for San Carlos that morning, a Major from 2 Para had sent a wireless signal to the LCUs, instructing them to prepare for a movement from Bluff Cove to Fitzroy. This was not what had been agreed with Southby-Tailyour. The LCU coxwains had been told about shipping 2 Para stores across Bluff Creek, but were otherwise ordered to stay put.

The Corporal who took the first radio message therefore replied correctly, 'Wait-Out', while he sent for his cox'n, a Colour Sergeant. The Major promptly came on the air again saying, 'I want a fucking answer, not a "Wait-Out".'

Matters then deteriorated sharply. The Parachute Major descended on the LCUs and proceeded to throw his weight about. When the cox'ns proved reluctant to disobey their original orders and added that anyway they had no charts for the transit to Fitzroy, had not been up there before, and the weather, as anyone could see, was foul, it is alleged – and not denied

– that a pistol was produced and the order to put to sea repeated.

It is not likely that brandishing a pistol in their faces had any real effect on the LCU coxwains; it seems hardly possible that the pistol would have been used. Nevertheless, the NCOs were in a dilemma. There was no senior officer to whom they could appeal, and in the end, since they were Sergeants and this was a Major and orders are orders, the coxwains took their craft to Fitzroy. Once at Fitzroy they were stormbound and unable to return.

Once again, 2 Para had taken the initiative but the effects of this one were to recoil on the Welsh Guards. It should also be remembered that radio communications between Fitzroy and San Carlos were non-existent – which is why Southby-Tailyour had to fly back there in the first place and send messages by helicopter. No one at San Carlos knew that the landing craft were missing and *Fearless* was meanwhile heading for the rendezvous.

Having no craft, Southby-Tailyour could not make the rendezvous that night and *Fearless* had only two loaded LCUs. *Fearless* duly arrived at the rendezvous at 0200 hrs but was unable to unload all her troops. HMS *Fearless* waited two hours at the rendezvous and then sent the two preloaded craft off to Bluff Cove before returning to San Carlos with the other half of the battalion, three hundred and fifty very disgruntled men of the 2nd Welsh Guards.

Guided by Major Tony Todd of the RCT, the two *Fearless* LCUs reached Bluff Cove shortly after dawn. There now remained the problem of shifting up the remainder of the Welsh Guards, now back at San Carlos. As Southby-Tailyour pointed out, 'We have got away with it for two nights running, but a third night approach might be pushing our luck.' Southby-Tailyour then embarked in one of the *Fearless* LCUs and sailed round to Fitzroy where he found his missing craft and heard what had happened. He was not best pleased, but this was no time for recriminations. The LSL *Sir Tristram* had arrived at Fitzroy full of ammunition and had to be unloaded. For this task Southby-Tailyour now had six LCUs, but orders soon arrived calling the four *Intrepid* LCUs back to San Carlos that night.

These craft duly sailed, and that night Ewen Southby-Tailyour lost another of his precious LCUs, 'Foxtrot 4', sent off to Darwin to collect 5 Brigade's radio equipment. This reduced his fleet to one vessel but with the unloading underway on *Sir Tristram* Southby-Tailyour turned in for a few hours sleep. At dawn he was up again, and coming up on deck saw, much to his surprise, the LSL *Sir Galahad* moored 200m away. More than that, he saw that the *Sir Galahad* was crammed with troops. The Welsh Guards had finally made it from San Carlos . . . but not to Bluff Cove.

It will be recalled that when the Welsh Guards returned to San Carlos, having failed to make a rendezvous with the missing LCUs, the *Sir Galahad* was there, loading No. 16 Field Ambulance and some Rapier missile launchers for Fitzroy. There was space available on *Sir Galahad* and it was therefore decided to put both Welsh Guards Companies on board and send them up, though the Company officers were not told that the ship was sailing for Fitzroy. These officers were therefore less than pleased to discover when the ship dropped anchor, that they were some distance from their final destination. With the two ships and the Welsh Guards at Fitzroy, all the elements for the *Sir Galahad* tragedy were now in place.

The departure of 'Foxrot 4' for Darwin had reduced the unloading capacity at Fitzroy to one LCU – 'Foxtrot 1' – and one mexefloat raft, plus the Sea King brought up on *Sir Galahad*. It was immediately obvious that it would take time to finish unloading *Sir Tristram* and unload whatever stores and equipment were on board *Sir Galahad*.

With dawn breaking over a calm sea and the possibility of Argentine air attacks growing by the minute, Southby-Tailyour hurried over to the *Sir Galahad*, his aim now to get the soldiers on board ashore to the comparative safety of the beach. This is not hindsight. Southby-Tailyour's diary notes, scribbled that morning, say: '*Not sure what we can unload Sir G with but whatever we do I think these ships are in grave danger.*'

On board the *Sir Galahad* he found soldiers milling about everywhere and was soon accosted by two Majors from the Welsh Guards, who asked him who was in charge of unloading the ships. This was actually Major Tony Todd, who was on the COMAW's Staff, but Southby-Tailyour was the man on the spot. Keeping to the approved chain of command, he explained to the officers that if they told Major Todd what they wanted he, Southby-Tailyour, would see what he could do. They replied that they wanted to go to Bluff Cove, by sea, at once.

'No one is going to Bluff Cove today, unless they walk,' said Southby-Tailyour, 'but the stores can be unloaded here just as soon as we finish unloading *Sir Tristram*.' He also suggested that if the Guards were prepared to wait until the LCU had finished the unloading tasks, he would run them round to Bluff Cove that night. Otherwise they could walk round to Bluff Cove over the now repaired bridge, but either way they must get off the ship NOW. The Guards officers refused. They wanted to go, by sea, to Bluff Cove and they wanted to go now, in the *Sir Galahad*.

'You can't,' said Southby-Tailyour patiently, 'there is no place to beach the *Sir Galahad* at Bluff Cove. We cannot put your men and stores ashore there without either landing craft or helicopters and the only two we have are needed here. We cannot sail to Bluff Cove in daylight anyway, as we would be passing right under the Argentine OPs.'

This explanation did not please the Guards officers. They had been told they were going to Bluff Cove in the *Sir Galahad* and instead they had been taken to Fitzroy. Now they were being told they must get off and walk. How were they to even get ashore? Southby-Tailyour pointed out the mexefloat raft and his remaining LCU and said, 'In those.'

'That is not acceptable,' said the officers. 'They are loaded with ammunition.'

'So is this ship,' pointed out Southby-Tailyour.

The Guards officers still refused to budge. They and their men would stay on the *Sir Galahad* and the ship could take them to Bluff Cove that night. Southby-Tailyour told them that if he took them anywhere that night it would be from off the beach; they HAD to go ashore. Major Tony Todd, who was on *Sir Galahad* at this time backed up everything Southby-Tailyour said but the Guards officers remained unconvinced. It is not hard to sympathise with these officers. All they wanted was to rejoin their battalion, but they had had been severely mucked about in recent days. They had had *enough*.

Also, as Julian Thompson points out: 'They had not experienced those five days of air attack at San Carlos, when ships were being attacked and bombed and sunk. Anyone who had been through that would have swum ashore rather than stay on board in daylight and risk air attack . . . and with every hour that passed the likelihood of air attack increased.

'By now it must have been obvious to the Argentine OPs that something was going on at Fitzroy. There were helicopters buzzing in and out, ship movements, the anchorage was under observation and there would have been a perceptible increase in radio traffic, if only from the ships and helicopters. The Argentines located my HQ through the radio traffic – and then bombed it – so no doubt they could do the same to 5 Brigade HQ.'

In the end, after much further argument, Southby-Tailyour gave the officers a direct order – to get their men off the ship. The Guards officers refused to accept the order, pointing out that they and Southby-Tailyour were of equal rank. Southby-Tailyour retorted that this was an amphibious matter and he urged them to take his advice if not his orders. They still refused.

Southby-Tailyour then went ashore and sought out Major Barnie Rolfe-Smith, a Staff Officer with 5 Brigade HQ. Southby-Tailyour told him what had happened and urged him to go on *Sir Galahad* and as the man responsible for getting 5 Brigade troops up, order the Welsh Guards off the ship at once. Later that day word reached Major Southby-Tailyour that the Guards were finally getting off but a further problem had now arisen and the Guards had left it just a little too late.

After the ammunition had been unloaded from *Sir Tristram*, the Lt.-Colonel in charge of 16 Field Ambulance stated that his unit must have priority over the Guards' disembarkation and he needed the services of 'Foxtrot One'. Getting his unit ashore took a full hour. Finally it was time to disembark the Welsh Guards but by then a further problem had arisen; the loading ramp on the landing craft had been damaged and could not be lowered to allow easy access for the troop baggage and heavy weapons. The troops were therefore kept on *Sir Galahad* while a crane was used to lower their heavy equipment into 'Foxtrot One'. This was still going on when, five full hours after the *Sir Galahad* had anchored at Fitzroy, Argentine aircraft swept in to the attack.

There were no anti-aircraft defences at Fitzroy, other than the Bofors and GP machine-guns on the two landing ships. The Rapier missile-launchers were ashore but had not yet been set up. The Rapiers that had already arrived were protecting Fitzroy settlement, not the landing area, and the Combat Air Patrol of two Harriers had gone off to engage a squadron of Argentine aircraft which had arrived over the islands and were seeking targets. Five of these aircraft had been vectored on to the Fitzroy ships by Argentine OPs on Mount Harriet and were racing in towards the anchorage.

The attack on Fitzroy therefore caught the defenders completely unawares as three of the aircraft attacked the *Sir Galahad* and two the *Sir Tristram*. Fortunately the ammunition on the *Sir Tristram* had been unloaded and the two bombs which hit that ship did little damage, though killing two Chinese seamen.

The three bombs that hit the *Sir Galahad* had a far more devastating effect. One bomb hit the officers' quarters killing one of the engineers; another hit the engine room, killing another Chinese crewman; the last bomb exploded on the tank deck, which was full of Guardsmen waiting to disembark. There were twenty tons of ammunition on this deck and a large quantity of petrol. Apart from the effects of the blast, much of the ammunition and petrol ignited, turning the tank deck into an inferno. Forty-eight men died in the bomb blast, thirty-two of them from the Welsh Guards; at least another one hundred and fifty were terribly burned in the fire which followed.

The order was given to 'Abandon Ship!' and within minutes men, many of them injured or supporting their injured comrades, were swarming down the scrambling nets. Helicopters from 825 and 846 Squadrons came out to help, quickly joined by helicopters from 847 and 656 Squadrons, and the cox'n of 'Foxtrot One' manoeuvred his craft alongside and took off survivors, the LCU's sides scorched by the heat. Other men scrambled on to the Mexefloat pontoon. On shore the men of 16 Field Ambulance and 2 Para found a stream of injured Guardsmen needing urgent attention, mostly for burns. Nearly one hundred and sixty casualties were flown out to the hospital ship *Uganda* later that day.

Like the battle at Goose Green, the Fitzroy disaster caused a great deal of anguish and in some quarters at least, the wish to apportion blame, but a series of events combined to cause this tragedy. The reluctance of weary troops to get off the *Sir Galahad* was perhaps the main cause but as one Royal Marine officer pointed out later, 'It's all a matter of experience. You or I or anyone with a knowledge of amphibious warfare would have got off that ship at any price and sprinted up the beach into cover; unfortunately, "amphibiosity" is not much needed on the North German plain.'

While the *Sir Galahad* tragedy was being digested in London and at San Carlos, plans were going ahead for the advance to the hills around Stanley. Reconnaissance teams and fighting patrols went out to observe the ground and harass the enemy and one possible threat was eliminated when twenty men of the Royal Marines Arctic and Mountain Warfare Cadre were lifted forward to attack a party of Argentine troops at Top Malo House, south of Teal Inlet, where they killed five Argentine soldiers and took twelve prisoners. Meanwhile 3 Para, 42 and 45 Commando continued to ease up on Stanley, until they were up against the Argentine perimeter on the hills around the town. All this was achieved within one week of 3 Commando Brigade leaving the beachhead at San Carlos.

Andrew Tubb of 45's Recce Troop went on several of these recce patrols, penetrating the Argentine positions on Two Sisters:

The Falklands terrain is like a harsh Dartmoor, or the Scottish Highlands, no trees, lots of long 'stone-runs' covered with moss, very slippery ... the weather was sunny to start with, crisp autumn-like, but always a wind. It never stopped blowing and then the rains came and stayed.

We were tasked for a twenty-six-man patrol to the Stanley side of Two Sisters ... saw five Argentines and called in artillery fire. We were actually inside the Argentine positions at the time, so we ended up shelling ourselves. On that first time we 'pepper-potted' – ran back singly or in small groups – for about four hundred metres to get out through the Argentine lines, firing 66-rockets to fight through and re-group. It took us well over an hour to get away but it seemed like a few minutes. We killed seventeen of them, and all we had was one bloke with a flesh wound. Then we had a seventeen kilometre march back to our own lines. Colonel Whitehead said he got a lot of information out of these patrols. He would always listen to what his Marines had to say and alter his plans accordingly. When the attack went in on Two Sisters the Colonel was right up there with us, just behind the leading Company.

Lt.-Colonel Whitehead: 'Our orders were to take Two Sisters by a two-phase, two-pronged attack with a "silent" approach. In other words, we had artillery support but they didn't fire until I said so – they altered the range, kept to a timed fire plan, did everything but pull the lever that fires the shell, while we worked our way up and got as close as we could to the enemy positions . . . and so we moved out towards Stanley.'

The Argentine forces defending the hills around Stanley still numbered between eight and nine thousand men, of whom about five thousand were infantry. They had had plenty of time to dig in and had surrounded their positions with mines. They had good night-sights and made excellent use of an abundance of heavy machine-guns. On the other hand their supply arrangements were poor, with very few rations getting forward to the troops in the trenches. Even so, the Argentine soldiers were still ready to fight.

General Jeremy Moore now had four front-line units ready for the Port Stanley battle, and three more close behind. To the south, in front of Bluff Cove, were the 2nd Bn., Scots Guards of 5 Brigade while to the north lay the units of 3 Commando Brigade. On the right flank, facing Mount Wall and Mount Harriet was 42 Commando. They were opposed by troops of the 4th Argentine Infantry Regiment. In the centre, 45 Commando faced Two Sisters, another 4th Regiment position, while on the left flank, 3 Para faced Mount Longdon, held by part of the 7th Infantry Regiment.

Close behind were the 1/7th Gurkhas, of 5 Brigade, and 2 Para. This last battalion was now in reserve but back under command of Thompson's 3 Commando Brigade. Also in reserve was 1st Bn., Welsh Guards, which had two companies of 40 Commando attached to make up the losses sustained on the *Sir Galahad*. The Argentine positions lay across a long strip of No-Man's-Land which varied in width from five miles in the north to two miles in the south. British patrols went out across No-Man's-Land into these positions every night, and suffered several casualties from mines.

General Moore's plan for the assault on the defences of Stanley called for a two-phase attack over two nights. 3 Commando Brigade were to attack Harriet, Longdon and Two Sisters on the first night, 11/12 June. On the next night, 12/13 June, the Scots Guards and 2 Para were to take Tumbledown, Wireless Ridge and the Gurkhas would take Mount William. If the Argentines continued to fight, then Sapper Hill, only a mile south of Stanley would be attacked on the third night. All these attacks were supported by artillery and naval gunfire.

The assault was begun by 3 Para, attacking Mount Longdon, which they took for the loss of eighteen men, including Sergeant Ian McKay, who won a posthumous VC for his gallantry during the action.

45 Commando moved against their objective, Two Sisters, south-west of Mount Longdon, at 2300 hrs local time, aiming to put in a two-phased attack on the Argentine positions. This attack was delayed because 'X' Company, which had to put in a flanking attack on the southern peak of Two Sisters, was seriously delayed by the rough going to their start line and the weight of their equipment. Lt.-Colonel Whitehead took advantage of this delay to order the two companies detailed for the attack on the northern summit, 'Y' and 'Z', to work their way forward. These two companies had advanced to within three hundred metres of the Argentine position before they were spotted and came under fire, at which moment 'X' Company attacked the southern feature. In the event the three rifle companies of 45 Commando attacked Two Sisters together.

A fire-fight below the northern crest caught the forward Troops of 'Z' Company out in the open, and they were soon under heavy fire. Lt. Dytor's 8 Troop of 'Z' Company then rose and charged the Argentine positions, with the rest of 'Z' following close behind, and 'Y' Company swinging in to take the southern edge of the northern feature. Meanwhile 'X' Company's Rifle Troops came leap-frogging up the steep southern slope. 45 took Two Sisters for the loss of four men killed and eight injured, killing, wounding or capturing a large number of Argentine soldiers.

Captain Gardiner of 'X' Company again:

> Taking Two Sisters was like fighting in a ruined city, set on a steep slope. What went wrong? Well, we got lost, that was one problem – then the men were carrying 80 lb each at least, and some had Milan rockets as well – we had 40 Commando's Anti-Tank Troop along. We were almost two hours late so eventually I broke radio silence and told the Colonel what had happened. He was marvellous about it; he said, 'Get in position, sort yourselves out, and then we'll go,' . . . and that's what we did.

'X' Company was to take three successive ridges on the south peak, so I put the Troops in one after the other to leapfrog up the hill; 1 Troop first, then 3, then 2. I stayed with my Tac-HQ, just behind the leading Troop. Lt. James Kelly's 1 Troop took the first objective unopposed – not a shot fired, so in went 3 Troop, Lt. Steward. They also took their objective unopposed – as they thought. In fact, they had only taken two-thirds of it, an easy mistake to make in the dark on that broken ground. Steward came on the radio and had just said, 'I've got into the position unopposed, shall I press on . . .?' when he ran into fire.

2 Troop were held up, so I said, 'Right, we'll withdraw you fifty yards and call in some artillery.' We could see a real ding-dong battle going on at Harriet, and the other 45 Companies were engaged ahead, so there wasn't enough artillery to go round, so what else? . . . mortars! I called for mortars. The mortars got off half-a-dozen rounds but on that boggy ground their baseplates and barrels sunk halfway into the ground. So, no mortars . . . Milans . . . right! I called up Lt. Steve Hughes with 40's Anti-Tank Troop. 'Can you see where I am?' He was two thousand yards away – and I also flashed a torch and they fired four or five rounds over our heads, which went off with a hell of a bang. Then Stewart and his 2 Troop went up the hill like banshees out of hell. The front was very narrow, only three or four men wide with no room to deploy, so the weight was on the Corporals and Marines, not on me.

2 Troop cleared their objective and we had one man wounded. We killed seven of the enemy and the rest legged it. I went up the hill and found 2 Troop eating Argentine rations and rooting around in their stores. When I looked back down that long, steep ridge, a massive objective over a thousand yards long, I could hardly believe it. We stayed up there for the next twenty-four to thirty-six hours and watched the Scots Guards take Tumbledown – they took a hell of a long time about it.

While 3 Para and 45 were tackling Longdon and Two Sisters, 42 Commando were attacking the Commando Brigade's final objective for that night, Mount Harriet. This was considered the most difficult task of the three, not least because the Argentine position was heavily protected by minefields. The CO of 42, Lt.-Colonel Nick Vaux, had sent several patrols to reconnoitre Mount Harriet, and they had finally found a relatively mine-free route to the south side of the mountain.

Lt.-Colonel Vaux therefore decided to attack the Argentine positions from the flank and rear, sending his rifle companies swinging on a four-mile approach march around the minefields, hoping their advance would not be detected. To achieve this, they would need to swing into 5 Brigade's area, and it was therefore agreed that their 'Start Line' for the attack should be secured by the Welsh Guards. While 42 were marching south, artillery fire would provide a diversion by falling on the western slopes of Mount Harriet. When 42 arrived at their Start Line they were less than amused to find the Welsh Guards Recce Platoon sitting behind a fence, chatting and smoking. Hard words were said and then the attack went in.

Nos. 2 and 3 Troops of 'K' Company, 42 Commando, led the attack up the south-eastern side of Harriet and were already among the Argentines before they were detected. Firing then broke out everywhere and in all directions as 'K' Company swept ahead, clearing enemy trenches and mortar pits, pushing their way up the mountain to the first dip, working their way forward in small groups, using Milan anti-tank missiles against heavy machine-gun posts. The forward troops of 'K' then crossed the saddle and took the forward slopes of the far ridge before 'I' Company came up to carry on the assault up the eastern slope. Here they met with considerable opposition from snipers and machine-gun posts.

One particularly persistent sniper was finally silenced by a direct hit from a Milan rocket, and after one last skirmish on the top of the feature, the Argentine resistance collapsed. 42 Commando took Mount Harriet after an eight-hour battle, at a cost of only one man killed and twenty wounded. Twenty-five Argentine soldiers died in the assault on Mount Harriet and 42 took over three hundred prisoners.

Brigadier Julian Thompson: '42's battle for Harriet was a real Commando battle. They infiltrated the Argentine positions and just rolled them up. 42 took more prisoners than they mustered in their assault companies – a real crafty, cunning attack, with all the Commando elements – quite brilliant.' It is some indication of the role played by junior NCOs in this battle that all three 'K' Company Corporals were awarded the Military Medal.

3 Commando Brigade had now pushed a hole in the defences

surrounding Stanley. The Marines and Paras were able to spend the following day removing Argentine casualties and consolidating their positions on those three features, because the follow-up attack, on the night of 12/13 June had to be postponed as the Scots Guards and Gurkhas had had insufficient time to recce their tasks. On the following night, 13/14 June, the Scots Guards attacked Tumbledown Mountain and took it after a fierce fight with the Argentine 5th Marines, which lasted almost until dawn. This delayed the planned Gurkhas' assault on Mount William, but 2 Para then attacked Wireless Ridge with naval gunfire and artillery support and took it for the loss of only one man killed and a handful wounded.

Major Philip Neame of 'D' Company, 2 Para takes up the story:

Let's go back a bit. After the battle we stayed about six days at Goose Green. During that time 5 Brigade arrived and we were attached to them, so that each Brigade now had four battalions. Tony Wilson, the Brigadier, came up to see us several times, and the 'Toms' were very amused that he always wore a different hat, one day a Greenjacket beret, next day an Army Air Corps helmet, next day a red Parachute beret. Come to think of it, they weren't very amused about that. Then we were sent forward in two helicopter lifts to Fitzroy and Bluff Cove but you know about that.

We were deployed on hills around Fitzroy and the first significant thing that happened there was shelling by a 155mm gun, which was a lot worse than shelling from a 105mm. We tended to work through 105mm fire but the 155mm had a real punch to it. The second thing was that the weather broke; it fairly teemed down for three or four days until we were like drowned rats and living in waterlogged trenches. The final thing was that our new CO, David Chaundler, arrived, fresh out from England.

We had now been put back under 3 Commando Brigade and were all very glad about that. Chaundler got off to a very good start by deciding that we were serving no useful purpose out on the hills and pulling us back into Fitzroy. We stayed in the sheep shearing sheds and managed to dry out a bit, but we were well deployed during daylight hours for fear of air attack. We were therefore on the spot when the *Sir Galahad* was hit and managed to get some useful kit off the Welsh Guards as they came ashore. We also had one FOO (Forward Observation Officer) accidentally shot by one of his mates; I think that was when I started to go off Gunners!

Anyway . . . Wireless Ridge. The battalion moved up behind Mount Longdon and were waiting there while 3 Para took it. By this time about half the battalion, including myself, had the trots. That was not too good for morale as you have enough to worry about without that. I can't say that we were thirsting for battle; far from it. There was no 'gung-ho' left in the battalion. The general feeling was that we had done our bit at Goose Green, so let some other bugger have a go. We were pretty apprehensive about going in again, though once we got in it was all right. We were also a more experienced, battle-hardened unit, better able to tell what was dangerous and what was only frightening.

Wireless Ridge is actually two hill features; the first is a low mound and the ridge proper, which actually is a ridge, and quite narrow, lies south of the mound and overlooks it. In addition, the entire Wireless Ridge position is overlooked and commanded by Tumbledown. Therefore, we could not attack the Ridge until the Scots Guards attacked Tumbledown on 13/14 June, so there was a bit of a delay.

We used this time to go up and visit 3 Para on Longdon, have a good look at the Wireless Ridge and get the artillery ranged on the enemy. This last was not too easy and we had an argument about one position on the map which 3 Para said was in their lines and we said was held by the Argentines and in the way of our attack. We settled the argument by shelling the feature and when 3 Para didn't complain we knew we were shelling the enemy.

Wireless Ridge was strongly held by an Argentine battalion from the 7th Infantry Regiment. This regiment had fought 3 Para on Longdon and had four full companies on the Wireless Ridge feature, dug in and well supplied with heavy weapons. Lt.-Colonel Chaundler elected for a two-stage attack, with the bulk of the battalion first taking the northern feature. Three rifle companies would then use that as a fire base to support Major Neame's 'D' Company, which would attack the southern ridge and sweep along it, rolling up the two Argentine positions there which had been codenamed 'Blueberry Pie' and 'Dirty Dozen'.

Colonel Chaundler had promised 2 Para that they would have

full support from naval guns, artillery and the light armour and this duly arrved, with the frigate HMS *Ambuscade* and Scorpion light tanks providing useful support. The artillery contribution was less helpful as Major Neave reveals:

H Hour was at 0300 and at first all went well. We over-ran the outlying position, the one we had shelled, and found it deserted. We cleared the trenches but there was no fighting or co-ordinated resistance and we moved up to the main southern ridge. It was a very cold night, bright and clear. We felt all right up on the ridge for we had 'B' Company ready to come in and support us if necessary, but really there was not enough room on the ridge for more than one company. There was no opposition on 'Blueberry Pie'. Plenty of signs of recent evacuation, empty trenches, kit lying about, weapons, including heavy weapons and abandoned ammunition but no troops. I don't think that the enemy knew we were up there.

We moved on along the ridge until we got somewhere between 'Blueberry Pie' and 'Dirty Dozen' and then I told our FOO to put down some fire on 'Dirty Dozen' before we attacked. That is when the trouble started. I should explain that in theory every Company should have an FOO, a Forward Observation Officr, who travels with the Company Tactical HQ to control artillery fire. Unfortunately, there was a shortage of FOOs and we didn't have one – or not a fully qualified one, who could handle radio procedure and read a map and know his job. We had a Signals Sergeant and when I told him to call down fire he gave the wrong reference. As a result a full artillery battery put down thirty airburst shells . . . on us.

We went to ground but we had one guy killed and another injured by our own artillery. There was no point in having a shouting match in the middle of a battle, so I told him to call up the correct reference. I don't know what he did but the shell fire came nowhere near the target and some shells fell on 'C' Company. There was then a considerable delay as we tried to get a grip on the artillery which was sending shells all over the place, including one gun which was right out of alignment and shelling 'B' Company. While that was going on Chaundler came on, somewhat irate, to ask what the delay was and why wasn't

I sending in 'sitreps' (Situation Reports) every fifteen minutes or so, in the approved School of Infantry fashion.

We finally got four guns firing on 'Dirty Dozen' and I said, to hell with it, we'll go with four. I should add that the light tanks were marvellous, hosing the ridge with fire. This was especially useful in diverting the enemy's attention since we were in plain view on the ridge for about an hour; we could see them and if it had not been for the fire coming in from the northern feature and the CVRTs we would have been in more trouble.

Anyway, the time had come for the big push and then, just as we were about to go, one of the Company set off an illuminating flare . . . and that blew it.

We had already lost momentum and a lot of fire came up at us. This fire drove us to ground and the troops were very reluctant to get up again. It all came down to junior leadership; I know I was shouting and swearing, but I don't know what I was saying; everyone else, the officers and NCOs were yelling, 'Come on' and 'Let's go' with a lot of effing and blinding. Frankly, I was scared shitless. Anyway, we got up and started advancing. As I got up I lost my signaller, who fell into a shell hole; I assumed he had been shot but he was carrying the rear link to Battalion and was the only signaller we had.

We took the 'Dirty Dozen' position at the trot, 10, 11 and 12 Platoons all deployed across the ridge. One of 11 walked into a trip mine but we could see the Argentines running so we kept moving, anxious to give them no time to stop, think and fight back. We had been told to stay up on the ridge and not go below the southern ridge line towards Moody Brook or beyond the telegraph wires at the end of the Ridge, as the SAS were having some sort of private party down there. We got to the end of the ridge and reorganised just as the Argentines put in the first counter-attack. We had lost our artillery signaller by then but 12 Platoon squashed that attack.

I noticed that there seemed to be a lot of fire following me about as I moved around the ridge, probably snipers; the Argentines had good night sights, better than anything we had. When I got up to 10 and 11 Platoons I found that my runner, Private Hanley, had already got a grip on things . . . a super chap, Hanley, so I had time to find my signaller and pacify the Colonel who was still demanding 'sitreps'. We then beat off a second counter-attack.

It was now getting light and there was constant small-arms fire from positions on the south slope towards Moody Brook but this petered out as the enemy fell back.

It was now full daylight and from the ridge we could see hundreds of Argentine troops streaming off Tumbledown, moving in long files like Scouts on a ramble, all heading back into Stanley, while other troops were coming out of Stanley and heading up Sapper Hill. We tried to get some artillery fire onto them but suddenly the artillery fire on us stopped and it was pretty clear to me that the Argentines had collapsed.

Chaundler came up and asked me why we were not firing on Sapper Hill and then Brigadier Thompson arrived, nattering on about the next phase of his battle, until he, too, saw what was happening. 'A' and 'B' Companies came through my position and we all got ready to push into Stanley. The 'Toms' took their helmets off, got their red berets out and one or two of the more excitable ones started to throw smoke grenades around until the Company Sergeant Major put a stop to it. We could see it was all over.

Major Neame was right. The time had arrived for a general advance on Stanley for the Argentine forces were disintegrating, abandoning their positions on the outskirts, and running back towards the town. 2 Para were ordered to speed this up by taking the road to Stanley, while 45 Commando went forward to dislodge any Argentine troops from the last objective, Sapper Hill. They arrived at the bottom of Sapper Hill to find the Welsh Guards landing by helicopter on the top, having been ordered forward by 5 Brigade. 'It was daylight,' says Colonel Whitehead, 'or our two units might have fired on each other.'

The Argentine Commander in Stanley, General Menendez, had already received surrender proposals from Major-General Moore. These were accepted at 20.59 on 14 June 1982, by which time most of the Argentine soldiers had already laid down their arms.

Jeremy Moore:

That morning I went up onto Goat Ridge, between Harriet and Two Sisters, to meet the two Brigadiers and decide what to do next. I told Julian to move his Brigade along the south of Stanley, but to stay out of the town. If we went in there was too great a risk of civilian casualties. We looked out to the south and saw some Argentines moving about one of their positions on Sapper Hill and shelled them.

I had hoped that when the Commando Brigades' attacks on Two Sisters, Harriet and Longdon all succeeded, that would convince them that they had to surrender, but no – so the Scots Guards went in and took Tumbledown and 2 Para took Wireless Ridge. Still nothing, so I went back to my TAC-HQ and thought about how we might get Menendez to call it off.

We had one great asset, Captain Rod Bell, who was invaluable; he had lived in South America, spoke the language, understood the mentality and he explained how we must handle them. We had been in communication with an Argentine Staff Officer in Stanley for some time because there could be situations, even during the battle, when we needed to talk – about evacuating civilians, or wounded, so contact existed. Rod explained that these people regard themselves as honourable soldiers, and their honour is very important to them – no one will surrender until they feel they have done their best. Our job was to persuade them that they could do no more and therefore, to save lives, surrender was the honourable course.

So, I was back at Fitzroy, kicking my heels against tufts of grass, thinking, 'Why doesn't this man see he's beaten?' when someone called out from the tent that white flags were appearing in Stanley. Then *Fearless* came on and said, 'They want to talk.' I went outside again and jumped about like a two-year-old – and quickly called off an air strike. I sent Michael Rose of the SAS and Roddie Bell into Stanley to discuss terms. The Government wanted the phrase 'Unconditional Surrender' in the document, but I saw no point in that. If we had won, we'd won, and that was an end of it. The Government insisted, so I told Michael and Roddie to put it in, but added that if Menendez jibs, take it out – and he did jib, so I crossed it out. I didn't want the war starting up again over a phrase, and we didn't want to seem to be glorying in their defeat – and that was that.

Julian Thompson: 'I remember the finish; a cold grey day with just a snowflake or two. Their 155 guns were still malleting our positions and I didn't see any of the white flags some people claimed to see. When it was over, my main emotion was relief that no more of these young men were going to die. The young men were remarkable. It did my morale good every time I saw them, with their cheerful dirty faces.'

Julian Thompson had already ordered his Brigade into Stanley, and so the final advance began, led by 2 Para and the light tanks of the Blues and Royals, with 3 Para close behind and 45 yomping yet again for Sapper Hill, where they started to dig in and stayed for two more days since Julian Thompson had no intention of letting his guard drop at the last moment.

42 Commando, which had been helicoptered forward to Tumbledown, then came forward into Stanley and were billeted in an old hangar on the western side of the town, which the Argentines had used as a dressing station. Several limbs and frozen pools of blood lay on the floor and a dead Argentine soldier lying in a wheelbarrow was gently wheeled outside. In these rather grisly surroundings, the Commando settled down to rest and clean up. 45 Commando left Sapper Hill to the Welsh Guards and two rifle companies of 40 Commando came on into the town later that day, arriving just as 2 Para were marching off to a Church Parade.

'Stanley was a mess,' recalls Marine Andrew Tubb. 'Telephone wires down, drains overflowing, a lot of Argentines floating about. We went up to the Town Hall and spent a few days organising working parties of prisoners to get the place cleaned up before they were repatriated back to Argentina and we went home again.

'I didn't fight for the Falklands. They could give the islands to Argentina tomorrow and it wouldn't bother me. I went because I was in the Royal Marines and my unit was sent there. Once there, I just wanted to do my bit and not let my mates down, but people don't understand that. When I got back home, all they asked was, "Did you kill anybody?" and there's no answer you want to make to that.'

The Falklands Task Force came home to a tumultuous reception. The welcome extended over several weeks as various units and ships sailed back into Portsmouth or Southampton, culminating in a somewhat controversial Victory parade through the City of London, with a triumphant Margaret Thatcher taking the salute. Thanks to that Falklands success, Mrs Thatcher's party won a victory at the next general election, but by that time the celebrations were over.

'2 Para flew home,' says Major Philip Neame, 'though we went back to Ascension on *Norland*, the ship we had sailed out on. There was a tremendous rapport between 2 Para and the crew of *Norland*. Before we went ashore the skipper, Captain Don Ellerby, wished us all the best, hoping that we would all survive to sail back with him and we would have liked to do that, even if it meant getting back a few weeks late.

'There was a bizarre event some months later, when the battalion got a vast bill from the NAAFI – about £12,000 – for the 'comforts', the daily bar of chocolate or packet of fags dished out to the troops in the field. We hadn't asked for this and had assumed it was free. We had no funds to pay and when they suggested we should levy a charge on the men who had served in the South Atlantic, we pointed out that quite a few had died there. In the end they dropped it.'

The other account from the Falklands War was rather higher. On the British side 255 men died and 777 were wounded. Four warships were sunk, as well as the *Atlantic Conveyor* and the RFA *Sir Galahad*. The Fleet Air Arm and RAF lost 34 aircraft, either fighters or helicopters. Argentine losses were 746 men killed and thousands wounded, 12,978 taken prisoner and repatriated to Argentina. Apart from the cruiser *Belgrano*, the submarine *Santa Fé* and several smaller ships were sunk and more than 100 Argentine aircraft were shot down.

The two nations are once again at peace, even discussing ways to exploit the mineral resources of the South Atlantic and share the profits but the original cause of the war that cost so many lives, the Argentine claim to 'Las Malvinas', has yet to be resolved.

20

The Troubles in Ireland: 1975–1996

'The problem with this bloody country is too much religion and not enough Christianity.'

An NCO of The Parachute Regiment, Belfast, 1980.

To continue the story of the war against the IRA it is necessary to go back a few years, to the time before the Falklands War came along to distract the British from the Northern Ireland troubles. The 1970s saw many changes in the IRA situation, but one factor remained constant – the use of terrorism. The object of terrorism is to terrorise and by constant practice the IRA became very good at that particular form of warfare.

The first five years of the Troubles in Ireland, from August 1969 to the end of 1974, can be regarded as the learning years, when both the IRA and the British Army were finding their feet in a new kind of war. The IRA were attempting to dominate the Catholic areas and retain Republican sympathies in Ireland and the USA, and in the pursuit of this aim they had certain assets. Among these was the wish of most Irish people for a United Ireland – if only because that would put a stop to all this IRA business – and in this the decent Irish also had the support of the majority of British people, with the proviso that a United Ireland could only come when a majority of the people in the north wished it.

The IRA were not concerned about that final point. Their aim was to shoot and bomb the Brits out of the north and shoot and bomb the Prods into the Republic, and that has remained their aim. In this ambition the IRA enjoyed unthinking support from more fervent Republicans, who could excuse any atrocity on the grounds that it advanced 'The Cause' and the Boys would not have murdered – or 'executed – that policeman or soldier or bombed that bar full of people if they had not had a good reason – and the British soldiers should not be here anyway.

The facts that the British Army were on British soil and that without them the Protestants would be down on the local Catholics in force, were not accepted as arguments. Arguments in Ireland tend to be dialogues of the deaf, with a great deal of talk and very little attempt at understanding.

The Army, on the other hand, was fighting with one hand tied behind its back. Its role was to help the RUC keep the peace, damp down intercommunal violence and, in what little time was left, deal with the hard men of the IRA who had the initiative, could attack at will and vanish back into the Catholic areas or across the Border when the killing was over. As the struggle went on, terrorism ceased to be a means to an end and became an end in itself, a way of life for the ever more sophisticated killers of the IRA.

The British Army was used to fighting terrorists. By the middle years of the 1970s British soldiers had been fighting terrorists in one country or another for thirty years. They knew all there was to know about stifling terrorists and winning the 'hearts and minds' of the civil population. Given that the methods of the IRA – murder, shootings, bombings, beatings, tarring and feathering, and the torture and maiming of those brave enough to oppose them – were anathema to all decent folk, winning the hearts and minds of the local people should have been easy, not least because the people of Northern Ireland live in a democracy.

To the soldiers from the Mainland, the people they met in the street, Catholic or Protestant, were their own kind of people ... or so it seemed. It took the soldiers some years to realise that this terrorist campaign was different from anything they had met before. Terrorist war had come home from the outposts of the Empire and was now being waged in the streets and villages of their own country for, let it be said again, until the majority of

Northern Ireland's people decide otherwise, the Province is a part of the United Kingdom.

This factor, the sense that 'it should not be this way', added to the bitterness that came to mark this conflict, providing an extra slice of horror to a war that was already bad enough. To be insulted, spat at, stoned and shot at by anyone is hardly pleasant, but when you find your neighbours doing it, the revulsion goes deep.

'If only they were wogs,' said Colour Sergeant Eric Blythe of the Royal Marines, 'we could sort this lot out in no time; but these are the sort of people we mix with back in Kilburn. There is no longer any need for it and if you want my opinion, they ought to be ashamed of themselves.'

Geordie Mather, another Marine who served with 40 Commando in Northern Ireland, also noticed the change from the campaigns fought in more far-flung regions: 'Belfast was a new experience for me. My "wars" had been out in the open, in the jebel or the jungle or the desert. Now our "patch" was on a housing estate, our "location" part of Musgrove Hospital, our "observation point" up a tower overlooking the M1 motorway and Andersonstown.'

Not only the location was new. Attitudes were different as well. It took a few years for the soldiers to grasp the fact that some of the local Irish were not only not ashamed of the IRA activity but positively proud of it. Once that had been accepted the Army dusted down its anti-terrorist experience and went to work on this new situation.

The first move was to reduce the level of confrontation on the street. The young soldiers on patrol faced a constant battery of insults and provocation, and had to be trained to endure it. Therefore, before battalions were sent on their four-month tours to Northern Ireland, the soldiers undertook an intensive six-week training programme to teach or remind them what they would be up against.

Geordie Mather again: 'As you know, units sent to Northern Ireland were first sent to a special camp in Kent, built to look just like a Northern Irish village. The idea was to get the lads used to the sort of situation they would have to face in the Province and we did the lot from street patrols to riot control.

'After a bit it got very sophisticated; they even had WRENS or women soldiers acting the part of housewives, screaming at us, throwing stones; the girls really got into it and were just like the real thing, quite frightening. We went through the whole routine until we knew it inside out and we did that before every tour. By the time we went onto the streets we were well prepared and that really helped the lads handle themselves when the locals cut up rough.'

The next main problem was a shortage of good intelligence. As other accounts in this book will have shown, accurate intelligence is vital in the successful prosecution of an anti-terrorist campaign. Given good intelligence the security forces can anticipate what the terrorists will do, and either prevent the attack or ambush the attackers. In Northern Ireland this sort of information was even more essential, not just to target the real terrorists but to reduce the need for sweeps and searches which only antagonised the uncommitted portion of the Catholic population. Targeting the terrorists – and by now there were Protestant terrorists at work as well – became a major priority for Army Intelligence.

The best source of good intelligence was through informers – 'touts' in IRA jargon. The IRA were afraid of 'touts' and anyone even suspected of informing on IRA operations faced a brutal interrogation and a bullet in the head. The bulk of the intelligence on IRA affairs and operations should have come from the Special Branch of the RUC. Unfortunately, their men were so well known and so unpopular that their activities were compromised and the information they provided unreliable.

Before long the Army had set up its own intelligence-gathering organisations. The first of these was a group of former IRA men who were willing to mix with and inform on their former colleagues. These men were known as the Military Reconnaissance Force or 'Freds'. Any 'Fred' taken by the IRA faced torture and death. Most of the Freds were eventually compromised and forced to flee with their families to some safe location abroad.

In 1974, Frank Kitson, now a Major-General, raised another intelligence-gathering force, the 14th Intelligence Company, which operated in plain clothes and roved about the country in unmarked cars. Details on this organisation are still obscure and most of those who served in it are unwilling to talk. One of the 14 Company officers was Philip Neame:

I cannot tell you much, but it was not a bit like James Bond. What you should know is that the operations of the regular battalions on the street were simply the icing on the cake, the 'aid to civil power', to keep life in Northern Ireland as normal as possible. The soldiers could not achieve much more than that and they knew it. After a while, a good battalion tour was one where you had no casualties and not much trouble. This was just a backdrop, a curtain if you like, to another war, the covert war, that went on beneath the surface . . . and I am not going to talk about that.

The covert war could be dangerous. In May 1977 Captain Robert Nairac, a Guards officer and a member of 14 Company, elected to meet a contact at a bar in South Armagh, close to the border. Captain Nairac was in plain clothes and alone. An IRA gang was waiting for him, attacked him in the car park, bundled him into a car and took him across the border where he was tortured and killed. His body has never been found.

While the covert war went on, the open war continued, with growing if more selective violence. Car bombs were used in city centres and when the British bomb-disposal squads became too good at defusing them, proxy bombing was introduced, the IRA kidnapping drivers or their families, forcing the driver to take his bomb-filled car to some city centre and abandon it there for detonation.

The bombing campaign continued into the 1990s, devastating the heart of towns like Colraine, Londonderry, Omagh, Dungannon and Strabane, and the erection of city centre barriers did little to prevent it. Seeking softer targets and more publicity, the IRA also switched some of its men to attacks in England. On 6 December 1975, four IRA men drove up Walton Street in Knightsbridge and machine-gunned Scott's Restaurant. This attack caused no casualties among the diners and the gunmen were eventually tracked to a flat on Balcombe Street in Central London. There they took two hostages, Mr and Mrs Matthews, but surrendered after a six-day siege culminated in the arrival of the SAS.

Violence continued in 1976 but in August of that year a tragic incident produced the first of several Peace Movements among the civilian population. On 10 August, a patrol of soldiers shot and killed Danny Lennon, a PIRA terrorist who had failed to stop his car at a road block. The car crashed into a group of children walking along the pavement, killing three of them. The children's aunt, Mairead Corrigan, and another woman, Betty Williams, began circulating a Peace Petition. The petition attracted international support and the two women were awarded the Nobel Peace Prize in the following year. The Petition did not, however, influence the IRA; their activists denounced the two women as supporters of British rule and the IRA violence went on.

During 1975 the violence spread to the prisons which were now full of IRA prisoners. In March 1975 the 'blanket' or 'dirty' protest began, when the IRA prisoners demanded the restoration of 'political status', smearing the walls of their cells with excrement, refusing to wash or wear prison clothes. This 'dirty protest' went on for three years but achieved nothing; the prisoners were not detained for their political views but because they had been tried and convicted of crimes ranging from assault to robbery, from murder to the possession of explosives.

Out of the 'blanket protest' came the hunger strikes, again over the question of political status. The first hunger strikers to die were Michael Gaughan and Frank Stagg, who starved themselves to death in Parkhurst prison in 1974 and 1976 respectively. Michael Gaughan was buried at Ballina in County Mayo, and the IRA fired a volley of pistol shots over his grave. Hunger strikes continued, culminating in the death of Bobbie Sands, a leading IRA activist who was also an elected Westminster MP. Sands and his kind were brave men but the democratic road was not one that interested them and the British Prime Minister, Margaret Thatcher, would not offer them political recognition as a reward for terrorism. In the end the IRA backed down and hunger striking ceased.

Catholics and Protestants were also fighting among themselves and intercommunal sectarian murders run like a bloody threat through the history of the Troubles. In January 1976 the IRA ordered ten Protestant building workers out of their mini-van and machine-gunned them. This 'two-for-one' atrocity followed the killing of five Catholics on the nearby Bessbrook estate. Protestant attacks were not confined to the north; in May 1974 bombs were planted in Dublin and Monaghan in the Republic, these two attacks alone killing thirty-one innocent people.

Protestant terror groups also murdered three Irish musicians, members of the Miami Showband, while 1974 and 1975 saw a string of horrific sectarian murders carried out by a Protestant terror group who came to be known as the 'Shankill Butchers'. The 'Butchers' roved the province, picking up Catholics and taking them away for torture and murder. This group was eventually broken up, eight 'Butchers' receiving five life sentences each for nineteen sectarian murders.

On 27 August 1979, 'Bloody Monday' was added to 'Bloody Friday' and 'Bloody Sunday', when the IRA killed the former Viceroy of India, Earl Mountbatten, while he and his family were out fishing in the bay of Mullaghmore in County Sligo. On the same day a bomb at Warrenpoint in Armagh killed eighteen soldiers of the 2nd Battalion, The Parachute Regiment. Ten years into the Troubles and the Army was still on the streets of Northern Ireland, with every battalion doing its tour of duty in that unhappy Province. Royal Marine Geordie Mather again:

We relieved the Fusiliers, the ones with a budgerigar in their berets. At one of the lectures before we left the UK, we asked who we were to relieve and said, 'That's OK, as long as its not the Paras'. No one in Ireland had a good word for the Paras and the Catholics hated them. The Army was not too fond of them either, because of their attitude. They didn't know the meaning of 'Hearts and Minds', they just kicked arse and got people's backs up and the next unit in got all the stick.

I was not too impressed with the RUC. It would take a patrol of Marines and a single RUC man to deliver a parking summons. I thought the local territorials, the UDR blokes (Ulster Defence Regiment) were brave, because they had to live among the locals and the neighbours knew who they were, so they were at risk from car bombs and ambush every day.

Andersonstown was a place where they really hated you anyway but the Marines just took it, the abuse and the kids chucking bricks. The young Marines controlled their patch, stayed polite, drove around in open-topped Landrovers, even stopped at pedestrian crossings, which you did not want to do in case of snipers. We had our share of bombs and bullets and we had to break a few heads but we never lost control of our patch.

When we left at the end of our tour, embarked on an LCL, it

was a lovely June evening and a pipe band played us away. The CO was saying goodbye to the civic leaders and we got a recommend. They said we had been hard but fair and could stay another four months . . . really! We could hardly wait to get on the ship but at least somebody had thanked us.

Every infantry regiment in the British Army sent troops to Northern Ireland and there was participation from artillery units serving in the infantry role and some armoured units, the latter usually working in scout cars. A good account of life for a soldier on the streets of Northern Ireland in the later years of the Troubles comes from Major Richard Nugee of the Royal Artillery:

One of the problems of Northern Ireland was a lack of continuity in the allocation of areas. A Company of soldiers could have enormous influence in a particular area, hence the so-called 'Para Diversion' which you know about, but it really helped if you knew your patch and the people on it. Whether the IRA liked it or not, contacts were eventually built up between the soldiers and the local civilians.

Paratroopers are disliked in Northern Ireland as they are believed to have an aggressive attitude – no doubt a sweeping generalisation, but the effect is there. When 7 RHA, a Parachute Gunner regiment, was next to us in Newtownbutler, they were told not to wear their red berets as it would unduly influence the locals against the regiment. Quite often the way the locals treated you was a direct result of the way you treated them.

Patrol hours varied enormously, according to the situation and the terrain. In Belfast you might spend one-and-a-half to two hours actually on patrol and probably an hour briefing and debriefing, with anything up to four hours between patrols. This can be exhausting if kept up for long periods, hence the need to vary the routine between foot patrols, mobile patrols, vehicle check points and sentry-duties. Most of the time not on patrol was spent sleeping. There were also video films, and in the North House Street Mill in Belfast, a twenty-four-hour kitchen to feed the men coming in or going out on patrol. In theory you could eat all day but in practice you did not want much food . . . too tired, usually. You never went out for a drink or a walk or a meal; for the four months of your tour you were in barracks or on duty.

In rural areas patrols tended to last much longer; three to four days in Fermanagh, mainly because of a shortage of helicopters and the distances involved. After a three-day patrol you might get twenty-four hours off to sleep and sort yourself out, clean your equipment and take care of your feet; sometimes you only got twelve hours and were out again. Three-day patrols were not liked or especially efficient as once the enemy knew where we were, and did not hear any helicopters, they could work out our radius of action and plan accordingly.

These patrols were also hard physically because of the weight we had to carry . . . especially the radio batteries. For some reason Army batteries are very heavy and do not last long; I tried to get replacement batteries flown in by helicopter at night if possible, but re-supply cut down on rest time as well. In Omagh we patrolled for eight hours a day on average; that was in 1988–89, before the six-months tour came in. The length of patrol was dictated by the availability of helicopters and many lasted between twelve and fourteen hours. Throw in debriefing and briefing and you got little change from an eighteen-hour day.

Most sections went out five times a week so we were working a ninety-hour week, week after week, for months. I once went out seven days on the trot with different sections but I know that on the last patrol I was so mentally tired that I began to take unnecessary risks; at least it taught me the importance of the commander getting enough rest.

In South Armagh we spent six weeks living in trenches while the observation towers were rebuilt. I worked out a roster of four hours on and eight hours off, which should have worked and given us enough rest but after five days of living in trenches with not much sleep to begin with, I was amazed at how long it took to recover after a patrol. The routine was to do one patrol from the trenches while the rest 'stagged on' resting or on guard, and although the patrol was only six hours the effect was tremendous. A man would do eight hours on guard then go on a six-hour patrol, then it took two hours debriefing and sorting out. Then a meal and a bit of sleep and the same again.

We were supplied by helicopter which brought in food, water, everything. Every so often we were lifted out for a shower at Crossmaglen. My first shower came after twenty-one days in the trenches and it was extremely pleasant; our clothes were washed and dried while we showered and a meal was cooked for us – until then we had been living for six weeks on compo rations, twenty-four hour ration packs – all Menu 'A'; I will never be able to eat compo chicken curry again.

What was life like on patrol? . . . Well, here again, it depended where you were. Some of the patrols went without meeting anyone, though we always tried to meet people, to let them know we were in the area. Around Omagh I used to put in a VCP late at night then speed-march the section to some other position to give the impression there were more of us on the ground than there actually were.

In Belfast our VCP once stopped Congressman Joseph Kennedy, one of the Kennedy family, over from America on a 'fact finding' mission, a young man who was particularly hostile to us. There is nothing more frustrating than being insulted by an American who has little understanding of the real situation and had come to Ireland 'to see oppression at first hand', as he put it.

The soldiers usually enjoyed VCPs as they enjoyed talking to people and it added a little variety. VCPs did not last long, often just a few minutes. I recall putting one on a very 'anti' village near Omagh; the locals were hostile and the village had been out of bounds for months. After about ten or fifteen minutes I noticed that the same cars were coming round again and again, all of them carrying known 'players', terrorists. We pulled back and watched and it became clear they were just looking for a shot at us.

Soldiers often preferred the urban areas, partly to meet people, partly because the patrols were shorter and there was more to concentrate on; concentration saved lives. One soldier got into the habit of counting telephone wires and noticed that while most telegraph poles carried twelve wires one on the road carried 13; we checked and found it was the command wire for a bomb. Another soldier constantly looked for dislodged bricks on walls, which might conceal a booby trap.

The urban environment was risky but more mentally stimulating. It was hard to keep up the necessary state of alertness when trudging over ploughed fields and climbing over fences. Derelict cars were a definite no-no, because of the risk of booby traps. Corrugated iron and 'wheelie-bins' for rubbish were also to be avoided and we always tried to walk on the far side of the road going past them, in the knowledge that this, too, might set us up for a sniper. It may sound nerve-wracking and it was, but if you thought you were in danger every time you went on patrol you would never finish a tour.

The local people? On the whole people were very polite to us. The real terrorists were always careful to give us no reason to pick them up or take them down to the police station but the general public, especially in Belfast, could be quite rude and insulting. The most abusive were often the women and the young lads. In the Falls Road youths would shout, 'Make like Captain Nairac,' and fall down on the pavement – a reminder to us that Captain Nairac had been captured, tortured and killed by the IRA. They were the exception, though. Most people in Republican areas were sullen but not deliberately unco-operative. The vast majority of the population were either resigned to our presence or accepted that we had a job to do.

So the fight went on, year after year, until almost every soldier and battalion in the British Army had seen service in Northern Ireland. The violence continued and became almost commonplace, a daily round of trouble often virtually unnoticed outside the Province, unless some particular atrocity caught the public attention for a few days.

The main aim was to sicken the British public with the Irish problem; the secondary aim was publicity for the Cause, and it was soon discovered that attacks on the mainland produced more TV coverage and column inches in the newspaper.

The IRA struck on the mainland at Brighton in 1984, when a bomb planted in the Grand Hotel nearly killed the British Prime Minister, Margaret Thatcher, and did kill five other people, three of them women. A bomb which killed eleven Royal Marine bandsmen in an attack at Deal in September 1988 also brought the Northern Ireland problem back to centre stage. Attacks in Great Britain were not easy, however; the terrorists had no border to flee across, no supportive community. The public were vigilant and the ASUs were swiftly tracked down, though others came across the Irish sea to keep up the campaign.

When these attacks became difficult or failed to generate publicity, the target area was switched to British Army camps in Continental Europe. Mainland attacks were concentrated against civilian targets, or on some prominent public figure, like the British MP Airey Neave, killed by a bomb in the House of Commons car park, the Ambassador to the Irish Republic, Christopher Ewart Biggs, shot dead in Dublin, or Lt.-General Sir Stuart Pringle, the Commandant General of the Royal Marines, who was blown up and severely injured outside his home in London in 1981. For a few days after such events the problem returned to the front pages of the newspapers. Otherwise the war just went on, with no end in sight and no political solution apparent.

By the end of the 1970s the main aim of military operations was to stay ahead of the IRA, track down and eliminate the known players and contain the violence. One step to that end was the commitment to the struggle of the 22 SAS Regiment.

The SAS have leapt to national and international prominence since SAS soldiers brought the 1980 siege of the Iranian Embassy in London to such a dramatic end, abseiling down the sides of the Embassy before a massed battery of televison cameras. In the 1970s the SAS was just another unit of the British Army, albeit one with a very specialist role and a high reputation. Only in later years was their role in Northern Ireland to become a cause of controversy.

The SAS first arrived in Northern Ireland in the early days of the Troubles. 'D' Squadron arrived at Bessbrook, in uniform, in August 1969 and one of their first acts was to hold a memorial parade in Newtownards cemetery at the grave of a wartime SAS hero, the Ulster soldier Lt.-Colonel Blair 'Paddy' Mayne. The squadron took part in normal IS duties before being withdrawn for service in Oman.

In 1974 the SAS returned to Northern Ireland and were stationed at Bessbrook Camp where their move into covert operations seems to have begun. 'I recall that when they arrived they wore their sand coloured berets but that soon changed,' says Julian Thompson, then CO of 40 Commando. 'While we were there they started to go about in green berets and when the Paras arrived they wore red berets; no doubt when the Jocks arrived the SAS wore Highland bonnets.'

Before long the SAS were running four-man car patrols about the Province, the men in civilian clothes but heavily armed. This faintly clandestine state of affairs lasted until 1976 when the British Prime

Minister announced that the SAS Regiment was to be deployed in Northern Ireland. This was after the SAS had been credited with ending the Balcombe Street siege in London and was seen as an attempt to tell the IRA that hard times were coming unless they reined in their gunmen. This deployment soon began to have an effect.

On 12 March an SAS patrol arrived at a police station in South Armagh bringing with them Sean McKenna, a noted 'player' who they claimed to have found wandering about drunk. McKenna claimed that he had been sound asleep in bed in the Republic when masked men entered his bedroom and took him back across the border. McKenna was duly tried for a long list of terrorist offences and sentenced to twenty-five years in gaol. A month later the SAS killed Patrick Cleary, another IRA activist who had ventured across the border to see his girlfriend and been ambushed by the SAS. Since someone was clearly feeding the SAS with contact information, the IRA became seriously worried.

The next piece of news about the SAS was less welcome to the Army authorities. A patrol of the Irish Police, the Gardai, stopped a car below the border which contained four armed SAS soldiers in plain clothes. These were arrested, released on bail, and returned later to Dublin for trial where each soldier was fined £100 for carrying arms in the Republic. The fine was small, the political embarrassment considerable.

In January 1977, the SAS followed another tip-off and mounted an ambush on a car parked near Crossmaglen. The ambush was kept in position for several days until an armed and masked man approached the car. He was challenged and shot down, at which a number of hidden IRA men opened fire on the SAS patrol. Fire was returned but there were no further casualties on either side before the IRA fled. It is more than probable that the SAS were working hand-in-glove with 14 Company, which was supplying them with contact information. This enabled the SAS to bring IRA gangs to battle but the results were not always entirely beneficial. The streets and villages of Northern Ireland are not the empty jebels of Arabia or the jungles of Borneo and all too often civilians strayed into the gunfire.

In June 1978 three IRA men walked into an SAS ambush in Ballyskillen and were killed when placing a bomb in a post office.

A fourth IRA man escaped the firing and was chased but in the pursuit the SAS – or perhaps a Special Patrol Group of the RUC – shot and killed Mr William Hanna, who was standing outside a pub. The IRA man escaped and Mr Hanna had no connection whatsoever with the IRA. An attempt by the Army Public Relations Department to cover up this accidental shooting, by claiming that Mr Hanna had been killed in a 'cross fire', was soon exposed as false. Another tragic shooting came a month later, in July 1977. The SAS were sent to ambush an IRA arms cache found and reported by a farmer's sixteen-year-old son, John Boyle. The ambush was set but unfortunately no one thought to tell the Boyle family that the cache site should be avoided. Young John therefore wandered down to see if the arms were still there and – according to the official report – picked up a rifle and pointed it at the SAS men, who promptly shot him dead. Two SAS men were arrested after this shooting, tried for murder and acquitted.

Other such incidents followed. In September 1977, James Taylor was out for a little rough shooting when he walked into an SAS patrol. Seeing his shotgun, the SAS shot him dead. In November of the same year the SAS entered a house in Londonderry which, according to a tip-off, contained a cache of arms. Patrick Duffy, a known terrorist but unarmed, entered the house, was challenged by the SAS and killed. Questions were raised as to why four SAS men were unable to overpower one unarmed terrorist without killing him.

So it went on, successful actions against the IRA, spiked with killings of unfortunate civilians who just happened to be in the way. The SAS too, had casualties; Captain Herbert Westmacott was killed in Belfast in May 1980 and in December 1984 another SAS soldier, Lance-Corporal Slater, was killed when he attempted to stop an IRA gang planting a bomb, two IRA men being killed in the gunfight that followed. The IRA were seriously concerned about this SAS activity and the Sinn Fein Press Office made great capital out of SAS mistakes.

In Febuary 1985 five IRA men drove into an SAS ambush near Strabane; three were killed, a fourth man was captured and the last one fled. It was then reported that the three men killed had also surrendered but been ordered to lie in the road and were then shot in the back. An inquest failed to find any evidence to support this allegation and brought in a verdict of lawful killing. A year later another civilian was killed, Frank Bradley, who was shot when he entered a yard under surveillance by an SAS patrol. At the inquest the soldiers pleaded that Mr Bradley had been shot dead when he failed to respond to a challenge. Other evidence at the inquest revealed that Frank Bradley had no terrorist connections, had reacted normally to the challenge – and been shot no fewer than eight times.

Incidents like these inevitably gave rise to the suspicion that the British Government, or the RUC, or the SAS, were operating a 'shoot-to-kill' policy. This accusation has always been strongly denied by the British Government but, as the IRA and the Sinn Fein Press Office point out, 'They would say that, wouldn't they?' A more cogent reason for rejecting the existence of an official 'shoot-to-kill' policy comes from 'Billy', an RUC officer from Coleraine, in conversation with the author in 1991:

'There is no "shoot-to-kill" policy. Don't be bloody daft. We know who the "players" are. We know all about them, where they live, where they go. If we had the evidence for a conviction they would be in the Maze but if there was a "shoot to kill" policy they would be all in their graves long ago. Forget this idea of a "shoot to kill" policy. There isn't one. Life is just bloody difficult out there on the streets . . . don't forget to put that in your book. We are not all murdering bastards over here; put that in your book as well.'

This seems an acceptable explanation and no evidence for an official 'shoot-to-kill' policy has ever been produced. The civilian deaths are due to accidents largely because the military and the IRA are fighting it out in public areas with high-velocity weapons. Even so, there have been too many of them and they cannot be excused by recalling IRA atrocities like the Enniskillen bombings of 8 November 1987.

This was Remembrance Day and a large crowd of civilians, mostly Protestant, had gathered at the War Memorial in Enniskillen to commemorate the dead of two World Wars. A bomb concealed close to the memorial went off by the speakers' platform, killing eleven people, all civilians, including women, and injuring sixty-three more. The IRA were roundly condemned for this attack but the attacks continued. In December the IRA killed two more civilians, both pensioners, and over the next six months they killed no fewer than seventeen civilians, young and old, in a series of 'mistakes'.

One of the most successful SAS ambushes took place in May 1987 outside the police station at Loughall in North Armagh. The SAS had clearly been tipped off about an impending attack, for on Friday 8 May they were in position long before the IRA gang arrived, some in a van, some on a yellow JCB excavator bearing a bomb in the bucket.

The idea was to ram the bomb through the fence around the police station, set it off and then storm the station and kill all those inside. Three IRA men jumped from the van to give covering fire as the JCB charged the wire and were met with a storm of fire from SAS soldiers hidden about the village; this killed three men riding on the JCB and the driver of the van. A survivor then detonated the bomb on the JCB which demolished half the police station – safely empty of police – and killed two more IRA men. Another was shot and killed as he took shelter under the van.

So far, a great success for the SAS, with eight armed IRA men dead . . . and then came tragedy. Just before the attack two brothers, Oliver and Tony Hughes, drove into the village. Both men were mechanics and wearing their working overalls, not unlike those worn by the IRA; when the firing started they tried to reverse their van out of the village, but the soldiers opened fire on the van, killing Tony and severely wounding his brother.

The inquest verdicts were 'lawful killing' for the IRA deaths and 'accidental death' for the unfortunate Tony Hughes. A year later came a far more controversial shooting, the 'Death on the Rock' affair in the Crown Colony of Gibraltar, on Sunday, 5 March 1988.

During the 1980s the IRA switched some of their gangs to targets on the Continent of Europe, attacking British Servicemen in Germany, ambushing cars with British number plates driving down the autobahn. The intense security kept around Army camps in Britain was therefore extended to those in Germany and the IRA began to look elsewhere. Eventually their eyes fell on the small Army garrison in Gibraltar.

British Intelligence gathering had greatly improved in recent years and they now maintained a close watch on known terrorists, tracing their movements and noting their contacts. In the autumn of 1987 two known 'players', Sean Savage and Daniel McCann, were located on the Costa del Sol, apparently on holiday. However, the pair returned to the Costa del Sol frequently in the following winter, which aroused suspicion that they were not there just to get a suntan. Since the obvious target for a bomb in Southern Spain was the British garrison of Gibraltar, a close surveillance team flew out there in early 1988 and drew up a list of possible targets on the Rock.

British Intelligence could evaluate targets from the IRA point of view and it was apparent that the 'best' form of attack would be a car bomb placed to destroy lives at one regular weekly event – the Changing the Guard at the Governor's Palace. During this parade, which was a popular tourist attraction, a military band and troops marched through the narrow streets and crowds gathered along the route. Military ceremonies had provided the IRA with several bloody opportunities in recent years, not least against the Greenjacket Band and the Horse Guards at Hyde Park, and the signs were that another atrocity was being planned for Gibraltar. It was also known that the IRA had developed a hand-held triggering device which could detonate a car bomb from a safe distance.

The third known terrorist, a woman, Maraid Farrell, now came on the scene. She arrived in Malaga on 4 March 1988 to complete the ASU and it seemed likely that the attack was about to take place quite soon. The Spanish police were aware of the situation and willing to cooperate in the search for the car bomb, and a sixteen-man team from the SAS, in plain clothes, was flown to Gibraltar on 3 March 1988. A full-scale security alert was then put in hand and given the codename of 'FLAVIUS'.

Anti-terrorist or Internal Security operations are only conducted by the Army when their aid is requested by the relevant civil authorities, under the general heading of 'Aid to the Civil Power'. The overall commander of 'FLAVIUS' was therefore the Gibraltar Police Commissioner, Joseph Canepa. His orders were that the terrorists should be arrested and their arms and bombs made safe. This instruction was declared at the subsequent enquiry, and the point is important because the Spanish police on the Costa del Sol had managed to lose track of the three terrorists.

This was a setback at this stage in 'FLAVIUS', but the pattern of the probable attack had already been worked out; the Intelligence Services had plenty of experience of IRA attacks. They knew what they were looking for, and how the attack would probably be mounted.

The IRA would use two cars. One car would enter Gibraltar from Spain and park somewhere on the route used by the military band and marching detachment. The role of this car was simply to occupy a space on the route to ensure that when the 'bomb car' arrived it would have somewhere to park. The most likely spot was in the plaza where the troops and band assembled for the Guard Changing, so a close watch for the first car was kept there. Meanwhile the Spanish police hunted up and down the Costa del Sol for the IRA terrorists and the bomb car. The bomb car was not located and the IRA terrorists managed to slip into Gibraltar and park a white Renault 5 in the plaza without being noticed. Regular street checks did, however, notice the parked car.

This car was examined early on the afternoon of Sunday, 5 March 1988 when it was suspected of being the bomb car. The guard would be changed on the following Tuesday morning and SAS troopers, in plain clothes and armed with Browning 9mm automatic pistols, were working eight-hour shifts in teams of four, ready to take a hand if required, when the terrorists were located.

The break came at 2 o'clock in the afternoon when a police surveillance team reported that Savage had been spotted at the Renault in the plaza, 'fiddling with something inside the car'. The reasonable assumption was that there was only one car and that Savage was priming the explosive charge for detonation by radio signal or by booby trap. Then another message came from the border check-point, that Farrell and McCann had crossed the border and were walking into the town. They continued into the town centre and met up with Savage, the three talking together before turning back towards the border.

There was then a great deal of hurried activity. An explosive expert took a careful look at the car and reported that it probably contained a bomb. The police chief, Commissioner Joseph Canepa, duly signed the order passing the operation over into the hands of the SAS. This order was signed at 1540 hours and SAS soldiers, in plain clothes and armed with 9mm automatic pistols, moved in on the IRA terrorists who were now walking back towards the border control post.

The road to the border at Gibraltar crosses the runway of the airport and here Savage left the other two to walk on and turned back towards the town centre. Four SAS soldiers in civilian clothes were within yards of the terrorists and two of them, later identified as Soldiers 'A' and 'B', continued with McCann and Farrell while the other two, Soldiers 'C' and 'D', shadowed Sean Savage. For a few more minutes these little groups walked on together. Then the shooting started.

The orders from Commissioner Canepa were that the IRA terrorists were to be arrested. The shooting seems to have been triggered by a police siren coming from a police vehicle which was attempting to get down through the heavy Sunday afternoon traffic to the border post where the SAS men were going to arrest the IRA. The police switched on the siren in an attempt to clear a way and this sound close on their heels clearly alarmed the two IRA terrorists, Farrell and McCann. According to the inquest, McCann, looking round suddenly, made 'eye contact' with Soldier 'A', about thirty feet behind him. McCann realised that the police or the security forces were on to them and Soldier 'A' realised that he had been spotted.

According to evidence given at the inquest, McCann put his hand inside his jacket, perhaps to grab a pistol or trigger the firing device for the car bomb in the plaza. Taking no chances on either outcome, Soldier 'A' drew his pistol and fired one round into McCann. Then – according to the evidence given at the inquest – seeing Farrell reach for her handbag, Soldier 'A' fired one round into her as well. He then switched aim and put another bullet into McCann. Soldier 'B' had meanwhile drawn his pistol and he fired a bullet into Maraid Farrell and another into McCann.

This burst of shooting was heard by the last IRA terrorist, Sean Savage who, again according to the evidence at the inquest, was seen to put his hand into his pocket. His shadowers, Soldiers 'C' and 'D', promptly opened fire and shot him dead. At 1606 hours the SAS handed control of the incident back to the police chief, Joseph Canepa. The entire incident had lasted just twenty-six minutes, three terrorists were dead and as far as the SAS were concerned the matter was closed. In fact the 'Death on the Rock' affair had hardly begun.

At first the British Press and public were very pleased and relieved when they heard of the Gibraltar affair. A statement issued from Gibraltar within an hour of the shootings claimed that a suspected bomb had been found in Gibraltar and three bombers shot by civilian police. A further Government statement issued at 2100hrs on Sunday night admitted that 'security forces' had been involved and had dealt with a suspect bomb.

Disquiet arose on the following day after a series of statements made by Ministers on the radio and in the House of Commons. On the morning of Monday, 7 March, the Armed Forces Minister claimed that a 'large bomb had been found in Gibraltar and defused'. However, later that day, when questioned in the House of Commons, the Foreign Secretary revealed that none of the terrorists had been armed or had a triggering device, and the car in the plaza did not contain a bomb. The 'bomb car' – full of Semtex explosive – was located on the following day, Tuesday, 8 March 1988, in a car park at Marbella on the Costa del Sol, but the effect of these varied statements was to start a series of Press enquiries.

On the day after the shooting the Press had hailed the Gibraltar shootings with delight, heaping praise on the expertise of the SAS. By the Tuesday morning most British newspapers had changed their tone completely. The SAS and the Government came in for a great deal of criticism, the first for the use of excessive force, the second for allegedly attempting a cover-up. A large proportion of the British public were also very unhappy about the Gibraltar affair and a TV programme, 'Death on the Rock' broadcast on 28 April, which went into the affair in detail, only served to increase public unease.

The official verdict brought in by the Gibraltar inquest in September 1988 was one of 'lawful killing'. This might have ended the speculation about what actually happened on that violent Sunday afternoon but attempts by sections of the Press and the Government to stifle comment on the Gibraltar shootings or blacken the reputation of witnesses at the inquest only helped to keep speculation alive. The Government attempted to stop the showing of 'Death on the Rock' and sections of the Press tried to blacken the character of one witness, Mrs Carmen Proetta, who, according to her evidence, had seen the killing of McCann and Farrell from the window of her flat, just across the road.

According to Mrs Proetta, her attention was attracted to events across the road by the sight of two people putting their hands in the air: 'These people were turning their heads to see what was happening and when they saw these men with guns in their hands they put their hands up. It looked as if the man was protecting the girl because he stood in front of her but there was no chance.' According to her evidence the SAS 'jumped in with their guns in their hands and just went and shot these people'. Another witness claimed that Farrell and McCann were shot again while lying on the ground.

This evidence contradicts that given by the SAS soldiers, who claimed that all three terrorists either put their hands to their pockets or, in Farrell's case, into her handbag. Thinking the terrorists were reaching for weapons or the bomb trigger, the soldiers drew their pistols and opened fire. The snag with that explanation is that since the three terrorists did not have weapons or a bomb trigger, they had nothing to reach for. A natural reaction would be to raise their hands in the air which, according to Mrs Proetta, is exactly what the two she saw did do. It must be conceded that the sight of hands being put in the air is more likely to attract attention from a lady sitting in a window across the street than a hand reaching for a handbag or into a pocket. British newspapers which attempted to disparage Mrs Proetta's evidence were later obliged to apologise and pay her large sums in damages.

There is no need to waste much sympathy on the three terrorists, McCann, Farrell and Savage. Had their plan succeeded the streets of Gibraltar would have run with innocent blood, been littered with shattered limbs and dead bodies; that was their intention and clearly they had to be stopped. The only question is, did they have to be killed?

That question raised a broader issue for a democratic society, on the use of armed soldiers, operating in civilian clothes, on the streets of British cities. Should units of the British Army be used for such tasks at all when armed police units are increasingly available? This is a question that the Army commanders, the politicians who instruct them and the SAS Regiment which carries out such tasks, will need to consider carefully.

Back in Ireland, the shootings in Gibraltar had ghastly consequences. There were riots and a spate of 'revenge' attacks culminating in another savage incident when the Gibraltar terrorists were buried at Milltown Cemetery in Belfast on 16 March 1988. A Protestant gunman, Michael Stone, opened fire on the mourners with a pistol and threw grenades over the cemetery wall, killing three people and injuring fifty more, supposedly in revenge for the Enniskillen bombing of the previous November. Three days after that, when a large crowd was returning from the funeral of one of Stone's victims, two British soldiers taking the wrong turning found themselves in the midst of the crowd. Their car was brought to a halt and the two men identified as British soldiers.

What followed was a lynching. The two men, Corporals Robert Howes and Derek Wood, were set upon by the crowd. Both men were armed with pistols but they did not open fire and attempt to shoot their way out. They were dragged from their car, spat on, punched, slapped, stripped naked and beaten, then hustled on to a piece of waste ground. Here the two young men were further abused until an IRA man appeared carrying a pistol. While hundreds looked on, he then murdered the two men, by firing shots into their heads.

This was not simply another IRA atrocity, one which the local people could dismiss or shrug off as none of their concern; everyone there that day played a part in these murders, and there were hundreds of them; no one lifted a hand or said a word to stop these young men being brutalised and done to death.

So the tragedy of Northern Ireland has continued. There have been many political moves in search of a settlement, most of which came to nothing. Great goodwill and a quantity of good intentions have been ground between the twin rocks of IRA and Republican demands for a United Ireland and the Unionist determination to keep Northern Ireland British.

In the mid-1980s the politicians moved towards a half-way house, which began with the Anglo-Irish Agreement of November 1985. This offered the Irish Government a say in Northern Ireland's affairs in return for increased cooperation in counter-terrorist activities. The IRA's response to these peace initiatives ranged from mortar attacks on 10 Downing Street in February 1991, to destroying the Baltic Exchange building in the City of London in April 1992 and the planting of bombs in the shopping streets of Warrington in Cheshire, which killed two small boys in March 1993.

The path to peace which began with the Anglo-Irish Agreement, led to the Downing Street Declaration of 1993, an offer of political debate drawn up by the British Prime Minister, John Major, and the Irish Prime Minister, Albert Reynolds, a declaration of intentions which aimed at finding 'a new political framework based on consent within Northern Ireland, within the whole island and within these islands.' Then followed meetings between John Hume, a Northern Ireland politician and Gerry Adams, a former IRA man and now spokesman for the IRA's political wing, Sinn Fein; the result of all this was the IRA 'cease-fire', declared on 31 August 1994. That cease-fire continued until February 1996, when the IRA restarted their campaign with a series of bomb explosions in London.

The eighteen month 'cease-fire' – though beatings and shooting continued – was supposed to lead to round-table talks between all the interested parties, including both Governments, representatives of Sinn Fein-IRA and the various Unionist parties. A precondition of the British Government was that the IRA should first surrender its arms. This the IRA refused to do and the precondition was then amended to a 'token surrender or decommissioning of arms'. This proposal too was bluntly rejected by the IRA.

The reason for this precondition is obvious. The IRA is a terrorist organisation and Sinn Fein is their mouthpiece. The IRA has been responsible for the deaths of over three thousand people in Northern Ireland over the last quarter-century and Sinn Fein-IRA cannot sit down and negotiate with democratic parties while their partners retain a military arsenal and the will to use it. By rejecting the precondition, and eventually restarting the violence, Sinn Fein-IRA made it clear that unless their demands are met in full, they will take up the gun again.

If the British and Irish Governments were to agree to this demand, the Unionists would refuse to attend the talks. This may indeed be what the IRA had in mind; to put the Unionists in the dock as intransigent Protestants who refuse to discuss peace. The fact remains that the Unionists represent the majority of Northern Ireland's population – Sinn Fein gathered less than 10 per cent of the vote in local elections – and without Unionist participation, both in the talks and in whatever settlement is eventually arrived at, the hopes for a long-term peace seem remote indeed.

The request for even a token decommissioning of arms was also turned down by the IRA. The American Government then became involved as 'honest brokers' and in an attempt to keep the peace process moving the British Government then agreed to the setting up of a decommissioning committee, the Mitchell Commission, which would operate half of a 'twin-track' approach, in which talks about the future of Northern Ireland could go on while the matter of arms was being debated. To underline the impartiality of the Commission, the chairman, Mr Mitchell, a former American senator, was appointed to the post by Bill Clinton, President of the United States.

The twin-track approach was generally seen as a fudge but it pleased Bill Clinton, who needed to play a peace-making role in Ireland to boost his 1996 re-election chances in the United States. Clinton visited Northern Ireland and the Republic just before Christmas 1995 and received a rapturous welcome on both sides of the border, from people weary of a generation of violence, and his popularity at home duly soared. Two days after he left, the IRA rejected the twin-track proposal and spurned the Mitchell Commission.

A further suggestion, by John Major, that Sinn Fein-IRA should demonstrate their interest in democracy and the peace process by participating in a Northern Ireland election, was also rejected and within days of that rejection, bombs were going off in the centre of London. The IRA have been quite frank on the decommissioning issue, and by resorting to the bomb again have made it clear that they will renew the 'armed struggle' whenever they do not get what they want. Such a position would make any talks pointless and the Troubles in Northern Ireland look set to continue, at least until Sinn Fein-IRA accept that violence is counter-productive. That may take time for the IRA have always flatly refused to give up their arms.

Just before the Mitchell Commission met for the first time in 1995, the IRA issued a statement on the arms issue. 'There is no question of the IRA meeting this ludicrous demand for the surrender of IRA weapons, either through the front or back door.'

The response of the Irish Foreign Minister, Dick Spring, to this IRA statement was interesting. He described it as 'hopeful', adding that he saw 'no reason' why talks could not still go ahead. The sub-text of that statement was summed up by Ireland's veteran political commentator, Conor Cruise O'Brien: 'Clearly, however badly the IRA behave, the failure of the talks will be the fault of the British.'

The comments of another Irish politician, Bertie Ahern, would tend to confirm this opinion. While he 'profoundly regretted the IRA statement', he had to add that 'the very unhelpful and uncompromising statements in recent days from the British Government and Unionist leaders have damaged the recent renewed climate of hope.' Then came the bombs in central London.

The politicians in Washington, Westminster and Dublin were shocked and disgusted when the IRA restarted their campaign in February 1996 and unanimous that talks with Sinn Fein could not continue unless the cease-fire were restored. This unanimity may not last for Bertie Ahern and his ilk on both sides of the Atlantic were clearly preparing the ground for a growing belief that only a complete surrender to the IRA will ensure the continuation of the Peace Process – was it for this that more than three thousand people died? As for the talks, what solution can they offer that the two main parties and their supporters – Unionist or Republican – will accept? The IRA want a United Ireland and will settle for nothing less, and the Northern Unionists will never agree to it; opinions on that point have not shifted an inch since 1969.

This is not a political history. No more politics have been included than are necessary to provide the background to the military situation but the problems of Northern Ireland will not be solved by military means. All the soldiers can do is hold the ring and contain the violence until wiser counsels prevail. That, too, is a faint hope. If reason had anything to do with the matter, the Troubles would have ended long ago, and the poison of the IRA rooted out of Ireland for ever.

The injustices that rightly brought the civil rights activists on to the streets in 1968–69 have largely been resolved and corrected. All that laws can do has been done and peace must be found where it ought to be anyway, in the hearts and minds of the local people. If it does not exist there, it will not be found at all.

Although they can and will fight the IRA or any of the Queen's enemies until the end of time, the British Army on the streets of Northern Ireland is not the answer to the problem. However, let the final, personal account of this campaign come from a soldier who served in Northern Ireland, Major Richard Nugee:

It is very difficult to comment on the difference between my tours in '87 and '93 because I was in a different location each time and that can change things. There is no doubt in my mind that as the impact of the Anglo-Irish Agreement sunk in, the Protestant community has become less friendly to the security forces, but only as part of a general trend. The other noticeable trend was a general 'war-weariness' among the local people.

A small example of this comes from Fermanagh. A local pub just south of Enniskillen had opened an extension and the local 'great and good', including the Mayor and the Police Chief, had been invited to the opening. On the following day the IRA blew up the extension, shattering the place and scattering glass all over the pub. This took place at about 0500 hours and before I could get a patrol down there – it was before dawn and helicopters were out – the locals had swept up the glass and cleared away the mess and got back to 'normal' life.

The publican, a Catholic, was fed-up with the IRA, and could not understand why they were damaging the communities they claimed to be defending. This loss of support for the IRA is linked to the growing belief that their campaign is futile. Certainly more people were ready to defy the IRA and talk to us, but as I said, each area is different.

In Belfast in '87 people around the Bull Ring and the Falls Road were openly hostile. Large dogs were trained to attack us and one of my patrol commanders once had to cock his rifle and threaten to shoot an Alsatian unless the owner called it off. Hardly 'hearts and minds', but that is the reality of the situation.

It never ceased to amaze me how young the children started being hostile. Six-year-olds were able to hit a vehicle with stones and twelve-year-olds could hit the soldiers standing at the back, obviously the result of years of practice. That stoning was on a normal patrol, not during a riot or any heightened tension, hence the need to wear visors at all times.

In Omagh the people were basically friendly and you will know that the Army was thinly spread. Northern Ireland is not an armed camp. I remember meeting two brothers up one valley, both in their seventies, who had only twice been to Londonderry and to Belfast just once, in their youth. They told me they had not seen any soldiers for two or three years and I could well believe it. We spent most of that snowy morning tobogganing down one of their fields on plastic rubbish sacks. Barely ten miles away at Greencastle, home of one of the IRA bombing cells, no one would speak to us – though some of the soldiers, those with the gift of the gab, took this as a challenge.

One of the most frustrating aspects of the job, especially for soldiers who did not understand the political dimension, was the lack of an identifiable enemy. Many of the soldiers did not understand why they had so much training only to meet so little activity . . . though when attacked the soldiers could react swiftly and aggressively.

On our last tour the CO told us to treat the locals like part of our families and win their confidence by displaying a professional and polite manner, while being always alert to the possibility of attack. Some soldiers, inevitably the more intelligent ones, proved much better at this than others and it became a difficult and therefore much sought after task, to talk to a known terrorist. This was usually done by the patrol commander, and the rest of the patrol got pretty bored.

One thing I did notice on my last tour was a determination among the troops to help the local communities. From sending Santa Claus in by helicopter to deliver presents to the kids at a school for mentally handicapped children – the bombardier who did it loved children and was very good as Santa – to raising money for a local old people's home, the Regiment sought to be involved as much as possible with the local people. For the annual 'Children in Need' Appeal our VCPs put out buckets at the check-points and raised over £1,000 from the motorists.

I suppose the best way to sum it up was that in the 1990s we felt we were there to help the local people not just guard them. The Mayor of Armagh and a number of people told us that our ability to get on with the local people was particularly noted. I don't want to generalise on any trend, but that is one I could mention.

The tragedy of Northern Ireland has existed for centuries. One can only hope that a permanent solution will eventually be found, even if the past offers the present no clues as to what that solution might be. Until that solution is found, the soldiers of the British Army will continue to do their duty.

The soldiers have been serving on the street of Northern Ireland for more than a quarter of a century with their usual patience and good humour, seldom thinking themselves hard done by, never thinking themselves brave. There have been mistakes certainly, but very few of them. Just now and then the people in Northern Ireland might pause and thank whatever God they believe in that their streets have been patrolled for nearly three decades by soldiers of the British Army, the finest and most tolerant Army on Earth.

Sniping, bombing, callous murders, stoning, spitting and constant verbal abuse have largely failed to brutalise or provoke the soldiers of the British Army, most of them young men in their late teens and twenties. Some public memorial, even word of thanks, for these years of patient service in Ireland or half a century of service to the dying Empire would not go amiss, but as Francis Quarles noted over four hundred years ago:

> God and the soldier, we alike adore
>   In times of trouble, not before.
> Troubles past, both are alike requited,
> God is forgotten, and the soldier slighted.

EPILOGUE

The British Empire, 1997

*'Paramountcy was a doctrine. You could not transfer
a doctrine. But if you can't transfer it, what can you do
with it? The answer is, nothing. It simply lapses.'*

Paul Scott, *A Division of the Spoils* ('The Raj Quartet',
1975).

The return of Hong Kong to China marks the end of the British
Empire. There will be a few remnants here and there, some fleeting
reminders of imperial splendour. The Governor of Burmuda will
still collect his Peppercorn Rent and the Governor of the Cayman
Islands will still present prizes at the local schools. The Governor
of the Falkland Islands will still see British troops going out to patrol
on Tumbledown Mountain and Wireless Ridge and will lay an annual
wreath at Goose Green. There will still be fifteen small, scattered,
British colonies dotted about the world, but in any larger sense the
British Empire is over.

Unlike many of the other territories in this book, the colony of
Hong Kong always had a limited life, for Hong Kong island is not
large or fertile and a large percentage of the territory was leased from
China. Only Hong Kong island was held in perpetuity and Queen
Victoria was highly amused when she obtained it by the Treaty of
Nanking in 1842. Not so her Prime Minister, Lord Palmerston, who
referred to this latest imperial territory as 'A barren island with

hardly a house upon it', though it proved to be a most profitable acquisition.

Over the next one hundred and fifty years Hong Kong developed into one of the most profitable and successful of all Britain's colonial possessions, a fact which must be largely attributed to the industry and intelligence of the Chinese population. The New Territories were obtained by Great Britain on a 99–year lease in 1898 and with the end of that lease the island alone is not viable.

Michael Wood, one of the last British officers to leave India in 1947, now lives in Hong Kong;

> Fifty years after India, history repeats itself for me. Some differences from India days, of course. To get here from Britain just twelve hours in the air instead of three weeks on a troopship, one of the civilians now and not in the military, and the countdown to handover is longer, thirteen years instead of just ten weeks. In India the British Raj was still powerful right to the end and all the expats were British. In Hong-Kong the commercial types run the place and the Government is not a dominating influence in people's lives though the Hong Kong Chinese do feel that the Brits let them down by negotiating a handover to China back in 1984.
>
> The takeover by a generally unwelcome neighbour has been looked forward to by very few, even though they do not believe that things will actually change much. Most people are too busy making money while the going is good. Those Chinese who can afford to, have taken up residence in the UK, Canada, Australia, or New Zealand, or have passports for these countries so they can move if the change proves unfavourable.
>
> Hong Kong had been ruled by the British for the last one hundred and fifty years without a word of complaint from the locals, mainly because the colony encouraged enterprise and the people were able to make money unhindered.
>
> The local Chinese are unmoved by worries over democracy; few of them even understand the concept of the ballot box. The mainland Chinese, of course, want to know what the rush is. Hong-Kong has not had democracy for the last one hundred and fifty years so why introduce it? The mainland Chinese have also made it pretty clear that they will dismantle much of what

the British Administration established. All memorials of British rule will be soon be removed and it will be made to seem that the British Empire has vanished.

There are those who maintain that the British Empire has not really disappeared but simply been transformed into a Commonwealth of Nations, and cite the role of the British monarch as 'Head of the Commonwealth' as some evidence of this fact. Other evidence does not support this view. Opinions also vary on the value of the Commonwealth connection. Some of the contributors to this book feel strongly that the Commonwealth, which now numbers fifty-two independent nations, including the former French colony of Cameroun, has some value and is a force for good in an uncertain world. Field Marshal Lord Bramall, a former Chief of the Defence Staff, is one who holds that view;

I would have to say that I am in favour of the Commonwealth. It does a lot of good and the links are still strong, for we have a lot in common with the people of the old Empire, rather like people who have been to the same school. Yes, there has been a lot of ranting about the British Empire over the years by some Commonwealth politicians but I think most of that was for home consumption.

On a personal level most of the Commonwealth leaders get on very well, and that has definite value. All in all, the Commonwealth exerts a good influence on world affairs. As for the Empire, I don't miss it at all. In fact, I feel a good deal more comfortable now it is gone.

That view is shared by many other contributors, including Captain John Masters, who worked in many parts of the Empire and also served in Zaire, the former Belgian Congo, an experience which provides him with a basis for comparison:

My task in Zaire was to re-establish some system for getting medical supplies into the interior, for like the rest of Africa, Zaire was undergoing change. There was a marked difference between the British colonies and the Congo. Unlike the British, the Belgians made no preparations whatsoever for the local people to run their own affairs. All the technicians, even to the lowest level, were sent out from Belgium, so there were few local doctors, lawyers, or administrators to run the place when the Belgians were driven out. The result has been ruin and chaos.

I conclude from this that the British can at least take some pride in their efforts to leave behind the bones of an administration that has formed the heart of many emerging nations. There were also those wonderful Colonial officials who became very protective of their charges and would take up the cause of the local people, even against their paymasters in Whitehall. We did not form an Empire for the good of the 'Natives', but for our own enrichment, and what happened in the Empire is history now and cannot be changed. I just hope that the members of the old Empire can share something more than just friendship, as for better or worse we are all members of the same family.

Major–General James Lunt thinks it is too early to take a view on the worth of the British Empire:

I believe the Empire has disappeared too recently to make valid judgements about it. It required the passing of many centuries before there could be balanced judgements about the Roman Empire, if indeed, it has ever been possible.

It was my good fortune to spend most of my thirty-five years in the Army serving with other races, Arabs, Indians, Burmese, Africans, so to that extent my perspective is different from that of the more orthodox soldier. From 1966 to 1969 I was John Freeman's Defence Adviser at the Embassy in New Delhi and I was astonished to find how faithfully the post-Independence Indian Army mirrored the Army under the British.

At the age of seventy-eight I can hardly claim a vested interest in the future, but for what it is worth, I think this country is drifting like a boat which has lost its rudder and sooner or later we will end up on the beach unless we do something about it. My grandsons, however, would probably not agree with me.

William Broadway, who served the Empire in West and East Africa, and in Egypt, is another supporter of the Commonwealth:

The Commonwealth has real value and in some ways is more effective than the United Nations. The Commonwealth is a group of nations, rich and poor, containing people of every colour and creed, and they have one very important thread which binds them together – Britain's democratic institutions which they inherited from the imperial power, though some may pay only lip-service to them to-day. Whether the Commonweath will survive after the present Queen dies, I am not sure, but if it collapses it will not be the fault of the institution itself, though I believe we should have stayed in most of the colonies for at least another ten years.

The Commonweath is not a post–Second World War creation. The credit for its invention can be given to the British Prime Minister Arthur Balfour who, in 1926, put forward the idea of the Empire becoming 'a Commonwealth united around free institutions'. This is the aim that the Commonweath as a whole has striven to achieve down the years since 1947, though anyone looking back on the post-colonial record of Nigeria, Uganda, Kenya, Sierra Leone, even Singapore, would not list 'free institutions' as one of the Commonwealth's most significant characteristics.

Now, seventy years after Balfour, after the long–running sore of South African apartheid has finally been healed, perhaps the Commonwealth will abandon its former enthusiasm for anti-Western, anti-British rhetoric and the member states will devote their energies and influence to encouraging, even enforcing, decent standards of government among all the member States. Steps to that end, by linking aid to improvements in human rights and the establishment of democratic rule, have begun and must continue.

The post-independence fate of the former colonies and territories covered in this book has been rather mixed. India and Pakistan have gone to war several times and a state of armed truce usually prevails between them, mainly caused by boundary disputes and arguments over Kashmir. Pakistan lost half its territory and endured another war when East Bengal opted out of Pakistan and became Bangladesh, another Commonwealth country but one of the poorest and least viable of nations. India remains the world's largest democracy and in the decades since the Raj ended has become one of the top ten industrial nations. Famine has been eliminated but the bulk of the population is still grindingly poor and the old problems of caste and corruption remain.

Democracy in Pakistan has trodden a more dangerous path, hemmed in between military dictatorships and the rising power of Islamic fundamentalism. One democratically elected Premier, Mr Bhutto, was deposed and hanged by the military junta, but Bhutto's daughter, Benazir, is currently occupying the precarious post of Prime Minister.

Malaysia survived the Indonesian Confrontation and is now a prosperous state, as is Singapore, though in both cases economic success has not been achieved without a certain curtailment of civil liberties. Freedom of speech has been significantly reduced and draconian punishments introduced for quite trivial offences, but these states have survived and will probably continue to prosper.

If the countries of Asia have done well, the countries of Africa have suffered terribly, from war, tribalism, nepotism and corruption. Kenya, once the jewel of Africa, has become a one-party state, where free speech is curtailed and the members or supporters of any opposition parties are threatened by the bully boys of the ruling élite. Kenya has been beggared by corruption and the rule of law has broken down. The wealth of the country has been dissipated, the mismanagement of the economy continues unchecked, and civil rights are steadily eroded. Here too, the world community has let the nation's leaders know that continued economic aid will be linked to improvements in human rights and the re-establishment of a full democratic process.

Compared with most other African countries, though, Kenya has enjoyed a peaceful period since independence, certainly compared with the experiences of some neighbouring countries, most notably the former Belgian Congo – now Zaire – and Rwanda, where corruption and tribal wars have ravaged the land and lead to deaths by the million. Tribal problems have also plagued many of the African nations formed from the former British colonies, provoking, among other tragedies, the Biafran War in Nigeria during the 1960s.

A similar disaster overcame the former British colony of Uganda. The first Prime Minister, later President, Milton Obote, was overthrown by an Army NCO, Idi Amin, in January 1971, while Obote was attending the Commonwealth Heads of Government Conference. Idi Amin ruled – or misruled – Uganda for the next eight years. During that time hundreds of thousands of Africans were murdered and the country sank into chaos and misery. The road to economic ruin was reached in 1972 when Amin gave Uganda's seventy thousand Asians just ninety days to leave the country, taking only the clothes they stood up in. This action was widely praised by the Africans, the Asian Commonwealth proved indifferent and most of the Ugandan Asians fled to Britain.

Amin then turned on the British expatriate community, nationalising their businesses without compensation and forcing foreign-owned companies to close. Finally, he went too far. In 1978 Amin invaded Tanzania, and laid claim to large tracks of Tanzanian land. The Tanzanian Army rapidly defeated Amin, who fled to Saudi Arabia, and Milton Obote returned in triumph, only to begin a second reign of terror against the hapless population. This provoked a rising led by Yoweri Muselveni and in 1986 Muselveni took over the country. Since then Uganda's future has looked brighter, as order has been restored and the shattered national infrastructure improved. After a quarter-century of terror, Uganda is enjoying a period of calm, and some of the Asian traders are starting to return.

Rhodesia became Zimbabwe in 1980 and has survived as a one-party state, though not without a steady decline in economic power and the growth of tribal problems. Many white settlers have left the country, the Matabele people have been harassed by the Army and there is speculation on what might happen when the ageing President, Robert Mugabe, dies. For the moment, however, Zimbabwe survives, though the white community continues to decline and with it the basis of the national economy.

Joan Mary McDowell is a doctor's wife who stayed in Rhodesia throughout UDI and saw a lot of hard times during the war there, as she recorded in a letter written in 1980:

If you lived in Rhodesia during those years you would endeavour to convince yourself that death has no consequence; we were surrounded by it. One day I sat next to Jackie Pearson, whose daughter was an air stewardess on the Viscount airliner shot down by Nkomo's rockets. A few weeks later one of our young friends was killed, and just after that Bindura was attacked. I sat on the floor in the hall, with shots flying around, but not frightened. Our cousin in the UK wrote and said we must leave but where could we go at our age? Besides, it is so lovely here and we have worked here for thirty-five years.

Well, finally we have independence and we live in Zimbabwe, not Rhodesia. Life here is lived day to day and we hope the teething troubles will eventually sort themselves out. One thing I do wish is that the papers and TV would stop telling us what rotten colonial racists we are. That is why so many have left and those of us who have stayed on are trying to adapt. Having never in my life been rude to a black person I feel sure that only a minority of whites are lousy. Mac, my husband, feels that this is still his country – he was born here – and we are too old to start again somewhere else, but all this mud-throwing is why our age group are leaving.

Israel, that state established on the ruins of mandated Palestine, has fought a series of wars, from the day the State was founded in 1948 almost to the present day. In all of these, the Idependence War, the Suez War, the Six-Day War, the Yom Kippur War, Israel has eventually emerged victorious but that has not stopped Arab and especially Palestine terrorists attacking Israel's frontiers and her citizens at home and abroad. Only in 1994 did the Palestinians and the Israelis finally sit down to talk peace and the development of an infant Palestine State on the West Bank and the Gaza Strip gives hope that fifty years of Arab–Israeli conflict is finally coming to a close.

Aden colony vanished into the grasp of South Yemen, and after a brief period as a Soviet satellite, when Aden was a base for the Russian Fleet, South Yemen has collapsed into anarchy, gripped by war between tribal or political factions, or with North Yemen. This is one problem that Britain has stayed well clear of, as warfare continues to rage in the old colony.

Cyprus is a tragedy. Britain retains her two bases in Cyprus, a country where independence began well but finished badly, and the future prospects are not bright. The EOKA campaign ended in 1959 and the three sides, British, Greek and Turkish, then met in Zurich to find a solution for Cyprus that would avoid either *enosis* – union with Greece – or partition.

The basis of eventual independence was a Tripartite Agreement by which the government of the island would be divided as 70 per cent Greek, 30 per cent Turkish, with Britain obtaining her two sovereign bases and the Greek and Turkish Governments having the right to intervene if the rights of their communities were threatened.

This Agreement specifically forbade *enosis* or any activity promoting it. On that basis Cyprus became independent in 1960 with Archbishop Makarios as President. This Agreement did not please Colonel Grivas who, on leaving the island for Greece, claimed that his EOKA fighters had defeated the British and should be given the reward of *enosis*.

This Agreement was not kept. The two communities remained highly suspicious of each other and friction between the civil servants and Government officials did not help. Within months there was deep disagreement between the two communities on the running of island affairs. Finally, in December 1963, the Greeks broke the Agreement and attacked the Turkish communities in Larnaca and Nicosia. Both sides had stockpiled arms and fighting between the two communities went on for three months, until the United Nations intervened. An uneasy peace, with frequent outbreaks of violence, prevailed until 1974, when heavy fighting broke out again.

Grivas was now back on the island as a General in the Greek Army, and under his leadership and that of a local man, Nicos Sampson, another former EOKA terrorist, the Greek National Guard – a properly uniformed and equipped Army, officered by Greeks from the mainland – staged a coup, ousted President Makarios and revived the demand for *enosis*. After several massacres of Turkish civilians and the steady reduction of the Turkish enclave in the north of the island, which the UN forces seemed unable to prevent, the Turkish Army invaded Cyprus in September 1974. The Turks had to do this to protect their own people, but the result has been partition.

Cyprus has been effectively partitioned since 1974 and while it is doubtful if the Tripartite Agreement would have worked in the long-term, the blame for breaking it so soon must be laid on the Greek Cypriots, General Grivas and the Greeks in general. That is not a popular view and the Turkish invasion of 1974 has been widely condemned but the Turkish Government had the legal right to intervene under the 1960 Agreement and were sorely provoked by the the Greeks before doing so.

If the problem of *enosis* could be solved or the demand for it laid aside, the Republic of Cyprus could be a great economic success. It has a fine climate, a small, industrious, educated population, a good infrastructure, a thriving tourist trade and a strategic position close to the markets of both the Middle East and Europe. Large sections of the Greek and Turkish communities now admit that the actions of the 1960s and 1970s did nothing but harm so perhaps the will is there for open-ended discussions, a new constitution and a fresh start. That would be the best solution, but the mistrust created by the past will make such a solution very hard to reach.

Britain's former colonies, even those that fought their way to independence through a maze of troubles, have managed to survive reasonably well, certainly when their independence struggles are compared with those of the French, Belgian, Dutch or Portuguese colonies. Britain and her former colonies have never faced or fought colonial wars on the scale fought by the French in Indo-China and Algeria, or seen massacres like those in the Belgian Congo in the 1960s, or had colonies collapse into anarchy and war of the type endured by the Portuguese in Angola and Mozambique. British expatriates have not been bundled out of their homes and murdered in the streets as the Dutch expatriates were in Indonesia.

In most of the places once under British rule, the Empire ended quietly and the story of what happened in those countries where there was a problem has been fully related in this book. The British record in the decolonisation decades stands comparison with any and is not one to be ashamed of. The problems of Northern Ireland remain unresolved but elsewhere the post-colonial signs are encouraging.

Now that the immediate post-independence period has passed, a new realism is emerging in the relationship between Britain and her former colonies. Insulting Britain is no longer fashionable at Commonwealth Heads of Government Conferences, and accusations of British imperialism, racism or neo-colonialism are not as common as they once were, though there are, and probably always will be, a few strident voices demanding compensation or apologies for the events of the past. That independence came too soon in many places can hardly be doubted, but independence is what the United States, the United Nations and the colonial territories demanded years ago and they must live with the consequences now.

Ian Aers, once a District Officer in Tanganyika, explained this to the local people at the time:

We arrived in Tanganyika in 1948 and were posted up-country. We spent at least ten days every month on walking safaris to meet the people and their chiefs and to check the record of cases heard in tribal courts and assess the need for food relief.

While I was DC (District Commissioner) at Kimba in the mid-50s, a police constable called William ran amok; he stabbed the police sergeant to death, burned a police corporal to death and then took to the bush with his rifle, where he killed about thirty-five men by shooting them at close range. Eventually we had thousands of beaters in the bush to flush him out and he was finally shot dead by the police commander from Mwanza. Shortly before he ran amok William had been on the Guard of Honour for Princess Margaret.

Anyway . . . independence. By the late 1950s the Tanganyika African National Union (TANU) was the only effective political voice in the country. TANU people would go around the district and hold meetings saying how well they would run the country after independence and how bad the British, and indeed the Chiefs, had treated the people. I used to follow a few days later and hold my own meetings and enrage TANU by telling the locals a fable. It sounds better in Swahili, but in English it goes like this:

'Once upon a time there was a colony of frogs who lived peacefully and flourished in the shade of a large tree. Then one day the frogs prayed to the Lord that the Tree King might be removed and a new King given to them, one that could walk and talk.

'The next morning the Tree had gone and there stood a large stork, and the frogs were delighted. The frogs were even more delighted when the stork began to walk and talk but later the same day the stork got hungry and started eating the frogs.

'The frogs now called on the Lord to remove the stork and give them their old king back, the shady, protecting tree, but the Lord said "You have chosen your own King and now you must live with him."'

Rodney Pringle presents another, more personal view of the old Empire:

Wandering through the wastes of a finished Empire, the ghosts of all those brave officers, decent administrators, good technicians, have haunted me every time someone has come up and said, 'Please Bwana, we have a problem. Please help.' I can't help because I am no longer the Bwana. I live somewhere else, in safety, in my own new world, which is acquisitive, indulgent, and requires wealth, and isn't concerned with simple people like him.

The Empire wasn't useless and it wasn't good, or bad, imperious or self-seeking, noble, wise or any of the other terms applied to it today, because it was British and we are special. We aren't all that special. Just a bit special. It was a human mechanism for encouraging unselfishness and could equally well have been operated by the Chinese, Germans, French, Americans or anyone else, caught at the right moment in their history. We did well with the mechanics when we were at the right moment, and felt it less well later, when we got a bit puffed up with our own goodness.

Really, it is miraculously simple. Take any man who is educated, civilised, technically well informed, who has an understanding that he is lucky to be just that, and a sense that he has not been put into the world just for himself. Tell him that for little pay and miserable conditions he is to live in a horrendous climate, away from civilised life, but that he is to be put in charge of thousands of his less lucky fellow men, to look after them, to nurture and protect them, to bring them into the light of day, and most important, to have the power to do those things. To play God, even though only a God in a pig sty!

What man or woman could ever reject that tremendous challenge? Who would worry even for a moment that the life would reduce him to a physical wreck, even knowing that in the end he would come home washed out and desolate, but proud. No wonder they got puffed up. It had to end, of course. A pity. The Empire was an excellent method of bamboozling people to do good.

The British Empire has gone, but what of the British people, their leaders and the Army? When considering the old Empire or dealing with the new Commonwealth, British politicians have finally managed to shed their 'post-colonial guilt'. They now feel able to speak openly and frankly about the problems in those independent countries that were once British colonies, and on the human rights record in far too many Commonwealth countries. Such plain speaking is long overdue and a very healthy development which ought to be encouraged. As for the British Army, it is praised wherever it goes and kept constantly employed.

The British Army, though much reduced in size, remains highly professional and well respected, plagued though it is by a seemingly-endless round of defence reviews and cuts. Field Marshal Lord Bramall again:

> The truth is that the British are rather good at military operations. We may have lost a lot in the last fifty years but we are still good at fighting. In fact, for our size and weight the British Army is the finest military force in the world. A lot of that is due to the character of the soldiers, their sense of humour and restraint. Other armies are quite good – the French are quite good – but some, like the Finns and the Danes and Canadians, are very good peacekeepers but perhaps not so good at the other business. The British soldier is good at peacekeeping, but he also knows how to fight . . . and enjoys it.

Finally, what of Britain and her people, fifty years after the end of the Raj? Much has changed. The Empire has gone, the Commonwealth is no longer the 'British' Commonwealth, the world map is no longer splashed with the pink that marked the wide grasp of the British people. There is trouble close to home in Ireland and murmurs about devolution or independence for Scotland, while Great Britain as a whole gets ever more entangled in the bureaucratic embrace of the European Community. What happens to Britain and the British, now that the Empire has gone?

Great Britain is hardly recognisable as the Imperial Power that emerged from the Second World War but the research for this book has found few signs that anyone regrets the loss of Empire or Britain's declining international status. There is, however, a great desire to restore a sense of national self-respect and rebuild the country's industrial base, to ensure lasting economic viability. Perhaps now, with the end of Empire, Britain can apply herself to those long-overdue tasks, but certain international pretensions still remain, not least in the corridors of Westminster and Whitehall.

Britain takes her fair share – some might say more than her fair share – in United Nations peacekeeping operations. Britain retains a seat on the UN Security Council, maintains a nuclear deterrent, and is still eager to support US actions around the world, and feels obliged to play a leading role in international affairs. All this is expensive and the nation's economic position remains uncertain. Fifty years after the Second World War Britain's industrial power cannot match that of many other nations, including that of her old adversaries, Germany and Japan. Without sound economic strength, political declarations or military adventures are mere posturing. Britain in 1997 has come a long way since the great days of Empire, most of it downhill.

There is, however, one ray of hope, one lesson from this examination of the recent past and the nation's splendid history. The British have always drawn strength from their history and the past can sometimes provide a signpost to the way ahead.

When Queen Elizabeth II came to the throne of her ancestors in June 1953, there was much harking back to the days of her great predecessor, Elizabeth I, and a lot of talk about the dawning of a 'New Elizabethan Age', when Britain would shake off her divisions and economic woes, raise her voice in the world and be a power among the nations yet again.

That dazzling prospect has not been realised but there is one lesson from the reign of the first Elizabeth which indicates that the loss of Empire may be no bad thing and certainly no reason for regret. Empires are not everything and the 'End of Empire' might signal a new beginning for the British people. At least the opportunity is there to grasp and the historic parallels encouraging.

When Elizabeth Tudor sat on the throne of this Kingdom, her seamen roamed the world and were the terror of the seas. Her soldiers challenged the might of the Spanish Empire, her explorers mapped the New World and travelled uncharted oceans, her dramatists left a mark on the arts that can never be erased. This truly was a 'Golden Age'.

Her predecessor, Mary Tudor, lost Calais, England's last possession in France, and the great Queen had been dead for four years before her successor, James I, established the settlement in Virginia. Mistress over part of one small island, Elizabeth I held a hostile world at bay for fifty turbulent years and her glory lives on . . . yet Elizabeth Tudor is the only British sovereign, from the Norman Conquest to the present day, who never laid claim to a single overseas colony.

SELECTED BIBLIOGRAPHY

Adkin, Mark, *Goose Green*, Leo Cooper, 1985.

Barnett, Corelli, *The Collapse of British Power*, Eyre Methuen, 1972.

Bethell, Nicolas, *The Palestine Triangle*, Deutsch, 1979.

Blake, Christopher, *A View from Within*, Mendip Publishing, 1990.

Bullock, Christopher, *Journeys Hazardous (Borneo 1965)*, Square One, 1994.

Campbell, A. F., *Jungle Green (Malaya)*, Allen and Unwin, 1953.

Carver, Michael, *Tightrope Walking; British Defence Policy since 1945*, Hutchinson, 1992.

——, *War since 1945*, Weidenfeld and Nicolson, 1980.

Clutterbuck, Richard, *The Long, Long War – The Emergency in Malaya*, Cassell, 1966.

Collins, Dominique and Larry, Lapierre, *Freedom at Midnight (India)*, Collins, 1975.

Coogan, Tim Pat, *The IRA: A History*, Roberts Reinhart, 1994.

Crockett, Anthony, *Green Beret, Red Star (Malaya)*, Eyre and Spottiswoode, 1954.

Cross, Colin, *The Fall of the British Empire*, Hodder & Stoughton, 1968.

De Butts, Freddie, *Now the Dust Has Settled*, Tabb House, 1995.

Dickens, Peter, *SAS: The Jungle Frontier*, Fontana Books, 1984.

Durrell, Lawrence, *Bitter Lemons (Cyprus)* Faber, 1957.

Farwell, Byron, *Armies of the Raj*, Norton, 1989.

——, *The Gurkhas*, Norton, 1984.

Frost, John, *2 Para Falklands*, Buchan and Enwright, 1983.

Grivas, George, *The Memoirs of General Grivas (Cyprus)*, Longmans, 1964.

Hastings, Max, and Jenkins, Simon, *The Battle for the Falklands*, Michael Joseph, 1983.

Hunter, Robin, *True Stories of the SAS*, Virgin Books, 1995.

Jackson, Sir William, *Withdrawal from Empire*, Batsford, 1986.

Jacobs, B. L., *Administrators in East Africa*, Authority Books, Entebbe, 1965.

James, Lawrence, *Rise and Fall of the British Empire*, Little, Brown, 1994.

Kitson, Frank, *Bunch of Fives*, Faber, 1977.

Kitson, Frank, *Gangs and Counter Gangs (Mau-Mau)*, Barrie and Jenkins, 1960.

Lapping, Brian, *End of Empire*, Granada Publishing, 1985.

MacArthur, Brian, *The Penguin Book of Historic Speeches*, Penguin, 1995.

Loch, John, *My First Alphabet*, privately published, 1994.

Lunt, James, *The Barren Rocks of Aden*, Barrie and Jenkins, 1966.

——, *Sixth (6th QEO Gurkha Rifles)*, Leo Cooper, 1994.

Majdalany, Fredrick, *State of Emergency (Kenya)*, Longmans, 1962.

Mansfield, Peter, *The British In Egypt*, Weidenfeld, 1971.

Masters, John, *Bohwani Junction*, Penguin, 1990.

——, *Bugles and a Tiger*, Viking, 1956.

Messenger, Charles, *The Steadfast Gurkha*, Leo Cooper, 1985.

Middlebrook, Martin, *Operation Corporate (Falklands, 1982)*, Viking, 1985.

Morris, James, *Pax Britannica and Farewell the Trumpets*, Penguin, 1979.

Neillands, Robin, *By Sea and Land (The Royal Marine Commandos, 1942–82)*, Weidenfeld & Nicolson, 1986.

Nutting, Anthony, *No End of a Lesson (Suez, 1956)*, Constable, 1967.

Paget, J., *Last Post: Aden, 1964–67*, Faber & Faber, 1969.

Pocock, Tom, *East and West of Suez*, Bodley Head, 1986.

——, *Fighting General (Sir Walter Walker)*, Collins, 1973.

Roberts, Andrew, *Eminent Churchillians*, Weidenfeld & Nicolson, 1994.

Scott, Paul, *The Raj Quartet* (four vols).

Short, Anthony, *The Communist Insurrection in Malaya*, Muller, 1975.

Southby-Tailyour, Ewen, *Reasons in Writing*, Leo Cooper, 1993.

Spear, Percival, *A History of India, Vol. 2*, Penguin, 1978.

Sykes, Christopher, *Crossroads to Israel (The Palestine Mandate)*, Mentor, 1967.

Thomas, Hugh, *The Suez Affair*, Weidenfeld and Nicolson, 1957.

Thompson, Julian, *No Picnic (Falklands War, 1982)*, Leo Cooper, 1985.

Townsend, Peter, *The Last Emperor (King George VI)*, Granada Publishing, 1978.

Tuker, Sir Francis, *While Memory Serves*, Cassell, 1950.

Young, David, *Four-Five (Commando)*, Leo Cooper, 1972.

Zeigler, Philip, *Mountbatten*, Collins, 1985.

INDEX